Second Edition

MANAGEMENT CONTROL SYSTEMS
Using Adaptive Systems to Attain Control

Joseph A. Maciariello, Ph.D.
Claremont Graduate School
Claremont and McKenna College

Calvin J. Kirby, Ph.D.
Vice President, Product Operations
GM Hughes Electronics

Prentice Hall, Englewood Cliffs, New Jersey 076

Library of Congress Cataloging-in-Publication Data

Maciariello, Joseph A.
    Management control systems : using adaptive systems to attain
control / JOSEPH A. MACIARIELLO, CALVIN J. KIRBY.—2nd ed.
        p.   cm.
    Includes bibliographical references and index.
    ISBN 0-13-098146-X
    1. Industrial management.   2. Managerial accounting.   I. Kirby,
Calvin J.   II. Title.
HD31.M28135   1994
658.15'11—dc20   93-29228

To Judy and Ann

Acquisitions editor: *Don Hull*
Editorial/production supervision interior design: *Edie Riker*
Cover design: *Maureen Eide*
Cover photo illustration: *Merle Krumper*
Production coordinator: *Patrice Fraccio*

© 1994 by Prentice-Hall, Inc.
A Paramount Communications Company
Englewood Cliffs, New Jersey 07632

Printed in the United States of America

10   9   8   7   6   5   4   3   2   1

ISBN 0-13-098146-X

Prentice-Hall International (UK) Limited, *London*
Prentice-Hall of Australia Pty. Limited, *Sydney*
Prentice-Hall Canada Inc., *Toronto*
Prentice-Hall Hispanoamericana, S.A., *Mexico*
Prentice-Hall of India Private Limited, *New Delhi*
Prentice-Hall of Japan, Inc., *Tokyo*
Simon & Schuster Asia Pte. Ltd., *Singapore*
Editora Prentice-Hall do Brasil, Ltda., *Rio de Janeiro*

CONTENTS

PART II   MUTUALLY SUPPORTIVE SYSTEMS MODEL (MSSM)
FOR THE DESIGN OF CONTROL SYSTEMS

PREFACE

Control systems are employed in all organizations. They are used by managers as they seek to bring unity of purpose out of the diverse efforts of organizational participants and steer their organizations towards its goals and objectives. As such, they are concerned with the work of **coordination, resource allocation, motivation** and **performance measurement**.

This text has been designed to present a comprehensive treatment of the theory and practice of management control and of the design of management control systems. The practice of management control and the design of management control systems draws upon a number of academic disciplines. Management control involves extensive measurement and it is therefore related to and requires contributions from *accounting* especially *management accounting*. Second, it involves resource allocation decisions and is therefore related to and requires contributions from *economics* especially *managerial economics*. Third, it involves communications, coordination, and motivation which means it is related to and must draw contributions from *social psychology* especially *organizational behavior*. The result is very much an interdisciplinary subject.

Dr. Calvin J. Kirby has become a coauthor of this edition, thus adding significant managerial experience and insight to all of the material in this book. Dr. Kirby is Vice President, Product Operations of GM Electronics–Hughes Aircraft Corporation. He is an expert in operations, including international operations, and in Total Quality Management. He brings significant managerial and international experience, and academic training to the field of management control systems.

The text has been written for both graduate and undergraduate students and for practicing managers, some of whom may also be students enrolled in executive management programs. Ideally, students will have had some prior exposure to accounting, economics, and behavioral science before taking this course. Students with little or no formal training in these areas but with significant professional experience should have little difficulty identifying with the issues raised in this text, although it is advisable that these students complete at least one course or a programmed instruction in accounting.

This revision represents a marked departure from the original edition. In many ways, it is a new text. Ten of the nineteen chapters are completely new; the remaining nine have undergone significant revision and updating to reflect the changes that have occurred over the past ten years. Thirty-three of the forty-four cases are new to this edition.

The drastic nature of the revision represents the equally drastic changes that have occurred within the field of management control systems itself. The biggest change is the relatively new emphasis many organizations are placing on the informal control system in general, and values and informal organizational arrangements in particular, and the resultant reduced role of formal control procedures. This revision seeks to achieve a balance between formal and informal control systems.

We have also sought to incorporate all of the other significant changes affecting the design of control systems. We have focused this revision strongly on the attributes of control systems that are required to serve **customers** and to achieve high levels of **quality, productivity**, and **innovation** while doing so. We see these as the key determinants of profitability over the long-run and not incompatible with achieving strong short-run results. Our emphasis is upon the design of control systems to achieve desired results on a continuous basis.

The book reflects the changes that are occurring in the design of organizations, and their impact on the design of control systems, such as flatter organizations and wider spans of control; empowerment and human motivation; teams, teamwork, and action-oriented learning; market-driven organizational structures; elimination of barriers among organizational units and among external stakeholders such as customers and suppliers; and the coordination and control of international operations. Issues of global coordination and competitiveness are discussed throughout the text. Our approach to the design of control systems is shown to be appropriate for both domestic and international operations.

The whole area of control by shared values receives extensive treatment throughout the book. Values are seen as control devices that may be more effective than formal controls if they are the right values for the environment and if they are shared widely and deeply. **Values such as customer focus, continuous learning and improvement, quality, ethical conduct, flexibility, teamwork, collegiality, plain dealing, honesty, trust, ownership, quick response, focus on reality and simplicity are shown to be instrumental to achieving competitive success.**

A number of communication and integration devices are emphasized to integrate diverse organizational units such as teams, organizational councils at various levels, committees, conflict resolution methods, training forums and programs, boundaryless organizations, information and communications technologies, and two-way communications.

Rewards emphasize the full range of rewards such as formal rewards-bonuses, stock options, promotions, and informal rewards-recognition, and promotion of and identification with organizational values. We emphasize the importance of tailoring rewards to the espoused values of the organization.

In the management control process, we emphasize the relatively new tools and processes that have been instituted to improve decisions made within the process and to improve the overall functioning of the control system and competitiveness of the organization. These newer tools include total quality management and continuous improvement tools; activity-based and target-costing techniques; best practice, benchmarking and benchtrending techniques; and just-in-time methods. Traditional control techniques such as budgeting, accounting, capital budgeting, and program-management techniques are also discussed and evaluated.

The importance of a number of performance measures are stressed such as customer satisfaction, employee satisfaction, productivity, supplier performance, direct measures of performance regarding quality, cycle time, and cycle-time reduction.

Finally, we consider the ethical dimension of control systems to be fundamental to the success of these systems. **Trust** is a key issue in organizations. Control systems increase trust when they are designed to promote **fairness** to all stakeholders of an organization. Trust, in turn, reduces the costs associated with control systems and increases their effectiveness. As a result, the ethical dimension of control systems is given significant attention in this revision.

With all of these changes, it is possible to miss the three changes we consider **absolutely fundamental** to the subject. First, there is the overall, **mutually supportive framework** for the design of the **formal** and **informal** dimensions of control systems. Second, we believe it is logical and completely consistent with management practice to subdivide the work of management control into **strategic**, long-term processes, and **operational**, short-term processes. Third, we emphasize the need to design the control system in such a way as to facilitate **organizational adaptation** to changing environments and conditions. Adaptation is an important requirement for organizations today and we envision it being an even more important requirement in the future. Innovation and continuous improvement are fundamental ingredients to adaptation. These three design features are fundamental to our approach and differentiate this text from others.

ACKNOWLEDGMENTS

Our debts on this textbook revision are many. The basic framework for the design of control systems used in this book was inspired by the work of Richard F. Vancil of the Harvard Business School. His work in describing the management systems in place at Texas Instruments Inc. (HBS Case 9-172-054) and in developing a series of additional case studies, teaching notes, and videos which were associated with a course module entitled *Implementing Strategy: The Role of Top Management* (HBS Course Module 9-983-001, 1982), was instrumental to the development of the overall approach taken in this revised edition. His related study of decentralization practices in U.S. industry, which was published earlier under the title *Decentralization: Managerial Ambiguity by Design* (Dow-Jones Irwin, 1979), has also significantly influenced our approach.

Many of the ideas in this text were worked out and applied in Executive Management classes at the Drucker Center of the Claremont Graduate School. The numerous references in the text to the work of Executive Management students attests to the impact these students have had on this book. In addition, the book has benefited from the results of a number of Ph.D. dissertations carried out in the Management Systems Area of the Executive Management Program over the past decade. We have tried to acknowledge all of these contributions within the text but we are sure that we have fallen short of giving these students the credit they richly deserve.

One of us (JM) benefited significantly from the generous sabbatical policies of both the Claremont Graduate School and Claremont McKenna College. Without two sabbaticals over a three-year period, it would not have been possible to complete this revision. We are grateful to both of these institutions.

One of us (CK) would like to thank Hughes Aircraft for providing an environment conducive to personal and professional growth. We also acknowledge the expert assistance of Wanda Denson-Low of Hughes Aircraft for her legal assistance in clearing the document for publication. We also acknowledge the work of Patrick Rodgers for leading the development of the Ethics Program at Hughes that has become the basis for our Chapter 19.

The content of the book itself reflects the assistance of many additional colleagues from industry and academe. We have benefited immensely from the work of these colleagues and we have tried to give recognition to each of them within the body of the book itself. While we are grateful for their contributions, only we are responsible for any inadequacies that may remain.

We are grateful to our secretaries, Shirley Renyer (Hughes Aircraft) and Elizabeth Rowe (Claremont Graduate School), for their extensive help in handling all the correspondence related to manuscript preparation, including correspondence between both of us. In addition, we would like to thank Leslie Alston, Debrah Maglica and Juliene Urain (of the Claremont Graduate School) for their help with various aspects of manuscript preparation.

Don Hull of Prentice Hall was a joy to work with throughout the editorial phase of this project, as was Edie Riker of East End Publishing Services throughout the production phase. We also would like to thank Joseph Heider and Linda Albeli of Prentice Hall for their help and support on the project.

Finally, and most importantly, we acknowledge the patience and assistance of our wives, Judy and Ann, during the past three years when this book occupied much of our attention and "free" time. We dedicate this book to them.

Joseph A. Maciariello
Calvin J. Kirby

INTRODUCTION TO MANAGEMENT CONTROL SYSTEMS

The purpose of this book is to provide a systematic and in-depth treatment of the subject of management control systems. The principal focus of this book is upon the work of complex and large organizations in the private sector of the economy, although the principles described here will be shown to be almost totally transferable to the public and not-for-profit sectors of the economy.

What is a Management Control System (MCS)? A MCS is a set of interrelated communication structures that facilitates the processing of information for the purpose of assisting managers in coordinating the parts and attaining the purpose of an organization on a continuous basis. All organizations use control systems. All but the smallest organizations require the use of formal control systems to function effectively. Many organizations use informal as well as formal control systems.

THE PURPOSE OF MANAGEMENT CONTROL SYSTEMS

The purpose of a management control system is to assist management in the **coordination** of the parts of an organization and the **steering** of those parts toward the achievement of its overall purposes, goals and objectives. A control system is designed to bring **unity out of the diverse activities** of an organization as it seeks to fulfill its overall purpose. It is a major tool of management for bringing about the cooperative effort that is at the very heart of the work of organizations.

In this book we shall use the term *purpose* to refer to the *mission* of the organization which is directed, first and foremost, toward meeting needs of customers and society. We shall use the term *objectives* to refer to specific, short-term, and predominantly quantitative pursuits of an organization. We shall use the term *goals* to refer to specific, long-term pursuits of an organization.

Each part of an organization has a purpose, objectives, and goals. The MCS knits the organization together so that each part, by exercising the *autonomy* given to it, fulfills a purpose that is consistent with and contributes to the fulfillment of the overall purpose of the organization.

Control systems should be designed so as to bring about unity of purpose through the use of diverse efforts of individuals in the organization. The task of management control is the achievement of unity through diversity by the use of communications and coordination, in pursuit of short-term objectives and long-term goals.

THE DOMAIN OF MANAGEMENT CONTROL SYSTEMS

There is some disagreement about the proper domain for control systems among authors in the field. Anthony, Dearden and Govindarajan,[1] for example, in an influential book consider strategic planning, management control, and task control as three separate but interrelated processes of planning and control. Management control is seen by them (p. 10) as "the process by which managers influence other members of the organization to implement the organization's strategies." In their view, the proper domain for management control systems is the successful implementation of strategy. They do not treat adaptation and innovation as an integral part of the managerial control process.

William Newman, on the other hand, in his very lucid development of the design and use of control systems,[2] considers the domain of control systems to be the control function of management and believes (p. 5) "Control is one of the basic phases of managing, along with planning, organizing, and leading." Control is seen as an essential part of the management process and a part of all the managerial efforts of an organization.

Our view of the domain of control systems is different; it is derived from the theory of cybernetics and is close to that described by Stafford Beer in his two books, *Cybernetics and Management* and *Decisions and Control*,[3] by Katz and Kahn in their important work, *Social Psychology of Organizations*[4] and by Griesinger in his paper "Toward a Cybernetic Theory of the Firm."[5] Here the entire organization is viewed as a control system. "Control" is seen as a characteristic or attribute of a control system; *it occurs when the organization is attaining its purpose*. Purpose and the attainment of purpose are central to the work of control systems.

Unlike the Anthony, Dearden, and Bedford view, our definition of managerial control considers both the *control of strategy* and *the control of operations*. Moreover, because it is concerned with the design of management systems used to steer an organization towards its purpose, it includes *aspects* of the *planning, organizing, and leading* functions of management, thus distinguishing it from Newman's definition. We believe our definition has face validity—it is based upon a strong theoretical foundation, consistent with management practice and quite natural. But you should be aware that authors differ in their approach to this subject.

This book adheres to our defined domain of control while freely incorporating many useful concepts from the other two approaches. It describes a management control framework which when implemented will enhance organizational adaptability and thus accelerate productivity and quality improvements. The framework is a tool for resolving inadequacies in current control systems, for coaxing organizations toward optimal performance, and for enhancing competitiveness. Like the systems found in Japanese industry, it seeks to increase individual cooperation, minimize suboptimization and stimulate responsiveness to changing conditions.

THE ORGANIZATIONAL CONTEXT OF MANAGERIAL CONTROL SYSTEMS

If we are to design control systems to assist managers in carrying out their functions, we must have a realistic description of the context within which organizations, managers and individuals function. In this book we use a model of organization and management based upon the one first described by Chester Barnard in his *Functions of the Executive.*

Organizations

Subunits

Organizations are usually divided into subunits. Subunits are comprised of individuals at particular locations who perform certain activities in order to fulfill a portion of the purpose of the organization. Subunits are organized to overcome the physical and biological limitations of individuals in dealing with their environment. Subunits are usually formed by using the principles of *specialization* and *division of labor.* By dividing labor into like activities, members can specialize on certain tasks, thus improving the efficiency of the subunits. For example, all activities that are concerned with building a product will likely be combined into a production department (a subunit).

The formation of subunits in an organization presents other challenges. A primary one is the achievement of efficient coordination of activities between subunits. The control system plays a major role in attempting to coordinate the efforts of these subunits. The cost of coordinating the efforts of these subunits may be referred to as *transaction costs.* Control systems designers try to design systems that help in reaching goals and objectives while minimizing these transaction costs. Inefficiencies in coordination result in *excess transaction costs.* For example, excess transaction costs occur when designs are produced in engineering that are not readily manufacturable, necessitating the need for rework or possibly creating lower than expected output yields in manufacturing.

The specialized subunits of complex organizations are established with varying degrees of autonomy. Each unit has a specific objective derived from the overall purpose of the organization and each is coordinated by another subunit in a superior–subordinate relationship. In the past, it was not considered important that the overall purpose of the organization be known or accepted by each subunit. More recently, however, the revival in recognition of the vital role of the informal organization has highlighted the value of general acceptance and understanding of the overall purpose and the supportive values of the organization.

Effectiveness and Efficiency

An organizational unit is said to be *effective* when it meets the overall purpose of the organization and fulfills a genuine need in society. On the other hand, it is said to be *efficient* when it is meeting all the needs of its constituents. Effectiveness relates to the social purpose of the organization, whereas efficiency relates to the personal motives of the stakeholders of the organization. An efficient organization achieves its purpose with minimum waste of resources. Effectiveness and efficiency are interrelated and are both necessary for long term prosperity.

Efficiency is necessary to attract, hold, and motivate individuals; without effectiveness an organization has no social purpose and will eventually lose its ability to meet the needs of its constituents. Many individuals contribute to the efforts of organizations, and an efficient organization will meet their expectations. For example, employees provide labor to produce the product. Investors provide funds for operations. Customers purchase products and services. Each of these stakeholders expect a reasonable return on their efforts and investments. The worker expects a competitive wage, the investor a competitive return, and the customer the satisfaction of a need.

The control system is designed to assist executives in meeting both the overall purpose of an organization and the requirements of its constituents. Both tasks must be met for the organization to remain viable.

Internal and External Stakeholders

Organizations are open systems and as such they must deal with a set of stakeholders including those inside and those outside the organization. Each stakeholder operates in an organized market. Managers must decide which activities it should perform inside the organization and which it should purchase in an outside market. If management decides to internalize these activities, it must acquire the resources in stakeholder markets to do so. In this case the control system is called upon to coordinate these external exchanges and resultant internal activities. If management decides to purchase activities in outside stakeholder markets (for example, vendors and consultants), the control system must be designed to integrate the efforts of the stakeholders performing these external activities.

The continued operations of a firm require that stakeholders be rewarded at market rates. Markets can change dramatically, and executives must quickly adapt to changes in these markets. For example, with the actual and projected decline in the budget of the U. S. Department of Defense [1993], engineers and scientists who only a few years ago were in high demand and thus received high compensation are in much less demand now. The challenge to executives in these organizations is to redeploy these technologists to other uses, reduce salaries, or lay off and rehire under new market compensation arrangements.

Executive Functions

In light of these characteristics of organizations and of stakeholder markets, it is quite logical to understand the functions of executives and the role of control systems in carrying out these functions. Barnard defined the essential managerial functions as three:

- Securing essential efforts
- Providing the system of organizational communication
- Formulating and defining purpose

These executive functions don't exist in isolation but rather are elements of an organic whole.

1. Securing essential efforts: inducing participation of stakeholders into the organization

The first function of management is to motivate participation and performance in the organization. This involves recruiting persons with proper character and ability and motivating them to use their capacities.

Selection of the right people for managerial positions is one of the most important functions of the executive. Individuals are recruited to the organization by offering *inducements* or rewards (monetary and nonmonetary) which are equal to or exceed those offered by competing organizations. Executives then motivate *contributions* from participants that generate income from which the inducements are paid. Participants include customers, employees, executives, owners, distributors, and suppliers.

2. Provide the system of organizational communication.

Once recruitment has been accomplished, the management function turns to the design and redesign of the *formal organization,* which is the basic communication system for carrying out the purpose of the organization. The job of defining a formal organization structure involves dividing the labor and creating specializations. The formal organization is defined in the organization chart.

Communication is the essence of organizations. The parts have to be related to the whole, purposes have to be identified and accepted, and the proper sequence of steps needs be maintained. This requires definition of management positions and finding personnel to fill them.

Communication patterns, those relevant and those irrelevant to organizational purpose, are present in all organizations. The aspect of communications most relevant to the management control systems designer is the *communications that are used to coordinate the various activities of the organization.* These coordinating activities may be either formal or informal.

a. Formal and informal organization

Formal communications follow the relationships given in the organization chart. Formal organizations are relatively permanent systems of communication for coordinating the activities of two or more individuals as they seek to fulfill a common purpose.

The informal organization is not tangible but is more something that is sensed. It consists of interpersonal relationships that are not shown on the organization chart. Barnard defines it as (p. 115) "the aggregate of personal contacts and interactions and the associated groupings of people. . . . Though common or joint purposes are excluded by definition, common or joint results of important character nevertheless come from such organizations." The formal organization provides the bare bones impersonal structure, whereas the informal provides the personal energy.

As a result, the informal organization is not defined in the organization chart but develops, both by design and spontaneously, as the organization performs. It gives life and vitality to the formal organization. It facilitates the development of mutual trust and personal understanding. It helps to *personalize* the organization and to ensure that persons are socially compatible.

Informal communications may occur at any time. For example, individuals in a manufacturing organization may share a common interest in bowling with those in engineering. Periodic meetings outside of the work place might lead to a good deal of work-related coordination activities as well.

3. Establish purpose, goals, and objectives

This is the job of the entire management team. Essentially, it involves delegation of responsibility to the various subunits of the organization for accomplishing the overall purposes of the organization. The overall purposes (ends) of the organization are redefined in terms of the subpurposes (means) that are applicable for each of the subunits. Each lower subunit purpose becomes the means to higher subunit purpose which is its end.

Organizational Survival and Control Systems

The conditions for organizational survival are as follows: the organization must provide inducements that are sufficient to attract the essential contributions from stakeholders, such as capital from investors, labor from employees, material resources from suppliers, and product purchases from customers. Inducements are effective if they are preferred by the stakeholder to inducements offered for comparable participation in competing organizations. Moreover, the *internal production processes* of the organization must be efficient enough to convert the contributions of these stakeholders into sufficient inducements to sustain stakeholder participation and cooperation and to achieve the purpose of the organization.

Survival requires that management process and act upon information in all stakeholder markets at least as efficiently as these outside markets do as it pursues organizational purpose. The well-run organization would have managerial controls that monitor the inducement–contribution balance for each stakeholder and decision processes that permit timely response to competitively induced changes threatening stakeholder participation. One structural manifestation of the need for the control of stakeholder relationships is the traditional functional organization, which assigns departmental status to the concerns of each strategic stakeholder such as the marketing department for customers, the personnel department for employees, the purchasing department for suppliers, and the treasury department for investors.

People in organizations must constantly adapt and change because organizations operate in dynamically changing markets. Competitive advantage is always threatened by competition. To maintain advantage and survive in a dynamic environment, control systems must facilitate *innovation, adaptation,* and *change.* Changes in these markets, such as rapid innovation by competitors in customer markets, rapid innovation in information systems impacting supplier and distributor relationships, and changes in global competition, have intensified the need for effective and adaptive control systems.

The real bottom line of the firm is to be able to convert the contributions of the principal stakeholders into potential inducements efficiently enough to meet present stakeholder requirements and also to provide sufficient resources to continue the *innovation process* so that the competitive challenges of the future will be met.

Our job as control systems designers is to design management systems that assist management in carrying out their functions so as to achieve the purpose of the organization. We turn now to a description of a framework for the design of two sets of five mutually supportive management systems, which in total comprise the overall approach to the design of adaptive management control systems. This framework provides the basic structure upon which the entire textbook is based.

Assumptions about Human Behavior

Control systems are designed to favorably influence human behavior as organizations pursue their goals and objectives. Therefore, it is not only necessary for designers to understand how organizations function but it is also necessary to understand something about human behavior. The work of the control systems designer must proceed based upon certain assumptions about the behavior of human beings. In this text, we shall make five assumptions about human drives.[6] They are

1. Basic rationality.   Human beings are basically rational and as such are able to reason, make plans, and control behavior.
2. Creativity.   A basic human instinct is the desire to be creative.
3. Mastery.   Humans desire to manage; therefore, the desire to be "in control" is innate.
4. Morality.   Human beings have strong moral instincts, although these instincts may not always dominate behavior.
5. Community.   Human beings have strong needs and desires for human associations.

These fundamental assumptions about human drives have a profound effect upon the philosophy that we employ in the design of control systems.

ADAPTIVE CONTROL SYSTEMS: TWO SETS
OF MUTUALLY SUPPORTIVE SYSTEMS[7]

A control system is a set of *formal* and *informal* systems that are designed to assist management in *steering* the organization toward the achievement of its purpose by *bringing unity out of the diverse efforts of subunits and of individuals*. These two sets of systems are distinct but highly interrelated, and sometimes indistinguishable, subdivisions of control systems. They are considered *adaptive* if the two systems are *internally consistent, consistent with one another*, and designed to *permit learning* that is effective in continuously meeting the competitive challenges in the environment.

Control systems come in many shapes and forms, and no two systems are exactly alike. Moreover, organizations differ as to the extent to which their systems are formal and informal. Yet it is possible to describe the general elements of comprehensive and effective control systems.

Throughout this text, we take the perspective of the control systems designer, who in practice might be a systems analyst, a controller, or a manager. These are normally the people who are most concerned with the design and operation of the management control system. You should understand that when we refer to the control system designer, we are referring to the persons who have the responsibility for the design and operation of the control system and that these persons may have different positions and titles in different organizations, but regardless of the organization, these are the people who are most concerned with the technical and behavioral issues involved in the design of these systems.

We also recognize in this text the strong relationship between the effectiveness of control systems and the leadership characteristics of the management of the organization. Control systems function in the midst of the dynamics of organizations, and these dynamics must be taken into account in the design of control systems.

Finally, in thinking about the work of control systems, we must be mindful that actions taken in an MCS influence people, and that control in organizations is accomplished by people through people.

THE FORMAL SYSTEMS

Formal systems make possible the delegation of authority in that formal systems make explicit the structure, policies, and procedures to be followed by members of the organization. Formal documentation of these structures, policies, and procedures assist members of the organization in performing their duties. Exhibit 1-1 contains an overview of a generic set of five mutually supportive management subsystems and is useful for describing the formal aspects of management control systems. This system of structures, procedures, and patterned responses assists management in planning and maintaining strategies to meet organizational goals in rather predictable environments. We refer to this model as the mutually supportive management systems model (MSSM).

Exhibit 1-1
Formal Control Systems

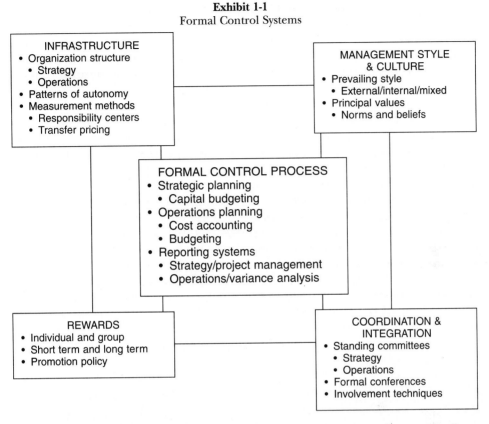

It is possible, at least in principle, to differentiate between what a control system "is" from what a control system "does." The formal structure of a control system is shown in Exhibit 1-1. The structure is the relatively permanent part of a control system. It consists of the following subsystems:

- Management style and culture of the organization
- Infrastructure
- Rewards
- Coordination and integration
- Control process

Each one of these subsystems is further subdivided into its components. Many of the important components of the formal control system are displayed in Exhibit 1-1.

The formal subsystems represented in Exhibit 1-1 are designed to focus upon the needs of customers and markets, to be consistent with the informal systems of the organization, and to be mutually supportive to each other. Moreover, each subsystem should contain explicit provision for managing both short-term concerns and the innovations necessary to remain viable in the long run.

THE INFORMAL SYSTEMS

All organizations have informal dimensions. These informal dimensions consist of interpersonal relationships that are not shown on the formal organization chart. Barnard[8] defines the informal organization as "the aggregate of personal contacts and interactions and the associated groupings of people."

A companion set of systems to the formal are the informal systems. The presentation of these systems as a complement to the formal systems was first proposed by Kirby and developed extensively by Maciariello and Kirby (1990). Informal systems complement the formal systems in a manner similar to the way the informal organization complements the formal organization.

Informal systems require of management a mind set that differs from that required to operate formal controls. "Formality" in these systems refers to the extent to which the behavior is segregated from the ongoing activities and is made explicit. "Informality" refers to the relaxation of sharp differentiation and explicit description of behaviors. In this respect formality leads to a pattern of defined behaviors, whereas informality leads to a pattern of interacting roles.[9]

Exhibit 1-2 contains a summary of the structure of a set of mutually supportive control subsystems that comprise the informal systems. This set is symmetrical to the formal set presented in Exhibit 1-1. Therefore, for the *formal infrastructure*

Exhibit 1-2
Informal Control Systems

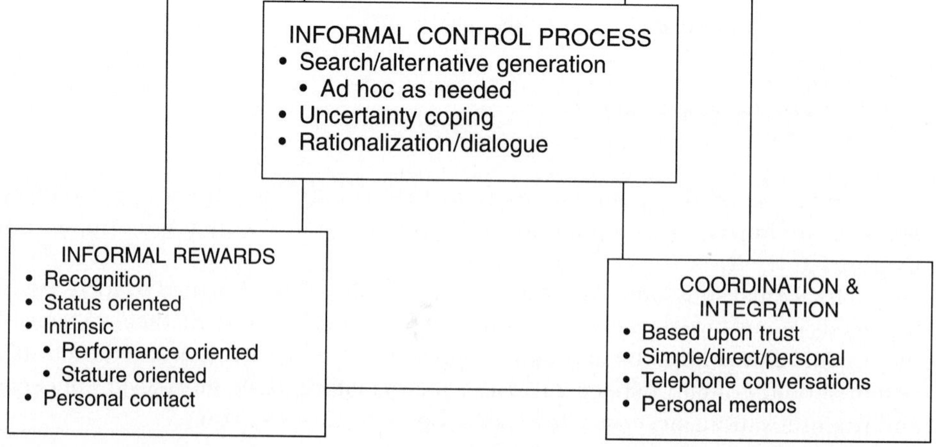

INFRASTRUCTURE
- Personal contacts
- Networks
  - Expertise oriented
  - Minimal structure
- Emergent roles

MANAGEMENT STYLE & CULTURE
- Prevailing style
  - External/internal/mixed
- Principal values
  - Norms and beliefs

INFORMAL CONTROL PROCESS
- Search/alternative generation
  - Ad hoc as needed
- Uncertainty coping
- Rationalization/dialogue

INFORMAL REWARDS
- Recognition
- Status oriented
- Intrinsic
  - Performance oriented
  - Stature oriented
- Personal contact

COORDINATION & INTEGRATION
- Based upon trust
- Simple/direct/personal
- Telephone conversations
- Personal memos

the informal counterpart is *emergent roles.* Emergent roles are the informal relationships and responsibilities that emerge based upon expertise, experience, and trust. Emergent roles are those that build cooperative norms through the development of informal contacts. These informal contacts promote personnel compatibility and encourage the "willingness to serve" organizational purposes.

The remaining three outer boxes are *recognition and rewards, informal coordinating mechanisms,* and *style and culture.* Recognition and rewards consist of personal feedback based upon performance. Informal coordinating mechanisms are cooperative networks of relationships that emerge as a result of socialization and mutual adjustment. Style and culture consist of the prevailing style of management and the principal values of the organization.

The informal control process consists of activities engaged in by members of the organization outside of the formal control process when encountering non-routine decision making such as realignment of goals or when seeking new information to increase their understanding of problem areas.

These informal systems supplement the formal systems by increasing the organization's ability to make adaptive responses. Informal controls usually develop as complex patterns of interpersonal activities or temporary structures controlled by the prevailing culture which support the management in adapting and maintaining the organization. Exhibit 1-2 identifies each of the five subsystems; again each subsystem should be mutually supportive and reinforcing.

In the presence of greater unpredictability, management should increase the use of informal controls and attempt to reduce reliance upon formal management controls.[10] More specifically, current environmental change, expanded competition, and the need for associated technical innovation have all increased the uncertainties to which today's organizations must adapt. Management gains the necessary flexibility by "backing away" from formal controls in order to explore alternative actions. In this way management shortens communication channels and depends upon expectations and key values of the organization to guide their behavior. Even during turbulent times, however, management must rely upon certain formal systems, such as clear charters, to prevent instability within subunits.

Exhibit 1-3 presents the activities and actions taken within the formal control system. These actions may be observed directly as the organization performs its tasks within the context of control systems. Formal actions include chartering activities, indoctrination in values, establishing and clarifying procedures, providing formal feedback, giving merit increases, and establishing lines of organizational communications among organizational subunits.

Exhibit 1-4 presents the activities and actions taken within the informal control system. These actions may also be observed directly as the organization performs its tasks. Informal actions include assuming responsibilities in addition to formal ones, searching for and gathering information, showing appreciation, and members checking with others in another organizational unit.

Most of the actions in an organization over a period of time consist of the repetitive steps and decisions that the organization must take to establish goals and objectives and to achieve them. These steps include:

Exhibit 1-3
Control Systems Actions Table

FORMAL ACTIONS BASED PRIMARILY UPON ASSUMPTIONS OF FORMAL AUTHORITY	
The Formal System	**If Actions Refer To**
Infrastructure	Chartering or appointing
	Establishing management support
	Setting a direction or mission
Style and Culture	Training in values, beliefs, or social dynamics
Planning and Control Process	Establishing procedures
	Clarifying procedures
	Documenting procedures
	Developing measurement metrics
	Reporting/providing feedback
Reward System	Giving a merit increase
Coordinating Mechanisms	Establishing communications among organizational units

- Establishing goals and objectives
- Evaluating performance
- Making decisions to keep the organization on track
- Implementing these decisions through people
- Obtaining feedback on the results of these decisions

The effectiveness of these decisions depends both on the support decision makers receive from the control system and upon the quality of the decision makers themselves.

Exhibit 1-4
Control Systems Actions Table

INFORMAL ACTIONS BASED PRIMARILY UPON ASSUMPTIONS OF PERCEIVED NEED BY THE INDIVIDUAL	
The Inormal System	**If Actions Refer To**
Emergent Roles	Becoming the expert
	Assuming new responsibilities
Style and Culture	Training in values, beliefs, or social dynamics
Active Planning	Searching and gathering information
and	Investigating and brainstorming
Control Process	exploring possibilities and potential solutions
	Discussing developments regarding problems, projects, & goals
Reward System	Showing appreciation
	Giving thanks
	Recognizing accomplishment
Coordinating Mechanisms	Members checking with others in other units

We turn now to describe the subsystems and components of both formal and informal control systems. We start with style and culture, because these are common to both formal and informal systems.

The Subsystems and Components of Control Systems

Style and Culture

Formal and informal control approaches must deal with style and culture. Control systems should support the prevailing method of "doing things" in an organization as well as the style of top management. A planning and control system must be blended into the way an organization and its management choose to do its work. It's one thing to know what kind of system is needed to improve the steering and coordination functions of the organization, but it is another thing to know how to implement the new system. The latter is usually the more difficult task because it requires changes in the way people make decisions and this occurs slowly.

Managerial styles may be summarized on a continuum between highly directive or autocratic styles (external styles) and highly participative (internal styles). Style influences the design of management systems in that these systems serve management and should fit the way management chooses to operate.

Well-developed and strong control systems tend to evolve over long periods of time and fit the prevailing culture of the organization. Since these systems are at the heart of the way things are done in an organization, they cannot be installed quickly because of the many changes in behavior required by a new set of systems. If a system requires behaviors that are counter to the culture of the organization, the system is likely to be by-passed in decision making.

What Is Corporate Culture?

Corporate culture consists of shared values, common perceptions, and common decision premises applied by organizational participants to the activities and problems of the organization. Most organizations tend to develop shared value systems and common decision premises and therefore can be said to have a corporate culture. The strength of a culture depends upon the number of key premises that are shared, how extensively they are shared, and how deep the commitment is to them.

Corporate Culture as a Coordination and Control Mechanism

The simplest and most effective form of coordination occurs when individual members of an organization share common values and beliefs. Common beliefs and values about the activities and problems of a business greatly facilitate control by:

- Internalizing in individuals key decision premises and directions
- Developing a sense of group loyalty
- Reducing dissonance and friction

A strong sense of shared values facilitates the control process. As a matter of fact, "self-control" through acceptance of common values is the most effective kind of control system that could possibly exist *so long as the values are the right values for the environment facing the organization at the time.*

Effectiveness of Corporate Culture as a Control Mechanism

To be effective as a coordinating mechanism, a corporate culture must be consistent with the requirements of the environment, and it must be widely accepted. Each functional group has its own perspective and consists of participants with similar backgrounds and training who in turn differ from participants in other functional groups. Steps must be taken by executives to reduce functional fixation, the potential insularity and subcultures of the various groups of the organization, and instill an organizational identity. It is also crucial for executives to develop a sense of trust among the various members of the organization. Trust reduces the transaction costs associated with coordination activities.

Example: Matching Corporate Culture and Management Systems to the Environment

For control systems to work effectively, they must be designed to be consistent with the way management chooses to operate and with the environment in which the organization functions. If the corporate culture is out of sync with the environment, the organization will not perform effectively. We turn to an example of the impact of corporate culture upon the effectiveness of an organization.

> The rapid decline in the Department of Defense budget [1993] has triggered various responses from the Aerospace Industry as companies recognize that overcapacity threatens competitiveness. Historically, these companies have had great difficulty adapting to the commercial business environment even though these companies possess exceptional technical resources.
>
> The difficulty of adaptation is caused by the culture these organizations have had to adopt to be successful in the defense business. The Department of Defense values deliberate if not slow development of product, being very risk adverse. In contrast commercial product development must be rushed to beat the competition. The DOD culture values the development of detailed specifications and documentation and wants to monitor the step by step development and production of a product. Commercial customers, on the other hand, want to be satisfied with the end product and they do not care about the internal procedures used by the firm. Each set of values is appropriate for the market served, but the values in play influence the type of management system employed in each market and one set of values and management systems is not appropriate for the other market. Therefore, for an Aerospace firm to convert to commercial business, it must adapt a new set of values and a corresponding new set of management systems.

Management Indoctrination and Skill Training

Formal indoctrination and training programs result from the need to impart a set of attitudes and skills to assist personnel in carrying out the control process of the organization. Indoctrination is the process used by the organization to socialize members to the values, policies, and procedures of the organization. Skill development involves imparting knowledge of methods used to perform various tasks required in the organization. The combination of indoctrination and skill development is crucial to the effective functioning of the control process.

We turn now to a description of the remaining subsystems and components of the formal control systems.

Formal Control Process

We subdivide our discussion of the formal control process into its planning and reporting dimensions. Then we consider an integration of the two interrelated processes.

Formal Planning Process

Two distinct but interrelated formal processes are represented in the middle box of Exhibit 1-1; one for strategic planning and one for operations planning. There are two budgets: one for operations and one for strategy. There are two sets of reports: one for strategic projects and one for operating activities. The formal planning and control processes in turn should support style and culture and be supported by infrastructure, rewards, and communication systems. Each of these subsystems should in turn be designed to focus both upon strategic and operational issues so as to balance long-term and short-term objectives.

A strategic planning system is necessary to assist in the planning and control of strategic thrusts or projects of an organization. It is the formal framework within which an organization decides upon its goals and objectives, key strategies, and capital allocations. These plans in turn guide the organization for the next five to ten years.

An operations planning system is necessary for the coordination of organizational activities in pursuit of the nearest term objectives. The cornerstone of the operations planning system is the budgeting process within which all the activities of the organization are planned for the upcoming year. Estimates to support the budgeting process are provided by all the functions of the organization.

The cost accounting system of the organization is used to provide crucial measurement information for both the operational and strategic planning processes of the organization.

Formal Reporting Process

Detailed reports are prepared to assess progress against both the strategic plans and the operational plans of the organization. Monthly, quarterly, and year-to-date comparisons are made and detailed operating variances are calculated to assess progress toward achieving operating plans. Reporting against strategic plans occurs by treating each strategic thrust and accompanying action programs as projects that are monitored over time.

Integrated Planning and Reporting Processes

Although two distinct planning and reporting processes exist, it is highly desirable that a fair amount of integration exist between these two processes. A number of natural interrelationships exist. First, most strategic programs are funded out of current operations. Second, most strategic plans and programs grow out of current activities. Third, strategic plans and programs eventually impact current operations and must be carefully monitored for their impact upon current operations.

Infrastructure

The infrastructure of formal control systems consists of the organization structure and patterns of autonomy. Patterns of autonomy in turn include designations of responsibility and accompanying measurement methods.

The corporate structure needs to embody provision for both the strategic and operational mode of operations. Two modes of operation are necessary within the same organization. One of the most common methods of placing responsibility for strategic business planning is to create strategic business units (SBU's) at various levels of the organization. An SBU is defined for those parts of a business that can relate to an established outside market, including competitors. Goals, strategies, and action programs are established at the SBU level.

Profit centers are then established at various levels at and below the SBU level of the organization where appropriate. Each of the profit centers acts like a small business organization with profit responsibility. Profit centers do much to develop a spirit of customer responsiveness, entrepreneurial management, and adaptation.

One of the key issues in the design of organization structure is where [that is, at what level(s)] to place formal responsibility for strategic planning. Even though all managers of an organization should participate in strategic planning, it is necessary to fix responsibility, and this is done in various ways and at various levels in organizations.

Rewards

It is essential for the executive to induce individuals to participate if there is to be a formal organization. The effectiveness of a given incentive is a function of the broader environment and the tailoring of the incentive to individual needs. The organization cannot pay out in inducements more than what it receives from its value-creating activity, so it must match incentives to the value contributions of individuals in the organization.

Incentives take the form of both materialistic and nonmaterialistic inducements and include all forms of monetary compensation, together with nonmonetary forms, such as organizational purpose, desirable associations, acceptance, status, increased autonomy, pride of workmanship, and desirable physical conditions.

The scheme of incentives is not stable over time. Barnard states regarding the stability of incentives: ". . . the scheme of incentives is probably the most unstable of the elements of the cooperative system, since invariably external conditions affect the possibilities of material incentives; and human motives are likewise highly variable." (pp. 158–159). The most stable of the incentives includes ideals of the organization that individuals identify with and find worthwhile.

Inculcation of motives involves the culture of the organization, which is in turn influenced by precept and example. The value of the reward to the recipient is important to consider. Personalized rewards tend to mean more to individuals receiving them. Management should seek to provide various rewards based upon the situation.

The difficulty of providing adequate incentives over time leads to pressure for growth. Expansion provides added wealth, which can be used to provide additional incentives to individuals over time, thus alleviating the pressure on existing resources.

Individual Rewards

The reward systems of an organization should emphasize both individual and group performance as well as operating and strategic performance. Formal reward programs are necessary to reward performance on all four dimensions.

Formal individual rewards, including compensation, should reflect individual contributions to performance regarding short-term objectives and long-term goals. Organizations compete with each other for the services of people, so rewards should be at market rates.

Group Rewards

Some of the most effective group awards are those tied to overall organizational performance. These group awards are often granted based upon short-term performance as well as long-term performance. Vesting of stock options, for instance, is made conditional upon the company's meeting a specified earnings per share target each year for a number of years hence.

Coordination and Integration Mechanisms

Specific management communication vehicles within the organization are necessary for coordination, for resource allocation decision making, for conflict resolution, for building identification with organizational purpose, and for developing commitment and trust within the organization.

The formal coordinating mechanisms vary in degree of formality. They are designed to provide lateral linkages throughout the organization. As such, they play a major role in bringing unity to the diverse efforts of the organization. Formal coordinating mechanisms are usually liaison groups explicitly chartered to increase decision-making capability across subunits of the organization.

All coordinating mechanisms are highly dependent upon timely and accurate information flows. In this age of decentralization and globalization, these communication mechanisms require sophisticated information and telecommunication systems. Effective information and telecommunication systems are therefore key strategic assets for assisting coordination activities.

Committees

Two management committees with overlapping membership are helpful for resource allocation decision making: one for operations and the other for strategy. The committees do many things, but one of their primary roles is to manage conflict in resource allocation—conflict resulting from short-run versus long-run tensions and conflicts resulting from intraperiod resource allocations.

Strategy Committee

This committee should consist of the top officers and managers of the organization as well as a number of top-level staff people. The agenda for their meetings should consist of a rigorous review of ongoing and new goals, strategies, and SBU plans and action programs. The extent of the reviews and the detail to which they are carried depend upon the degree of decentralization present in the organization and the uncertainty that is present in the marketplace. Specifically, the agenda might consist of a determination of the appropriateness of various corporate or business goals in light of current information, progress in the strategic development of a goal, actions to be taken at the corporate level to speed up or modify a given goal, consideration of new goals, and progress reviews of key action programs.

The Operating Management Committee

This committee should have nearly the same composition as the strategy committee. It treats operational issues and the allocation of resources between the operating and strategic mode.

Formal Conferences

Formal meetings of the key managers of the organization including those at the profit center level are held periodically. The purpose is to formalize the results of the planning process, to enhance communication so as to help keep the corporation knit together, and to have each manager make a public commitment of what is proposed for the next year.

We turn now to a detailed explanation of the informal subsystems.

Informal Organization Structure and Emergent Roles

All organizations have informal dimensions that are not shown on the organizational chart. The informal dimensions of structures or the *soft structure*, are difficult to define, yet all organizations have them. Informal organizations come about as a result of interactions among people. These interactions include person-to-person contacts, networks, ad hoc teams, and available expert resources.

The informal structure and emergent roles come into play especially when management perceives a need to increase the adaptability of the organization. Temporary subsets of individuals may form for the purpose of coping with uncertainty. The purpose of these subsets is to develop new goals and objectives, remove barriers to goal attainment, attain organizational purpose, and increase adaptability.

For example, the management of an organization that begins missing shipments and incurring large cost overruns will most likely search for appropriate actions. Management will utilize informal structures to accelerate improvement. They might establish an action team, hold "off-line" discussions, off-site strategy sessions, one-on-one discussions, and so on. They will strive to gather information, quantify risks, assess constraints, and finally, establish new recovery plans and goals.

Informal Control Processes

Management decisions are based upon experience, intuition, and feeling. Successful decision making involves sensing the whole and the impact of the decision upon the whole.

Management facilitates decision making in various ways. Insights into the decision-making process used to adapt and steer the organization can be gained by utilizing the cybernetic perspective. An adaptive cybernetic system is structured to: (1) exact information from the environment, (2) form and adopt goals, (3) select and emit goal-directed behavior, and (4) learn to adapt.[11]

Limitations exist, however, upon the conditions in which this goal-directed behavior is effective. The cybernetic paradigm lacks steerability in those instances in which environmental disturbance is significant enough to require the rapid development of new goals; so rapid that decisions and feedback information cannot be acquired fast enough to determine whether control is being attained. When managers make decisions during environmental disturbances, they tend to use more informal decision-making frameworks. In these situations, key values and informal planning processes take over as members search for meaning to the current situation in order to determine future directions. These processes involve data gathering, contacting experts, recalling past experiences, and in general seeking to increase understanding.

Even under these conditions part or all of the cybernetic process is followed in the informal system. Management does not usually consider completely new business behaviors; past experiences are applicable, and pure prediction is not required. Also, various skills are still valuable, key success factors are known, and similar business situations can most likely be examined. But these situations can require a complex array of data. Structured techniques of analysis may also be used.

The added flexibility afforded to the manager when the informal control system is used allows for the temporary selection of a tailored set of skills, knowledge, and experience in order to provide the resources needed to maximize decision-making rationality. In this way, management can aggressively search for new insights and information, gather data from various sources, and test new ideas.

From an adaptive control perspective, dominant values and expectations control this process, in much the way that goals and objectives direct behavior under stable conditions. Under conditions of uncertainty, management tends to (1) accelerate information gathering, (2) search for alternative goals, purposes, or strategies, (3) compare their selection to values, beliefs, and expectations, and (4) adapt to new conditions. If the overall purpose of the organization is actually being challenged during periods of change, then more deeply seated values, beliefs, and expectations will likely come into effect and the behavior selection process can be very disruptive indeed.

As an example, as the mainframe computer business diminishes in importance [1993] and as the personal computer business has become much more competitive, IBM has been forced to change the way it conceives of its business and its values. In particular, it has been forced to think of itself more as a software and service company than a hardware company, and it has been forced into nonvoluntary reductions in its work force, thus violating its commitment to job security. These changes are being accomplished by both formal and informal means.

Informal Recognition and Rewards

Formal rewards, including basic compensation, incentive compensation, and promotions, get much more management attention than informal rewards. As important as formal rewards are, however, informal rewards contribute significantly to organization success.

Informal rewards are stature oriented. These rewards are bestowed upon the key team members within the informal system. They are usually more intrinsic in nature. Individuals are shown respect for their ability to operate within the informal control system and the team itself shares in the recognition. Informal teams and networks also tend to bestow respect upon their own members.

Informal recognition and rewards are effective because of the personal involvement of the giver. They are to be contrasted with rewards that are impersonal and standardized, and those that are perceived as entitlements. Examples are schemes to recognize superior performance with highly visible, but not financial, forms of recognition.

A challenge for management is to ensure that formal rewards are also bestowed appropriately upon organization members who are recognized informally.

Informal Coordinating Mechanisms

The formal system of communication can be identified by the structure of the organization. Specific management communication vehicles within the organization are necessary for coordination, resource allocation, conflict resolution, and building identification with the organization and its goals and objectives. Informal communication systems evolve as people develop working relationships. They depend upon interpersonal relationships and, as such, are quite adaptable, growing and changing to meet the perceived needs of organizational members. Communications tend to be less guarded during informal communications, leading to discussions of more sensitive issues. They are especially helpful in supporting key values of the organization. Fostering informal communications is critical to the development and maintenance of effective adaptive controls.

The recent use of ad hoc teams to solve problems, improve productivity, and achieve organizational change reflects the growing importance of informal coordinating mechanisms. Informal teams often consist of cross-organizational groups, groups made up of members from different organizational units that focus on problems related to particular clients, products, and markets. An example is the formation of *concurrent engineering teams,* which are assembled to focus on the design products and processes. The desire is to design products in a more effective and efficient manner—to better reflect market requirements and to do so in a shorter time period.

Interaction Between Formal and Informal Systems

Control systems must support organizational activity during periods of both environmental stability and instability. Both formal and informal systems are always present. The association between the informal and formal changes with the degree of uncertainty and the strength of the organizational culture. As stability and predictability increase, the use of formal systems increases.

In times of major change the informal system may be the dominant management system. The formal system, that is, the policies and procedures which applied to the past products and customers, may actually be looked upon by management as potential barriers. Conversely, when the environment settles into more predictable patterns of activities, management tends to formalize procedures, utilize formal controls, and track progress via formal status reporting methods.

In the more stable situation the formal system should become dominant. The informal system then serves a maintenance function by securing personal relationships, adjusting to personal needs, and sharing current information.

Control activities in the organization vary in degree of formality depending upon the situation. For example, active planning can result from a chance meeting of a few members who "kick around a few ideas" about a new objective—a very informal situation. Conversely, a periodic meeting is held to search for an appropriate objective. Although informal, the periodic meeting is a more formal activity than the first meeting. Therefore, formal and informal systems actually overlap somewhat. The degree of formality is neither better or worse. The key is to use the degree of formality that appears appropriate for the situation at hand.

Management must insure that each subsystem and both sets of subsystems are mutually supportable. One improperly designed system can block desirable activities in the other system. For example, a manager with an autocratic style can block desirable informal active planning activities.

Adaptive Controls and Individual Actions

How can a systems designer identify various control system actions and related subsystems? The question is pertinent to the control systems designer who wants to observe and evaluate a control system design. Each action in the formal and informal control system can be identified by using "control action tables." Such tables were presented previously in Exhibits 1-3 and 1-4. Each action in these tables refers to an activity in one of the two control systems. By observing the actions taken in an organization and categorizing them according to the definitions in the table, the designer can determine if the control system is predominately formal or informal and then can begin to suggest an appropriate strategy for redesign if necessary. A large-scale demonstration of the successful use of these action tables in the evaluation of formal and informal control systems appears in Kirby (1992).

SUMMARY

This chapter has described the overall approach we will take to the design of control systems in this book. We have studied the domain and purpose of control systems and the organizational context within which they must operate to be effective. We then described the overall elements of a comprehensive control system for an entire organization. These two mutually supportive system models and related actions comprise the basic overall framework for the development of adaptive controls. They include provision for formal and informal communications, selecting and rewarding people, formulating purpose and objectives, allocating resources, measuring performance, and providing feedback. These systems when appropriately implemented support management in aggressively seizing market opportunities and improving current operations on one hand while concurrently maintaining optimum controls over current operations on the other. We are now in a position to study the subsystems and components in much more detail.

REFERENCES

BARNARD, CHESTER I., *The Functions of the Executive.* Cambridge, Mass.: Harvard University Press, 1938.

DRUCKER, PETER F., *Management* (abridged and revised version of *Management: Tasks, Responsibilities, Practices*). London: Pan Books Ltd, 1979.

GRIESINGER, DONALD W., *Innovation for Stakeholder Advantage: A Stakeholder Approach.* Graduate Management Center, GMC 8401, Claremont Graduate School, Claremont, California, 1984.

GRIESINGER, DONALD W,. "Toward a Cybernetic Theory of the Firm," draft, the Peter F. Drucker Management Center, The Claremont Graduate School, Claremont, Calif., 1992.

KIRBY, CALVIN J., *Performance Improvement Teams: A Study from the Adaptive Controls Perspective*, Ph.D. dissertation, Claremont Graduate School, Claremont, Calif., 1992.

MACIARIELLO, JOSEPH A., and CALVIN J. KIRBY, "Adaptive Control Systems," Draft Paper, Claremont Graduate School, 1990.

MINTZBERG, Henry, *The Structuring of Organizations.* Englewood Cliffs, N.J.: Prentice Hall, 1979.

SALTER, MALCOLM S., AND WOLF A. WEINHOLD, *Value Creation and General Management*, Case No. 9-384-080, Harvard Business School, Cambridge, Mass., 1983.

SATHE, VIJAY, *Culture and Related Corporate Realities.* Homewood, Ill.: Irwin, 1985.

TUSHMAN, MICHAEL L., and DAVID A. NADLER, "Information Processing as an Integrative Concept in Organizational Design," *Academy of Management Review,* Vol. 3., 1978.

WATSON, THOMAS J., *A Business and Its Beliefs.* New York: McGraw-Hill, 1963.

WOLF, WILLIAM B., *The Basic Barnard: An Introduction to Chester I. Barnard and His Theories of Organization and Management.* Ithaca: New York State School of Industrial and Labor Relations, Cornell University, ILR Paperback 14, 1974.

NOTES

1. Their description of the domain of management control is found in Chapter 1, pages 3–23 of their book *Management Control Systems,* 7th ed. (Homewood, Ill.: Richard D. Irwin, 1992).

2. See William H. Newman, *Constructive Control: Design and Use of Control Systems* (Englewood Cliffs, N.J.: Prentice Hall, 1975).

3. See Stafford Beer, *Cybernetics and Management* (New York: John Wiley & Sons, 1959) and *Decision and Control* (New York: John Wiley & Sons, 1966). These two books are quite abstract for the practicing manager, but they do provide deep insight into the relevant domain for control systems. One of us has worked out this view of control in great detail in Joseph Maciariello, *Management Control Systems* (Englewood Cliffs, N.J.: Prentice Hall, 1984).

4. Daniel Katz and Robert L. Kahn, *The Social Psychology of Organizations,* 2nd ed. (New York: John Wiley & Sons, Inc., 1978). See especially Chapter 2, "Organizations and the Systems Concept," pp. 17–34.

5. Donald W. Griesinger, "Toward A Cybernetic Theory of the Firm," draft paper, Peter F. Drucker Graduate Management Center, The Claremont Graduate School, Claremont, Calif., 1992.

6. Used by permission of Good News Publishers/Crossway Books, 1300 Crescent St., Wheaton, Illinois 60187.

7. The basic five-part chart used for the two mutually supportive systems models is developed and generalized based upon the systems in place at Texas Instruments as described in Harvard Business School Case 9-172-054, May 1982 Revision; P. Lorange and R. F. Vancil, *Teachers Manual, Strategic Planning Systems* (Englewood Cliffs, N.J.: Prentice Hall, 1977), pp. 68–80; an address by E. W. Helms, Manager, Corporate Engineering Center, Texas Instruments, given at The Instituto Panamericano de Alta Direccion de Empresa, Mexico, entitled "Texas Instruments: Objectives, Strategies and Tactics Systems," May 1980; and *Management Philosophies and Practices of Texas Instruments Inc.,* presentations by P. E. Haggerty, Texas Instruments Inc., Dallas, Texas, 1965. The five-part chart is adapted by permission of Prentice Hall.

8. Chester I. Barnard, *The Functions of the Executive* (Cambridge, Mass.: Harvard University Press, 1938), p. 115.

9. Vijay Sathe, *Culture and Related Realities* (Homewood, Ill.: Richard D. Irwin, Inc., 1985), pp. 227–229.

10. Henry Mintzberg, *The Structuring of Organizations* (Englewood Cliffs, N. J.: Prentice Hall, 1979), p. 270.

11. Donald W. Griesinger, "Management Theory: A Cybernetic Perspective," GMC 8601 working paper, January 1986.

Case 1-1 Logistics Systems Limited

We bought Logistics Systems five years ago. We underestimated the future challenges they would face in the global airline industry. We also underestimated the depth of their culture and the resultant difficulties of making the changes in their management systems that would be necessary to compete in this new environment.
Micheal Jenkins

BACKGROUND

Logistics Systems Limited (LSL) is a commercial electronics company located within the European Economic Community (EEC). The company was founded in 1968 by a team of technical personnel for the purpose of supplying logistics and training systems to the airline industry. The early success of the company derived from several patents which protected certain of their key products. Their products included computer-aided inventory controls, training devices for pilots and other airline personnel, and spare parts for aircrafts.

From 1970 to 1988 the global airline industry was in a growth phase, and as a result LSL experienced little pressure. In addition, the company did not have a strong desire to innovate or to grow. The combination of success and limited growth aspirations resulted in a fairly relaxed environment for the company's managers and employees.

In 1989, however, the company was purchased by an aggressive electronics firm whose management believed that LSL should innovate, grow, and improve its return on assets employed in the business. The management proceeded to develop investment and growth plans. After three years of modest growth and substantial investment in buildings, plant, and equipment, the structure of the airline industry changed dramatically.

The airline industry was forced into cost-cutting moves by the advent of deregulation, the recession, and the outbreak of the war in Iraq. The end of patent protection allowed competitors to close the functional gap between their products and those of LSL and to compete with LSL on the basis of cost, quality, and service.

Both the size of the market served by LSL and their share of the market declined. The company began to lose money, and the CEO initiated a massive recovery plan, which in turn was followed by the development of a second and third plan. About half of the management team was unable to improve performance even though they held planning meetings, issued instructions for change, and discharged "nonperformers." The remainder of

---

This case is an integrating case for all issues discussed in this book pertaining to the framework used to design adaptive control systems. We shall refer back to it in this textbook. LSL is not a unique situation but is typical of many technologically oriented companies that face increased competition from globalization and improved operational efficiencies brought about by TQM and related tools.

the management staff were able to initiate some improvements, but they underestimated the depth and the length of the downturn in the airline industry, thinking it would be like other periodic downturns in the past.

Exhibit 1-5 presents the organization chart for LSL. Total number of employees at the time of the case was 2640. The human resource, finance, and marketing managers were located in the main corporate office building. The engineering organization along with two of the business units were located near the corporate office building. The third business unit was located in another building three kilometers away. Manufacturing was also performed in two other buildings about ten kilometers away from corporate headquarters. Exhibit 1-6 presents eight years of data on revenue and profit and loss.

patched a specialist in management systems, Micheal Jenkins, to review the entire operation. Jenkins was charged with responsibility to review:

1. Management structures and processes at LSL
2. Business and operating systems
3. Personnel competency and attitude
4. Status of both operating and performance improvement objectives.

The review was completed in three weeks' time, and Jenkins presented his findings in a report. He was now considering his recommendations to top management. His report is summarized below.

REPORT ON AN AUDIT OF LSL's MANAGEMENT SYSTEMS

ANALYSIS OF LSL MANAGEMENT SYSTEMS

MANAGEMENT SYSTEMS

As the company continued to experience reductions in profit, the parent company dispatched ment systems presently in place at LSL.

Exhibits 1-7 and 1-8 represent the management systems presently in place at LSL.

Exhibit 1-5
LSL Organization Chart

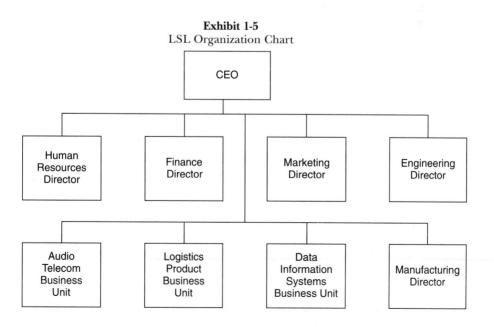

Exhibit 1-6
LSL Revenue and Profits

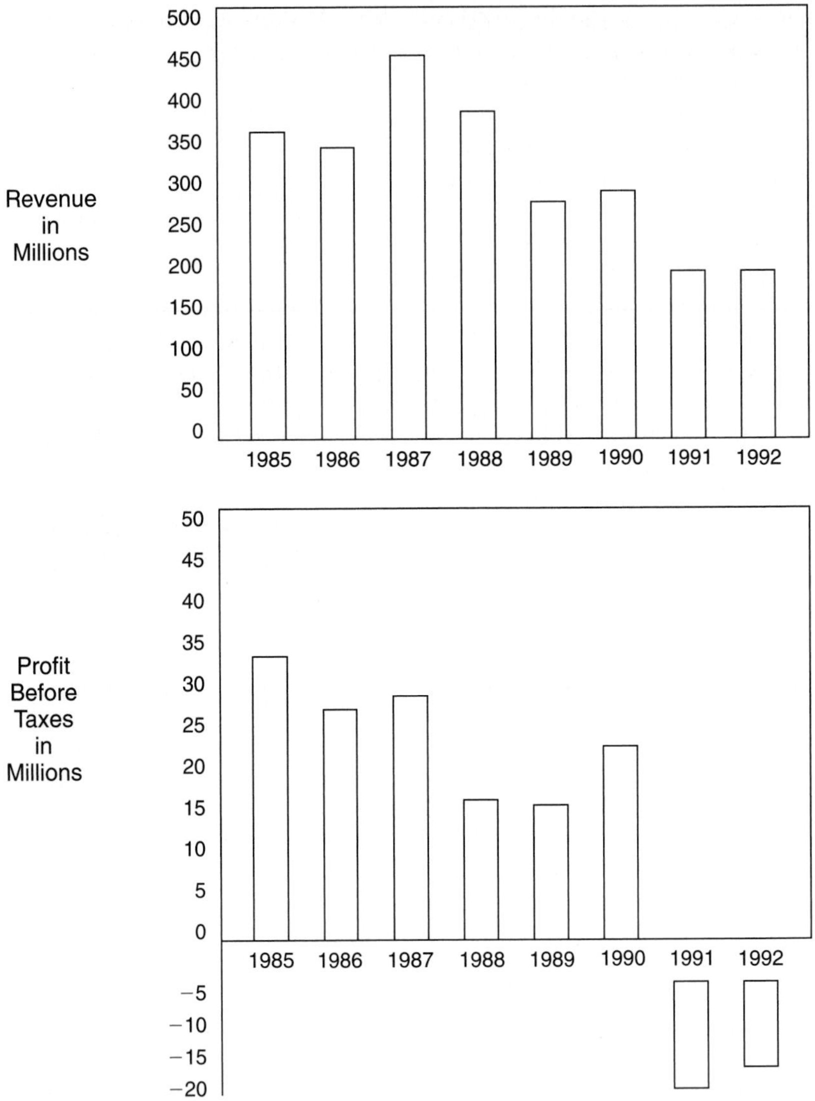

Revenue
in
Millions

Profit
Before
Taxes
in
Millions

Each subsystem is described in turn. I shall begin first with style and culture, and then I will describe the formal and informal subsystems.

Style and Culture

The style and culture at LSL is typified by a lack of trust. Managers believe that they have to protect themselves by complaining to their superiors about the problems of their peers. They are quick to cast blame on others. Conversely, employees are reluctant to complain about their superiors because they fear retaliation. As a consequence of this "climate," employees are reluctant to take actions or to implement change. Instead they engage in endless discussions and intellectual debate about issues. Employees also resist the assignment of accountability and take every opportunity to exploit "loopholes" in formal reporting procedures.

Managers are quite bureaucratic. They do not attempt to skip levels in the organization to accelerate individual actions. The style of first-line supervision is authoritative.

Supervisors refrain from involving workers in decision processes.

There is no systematic training in management skills or in worker techniques. The primary method of training and indoctrination at all levels is "on the job" training.

Formal Subsystems

Infrastructure

The infrastructure is characterized by a high degree of vertical integration and by powerful directors of engineering and manufacturing. Directors of strategic business units (SBU's) are less powerful, but all directors run their own organization in an insular manner.

Exhibit 1-7
Formal Control Systems
Logistics Systems Limited

INFRASTRUCTURE	MANAGEMENT STYLE & CULTURE
• Strong vertical integration • Powerful directors • Weak program management • Strong unions	• Authoritative • Status conscious • Technical dominance • Values intellectual debate • Lack of trust • Knows better than the customer

FORMAL CONTROL PROCESS
• No formal planning method
• Minimal formal reporting
• Data scrubbed
• No audits
• Old systems

REWARDS	COORDINATION & INTEGRATION
• Little pay for performance • Many confusing overtime rates • Controlled by human resources	• Weekly directors meetings • Communications considered job of human resources • Committees not supported by management

Some employees at LSL are unionized. Management does not communicate with employees other than for purposes of direction. No cross-functional teams exist.

Planning and Control Process

The formal planning and control process is actually designed to reduce accountability. Management routinely "cleanses" reports of any embarrassing data. No financial planning is performed; instead budgets are prepared in terms of "hours to do a job." No independent auditing of activities is performed.

Rewards

The formal reward system is not based upon performance. Instead, everyone receives the same percentage increase "so no one will complain." Also, a very generous but complex set of rules exists for the payment of overtime.

Coordination Mechanisms

Formal meetings of directors take place weekly, at which time cooperation among directors is nil. They merely defend their own functions. Only one committee is for-

Exhibit 1-8
Informal Control Systems
Logistics Systems Limited

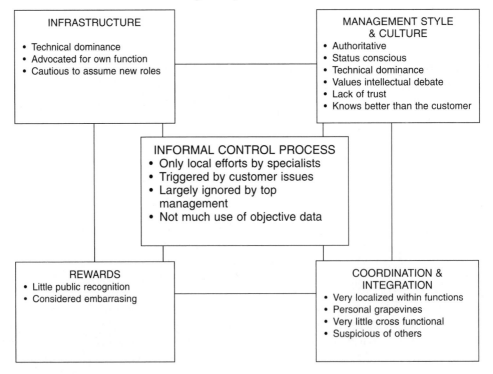

mally chartered, the systems improvement committee. The output of this committee is ignored almost completely by management. The CEO prefers to coordinate activities separately with each director but does not want to involve lower-level managers.

Management has set up a company newsletter and a one-page letter that is read at all staff meetings. All messages to employees are reviewed by the Director of Human Resources, who is formally placed in charge of all communications to employees. Management is instructed not to deviate from the "written text" in meetings with their staff.

The formal systems reflect years of stagnation due to lack of pressures to improve. Managers have built in much slack as a result of operating so autonomously, avoiding conflict, not sharing information, nor openly coordinating work. The inefficient formal systems are supported by the CEO, who wishes to operate through individual contacts rather than by team management. The subsystems have become entrenched; as a result it is difficult for any one member of the organization to bring change.

I now discuss the complementary informal subsystems. In the process, you will observe just how the informal subsystems evolved and influenced the formal subsystems. In describing both the formal and informal subsystems, I am trying to identify not only weaknesses but also strengths, believing that the strengths are the basis for suggesting improvements.

Emergent Roles

The best examples of emergent roles are found amongst the technical experts. As a group, they are very independent, dominate the management of programs, and appear arrogant to customers. In addition to the technical experts, functional managers have emerged as strong advocates for their functions.

Moreover, they do not consider purchasing components even when outside sources are known to be superior and less costly.

Informal Planning and Control

Active planning is kept to a minimum. Management, in general, does not want objective data displayed for "everyone to see." Members of the organization do not feel comfortable searching for data except in their local areas, where the information often remains.

Informal Recognition and Rewards

Managers are generally embarrassed to give or receive recognition in public. So, managers consider outstanding efforts to simply be "part of our jobs." These efforts usually take place just prior to the delivery of a major system when many problems are being uncovered, time is short, and the customer is irritated.

Informal Coordination Mechanisms

The resultant impact on informal coordination mechanisms is almost predictable. As a consequence of the lack of trust and strict adherence to "channels" of communications, all problems are passed up the chain of command to a director, communicated across functions to another director, and then down the chain to the worker on the shop floor. For example, it takes days for a product engineer on a product to learn of low manufacturing yields on that product. Cross functional, ad hoc coordination is minimal, strongly limited by the belief that each area has to protect itself from blame. Ad hoc teaming is nonexistent. Informal networks ("grapevines") are well developed but based upon individual pairings. For example, a secretary has a friend or two with whom she cautiously shares information. A like situation exists with the various managers and union workers.

As Jenkins reviewed this report, he began to ponder the recommendations he would make to corporate management regarding LSL.

QUESTIONS

Assume that Jenkins, in attempting to return LSL to competitiveness, recommended that LSL should:

1. Begin implementing a new business information system.
2. Establish a companywide process improvement team to begin improving operating processes.
3. Organize a new bidding and proposal process to improve the accuracy of new product bid proposals.
4. Train all personnel in total quality management concepts.

Discuss the impact each action will have upon organizational adaptiveness.

Case 1-2 Central Hospital

It's the fall of the year, 1992, and a relatively worrisome time for Jack Weber. Weber, 41, had been the hospital's administrator for about six months after having been assistant administrator for about five years. The fall months are traditionally slow periods of time and the tendency at Central had been to panic into thinking that business would never pick up and that the hospital would have to close down. This was the time of the year when there was a great deal of thinking about the strategic course of the hospital; many questions were typically asked but few solutions were found.

HISTORICAL AND ENVIRONMENTAL DATA

Jack Weber found himself facing a situation of increasing change and turmoil. On one hand, competition was being introduced into the hospital system, while on the other hand, regulation was still an important factor.

Hospitals faced a highly competitive environment because of the current oversupply of hospital beds. In this environment, it was no longer enough to simply "administrate" a hospital; executives had to give as much attention to the future viability of their organization as executives of other kinds of organizations. There were predictions that some twenty-five percent of U.S. hospitals would face bankruptcy in the next five to ten years. Many small and, for that matter, large hospitals have encountered severe financial difficulties in the past few years.

Central Hospital is a 120-bed acute care community hospital located in an affluent residential area of the city of Oakmont. A nonprofit institution, Central Hospital was founded in 1908. At the time of the case, the hospital had approximately $22 million in revenues and employed 400 people.

The hospital provided basic medical and surgical services and had also specialized in opthamological surgery for many years. It had the typical departments associated with medical/surgical services, a six-bed intensive care unit (ICU), coronary care unit (CCU), a laboratory, a radiological unit, a pharmacy, a respiratory therapy unit, facilities for physical, occupational, and speech therapy, and an emergency room. Although a relatively small hospital, Central Hospital had attempted to maintain an advanced technological approach to the services it did offer. It had purchased the first CT and MRI scanners in the Oakmont area, and it had been on the forefront of laser technology, employing seven lasers for diverse surgical procedures.

However, two other acute-care hospitals in the Oakmont area provided a very competitive environment—Founders Hospital, with 502 licensed beds, and Valley Community Hospital, with 165 licensed beds. All three hospitals had seen very substantial decreases in in-patient census in the previous five years; Founders Hospital had maintained the highest occupancy rate (approximately 50 percent) during the past year.

At one time, Founders and Central Hospital were equal in size and stature in the community. However, in the 1960s, Founders used the Hill–Burton funding program to expand bed capacity and programs, while Central Hospital simply treaded water. Thus, Founders Hospital was now the largest facility in Oakmont and provided many hospital services not offered by Central Hospital. There had also been an extensive shift to outpatient care in the Oakmont area. Two major clinics had been gaining substantial market share over the last five to ten years, and one was planning to build a freestanding outpatient surgical center. Moreover, a number of freestanding emergency centers had already been opened by young physicians, and these had reduced business at each hospital's emergency room. Finally, the oversupply of physicians in the community had led them to perform more procedures in their offices that would have previously been done in hospitals in order to employ their excess capacity.

HOSPITAL REIMBURSEMENT AND REGULATIONS

The hospital reimbursement situation had changed greatly over the last five years. All

payers of hospital charges had begun to control their costs by reducing the amounts of money that they paid to hospitals. Most had attempted to accomplish this by a combination of enhanced utilization review and discounts in hospital charges. The federal government had led the way by changing its reimbursement method from one based on cost to a prospective rate-setting system based upon Diagnostic Related Groups (DRG). It had also been aggressive in forcing patients to have certain surgical procedures done as outpatients rather than as inpatients. In the same manner, managed care programs, which were growing in popularity, had reduced the number of hospitalized patients.

Another major reimbursement problem was indigent care. The number of people entering hospitals without adequate financial support had been increasing, and hospitals found themselves unable to recover the costs of their care. In addition, concern over malpractice suits and ethical issues such as how long to continue life support often led to overuse of hospital resources, driving up the cost of care. And, of course, regulations in the hospital field continued to increase at a rapid rate. The amount of time and manpower devoted to meeting these numerous rules and requirements was staggering. How could hospitals respond to the many reports and forms required by regulators while at the same time attempting to reduce staff expenses?

TRENDS

An analysis of Central Hospital's inpatient census showed a substantial decrease in bed utilization over the last five fiscal years. Patient days had decreased markedly during that time due to a decrease both in the number of patients and in their average length of stay. One of the reasons for these declines was a shift to outpatient surgery. Although surgical activity at Central Hospital had increased, that increase had come from outpatient surgery, and inpatient surgery had actually decreased.

Emergency room use had declined from 1987 to 1989 as a result of competition from freestanding urgent-care centers. Although this trend had reversed in 1991, approximately 50 percent of the hospital's emergency room charges were not reimbursed.

The hospital captured a large amount of outpatient revenue in the early 1980s because of its body scanner. When four other body scanners were purchased by the two other hospitals in Oakmont in 1982, however, Central Hospital's outpatient scanner revenue decreased precipitously. Fortunately, at that time outpatient surgery had increased, enabling the hospital to maintain total outpatient revenue.

Central Hospital's balance sheets showed a good cash position, and it benefited substantially from donations, interest income, and property sales. The hospital had no long-term debts. It was, however, in the middle of an $11 million construction project that would put pressure on its cash flow. The primary concern was that its operating income had turned negative and was progressively deteriorating. Clearly, Central Hospital had to correct this problem, or it would soon be unable to operate as an acute-care hospital.

MANAGEMENT'S STYLE AND CULTURE

The centralized style and philosophy of management no longer served the institution well. They had developed over the years and had been influenced by many factors, including the conservative nature of the city of Oakmont. This philosophy was pervasive throughout the hospital and affected almost all day-to-day operations. The board of directors, chosen for their prestige and their ability to raise funds, were conservative members of the community. They did not encourage risk taking or unconventional methods of delivering health care. Change was therefore difficult to implement.

The executive vice-president had worked at Central Hospital for over twenty years. He had been its administrator for 15 years and moved on to become executive director when another administrator was hired. His influence on the culture and operations of the hospital had been formidable. He had been responsible for two large additions to the hospital and had been very successful in fund raising for capital expenditures. His conservative nature and desire for total control of the operations of the institution had reinforced the tradition of centralized decision making that had existed even before his arrival.

Fortified with a demanding character, he had maintained very strict standards of performance for all employees and had enhanced the appearance and services of the hospital despite its age. His ability to work a seven-day week had made his presence at the hospital an extraordinary one, although his preference for centralized decision making had created some problems for the administrators who were responsible for the operations of the hospital.

The hospital's administrator and executive vice-president retained tight control of decision making. Individuals at the lower levels of the organization were seldom able to influence policies. The hospital administrator at one point had attempted to introduce a more participative style of management, but little had come of the initiative because of the hospital's long tradition of autocratic management. Central Hospital had made no provisions for strategic business units in the past, although recently a freestanding retail pharmacy had been opened. Its manager had been granted a substantial amount of freedom to manage revenue and expenses.

The management of the hospital had not increased the number of beds available despite growth by many other nearby institutions. This made it easy to maintain a centralized management approach and to ensure that employees concentrated on providing the most personal service possible to patients. Although there was a 25 to 30 percent turnover in employees each year, 50 percent of the employees had been at the hospital for more than four years. The hospital had long had a policy of promoting from within whenever possible, which had also increased the loyalty of its employees.

With less than 400 employees, Central Hospital was known for the family atmosphere that existed among staff and patients. It just seemed to be pervasive throughout the organization. Most employees knew each other and called each other by their first names.

COMMUNICATION SYSTEMS

Formal managerial communication was accomplished at Central Hospital through meetings of the board of directors, the management council, department heads, and individual departments. Central Hospital had a 15-member board of directors that met quarterly. Most of the work of the board, however, was performed at the committee level and was synthesized at the full board meetings. The board's major committees were the executive, planning, and finance committees. Of these three, only the executive and finance committees met regularly. The planning committee had met frequently when a formal long-range plan was being prepared by a consulting firm. The hospital had not engaged in much strategic planning after that, so the committee had become inactive. But it had recently been revived, and the intention was to meet regularly with the idea of engaging in strategic planning on an ongoing basis. This committee consisted of four board members, the executive vice-president, three medical staff members, and the administrator. Recommendations of the planning committee were always brought to the full board for action.

Management of the hospital was in the hands of the executive vice-president, the administrator, and three assistant administrators. The hospital was organized into functional departments led mostly by technical personnel who had come up through the ranks. Few of the managerial personnel had formal management training prior to assuming their current positions. It was assumed that they would learn on the job and would also attend seminars and programs. There was no planning staff at Central Hospital.

Departmental managers had been given responsibility for their individual departments, but had little authority to manage as they saw fit. In other words, responsibility exceeded authority. Each manager prepared his or her budget every year, but budgets were usually adjusted to meet top management's wishes. Departmental managers had little authority to set their employees' salaries, increase employment, change prices, or develop new products without approaching top management first. The autonomy of assistant administrators and other managers was limited. This had caused some conflict in that assistant administrators felt they should have sufficient authority to carry out their responsibilities.

The members of the management council were the executive vice-president, the administrator, the chief financial officer, the director of nursing, the assistant administrator, and the director of personnel. Meetings were supposed to be held once a week but were frequently canceled. The purpose of the management council was to share information among the top managers of the hospital and to help make decisions about issues that would impact the entire hospital.

The department head meetings were held for the same reasons as the management council meetings but were mainly for middle-management personnel. The managers of the functional departments met with top management once a month. Department heads were also supposed to meet formally with their staffs on a monthly basis, to discuss items of importance to the group.

There were a number of secondary communication vehicles that were sometimes quite effective in eliciting and generating information. These consisted of such items as an open-door policy to the top managers, phone calls and visits to departments by upper management, and a bimonthly newsletter about the affairs of the hospital put out by the personnel department. Management seldom used memoranda to communicate with employees, but because of regulatory requirements, the hospital had massive quantities of written policies and procedures in each department.

PLANNING AND CONTROL PROCESSES

Planning for operations at Central Hospital had always been from the top down. It had been the exclusive prerogative of the administrator or the administrator and executive vice-president for many years. Recommendations from the medical and employee staff were welcome but had never been officially solicited. Staff input was usually requested when top management had already decided on a project. Planning at this and at most other hospitals had focused on buildings. The challenge used to be to configure hospital buildings so as to handle the changing nature of hospital care. Physicians made the decisions about patient care, and the hospitals worked with physicians in organizing their buildings as effectively as possible.

Central Hospital had produced a mission statement, which is shown in Exhibit 1. However, the next step of setting goals and objectives for the organization had not been taken. Among other things, long-time managers remembered that when management by objectives had been attempted in the distant past, it had not been successful. At any

Exhibit 1

> ## MISSION STATEMENT OF CENTRAL HOSPITAL
>
> Central Hospital of Oakmont has been founded to meet human needs. We contribute to the physical, psychological, and social well-being of the patients and community we serve. We adhere to the highest ethical standards of the healing professions. Central Hospital seeks to communicate and collaborate with private and public agencies and organizations of the people we serve.
>
> We are a nonprofit, acute-care hospital offering generalized and specialized inpatient and outpatient health care services within the limits of our resources. We respect all persons, including medical staff, employees, and volunteers who serve in any capacity in our hospital. Quality of care is continuously monitored and evaluated. To perpetuate the institution and to fulfill our mission, we utilize principles of sound management.

rate, it had become difficult or impossible to require that departmental managers set goals and be judged by their success in meeting goals.

Department heads provided the typical excuse that it is too difficult to run the day-to-day operations of their departments and still find time to plan formally for the future. Innovative ideas seldom came from department managers. Either their ideas had been rejected in the past and they were reluctant to suggest new ones, or they truly were unable to focus on anything other than the crises of the day.

The only formal planning process implemented at Central Hospital occurred in 1980 and consisted of a plan produced by a consulting firm. The firm had been engaged by the planning committee to complete a long-range master plan. It followed traditional methods of planning, interviewed members of the community and of the medical and hospital staffs, and examined the hospital's current situation and possible future trends in health care. Once the plan was finished, however, the process did not continue even though the basic methods had been established.

The hospital therefore made no effort to allocate its scarce resources through any formal strategic planning process. Rather, resources were allocated through an annual budgeting process focused on maintaining the operations as performed in the past. Department managers submitted operating and capital budgets in April each year, but the budgets were often arbitrarily changed by top management. Therefore, many department heads felt that they must ask for more funds than they needed in order to receive what they really wanted.

After review and revision by the administrator and director of finance, the budgets were submitted to the finance committee and board of directors for approval. Even after approval of budgets, request for replacement personnel had to be approved by the administrator. Capital items, which were defined as durable property, plant, and equipment items over $150, also had to be approved by the administrator before purchase. It was only supplies that department heads could acquire without approval.

Capital budgets focused on equipment, especially replacement equipment, but a financial analysis of these purchases was seldom required. Only once was an analysis of net present value and internal rate of return made on requested capital items. In other words, Central Hospital did not compare returns in different capital projects as a means of choosing among them. As a result, there could be no assurance that capital resources were being allocated economically in this difficult environment.

Because it lacked a formal planning system, the hospital had initiated very few innovative new programs. The recommendations contained in the plan formulated in 1980 were followed, but those recommendations focused on buildings. The plan had identified the need for a new surgery department and ICU, and the new surgery wing was nearing completion five years later. Financial analysis played no role in planning for the new surgery department. It was simply felt that this was a major department in the hospital that needed to be updated. The only new program the hospital had developed in the last five years was outpatient surgery, and this was in response to suggestions by physicians.

REPORTING

Each department head received a monthly financial statement that listed revenue and expenses for his or her department. Comparisons were made against the previous year and against the budgeted figures for the month and the year to date. Typical financial statements showed only direct expenses and revenues. Not all the managers gave the same amount of attention to these financial statements. Quarterly meetings were held to review departmental financial performance. The administrator, assistant administrator, director of finance, and controller participated in the evaluation of each manager's performance for the quarter. The board of directors reviewed the hospital's overall income statement at each meeting.

REWARD SYSTEM

All Central Hospital employees, including managers, were evaluated once a year, except during their first year, when they were evaluated after three and six months. Performance evaluation criteria were very subjective and ambiguous.

The salary system at the hospital was based on longevity for nonmanagerial employees. All these employees were paid on an hourly basis. They received 5 percent salary increases at their six-month and one-year anniversaries and annually thereafter until their fourth year. Beyond that, they had to rely on annual cost-of-living increases. Managerial employees were on salary scales. Their salaries were based on their experience and education at the time of being hired. Salaries were increased initially at six- and twelve-month anniversaries and annually thereafter. Managers usually received an annual cost-of-living increase plus 1 percent. The salary structure contained few or no merit components. Salaries for all employees were based, primarily, upon the going rate at other hospitals in the metropolitan area and especially in Oakmont. Central Hospital had no bonus system.

Promotion opportunities were limited in the hospital. Employees were able to rise through the ranks of their own departments but were usually unable to transfer to other managerial positions with greater pay. For example, a respiratory therapist could become a senior therapist and then a chief therapist, but it was very rare for such a person to move into upper-management levels.

QUESTIONS

1. What are the strengths of the management systems in place at Central Hospital? What are the weaknesses?
2. Advise Weber on actions he should make regarding revisions to the formal and informal management systems at Central Hospital so as to meet the challenges facing the Hospital.

2

DESIGNING THE CONTROL PROCESS AND MANAGERIAL CONTROLS

INTRODUCTION

An MCS was defined in Chapter 1 as a set of interrelated communication structures that facilitate the processing of information for the purpose of assisting managers in coordinating the parts and attaining the purpose of an organization on a continuous basis. When properly designed, each subsystem of the control model is *mutually supportive.* Mutually supportive means that the elements of both formal and informal systems should be designed to exhibit reinforcing behavior in support of the goals of the organization.

Another term that captures the dynamic nature of the positive reinforcing behavior of supportive systems is "snowball effect." Conversely, if improperly designed, individual elements can block organizational progress towards goals. This may be referred to as a "downward spiral." The implications are that the interactions among subsystems must be carefully considered in design and redesign efforts.

These communication structures were described in Chapter 1 by the use of the mutually supportive subsystems model of control. When the subsystems are properly designed, they provide the basis for an organizational control system that may also be described as an adaptive control system.

This chapter describes the control processes and related managerial controls that must be supported by the management systems as the organization seeks to attain control. We will describe the control process in this chapter using a somewhat static model. In the next chapter, we will examine a model of the dynamics of the control process. A fundamental understanding of both the statics and the dynamics of the control process is essential to the design and redesign of control systems.

We begin this chapter with the definition of terms used in our discussion of control systems in this and future chapters.

ATTRIBUTES OF SYSTEMS

A *system* is an association of parts that are related to each other. It is the relationship of parts that defines a system. The boundary for any one system is entirely arbitrary. We may expand or contract the parts that make up a system. *Control systems design* is the process of designing the parts of the system so that the system is able to attain its purpose. In this text, we consider a system as "open" in the sense that the external environment reacts upon the system across its boundaries, requiring the system to adapt to these changes and "open" in the sense that the system attempts to predict and control these reactions.

A *managerial control system* is a set of interrelated communication structures that facilitate the processing of information in an attempt to assist managers in achieving the purpose(s) of the organization. Each subunit has a purpose and the subunits are linked together by a *macrostructure* defining the relationships of the parts.

Autonomy is an attribute of the macrostructure. The parts of the organization are linked to each other by communication links. Each unit operates its decision functions with a certain amount of local autonomy and is linked to the organization as a whole by communication links. The degree of autonomy in the decision linkages is either designed or allowed to evolve by top management. Autonomy, which manifests itself in degrees of decentralization, is strongly related to the style and philosophy of top management.

An essential feature of a cybernetic system is the concept of *feedback*. Feedback is both *negative* and *positive*. Negative feedback is the process whereby a system emits a signal that displays deviation from a desired result of the system and suggests a change in behavior. Positive feedback, on the other hand, is a process whereby a system emits a signal that leads to an action that reinforces the current system action and thus suggests behavior in the same direction as past behavior. A self-regulating (that is, homeostatic) system requires the presence of both *negative and positive feedback* to achieve its objectives and goals.

By using feedback to reward and encourage desirable behavior and penalize and discourage undesirable behavior, managers can use control systems to achieve organizational purpose.

Control systems function by establishing numerous *controls* or *homeostats* for each of the key success variables that must be held within desired limits. Unlike natural biological and physical systems, which are self-regulating and hold their variables within prescribed limits automatically, organizations are contrived social systems. "Controls" and control systems must be designed for organizations, because achieving purpose is not automatic.

If organizations are left to their own devices, disorder and chaos result. That is, they move towards a state called *entropy*. Entropy is the tendency for systems to run down and become chaotic. A managerial control system seeks to reduce *chaos* and *uncertainty* by bringing unity out of the diverse efforts of the various parts of an organization as it seeks to fulfill its purpose. By the use of numerous controls it seeks to keep the key variables of the organization within prescribed limits, thereby reducing uncertainty. Limits may be set on the value of key variables; the values of these variables can be monitored, and through the use of feedback chaos and uncertainty can be reduced.

A complete understanding of the meaning of feedback information requires an understanding of the cause and effect relationship between the measurement taken and the value of the variable being measured. This is the most desirable state as we try to achieve control. But, in the absence of cause and effect information, statistical inference is called for in order to achieve control.

A purely mechanical control system such as a machine or a thermostat can achieve control only within the range of disturbance that it was designed to handle. Managerial control systems, on the other hand, must be designed to handle problems that are not known at the time of design—that is, managerial control systems must be *adaptive* in nature. Adaptation requires that managers *learn behaviors* that are functional and differentiate those that are functional from those that are dysfunctional regarding the purpose of the organization. Therefore, quantitative, formal controls similar to those used in mechanical systems are necessary but not sufficient for gaining control in social organizations. Social organizations need informal controls such as values and principles in order to adapt to states of high uncertainty.

Adaptive control requires that the system allow for sufficient *variety* of behavior to accommodate the alternate states of the environment that can affect the organization. Also, adaptation requires establishment of sufficient interfaces between the organization and the environment so as to acquire necessary information. The acquisition of information about the environment and the acquisition of information concerning alternative behaviors tend to reduce uncertainty and make the system more predictable and controllable.

An adaptive control system will not allow for behaviors necessary to counteract all potential environmental conditions. It will, however, provide the capability for gathering more information, and for searching for new behaviors that will allow the system *to find or learn to find answers* to problems it encounters. A tightly controlled macrostructure with low levels of autonomy will not have the adaptive capacity to meet a great deal of environmental disturbance.

THE CYBERNETIC PARADIGM OF CONTROL

We shall follow a long-standing tradition in the field of MCS and employ the *cybernetic paradigm of organizational control* as a theoretical model of the control process. In Chapter 3, we shall expand upon traditional control theory by relating the concepts of systems dynamics [see Senge, 1990] to the subsystems of the adaptive control model.

Hofstede reports (1978, p. 451) that "a review of nearly 100 books and articles on management control theory issued between 1900 and 1972 reflects entirely the cybernetic paradigm." Cybernetics is derived from the Greek word *kybernetes,* which means "steersman." A steersman is a person who directs or governs a ship and corrects deviations from planned course as they occur.

The study of cybernetics was formalized and extended by the mathematician, Norbert Weiner, in his book *Cybernetics* published in 1947. Weiner and his colleagues were originally concerned with the common processes of communication and control in people and machines that were used to attain desirable goals and objectives. From the beginning, cybernetics was concerned with *mapping* the self-regulating principles underlying the human biological system onto systems of machines. Others have attempted to adapt these self-regulating principles found in the human brain to organizations. Most notably perhaps in this area is the work of Stafford Beer, which appears in his *Cybernetics and Management* (1959) and in his *Decision and Control* (1966).

The predominant view of the human brain in cybernetics is one of great complexity. It is seen as containing processes that lead to the regulation of body functions, although its operation is largely unknown. It is thought to be probabilistic and highly complex. Therefore, since organizations are collections of individuals, they are even more complex and probabilistic in their behavior. If the human brain is a "black box," how much more so is an organization? But, following the biological analogy, if we can discover inputs that lead to desirable outputs, we can formulate principles of self-regulation *without* knowing the exact nature of all the causal relationships between inputs and outputs. Although we try to improve our knowledge of causal relationships, it is not necessary to have complete knowledge to achieve control.

In this text, we will use insights from the cybernetic paradigm both to *design individual controls* and to *design complete control systems*. We also use the paradigm to capture the essential elements of the *control process*. We then use the results of our analysis to guide the design and redesign activities of the control process so as to improve the control processes we find in reality. We shall use the paradigm to describe control processes and systems and to improve these control processes and systems.

THE CYBERNETIC PARADIGM AND THE CONTROL PROCESS

We shall use the cybernetic paradigm in this text to represent the control process and the information systems which support it. Exhibit 2-1 represents the control process used in this book. This particular version of the paradigm has been devised by Griesinger (1979); it not only captures all the elements of the control process but does so with an economy found to be remarkable.

The cybernetic paradigm represented in Exhibit 2-1 allows us to capture the essential elements of the repetitive control process, which may be enumerated as follows:

1. Set goals and performance measures.
2. Measure achievement.
3. Compare achievement with goals.
4. Compute the variances as the result of the preceding comparison.
5. Report the variances.

6. Determine cause(s) of the variances.
7. Take action to eliminate the variances.
8. Follow up to ensure that goals are met.

These eight elements of the control process are captured in the cybernetic paradigm. The paradigm begins with the assumption that decisions are explained as the result of the interaction between the manager/decision maker and the environment faced by the decision maker. Each subunit or responsibility center of the organization operates within an environment. The environment includes the "outside world" (that is, the external environment) as well as other organizational units internal to the firm (that is, the internal environment). Each responsibility center must be responsive to changes in its external environment as well as to the goals, strategies, policies, decisions, and management style of its superior responsibility center (that is, its internal environment).

Each manager of an organizational unit scans the environment either formally or informally, so as to absorb information or feedback pertaining to its condition. The manager comes into contact with the environment through the sensors of the organization. Sensors are mechanisms used by managers to collect data. The mechanisms include reports that are reproduced as a result of formal attempts to scan the environment as well as "informal reports" that come to the attention of the manager through his or her sense of hearing and seeing. The sensors collect data both on changes that are occurring in the external environment as well as on the internal performance of the responsibility center.

The manager constructs from these data certain beliefs concerning performance and the state of the external environment. These beliefs are referred to as *factual premises*. Factual premises are formed by passing these data through a cognitive process referred to as *perception*. We use the word "perception" broadly to refer to the psychological processes of extracting information from data and of

Exhibit 2-1
The Cybernetic Paradigm of the Control Process

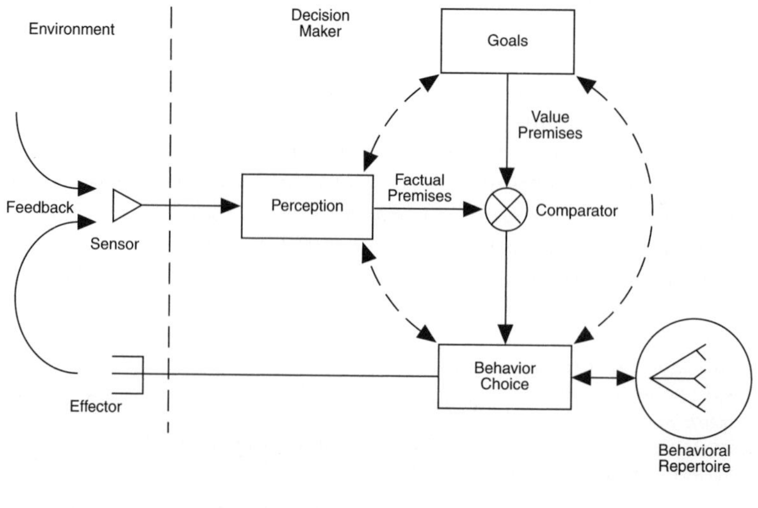

interpreting the meaning of that information. Cognitive limitations prohibit decision makers from assimilating all data in the environment, so the decision maker uses past experience, organizational goals, and personal and organizational aspirations to arrive at these beliefs about the actual state of the environment.

The manager uses these factual premises in a comparison process with organizational goals and performance measures. *Goals* are themselves a result of past learning concerning performance and accomplishments and represent the desired state for the manager. When a difference is determined to exist between what decision makers desire (that is, *value premises*) and their beliefs about the environment (that is, *factual premises*), they are motivated to seek to close the gap. The *comparator* represents the comparison process that takes place between performance measures and performance information.

When a performance gap exists, decision makers are motivated to search for courses of action that will move them closer to their goals. This choice is referred to as *behavioral choice* and is made by evoking from experience a limited set of alternatives that have been successful in solving similar problems in the past. The content of the set of alternatives evoked from the decision maker's *behavioral repertoire* is itself a function of goals, past experience, and the decision maker's perception as to the state of the environment. Search procedures are also included in the behavioral repertoire.

Alternative solutions are evoked from the behavioral repertoire according to established or learned search procedures. The first alternative during the search that is believed to solve the problem is normally selected so long as it meets general budget and return constraints. In the event that two or more alternatives are generated by the search procedure as potential solutions to the problem, the feasible alternative with the highest *subjective expected utility* that closes the gap will be chosen.

An alternative will be chosen only if it is expected to meet the goals of the decision maker. If no alternative is expected to reduce or close the gap, the decision maker will expand the search process. The search process is motivated by the presence of a gap and will stop when a feasible alternative is found that will close the gap. Simon refers to this decision-making procedure as *satisficing* (1978, p. 272).

Decisions require implementation. The *effector*, a manager, activates the decision, thus serving as a change agent. Control is brought about by action taken by the manager, who next seeks to determine the effects of the action. This new information is referred to as *feedback*. If the new behavior leads to a reduction or elimination of the gap, the behavior is likely to be repeated in the future under similar circumstances. If goals are being met routinely, it is likely that the organization will eventually seek higher levels of performance.

Feedback has the long-term effect of producing learning in the organization. Goals and performance measures adapt to actual performance. Search and decision rules adapt to experience, with those found most effective being used earlier in similar circumstances in the future and those found least effective being dropped from the behavior repertoire.

In the event that goals are not achieved, the manager will repeat the process. If after repeated attempts the goals are not achieved, the manager will either alter the performance measures that are attended to and thereby distort his or her perceptions of reality or reduce his or her goals. In either case, the performance gap is ultimately closed.

A certain amount of interaction takes place during the control process among the variables in the cybernetic paradigm. Goals direct the part of the environment that is perceived by managers. Perceptions about past performance influence current goals. We perceive that part of the environment that pertains to our goals. If decisions cannot be found that meet our goals, we change goals. Additional information may be introduced during the search process that can alter goals and alternatives considered as well as the part of the environment that is attended to (perceptions).

Decision makers and collections of decision makers learn as a result of their past experiences and adapt to new problems based upon their cumulative experiences and training. While individuals and organizations have vast long-term memories to draw on, evidence indicates that they have limited information-processing abilities, which severely restrict the number of goals that are operative at any one time as well as the number of alternatives that may be evaluated to solve a problem.

This leads to the conclusion that there will be strong tendencies among managers of responsibility centers to consider only local objectives and goals when making decisions. That is, there will be a tendency, barring the workings of other aspects of the control system, toward decisions that are only locally optimal. Moreover, it suggests that only a few alternatives will be considered at any one time to solve a problem and that the best of the few will be chosen.

DESIGNING MANAGEMENT CONTROLS

All goal-oriented controls should reflect the basic elements of the cybernetic paradigm. But there are many subtleties to observe in designing effective performance measures, that is, in designing individual controls for an activity. We turn now to a discussion of these issues.[1]

1. We should view the process of establishing controls as a *constructive* exercise, not a punitive one. Our efforts should focus upon the use of controls to assist people in attaining the goals and objectives for which they are responsible. Controls should be viewed by all participants as "fair," important indicators of the real purpose of the activity, and "constructive" as to the help they provide in achieving the purpose of the activity. Standards should be challenging but attainable. Support for the controls should exist in the informal organization, especially among informal leaders.
2. Objectives should be expressed in *measurable terms* whenever possible. If we can't measure a variable, we can't evaluate how we are doing in achieving results; it thus frustrates the control process.
3. Controls should focus upon the objectives and key results of an activity and should be limited in number.
4. In establishing controls we should seek to establish *balance* among the various aspects of the activity being controlled. Easily measurable factors (for example, financial variables) and short-run variables tend to get too much attention unless we guard against these pressures by actively seeking balance.

5. A single individual should be assigned responsibility for achieving desired results for an objective.
6. True control is achieved as a result of comparing *projected performance* regarding an objective to desired results. Comparing actual performance to desired results might be useful for achieving control in the next period but will not be helpful for achieving control in the current period.
7. In establishing controls, we should try to identify *early warning predictors* of the variables we seek to control. For example, inquiries (process) may be a good predictor of future orders; symptoms such as absenteeism and tardiness may indicate morale problems; the sophistication of the process may be a reliable indicator of the result, as, for example, good lesson plans are an indicator of the quality of an educational experience.
8. It may be possible and desirable to *sample* the variable that is being controlled. Sampling may be done by direct observation, by walking around, or statistically.
9. We should establish an *acceptable range of variation* for the value of each variable whose value we seek to control.
10. Reports should focus upon *exceptions* to desired results and be made promptly to the person who is responsible.
11. The *severity* of the problem should be confirmed by independent means. The *cause* of the problem needs to be identified and corrective action taken. *Results* of the corrective action should be monitored and compared to expectations.
12. We should develop a *discerning view* of controls, and apply judgement in establishing them and in interpreting results.

THE CONTROL PROCESS HIERARCHY

The organization is, of course, more than one responsibility center; in fact, it consists of many responsibility centers. The control process paradigm, therefore, must be expanded to include superior–subordinate behavior as well. To do so, it is desirable to view the relationship between a superior and subordinate as a means–end chain or relationship. The goals or ends of the superior are communicated to the subordinate, who in turn devises means that are appropriate to achieve those ends. These means in turn become ends for the subordinate, which in turn become the basis for more detailed means for the next level of supervision. An illustration of a means–end chain is provided in Exhibit 2-2.

The overall goal (G) or end of the organization becomes the basis for goals

$$(G_1, G_2, G_3, \text{ and } G_4)$$

at the next level. The goals or ends at the second level serve as ends for that level as well as the basis for developing means for the third level. These means in turn become ends or goals for level 3, and so on.

Expanding the control process to include superior–subordinate relationships, we find that the subordinate should set goals in response to the goals of the superior as a result of a communication process that, depending upon the autonomy given to managers of the organization and the style of management employed in the organization, may include negotiations. This is illustrated in Exhibit 2-3 by a feedback–communication relationship between superior and subordinate responsibility centers.

Exhibit 2-2
Means-End Analysis

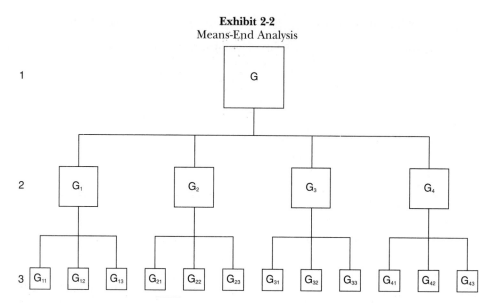

The goals of the superior include those of the subordinate, although this does not suggest that the goals of the superior are merely the sum of the goals of the subordinate. The subordinate is subject to corrective actions taken by the superior, thus the feedback loop from the effector of the superior to the sensor of the subordinate. This feedback can lead to changes in perceptions, goals, or choices.

The goal-oriented process described above requires that members of the organization collaborate in making plans and establishing social contracts. Details are different for different organizations, although the basic elements are usually the same.

ILLUSTRATION OF THE CONTROL PROCESS RELATING SUPERIOR AND SUBORDINATE

The following scenario illustrates the basic nature of the control process relating the supervisor and the subordinate. We assume a hierarchical organization consisting of appropriate decentralization of authority and responsibility.

For purposes of this discussion, the control process begins when a superior meets with a subordinate to review past performance and negotiate goals, new objectives, and targets for key variables for the next year. Once goals are negotiated, the subordinate will track actual performance at periodic intervals.

The superior meets with the subordinate periodically during the period to review performance. They agree on that portion of performance that is satisfactory (that is, where targets are being met) and on those areas where improvement is necessary. For those areas where performance has not been satisfactory, they seek to discover the reasons why. Once they identify the probable causes of the shortfall in performance, they agree on a plan of correction.

At the next review session, they review the results of past corrective action together with current performance to arrive at targets and actions for the next period. The process continues in a repetitive manner for each period throughout

Exhibit 2-3
Control Hierarchy: The Structure of Control

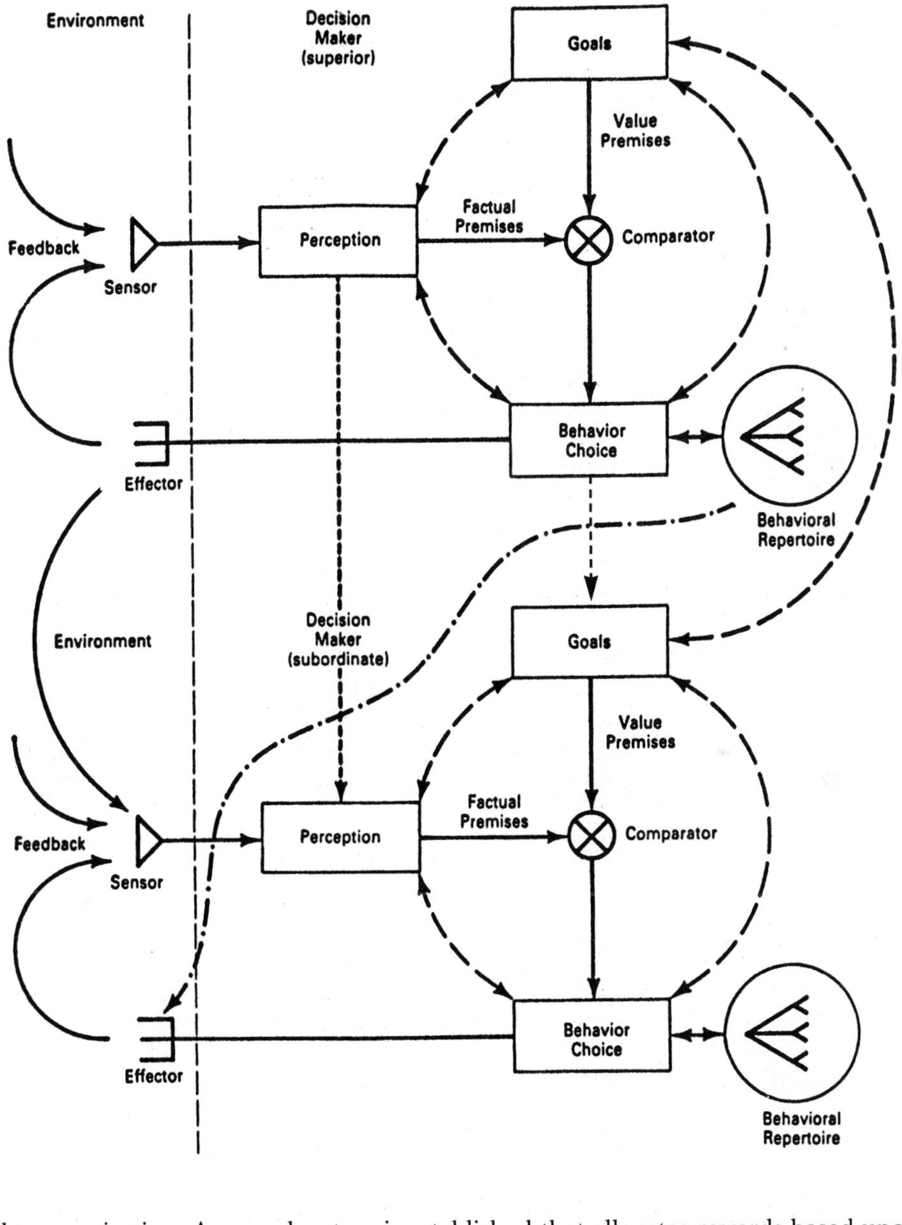

the organization. A reward system is established that allocates rewards based upon performance and improvement in performance.

The targets of the superior are negotiated before the superior negotiates with subordinates and may be altered based upon the negotiations with subordinates. The subordinates' objectives should contribute toward the fulfillment of the goals and objectives of the superior. The objectives of the superior should be less a summation of the objectives of all subordinates than guides for giving purpose to pursuits of subordinates.

All targets should be specific and if possible measurable. They should be limited (for example, to no more than seven key targets per manager) in number, given the information-processing limits of managers. Finally, they should include variables that cannot be measured in financial terms and variables that are qualitative in nature (for example, work force development and product quality). Often quantitative surrogates may be developed for qualitative variables.

Other interactions almost certainly occur between superior and subordinate. Some of these are captured explicitly within Exhibit 2-3. For example, the extent to which a subordinate has managerial autonomy in decisions depends upon how much influence on the subordinate's behavior is exerted by the superior's effector. Moreover, the perceptions of a superior in assessing a given problem faced by a subordinate may influence the perceptions of subordinates. We may call these influences the influences of managerial style and behavior upon subordinate behavior.

This is an example of what we mean when we discuss the control process. It is a behavioral process that requires information about the environment, plans, and results to function, but it is itself inherently a behavioral process.

To summarize, the goal-oriented control process follows the cybernetic paradigm, and it includes the essential elements of planning (goals), decision making (behavioral choice), and control (comparator-feedback). It operates within the control structure (a hierarchy of control paradigms) and has as its purpose the continuous attainment of organizational goals and objectives. Responsibility centers are linked to one another by their control processes in a hierarchical structure of control according to reporting relationships. In this manner, each organizational subunit is linked to the whole by myriad interlacing relationships.

DECENTRALIZATION, LOOSE COUPLING, AND ORGANIZATIONAL SLACK

THE NEED FOR DECENTRALIZATION

Decision makers are known to have severe limitations upon their information-processing ability, being able to process seven plus or minus two chunks of information at one time (see Miller, 1956). This limitation on the information-processing ability of decision makers creates the need to decentralize decision-making authority, to establish subgoals, and to hold each decision maker responsible for only one small portion of overall organizational purposes. Even with this decentralization of decision-making authority, decision makers must find ways to deal with the complexity they find in their environment, given their limited information-processing ability.

LOOSE COUPLING

The very nature of a hierarchical responsibility center structure implies a multiplicity of goals and objectives, each subunit having its local set following the means–end chain described previously. Indeed, a major purpose of the MCS is to knit these organizational subunits together, bringing unity out of diversity. Yet decentralization into responsibility centers does mean that profit, return on investment, or any other overall corporate goal will enter only indirectly, through a means–end chain, into the decision making of most subunits.

Herbert Simon (1976, p. 278) summarizes these ideas as follows:

Since there are large elements of decentralization in the decision making in any large organization, different constraints may define the decision problems of different positions or specific units. For example, "profit" may not enter directly into the decision making of most members of a business organization. Again this does not mean that it is improper or meaningless to regard profit as a principal goal of the business unit. It simply means that the decision-making mechanism is a loosely coupled system in which the profit constraint is only one among a number of constraints and enters into most subsystems only in indirect ways.

ORGANIZATIONAL SLACK

The purpose of the MCS is to facilitate achievement of the objectives and goals of the organization. It is quite possible and likely that goals and objectives of an organization can be achieved without achieving maximum efficiency. In other words, there will almost always be opportunities to improve performance. So long as goals are being met, and *competition allows*, great pressure will not exist to improve performance. This follows directly from the cybernetic paradigm of the control process—the pressure to improve performance ceases when goals are achieved.

If a firm has been successful in achieving its objectives and goals, there will not be significant pressure to tighten the congruence or *coupling* between the goals and objectives of the organization and the goals of each subunit. And tightening will not occur automatically. This means that the firm will often be underexploiting its environment.

This underexploitation will manifest itself in a variety of ways. Costs, including salaries, wages, and perquisites, may be higher than necessary to carry out the goals and objectives of the firm. Prices may be lower than those that will maximize profits. Dividends may be higher than absolutely necessary to maintain the confidence of the shareholders. Cyert and March (1963, p. 36) define this difference between total payments to organizational participants and total necessary payments (that is, money, perquisites, policies, personal treatment) as *organizational slack*. Organizational slack can also include the maintenance of costly support services, extra inventories, or longer product time to market.

Looked at strictly from the point of view of profit-maximizing behavior (that is, the normal point of view of the economist), the existence of organizational slack resembles dysfunctional behavior. But, in terms of the MCS, a small amount of slack creates a cushion against the variability of the environment, and it provides resources for innovation and adaptation in various stakeholder areas. Slack absorbs a substantial amount of the variability, and it brings stability to the organization. Slack is costly. Management must make sure slack resources have strategic value and are not simply idle resources.

Before the movement towards total quality management (TQM) and the rapid development of information-processing capability, the presence of slack allowed conflict among responsibility centers to remain latent. For example, if the marketing organization pursued revenue in its decision making, it would have been interested in the production of many different products and styles of products. This desire often ran counter to the interests of the manufacturing organization, which pursued cost as its primary objective. Thus there was potential conflict. Since these objectives were set by different responsibility centers and since the firm was simply trying to attain a profit objective, revenue in the marketing organization may have been lower and cost in the manufacturing organization higher than under a profit-maximizing solution. The production organization may have had production-smoothing goals that allowed it to achieve its cost standards, whereas the marketing organization may have had sales volume and product mix goals which allowed it to achieve its revenue standards.

As competitive pressures have increased, information-processing capability has improved dramatically and total quality management values have become more prominent, organizations are attempting to forge common overarching goals for all subunits. The result is a reduction in the desire to maintain large amounts of slack. An increase in the use of liaison activities such as concurrent engineering and techniques such as quality function deployment, which include encouraging participation by all functions including marketing and manufacturing in design and manufacturing activities, have resulted in attempts to reduce slack. Common goal development reinforced by reward systems based upon overall performance of the entire organization also tend to encourage more closely coupled behaviors.

As an example of attempts towards tighter coupling, consider the impact of just-in-time (JIT) inventory control. JIT results in reductions in unnecessary (that is, slack) inventories by having small amounts of material delivered only when needed by the manufacturing process. As a result, JIT puts more pressure on the purchasing department to get purchases to manufacturing on time, and it puts more pressure on manufacturing to maintain production yields at a high level to meet customer demands and to avoid shortages. With use of common goals, cross-functional work teams, and statistical process control techniques, a competitive advantage can be maintained with less slack.

EXAMPLES OF DECENTRALIZATION, LOOSE COUPLING, AND ORGANIZATIONAL SLACK

Let us consider some extended examples of how these concepts impact control systems.

The production unit of an organization may not have much influence over revenue and investment variables that determine profitability, yet it is necessary in the design of responsibility centers to translate the overall profit and return objectives down to the level of the production unit so that the production unit is "knit" into the overall purpose of the organization. There may be many levels of the hierarchy separating the production organization from top management; nevertheless, production must be grafted into the whole organization by its responsibility center designation and performance measures.

Let us assume that management concludes as the result of a means–end analysis that the production unit can best contribute to the overall goals of the firm by producing its planned production *efficiently* and at a level of *quality* necessary to fully meet customer requirements. The production manager agrees that it would indeed be fair to be held responsible for cost, schedule, and quality of output, since the manager is convinced that he or she has sufficient influence over cost and quality variables to "control" their values to predetermined objectives. Therefore, the organizational subunit is designated as a standard cost, schedule, and quality responsibility center. In practice, management may simply refer to the production unit as a cost center.

In establishing a cost budget for the production unit, the controller would take planned production levels and multiply them by unit costs of production to arrive at an appropriate cost budget. The overall goals of the firm thus affect the production manager as *cost, schedule, and quality objectives.* While it may be desirable to improve the cost budget, the goals of the firm are translated in such a way that the goals appear to the production manager as a set objectives to be met. These objectives will guide the decisions of the production manager.

Quality objectives are set by two means: the first is aimed at *efficiency.* These quality objectives are usually expressed as yields, product returns, and scrappage. The second set of quality objectives are aimed at *effectiveness.* These objectives are related to the production process characteristics of the product that are most valued by the customer.

Let us next consider the research and development department. The relationship between its output and the goals of the overall organization is not known precisely. The "proper" amount and type of R&D is established by negotiation between the management of the firm and the R&D department. It is heavily influenced by market conditions and organizational strategy. Specific factors influencing the R&D budget are rate of technical innovation, impacts from new technology, and competitive pressures. Once the budget is established, the engineers and scientists begin to execute their research plans subject to their expense budgets. Again, the overall goals and objectives of the firm are translated to the R&D department as technical and expense objectives.

Similarly, the marketing organization may be held responsible for revenue and market share. Since it often has little control over the variables that influence cost, it is normally unfair to hold the marketing organization responsible for profit. It should, however, provide trend data for planned price–cost ratios, and it is expected to provide customer feedback to the organization. Both of these functions are important determinants of profitability. Nevertheless, even its work force levels may be set for it by upper management, taking away a major variable influencing profitability. It proceeds to sell the firm's products and is guided in its efforts by its revenue and share budgets. Profit, in this example, does not enter directly into the calculations of the marketing manager, only revenue and market share; and these enter not as variables to be maximized but as fixed objectives to be met.

These three responsibility centers may all report to one divisional profit center. In the context of the control systems framework, the profit center has a profit and share budget to meet. It attempts to achieve its goals by coordinating the activities of its various organization units. It does so by breaking down its goals into cost, schedule, and quality budgets for production and R&D; and a revenue and share budget for marketing.

As responsibility for achieving the profit and share goals is decentralized, we notice that the goals appear to the three organization units as cost, schedule, quality, revenue, and share objectives. Profit does not enter directly into the decisions of any of these three responsibility centers. Since most of the responsibility centers of the organization are other than profit centers, we conclude that profit enters into the decision making of most responsibility centers very indirectly indeed. Most decisions, therefore, are likely to be motivated by discrepancies produced in the comparator between *actual* cost, schedule, quality, revenue, or share performance and *desired* performance.

While profit center projections will be present in the development of market projections, strategies, and associated cost estimates, because of the substantial decentralization of decision making that exists in organizations, most decisions will be motivated by subgoals that are only loosely coupled with profit or any other corporate goal. It is a loose coupling of actions among organizational subunits.

STAKEHOLDER CONTROLS

To achieve control the organization must meet the needs of *stakeholders*, who include investors, customers, employees, suppliers, and the general public. It is therefore both necessary and proper to establish goals, objectives, performance measures, and standards for each of these groups. The functional organization structure associates each of the major stakeholders to department status. We then design managerial controls and control systems for each of these departments. In this manner, we attempt to establish control of stakeholder relationships.

One of the primary functions of the executive (Barnard, 1938, pp. 139–160), is to take the contributions of the various stakeholders and convert them into inducements sufficient to maintain their cooperation in achieving the overall purposes of the organization. Given the various markets for stakeholder services, management must not only convert contributions to inducements but because of competition it must do so in an *efficient manner*. Inducements include material rewards, prestige, power, distinction, physical conditions, altruism, association, and enlarged participation. Contributions include capital, revenue, performance, materials and services, and community support.

An analysis of stakeholder relationships begins by first identifying *all* the stakeholders. Next, we should isolate the crucial stakeholders. These are groups that are most affected by the organization and have the most power to affect the organization. Then, we might look at their contributions and the inducements we offer them. Finally, we should look at the competition for the particular stakeholder.

This kind of analysis will assist us in identifying crucial stakeholder variables whose values we will want to monitor and influence in the control process in order to insure the long-run viability of the firm.

COMMUNICATION STRUCTURES IN SUPPORT
OF THE CONTROL PROCESS

The control process described in this chapter is distinguishable from the communication structures (described in Chapter 1) that support it, although it is not always easy to separate them in practice, since they are intertwined.

The cybernetic model of the control process is an information-processing or communications model. The control systems designer is concerned with designing an information-processing system that allows the control process to function effectively. The elements of the information system that are required to support the control process (that is, the detailed elements of the formal and informal control process of the MSSM) may be identified by examining the cybernetic paradigm.

The first element of the information system is a formal or informal process that scans the environment facing an organizational subunit. We might refer to this element as *environmental scanning*. It is concerned with sensing the condition of the environment as it pertains to the pursuits of the subunit and providing data for the purpose of formulating goals, plans, and decisions. Next, the organization requires a planning process wherein goals, objectives, and performance measures are set.

Feedback comes to the responsibility center from external sources through an environmental scanning process and from internal sources from a *performance measurement system*. The performance measurement system is normally developed from the internal accounting system of the organization. More recently, with the advent of direct and indirect measures of quality and customer satisfaction, the internal accounting systems of U.S. firms are being expanded to include nonfinancial measures as well as financial measures.

The internal accounting system not only measures the performance of the organizational subunit, but it compares performance with key performance measures and provides *reports*. It thus serves as both a sensor and a comparator, and it provides analyses of performance against goals and objectives.

The *decision-making procedures* of an organizational subunit may include standard operating procedures for meeting various recurring but not necessarily repetitive problems and a cost–benefit procedure for comparing alternatives for their feasibility and acceptability. Procedures are also required to monitor the implementation of decisions.

The planning process may itself include as many as four subprocesses. *Strategic planning* is concerned with developing and sustaining the organization's competitive advantage; *business planning* is concerned with resource allocation decisions concerning a corporation's "portfolio" of businesses or product lines; *long-range planning*, sometimes referred to as *programming*, is concerned with forecasting existing operations and planning new programs to achieve goals and objectives; and *operating budgeting* deals with the upcoming periods' operating and profit plans.

We should expect to find all four processes well developed only in large, diversified corporations. Yet it is important for almost all organizations to have a planning process that is both market driven and concerned with issues relating to the allocation of resources directed both toward long-term and short-term goals.

In addition to the information flows just discussed, there are informal and formal communications within the hierarchy of control, including meetings, day-to-day contacts among managers, the "grapevine," body language, ad hoc teams, and so on that are often crucial to understanding and improving the control process of an organization.

IMPACT OF INFORMATION TECHNOLOGY (IT) ON CONTROL SYSTEMS

Improvements in information technology have had and will continue to have profound effects upon the efficiency and effectiveness of control systems. This is readily apparent as we look at some examples of the impact of IT on two of the main functions of control systems.

Bringing Unity Out of Diversity

Improvements in IT permit a broader span of managerial control, thus permitting the elimination of many layers of the organization and reducing the filtering of information that occurs as information passes from one level of the organization to another. Voice and electronic mail have also made the coordination functions among all organizational participants more efficient.

New and improved order entry and inventory tracking systems result in shifting many of the pricing decisions closer to the customer while retaining central control of records of transactions. These systems also facilitate rapid communications with suppliers regarding product requirements.

Spread-sheet technology speeds up the coordination activities that take place during the budgeting and strategic planning process. It facilitates the rapid development of "what if" scenarios for the business, which results in shortening response times to changes in the internal and external environment.

Automatic performance measurement systems are being designed into production equipment and into service operations. In these cases, incentives may be based upon some of these automated performance measures such as quality of output and the number of defects. Electronic scoreboards are being designed for service performance using measures such as customer satisfaction, and incentives may be attached automatically.

Providing Information for Operational and Strategic Decision Making

The rapid decrease in the cost of information processing is one of the main factors contributing to the rise of activity based costing (ABC) systems. ABC systems are providing much more accurate cost data for the major operational and strategic decisions faced by an organization, such as make versus buy, product pricing, product emphasis, capital investment, and transfer pricing decisions.

In addition, the wide-scale availability of optical scanning equipment has not only improved inventory control in retailing environments, but it has also provided a vehicle to conduct market research by noting customer demand patterns and by noting the relationship between demand patterns for products and various promotional schemes.

MICRO, INTERMEDIATE, AND MACRO CONTROL FRAMEWORKS

Often in this text we will consider a particular control problem having to do with a specific situation in which it will be necessary to establish "controls" or performance measures for a particular problem area. The cybernetic paradigm (Exhibit 2-1) will be our guide in these situations. We shall refer to these problems as *micro* control problems.

At other times we shall be considering issues related to the design of mutually supportive management systems. In these instances the overall framework for the design of these systems described in Exhibit 1-1 (i.e., the MSSM) will be useful as a guide. Exhibit 1-1 is an *intermediate* framework for the design of control systems.

In addition, it is desirable to consider a *macro* cybernetic framework that incorporates all aspects of the design of control systems including the MSSM framework. Exhibit 2-4 is such a macro framework that places the entire task of control system design within the cybernetic framework. The framework can be understood by viewing it from left to right.

The initial conditions (or state) of the organization are taken as given. Stakeholder goals and strategies for attaining them are elicited. Critical success factors and impediments are identified by the designer, leading to the identification of appropriate performance measures. The MSSM is designed to exert control over the factors that can be controlled, to predict the uncontrollable factors,

Exhibit 2-4
Macro Cybernetic Control Systems Framework[2]

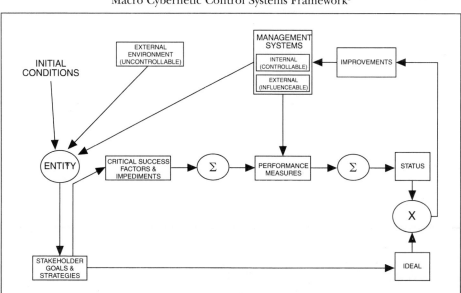

and to influence those external factors that cannot be controlled. Status reports are prepared periodically, comparing actual performance against ideal performance. Gaps are a signal that changes must be made and improvements sought.

Each of these three frameworks will be used throughout the text. Most of the control issues discussed in this text can be related to one of these three frameworks.

SUMMARY

This chapter has reviewed many of the underpinnings of the design of control systems. The cybernetic paradigm was described as the underlying model for the control process. The paradigm instructs us as to the important elements of the control process and control systems and helps us to achieve effective managerial control in all stakeholder relationships.

REFERENCES

ANTHONY, ROBERT N., *The Management Control Function.* Cambridge, Mass.: Harvard University Press, 1988.

BEER, STAFFORD, *The Cybernetics of Management.* New York: John Wiley and Sons, 1966.

_____, *Decision and Control.* New York: John Wiley and Sons, 1966.

FREEMAN, E. R., *Strategic Management: A Stakeholder Approach.* Mansfield, Mass.: Pittman, 1984.

CYERT, RICHARD M., AND JAMES G. MARCH, *A Behavioral Theory of the Firm.* Englewood Cliffs, N.J.: Prentice-Hall, 1963.

GRIESINGER, DONALD W., *Management Theory: A Cybernetic Perspective.* Graduate Management Center, The Claremont Graduate School, Claremont, Calif., January 1986.

_____, "Toward a Cybernetic Theory of the Firm," draft, Peter F. Drucker Management Center, The Claremont Graduate School, Claremont, Calif., 1992.

HOFSTEDE, GEERT, "The Poverty of Management Control Philosophy," *The Academy of Management Review,* July 1978, pp. 450–461.

KATZ, DANIEL, AND ROBERT L. KAHN, *The Social Psychology of Organizations,* 2nd ed. New York: John Wiley and Sons, 1986.

MARCH, JAMES G., AND HERBERT A. SIMON, *Organizations.* New York: John Wiley, 1958.

MILLER, GEORGE A., "The Magical Number Seven, Plus or Minus Two: Some Limits on our Capacity for Processing Information," *Psychological Review,* 63 (1956), pp. 81–97.

NEWMAN, WILLIAM H., *Constructive Control: Design and Use of Control Systems.* Englewood Cliffs, N.J.: Prentice Hall, 1975.

SIMON, HERBERT A., *Administrative Behavior,* 3rd ed. New York: The Free Press, 1976.

NOTES

1. This section has been adapted by permission from William H. Newman, *Constructive Control: Design and Use of Control Systems.* Englewood Cliffs, N.J.: Prentice Hall, 1975.

2. We are grateful for the help of Karen Higgins in devising this framework diagram.

Case 2-1 Leon Horn Efficiency Expert

Jeffrey McKlintock, Controller of Johnson Manufacturing, was pondering the developments with Leon Horn at the Cherry Hill Plant. He had supervised the design and installation of the standard cost system at Cherry Hill and although he had heard some reports of trouble, he was under the impression that the problems there had been basically solved. As a result, he is perplexed about the recent developments at Cherry Hill and is eager to avoid any future problems of this kind.

Johnson Manufacturing Company was a large producer of manufactured parts. It produced stampings, machined castings, and assemblies of stamped and machined parts that it sold to various manufacturers nationwide. Most of Johnson's parts were used in final assemblies of products such as automobiles, refrigerators, ranges, and home appliances. Johnson Manufacturing had 32 manufacturing plants. Annual sales were approximately one billion dollars.

THE CONTROL SYSTEM AT JOHNSON'S PLANTS

For many years, Johnson had no control system for its manufacturing plants. The plants had an actual cost-accounting system, and reports on cost performance were submitted monthly to the central office in the Midwest. Nothing much was done with these reports so long as plant managers met their production schedules.

In the late 1980s, however, competition became fierce in the markets Johnson served. As a result profit margins were severely squeezed. Management reacted by asking its central control group to install a system for the control of manufacturing costs in each of its plants. The result was the installation of a standard cost system for manufacturing and strong cost and employment controls over discretionary expenditures in plants.

RESULTS OF THE CONTROL SYSTEM

The immediate effect of the new control system was to reduce manufacturing costs significantly. This occurred because plant managers and supervisors became very sensitive to cost control since it became the predominant measure of performance in plants. The control system, however, was not without its problems. We turn now to examine one such problem that surfaced within a few years time.

THE CHERRY HILL PLANT

The Cherry Hill plant produced machined parts and assemblies for the automobile industry. At about the time of the introduction of the new control system, a new plant manager, Leon Horn, was hired to manage the Cherry Hill plant. Leon was recruited from a competitor where he had acquired a reputation as a "no-frills," "no-nonsense" production manager.

Horn was shocked to see the "fat" which had accumulated at the Cherry Hill plant. His response was to begin an ongoing program of cost cutting. His first budget for the plant was 15 percent below actual expenses of the previous year. He managed the budget continuously and was able to hold actual costs to 95 percent of budget. Leon was promptly rewarded by management with a large bonus and he was singled out for praise at the company's annual awards banquet for plant managers.

Needless to say, Horn went right on cutting costs. His budget for his second year was approximately 10 percent below the actual costs of the previous year.

Some of Horn's initial cuts were savings that were realized as a consequence of reductions in direct costs. These cuts were largely a by-product of the new standard cost system. The more recent cuts, however, were in indirect costs. These included employment reductions in manufacturing and industrial engineering, production control, purchasing, training, and maintenance. Horn's budget for the second year was approximately 50 percent lower in the overhead category than it was when he assumed the duties of plant manager at Cherry Hill. Moreover, Horn's actual cost performance was under budget well into the second year.

There were very few design changes in the parts produced at Cherry Hill during Horn's first year. The same parts were produced with only minor modification. The second year was much different. Every large automobile producer made changes in its specifications for the assemblies which were manufactured at Cherry Hill. To make matters worse, the automobile producers made numerous design changes to the parts as the year unfolded. Because of staff reductions in the engineering, purchasing, production supervision, and production control areas, Horn was unable to respond rapidly to these new and changing designs and missed a number of schedule commitments. As a result, the Cherry Hill plant lost much of its business as manufacturers became impatient and sought out other sources of supply. Profits turned to big losses. Johnson management reacted by firing Horn.

QUESTIONS

1. Diagnose the developments of the problem with Leon Horn in terms of the cybernetic paradigm of the control process.
2. Assume that you are McKlintock. In a report to the president of Johnson, describe the subsystems and elements of the control system that need to be redesigned in order to prevent similar problems from developing in the future.

Case 2-2 "Racy" Jones

For "Racy" Jones, attendance at State University will be possible only with financial help. The university is 160 miles from Racy's home, so there will be living expenses as well as other costs. Racy's father died one year ago, and the two brothers eat up most of the meager income that their mother can provide. Fortunately, Uncle Kirby offers to help —if Racy is really serious about professional education.

Racy's S.A.T. scores are quite good— much more impressive, in fact, than his high school grades. Racy's attention has vacillated between track (the source of the nickname), hi-fi, love, and parental reform—with book learning coming in big gulps just before tests. The overall record, however, is good enough to secure admission to State University next fall.

"My father's death made me take another look at what I wanted to do," says Racy. "Running around the track is fun for me, but it's no way to earn a living. So, at State University I guess I'll have to major in business administration, with only a minor

in physical education. Besides, that fits in with Uncle Kirby's talk of 'facing life's responsibilities,' and he is going to pay most of the bills the first year."

Uncle Kirby, a minister of the Gospel, has a church 200 miles from State University. He has young children of his own and helping Racy will put an unexpected strain on his family finances. Consequently, Uncle Kirby is loath to see his money "wasted."

What little Uncle Kirby knows about Racy's behavior to date does not inspire him with confidence. Instead he wants assurance that his money is well spent.

QUESTIONS

1. Assume that Uncle Kirby has asked you for advice on the kinds of controls he should establish on Racy's activities at State University. What do you recommend to Uncle Kirby?
2. In framing your answer, consider each of the 12 steps for establishing managerial controls discussed in the chapter.

This case was written by William H. Newman and is reproduced by permission.

Case 2-3 Fairfield Inn (A)

Mike Ruffer, the vice president and general manager of Fairfield Inn, Marriott's new entry into the economy limited service motel industry, summarized the dilemma facing Fairfield Inn's top executives in 1989:

> How does a new chain with limited ad dollars take on competitors like Days Inn, Hampton Inn and Red Roof Inn—each with more than 200 units already operating? When we started Fairfield Inn, we knew that it was going to be a distribution game, but now in the face of rapid room supply increases and greater competition, the established players are making it a marketing and ad spending game as well.

Ruffer paused and looked out of his window at Marriott's corporate headquarters located about a half mile away in a Bethesda, Maryland office park. He continued:

> The dynamics of the business have changed considerably in the past 2½ years. Our original recommendation called for a portion of our unit growth to come from franchising. Yet, when Bill Marriott nixed the idea because of his desire to have full control over the operations, we were still confident that we could successfully establish a meaningful presence and achieve good unit distribution.
>
> Since then, however, the economy category has experienced annual, double-digit growth in room supply—most of it occurring in the chains that are predominantly franchise focused. Good sites which have

typically been scarce and costly are becoming more so. And due to the rapid growth of other chains, we not only run the risk of being preempted from entering markets, but the growth of these other competitors greatly increases the size of their marketing "war chest" in the battle for the customer.

> Our preference in Marriott has historically been to manage our own operations rather than employ a franchising strategy. Yet, if we aren't able to increase our rollout rate, the true unit potential of this new business may never be fully realized.

COMPANY BACKGROUND

Fairfield Inn, with 25 properties open in March 1989, was the newest concept in Marriott's lodging and food services empire. In 1988, the Marriott Corporation had sales of over $7.3 billion, an operating income of $398 million and a net income of $232 million. (In the past year, Marriott stock had traded in a range of $26 to $35, and there were 108.7 million shares outstanding.)

Marriott Corporation traced its roots back to the peak of the Great Depression. On May 20, 1927, Charles Lindbergh took off in the Spirit of St. Louis on his historic trans-Atlantic flight, Babe Ruth was in the midst of his 60-home-run year, and J. Willard Marriott and his wife Alice opened a nine-stool root beer stand named The Hot Shoppe in Washington, D.C.

Kenneth Ray prepared this case under the supervision of Professor James L. Heskett as the basis for class discussion rather than to illustrate either effective or ineffective handling of an administrative situation. Copyright © 1989 by the President and Fellows of Harvard College. Harvard Business School Case 9-689-092. Reprinted by permission.

By 1989, the Marriott Corporation had over 230,000 employees, was serving more than 5 million meals daily, and was developing over $1 billion of real estate every year as one of the ten largest real estate developers in the United States. The corporation was divided into three major divisions: Contract Services, Restaurants, and Lodging.

CONTRACT SERVICES

Marriott's Contract Services provided 44% of the company sales and 32% of its operating income in 1988. The best known of these services was probably Marriott's In-Flite Services, the company's airline catering operations. Marriott pioneered this business in 1939 and by 1989 provided food and other services to over 140 airlines at 92 flight kitchens located in 70 airports throughout the world. Marriott's Contract Services also included Education Services that provided food services to 585 colleges and high schools. Health Care Services handled food services at over 400 hospitals and retirement centers.

RESTAURANTS

J. Willard and Alice Marriott's single Hot Shoppe had been expanded to a restaurant operation encompassing over 1,000 owned and franchised popularly priced restaurants that included Bob's Big Boy, Roy Rogers, Hot Shoppes, and Travel Plazas by Marriott. In 1988, this division delivered 13% of Marriott's sales and 16% of its operating income.

LODGING

Marriott's Lodging Group encompassed 451 hotels with over 118,000 rooms. Marriott was America's leading operator (as opposed to franchisor) of hotel rooms. Lodging operations represented 43% of sales and 52% of operating income in 1988. The lodging group, including Fairfield Inn, was subdivided into five distinct segments.

Marriott Hotels and Resorts were full-service hotels in the luxury/quality segment. In 1988, the system included 192 hotels in 38 states and 13 countries and totaled over 83,000 rooms. The cost of a room ranged between $75 and $195 a night.

The first Marriott Suites hotel opened in early 1987 in Atlanta. This full-service chain provided guests with their choice of one- and two-bedroom suites, a restaurant, a lounge and several meeting rooms. Three more Marriott Suite hotels opened in 1988, and the company planned to have a total of 40 open by 1993. Room rates typically ranged from $85 to $125.

Residence Inn by Marriott was America's leading moderate-price extended stay suite concept and was acquired by Marriott in July 1987. The typical Residence Inn guest stayed for five or more consecutive nights. Guests were usually corporate employees who were in the process of being relocated to a new city, on some sort of temporary project assignment, or working in some kind of consulting capacity. At the end of 1988, there were 130 Residence Inns in 37 states with nearly 15,000 suites. Room rates ranged between $65 and $90.

Courtyard by Marriott was a lodging concept that was only six years old and focused on the *moderate-price segment* of the hotel industry. A property normally had 150 rooms, a restaurant, a lounge and several meeting rooms. In 1988, Courtyard had 111 properties with 16,000 rooms in 27 states. Rates ranged from $50 to $88 each night.

THE FAIRFIELD INN DECISION

The decision to venture into the economy/limited service (ELS) segment (below $45 a night) was not an easy one and raised several questions for Marriott's senior management. They included the following:

1. Could Marriott compete as a late entry into a market segment already crowded with Red Roof Inns, Holiday Corporation's Hampton Inn, Days Inn, La Quinta, Comfort Inns, and over 45 other regional or state chains?
2. Would Marriott be jeopardizing its Courtyard clientele or cannibalizing some of its existing business by selling guests down to an economy-priced product?
3. Could Marriott design a product and property that was attractive enough to build a thriving business, yet cost effective enough to meet Marriott's corporate net present value goals and its 12% target internal rate of return for new development projects?

Mark Pacala, Fairfield's vice president of operations, was one of the strategists with Marriott's Corporate Planning Department who first looked at the ELS segment in 1985 as a possible growth opportunity for Marriott. According to him:

> Going ahead with Fairfield Inn was a very tough decision. The market was growing rapidly and established competitors had already built strong brand names with a consistent product. We knew we'd be walking into the middle of a share grab game.
>
> The no-go position was that we didn't know anything about this market segment, Marriott was too quality-oriented, we might tend to overinvest (hence, couldn't meet IRR goals because of high costs), and we would be entering too late into this market.
>
> The go position was that it's the second biggest segment in the lodging industry and the fastest growing. It would allow us to diversify. There was no one dominant national player, so we could take a little bit of share from everybody. Lastly, if things didn't work out, we projected that we could recover our costs by selling out to one of the established chains.

Despite their initial reservations, Marriott's Corporate Finance Committee approved the Fairfield Inn planning group's original request for $10.0 million to develop two five-property ELS test markets. In December 1985 approval was given, and in October 1987 the first Fairfield Inn opened in Atlanta.

THE ECONOMY, LIMITED-SERVICE (ELS) HOTEL BUSINESS

The economy segment of the U.S. lodging industry accounted for as much as 28% of all available rooms in 1988. Economy properties' room rents normally fell in the $25 to $45 per-night range. Economy hotels typically did not have restaurants, luxurious lobbies, or extensive meeting facilities. One authority estimated that for these reasons, economy hotels could break even with occupancy rates between 52% and 55%, about 10 to 12 occupancy points below the level at which full service properties tended to break even.

The top 50 ELS lodging chains had a combined total of 5,042 properties and 498,800 rooms at the end of 1987, a year in which occupancy rates for the entire ELS segment firmed up. Occupancies are shown in Exhibit 1.

The ELS segment was the fastest growing part of the U.S. lodging industry. In 1987, the segment expanded with 606 properties and 67,800 rooms. This translated to growth rates of 13.7% and 15.6%, respectively, in number of properties and number of rooms. In 1988, market experts anticipated that just over 1,000 properties with

Exhibit 1
Occupancy Rates, Lodging Industry and
Economy/Limited Service Segment, 1982–1987

Year	Entire Lodging Industry	Economy/Limited Service Segment
1982	64.6%	65.6%
1983	65.2	65.3
1984	65.9	65.2
1985	64.4	64.0
1986	64.7	62.7
1987	65.6	63.5

102,200 rooms would be added to the ELS segment. Projected growth rates for several of the leading chains in the segment are included in Exhibit 2.

The expansion of the segment paralleled corporate America's increased emphasis on controlling travel and entertainment (T&E) expenses. American Express' biennial Survey of Business Travel Management noted that "the number of chief executive officers and senior financial managers who rate rising T&E costs as a 'top concern' has risen from 45% to 55% in the past two years."

In 1990, industry experts estimated that American companies would spend at least $115 billion on T&E expenses, up from the $95 billion spent in 1988. While air travel costs were the largest single expenditure, responsible for 40% of every T&E dollar, lodging was next, accounting for 23% of every T&E dollar.

ESTABLISHED COMPETITION

Days Inn of America, based in Atlanta, Georgia, with 84,800 rooms and 590 properties throughout America, was the largest ELS chain in 1987. It owned 12% of its hotels and franchised the rest. In 1988, Days Inn opened 163 new properties and added 22,000 rooms. Occupancy rates for the chain were between 63% to 68%. Although Days Inn room rates averaged between $35 and $40 dollars per night, published room rates varied from $18 to $109 a night depending on the location of the property. Days Inn accounted for 17% of all rooms in the ELS segment in 1987.

Motel 6's 48,800 rooms and 431 properties ranked it as the second largest economy chain in the U.S. in 1988. All of the properties were owned and operated by Motel 6. Occupancies ranged from 70% to 75%, and its published room rates ranged from $17.95 to $28.95. In 1987, Motel 6 initiated a major radio advertising campaign that had spokesperson Tom Bodette telling travelers that "We'll leave a light on for you." Bodette's folksy voice and inviting manner increased the awareness levels of Motel 6 within its target market.

Comfort Inn, headquartered in Silver Spring, Maryland, was the third largest ELS chain in the U.S. with 375 properties and 33,700 rooms. Comfort Inns were 100% franchised. Its unit's occupancies varied between 65% and 70%, and published room rates were from $30 to $50 per night.

Exhibit 2
Projected Economy Lodging Capacities

	Number of Rooms 1986[a]	Number of Rooms 1987	Number of Rooms 1988	Number of Rooms 1989[b]	Number of Rooms 1995[c]	Annual Growth Rate[d]
Days Inn	49,500	66,400	84,800	69,000	137,000	12%
Hampton	11,600	13,400	19,100	23,000	85,000	25
La Quinta	24,100	23,500	25,200	25,700	85,000	15
Comfort Inn	18,200	23,800	33,100	44,500	64,000	15
Red Roof	16,500	17,600	19,500	21,500	50,000	13
Fairfield	—	NA	265	2,400	49,500	—

[a]As of January 1, based on annual information prepared by Laventhal and Horwath and published in *Hotel and Motel Management* magazine.

[b]The number of rooms for Days Inn was adjusted downward to reflect the amount of their room inventory that is effectively being sold at less than $45 per night, comparable to economy lodging.

[c]Estimates made in 1986.

[d]For three years prior to January 1, 1986.

Red Roof Inn was founded in Ohio in 1964 and opened its 200th property in Orlando in 1989. All Red Roof Inns were owned by the company. New Red Roof Inns had been opened at the rate of about 15 a year for the past three years. Its occupancies ranged from 77% to 82%, and room rates averaged between $35 and $40 a night.

Holiday Corporation's Hampton Inn had the most ambitious growth plans of all ELS chains. By 1988, Hampton Inn had 152 properties and more than 19,000 rooms. Holiday Corp. retained direct ownership of 12% of the properties and franchised 88% of the chain. Room rates ranged from $29 to $68 a night.

In a 1986 meeting of the Holiday Corp.'s limited-service hotel division, Ray Schultz, Hampton Inn's president, told managers, owners, and operators in attendance that, "We're not the biggest yet, but we will be. . . . Don't get greedy. Stay away from raising rates. Operate lean and efficiently. And hire, train, and motivate good people."[1]

Michael Rose, chairman and CEO of Hampton's parent company, emphasized that, "In a survey of Hampton customers, 98% said they would use a Hampton Inn again. Two-thirds said they would actually go out of their way to stay at a Hampton Inn hotel. . . . Design has been an important factor, but in the long term, outstanding customer service is the key to success."[2]

According to Hampton's President Schultz:

> We basically are competing in the upper and middle ranges of the limited-service segment. We see our main competitor (as of 1986) as being the La Quintas, the Comforts, the Days Inns. . . . We're going into a "burst" mode of advertising, where periodically we'll attempt to make travelers aware of our product. We're aiming for national awareness. . . . We're finding that new inns are running in the high 50s or low

60s percentagewise (in occupancy). After about six months, they're in the middle 60s. After a year, occupancy rates are typically in the 70-percent range. . . . We made aggressive plans, and we're fulfilling them, so I'm not so surprised that we're growing so fast. The competitors around us are the ones who are surprised.[3]

MARKET ANALYSIS AND FAIRFIELD'S POSITIONING

The size of the entire ELS segment was estimated at 285 million room nights annually in 1985. The market was broadly divided into business travelers who accounted for 178 million room nights and pleasure travelers who purchased 107 million room nights. (See Exhibit 3.) Overall demand growth in the ELS segment was expected to range from four to six percent each year throughout the next decade. Fairfield Inn was designed for the transient market, business and pleasure travelers who were seeking clean, comfortable, and convenient lodging in the $30 to $40 price range. Its anticipated guest mix was 65% business transients and 35% pleasure transients.

Business travelers in the economy segment usually traveled by auto and followed regional drive patterns in the course of their business and sales calls. When deciding where to stay for the night, the most important attributes for these travelers were cleanliness; overall value for the money spent; secure feeling; friendly, efficient employees; and overall service. Traveler comments obtained from focus group interviews conducted for Fairfield Inn's management appear in Exhibit 3.

According to Marriott's in-house research, business travelers could be subdivided into two basic traveler segments, "functional travelers" and "stylish travelers." Fairfield Inn's strategy was to make the functional business traveler the primary customer group; in 1985, this seg-

Exhibit 3
Customer Comments Regarding Fairfield Inn from Business Travelers

About the importance of price. . . .

"The company sets the limit for us. They say 'Anything over $45 and you pay the difference.'"

"I often work on a per diem basis. You can go to a really nice hotel and eat at McDonald's or you can stay at a cheap place and eat steak."

"I don't have any limit, but I don't spend an extra $30 for something I don't think I need. I might find something better to spend it for."

"I'm on straight commission. I'm an independent contractor, so I set my own limit and I look for a fair price."

Selecting a place to stay. . . .

"I've been on the highways for 40 years, and it gets to where you can pretty well drive by them and tell which ones are good."

"I want to drive up to the room. I don't like all these places they're making now where you've got to walk through the lobby, drag all your junk with you and drag it all back out with you."

"I want the convenience of being able to carry my files in and being able to do my paperwork in the evening."

"Some places go out of their way to make you feel at home and you want to go after a place like that. That means a lot."

About the Competition. . . .

"I prefer Hampton over Red Roof. The rooms were much nicer—they were much prettier. I just like the way the rooms were done. They have more luxury than Red Roof. I don't think Hampton is considered a budget hotel."

"Knights Inn transcends tackiness—purple bed sheets . . . I won't go back."

"One thing I like about Knights Inn is you can pack right at your door."

"It's like a White Castle that jumps right out at you . . . that red roof. They have a good sign that catches your eye."

"Red Roofs are at good locations. They work the exits very well."

Choosing a place to stay. . . .

"It's all a matter of economics. When you're traveling to a location and not planning on spending the whole day at a motel, you drive till you sleep, sleep, then you get up and go again."

"My wife gives the final say on where we'll stay."

"I really like the little book with the little map that says 'here it is,' you go down this street and turn and there it is!"

"I look at billboards. As you're driving into town you're trying to spot something that might ring a bell in your mind—somewhere you've stayed before or something you've heard."

"If the outside of the hotel is shabby looking, I always think the inside is going to be like that. I'm not talking real fancy. It can be just a neat appearance on the outside and all the lights are working. Normally, the inside will be neat also."

Some expectations. . . .

"Whether it's $29.95 or $49.94 or $95.99 a night, you want your motel to be as comfortable as home, if possible. That's what you're looking for. You don't want to get hassled when you complain about a drippy faucet. You want a place that's managed."

"Courteous people at the desk. If they have to pay those people a little more money, they're going to be nice to me—especially when there's a problem. That's one of my biggies."

"It doesn't matter if they're a clerk or a manager, they ought to be polite."

About the rooms. . . .

"As long as it's clean and it's tidy and it's sanitary, I have no problem."

"If I'm staying just a short while, all I really want is a good bed to sleep in and a clean bathroom to take care of business the next morning, and I don't need lots of space. Even with children you don't need lots of space."

"Once you close your eyes, all rooms are the same size anyway."

ment was estimated to comprise 66% of business travelers purchasing 72% of room nights occupied by business travelers.

Functional and stylish travelers possessed different attitudes toward lodging and had different demographic and travel profiles. The functional business traveler wanted the basic amenities (clean room, good price/value, and consistency) but didn't need lots of extras. Functional travelers preferred motels like Fairfield Inn, Red Roof, and Knights Inn. Stylish travelers wanted the basics plus some food and beverage service, business services and meeting rooms, and recreational facilities. Stylish travelers tended to prefer motels like Hampton Inn, Signature Inn, and La Quinta Motor Inn.

Fairfield Inn targeted the functional traveler group because this group was composed of the most frequent travelers, was the largest economy consumer group, and generated the most potential new room nights. Market research indicated that the vast majority of travelers within this price segment were new Marriott customers and not established Courtyard clientele. Also, the weekend pleasure customers' lodging needs were quite similar to those of the functional business traveler, so Fairfield's product and price allowed Marriott's new brand to attract the weekend pleasure traveler.

Market analyses conducted by Fairfield Inn's management showed four key customer target groups among frequent automobile travelers who were current users of other economy price hotels:

1. Traveling salespeople or regional managers were travelers with an assigned territory to cover. They had fairly strict per diem allowances for travel and lodging. They desired a good clean room that was also conducive to working at night.
2. Government and military employees had a rigid per diem budget that they were allowed to spend on lodging. Economy hotels met their needs quite well.
3. Self-employed businesspeople tried to minimize expenses by staying in reasonably-priced lodging. Since all bills were paid out of their "own pockets," members of this group were rate-sensitive and didn't want to be charged for services not used.
4. Extended stayers were defined as guests staying more than a week. Typically, these people were relocating or part of a project team.

Additionally, Fairfield Inn's management wanted to set a price high enough to discourage truckers and construction crews as guests. They wanted to exude the image of being a businessperson's hotel during the week.

Guest tracking surveys conducted in 1988 confirmed that Marriott's first 15 ELS properties were reaching their target customers. Fairfield Inn's weekday guest was an over-the-road (as opposed to air traveling) salesperson who was about 40 years old, made 33 business trips a year, and had a personal income of $52,600.

Focus groups conducted with ELS hotel customers indicated that pleasure travelers wanted a well-run, secure, inexpensive place to spend the night while on the road to some other destination or to use as a "base-camp" for visiting friends or family within the local area.

The ELS pleasure traveler represented a broad segment of the U.S. population. Marriott researchers estimated that 25% of U.S. families stayed in economy lodging at least one night each year for pleasure travel. Broadly speaking, these customers lived within a 300-mile radius of the hotel and drove there with their family. Marriott's research showed that many travelers who stayed in higher-priced lodging while on business also preferred to stay in ELS lodging when traveling for pleasure. The typical weekend guest at Fairfield Inn was 40 years of age, but had a lower personal income than weekday guests.

THE FAIRFIELD INN CONCEPT

After completing the initial feasibility studies, the real challenge for Fairfield Inn's operating managers was in designing, producing, implementing, and operating a Fairfield Inn concept. Mike Ruffer clearly delineated the expectations for Fairfield Inn:

In any lodging segment that we or Marriott compete in our objective going in is not to be the biggest; we do however want to be best of the class. Our long-term success is more dependent upon how well we serve our guests time and again. Consistently. Superior hospitality and execution day-to-day will let us "win" over time.

The mission statement that was developed by Fairfield Inn's management team reflected a desire to be the best:

At Fairfield Inn, our team's mission is to

- Impress our guests.
- Have committed employees pursuing excellence.
- Recognize and reward excellent performance.

Mel Warriner, vice-president of human resources, commented, "You'll notice we don't use the word satisfy. It's too mediocre. We are hanging our strategic hat on service. We want the guest to leave and say 'Wow, this was different.'"

Fairfield Inn's rooms rented for $36 per night, and each property had about 130 rooms. Fairfield Inn management anticipated that established properties would have an annual occupancy rate of 78%.

Fairfield Inn's amenities package was designed using surveys that asked experienced ELS customers what they wanted. According to Bob Ziegler, Fairfield's director of marketing communications: "We sampled more than 600 people. We screened them on several criteria, whether they took 6 or more business trips a year, expected to pay between $20 and $45 a night when they were paying for their own lodging, and stayed in competitive hotels during the past year.

Each Fairfield Inn offered guests king-size beds, free cable television, remote-control television, thick towels, free local phone calls, large comfortable chair, large work desk (45 × 28 inches), alarm clock, free coffee and tea in the lobby, swimming pool, inside or outside room entry, smoking or non-smoking rooms, long-cord telephones, separate full-length mirror, a meeting room just off the lobby, and vending machines with a variety of snacks, juices, and soft drinks.

Fairfield Inn's top management realized early on that if its concept was going to succeed in an already-crowded ELS segment, it would have to successfully combine an efficient, attractive property with a highly motivated staff. As Mel Warriner put it, "Too often employees are just marking time. At Fairfield, we are committing ourselves to reducing turnover in the housekeeping and lower staff levels dramatically below the industry's 150%–200% per year average. We hire people who like to make people smile. We have designed what we feel is an innovative pay-for-performance system that encourages the pursuit of excellence." Management called this the Scorecard System.

THE SCORECARD SYSTEM

According to Robert J. McCarthy, Fairfield's vice president of marketing, "Scorecard is the single most unique thing we are doing. It's not a typical hotel amenity, but it may be our most powerful amenity."

Each Fairfield Inn check-out counter was equipped with two Scorecard computer monitors. When a guest checked out, it was the guest service representative's (or GSR, the equivalent of a front desk clerk at Fairfield) responsibility to cheerfully ask the customer to please rate the quality of his or her stay and the services he or she received by entering either excellent, average or poor on the Scoreboard monitor's keypad.

The complete Scorecard system involved six questions (listed in Exhibit 4), but customers only answered four questions during each checkout. The question about the clean-

liness of the room was answered by every guest, while the software program rotated the remaining five questions in the other three Scorecard slots. These other questions queried the guest about the friendliness and efficiency of the clerk at arrival and checkout, an overall rating of this Fairfield Inn, value for the price paid and an overall rating of cleanliness and staff hospitality.

In order to facilitate use of the Scorecard, each GSR and guest room attendant (GRA or housekeeper) was assigned a special employee code number. Scorecard's software system automatically matched each guest's rating for every question to the appropriate service personnel. In this way, the ratings produced a performance "scorecard" for the property and every employee on the property who regularly came in contact with guests, as shown in Exhibit 4.

The Scorecard ratings played a major role in the incentive compensation levels of each employee at the Inn. They were published monthly and posted in the break room at each Fairfield Inn. A GSR or GRA was able to earn a bonus of up to 10% of salary every quarter with 50% of the bonus based on individual performance and 50% based on the entire staff's performance at each property. Fairfield Inn's base wages for each position ranked in the top quarter among salaries offered by local hotels and motels.

Joanne Eckhardt, a GSR in Detroit, commented:

> Scorecard gives corporate an immediate rating on a guest stay since we're all logged in. It gives credit where credit is due. You're not getting the same amount of pay as everyone else. It's very fair. With Holiday Inn (her previous employer) there was no incentive and no option to progress within the system. It was like you were expendable. Here at Fairfield Inn, I've seen them promote front desk clerks into management, or if you're happy doing what you're doing, they recognize and reward you.

Exhibit 4
Guest Scorecard Period Report: Atlanta Report

Report GSIRPT-04 *Run on 01/09/89*	Period 13: Quarter 4					Fiscal Week 13-1-89 to 01-07-90 Previous Period Average	Quarter to Date Average
Question	Number of Responses	Number Excellent	Number Average This Period	Number Poor	Average		
Friendliness and Efficiency of clerk at check-in	299	287	12	0	98.0	95.5	96.6
Friendliness and efficiency of clerk at checkout	308	300	7	1	98.5	96.8	97.6
Cleanliness of room	510	482	27	1	97.2	95.7	96.9
Overall rating of this Fairfield Inn	319	290	29	0	95.5	92.9	94.2
Value for the price paid	301	256	42	3	92.0	89.2	91.3
Overall Inn cleanliness and staff hospitality	286	272	14	0	97.6	95.9	96.8
Capture rate (responses/checkouts)					42.4%	26.7%	36.2%

Current period capture rate calculation

$$\frac{1128 \text{ checkouts with responses}}{2660 \text{ total checkouts}}$$

Linda Wilson, another GSR, said:

I love to see it when guests checking out push excellent. At Signature Inn, the only people who ever got a bonus check were the front desk crew and the manager. Housekeeping, maintenance and laundry got absolutely nothing. They tried to keep bonuses really hush-hush. Back then, I was assistant supervisor of housecleaning and it really made me mad that the front desk got a bonus and we didn't. They said that front desk sells the hotel, but what do you think happens if the guest walks into a room that's dirty. At Fairfield, we're a team.

According to Deneige Teague, a guest linen attendant (laundry room):

The money is nice. No other hotel company offers it. My bonus is based on the Inn's overall rating. Here, we are very proud of what we do. It's our property. When someone walks in that room we all have the same idea—to make sure they get a great room and come back again.

Scorecard ratings seemed to serve as a focal point for some good-natured competition among each Inn's staff and across the various Fairfield locations. Joyce Smith, a GRA, said, "Every time the ratings get posted we all rush up to see how well we did. Everybody takes care of their own section of rooms and wants to have the cleanest rooms in the hotel."

Rob Munro, a guest room supervisor, added:

> Scorecard is an incentive. We try and encourage the GRA's to take great pride in their work. Each day I will review two rooms (out of the 14 assigned daily to each GRA) with the person. I try to be really positive because we want to keep the person from getting discouraged. They are going to make a lot of mistakes initially—water spotted chrome, a stopper not in the tub, or dust on the chair legs. Fairfield is very particular. We don't have a lot of extras, so we want everything to be absolutely clean. Some of our high standards come from our hiring. We get people with good attitudes and good personalities. But it's up to the supervisors and managers to provide the right working environment.

PERSONNEL SELECTION

The Scorecard system and Fairfield's focus on hospitality was based upon hiring good people from the start and developing a strong relationship among the entire staff during the pre-opening stages of a property.

Fairfield Inn managers made their employee selections after evaluating the potential candidates in a series of personal interviews (as many as three rounds) and on the basis of a personality skills profile test designed by Selection Research Institute.

"Generally, we like to hire people who enjoy pleasing other people. For GRA's, we try to identify people who like to clean and enjoy housework. Similarly, for our maintenance jobs we focus on finding people who enjoy fixing things. Part of the six-to-eight-week training program for Fairfield managers is a three-day seminar on how to interview job candidates and how to evaluate the personality skills test," commented Mark Pacala.

Sue Graves, Fairfield's Detroit area manager, who supervised six area properties, remembered opening up the airport property a year earlier: "When we opened that Detroit property we were running about two weeks behind (in construction and finishing)

so that allowed me and the assistant managers to interview more people," she said. "We interviewed over 500 people to fill 19 positions at the first property, and in the last 90 days we haven't had any turnover."

Another way that Fairfield management had generated a tremendous amount of enthusiasm among the hourly employees at each hotel was through a team-building exercise in the pre-opening meeting where management and hourly employees had a round-table discussion of mutual expectations.

The team-building discussion began with employees and management generating a list of what they would want if they each were a guest at this Fairfield Inn. The next segment of the team-building exercise encouraged hourly employees to generate a list of expectations for each other. At the Warren property, a suburb of Detroit, the employee promises to each other were: dependability, teamwork, positivity, consideration, honesty, reliability, loyalty, integrity, encourage others, pats on the back, caring, understanding, jokes, a sense of humor, camaraderie, friendship, communication, light-heartedness, and to not sweat the small stuff.

Next, the hourly employees generated a list of their expectations from management. At Canton, these expectations included: sensitivity, respect, a second chance, empathy, fairness, friendship, protection, creativity, teach us, keep us informed, keep us a part of decisions, stand by us, listen to our ideas, money, sense of humor, understanding, support and patience.

At each Fairfield Inn, the posters that had been generated in the team-building exercise were prominently displayed in the employee break room located next to the property manager's office.

ORGANIZATION

Each Fairfield Inn had a staff of about 21 employees to run the property. The staff was composed of a manager, assistant manager and 19 hourly employees: four GSRs, 11 GRAs, one guest room supervisor, one maintenance chief, one custodial facility attendant, and one guest linen attendant.

The regional support group for each cluster of 10 to 12 Fairfield Inns was composed of a field marketing manager and an area manager. The area manager was directly responsible to headquarters for the performance of each Inn in his or her region.

Fairfield's decentralized organization was combined with a highly centralized operations system. Each Fairfield Inn was directly linked to a central computer at the Bethesda headquarters through an in-house system known as "The Coordinator." The resulting "flat" organization structure allowed each property manager to focus on "impressing the guest."

"The administrative load is really minimal. It's like night-and-day when compared to the inventory and labor reports I had to complete in another Marriott group. Not having tons of paperwork allows you to be out with your guests. Every morning, I try to be out at the front desk or lobby between 7:30 a.m. and 9:00 a.m. so I can personally greet and get to know our guests," commented Norm Bartlemay, the manager at Detroit's Canton property.

GUEST AND EMPLOYEE INCENTIVES

Another program developed by Fairfield Inn in 1988 was the creation of a discretionary promotions fund. The fund gave property managers the opportunity to provide special events and promotions for both their employees and guests. Each manager was allocated $175 every month to spend on employee incentives and $125 to use on guest incentives.

At the Detroit airport property, a "hospitality committee" composed of the mainte-nance chief, one guest room attendant, and an assistant manager determined how to allocate the money for guest incentives. In recent months, regular guests had been surprised with gift certificates to Bob Evans restaurants, green carnations on St. Patrick's Day and Easter baskets full of jelly beans in their rooms.

For the employees, incentives usually took the form of cash bonuses and gift certificates. For example, in March 1989 at the Warren property, the winner of the month's "White Glove Award," the person scoring highest on daily room inspections, had his/her choice of $25 cash, a $25 dinner certificate for a local restaurant or an equivalent amount of movie passes. Additionally, the winner's name was prominently displayed in the break room for the next month.

At the Madison Heights property, Manager Joan Susinskas handed out Easter baskets hand-stuffed with goodies to each of the team members when the employees came into her office to pick up their weekly paychecks. At the Warren property, people were talking about the employee Easter Egg hunt scheduled for the next day. Associate Manager Mary Von Koughnett had already generated a great deal of excitement by announcing that plastic eggs stuffed with various amounts of cash would be scattered throughout the property. After the "hunt," a coffee-and-donuts breakfast was scheduled for all employees. According to Koughnett, "With a staff of 15, it's real important to know how to deal with each one individually as well as in a group. You've got to make your employees feel like they are kings and queens. If someone calls in sick, we want to call back later in the day to see if anyone can bring over anything. We've become a really close group that cares about each other. At this property, our turnover has been almost nil. Last week, I had to hire the first new person since we opened last August (eight months previously)."

Fairfield Inn also had developed a unique paid leave program for its employees. The program was designed to reduce the industry's traditionally high absenteeism and high turnover rates among GRAs and GSRs.

Each employee was initially given a week of vacation per year. For every month with perfect attendance (not missing any scheduled work days or not failing to arrange for a substitute), the employee would "earn" a half day of paid leave. Perfect attendance for a quarter would earn the employee one full day of paid leave in addition to the three half days already earned for perfect attendance during each month of the quarter. Thus, an employee who had perfect attendance for a year would earn ten extra days of paid leave (4 quarters × 2.5 earned days), for a total of three weeks of vacation and paid leave.

Although the paid leave program had been in effect for less than a year in 1989, it appeared that Fairfield Inn had been successful in reducing its turnover versus the industry average. Mel Warriner reported, "Rough numbers from last quarter indicated that the annualized turnover of our hourly employees was about 91%, or approximately half the industry rate. Additionally, 85% to 90% of the eligible employees had earned some bonus leave during the last quarter. The turnover among our managers was four percent compared to the 15% management turnover rate that is normal in Marriott's full-service chains."

Another incentive designed to help Fairfield managers compensate for the inevitable GRA staffing problems was the Bonus Pay Program. Normally, GRAs were expected to clean 14 rooms during a seven-hour shift. However, GRAs were given the opportunity to clean additional rooms when unexpectedly high occupancies or a GRA's absence required that more rooms be cleaned per GRA. If the GRAs were able to complete cleaning the additional rooms during their shift, they would be compensated in cash at the end of the shift. The bonus was equal to one-half the employee's hourly rate for each room cleaned. Instead of the cash bonus, the employee could also choose to remain on the time clock for 30 minutes longer for each additional room assigned.

ECONOMICS

Occupancy rates, room rates, operating expenses, and investment costs were the major variables determining whether or not a Fairfield Inn property would be successful.

Fairfield Inn's development costs for a particular site were typically between $4.5 and $5.0 million. This included land (2.1 acres versus the 4 acres needed for a Courtyard), building and systems, FF&E (furniture, fixtures, and equipment), opening inventory, fees, and construction interest. Marriott usually funded 100% of the investment internally, then sold the entire property to outside investors (e.g., through a real estate syndication), and retained a management contract for operating the property. (Pro forma operating statements for a typical Inn are shown in Exhibits 5 and 6).

OPTIONS FOR FUTURE GROWTH

In 1989, Mike Ruffer and the rest of the Fairfield Inn management team were faced with three basic questions regarding the growth of Marriott's newest hotel chain: (1) Do we follow the traditional Marriott strategy of operating but not owning facilities? (2) If we don't, should we use a "standard" franchising approach (like Hampton Inn), or do we use a "McDonald's approach" to franchising? (3) Is there some appropriate mix of these alternatives?

The decision to grow internally versus expanding through franchising would have a large effect on the ultimate size of the Fairfield Inn chain. In 1986, an internal

Exhibit 5
Fairfield Inn Investment Assumptions
(105-room inn)

	Fairfield Low	Fairfield High	Per Room Low	Per Room High
Land	$ 528,000	$1,410,000	$ 5,029	$13,429
Buildings and systems	2,425,000	3,190,000	23,095	30,381
FF&E[a]	480,000	480,000	4,571	4,571
Fees	140,000	160,000	1,333	1,524
Construction interest	140,000	270,000	1,333	2,571
Total	$3,713,000	$5,510,000	$35,361	$52,476
Pre-opening expenses	135,000	135,000		
Working Capital	15,000	15,000		
Capitalized development	56,000	56,000		
Total	$3,919,000	$5,716,000		

[a]Fixtures, furniture, and equipment.

Marriott group completed an intensive study of site opportunities for an ELS chain. The report concluded that Fairfield Inn could grow to 350 units in a company-managed scenario or to 500 units in a franchising scenario.

Franchising would give Fairfield Inn access to many good undeveloped locations that were owned by developers and individuals unwilling to sell, but who wanted to use their land as an equity stake in a commercial project.

FRANCHISING OPTIONS

The Fairfield Inn concept seemed to be an ideal candidate for franchising. The product was relatively simple, a hotel without food and beverage operations where furniture, fixtures, and equipment could be controlled through a tightly-worded franchise agreement. Additionally, Marriott's history showed that the company was able to successfully manage "formula systems." Lastly, by linking the franchisee with ancillary support services (property management system, reservations network, group health insurance, etc.), Fairfield corporate would be able to maintain leverage with future franchisees and provide operations expertise.

Fairfield's ancillary services would create additional value for franchisees by providing them with benefits unavailable to an independent operator. Fairfield's management would in all likelihood price these services at a break-even level for Marriott. By pricing at its cost, Marriott could not be accused of "tying arrangements."[4] In fast food restaurants, McDonald's had successfully used a similar strategy to increase the real and perceived value of the McDonald's system for its franchisees.

However, under a franchise system, Fairfield Inn would lose control over prices. Federal laws dictated that franchisees had to be able to set their own prices.[5] One challenge for management under franchising would be to influence pricing among franchisees so that their room rates were consistent with Fairfield's desired position in the ELS segment.

Franchising would also impact the revenues that Fairfield Inn would deliver to Marriott. Fairfield Inn's competitors offered a variety of franchise packages. This suggested that Mike Ruffer and his management team would have a tremendous amount of flexibility in structuring any franchise agreement if they elected to franchise.

Exhibit 6
Fairfield Inn (A)

Fairfield Inn Economics
(105-room inn)
(Percentages of total revenues—year 4 of stabilized operations)

Revenues					
Rooms	96.0%				
Telephone	3.0				
Other	1.0				
Total	100.0%				
Department profits[a]					
Rooms	74.6				
Telephone and other	32.1				
Total (average of the two)	72.9%				
Deductions					
General and administration	7.3				
Heat, light, and power	4.8				
Repair and maintenance	3.6				
Group insurance	1.6				
Reservations	1.4				
National marketing	2.5				
Local marketing	3.3				
Other	4.0				
Total	28.5%				
House profit	44.4%				

• *Owned*		• *Syndicated*		• *Franchised*	
House profit	44.4%	Management fee	4.0%	Royalties	4.0%
Depreciation	(10.8)	Chain services fee[b]	1.5	Franchising	
Property taxes	(4.4)	Incentive fee	4.5	overhead	(1.2)
Corporate and		Corporate and			
division overhead	(4.0)	division overhead	(4.0)		
Interest	(20.0)				
Total	5.2%		6.0%		2.8%

[a]After direct costs of labor, material, and commissions.
[b]The chain services fee is a "cost pass through" to cover costs of area managers and central accounting functions.

Under franchising, Fairfield Inn's management group estimated the net present value generated by each property was approximately $400,000 for Marriott in 1988 dollars while also delivering an 18.0% cash-on-cash return to the franchisee. (This compared with an estimated net present value for a Marriott-owned property of $450,000 in 1988 dollars.) Under franchising, Marriott's initial investment would be reduced significantly.

Two potential franchising approaches were known in-house as the "Standard" and the "McDonald's" franchising plans.

THE STANDARD PLAN

The primary target under a "standard plan" would be management companies with in-house development and construction management abilities as well as lodging operations experience. Existing franchisees of other Marriott lodging concepts would provide a core of qualified franchisees who could finance, develop, construct, and staff their properties. The franchise terms would be a 20-year agreement with no renewal. Marriott would receive a 4% royalty on gross revenues and a $45,000 application fee.

Under the Standard plan, the overall number of projects developed would be increased because of sites brought in by franchisees. Only franchisees who were meeting operational performance criteria would be encouraged to build additional properties. The franchisee would manage construction, and Marriott would approve a general contractor. Marriott would control construction quality with a thorough design guide and with inspection visits to the construction site during key phases of development. The granting of the actual franchise would be contingent on the construction being completed satisfactorily.

A franchisee would need to arrange his or her own financing.

THE "McDONALD'S" PLAN

Under this plan, the primary target would be experienced hotel operators wanting to acquire their own property. These franchisees would have a demonstrated ability to meet Marriott operating standards. They would be required to personally participate in the business, thus most likely limiting them to one inn each. The franchise agreement would be for 20 years with no renewal. Marriott would receive a 4% royalty of gross revenues plus lease payments for the land and building. A $45,000 fee would be payable with application for a franchise.

Marriott would handle virtually all development. This would include analyzing market potential, conducting feasibility studies, and site selection and the approval process. Additionally, Marriott would construct each inn.

Marriott would retain title to the land and building while the property would be leased to the franchisee. Franchisees would finance the remainder of the investment on their own.

SYNDICATION

Fairfield Inn's third option for future growth was to follow a frequently-used Marriott strategy of syndicating the properties.

As Bill Marriott, Jr. explained in his 1988 letter to shareholders, "We extend our competitive advantage by using innovative financing techniques to minimize internal capital needs and access the lowest cost of capital available. We have 'decapitalized' our lodging business by selling hotels while retaining operating control under long-term agreements. We earn development fees by designing and constructing hotels for sales to investors and management fees for operating the hotels successfully."

A simplified syndication process followed these steps:

1. Marriott buys the land and develops the sites.
2. Marriott builds a Fairfield Inn on each piece of land.
3. When properties are open, they are sold via a public or private syndication, in groups.
4. After the sale, a syndication of investors has ownership of all properties in the block while Marriott staffs the hotel with its own employees for a management fee of four to five percent of revenues and an incentive fee based on operating results.

Each syndication by Marriott was different, but it was becoming typical for Marriott to offer a guaranteed return for the first three years to the investors. If Fairfield was going to syndicate, investors would expect about a 9% cash-on-cash return after-tax according to Richard Palmer, Fairfield Inn's vice president of finance. In the case of a cash flow shortfall for the properties, Marriott's syndication agreement usually guaranteed covering the debt-service payments for the first three years in addition to the guaranteed return to investors.

In a syndication, Marriott would earn development fees ranging from two to five percent based on a $5 million investment for each property. However, the transaction costs of a syndication, which included investment banker fees, printing and distribution costs, and closing costs, were estimated by Palmer to be in the neighborhood of 5% of the value of the properties to be syndicated. The syndication option had virtually the same corporate overhead costs as the owned option. Franchising would require less overhead per property.

Under a syndication scenario, Fairfield Inn's internal growth would provide a working environment with numerous opportunities for employees at every level to move up. However, it would also stretch the organization to find, hire, and train enough people to staff each property. Lastly, under a rapid expansion strategy, whether syndicated or franchised, Fairfield Inn would be challenged to insure that standards of excellence for customer service were consistent across the chain at each new property.

Mark Pacala commented:

It seems that the most important issue facing Fairfield Inn is how committed the employees will be to guest service under each growth option. Right now, we've created a very special environment for employ-ees. We're new, it's exciting, and we've only got 25 properties. There seem to be three components that are of critical importance to our future. First, can we require that franchisees use Scorecard? Second, can we insist that they compensate their people based on Scorecard performance? Third, can we get them to recruit based on the Fairfield Inn selection techniques that we use? The culture of Fairfield Inn will ultimately determine how successful we are in the ELS segment.

NOTES

1. Bill Gillette, "Hampton Plans to Rule Limited-Service Market," *Hotel and Motel Management*, June 30, 1986, p. 2.
2. *Ibid.*
3. Bill Gillette, "Schultz Leading Chain's Growth," *Hotel and Motel Management*, June 30, 1986, p. 38.
4. A tying arrangement is one in which the seller, with market power, conditions the sale of one product (the franchise) on the purchase from the seller (or a third party in which the seller has an interest) of a separate product, at a higher price than the buyer would have paid had both tying and tied products been purchased from other sources. Tying arrangements are violations of the antitrust laws and are not subject to economic justification.
5. As of 1989, establishment by a franchisor of the prices which franchisees charge for any product was a violation of Section 1 of the Sherman Act, regardless of whether the purpose of the arrangement was to raise, lower or stabilize retail prices. A franchisor could suggest retail prices so long as it did not attempt to coerce franchisees to comply with its "suggestions."

QUESTIONS

1. What are the strengths and weaknesses of scorecard?
2. Which other aspects of the control systems at Marriott and Fairfield support Scorecard in meeting customer service goals?

3

KEY SUCCESS VARIABLES AND PERFORMANCE MEASURES

INTRODUCTION

The hierarchical structure of an organization is a response to the limited information-processing ability of decision makers. The result is an organization consisting of subunits. The firm uses responsibility center designations to coordinate and control each subunit in pursuit of overall ends.

Separate responsibility designations are assigned based upon the key success factors of a business over which a particular subunit has control. Each responsibility center has its own goals derived from overall organizational goals according to means–end relationships. The degree of goal congruence that exists between the goals of the subunits and overall organizational goals will be much or little, depending upon the rationality of the control structure, including responsibility center designations and the efficiency with which the subunit manager attends to the key success factors affecting his or her goals. Although certain inefficiencies or dysfunctionalities are bound to exist, the question is: have we held them to a practical minimum?

We know from our discussion of perception in Chapter 2 that managers are cognitively limited. These cognitive limitations impose limits on the amount of data they can process at any one time. Managers of responsibility centers are unable to assimilate all the data in their environment, so they become selective in their perception of data. Information to the manager is developed by a process of perception whereby the manager focuses upon those data that seem to be important for the achievement of the manager's goals and objectives. What seems important to measure is itself based on the manager's perceptions of the environment being faced, perceptions that are themselves imperfect. We should expect two managers to differ with regard to their perceptions of the environment, since perceptions are influenced by experience, education, and position in the firm.

The measures selected and the standards established then become the basis for reports (that is, sensors), which are in turn the basis upon which the manager interprets the environment facing the responsibility center. These perceptions become the basis for decision making.

The importance of identifying those relatively few variables that are crucial to the attainment of strategy, goals, and objectives then is ultimately derived from the limited information-processing ability of the manager. We call these crucial variables *key variables* or *key success factors*. It is necessary to establish them for each responsibility center; they are instrumental for achieving the goals and objectives of the responsibility center. They in turn become the basis for the establishment of appropriate performance measures, responsibility center designations, reward structures, and resource allocation procedures. Once the key success variables are identified, the control system is given *focus*.

This chapter deals with principles of identifying key success variables, of setting performance measures that reflect the importance of these variables, and of establishing control structures that exert positive influence over the values of these variables. A number of examples are provided to reinforce the principles.

IDENTIFICATION OF KEY SUCCESS VARIABLES[1]

Key success variables are those variables in the external environment to which the goals, objectives, and strategy of managers are most sensitive. These are the key variables of the business and are the ones for which we should establish managerial controls.

TYPES OF KEY SUCCESS VARIABLES

The values of some of these key variables may be partially influenced by actions of managers of the firm, whereas still others are completely outside a firm's control. Examples of those variables that are either mostly or completely outside a firm's control are macroeconomic variables, the behavior of competitors (including prices and products), deliveries of some supplies, and actions of government. Examples of some key success factors that are at least partially under the control of the manager are product quality, cost, and demand variables. The quality and cost variables are not totally determined by the actions of management but rather by the interaction of many internal and external factors. Therefore, they must be monitored closely. If the key variables are completely outside the control of the decision maker, the task becomes one of monitoring the values of these variables, predicting or attempting to predict future values of these variable and adapting to the predicted future values of these variables.

Key success variables are also influenced by strategy. A firm or responsibility center following a low-cost strategy must be concerned with variables that are crucial to the success of that strategy in addition to those variables that are generic to the industry as a whole. The variables that are important for a cost strategy will include unit cost performance relative to competitors, capacity utilization factors, and cost of discretionary or overhead activities.

Potential key success variables influencing differentiation are more numerous and differ from firm to firm. Differentiation can be achieved through product performance, services provided, quality of raw materials, quality of labor, and technology used, or by the policies and procedures of the organization. Choices of variables to differentiate should be made on the basis of benefit–cost analysis with characteristics of the business in mind. The values of the variables that are to be differentiated should then be monitored and indicators of performance devised.

To summarize, key success factors are those variables that are at least partially out of the control of management and to whose values the strategy, goals, and objectives of an organization are most sensitive. They differ by industry, and appropriate indicators of performance also differ by application.

For example, the quality of its investments, measured by the incidence of default on principal and interest, is important to a life insurance company. The quality of customer relations, measured by repeat business, is vital to an automobile distributorship. One indicator of product quality is reorders, another is returns, and still another is complaints.

SOURCE OF KEY SUCCESS VARIABLES

Key variables come from five sources.[2] They are:

1. *Industry characteristics.*   There are certain general requirements for success in each industry. For example, costs are often critical in manufacturing industries; investment performance is critical for insurance companies; and circulation to specific socioeconomic groups is critical for magazine publishers.
2. *Competitive strategy.*   The choice of strategy further determines the variables that must be monitored and emphasized. A strategy to be the low-cost producer must in turn focus upon a detailed analysis of the product cost structure.
3. *Environmental forces.*   The obvious environmental ones are the economy and political climate. Changes in interest rates have a dramatic affect on purchases of consumer durable goods. Defense firms are critically dependent upon the procurement policy of the Defense Department. Health care organizations are dependent upon Medicare reimbursement rates. Publishers are critically affected by postal rates.
4. *Significant problems.*   Unusual problems having to do with key stakeholders such as customers, executives, suppliers, or creditors.
5. *Functional issues.*   Each functional manager has a number of key variables related specifically to that function. The treasurer is very concerned about the structure of interest rates. The operations manager is concerned about quality of goods produced.

Key variables are sometimes obvious, but in other instances they are imbedded within the dynamics of an industry and a firm and may require elaborate methods for their identification.

EXAMPLE: IDENTIFYING KEY SUCCESS FACTORS FOR A MAGAZINE PUBLISHING FIRM

The dynamics of variables affecting a goal (for example, profit) are sometimes very complex. To identify key success factors, we must identify those environmental variables whose values are crucial to the goal. This may be done by examining the matter with those managers who have had long and successful experience in a particular business. It may also be accomplished through the use of computer modeling and simulation. Moreover, these two techniques are not mutually exclusive, nor are they error free. We turn now to a simple example of the use of computer modeling as an aid for the identification of key success factors. The example is drawn from the magazine publishing industry and will provide insight into the process of establishing key success variables in businesses that are embedded in dynamic interacting relationships. This industry is particularly interesting for the subject of management control because three large magazines, the *Saturday Evening Post*, *Life*, and *Look*, were discontinued in their original form. Moreover, at the time of their initial crisis their circulation's and revenues were near peak levels!

Roger Hall (1973, 1976) has applied the methodology of systems dynamics to the modeling of a typical, large magazine publishing firm. He tested the assumptions of the model empirically with 20 years of data (1940 to 1960) from the old—and now defunct—*Saturday Evening Post* magazine. The empirical tests of the key relationships included in the general model (coefficient of determination and statistics) were impressive.

DECISION VARIABLES

Hall found that publishers and business managers of magazine publishing firms ordinarily have five variables that are subject to manipulation by a conscious decision-making process. These five variables are

1. The annual price of the magazine to the reader (that is, the annual subscription rate).
2. The price charged advertisers for each page of advertising copy (the price per insertion). This price carries a guaranteed level of circulation.
3. Annual expenditures for the promotion of subscription sales, both for trial and regular subscriptions.
4. Annual expenditures for the promotion of advertising sales.
5. The volume of the magazine (that is, pages per issue).

Hall then pointed out that variables 4 and 5 were set by policy. It is customary in this industry for the publisher to pay advertising sales agents commissions on the sale of advertising pages. The commission schedule is fairly standard throughout the industry. Once the publisher has contracted with the advertising sales agent, variable 4 is pretty much set and not subject to further manipulation.

Moreover, most publishers establish a ratio between the number of advertising pages and the total size of the magazine. This ratio determines the volume of the magazine by policy so as to remove variable 5 from management discretion.

The ratio is set to achieve a balance between editorial and advertising pages. If advertising pages expand, so must editorial pages so as to retain the editorial–advertising balance. The publisher of *Atlantic Monthly* (Harvard Business School, 1977) has reported handling variables 4 and 5 in approximately the same way as Hall has assumed for the industry.

To summarize to this point, Hall assumed that there were three active decision variables available to the management of a magazine publishing firm without altering established policy. Hall assumed that these three variables would be manipulated by the management in response to changes in one or more of the performance measures (that is, profit, circulation, and advertising revenues) that are used by the management to judge the performance of the magazine.

INTERACTIONS WITH THE ENVIRONMENT

Using regression analysis, Hall found four critical relationships concerning the interaction of a typical magazine publishing firm with its environment. We turn now to examine these relationships in order to begin to unravel some of the dynamics of magazine publishing. We shall formalize these relationships according to the qualitative description he provided.

The first relationship specified the demand for advertising pages (A_s) as a function of the price or rate charged advertisers per thousand of paid circulation (AR_k). It is given in equation (1).

$$A_s = f(AR_k) \tag{1}$$

Hall found a negative relationship between advertising sales and price, which we expect to be quite normal. This simply says that all things being equal, as the price per insertion falls, demand for advertising pages should rise.

The second relationship has to do with the demand for regular subscriptions (RS). The demand for regular subscriptions was assumed to be related to the number of trial and regular subscriptions that were expiring and are therefore potentially renewable (RT_e), the volume of the magazine (MV), and the rate charged annual subscribers (S_r). This relationship is formalized in equation (2).

$$RS = f(RT_e, MV, S_r) \tag{2}$$

Relationship (3) is concerned with the sale of trial subscriptions. The sale of trials (TS) was found to be a function of expenditures on circulation promotion (CP_e) and on magazine volume (MV) and is formalized in equation (3).

$$TS = f(CP_e, MV) \tag{3}$$

The last relationship concerns the total cost (TC) of producing the magazine, which Hall found is primarily a function of the total number of pages (TP) delivered to the readers. It is given as follows:

$$TC = f(TP) \tag{4}$$

These four equations relate the magazine publishing firm to its environment. You should notice that at least one of the five decision and policy variables appears in each of the four equations.

In addition to these four relationships, one more had to be defined. The computation of AR_k, the advertising rate per thousand, which appears in equation (1), is found by dividing the price per insertion (PPI) per page of advertising by the total paid circulation guarantee (PCG) of the magazine as follows:

$$AR_k = \frac{PPI}{PCG} \tag{5}$$

We proceed now to use these five relationships to demonstrate the dynamics of the magazine publishing industry as modeled by Hall so as to gain insight into the key success factors and performance measures that are necessary to reflect the dynamic characteristics of the business.

DYNAMICS OF MAGAZINE PUBLISHING

This model was simulated and allowed to run freely, using 20 years (1940–1960) of empirical data from the *Saturday Evening Post*. Decision variables 1 through 3 (subscription rate, advertising price per insertion, and circulation promotion expense) were fixed at their 1940 values for the entire 20-year simulation period. Decision variables 4 and 5 (advertising sales expenses and the volume of the magazine) were modified according to the values of the variables they depended upon. Please refer back to equations (1)–(5) as we review the dynamics of this model.

By fixing the decision variables and running the simulation one can get an idea of the intrinsic dynamics of an "uncontrolled" firm in this industry. Then one may evaluate alternative decisions taken to achieve control and observe their effects upon performance measures. This was the strategy followed by Hall.

Hall found that annual expenditures to promote circulation (CP_e) were large enough to yield new trial subscriptions (TS) in a quantity more than sufficient to offset the natural loss of readers from expiring subscriptions. Therefore, the total readership *grew slowly*.

With the total number of readers growing slowly, the advertising rate per thousand fell, since the price per insertion (PPI) was held constant. Given (assumed) constant magazine quality, advertisers made their choices regarding advertising media based upon the advertising rates per thousand of paid circulation (AR_k). Therefore, by equation (5) as PCG increased, AR_k fell, and advertising demand increased according to equation (1). As the number of advertising pages per issue increased, editorial pages also increased. This occurred as a result of the previously assumed management policy that attempted to maintain a constant balance between advertising and editorial page volume. As magazine volume (MV) increased, both regular subscriptions and trial subscriptions increased, according to equations (2) and (3). Total cost (TC) increased according to equation (4) as magazine volume increased. This because a bigger magazine required more paper, extra printing, and higher editorial and distribution costs.

The feedback process did not stop there. Because paid circulation increased as a result of circulation promotion, the feedback of the resultant lower advertising rates [that is, by Eq. (5)] raised magazine volume because of the policy that kept the number of advertising and editorial pages in balance. As the magazine volume rose, the demand for regular and trial subscriptions increased according to equations (2) and (3). The sequence was as follows: the initial increase in circulation reduced the advertising rate per thousand [equation (5)], which in turn increased the sale of advertising pages [equation (1)], which in turn raised magazine volume (as a result of policy), which in turn raised total cost [equation (4)] and increased the sales of regular subscriptions [equation (2)] as well as trial subscriptions [equation (3)]. This feedback process continued indefinitely and gradually expanded circulation, advertising, and the volume of the magazine.

This all looks fine as long as total revenues are expanding faster than total costs. That did not happen, however, in Hall's model. As these feedback processes unfolded, long-run costs rose faster than long-run revenues. To make correct decisions, it was necessary that management understand these intricate feedback relationships and the impact of current decisions on long-term results. This is the lesson one learns from the observation of the behavior of complex systems and from looking at what actually happened in the case of the *Saturday Evening Post.*

As profit margins fell, management had a number of options. They could have raised the annual price of a subscription (S_r). The immediate effect of that move would have been an increase in profit margins. By equation (2), however, we see that another effect of this decision would have been reduced demand for regular subscriptions. This in turn would have resulted in an increase in the advertising rate through equation (5). This because the subscription price increase would have reduced paid circulation, which, given a constant price per insertion, resulted in an increase in the advertising rate per thousand of paid circulation. The increase in the advertising rate per thousand would have resulted in the sale of fewer pages of advertising per issue, which through the influence of the policy relationship that attempted to keep the ratio of advertising to editorial pages constant, resulted in a decrease in the number of editorial pages, and a decrease in the size of the magazine. As magazine volume (*MV*) fell, so would the sale of regular and trial subscriptions through equations (2) and (3). This in turn would result in a further reduction in the number of advertising pages sold, and the dynamic feedback process would continue downward.

The price increase, as Hall contended and as seems plausible, struck at the core of the publisher's most valuable asset, its readership. It was a palliative that didn't solve the problem of falling profit margins. Whether it is a disaster or not for a particular magazine, however, depends upon just how long-term revenues and costs are affected by the price increase.

To see just how treacherous these feedback relationships can be, consider a decision to increase advertising rates. An increase in the price per insertion for a page of advertising (*PPI*) raised the advertising rate through equation (5) and, ultimately because of the policy with regard to magazine volume, led to a reduction in the volume of the magazine. Furthermore, a reduction in the volume of the magazine set off a decline in readership through equations (2) and (3), further increased the advertising rate through equation (5), further reduced advertising pages through equation (1), and reduced magazine volume, by the policy that kept a balance between advertising and editorial pages, which in turn led to even further declines in readership.

Profit margins rose at first because of the rate increase and the reduction in manufacturing expenses. But after a short reprieve, margins declined again. Again, the increase in the advertising rate was a mere palliative and did not prevent the deterioration of profit margins.

A third potential remedy to falling profit margins was to reduce circulation promotion expense. The immediate effect was to reduce total expenses and to increase profit margins, but that state did not last long either. The reduction of expenditures on circulation promotion predictably resulted in fewer trial subscribers [equation (3)], which brought a decline in the growth of regular subscriptions [equation (2)]. This in turn increased the advertising rate per thousand [equation (5)] and resulted in a decline in advertising pages [equation (1)], magazine volume, and production costs [equation (4)]. The reinforcing feedback loop continued to produce still lower subscriptions, higher advertising rates, lower sales of advertising pages, lower production expenses, and so on. The result is a decline in profit margins after three years of increases.

Given the dismal long-term prospects for the three decisions examined, the question is: *Is there a way to stabilize profit margins and achieve control, given the dynamics of the business?* Hall suggests that a way out of the dilemma is to keep the advertising rate per thousand (AR_k) constant by adjusting the price per insertion (PPI) accordingly as paid circulation guarantee (PCG) changes. This policy change results in a gently rising profit margin, but growth in revenue and growth in circulation are constant and are much slower than in any other alternative! This approach by limiting growth in circulation and revenue may run counter to other goals and objectives. It is directed toward improving profits, not revenues.

From the dynamics of this industry (that is, industry characteristics), we can see just how important certain variables are to the success of a publisher. While the firm may recognize the importance of circulation, advertising, and manufacturing costs to the success of the enterprise, it is important to recognize just how these variables interact together over time. It is clear that maximum incentives should be established in the control system to keep manufacturing costs in line as a percentage of revenues in order to maintain good profit margins.

The crucial importance of the perceived quality of the magazine to readers and advertisers is also highlighted by our analysis. Quality affects the demand for subscriptions. Advertising appears to be the name of the game in the publishing business. But success in appealing to advertisers comes through the size and characteristics of the readership. Quality is a key success variable that is derived from both industry characteristics and competitive strategy.

While we may agree that quality of the magazine is crucial to the success of the magazine, we must also readily admit that it really is a variable that is both subjective and in the eye of the beholder. Nevertheless, it is possible to identify quantitative surrogates for quality. To measure quality, management may attempt to survey its readership periodically. It may also use renewal figures as indicators of perceived quality. For example, the publisher may monitor the percentage of regular subscribers who renew and monitor this fraction over time.

As we look at the cost structure of magazines, we see the importance of the cost of paper and the cost associated with distribution. Paper costs depend on external factors, such as the supply and demand for timber (that is, environmental forces). Distribution costs, on the other hand, depend on postal costs (environmental), which in turn depend upon political factors (environmental). Printing costs may depend upon labor negotiations. Editorial costs may be almost totally under the control of the publisher.

Exhibit 3-1 captures these dynamic relationships of a magazine publishing firm in a causal diagram. Four categories of variables are included in this control model: *decision variables, policy variables, accounting flows,* and *performance measures.* The diagram utilizes the same symbols for variables as used in equations (1) through (5) above. In addition, three accounting flows (that is, total revenue, advertising revenue, and subscription revenue) and one performance measure (that is, profit) are included on the left side of the diagram. The positive $(+)$ and negative $(-)$

Exhibit 3-1
Causal Diagram of a Magazine Publishing Firm

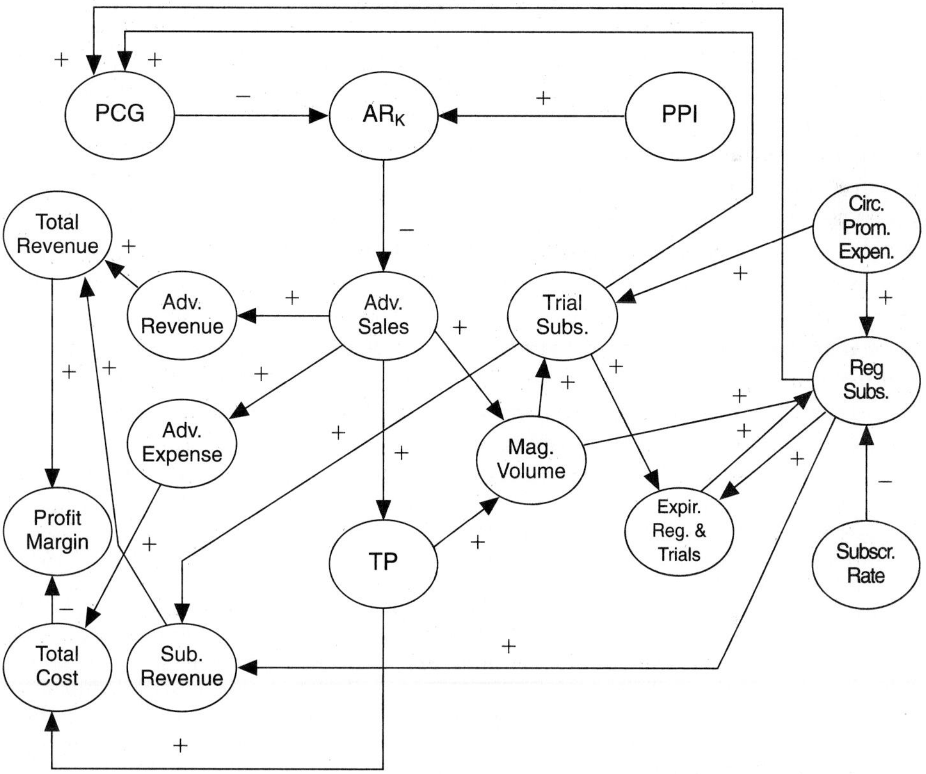

signs indicate relational directions. For example, as the advertising rate per thousand (AR_k) rises, advertising sales (AS) fall thus indicating an opposite or negative relationship between these two variables. Conversely, if the advertising rate falls, advertising sales rise. A negative sign indicates that the variables move in opposite directions in relation to each other, whereas a positive sign indicates that the variables move in the same direction in relation to each other.

Let's start from the bottom right-hand side of the exhibit and describe all of the causal relationships in the diagram. As the rate charged annual subscribers (S_r) rises, the sale of regular subscriptions (RS) falls. As the number of regular and trial subscribers expiring (RT_e) increases, so does the number of regular subscriptions (RS) increase. Likewise, as the number of regular subscribers increases (RS), so does the number expiring (RT_e).

Regular and trials expiring (RT_e) also increase as trial subscriptions (TS) increase. The number of regular and trial subscriptions (RS) increases as circulation promotion (CP_e) increases.

As magazine volume increases, so do trial subscriptions (TS) and regular subscriptions (RS). Also affecting magazine volume in a positive direction are advertising sales (AS) and total pages of the magazine (TP). As advertising sales rise (AS), so do total pages (TP).

Going to the top of the diagram, we see that price per insertion (PPI) in and of itself is positively related to the advertising rate per thousand (AR_k) whereas paid circulation guarantee (PCG) is itself negatively related to advertising rate per thousand (AR_k). That means that if the paid circulation guarantee rose without a change in the price per insertion, the advertising rate per thousand would fall. An increase in regular subscriptions (RS) and trial subscriptions (TS) leads to an increase in paid circulation guarantee (PCG).

We now turn to the left side of the diagram. Advertising sales (AS) raise advertising revenue, which in turn raises total revenue. As advertising sales (AS) increase, so do advertising expenses (AE), which in turn raise total cost (TC). As total pages (TP) increase so does total cost. Subscription revenue increases as trial subscriptions (TS) and regular subscriptions (RS) increase. As subscriptions revenue increases, so do total revenues. Profit is positively related to total revenue and negatively related to total cost (TC).

There are five major lessons to be learned from a dynamic analysis of the variables affecting a complex business:

1. When these variables are simulated it is possible to identify the variables to which the objectives and goals are most sensitive. That is, it is possible through this type of analysis to identify key success factors.
2. Goals and objectives may be in serious conflict with one another, and this may be counter to the intuition of management. In our example above, survival actually required lower circulation and revenue objectives than set by the *Saturday Evening Post*, *Look*, and *Life*. The circulation war was actually detrimental to each company.
3. If the management is not aware of the dynamic feedback relationships affecting a business, it can be misled into taking short-term corrective actions that can make matters worse in the long term even though these actions appear helpful for a time. Intuitive solutions to problems are often wrong.

4. Search for solutions to pressing problems tends to be simple-minded. It tends to reflect simple concepts of causality such as search in the neighborhood of: (a) the symptom to the problem and (b) a recent alternative that seems to have worked.
5. It is unlikely that mental models of complex business situations can alone provide a correct analysis of key success variables.

A causal diagram like Exhibit 3-1 indicating dynamic relationships is the first step in conducting an actual control study like the one reported above. From the flow chart, we may develop mathematical equations. Next, the model is simulated in free-running form. Finally, once we have confidence in the model, we seek improved policies and decisions for achieving control.

In a modeling effort of this kind, it is essential that management participate in the development of the model and come to a point of believing it represents reality fairly well. The primary purpose of the model is to deepen understanding of the interdependent nature of the firm's activities in order to improve policies and practices. There should be no rush to implement ideas before they are fully tested.

IMPLICATIONS FOR THE CONTROL STRUCTURE

Let us assume that we are dealing with a publishing firm that is organized according to the chart in Exhibit 3-2.

We know from our discussion of key success factors that editorial quality is crucial. The editor may have more influence over the long-term future of the business than any other manager, since the editor has a significant influence over the quality variable. The publisher may therefore decide to give the editor profit responsibility even though the editor does not influence manufacturing costs and has no responsibility for circulation. One way to do this is to establish standard costs for the magazines sold and compute profit as actual revenue minus standard cost. In that way, the editor will not be held responsible for variances from standard cost, which are the responsibility of the production manager.

Exhibit 3-2
Organization Chart for a Magazine Firm

The publisher may also conclude that the circulation manager by his or her choice of promotion strategies has a great deal of influence over circulation revenue as well as distribution costs. The publisher may decide also to hold the circulation manager responsible for profit, since the latter has at least partial control over revenue and cost variables.

The production manager is clearly responsible for costs and quality of production and should be held accountable for cost performance while not neglecting the quality of the product. Strong incentives should be established on the control of production costs. Margins must be maintained and the production manager has control over many of the costs that determine margin.

The distribution manager has control over the distribution channels that are utilized (a functional issue) and should also be held responsible for cost performance. If the advertising manager simply deals with the advertising sales agency and sets advertising rates according to a predetermined policy formula, this manager may not have much discretion over advertising revenue. He or she may, however, have a significant influence over the manufacturing cost of advertising pages. Under these conditions, the publisher might decide to hold the advertising manager responsible for cost performance.

The idea behind the responsibility center structure is to provide incentives to the executives of the firm to exert maximum influence over the variables considered crucial for the success of the magazine. Each responsibility center would then take a part of the overall goal of the firm and attempt to meet preestablished targets for these variables. In this way each of the success factors becomes a goal for various responsibility centers. The attainment of each goal is then met by establishing more detailed key success factors in each responsibility center and so on down the organizational chart.

Key Success Variables and the Control Paradigm

The hierarchical structure established by the publisher is a response to his or her inability to process all the information pertaining to the key success factors and to make appropriate business decisions. Through decentralization, the management gives a degree of autonomy of decision making to its subordinates. The firm uses responsibility centers to coordinate and control each subunit in pursuit of overall ends. Too few responsibility centers result in overloading the publisher and some of the subordinates. Too many responsibility centers result in conflict over the limited number of decisions to be made in the firm.

Responsibility center designations are assigned based upon key success factors of a business over which a subunit has control. Each responsibility center has its own goals derived from overall organizational goals and strategies. The congruence between subunit goals and overall organizational goals will be much or little, depending upon the effectiveness of the control structure, including responsibility center designations and the efficiency with which the subunit managers attend to the key success factors affecting their goals. This process will always produce dysfunctionalities; however, the objective is to minimize them by a sound design.

To summarize this discussion, consider another quotation from Professor Simon (1976, pp. xxxiv–xxxv):

> High-level goals provide little guide for action because it is difficult to measure the effects of concrete actions upon them. The broad goals (for example, "long-term profit," "public welfare," and so on) are thus not operative—nor do they provide the common numerator—to a choice among alternatives.
>
> Decisions tend to be made, consequently, in terms of the highest-level goals that are operative—the most general goals to which action can be related in a fairly definite way and those that provide some basis for assessing accomplishment. The operative goals provide the seed around which the administrator's simplified model of the world crystallizes. He takes into account those matters that are reasonably directly related to those goals and discounts or ignores others.
>
> Not only do his subgoals cause the administrator to attend selectively to his environment, but the administrative structures and communication channels he erects to attain these goals expose him to particular kinds of information and shield him from others. Yet, because of the complexity of the information that does reach him, even this selected information is analyzed only partially and incompletely.

In summary, it is important that control systems designers establish critical success factors that help managers achieve their subunit goals while also minimizing the suboptimization to overall corporate goals.

CRITICAL SUCCESS FACTORS IN GROWING RESTAURANT CHAINS

Calfas (1990) designed a financial simulation model of growing restaurant chains and used it as a tool to understand the dynamics of specialty/family restaurants (as contrasted to fast food and gourmet restaurants).

The model accurately replicated key financial variables for more than a decade for two restaurant chains that expanded rapidly and then failed. He used the insights gained from these two chains to test future policy decisions of a third restaurant chain that had similar dynamics but had not yet encountered difficulty. The idea was to advise company executives of this third chain of the steps that could be taken to prevent any pathological tendencies from developing.

The model was designed in four interrelated sectors: *financial, human resources, competitive,* and *business fundamentals.* Each sector added explanatory power to the results. The financial sector was concerned with the sources of debt and equity capital of growing restaurant chains and their relationship to the number of restaurant sites in operation. The human resource sector dealt with the rate of development of managers to run the growing sites, including the impact of training and incentives on efficiency of operations. The competitive sector dealt with changes in the number of customers that occurred over time as a result of customer service and competition. Finally, business fundamentals attempted to capture the impact of key business variables on the customer base, including site selection, advertising, product quality, perceived value, cleanliness, and service.

The inputs to the model included accumulated statistical information as well as "softer" information from interviews and trade data. Many of the relationships of the model were validated statistically. The outputs of the model were also compared to actual results; the fit was very close in all cases, lending credibility to the results. Restaurant executives were then asked about the credibility of the results and confirmed the relationships and the results indicated by the model.

KEY SUCCESS FACTORS FOR RESTAURANTS

The model identified a number of critical success factors that were common to each of the three restaurant chains studied (Calfas, pp. 170–171). They may be grouped into four categories:

- *Customer focus.* Success comes by focusing on the changing needs and preferences of customers. These environmental variables must be monitored carefully.
- *Excellence in human relations.* Growing restaurant chains need a growing number of competent managers. The success of these chains is contingent upon recruiting and retaining competent store managers. This requires good recruitment techniques as well as good incentive programs relative to the competition.
- *Adaptability.* Changing customer preferences require a firm to be constantly repositioning. This needs to be seen as a fundamental part of the business.
- *Value.* Successful chains deliver superior value to the customer in comparison to price, thus making the ratio of value to price a key success variable.

Calfas predicted that by managing the values of these four groups of key success variables within a desirable range, the management of this type of restaurant would succeed.

DETERMINING KEY SUCCESS VARIABLES BY ANALYSIS AND INTERVIEW

Control systems designers should thoroughly understand the industry before attempting to identify key success variables. This includes knowledge of the competition and of environmental forces impacting the industry. In addition, the designer must thoroughly understand the particular company, its history, culture, and strategy.

With this background information, the designer then may use interviews to identify key success factors at each organizational level. After discussing a manager's overall goals, objectives, and strategies, the designer may ask a few critical questions in order to zero in on true key success variables. Designers who have had extensive experience in identifying key success variables recommend that the following three questions be asked of managers in order to identify key success factors[3]:

> Will you please tell me, in whatever order they come to mind, those things that you see as critical success factors in your job at this time?
>
> Let me ask the same question concerning critical success factors in another way. In what one, two, or three areas would failure to perform hurt you the most? In short, where would you most hate to see something go wrong?
>
> Assume you are placed in a dark room with no access to the outside world, except for food and water, today. What would you most want to know about the business when you came out two weeks later?

If a business area is well understood by management, the three questions should elicit reasonably accurate key success factors. If not, the questions may lead to answers that mislead the designer.

DYNAMICS OF THE CONTROL PROCESS[4]

Previous sections of this chapter have considered the process of identifying the economic key success variables of the firm. It is also possible to examine the dynamics of the control system itself by using our two sets of mutually supportive systems. These dynamics also have a significant influence on the ability of the organization to achieve control. As the organization progresses in time, the various aspects of the subsystems interact. These interactions can be described as various patterns of cause and effect relationships. When the subsystems are appropriately aligned, they produce mutually supportive interactions that contribute to the efforts to achieve control. In contrast, when they are out of alignment they frustrate attempts to achieve control.

Patterns of cause and effect in systems often are circular or "linking back" to the first variable. We call these circles of causality *causal loops*. Exhibit 3-3 is an example of a causal loop. Activity A influences B, which in turn influences C, which then influences A. We actually used such loops in the magazine publishing example above. Let's review another example of how such a causal loop works but this time in the context of the dynamics of the control process.

Let's assume that a member of the organization expresses trust in another member (action A). The second member, influenced by this action, might take on expanded responsibilities to ensure that an expected outcome is achieved (action B). The improved outcome might lead a third member to comment to the first that the second member can be counted on to perform, thus increasing A's trust (action C). This is an example of a *reinforcing* causal loop in a positive direction. The opposite can also occur. Reducing trust might cause a member to reduce

Exhibit 3-3
Reinforcing Causal Diagram

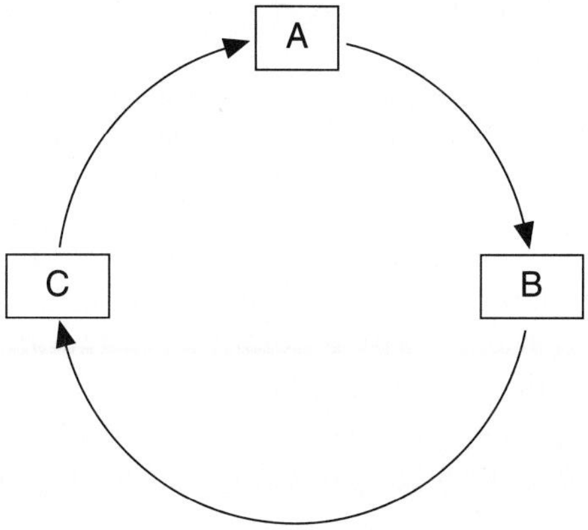

effort, thus further reducing trust. This too is a reinforcing spiral but in a downward direction.

A reinforcing loop does not occur forever. Limiting forces materialize. Systems thinking recognizes that a change in one variable can cause changes in secondary variables. These secondary changes, not so obvious at first, can begin to feed back influences over time that limit the reinforcement process. For example, if a third party overheard the lack of trust member A has in member B, he or she might begin expressing trust in B, thus *balancing* the downward spiral. The second causal loop thus balances the first.

The second causal loop took some time to take effect. The *delay* is the third building block of systems thinking along with *reinforcing* and *balancing* loops. Many of the dynamics we observe are due to unforeseen delays. From a management control perspective, the designer can use this kind of dynamic systems thinking to enhance the mutually supportive and adaptive dimensions of the control system.

A general principle to note based on the preceding discussion is

When a reinforcing process is set into motion in order to achieve a desired result, it also sets into motion secondary effects, which usually slow down the primary effect.

When a subsystem or element is changed in the MSSM, each other subsystem and element should be examined to understand the secondary effects. For example, to reduce costs, the management could reduce the number of phones in the entire organization. If informal communications were carried out in the organization by phone messages, the loss of efficiency due to reduced coordination might increase costs more than the reduction due to lower phone costs.

A second class of problems can be explained with a systems paradigm Senge calls the "Quick Fix"; an easy action is taken which only solves the problem temporarily but makes matters worse in the long run, like many of the proposed solutions we reviewed in the magazine publishing industry above. Another example is the behavior of a dominant team member who blocks or curtails informal planning efforts with a pet solution to a new problem. An open environment coupled with a rigorous search for information and a thorough analysis of data is crucial to minimizing reliance on the Quick Fix.

Another problem, this one caused by delays, occurs frequently in the control process when management tends to *overreact* to a problem. Still another dynamic problem involves *lowering expectations.* This situation occurs when a problem is complex and management lacks resolve. Eroding goals reduce tension to resolve the gap between performance and expectations. This relaxation typically results in lowered accomplishments.

Senge (1990) and Kirby (1992) have shown that these dynamic control problems can be minimized by creating a *learning* (that is, *adaptive*) *organization.* As discussed in these two studies, a learning organization requires the development of a shared vision of what the organization wants to accomplish, an environment that is continuously open to new ideas, one that encourages individual learning and mastery, and leadership by example.

The management style most supportive of the learning organization is a participative one. The use of multidisciplinary teams (that is, coordinating mechanisms) for problem solving also fosters learning. Executive staffs, policy committees, concurrent engineering groups, and planning groups all include cross unit membership and can represent team-like coordinating mechanisms. An example of goal-congruent team dynamics in terms of our adaptive control framework is given below.

THE DYNAMICS OF CONTROLLING A MANAGEMENT TEAM

The first step a newly formed team must take is to develop a shared vision for its goal or objective. Then they must assess the current situation in terms of the vision. To do this they must gather information to refine their understanding of the current situation and then determine appropriate action. As a result of the process of implementing the actions and gathering more feedback, members emerge in different roles more suited to the needs of the goal and vision. The team essentially learns to be effective. Each one of these steps requires support from the control system.

Using findings from Kirby's study of successful and unsuccessful teams, Exhibit 3-4 shows the reinforcing system of informal activities that allowed the most successful teams to achieve their goals. The key environmental issue found in the most successful teams was a culture of trust and openness. The leader of these teams had few preconceived assumptions or beliefs about the "best way" to perform any given action. The groups used a free interchange of ideas in their search procedures to weigh the benefits of any suggested actions. This culture led to the development of a shared vision of the desired objective and a search for the processes that optimize output. These activities represent informal planning activities. Once the process of making improvements was underway, team members assumed roles that better supported the process of further improvement. This led to an environment that fostered team or staff learning. After operating in this environment for

Exhibit 3-4
Reinforcing System of Informal Activities

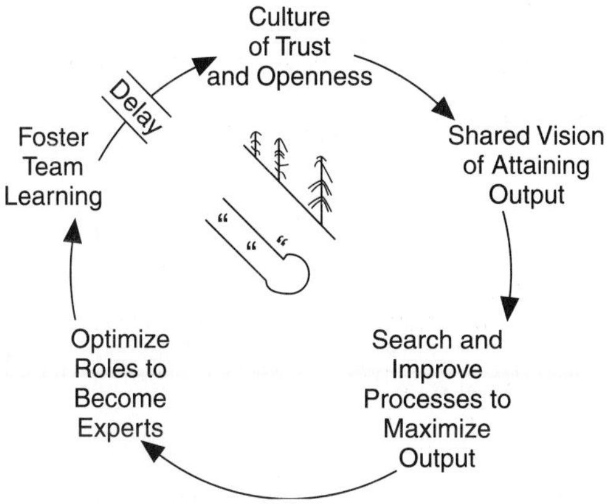

some time, during which the teams developed and refined these skills, the process began to provide reinforcing feedback for increasing the level of trust and openness. This further reinforced the other activities, thus accelerating their efficiency.

Unfortunately, neither management staffs nor improvement teams will continue to improve their output endlessly. Exhibit 3-5 introduces the key limiting or balancing factors to this learning engine. There seem to be five such limiting factors. They should be expected in poorly performing teams and to some extent, eventually, in successful teams.

Teams that begin to fail or fail often have a leader or *dominant member* who carries strong preconceived beliefs about how the management team should act. This situation seems to block the discovery and ownership attributes present in the open dialogue of goal-seeking groups and balances the culture of openness and trust.

Clockwise along the reinforcing loop, the next limiting factor is a gradual *erosion of the commitment* to the goals of the team, which erodes the common vision. There are various degrees of commitment, the minimum being apathy and the maximum being total commitment. As levels of commitment fall, the amount of energy devoted to the goal falls.

Even if a staff remains committed to a goal and retains a culture of openness and trust, it can still be unsuccessful if it lacks an *adequate model of cause and effect*. These models are necessary to understand the meaning of data and in order to facilitate specific actions. The models available include many of the techniques associated with total quality management (TQM).

Exhibit 3-5
Reinforcing System of Informal Activities
with Balancing Items

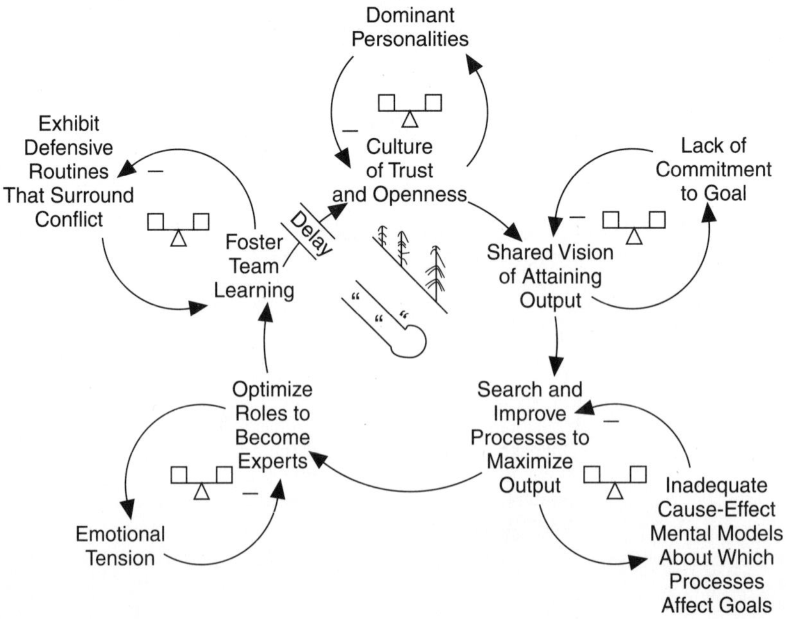

As team members seek to optimize their roles and become experts, a source of motivating energy propels them to close the gap between current performance and their goal. Senge calls this *creative tension;* the opposite of creative tension is *emotional tension.* Emotional tension distracts members from pursuit of their goal by forcing them to spend increasingly larger amounts of time in ambiguous roles. The matrix structure is particularly prone to role ambiguity because of the competing and often ambiguous instructions given to program participants by program and functional managers. Emotional tension tends to balance the positive forces that encourage mutually supportive emergent roles. Similarly, when staffs or teams exhibit *defensive routines* in reaction to team conflicts, team learning is curtailed. How teams respond to conflict frequently separates the excellent from the mediocre teams.

In summary, our analysis indicates that team learning is facilitated by the informal subsystems of control. But the formal elements of the control system also interact with the informal elements. Exhibit 3-6 shows the interaction of the informal with the formal elements of the control process.

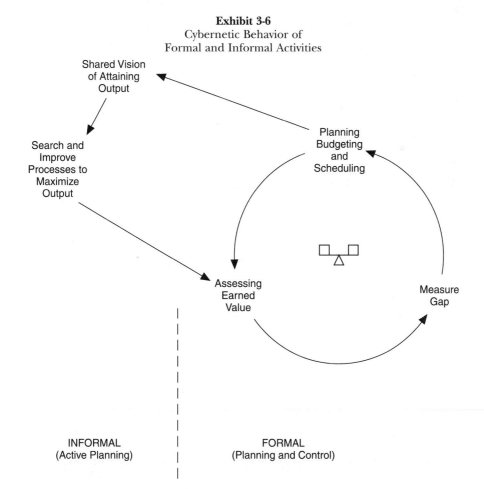

Exhibit 3-6
Cybernetic Behavior of
Formal and Informal Activities

Shared Vision
of Attaining
Output

Planning
Budgeting
and
Scheduling

Search and
Improve
Processes to
Maximize
Output

Assessing
Earned
Value

Measure
Gap

INFORMAL
(Active Planning)

FORMAL
(Planning and Control)

Exhibit 3-6 illustrates the cybernetic behavior of both the informal and formal planning activities for a team working on an improvement project. The two activities shown on the left come from the informal systems and involve searching for data, seeking new directions, and formulating plans. These activities are most prevalent during times when teams are searching for data, seeking new directions, and formulating plans. The balancing feedback on the right illustrates the relationships of formal and informal processes. Formal planning and control processes are seen as the formal aspects of attaining output goals through shared vision, assessing the gap between performance and the vision, and taking steps in the planning and budgeting process to close the gap. The formal interacts with the informal to allow the team to achieve its goals. The formal gap-measuring activities allow the team to steer its efforts towards goals.

Showing the formal and informal control activities within the context of the entire control system produces a mutually supportive reinforcing learning system. Exhibit 3-7 displays a reinforcing loop which we might call the *adaptive control* or *learning engine.* The reinforcing loop shows the additional influence of formal and informal rewards (as a result of measurement) on team learning, thus linking the structural aspects of the control system to the process aspects.

Finally, we are in a position to view the entire dynamics of the control system as it affects team performance. Exhibit 3-8 is such a view. Two elements of the control structure not previously discussed are included at the top left. Both set the initial conditions for teams. Prior training or indoctrination for the team is one element, and infrastructure or formal chartering of the team is the other.

The familiar reinforcing loop of culture, vision, search, and so on is the upper reinforcing loop along with the five potentially balancing items shown along the outside. The formal control balancing activities support the informal planning processes. The outer loop of measurement and rewards reinforces team learning at the bottom of the structure.

Exhibit 3-7
The Adaptive Control Engine

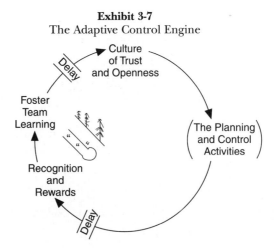

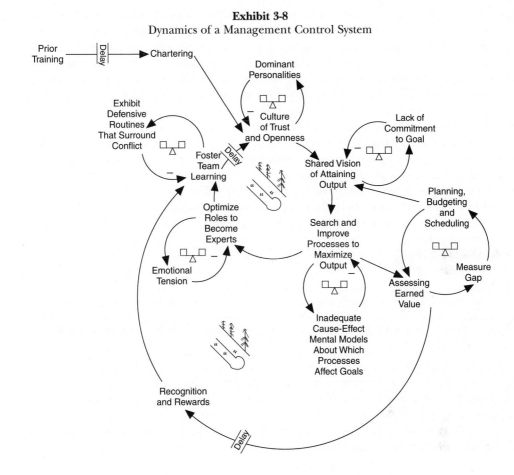

Exhibit 3-8
Dynamics of a Management Control System

The progress of the team is determined largely by how closely the leadership of the team can come to creating the mutually supporting reinforcing loops by using appropriate elements of the control subsystems in a dynamic manner. At any given moment, some loops are rapidly cycling while others are sitting idle.

COMPREHENSIVE PERFORMANCE INDICATORS

We want to identify the variables that influence success at each level of the organization so that we can monitor and predict the values they take. The idea is to influence them toward desirable values or, if that is not possible, to adapt our actions to the values taken by these key variables so as to attempt to compensate appropriately. The variables that we want to monitor are those that are causally related to our goals, objectives, and strategy. They should be identified at each level and for each responsibility center of the organization.

There is a big danger when we approach the problem of measurement, which is concerned with both the key variables that are included within the measurements and those that are excluded. The danger is that the variables that are easy to measure will be those that get all the attention. This tends to shift the attention of everyone to the values taken by these variables to the exclusion of those values that are difficult to measure but no less and perhaps more important to the achievement of long-run goals. The classic case, of course, is one where the firm emphasizes short-run profit in its measurements to a point where managers are encouraged to produce good "numbers" regardless of the effects upon the long-run welfare of the business. This often results in the reduction of discretionary expenses such as research and development, maintenance, employee development, and others that have no immediate effect upon performance but do contribute significantly to the accomplishment of long-range goals.

What we learn from these experiences is that what we choose to measure in our control systems is neither neutral nor objective. Drucker (1973, p. 496) puts it this way:

> In a perceptual situation of complexity, that is, in any social situation of the kind we deal with in business enterprise, the act of measurement is, however, neither objective nor neutral. It is subjective and necessarily biased. It changes both the event and the observer. For it changes the perception of the observer—if it does not altogether create his perception. Events in a social situation acquire value by the fact that they are being singled out for the attention of being measured. . . . controls create vision. They change both the events measured and the observer. They endow events not only with meaning but with value. And this means that the basic question is not "How do we control?" but "What do we measure in our control system?"

This should lead us to a number of precautions with regard to the measurements used in any responsibility center. First, the variables that are measured should be those that are important given the strategy we have selected in pursuit of our goals and objectives. Second, to prevent confusion, only those variables that are crucial should be measured, and they should be "measured" even if they are qualitative. Qualitative key variables may have quantitative surrogates. If they do not, we simply must form judgments about them. In these latter cases, managerial discretion is imperative in evaluating performance. *Key success factors should not be omitted from the control system because they are qualitative.* Third, the measurements should be developed as a system so as to ensure that measures taken in the short term speak to both short-term objectives and long-term goals. These points will be demonstrated increasingly as we proceed through the text.

We proceed on the topic of measurement by considering a detailed example of a previous attempt by the General Electric Company to develop comprehensive indicators of performance (as opposed to key success variables) at the department level. We shall use published information of this "measurement program" as the basis for our treatment of the subject. This example is particularly noteworthy in that it establishes performance measures at the department level for both long-term goals and short-term objectives as well as for all of the stakeholders of the organization.

THE G.E. MEASUREMENT PROJECT[5]

General Electric subdivided the measurement project into three subprojects:

1. Those designed to measure overall performance of the department as an economic entity
2. Those designed to measure performance of the functional organizations, such as engineering, production, marketing, finance, employee relations, and community relations
3. Those designed to measure the performance of management of the departments

The principles that guided the measurement program at General Electric are as follows:

1. Measures were designed to provide factual knowledge to support judgment in performance appraisal of departments.
2. Measures were to be put together so as to provide performance information concerning both short-run objectives as well as long-term goals.
3. A minimum number of measures were to be used at each level of the organization.

The following test was applied to variables to determine if they qualified as performance indicators:

Will continued failure in this area prevent the attainment of management's responsibility for advancing General Electric as a leader in a strong, competitive economy, even though results in all other areas are good?

In other words, General Electric applied its goal criterion to the determination of performance indicators. The long-term, endless goal of the company was stated to be leadership in the markets it served.

As a result of this analysis, G. E. developed the following performance measures for each of its departments:

1. Short-term profitability
2. Market share
3. Productivity
4. Product leadership
5. Personnel development
6. Employee attitudes
7. Public responsibility
8. Balance between short-range objectives and long-range goals

These performance measures at the department level formed the basis for the development of key success factors at the functional and management levels. We shall say more about that later. Now we shall turn to the methods G.E. used to operationalize each of these measures.

SHORT-RUN PROFITABILITY

General Electric considered many measures for short-term profitability. The potential measures considered were return on investment (ROI), profit as a percentage of sales, and a number of other indexes, such as profit as a percentage of value added. The test used for the development of a profitability measure was its ability to guide decision makers to make decisions that were in the best interest of the overall company, that is, to make goal-congruent decisions. In addition, the measure had to incorporate the contribution of both human and capital resources, and it had to be realistic and fair to the managers involved.

These criteria led G. E. to the use of the concept of residual income to measure short-term profitability at the department level. Residual income is simply net income as computed from the departmental income statement minus a capital charge. The capital charge is a charge for the opportunity cost associated with the capital that the corporation invested in the assets of the department as determined from an analysis of the departmental balance sheet. The profitability of each department is therefore based upon its full cost of doing business, including the cost of capital used by the managers of the department. Residual Income (RI) is an excellent measure of short-term profitability, much superior to Return on Investment (ROI).

Market Share

Market share is concerned with measuring the degree to which G. E. is attaining its leadership goal in various markets. It thus becomes a good example of a measure computed in the present that speaks to the attainment of the longer-term goal of leadership.

The first step in the process of computing market share is to define the market to be served. A number of questions must be answered to define the market to be served. These questions are as follows:

1. Does the definition of "the market" include directly competing products, such as electric ranges, or does it include all ranges, such as gas ranges?
2. Does the market include imports and export sales?
3. Does the market include sales to other G. E. departments?
4. Does the market include sales to retailers, wholesalers, and the final consumer?

A limited view of the market as far as performance measures are concerned has real dangers, and these dangers were recognized in the measurement system at G. E. A market concept that is not derived from a point of view that reflects a customer need may misdirect the efforts of the organization and damage the company. The waxed-paper industry is an example of an industry that lost most of its market to aluminum and plastic producers!

To quote the company (Greenwood, 1974, p. 71):

> In many of the markets in which our departments may participate, the products of more than one industry compete to satisfy the customer wants which that market represents. Because of the fact that in some of these instances it is unlikely that we would engage in the marketing of nonelectrical products, it is imperative that we would be constantly alert to the relative status of electrical and nonelectrical products in the market place.

The market share index is then computed as the ratio of departmental sales to total sales in the market served by the products.

PRODUCTIVITY

Productivity is an efficiency measure that relates output of a given department to the inputs used in the production of the outputs. As output per a given unit of input rises, unit costs of production fall. In the long term, prices adjust to reflect the cost of production. Therefore, productivity is a key measure of the relative cost competitiveness of a department. Trends in productivity indicate the efficiency with which the department is utilizing its labor and capital resources.

Productivity for the economy as a whole is computed by relating national output to labor and capital inputs. When national output is related to labor input, it is referred to as *labor productivity*. When national output is related to both labor and capital inputs, it is referred to as *total factor productivity*.

General Electric considered a number of indexes for computing productivity at the department level but settled on a total factor productivity index computed as follows:

$$\text{Departmental productivity} = \frac{\text{value added}}{\text{labor} + \text{capital inputs}}$$

Value added is computed by subtracting from departmental sales the input costs of all materials and services. In other words, all intermediate goods that have been purchased outside the department are subtracted from sales to arrive at value added. Labor dollars are simply the sum of all wages and salaries paid by the department, and capital inputs are estimated to be equal to depreciation expense computed on the departmental income statement.

PRODUCT LEADERSHIP

This measure relates to the extent that the products of a given department were originated by G. E., including the origination of research and development that led to the product. It is also concerned with a comparative analysis of G. E.'s products in relation to competitors'. As a measure, it is more qualitative than the previous ones. The measure is put together as a result of a detailed review of each major product by internal experts from marketing, engineering, and manufacturing. This measure clearly speaks to the accomplishment of the long-run goal of G. E., which is product leadership.

PERSONNEL DEVELOPMENT

This measure is concerned with the effectiveness of the personnel development program in the department. It measures the effectiveness of the company's investment in its human resources. This is done by first forecasting the demand for human resources in the department by type and then by forecasting the supply of talent by type. An attempt is made to promote in a timely manner personnel who are identified as promotable. Moreover, the contribution of employee development programs to promotions is monitored closely by reviewing the extent to which those people promoted were influenced by company-sponsored training programs. This in turn helps to evaluate the effectiveness of company-sponsored training programs.

The people decisions that the management of an organization makes with regard to selection, placement, and rewards are among the key influences on the control of the organization. In Drucker's words (1973, p. 460), people decisions "are the true control of an organization. They far more than the accountant's figures and reports model and mold behavior. For the people decisions signal to every member of the organization what it is that management really wants, really values, really rewards."

These employee development measures, therefore, are among the most important for the control and the future development of the organization.

EMPLOYEE ATTITUDES

Employee attitudes are defined by Lewis (1955, p. 13) as "the disposition of the employees to discharge their duties voluntarily to the full extent of their ability and in the best interest of the business."

Employee attitudes are measured by the traditional measures including labor turnover, tardiness, absenteeism, safety, and suggestions, and by the use of periodic surveys that attempt to sample the attitudes of employees toward their work and toward the company.

This measure attempts to assess the extent to which the needs of employees (for example, safety, security, acceptance, belonging, creativity, and growth) that can be met on the job are being met.

PUBLIC RESPONSIBILITY

General Electric expressed a desire to be a good corporate citizen and translated this responsibility to each of its departments. Measures were developed for employees in terms of the stability of employment and standard of living, for vendors' surveys taken to determine the relative attractiveness of doing business with G. E., and for the local community by measures that indicate the impact of the local business on the community such as contributions to local charities and nonprofit institutions; participation of managers in the civic, cultural, and religious affairs of the community; and volume of local purchases from the merchants of the community.

BALANCE BETWEEN SHORT-RANGE AND LONG-RANGE MEASURES

The seven measures just outlined represent a combination of measures toward short-term objectives of profit and growth and the long-term goals of business leadership. The question is How should each of these measures be weighted in the priority structure of the management? This question needs to be answered for each department to get the proper balance between short-range objectives and long-range goals. The weighting depends upon the strategy of the business involved and an analysis of crucial stakeholders. The weighting will be different from department to department.

Once the measures have been established for each department, they may in turn be established for each functional organization. Each department may have its own unique key success factors that it wishes to forecast and to monitor. Moreover, the performance of departmental management may be measured at least in part according to standards established for various performance measures. These standards, in turn, depend upon the particular characteristics of the business, including its strategy.

INADEQUACY OF "ACCOUNTING PROFIT" AS A MEASURE OF PERFORMANCE

Accounting profit is a readily available measure of performance, and in the absence of any other performance measure, it is most likely to be weighted very heavily in the evaluation of managers. From the foregoing analysis, the reader should recognize that accounting profit is inadequate as a measure of performance for a responsibility center that has "profit" responsibility. It does not measure the impact of the business upon all the constituencies that are important to the success of the business (for example, employees, suppliers, government, and the public). These other constituencies place demands or constraints upon the operation of the firm that must be met if the firm is to be successful in the long run. Short-run accounting measures miss the contributions made by many of the members of the coalition whose needs must be satisfied for the firm to survive and prosper in the long run. The impact of the business upon these members should be assessed periodically in any well-designed control system.

The last problem with using accounting profits as a sole measure of performance is that they do not always reflect the economic realities of the business. Many of the generally accepted accounting principles (GAAP) are inconsistent with the economic principles of performance evaluation that should be applied for internal accounting. The so-called "cost" and "objectivity" principles cause the biggest problem, since they preclude the recognition of changes in inventory and asset values as a result of changes in the specific economic environment facing the firm other than at predetermined rates and prices. Moreover, the accounting statements prepared according to GAAP do not reflect accurately the future economic prospects of the firm.

REFERENCES

BULLEN, CHRISTINE V., and JOHN F. ROCKART, "A Primer on Critical Success Factors," *The Rise of Managerial Computing*, Homewood, Ill.: Richard D. Irwin, 1986.

BURKE, JEFFREY, *Using Computer Modeling to Control a Magazine Publishing Firm*, Ph.D. dissertation. Claremont, Calif.: Claremont Graduate School, 1991.

CALFAS, ROBERT A., *Why Growing Restaurant Chains Can Fail: A Computer Simulation Model*, Ph.D. dissertation. Claremont, Calif.: Claremont Graduate School, 1991.

DRUCKER, PETER F., *Management: Tasks, Responsibilities, and Practices*. New York: Harper & Row, 1973.

FORRESTER, JAY W., "Counterintuitive Behavior of Social Systems," *Simulation*, 16, 1 (January 1971), pp. 61–76.

GREENWOOD, RONALD G,. *Managerial Decentralization: A Study of the General Electric Philosophy*. Lexington, Mass.: D.C. Heath, 1974.

HALL, ROGER I., "A Systems Simulation Model of a Magazine Publishing Company," *Proceedings of the Summer Computer Simulation Conference*, Montreal, Canada, 1973.

———, "A System Pathology of an Organization: The Rise and Fall of the Old Saturday Evening Post." *Administrative Science Quarterly*, 21 (June 1976), pp. 1–211.

Harvard Business School, Intercollegiate Case Clearing House. *Atlantic Monthly* (A) (ICCH No. 6-109-0114). Boston: Soldiers Field, rev. 1977.

LAWLER, EDWARD E., III, and JOHN GRANT RHODE, *Information and Control in Organ-ization*. Santa Monica, Calif.: Goodyear, 1976.

LEWIS, ROBERT W., "Measuring, Reporting, and Appraising Results of Operations with Reference to Goals, Plans, and Budgets," *Planning, Managing, and Measuring: A Case Study of Management Planning and Control at General Electric Company*. New York: The Controllership Foundation, 1955.

NEWMAN, WILLIAM H., *Constructive Control*. Englewood, Cliffs, N.J.: Prentice Hall, 1975.

MACIARIELLO, JOSEPH A., *Dynamic Benefit-Cost Analysis*. Lexington, Mass.: D. C. Heath, 1975.

SENGE, PETER M., *The Fifth Discipline*. New York: Doubleday/Currency, 1990.

SEVERINO, ROBERT A., "Systems Dynamics, Team Learning, and Paradigm Shifts for Program Managers," unpublished paper, Executive Management Program, The Claremont Graduate School, Claremont, Calif., 1992

ROCKART, JOHN F. and DAVID W. DE LONG, *Executive Support Systems*. Homewood, Ill.: Dow Jones Irwin, 1988.

SIMON, HERBERT A. *Administrative Behavior*, 3rd ed. New York: The Free Press, 1976.

SOLOMONS, DAVID,. *Divisional Performance: Measurement and Control*. New York: Financial Executives Research Foundation, 1965.

VANCIL, RICHARD F., "What Kind of Management Control Do You Need?" *Harvard Business Review*, March–April, 1973, pp. 75–86.

NOTES

1. Students often fall into the trap of mixing up key success factors with variables that management sets (that is, discretionary variables such as price or advertising). A key variable is one whose value is determined as a result of interactions with either the internal or external environment.

2. This list is adapted by permission from Bullen and Rockart, "A Primer on Critical Success Factors," *The Rise of Managerial Computing*, pp. 390–391, Homeward, Ill: Richard D. Irwin, 1986.

3. Bullen and Rockart (1986), p. 419.

4. This section was written by Kirby, Maciariello, and Robert Severino. The concepts used here draw heavily upon the work of Senge (1990), Severino (1992), and Kirby (1992).

5. This discussion is based on the extensive studies of the G.E. measurement system by Greenwood (1974) and Lewis (1955). It is also very similar to the one described by Drucker (1973, Chapter 9).

Case 3-1 Fairfield Inn (A)

Refer back to the Fairfield Inn Case (Case 2-3 on pp. 60–76).

QUESTION

The manager of the local Fairfield Inn asks you as a Control Systems Designer to identify the variables that should be monitored in a control system for his franchised inn.

1. How would you go about the task?
2. In preparation for this task, develop a "first cut" list of key success factors for this inn.

Case 3-2 The Beer Game

Imagine that you are a retail merchant, a mom-and-pop grocery store. Beer is the cornerstone of your business. You stock at least a dozen different brands of beer, and you keep a rough tally of how many cases of each are in your back room, which is where you keep your inventory.

Once a week a trucker arrives to take your order on an order form that you fill out. How many cases of each brand do you want delivered? The trucker returns the orders to the beer wholesaler, who then processes it and ships the appropriate order to your store. A delivery of beer generally arrives in your store about four weeks after you order it.

One of your steadiest beer brands is called Lover's Beer. It's not a super popular brand; in fact, the brewery doesn't advertise at all. But every week, four cases of Lover's Beer sell from the shelves.

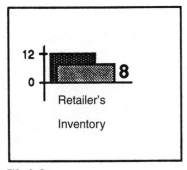

Week 2

To make sure you always have enough of Lover's Beer, you try to keep 12 cases in the store at any time. That means ordering 4 cases each Monday, when the beer truck comes. Week after week.

Week 2. Without warning, one week in October (let's call it Week 2), sales of the beer double. They jump from four cases to eight. That's all right, you figure; you have an eight-case surplus in your store. But to replace those extra cases, you raise your order to eight. That will bring your inventory back to normal.

Week 3. Strangely enough, you also sell eight cases of Lover's Beer the next week. At the moment the deliveryman comes, you're still not thinking much about Lover's Beer, but you look down at your sheet and see that he's brought only four cases this time. (It's from the order you placed four weeks ago.) You have only four cases in stock, which means—unless there's a drop-back in sales—you're going to sell out all your Lover's Beer this week. Prudence dictates an order of at least eight cases to keep up with sales. Just to be on the safe side, you order 12 so you can rebuild your inventory.

Week 4. You find time on Tuesday to quiz one or two of your younger customers. It turns out that a new music video appeared a month or so back on the popular cable channel and used the name of Lover's Beer on it.

This case has been adapted, by permission, from *The Fifth Discipline,* by Peter M. Senge. Copyright © 1990 by Peter M. Senge. Used by permission of Doubleday, a division of Bantam Doubleday Dell Publishing Group, Inc.

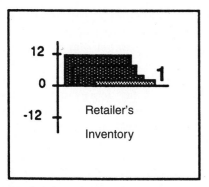

Week 4

When the next delivery of beer comes in, only five cases of Lover's arrive. You're chagrined now, because you have only one case in stock. You're almost sold out. And thanks to this video, demand might go up even further. Still, you know you have some extra cases on order, but you're not sure exactly how many. Better order at least 16 more.

Week 5. Your one case sells out Monday morning. Fortunately, you receive a shipment of seven more cases of Lover's (apparently your wholesaler is starting to respond to your higher orders). But all are sold by the end of the week, leaving you with absolutely zero inventory. Better order another 16 cases. You don't want to get a reputation for being out of stock of popular beers.

Week 6. Sure enough, customers start coming at the beginning of the week, looking for Lover's. Only six cases arrive in the next shipment. You call your "backlogged" customers. They stop in and buy their shares; and the rest of the beer sells out before the end of the week. Seems there's been a run on the beer; none of the stores in the area have it. The beer's hot!

After two days of watching the empty shelf, it doesn't seem right to order any less than 16 cases.

Week 7. The delivery truck brings only five cases this week, which means you're facing another week of empty shelves and back-

log orders. You order another 16 cases and silently pray that your big orders will start arriving.

Week 8. Eagerly, you wait for the trucker to bring in the 16 cases you expect. He brings only five. You place an order for 24 more cases. What is the Wholesaler doing to me, you wonder?

THE WHOLESALER

As a manager of a wholesale distributing firm, beer is your life. You're not the only beer wholesaler in your region but you are well established. For several small brands, including Lover's Beer, you are the only distributor in the area.

Mostly, you communicate with the brewery through the same method that retailers use to reach you. You scribble numbers onto a form, which you hand your driver each week. Four weeks later on average the beer arrives to fill that order. Instead of ordering by the case, however, you order by the gross. Each gross is about enough to fill a small truck, so you think of them as truckloads. You order four truckloads from the brewer week after week. That's enough to give you an inventory of twelve truckloads at any time.

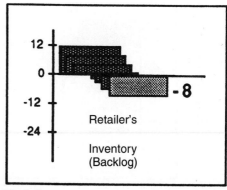

Week 8

By *Week 8* you had become almost as frustrated as your retailers. At first, you had easily filled the extra orders from your inventory in the warehouse. As you saw the trend developing for Lover's, you raised your orders from four to 20 truckloads by *Week 6*. By *Week 6*, however, you were out of beer and had developed a backlog of orders.

In *Week 8*, you called the brewery to ask if there was any way to speed up deliveries. They were just learning of the increase in demand.

Now it's *Week 9*. You're getting orders for 20 truckloads' from your retailers, but you still don't have it. You're confident that the 20 truckloads you have ordered will arrive. However, only six truckloads arrive.

Week 10 is infuriating. The extra beer you were expecting doesn't show. The brewery just couldn't ramp up production that fast. They send you only eight truckloads. Meanwhile, the stores are selling the stuff at unprecedented rates. What if they can't get any beer and they go to your competitors? You order 40 truckloads from the brewery.

In *Week 11*, only 12 loads of Lover's Beer arrives. You still can't reach anybody at the brewery. And you have 77 truckloads in backlog, and another 28 truckloads' worth of orders from the stores that you received this week. You've got to get that beer: you order another 40 truckloads from the brewery.

By *Week 12*, it is clear. The new demand for Lover's is far more major than you thought. You order 60 more truckloads. For the next four weeks, the demand continues to outstrip your supply. You can't reduce your backlog at all in *Week 13*. You finally start receiving larger shipments from the brewery in *Weeks 14 and 15*. At the same time, orders from your stores drop off a bit.

In *Week 16*, you finally get almost all the beer you asked for weeks ago. Throughout the week you wait for stores' orders. Zero. Zero. Zero. You catch the trucker and cancel the order you just placed for 24 truckloads.

Week 17. Sixty more truckloads arrive. The stores ask for—zero. One hundred and nine truckloads of the stuff sit in your warehouse. And again, the retailers order zero cases of Lover's Beer from you. You, in turn, order zero truckloads from the brewery. And yet, the brewery continues to deliver beer. Sixty more truckloads appear on your dock this week.

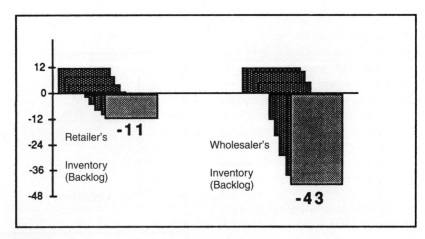

Week 9

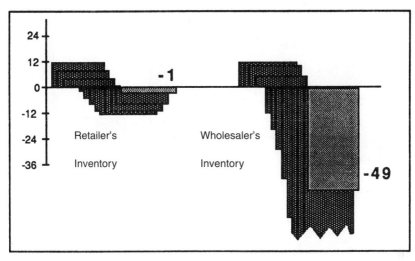

Week 14

THE BREWERY

Imagine that you were hired four months ago to manage distribution and marketing at the brewery. Clearly, you have been doing something right. Because in only your second month new orders have begun to rise dramatically.

You keep a few weeks' worth of beer in your warehouse, but those stocks were exhausted by *Week 7*, only two weeks after the rising orders came in. The next week, while

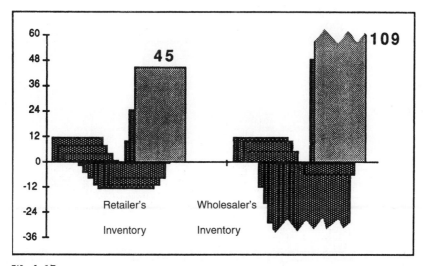

Week 17

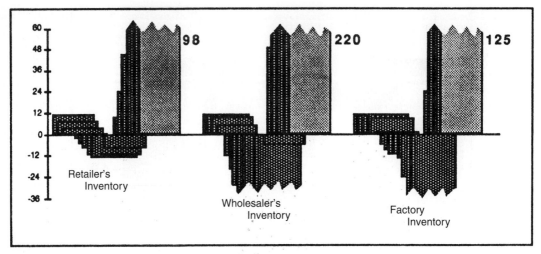

Week 21

you had back orders for nine gross and another 24 gross, you could send out only 22 gross. By that time you were a hero within your company, and the plant manager was interviewing new help.

Finally, you caught up with the backlog in *Week 16*. But the next week, your distribu-

tors asked for only 19 gross. And last week, *Week 18*, they did not ask for any more beer. Some of the order slips were actually cancelled.

Now it's *Week 19*. You have 100 gross in inventory. And the orders, once again, ask for no new deliveries. Zero beer. Meanwhile the beer you've been brewing keeps rolling

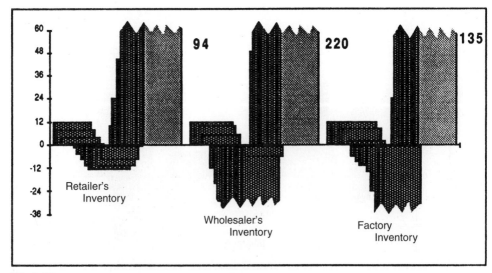

Week 24

in. You tell your boss to stop production—silence on the other end. The same pattern continues for four more weeks.

In *Week 24* you decide to visit the wholesaler. "Look," he says, "we still have 220 truckloads here." On the way home, you decide to stop at a store of a retailer you pass along the way. "Look," the retailer says, "we are stuck with 93 cases in our back room. At this rate it's going to be another six weeks before we order any more." Then you think to yourself, "if every retailer waits six weeks before ordering, it's going to take a year or more before they put a dent in those 220 truckloads sitting at the warehouse."

On your trip back, you plan the wording of your resignation notice.

QUESTION

1. Who created this instability in the system?
2. How do performance measures interact with decisions to create the dynamics we observe in this case?
3. What are the *points of leverage* for eliminating these instabilities in the relationships among the retailer, the distributor, and the brewer?
4. Using the MSSM as a framework, what can be done to improve the stability of the system?

Case 3-3 Mercury Stores

Mercury Stores, Inc., is a drug chain that sells prescription and nonprescription drugs and a wide line of merchandise similar to that handled in 5¢ and 10¢ variety stores. Customers can buy everything from vitamins to Pyrex coffeemakers, household mops, and hand luggage in any one of the company's 80 supermarket-type branches located in a fast-growing region of the United States.

The chain was founded 37 years ago and has grown steadily through merging, purchasing local drugstores, and rapidly increasing sales in an area characterized by local newspapers as one of "population explosion in America's finest economic and geographical climate."

Last year's sales of $136 million produced a net income before taxes of $9.6 million. Twelve new stores were opened during that period, and two small out-of-date facilities were closed. Average sales per store amounted to $1,688,000 per year, a figure that management would like to increase to over two million dollars. Present assets amount to $48 million.

The officers of the company have, from the start, operated under the principle that mass advertising, public relations, and superior supermarket facilities are the keys to success over competiton. They believe that the public wants fast, efficient, low-cost service in the most modern and up-to-date stores. Coupled with these top objectivers, the offi-

cers have added another objective that is "almost as important."

In the words of the president, "It's not enough to have low-cost, high-quality merchandise in fine stores, unless the public is kept constantly aware of our name and has a good feeling toward our organization. Especially since two other chains have arisen in our market area in the last 10 years whose facilities and services are just as up-to-date as ours. We must have the additional objective of keeping the public informed of our facilities and services and developing the feeling on the citizens' part that we too are a good citizen in the community."

PUBLIC RECOGNITION AND PUBLIC GOODWILL IN "ONE-STORE CITIES"

This case concerns the problem faced by Mercury's top management in implementing that objective in cities where the company operates only one large store. Management feels that the problems of public awareness of the name and of public "good feeling" toward the organization are different in cities where 5 or 10 stores are located.

There are 21 "one-store city" branches in the whole Mercury complex. The cities in which these stores are located range in populations from 40,000 to 150,000. Each branch is headed by a store manager, who reports on

Exhibit 1
Proposed Report System for Public Relations
(Prepared by F. K. Simms)

1. The branch manager will be evaluated once a year on his ability to produce good public relations results. These evaluations will be performed by the director of public relations, on the basis of the reports and information described below.
2. By January 10 of each year, branch managers will submit a report for the preceding year showing
   a. The number of visits made by the manager with municipal or county officials in his city (3 per year is satisfactory).
   b. The number of newspaper articles in his city in which the company name was mentioned, either favorably or unfavorably (8 favorable articles per year is satisfactory).
   c. The number of newspaper articles, other than paid advertising, written in city newspapers exclusively about the company or its branches (2 per year is satisfactory).
   d. The number of speeches made by the manager to local clubs, schools, or other organizations (2 per year is satisfactory).
   e. The number of training sessions that the branch manager holds with key store employees on the subject of courteous actions of store personnel (2 per year is satisfactory).
   f. The number of complaints received by the store because of poor service during the year.
   g. The number of unsoliciteted written compliments to the store, its personnel, and the company as a whole, received during the year (30 is satisfactory).
   h. The number of serious difficulties encountered with the public, other than minor complaints, during the year. This might include such things as threats of legal action, public criticism, and so on.
3. This report will be sent to the director of public relations, with a copy to the division managers for their information. The director of public relations will be responsible for visiting each branch manager during the year to discuss the results indicated on the reports. The public relations director will submit to the president a short summary of the statistics for all branches as a consolidated summary and a verbal summary of the "state of public opinion" in the company.
4. Division managers will receive copies of yearly reports of branch managers and yearly reports of the director of public relations.

the organization chart to a division manager. There are two division managers over the one-store city branches, one in the northern area and one in the southern area. These men report to the president.

Three years ago, D. M. James, Mercury president, called F. K. Simms, director of public relations for the company, into his office. He told Simms that the top management had never taken any steps to see whether branch managers are actually developing a public awareness of the company name or creating good feeling toward the company.

"We have published a list of our corporate objectives, with this one included, and I assume that managers are running their internal store operations so that we do get a certain amount of good public recognition. We have no way of knowing, however, the *degree* to which this is happening: Is public feeling deficient? Is it adequate? Or is it actually very high, in relation to what can be done? Are the managers doing all they can?

Exhibit 2
Proposed Plan for Control over Public Relations
(Prepared by Robert Flood)

1. Every three months division managers should visit with branch managers in their area so that the latter can report verbally on what they have done to improve public recognition and public goodwill in their cities.
2. The store manager's performance in public relations will be deemed satisfactory when
   a. He can show an overall plan of what he expects to accomplish during the next three months in the way of public relations activities.
   b. There is evidence that he has handled customer complaints in a friendly, courteous manner.
   c. He shows that he has a systematic plan for various advertising and promotional activities, within a lump-sum budget allocation of 4 percent of sales.
   d. He shows that he has participated in such outside relationships with the public as he deems advantageous in improving the prestige of the company.
   e. Public satisfaction ratios fall in the ranges specified below, as measured by Johnson and Leeds (this ratio is explained in point 4).
3. The first four items are to be reviewed by the division manager every three months in a personal discussion with the division manager. In addition, the store managers will send a brief written report of the four points once each year to the director of public relations to be used in discovering unique methods of public relations that might be of interest to other branch managers. The fifth point, results of the biannual Johnson and Leeds survey, will be sent to the president and public relations director.
4. Johnson and Leeds, public opinion consultants, should be employed to interview a random sample of citizens in one-store cities every two years. To keep costs down (the firm estimates that they will do the job for $4,500 per store per survey), one summary question will be asked:
   "Considering all of the drug outlets in (name of the city), which of the following statements most nearly describes your opinion of the store?"

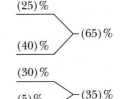

   a. "A highly satisfactory company—best   (25)%
      in town"
   b. "A good company—I'm glad they are in   (65)%
      (name of city)   (40)%
   c. "I don't know. They are about the same
      as other drugstores"   (30)%
   d. "I believe they are not a satisfactory
      company to do business with"   (5)%   (35)%

   The figures in the right column show what percentage of total persons interviewed should check this answer. Branch managers' performance will be satisfactory if levels specified above are maintained. Cumulative totals of the top two and bottom two categories are also significant.

I am a little concerned because we've grown so big, and a manager has his hands full running the store, and some of these managers may not be as conscious of public opinion as others, and may not have an inherent interest in giving special attention to this area."

As a result of this conversation, Mr Simms got an assignment to draw up a list of control reports that would give the top management some indication of the recognition of the company, and good feelings toward it on the part of the public in one-store cities

James also told Simms that he was asking Bob Flood, a branch manager, to perform a similar assignment; he said, however, that he would like the two projects to be done independently, so that the two proposed report systems could be compared with an eye to drawing on the best features of each. Flood was to be given a short leave of absence from managing one of the largest one-branch city stores in order to prepare his report. The president also told the two men that he wanted (1) a general statement of what information management should get, (2) an indication of which executives should receive various kinds of information, and (3) a statement of how often control information should be sent in. The essential features of the proposals submitted by the two men appear in Exhibits 1 (Simms's proposal) and 2 (Flood's).

THE PRESIDENT'S REVIEW OF THE PROPOSALS

When both proposals were completed, Mr. James studied them with, he says, a "constructively critical attitude." Regarding Simm's proposal, he wondered why three, instead of two or four, was selected as the number of visits of branch managers with public officials. Simms replied that a definite, quantitative result, known in advance, would eliminate the otherwise inevitable gripes of branch managers. "If we simply appraised and judged them on their relations with officials in a general way, *we* would have to say they are "good" or "bad." This way, both sides know what is satisfactory beforehand—they either do or don't carry out this task, and if they don't, all we do is point at the standard; we don't sit and argue about what "satisfactory is." Mr. James asked similar questions about some of the other standards (eight newspaper articles, two speeches, and so on), and Simm's arguments in support of the absolute standards were the same. Flood, who also was present at the meeting for studying the proposals, raised the question whether this arbitrariness might not stifle the initiative of managers who may want to make more visits or speeches and who were inclined to produce more newspaper articles.

Regarding Flood's report, James expressed some reservation about the ability of branch managers to draw up their own programs for public relations activities. He said that his long experience in operating stores and Simm's expertise in public relations practices were such that they should possibly lay out in specific terms just what activities managers should perform. For example, he cited the kind of things Simms had listed but said that even Simms had left out some important facets of public relations activities, such as membership on charity drives, membership in Rotary and other service clubs, and so on. James also expressed some concern that the director of public relations would receive reports only once a year under Flood's plan and that he himself would receive reports only every two years. Flood answered Mr. James's questions by saying that the situation in public relations is quite different from city to city and that all managers need not, for instance, concentrate on visits to public officials in any one year if in one branch the relations with the city and county were already good, or if a manager's time were needed in training employees for courteous service instead.

Recognizing that there were certain pros and cons of each plan, all three men agreed that a two-year test in four selected stores—two using each plan—would be advisable. Four cities of about 100,000 population were chosen where store sales ran between $600,000 and $800,000 annually. During the two years the president asked all four branch managers, their two division managers, and the director of public relations to forward to his office all problems that arose in connection with the systems. One of the president's administrative assistants kept a file of this correspondence and of memos the president dictated after he, from time to time, conferred personally with the various men involved.

There was, of course, a voluminous amount of material concerning problems that arose during the two years. Following are some significant examples of these problems, drawn from the experiences of the managers in various cities: Miller (City 1) and Jones (City 2), who operated under Simms's proposal, and Fry (City 3) and Kesler (City 4), who operated under Flood's proposal.

RESULTS UNDER THE SIMMS PLAN

Miller complained to the president at the beginning of the study that his branch city had always shown public acceptance of the company and that listing the number of speeches and "political calls" for him to make was going against the spirit of independence that the store managers had always been guaranteed. At the outset, Miller also said he thought getting newspaper articles, and reporting number of complaints and compliments, were good ideas and that he did not object to these points (2, 3, 6, 7 in Exhibit 1).

Jones made a number of statements throughout the two years in support of the system, stating that he was enthusiastic about it and thought the appraisal points were good. He did admit, privately to the president, that he had been "rubbed the wrong way" by Simms, who appeared only infrequently from company headquarters and did not seem to understand the pressure on a branch manager's time. Jones also said that "the system helped remind me, and even force me, to take the time to do things I've always known I should do but didn't always get around to." His principal complaint was that the newspaper editors in his town were very sensitive to efforts to try to get men-

tioned in the paper's news stories (as opposed to advertisements), and they took every precaution not to offend competing drug companies by appearing to show favoritism in free publicity. Therefore, Jones thought that he would be put at an unfair advantage with most branch managers when no such articles appeared in the paper.

At the end of the study, when the Johnson and Leeds figures were in (see Exhibit 2), Fry came to headquarters apparently upset and said to the president that although he did not know what the ratios were, he knew he was bound to show up poorly. He said he had come to City 3 only 26 months ago, following a long tenure by Mr. Forrest, a branch manager who was noted for his abrupt manner and lack of interest in community affairs. Mr. James knew this to be true and agreed that the J&L survey results would include influences left as legacy by Forrest that would affect Fry's incumbency. James wondered how many other managers would be in the same position.

Another thing puzzled James when he saw the result of the survey. He noted that City 4 had 67 percent in the top two categories (highly satisfactory and good). He wondered, "How do I know what this means— are they doing their best in City 4? How do I know it couldn't be 75 percent . . . 80 percent . . . ? I haven't anything to measure it against."

Kesler, in City 4, reported to his division manager that, in carrying out appraisal point 1 (Exhibit 2), he expected to attend the meeting of his Chamber of Commerce each month and that this, with his very active role in the church to which he belonged, was as much as his work pressures, and genuine interests, would allow. He showed the division manager three letters registering minor complaints, together with his replies, as evidence referred to in point 2.

Finally Kesler reported that the standard 4 percent ratio of advertising to sale (see points 2 and 3 in the Flood proposal) was an unjust measurement of his effectiveness in City 4. He said that City 4 had five large supermarket-type drugstores, three of which were operated by the strongest competitors of Mercury. It was his opinion that no other one-store city had such tough competition and that he needed a larger advertising budget in the face of such strong competitors.

FUTURE COURSE OF ACTION

After reviewing all the materials in the experience file, the president decided that there should be another study of the control problem in the area of public relations, one that would (1) be creative in listing the public relations activities of branch managers that would benefit the company and that did not appear in the proposals, (2) strive to make these listings as precise as possible, yet keep them valid, (3) overcome some of the problems encountered in the experiments, and (4) give special attention to the problem of what information goes to which executives and how often.

QUESTIONS

1. Assume that Mr. James believes that a good public image is a means to Mercury's ultimate objectives of sales and profit growth. In light of these overall goals, what should the goals be for the public relations activity at Mercury stores?
2. Given your answer to question 1, identify the key success variables for attaining those goals?
3. How shoud these key success variables be measured? How should reporting performance on these variables take place?

4

STYLE AND CULTURE AND THE DESIGN OF CONTROL SYSTEMS

INTRODUCTION

This chapter considers the important influence of managerial style and corporate culture on the design of control systems. Managerial style and corporate culture are related, but it is important to recognize the crucial role of each for designing systems.

Management style is something that we associate with individual managers, whereas corporate culture is pervasive and it is an organizational concept. The style of top management has a slow but steady influence upon the style of other managers and upon the culture of organizations. On the other hand, the culture influences the prevailing style of management. They are in fact intertwined and it is not always easy to separate them. But they are separate concepts and they have independent effects upon control systems design.

Culture consists of shared values, beliefs, and norms of the organization, which grow over time based upon the assumptions of what it takes to be successful. Therefore, management reinforces its values every time it achieves a successful outcome. Managers essentially learn how to act to be successful. Problems occur when the environment changes sufficiently to render those past assumptions invalid. Then management actions will not necessarily be appropriate for the new environment.

An example of this latter situation is General Motors. Blessed with a stable market environment and limited competition, General Motors had several decades to develop a culture based upon being successful in a benign market. Without competitive pressure managers focused upon internal operations, specifically financial operations.

Successful managers at General Motors learned to value stability and cooperation at the expense of customer needs. Management control structures and processes were influenced by the culture and became formal and rigid. This helped maintain stability but at the expense of adaptability. As a result, marketing was not valued highly. After all, the customer had little choice! Little effort was spent to determine customer needs and to investigate changes in consumer preferences.

During the 1970s, the marketing environment changed rapidly. Foreign competition focused squarely upon customer needs. Competition focused upon customer satisfaction, used teams extensively to solve problems, and attempted to constantly adapt to current market opportunities.

During this period, the culture at General Motors remained constant. In fact, the culture became a barrier to change—the control system still focused upon internal operations instead of upon the customer. Engineers often complained that customer-oriented design features were altered to conform more closely to past designs in order to meet cost targets dictated by the control system.

As a result of the failures of the existing culture in the new competitive environment, management has restructured the organization, retrained personnel, and introduced total quality techniques. A customer-oriented focus and new control systems to support that focus have become a top management priority. The development of a new culture and related adaptive management controls continues at this time, attesting to the importance and the difficulty of bringing about the change.

Managers unlearn past beliefs and values more readily if they are systematically exposed to objective data and can openly discuss the meaning of these data for the current situation. Therefore, cultural values that encourage "openness" facilitate the rationalization of new data and facilitate change in assumptions and values.

MANAGERIAL STYLES AND THE DESIGN OF CONTROL SYSTEMS[1]

Executives have different styles of managing, and these styles have a great deal of influence upon the design of control systems. Control systems should be designed to support managers. Style thus becomes one of the most important determinants in the design of control systems. This section describes the influence of managerial style upon each of the subsystems of control.

Managerial style is important to the design of control systems because:

1. Control systems influence the behavior of those controlled in that the controllee focuses his or her energies on the matters "that count" because this is the manner in which performance is evaluated.
2. The precise manner in which the control system influences behavior depends on how the systems are used by managers.
3. Managers differ in their use of control systems; that is, they have different styles of control.

There are an infinite number of managerial control styles. Yet it is possible in principle to describe three *pure* types of managerial styles in terms of their influence on the design of control systems. They are:

1. the *external* control style
2. the *internal* control style
3. the *mixed* control style

Under the external style the decision-making mechanism is maintained by top executives after data are gathered at lower levels in the organization. The external style uses a rather mechanical, authoritative, control system whereby goals are set at a demanding level, comprehensive formal measures are developed so as to cover completely areas of performance, the measurement system is designed so as to prevent manipulatory behavior on the part of controllees, and rewards are tied very closely to performance measures. This style is likely to produce considerable tension and will limit the flow of negative information from subordinates to the superior.

Harold Geneen[2] is an example of a successful manager who used predominantly an external control style while at ITT. His style led to the design of a control system for ITT with the following characteristics:

1. Infrastructure.   Powerful central management group, semiautonomous divisions and a highly refined formal system of goals and controls. Product managers were used to do worldwide product planning and marketing.

Geneen was very accessible to subordinates and viewed them as extensions of himself. He developed a strong controller organization. Controllers reported directly to the division controllers. The corporate controller checked the movement of inventories, payables, and receivables and detected the first sign of incipient losses, excessive stocks, or unprofitable products. ITT line managers were under the close surveillance of a large staff. Task forces were used whenever problems surfaced in the company.

2. Rewards.   Positive incentives and big bonuses were used effectively to motivate superior performance. Bonuses were 30 percent or more of salary. Managers were paid 12 percent more than the market rate. Competition was intense among executives. Employees occasionally transgressed the boundaries of legitimate business to insure that results were achieved.
3. Communications and integration.   He constantly scrutinized subordinates through the use of staff and through the use of frequent meetings. Geneen and executives spent the equivalent of three months per year in meetings solving problems. The meetings were often attended by many staff and line personnel. Parallel channels of information were used from the line and staff to monitor operations.
4. Control process.   A highly detailed formal planning and control process was used to provide the "facts" in a variety of ways. Managers submitted thick five-year and one-year plans. Weekly, monthly, and quarterly reports measured progress against plans. The planning process nailed down a manager's commitment and the reporting system measured the degree to which that commitment was fulfilled. Internal controls, monthly management reviews, constant pressures, and sampling were used to measure progress. Comprehensive analyses were performed on policies and plans as to sales, returns, and capital requirements.

Geneen's style had some significant costs associated with it. There was significant tensions between line and staff. It was difficult to justify any innovation that required faith, and it was for many managers too tension-filled an environment to develop and succeed.

The internal style is more participative and attempts to capitalize upon the internal needs and motivations of the subordinate, such as the need for accomplishment, mastery, socialization, power, and self-esteem in an attempt to build internal commitment for organizational goals. The formal and informal controls then emphasize self-control and steering control. The informal control system is much more important under this style of control that under the external style. Plans are set and problems are solved in a participative manner. The reward system emphasizes broader measures, including progress toward long-term goals of the organizational unit.

The internal control style should reduce dysfunctional "game playing," and it should encourage quick reporting of problems, since a more open atmosphere is created. On the other hand, this style may lead to the establishment of goals that are easily met. There is no *outward* pressure for above-average performance.

Ed Carlson, former chief executive officer of United Airlines, provides a good example of a successful manager who used predominantly an internal control style. His style led to the following control system characteristics:

1. Infrastructure.   Pushed responsibility down the organization to those closest to problems and sought to cut "red tape" out of the organization. Sought personal initiative throughout the organization. Did not insist on centralized control but rather placed his confidence in the trustworthiness and motives of his managers. He sought ways of being involved in operations without becoming excessively pivotal. Developed the profit center concept after extensive consultation. Developed over 1700 cost and revenue centers. He employed a small staff and used task forces to solve problems.
2. Rewards.   Bonuses were paid in relation to performance against plan. Competition was encouraged among executives.
3. Communications and integration.   Used extensive personal communications and a consultative approach to knit the organization together. Emphasized teamwork in problem solving and harmony in conflict resolution. Rotated top managers to eliminate boredom and provincial vision. Raised points of contention in an atmosphere in which peers worked as a team to resolve their differences.
4. Control process.   Used a highly detailed system that focused on results and people. Aspirations and commitments were established from the bottom up. Managers were held responsible for the commitments they originated.

Carlson was quite successful in turning United Airlines around, but his style did have problems also. It was extremely difficult to establish shared goals for an organization as large as United Airlines with such a participative control style.

The modified style includes a wide spectrum of styles consisting of a combination of the two extreme styles. It seeks participation without abandoning central direction. The rewards emphasize performance based upon both objective and subjective measures. The atmosphere is open, but there is also insistence that performance attain certain levels.

Roy Ash, co-founder and president of Litton Industries, achieved enormous growth in sales and profit during his reign. Ash's control style was clearly a mixed one. His style consisted of the following elements:

1. Infrastructure. Ash used an analytical approach to decision making and management. Litton was a highly diversified conglomerate like ITT. Unlike Geneen, Ash had loose reins on the conglomerate and gave considerable latitude to the operating divisions. Ash saw Litton as an entrepreneurial company. He was very aloof in his dealings with subordinates and made decisions through a deductive process involving few people. He possessed strong analytical powers and chose subordinates with similar analytical and strategic skills. He had a relatively small staff at headquarters and did not seek multiple sources of input on operations.
2. Rewards.   He hired and promoted the best people and gave them their heads.
3. Communication and integration.   Ash used numerous small meetings to obtain all the information he needed and to solve problems.
4. Control process.   Litton's financial plan was presented yearly and updated monthly and quarterly. Weekly performance reports against plan and cash flow statements were also prepared. Ash made extensive use of a return on investment measure of performance. He sought fewer numerical reports than Geneen.

Ash's analytical approach and emphasis upon return on gross assets (ROGA) was not without its problems. It motivated division managers to underspend on research and development and plant modernization.

We can see from this discussion that each control style has a set of mutually supportive systems that are consistent with it. Management must ensure that it attains a certain level of *internal consistency* between its control style and the remainder of the control system. For example, an external control style would be inconsistent with the use of loose or unreliable performance measures.

Finally, managerial style should be adapted to the type of people who are being controlled. If the employees show a high level of commitment or if the task is very complex and difficult to measure appropriately, it would probably be dysfunctional to use an external style exclusively.

Here again we can probably make some generalizations. A modified control strategy, it might be said, is almost always appropriate. Rarely can a situation be controlled *exclusively* by formal quantitative measurements. Tasks are almost always too complex to allow this. On the other hand, given human nature, checks and balances are required on behavior, and formal measurements provide some of these checks. Therefore, a control style based exclusively upon intrinsic motivation seems to be naive. One based entirely upon measurements seems heroic!

Although the case has been made for a modified style emphasizing both a system of measurement together with management procedures that attempt to build and capitalize upon implicit motivation, there are many styles that may be used along this continuum, and the control systems designer must be aware of the impact of style upon control systems design.

CORPORATE CULTURE AND THE DESIGN OF CONTROL SYSTEMS

Corporate culture consists of shared values, common perceptions, and common premises that members of an organization apply to its activities and problems. Culture influences many of the basic processes involved in organization life and thus has a major influence on the design of control systems. Control systems are both influenced and constrained by corporate culture. Let's look at the relationship.

At the top level, it is possible to identify three different types of corporate control mechanisms: bureaucracies, markets, and clans. Bureaucracies depend upon formal rules, procedures, and directives. Organizations that are very market oriented attempt to create market incentives within the organization in order to motivate performance. Clan-driven organizations depend upon values and beliefs (that is, culture) to steer their performance.

Normally, an organization uses all three corporate control mechanisms to varying degrees, so what we find in practice is some combination of bureaucratic, market, and clan-based control mechanisms. This section explores the use of clan- or culture-based control mechanisms.

Most organizations use values as an important part of their overall coordination and control process. The simplest and most effective coordination occurs when individual members of an organization share common goals and values. In such cases the problems of a business are minimized and a strong sense of group loyalty prevails. Indeed, the acceptance of common values constitutes the most effective kind of control process because it operates without any external influence. The values, however, must be the right ones for the environment in which the organization finds itself if the organization is to prosper.

Great organizations owe their resiliency to the power of their beliefs and the appeal that those beliefs have for their people. This set of beliefs is the premise on which all their policies and actions are based. Let's look at a very powerful example where values and beliefs were the key to success for many years but when markets were changed these values did not encourage rapid adaptation to the new realities.

INTERNATIONAL BUSINESS MACHINES (IBM)[3]

Thomas J. Watson, the founder of IBM, attributed his company's success primarily to the power of its beliefs—beliefs that he instilled in IBM and that became the basis for its culture. These beliefs included respect for the individual, customer service, and dedication to excellence. Historically, IBM has functioned so effectively that it is worth reviewing its belief system in detail. More recently, it has encountered severe problems. As a result, it is also desirable to review changes that it is seeking to make in its culture and in its formal and informal systems.

Respect for the Individual

Watson promoted respect for the individual at IBM in a number of ways. IBM has always seen *job security* as an important need of the individual. As a result, the company has done everything possible throughout the years to avoid layoffs. Job security was further enhanced by stressing the responsibility of managers to work with their people, to train them, and to help improve and enlarge their jobs.

The company instituted an open-door policy as a key element of respect for the individual. Its mere existence exercised a moderating influence on management. Whenever managers made decisions affecting any of their people, they knew they would be held accountable to higher management for the fairness of those decisions.

A strong spirit of social and intellectual freedom was instilled in employees. The organization did not want to hobble and constrain them, for Watson felt the need to maintain "wild ducks" in the organization as a way of continually challenging the status quo.

Customer Service

Virtually all decisions at IBM reflect a dedication to customer service, and almost all IBM executives have at one time or another found themselves in the field solving customer problems. IBM has always wanted to give the best customer service of any company in the world. Watson saw the value of the Golden Rule in business, believing that many people buy products on the basis of what other customers had to say about those products. IBM learned that the best way to serve customers was to provide equipment adapted to their requirements. The Watsons (Jr. and Sr.) instilled the value of putting the customer first and did it with real conviction. This simple but profound value, if carried out with conviction, can make a great deal of difference in the destiny of a company.

Dedication to Excellence

Watson believed that an organization should pursue all tasks with the idea that they can be accomplished in a superior manner. "It's better to aim at perfection and miss than it is to aim at imperfection and hit it" (Watson, 1963, p. 34). Believing in success can help make it a reality. If IBM executives thought they were second best to a competitor when introducing a new machine, they took it as a personal affront and doubled their efforts to be more responsive to customer needs.

Watson pointed out that some division managers at times became so profit minded that they would lose track of IBM's core beliefs unless constantly reminded of them by top management. This loss of customer focus is one of the potential difficulties of the use of profit centers that should be avoided. If profit centers are used, top managers should reinforce the idea that the best way to achieve high profits is to persistently apply customer-oriented values.

Watson's philosophy—respect for the individual, customer service, and dedication to excellence—was instilled into the organization by his precept and by example. These strong cultural values can be the foundation for the culture of any organization. If instilled with conviction so that they affect behavior on a repetitive basis, they can have a profound effect upon the actions and the results of organizations.

More Recent Experiences at IBM: A Company in Transition

During the past four years, IBM has been a company in transition. Early in the information technology revolution, hardware, software, and highly trained technical people were the critical success factors in the computer industry. Today, information technology can redefine the way operations are conducted. Two dramatic examples are the American Airlines Sabre (airline reservation) System and the Federal Express Package Tracking System. As a result, the critical success variables for a computer company have changed from manufacturing hardware and developing software to the provision of services delivered to the customer. Moreover, IBM's dominance has been in hardware and software, and it is also encountering stiff competition in these markets. As a result, it has started to incur massive losses; it restructured itself organizationally, and its CEO has resigned. We must ask, What went wrong?

We don't believe the problem lies entirely with its culture, narrowly defined to be its three principal values. Rather, we believe the slowness with which it has adapted to changes in its markets is as much the result of its traditional managerial style, its functional organization structure, and its vertical integration which isolated some of its divisions, such as the semiconductor division from the vigorous competition which was needed to create pressures for adaptation. Historically, IBM has been a hierarchical functional organization with most of its managers having very limited business autonomy. As a result, its resource allocation decision processes have been relatively slow to react to the changes in the computer market. The reorganizations of the last few years have reorganized the company into 13 separate companies, each with profit responsibility. In a word, the company has *decentralized* business responsibility and granted more autonomy to its division and department managers. Nine of the 13 companies are product/market based, and four are geographic marketing companies covering world markets.

Along with the new decentralized organization, IBM has added a new value of "total quality and empowerment of its people" a value that is entirely consistent with the three mentioned above. Also, in its restructuring it is being forced to revise its value of "lifelong employment" and it has begun forced layoffs of people. The loyalty the company has earned amongst its employees over its 75-year history, however, has helped it make these drastic adjustments. Time will tell whether these changes are sufficient to meet the demands of its new environment.

One final note on IBM. As it has changed its style of management from centralized to decentralized, it has been forced to redesign its management systems to support this new level of autonomy, thus illustrating the mutually supportive nature of management systems.

CORPORATE CULTURE: ASSET OR LIABILITY?

Corporate culture may be either a major asset or a major liability (the case of IBM illustrates both). If the culture is strong, lined up with the needs of the environment, and adaptable to changes in the environment, it is a significant asset for achieving adaptive control. If the culture is strong and poorly adapted to the needs of environment faced by the firm, control may be very difficult or impossible to achieve without culture change. If it is weak, it will have very little influence, good or bad.

Deciphering Corporate Culture[4]

The strength of a corporate culture depends upon:

1. Its "thickness": how many important assumptions are shared by the organization.
2. How widely the assumptions are shared.
3. The "clarity" of the ordering: how clear it is that some assumptions are more important than others.

We may infer the content of a corporate culture by learning of the background of the founders of the organization and other key leaders who followed the founders. We should pay particular attention to the purposes they had in mind in bringing the organization into existence.

Values brought into existence by founders tend to be refined and altered by crises the organization has faced during its history. As a result, we can infer the values of an organization by noting how it responded to crises and what was learned from these crises.

Finally, we can infer the values of an organization by noting what the organization considers deviant behavior and how it responds to such behavior.

Steps in Imposing Cultural Change

Because culture involves values and beliefs, cultural change is very difficult to bring about. As a result, management should do everything it can before attempting cultural change. In some instances, however, the gap between performance and expectations may be simply too large. *It may not be possible to achieve control without cultural change.*

Cultures seem to be formed early in excellent organizations and are reinforced by succeeding generations. Change is instituted only when growth or socioeconomic conditions force management to reevaluate the prevailing culture. When management needs to overcome resistance to cultural change, it can take the following steps (Sathe, pp. 386–393):

1. Promote intrinsic motivation by getting people to see the inherent worth of what they are being asked to do.
2. Nullify inappropriate justifications for retaining the old beliefs by giving people a way out.
3. Communicate the new pattern of beliefs and values by appropriate timing and by achieving consensus through identification with respected associates and by challenging them with the "try it, you'll like it" approach.

Other steps include giving rewards to employees who are contributing to cultural change and penalties to those who are not. Identifying, recognizing, and rewarding individuals who are trying to adapt to change reinforces desirable attitudes and behaviors. Cultural change can be a "messy" process in which the above steps are undertaken concurrently with actions that seem to be achieving new goals rewarded appropriately.

There may be times when a change of culture is required by environmental circumstances but people are unable to accept change. In such cases, the only alternative may be to replace the leaders of the "resistance movement."

Finally, once cultural change is begun, management must be sure that other sub systems of the control system are changed to properly implement the cultural change in the control system.

IMPACT OF CORPORATE CULTURE UPON CONTROL SYSTEMS

Control systems must be designed to fit and support the prevailing culture of an organization. The values that management wants to stress should be measured and rewarded. These values should be the focal points of the control system.

Major cultural change is unlikely to be produced by changes in the control subsystems alone since changes in the control subsystems will not alter values. The danger of such an approach is that if the control subsystems are changed without an appropriate change in values, behavior will remain unaffected. On the other hand, there are reported instances of formal control systems preventing the adoption of desirable values. One may have to change formal control systems, in some cases, in order to permit new values to emerge!

AN ILLUSTRATION: CULTURAL CHANGES AND THEIR IMPACT UPON ADAPTIVE CONTROL SYSTEMS—GENERAL ELECTRIC COMPANY[5]

General Electric, under the chairmanship of Jack Welch, has changed its culture and control systems to become more adaptable, tolerant of change, and agile. Welch has established a globally oriented vision of becoming either number one or number two in all markets in which General Electric competes. He has clearly communicated this purpose to General Electric employees. New supportive values also have been communicated and followed by top management.

Given this redirection of purpose and values, changes in organizational controls would be expected. That is exactly what has occurred. Communication links have been shortened, ad hoc meetings and one-on-one interactions have increased, while formal control systems have been modified to reduce rigidity.

Exhibits 4-1 and 4-2 summarize key changes made by Welch both in the formal and informal systems within the General Electric Company since 1981, using our adaptive control perspective. Indeed, Welch has strengthened the *informal systems*, while reducing procedurally oriented formal controls. These changes have permitted adaptation in values and systems elsewhere in the company as well.

A recent case involving the manufacture of compressors for refrigerators at the General Electric Company's Louisville plant further illustrates the relationships between changes in purpose, changes in values, and formal and informal controls.[6]

Exhibit 4-1
Formal Control Systems
General Electric under Welch

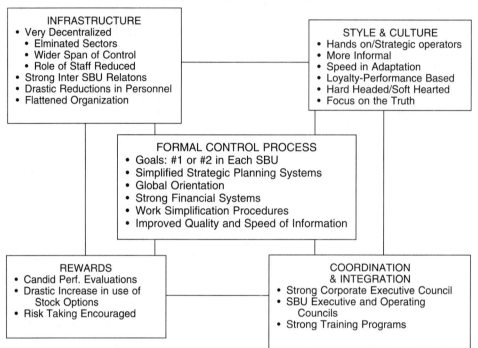

General Electric's formal systems were signaling problems in the refrigerator market. Profits were off. Market share was falling. Competitors were gaining on a number of fronts. Matsushita was making higher-quality and less expensive compressors. Mitsubishi was manufacturing advanced technology rotary compressors. Whirlpool, GE's chief competitor in refrigerators, was moving its compressor manufacturing facilities to Brazil to take advantage of very low-cost labor. Finally, Matsushita and Necchi began to offer compressors to GE at a much lower price than GE's cost of manufacture. All signals from the formal system pointed to a very significant problem.

A consensus was building in support of purchasing compressors abroad in order to address these competitive problems. This meant closing the compressor plant in Louisville. The consensus was supported by the prevailing opinion that the Japanese were manufacturing geniuses and that GE could not compete with them in compressors.

As a consensus built for sourcing, the manager of advanced manufacturing for the major appliance business group (MABG) began to have serious misgivings about going outside for the major component of MABG's largest product group. The compressor, he reasoned, is the heart of the refrigerator, and the refrigerator is the heart of MABG, and "you don't give away your heart." This in turn led to a more expansive search for an adaptive competitive solution that would preserve

Exhibit 4-2
Informal Control Systems
General Electric under Welch

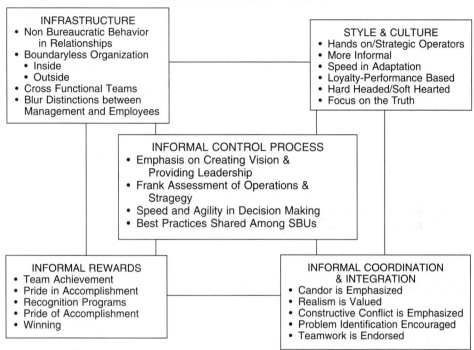

GE's competence in manufacturing. The search that followed was carried out largely in the informal control system. That is, interdisciplinary teams were established to look for solutions.

A value shift was beginning to occur at GE. The result was to define the problem in compressors as a gap in value terms, purely and simply in terms of manufacturing competitiveness. Through the use of consultants GE discovered that:

1. It cost GE over $48 to make a compressor, compared with costs of from $24 to $38 for international competitors.
2. General Electric was paying wage and benefit costs averaging $17 per hour for labor, whereas competitors were paying $1.70 per hour in Singapore and $1.40 in Brazil.
3. Productivity was also significantly lower at GE Louisville. It took 65 minutes to make a compressor in Louisville; 35 minutes in Italy (Necchi) and Japan; and 25 minutes in Brazil.

Three options existed: (1) the original option to purchase compressors, (2) build a factory in a low-wage country, or (3) invest in a new and more efficient factory in the United States. The option to build a plant in the United States included an option to utilize Japanese expertise to assist in factory design and construction.

Louisville management believed that they could build a more efficient plant if the talents of GE's MABG engineers were unleashed. A proposal followed to build a plant without the Japanese. A new goal and a new set of values emerged.

These goals and values were consistent with the overall purpose of the General Electric Company, as shown in Exhibits 4-1 and 4-2.

The goal was to make compressors more cheaply than any other producer in the world and the second was to prove that the United States could still be a world leader in manufacturing competitiveness. A new set of values were required to support the goal.

First, if the engineers at Louisville were to design a world-class plant, they had to believe they could do it. So the first step for management was to strengthen the morale of the engineers by positive statements as to their individual and collective abilities. Management would never let it be said that "it couldn't be done."

Second, the only way to build a plant to compete with $1.40-per-hour labor when GE was paying $17 per hour was to automate. The new value, based upon this assumption for success, was not simply automation but the concept of designing the plant and the product together. To that end, management physically moved the product engineers and manufacturing engineers together and encouraged constant informal interaction between the two groups.

Third, every piece of machinery in the plant would have to be American made. Fourth, additional value changes were needed for workers. They all had to be retrained so as to operate the automated equipment. The training was offered on a volunteer basis and on employee time. Fifth, workers and engineers were brought together in an informal way to discuss the steps that needed to be taken to improve efficiency and quality with the new equipment.

Once the plant was designed and built and placed into operation, the formal measurement systems needed to be changed to monitor cost, quality, and productivity. The measurements on these variables were themselves automated as a part of the automation on the new plant.

LESSONS IN THE USE OF VALUES AND SUPPORTIVE SYSTEMS IN ADAPTATION

General Electric's goal of low-cost production with high-cost labor was attained. This case illustrates how a successful strategic change leading to a dramatically improved competitive position is supported by changes in values in the control system. The new values emerged as a part of the adaptive control process. Emerging cultural values at the corporate level did permit such change in the refrigerator case. New formal controls were also necessary as a result of the adaptation process.

AFTERMATH OF THE DECISION[7]

Although it would be nice to report that life was happy ever after in the rotary compressor business of GE, it would not be accurate. The new compressors appeared in 1986 and with their help, GE's market share for refrigerators rose two points. But, in 1987, one of the rotary compressor refrigerators broke down and then others failed. Investigation of the problem detected that certain critical parts of the compressor were less durable than previously thought. The result was that

GE replaced all the new compressors with compressors purchased from another manufacturer. The result was a $500 million pretax disaster for GE.

However, this is not the end of it. The new values and revised control subsystems at GE took over, and other divisions of GE got involved in solving the problem with the compressors and making up most of the shortfall in earnings for 1988. Welch had revised the reward structure at the top to encourage teamwork and problem solving. A potential disaster was averted.

ESTABLISHING A CUSTOMER-FOCUSED TOTAL QUALITY CULTURE

In many cases, the customer is the most critical or mission stakeholder of an organization. This is especially true in very competitive markets where buyers have many choices. For example, customers currently have more automobile models to choose from at a wider variety of prices than ever before. As a result, the prospective customer can look for complete satisfaction before purchasing.

Situations like this present management with a tremendous challenge. On the one hand, they must focus upon meeting *customer needs*. On the other hand, they must *increase efficiencies* to remain competitive. It can be very difficult to reflect customer needs in the product while simultaneously meeting efficiency targets.

One widely used set of management systems for meeting both aspects of the problem is called *total quality management* (TQM). The next section will provide you with an overall understanding of the definition, history, and implementation procedures for this system of management.[8] We will then relate it to the adaptive control model set out previously in this text.

Total quality management requires that management develop a culture that will instill the belief that customer satisfaction, defined both externally and internally, is important; a set of management systems to support the culture; and techniques to carry out the steps of quality improvement.

The Definition of Total Quality

In this text, *total quality* is defined as *a management system that seeks the efficient achievement of all stakeholder expectations by focusing the efforts of every member of the organization on customer satisfaction and by using quality techniques in each of the management subsystems of the organization.* Customers are defined as the receivers of the output or services of individuals in an organization.

The challenge for an organization that seeks to become a total quality organization is to achieve a zero gap between customer expectations and performance, or to deliver a product or service that exceeds customer expectations. Quality expectations on the part of customers are influenced by:

1. The quality image of the industry
2. The perception of value created by the product or services of the organization
3. The experience of doing business with the organization.

Note that the definition of TQM includes three elements:

1. A statement of values or philosophy
2. Management systems to focus efforts
3. Set of techniques

The quality strategy of many world-class organizations has focused upon achieving customer satisfaction by carefully determining key determinants of customer satisfaction for each product or service and then translating each determinant into internal requirements. Quality specialists provide techniques and training to all employees for accomplishing these tasks. Companies that have used this strategy effectively have enhanced their competitiveness.

Under TQM each member of the organization is viewed as a supplier. The use of efficiency techniques that improve customer satisfaction is viewed as the responsibility of each member of the organization. *Benchmarking* (Chapter 15) world-class organizations in each of the relevant functions, under the guidance of quality specialists, is the responsibility of each member of the organization.

Background of Total Quality

The modern TQM movement traces its origin back to the quality control specialist, whose job it was to determine if the parameters of a product were within an acceptable range. The specialist was first required to establish specifications and then to inspect a product to determine acceptability. The methodology, called *statistical process control,* was developed by Shewart in 1931. The *control chart* was the basic tool of the quality movement for many years.

It is interesting to examine the assumptions about human behavior underlying statistical process control. It implied an inherent distrust for the quality of work produced by the worker. It ignored centuries of history showing that artisans all over the world had maintained high levels of quality with no outside supervision. The role of the worker under statistical process control did not necessarily include responsibility for quality. The worker concentrated upon schedule attainment and left the issue of quality control up to the specialist and to the formal control process.

Later, management perceived the need to shift responsibility for quality onto the internal controls of the worker. Armand Figenbaum first introduced the concept of TQM in 1951. Having been a manager of quality at the Schenectady, N.Y. General Electric plant, he noted that the cost of poor quality could occur both from errors in the design of the product as well as in the production of the product. He defined total quality as follows (1951):

> An effective system for integrating the quality development, quality maintenance, and quality improvement efforts of the various groups of an organization so as to enable production and service at the most economical levels which allow for full satisfaction.

He defined quality control as the process of setting standards, appraising conformance to these standards, acting when standards are exceeded, and planning for improvements in the standards. He did, however, support the idea of maintaining a production control department, believing that when quality becomes everyone's job it becomes no one's job! Nevertheless, he did establish customer satisfaction as the focus of quality efforts and he included concern for the activities of the entire organization in his quality focus. The major quality techniques in practice at that time were the statistical process control techniques.

At the same time, Deming presented a series of lectures on statistical process control both in the United States and in Japan. This included many examples of statistical applications of quality control to many production settings. The impact of Deming's lectures was minimal in the United States but profound in Japan. Not only did quality specialists become experts in applying Deming's techniques, but more importantly, so did supervisors, engineers, and manufacturing workers. As a result, manufacturing yields increased dramatically in Japan over a 20-year period from 1970 to 1990 as workers gained more effective control of the processes.

During the 1960s, Juran presented another approach to the management of quality. Juran recognized the need for management to be involved in the achievement of quality. He recommended that finance and control groups measure the cost of waste due to poor quality and report it to management and that management involve themselves directly in those efforts. He also introduced the concept of close customer/supplier relationships. He noted that each member of the organization has a customer (internal or external). Each recipient of an activity of the organization expects a product "fit for use." This concept of TQM places responsibility for quality on each worker and places responsibility for achieving quality onto management.

Leadership in the development of TQM then moved to Japan. Ishikawa (1985) published a guide to total quality control that expanded the array of techniques available for workers to improve product quality.

The next series of advances, which occurred in Japan, were extremely important. All the elements of TQM were in place except that designers lacked good techniques for translating customer requirements into requirements for products and processes. Also, coordinating mechanisms and techniques that allowed for close, efficient coupling of subunits and thus the reduction of costly slack, did not exist.

Quality function deployment (QFD) was the set of techniques developed for translating customer requirements into product characteristics and product characteristics into design requirements, and design requirements into process specifications. Initially developed by Kobe Iron Works, QFD was later refined by Toyota.

Under QFD, a multidisciplinary team of marketing, engineering, production, and support departments is chartered to develop both product and process specifications. Quality function deployment employs a matrix like a checkerboard. In the rows, the team lists the key expectations of the customer, which have been gathered by various means. Next, the team conducts a series of brainstorming sessions to identify the functions the product must have to achieve these customer expectations. These functions become the entries on the columns of the matrix.

Then the team discusses which product functions affect each customer expectation. In other words, the team attempts to match the columns with the appropriate rows together with an assessment of the strength of the affect of the columns on the rows. Once the priority is established on product functions, design specifications are considered for each function. The process continues until the actual production process is determined.

Another powerful quality technique is the *Taguchi loss function*. Taguchi, a design engineer for Nippon Telephone and Telegraph, developed a technique that facilitates the precise development of the production process, making the methods of establishing broad production tolerances obsolete. Others also developed techniques to minimize inventory such as Just-In-Time (JIT). All of these techniques are associated with TQM management systems. Currently, there exist over thirty techniques associated with TQM, and the number continues to increase.

We now look at the integration of TQM into the control systems of an organization.

TQM AND THE MANAGEMENT SYSTEMS OF AN ORGANIZATION STYLE AND CULTURE

Total quality management approaches usually share a common set of management styles and cultures. The following elements are usually present in some form:

1. A customer-oriented decision process aimed at satisfying both internal and external customers.
2. A management style that supports empowering the individual and encourages goal-oriented team activity.
3. A belief in continuous improvement by every individual both through incremental and breakthrough approaches.
4. The emphasis on gathering objective data to support decision making.
5. Constantly seeking new techniques to support quality improvement.
6. A belief in every member as to the importance of achieving excellence in all activities.

SUPPORTING MANAGEMENT SUBSYSTEMS

The work of TQM follows the cybernetic paradigm in solving problems, although team involvement makes the control process more informal than formal. Here are the impacts on management subsystems:

1. Top management must clearly charter the organization in TQM by formally establishing the policy for total quality. The policy should spell out the key philosophical principles of TQM in the organization.
2. Top management then establishes a company-wide quality improvement team. The task of the team is to communicate philosophy, develop experts to facilitate use of the appropriate techniques, and charter subunit teams in a hierarchical fashion with the same mission. These teams report progress to the corporate team.
3. Each team then establishes requirements for products and services, detailed process measurements for each product, and gaps between outputs and customer requirements. The teams employ appropriate quality techniques, analyze data, and continue to set even higher objectives as the previous ones are met.

A hierarchy of informally organized, but formally chartered, improvement teams is the result of this effort. The informal team organization is more adaptable than the formal structure and concentrates its efforts on cost or profit goals and schedules. Both formal and informal control processes are required. The informal facilitates the active planning and coordination, while the formal documents the planning and keeps the team focused on the objective at hand.

Teams are different for different functions. Engineering typically employs *concurrent engineering teams*. The objective of these teams is to include all major functions on the team—manufacturing, purchasing, design, and process engineering—for the purpose of designing both the product and the process concurrently. The practice of co-locating professional personnel shortens the communication channels and facilitates training in quality techniques.

Manufacturing- and process-oriented functions use *work cells*, self-managed teams of workers which emphasize resolution of local issues. The emphasis is upon trusting workers to produce high-quality products and the use of internal informal feedback as well as statistical analysis to improve efficiency.

Ad hoc teams are also organized to resolve specific issues. The emphasis here is to select appropriate members with expertise to gather specific data and to disband after achieving the objective. These ad hoc teams may be chartered by management or established by workers who are empowered to do so.

QUALITY TECHNIQUES

Quality techniques are different for different functions. The most important techniques are those used to relate product specifications to customer expectations, to analyze data to determine courses of action, or to optimize production processes. For example, engineering uses quality function deployment in support of its concurrent engineering efforts. Manufacturing uses statistical process controls, cause and effect analyses (fishbone charts) and self-checks among team members to support work cells. Management uses benchmarking (Chapter 15) to determine competitive standards in various functions and *brainstorming* to determine different approaches to solve problems and raise quality.

IMPLEMENTING TOTAL QUALITY

The successful implementation of TQM, including style and culture changes, management systems changes, and training in systems and quality techniques, is a long process, taking as much as seven years to complete. Again, methods of implementation will vary but certain procedures have been found effective.

Top management must drive the implementation process. It must first issue a policy statement and it must seek to develop expert trainers in the techniques of TQM. Next, it must attend TQM training and start pilot improvement teams in subunits. Successes should be publicized.

Next, it should start a cascading training program in TQM throughout the organization, and it should assist in developing quality improvement teams. It should then ask for improvement objectives from the teams, providing personal recognition and formal rewards for successful efforts at all organizational levels. Top management must repeatedly perform these tasks to reinforce desirable behavior.

Middle management must translate the policy into improvement-oriented initiatives. Their task is to ensure that an environment for continuous improvement is established and to ensure that TQM doesn't become a mere slogan or program, but becomes a way of life.

First-level members of the organization must accept the expanded role, which includes responsibility for learning their customer requirements and acting on this information to increase customer satisfaction. They must also take the initiative to learn quality techniques.

Exhibit 4-3 is a summary of both the formal and informal systems necessary to support a TQM program according to our basic framework for the design of control systems.

Exhibit 4-3
Management Systems for
Total Quality

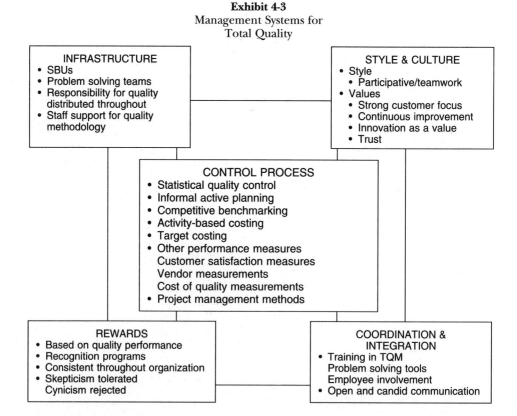

INFRASTRUCTURE
- SBUs
- Problem solving teams
- Responsibility for quality distributed throughout
- Staff support for quality methodology

STYLE & CULTURE
- Style
  - Participative/teamwork
- Values
  - Strong customer focus
  - Continuous improvement
  - Innovation as a value
  - Trust

CONTROL PROCESS
- Statistical quality control
- Informal active planning
- Competitive benchmarking
- Activity-based costing
- Target costing
- Other performance measures
  Customer satisfaction measures
  Vendor measurements
  Cost of quality measurements
- Project management methods

REWARDS
- Based on quality performance
- Recognition programs
- Consistent throughout organization
- Skepticism tolerated
  Cynicism rejected

COORDINATION & INTEGRATION
- Training in TQM
  Problem solving tools
  Employee involvement
- Open and candid communication

REFERENCES

CAMMANN, CORTLANDT, AND DAVID A. NADLER, "Fit Control Systems to Your Managerial Style," *Harvard Business Review,* January–February 1976, pp. 65–72.

FIGENBAUM, ARMAND V., *Total Quality Control, Engineering and Management.* New York: McGraw-Hill, 1951.

ISHIKAWA, KAORU, *What Is Total Quality Control? The Japanese Way.* Englewood Cliffs, N.J.: Prentice Hall, 1985.

KILMANN, R. H., SERPA R. SAXTON, AND ASSOCIATES, *Gaining Control of the Corporate Culture.* San Francisco: Jossey-Bass, 1985.

PASCALE, RICHARD T., "Three Chief Executives: How Style Effects Results," Research Paper No. 357 revised, Research Paper Series, Stanford University, Graduate School of Business, February 1977.

SATHE, VIJAY, *Culture and Related Realities.* Homewood, Ill.: Irwin, 1985.

SCHEIN, E. H., *Organizational Culture and Leadership: A Dynamic View.* San Francisco: Jossey-Bass, 1985.

SHEWART, W. A., *Economic Control of Manufactured Products.* Princeton, N.J.: D. Van Nostrand, 1931.

TICHY, NOEL M., and Stafford Sherman, *Control Your Own Destiny or Someone Else Will.* New York: Currency and Doubleday, 1993.

WATSON, THOMAS J., JR., *A Business and Its Beliefs.* New York: McGraw-Hill, 1963.

NOTES

1. Cammann and Nadler (1976) have summarized these influences very well. This section of the chapter has been adapted from their work.
2. The three examples of control style used in this section have been adapted from Richard T. Pascale, "Three Chief Executives: How Style Affects Results," Research Paper No. 357 Revised, Research Paper Series, Stanford University, Graduate School of Business, February 1977.
3. This section is adapted by permission from Thomas J. Watson, Jr., *A Business and Its Beliefs* (New York: McGraw-Hill, 1963).
4. The material in this section is adapted by permission from Vijay Sathe, "How to Decipher and Change Corporate Culture" in Kilmann, Saxton and Serpa, *Gaining Control of Corporate Culture.* pp. 230–261. Copyright 1985 by Jossey-Bass Inc., Publishers, San Francisco.
5. The General Electric example has been developed on the basis of extensive published materials. See, for example, Noel Tiscy and Ram Charan, "Speed, Simplicity, Self Confidence: An Interview with Jack Welch," *Harvard Business Review,* September–October, 1989, pp. 112–120, and Ira C. Magaziner and Mark Patinkin, "Cold Competition: GE Wages the Refrigerator War," *Harvard Business Review,* March–April 1989, pp. 114–124.
6. This example is adapted by permission from the article by Ira C. Magaziner and Mark Patinkin, "Cold Competition: GE Wages the Refrigerator War," *Harvard Business Review,* March–April 1989, pp. 114–124. Reprinted by permission of Random House, Inc.
7. This material on the aftermath of the decision is based on the account of the incident on pages 164–166 of Tichy and Sherman (1993).
8. One of the authors (Kirby) has had over twenty years' experience in applying TQM principles to complex organizations.

Case Data: 21st Century Electronics Performance Improvement Teams

This section of the course employs actual case data from six improvement teams. The performance of each team has been described in case vignettes that are distributed throughout the remainder of the book, according to their principal features.

21st Century Electronics designs and manufactures electrical and mechanical systems. The systems range from individually held radios to country-wide air traffic control systems.

The individual case studies are taken from various departments of one major division of the firm. Each team was formally chartered by management. Team actions were then observed weekly and classified according to the controlling actions taken (controlling actions are those described in Exhibit 1-3 on p. 12). Observations were made by an independent trained observer.

The objective of the study was to determine which specific controlling actions lead to successful team behavior. These findings are valuable for exploring the dynamic relationships of controlling actions.

A similar format is used to describe the activities of each team. First, the controlling actions of the team are described and the results are described. You are then asked to use your knowledge of the design of control systems to identify the factors leading to success or failure of the team to achieve its goal.

The findings are applicable to the work of all kinds of coordinating groups, such as management staffs, councils, policy boards, and committees. Multidisciplinary teams are widely used in management practice, especially in total quality environments.

Case 4-1   21st Century Electronics: Receiving Department

The receiving department of 21st Century Electronics was responsible for accepting incoming parts for internal manufacture and moving them from the receiving dock to the storeroom. This task involved logging, inspecting, and transporting small components and large structural parts to stores inventory. The department consisted of 25 people

Management wanted to reduce average receiving time in this department. Benchmarking studies of excellent firms showed that average receiving time was under 3.5 days for a shipment. The average time for receiving at 21st Century was 6.9 days. As a result, a team of ten members from the various functions involved in the dock-to-stores function was officially chartered by management with the objective of improving receiving time for materials received from vendors.

The team went right to work. Goals were set as a result of team members expressing strong individual "beliefs" about the problems associated with average receiving time. The team believed that their existing process was basically sound. These beliefs led to the definition of the problem as *the inability to find purchase orders for parts received.* At 21st Century purchase orders were placed by the originating department through purchasing, although in some cases electronic purchasing was employed. A copy of the purchase order did not always find its way to receiving. The emergence of these strong beliefs blocked the informal search for data for the purpose of better understanding the range of problems impacting performance.

At the second meeting, team members again focused upon discussing their beliefs about the seriousness of the problem, the perceived aggressiveness of other team members, philosophies for action, and past experiences. They concluded that a buyer should not consider his or her actions complete until certain steps had been taken, that is, until purchasing information had been forwarded to receiving and until progress of the purchased item had been monitored sufficiently.

In meeting three, a team member's suggestion of the use of TQM techniques for analyzing aspects of the problem was ignored. Team members *believed* they knew the situation well enough to settle upon concrete actions immediately. The team then attempted to implement changes based upon their perceptions of the solution. The team avoided collecting data or setting operational metrics. Finally after several more meetings, the team declared themselves successful based upon their perception of having reduced average receiving time to 5.6 days. Department management, however, perceived the team as being only marginally successful. In fact, this team ranked as the lowest performing of all ten teams chartered by management during this time.

QUESTION

Why did this team fail to meet its improvement goals? (*Hint:* see the dynamics of the control process discussed in Chapter 3 and the material on style and culture in Chapter 4).

Case 4-2   21st Century Electronics: Shipping Department

Top management of 21st Century Electronics chartered a team of seven members representing major functions within the shipping department of the firm. Management wanted the team to develop *appropriate shipping measurements* to be used for measuring and improving performance of the shipping department. The expectations was that improved measurements would lead to improved performance. The shipping department was a department of about 40 people. Their function was to package, label, and arrange the products of several divisions for transportation.

Jack, the leader of the team, began the first meeting by telling members that he expected them to set the standard for all improvement teams. He then explained the roles of each individual and the importance of their involvement in the teams effort. He stressed the importance of "an attitude of improvement among team members." The members then agreed that confusion did occur when the measurements from the department were unclear; they then agreed on a specific mission for the team which was to focus on establishing and using a "cost" measure of shipping costs to evaluate and improve performance.

This team was clearly chartered in meeting one, establishing both the roles of each member and the goals for the team. The value of the improvement effort was also established by the team leader and by team members.

At subsequent meetings, the team discussed data related directly to the overall goal. Various actions were established to bet-ter understand specific issues. As the process moved forward, team members volunteered to be the coordinating point between important support areas. Also, team members carefully evaluated the appropriateness of the existing formal reporting system for assessing shipping status and considered the type of reports and data that would be most useful for assessing status.

Issues were discussed and eventually resolved by gathering and analyzing data. Formal reports were used throughout the process to keep the effort focused upon the mission, mainly through reviewing progress and assessing new actions. The reviews tended to trigger informal planning activities. The team tended to work around formal structures and processes, but did attempt to change them when they didn't support a specific action. For example, the current reporting systems had invalid data in them and this became a corrective action.

The department manager periodically met with the team to discuss results and to provide encouragement. The leader maintained expectations that the team would meet its mission. As a result, the team's progress through final steps was perceived to largely complete its mission. The following patterns of management control actions were noted on this team:

1. The team was formally chartered and roles were established.
2. Norms and expectations perceived useful were established by the team leader.
3. Informal planning was used during initial

meetings to formulate the goals of the team, understand the issues involved, and establish direction as members actively sought out data.

4. The formal planning and reporting process was used to maintain focus on goals of the team. The team members formalized procedures and documented new methods. The leader continued to remind the team of the goals when discussions were "off track."

The performance of the shipping team was ranked first by top management as far as goal attainment was concerned. They were perceived to have met all of their goals.

QUESTION

What were the characteristics of the performance of the shipping department team that led to so much better performance than the receiving department team in Case 4-1?

Case 4-3 Logistics Systems Limited

Please refer back to Case 1-1, Logistics Systems Limited.

QUESTION

Assume that Michael Jenkins is about to recommend to top management of the parent company a major change in the culture of LSL to better fit the current and projected environment of the company. What values or beliefs[1] should he recommend they develop? How would you go about implementing this change in culture at LSL?

NOTE

1. It is sometimes desirable to distinguish between values and beliefs. A *value* is a desired end state, such as the value of truthfulness. A *belief* is the way to achieve the value, such as the belief that not killing the messenger will lead to more truthfulness.

Case 4-4

Please refer back to Case 1-2, Central Hospital.

QUESTION

Assume that Jack Weber is about to recommend to top management and the board of Central Hospital a change in the culture of Central Hospital to better fit the current and projected environment of the hospital. What values should they change? How would you go about implementing this change in culture at Central Hospital?

5

INFRASTRUCTURE I: ORGANIZING FOR ADAPTIVE CONTROL

INTRODUCTION

In Chapter 1, we defined a management control system as a set of interrelated *communication structures* that facilitates the processing of information for the purpose of assisting managers in *coordinating* the parts and attaining the *purpose* of an organization on a continuous basis.

It is necessary to design the elements of the *control system infrastructure*, that is, the organization structure, responsibility centers, performance measures, and rewards, in a mutually supportive and adaptive way so as to effectively implement the goals of the overall organization. A properly designed infrastructure is crucial to ensure that resources will be allocated effectively in decentralized decision making in pursuit of organizational goals.

The formal organization structure is a communication structure that is established to process information for the purpose of attaining the purpose for which the organization is established. As such, it is right at the heart of the control system. To achieve coordinated control, an organization must process information and reciprocal communications.

An organization's ability to achieve and maintain control is directly proportional to its information processing and communications capability. Any management practice or innovation that improves the ability of the organization to process information will ultimately reduce the weight placed upon the formal organization in pursuit of control. For example, recent improvements in the technology of information processing that speed up information processing have resulted in increases in the span of control in organizations. The organizational hierarchy shrinks, and fewer layers of organization are the result. As another illustration, the stronger the culture of an organization, the greater the amount of "self-control" and the less reliance on the need for supervision and information-processing. Therefore, information-processing innovations and the development of strong values are in part substitutes for formal organization structure in terms of the requirements for achieving control. The more rapidly and accurately information is processed and the more strongly held key values are, the less the dependence the control system has on the formal organization structure.

With these tradeoffs in mind, we will in this chapter be concerned with the dimensions of adaptive control systems that are related to and influenced by the formal organization and informal structure. Topics discussed include the influence of strategy upon organization structure and control requirements; the evolution of the multidivisional structure in response to changes in control requirements; the evolution of the matrix in response to strategies with more demanding coordination and control requirements; the importance and organization of the controller's function; and the characteristics of the adaptive organization. We omit discussions of the influence of managerial style upon organization, since that is discussed extensively in Chapters 4 and 6.

STRATEGY, STRUCTURE, AND CONTROL

A major conclusion of Chandler (1962) in his historical study of the growth and development of American industrial enterprise was that changes in the design of organization structure were normally a response to changes in the strategy of an organization. The movement of American enterprise to the multidivisional structure, for example, was a response to the strategy of growth by geographical expansion and was brought about by the need to maintain coordination and control of expanding operations. Chandler (1962, p. 297) summarizes these ideas as follows:

> The lack of time, of information, and of psychological commitment to an overall entrepreneurial viewpoint were not necessarily serious handicaps if the company's basic activities remained stable, that is, if its sources of raw materials and supplies, its manufacturing technology, its markets, and the nature of its products and product lines stayed relatively unchanged. But when further expansion into new functions, into new geographical areas, into new product lines greatly increased all types of administrative decision, then the executives in the central office became overworked and their administrative performance less efficient. These increasing pressures, in turn, created the need for the building or adoption of the multidivisional structure with its general office and autonomous operating divisions.[1]

Chandler found that the strategy of geographical and product line expansion overtaxed the information-processing ability of chief executives of major companies he studied, and this created the need for the multidivisional structure and for new management systems. The multidivisional structure is a decentralized structure wherein divisional managers have a fair degree of autonomy in decision making and are held accountable for profit as well as asset utilization.

The multidivisional organization structure improved the overall process of planning and control. Again to quote Chandler (p. 295),

> In these new and rapidly expanding automotive enterprises, the President or General Manager tended to become involved in detailed operating duties. This tendency was, in fact, a basic weakness of the central office structure developed in these several enterprises. Executives responsible for over-all planning, coordination, and appraisal became increasingly enmeshed in operational activities. They had neither the time, the information, nor the inclination necessary to stick to entrepreneurial and strategic decision making.

The decentralized multidivisional structure also improved the ability of chief executives to evaluate the economic performance of their enterprise, since each division was more or less a "complete business" unto itself and could be held responsible for *profit* and *asset* utilization. Thus the rise in importance of profit and investment centers in organization.

The decentralized form of organization has since spread rapidly in American business enterprise. According to Vancil (1979, p. 25),

> If decentralization was a managerial invention in 1920, it was an articulated philosophy by 1950, a reorganizational trend by 1960, and a universal practice by 1970.

Decentralization versus Centralization

The very fact that conditions exist which create the need for a decentralized organization structure indicates that the complex organization will not make decisions through a central decision-making process but rather through a diffuse one. The responsibility for controlling significant amounts of resources is delegated in modern complex organizations. Given these elements of decentralization in decision making, measures of performance need to be established for organizational subunits that "link" each subunit to the whole. We call these organizational subunits *centers of responsibility* or *responsibility centers.* Each will face different constraints, and while the organization as a whole attempts to pursue certain short-range objectives and long-range goals, a large number of decision makers will not be motivated directly by these overall objectives and goals.

The pattern of resource allocation in the organization will be influenced significantly by decisions made in these subunits of the organization, and managers making these decisions will be under the strong influence of local goals.

Organization units are not normally part of a given corporation unless they share some common characteristics with other organization units. These characteristics include what Porter (1985, Chapter 9) calls tangible or intangible interrelationships. Tangible relationships are opportunities to share activities among business units because of the presence of common buyers or suppliers, technologies, channels of distribution, production processes, or other business activities. Intangible interrelationships arise from the application to different business units of similar managerial skills because of the presence of similar buyers or similar manufacturing processes. As a result of these tangible and intangible interrelationships, complete or radical decentralization almost never fully exploits the strengths of the entire organization.

Sharing activities by two or more organization units also introduces some costs. These costs include coordination of the activities of different units, compromises made to fit similar activities into identical processes, and the resultant inflexibility created by sharing an activity among business units.

Organizational decentralization of profit and investment responsibility has significant benefits. It allows closer control and supervision within the division than does centralization. It facilitates information processing, since it permits analysis of trade-offs among cost, revenue, and investment at lower levels of management closer to the impact of the decision. It produces greater managerial motivation as general managers of divisions run their own business, given only broad constraints in terms of company goals, objectives, strategies, and policies. Decentralization also permits better overall performance evaluation of the various organizational units of the business. As a by-product, these characteristics of decentralization provide the environment wherein general managers may be trained.

Decentralization, although it can reduce the dysfunctionalities associated with centralization that basically have to do with information-processing limitations and the resultant lack of responsiveness of central management to specific markets and activities, exposes the organization to other potential dysfunctionalities which are themselves associated with the decentralized decision-making process. These dysfunctionalities occur because only local goals enter the decision-making process of decentralized subunits. A balancing of the costs associated with decentralization versus those associated with centralization should in fact determine the appropriate choice of organizational form.

For some organizations, the incremental costs associated with inefficiencies of decentralization (that is, loss of scale economies, increased costs, and dysfunctional performance) are less than the incremental benefits derived from improved information processing, planning, decision making, and motivation. To others, however, the benefits of decentralization are less than the costs, so consequently they remain highly centralized.

The fewer and more homogeneous the markets, and the more homogeneous the product, the easier it is to plan, administer, and coordinate functional departmental activities, and, therefore, the greater the advantage of centralization. Organizations that sell many variations of one major line of product, in high volume, to a large number of industries and businesses (for example, the copper and nickel industries) have consistently centralized the control of their activities. Those making and selling quite differentiated lines to increasingly differentiated groups of customers (for example, the oil industry) have turned to the multidivisional structure. In any case, each of the organization forms has its costs and its benefits, and the decision as to which form to use is based significantly upon economic and control factors.

We turn now in this chapter to some examples of trends in strategy and their implication for the design of organization structure. This chapter does not purport to contain a complete discussion of the organizing function of management. Rather, it seeks to draw out some of the control system implications of corporate strategy for organizing. There are indeed many additional considerations required in addition to the control considerations before the appropriate organizational structure is decided upon. These additional considerations, however, are beyond the scope of this text. They are properly covered in courses concerned with the management process and with organizational design.

ANOTHER RESPONSE OF STRUCTURE TO STRATEGY: EVOLUTION OF THE MATRIX STRUCTURE

The process identified by Chandler in his landmark study wherein organization structure was shown to follow organizational strategy has taken still another twist over the past 25 to 30 years. This twist has been the evolution of the matrix structure in response to the strategy followed by organizations that pursue high-technology projects, complex products and services, and multinational business. We shall explore these developments at length in this chapter, given that the U.S. economy as well as other advanced economies increasingly will be characterized by these categories of business.

High-technology projects require an organization to maintain a high degree of technical excellence in multiple disciplines, which in turn calls for division of labor and specialization. Division of labor and specialization are of course fostered by the functional organization, as illustrated in Exhibit 5-1. A strategy that has the organization pursuing high-technology projects requires for its success policies that facilitate recruitment and maintenance of a staff that is working at or beyond the current state of the technological art.

To build a functional organization that is at the state of the art, many disciplines and subdisciplines must be represented. To utilize each specialty fully, there must be a number of projects where these specialized talents are employed. This generally means that an organization engaged in high-technology work will be managing multiple projects simultaneously. The management of multiple, high-technology projects places a strain on the coordinating and control mechanisms of the functional organization. This strain occurs not only because of the number of

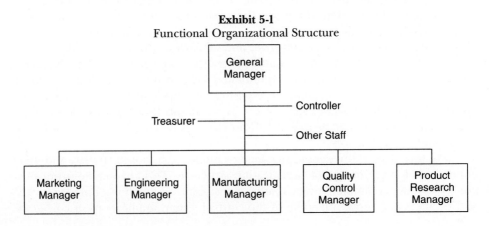

Exhibit 5-1
Functional Organizational Structure

projects to be coordinated by general management but because of the additional difficulties encountered in integrating multiple high-technology disciplines.

The coordination and control problem may be resolved easily enough if the projects are sufficiently large to support a permanent functional organization of their own and simultaneously allow for scale economies in the functional organization. In that case the decentralized organization of Exhibit 5-2 will do the job. This organization structure, which is patterned after the divisional organization, will allow the firm to achieve the coordination and control required for the project while not foregoing the technical excellence and the scale economies of the functional organization.

The decentralized divisional structure, however, should be used only when the project is large enough to support on a permanent basis a functional staff that is of approximately optimal size so far as achieving technical excellence and scale economies are concerned. Normally, the organization will be managing multiple small projects with short durations. In this case, the decentralized "project" organization cannot be supported, yet there remains a need for both the excellence and scale economies of the functional organization as well as the coordination and control of the decentralized project organization.

The resolution of these demands for control and functional excellence has led to the use of the so-called *matrix organization*. The matrix organization maintains the functional organization and superimposes matrix managers for each project. This is illustrated in Exhibit 5-3.

The matrix project managers have responsibility for achieving the goals and objectives of the project but must share resources for the attainment of these goals and objectives. While at first glance this appears to be a radical departure from the

Exhibit 5-2
Decentralized Organization Structure

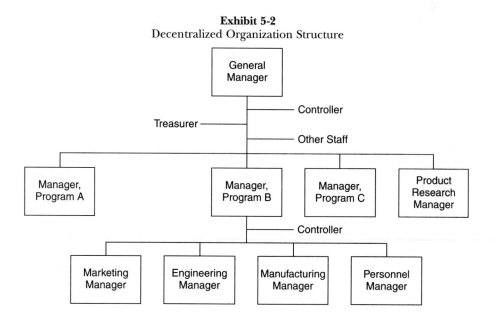

Exhibit 5-3
Project Matrix Organization Structure

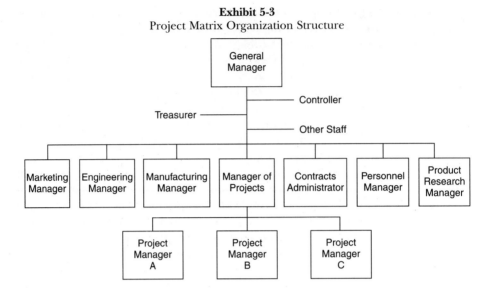

decentralized project organization, a closer examination of virtually all decentralized divisional organizations reveals that they share at least some of their resources with other divisions. Some staff groups, for example, remain centralized and are shared by the entire organization. Moreover, even in the matrix organization the project managers normally have some staff reporting directly to the project office.

The matrix organization is still another example of structural change following strategy to improve control. It has, however, been an evolutionary rather than a revolutionary change. To date, the most extensive use of the matrix structure has taken place in the management of complex projects, primarily by aerospace and defense contractors and subcontractors.

Project Organizations

Project organizations are concerned with planning, coordinating, and controlling complex projects of an organization; projects require many activities proceeding both serially and simultaneously toward an ultimate goal and continuous and intricate interaction among many different functional personnel of an organization. The objectives and goals for each project ordinarily include profit, either short term (that is, the project only) or long term (that is, future business), growth in the kind of business represented by the project, and development of expertise.

The goals and objectives are met by achieving agreed-upon performance with respect to cost, quality, and time variables. Therefore, cost, quality, and schedule are ordinarily the key success variables for a project. Upon completion of all activities, the life of the project ceases and the organization is dissolved. The formal organization chart for the matrix structure given in Exhibit 5-3 does not clearly illustrate the dual dimensions of management embodied within the matrix structure. These dual dimensions are clarified by comparing Exhibits 5-3 and 5-4.

Regardless of the nature of the firm employing this hybrid organization form, it may be described by using a matrix as shown in Exhibit 5-4, with the various products, projects, or services identified in the columns of the matrix and the functions identified in the rows.

The matrix depicts an organization with n programs. These programs represent the primary output of the organization and therefore place demands upon the various functions. The functions, represented in the rows of the matrix, supply resources to various programs within the organization. The total output of a function for any particular period of time is found in the last column of the matrix and consists of the sum of all the contributions of a particular function to various programs. Each row of the last column represents the demand placed upon one function by multiple programs. This demand may be measured in physical units of input, such as hours, or in monetary units. Functional contributions that are indirect, such as research and development, contract administration, personnel, business planning, public relations, and finances, are included in the overhead row of the matrix.

The matrix diagram itself, however, does not uniquely define the distinguishing characteristics of the matrix organization. Any organization may be described as a matrix; it need not be a hybrid form. All organizations produce outputs that may be identified in the columns of a matrix and utilize inputs that may be identified in the rows of the matrix. That is, all organizations have a purpose and utilize inputs or processes to fulfill the purpose. The truly distinguishing characteristics of the matrix organization structure, in all its variations, lie in the dual dimensions of management embodied within it and the allocation of responsibility and authority resulting from the dual management dimensions.

The matrix organization employs two overlapping dimensions of management, each of which may be identified within the matrix. Under the matrix orga-

Exhibit 5-4
The Structure of a Matrix Organization

Programs Functions	Program 1	Program 2	Program 3	Program 4	Total Functional Output
Engineering					
Procurement					
Quality assurance					
Logistics support					
Manufacturing					
Program control					
Program management					
Overhead	_____	_____	_____	_____	
Total program requirements					

nization structure, full responsibility is identified by the column dimension of Exhibit 5-4. However, functional personnel who perform the work on the programs of an organization receive technical direction from functional management under the matrix structure, thus providing the second and overlapping dimension of management for the programs of the organization. The functional dimension of management is identified by the rows of the matrix in Exhibit 5-4.

Therefore, although the program manager assumes full responsibility for delivery of a product which meets performance specifications on a timely basis and in accordance with contractual resource limits, he or she does not have direct authority over the functional organizations that actually perform the work. If the manager did have such authority, the organization would not be a hybrid at all; it would be simply a decentralized form. The distinguishing feature of the matrix organization, therefore, is the separation of the responsibility for the goals of a program from the authority to direct the work necessary to achieve those goals.

Furthermore, functional personnel actually do operate subject to dual sources of authority under the matrix: the knowledge-based authority within the function and the resource-based authority (i.e., the program manager does have control over program budgets) of the program manager. Unity of command is thus broken.

Even though the hallmark of the matrix is the separation of responsibility and authority, in practice we find that rather than a clear separation of responsibility and authority we have formal and informal relationships among program and functional personnel which lead to a distribution of responsibility and authority. Formal and informal relationships, however, vary depending upon the application and personalities involved.

We turn now to three simplified, but realistic, cases illustrating the use of this organization structure in the management of products, services, and multinational organizations.

Product Organizations

The matrix structure has been used for the introduction of new products as well as for ongoing administration of projects. The matrix structure is appropriate for the management of products when (1) the number of products of an organization grows to be relatively large, (2) products require close coordination among many specialized disciplines, and (3) markets are too small to justify separate divisions for each product. In addition, the matrix structure often is appropriate for organizations that serve markets differing significantly from one another. In this last case, the two dimensions of management embodied within the matrix are the markets and the products of an organization. When the matrix structure and the program control process are applied to the management of products, we refer to the management control system as a *product control system.*

Exhibit 5-5 illustrates the structure of a product organization with the matrix structure superimposed. The matrix structure preserves the economies of scale in each discipline, while providing total management of each product, thus attempting to achieve a high level of both efficiency and coordination. As under product management, each functional specialist employed on a given product reports to

Exhibit 5-5
Product Matrix Organization

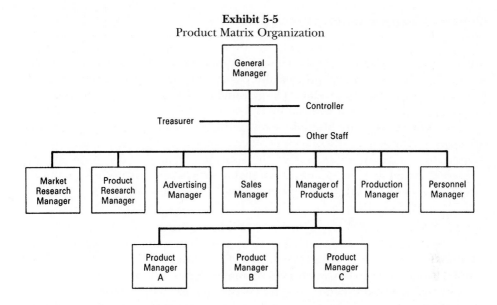

the respective functional manager and not to the product manager. Unlike projects, however, products normally have a very long life expectancy.

Generally, product managers are responsible for the planning and coordination of functional efforts required to introduce new products, modify existing products, and make changes to the advertising programs of any established product. A hypothetical, but realistic, example of the product management process appears in the paragraphs that follow.

> For a new product, the product manager first negotiates with contributors from marketing research to determine the size of the market at alternative prices for the new product idea; product research then determines the feasibility of converting the idea into a product. The production organization is consulted by the product manager regarding the cost of production to be sure that it is feasible to produce the product within limits of cost that would also allow the firm a profit.
>
> If all signs are positive, the product manager begins to test the market for the product; therefore, the product must be produced, but in limited quantity only. Sales concepts then must be developed by the marketing research and advertising functions in conjunction with the product manager to provide the sales force with the tools necessary to sell the product. Results of the test market are evaluated by the product manager in conjunction with the controller to determine if the new product is potentially a profitable venture. These data and evaluations are then passed up the organization for approval.

For a complex product this entire process requires close coordination among virtually all functions; such coordination is nearly impossible to obtain without the total management that the matrix structure allows. Moreover, because individual contributions to any one product from the various functions are usually relatively short in duration, it is wise to maintain highly centralized functional groups to obtain scale economies. Program managers then purchase services as needed from these functional groups.

Service Organizations

The service sector of the economy now accounts for more than 60 percent of total national employment in the United States. Services such as government, education, health, accounting, and consulting comprise a large part of the service sector. These organizations produce a large number of services that require for their provision coordination of contributions from many highly skilled and diverse disciplines. Where there are multiple services offered through the close cooperation of many highly skilled disciplines to many customers, often geographically dispersed, the matrix structure may be the appropriate organization form. We turn now to an example of an application of such a structure to a hypothetical, but representative, large CPA firm, doing business on a national basis.

Hypothetical CPA Firm

This firm provides a variety of services to its clients, including financial audits and tax reports that are mandated by law. In addition, the firm offers its clients certain consulting services, such as economic forecasting; the design of financial control and other information systems; analysis and evaluation of production, marketing, and other operations; and evaluation of potential acquisitions and mergers. Clients include business, government, and private nonprofit organizations.

To offer such a diversity of professional services to clients on a national basis, it is necessary for the firm to maintain a large staff of highly specialized personnel, including accountants, auditors, economists, tax lawyers, finance specialists, systems analysts, programmers, industrial engineers, operations researchers, and general management consultants. Furthermore, clients demand very high-quality work, and it is general industry practice to meet these standards.

Even though a functional organization is desired to meet these high-quality standards in diverse areas, the focal point of demand for the firm's service is the client and the client's demand for services provided by many diverse functions. Furthermore, much of the firm's business in the nonauditing and tax areas results from contacts with clients regarding the two legally mandated services. The client is a primary source of growth for the business, and the development of client services is vital for the firm's health and growth.

Clients are served best if a local office provides all the services required, when they are required, and in a high-quality manner. For these reasons, the firm finds it desirable to establish local offices in major metropolitan areas to service client needs.

Therefore, highly skilled functional specialties are needed to meet desired quality standards in diverse fields. Local offices are needed to meet client requirements. Moreover, local offices require some functional contributions sporadically, only when a need is identified.

The matrix structure allows us to achieve high-quality standards and economies of scale in each function while providing coordinated services for clients. We may describe such a structure for this hypothetical CPA firm with the help of Exhibit 5-6.

Exhibit 5-6
Service Matrix Organization Structure

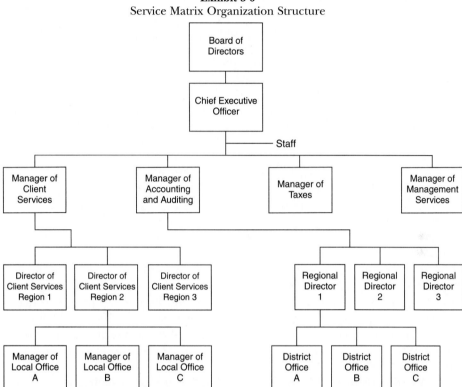

As was the case for product management, the functional groups supply each local (program) office with its services as the need arises; the local office provides facilities and resources to market, plan, and control client services in a given metropolitan area. The functional personnel, however, report directly to functional managers, and local office managers contract for the services of functional resources in a manner identical to that of project and product managers. Regional client centers as well as functional offices exist to plan, direct, and control the work of a given region. Regional functional offices are large enough to reap all the scale economies. In addition, these regional units adhere to the standards formulated at the national level for a given function.

We have now introduced the hybrid matrix structure into project, product, and service organizations. There are also many potential uses of the matrix structure in multinational corporations engaged in the provision of products, projects, or services. In the multinational firm, however, the dimensions of the matrix normally change from program and function to area and program. In fact, a multinational matrix may have any two of the following three dimensions: area, program, and function.

The Matrix Structure and the Multinational Firm

The problems of achieving coordination and efficiency in multinational enterprises differ from those found in domestic product organizations in two ways. First, there is a greater geographical dispersion of various units of the enterprise. As a result, multinational firms often subdivide their organization by area of the world; each division is responsible for all products in each geographical area. The divisions are often large enough so as to employ fully each of the functions within the division and achieve significant functional economies of scale, with some loose coordination of each function among various divisions taking place at headquarters.

The second difference between a multinational and a domestic firm closely relates to the first. Since each division of a multinational firm is responsible for sale and sometimes production of all the company's products in a given area of the world, little attention can be given to the development, introduction, and coordination of a given product for the company as a whole. This second distinction between the domestic and multinational firm intensifies the need for the matrix structure.

In a multinational enterprise, therefore, the two dimensions of management that must be considered in the design of the organization structure are market area and product rather than product and function, although it may be necessary depending upon the size of the organization to include a third, the functional dimension. Exhibit 5-7 depicts the evolution of a matrix organization structure by area and product from either a product division structure or from an area division structure.

We will not deal with triadic organizational designs (that is, area, product, and function) in this chapter, because they are beset by many potential problems in addition to those of the two-dimensional matrix organization. We should note, however, the tendency to centralize certain functional activities, most notably manufacturing and engineering, in multinational firms, thus creating at least the potential for triadic organizational designs.

It is not always appropriate for the multinational organization to establish the matrix structure. If the design of a product is considered standard and fixed for the foreseeable future, management's concentration should be placed upon markets only, given that scale economies are achieved in the functional organization. On the other hand, if worldwide markets for the products of the organization are considered to possess homogeneous characteristics, perhaps only the product-management dimension is called for, assuming that scale economies can be achieved under this organizational design.

We should not expect these two conditions to occur often for multinational firms, however, since a primary cause of the multinational business phenomenon lies in the technology embodied within certain products, which makes the incremental cost of production low relative to total costs and which makes large-scale economies possible. These two conditions make it profitable to export these products even though transportation costs and trade barriers exist. Moreover, market characteristics as well as basic labor costs are very different for most products in various parts of the world, and organizations as a result have found it necessary to

Exhibit 5-7
Evolution of Multinational Matrix Structure from Worldwide Product Structure
or from Worldwide Area Structure, Simplified

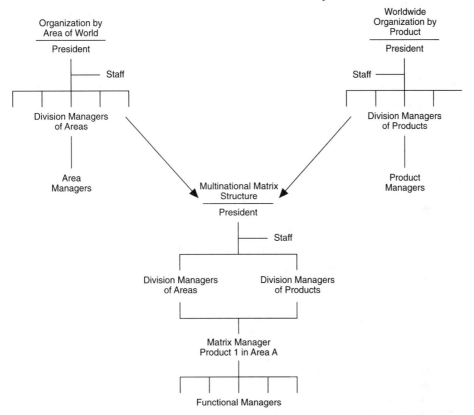

Source: Stanley M. Davis, *Matrix Organization and Behavior in Domestic and Multinational Enterprise,* Harvard Business School Case 9-474-036, 1973, p. 32. Copyright © 1973 by the President and Fellows of Harvard College. Reprinted by permission.

differentiate markets. Therefore, many multinational firms are forced to consider both the geographical and product dimensions of management.

The matrix organization provides us with a dual structure for managing both the product and market dimensions in the multinational firm. Under the matrix structure, a product manager is appointed for each product or product group, along with an area manager for each geographical area. Then the question becomes: What should be the division of responsibility and authority between product managers and area managers for a given product?

The product manager often assumes a role similar to that of the program manager, having full responsibility for the profitability of the product on a worldwide basis and yet no formal authority over the functional disciplines employed on the product. The area manager has responsibility for overall profitability of his or her division and full authority over functional personnel assigned to that division.

Product managers for multinational firms are generally concerned with current business, new business, and technological developments for their product. They usually use their technical and business knowledge, together with their influence and credibility, to convince corporate and area managers of technical and business programs that will improve the profitability of their product line on a worldwide basis. The product manager becomes the advocate for his or her product or product line in each geographical organization to make sure that it gets the correct amount of attention by the area manager. The product manager may also coordinate distribution, production, and interarea transfers of his or her product among area divisions to alleviate bottlenecks and improve worldwide sales.

Clearly products differ in their key success variables. Some products require a marketing emphasis, whereas others require an engineering or production emphasis, and it is generally up to the product managers to see to it that their product lines get the proper emphasis by the divisions. Furthermore, an identical product might be more profitable in one area than in another, and product managers must see to it that production and sales resources are allocated to divisions for their products according to profitability. It may be necessary to drop a product in one division, while expanding its sales in another. Perhaps most important, where a product is experiencing rapid technological change, the product manager should seek to forecast such change and to have it incorporated into the product in each area division.

As has been the case for all our applications of the matrix structure, the principal ingredients for its success in multinational organizations are behavioral adjustments on the part of both area and product managers. Pyramidal thinking must be replaced by matrix thinking, and we should not expect the informal relationship required under the matrix structure to develop overnight.

It is obvious even to the most casual observer of business that multinational enterprises have grown very rapidly during the past two decades, so much so that large U.S. corporations, such as the International Businesses Machines Corporation and the General Electric Company, currently derive over half of their revenue from foreign operations. The multinational corporation thus presents a large and growing entity for application of the matrix structure. In addition, the introduction of new high-technology products on a multinational scale through many area divisions is certainly a challenging task for the matrix and even triadic forms.

To summarize to this point, the history of American industrial enterprise seems to bear out the thesis that organization structure evolves to meet the ever-changing demand for planning, coordination, and control created by strategy and changes in strategy. The decision as to the appropriate organization form for purposes of control may be placed within an economic framework. We turn to examine this framework as applied to the matrix structure. We use the matrix structure in its application to complex programs because it is an increasingly common application and because it illustrates the control trade-offs of various organizational forms quite explicitly. The framework of analysis presented next, however, is quite general in application.

Still Another Response of Structure to Strategy: The Use of Teams

Recent emphasis on total quality management strategies have resulted in the wide-spread use of teams. Teams are defined as cross-unit groups that are made up of task-relevant representatives who meet periodically to focus on particular clients, products, markets, or problems. These groups may be formal or informal, permanent or temporary, and may include appropriate membership to ensure that relevant expertise is available to deal with the task or goal. In this book, most of our interest will be upon the use of quality improvement teams. Because teams are formed for the purpose of achieving certain project work, their operations are similar in nature to matrix organizations formed to perform project work, although they are usually more temporary and informal than matrix organizations. Team actions may be classified according to the controlling actions table presented in Exhibit 1-3.

EVALUATION OF THE CONTROL FACTORS IN ORGANIZATIONAL DESIGN

Three principal organizational designs have been identified that may be used to manage organizational activity: a centralized functional organization, in which the ultimate responsibility and authority for all products, projects, and services rests with top management; a decentralized program organization, in which the division, department, or program group has its own management, which is responsible for performance and has complete authority over the functional organizations that perform program work; and a matrix structure, a hybrid structure within which we attempt to capture the benefits of each of the other forms and reject the assumption of classical organization theory that a trade-off must be made between the benefits of scale economies and those of coordination.

The objective of our analysis in this section is to choose the organization form, among the three alternative forms, that produces the highest net benefit to the organization. We should not expect, however, to devise a quantitative measure of net benefits, since most of the benefits of each form and some of the costs remain unquantifiable. Moreover, although we consider only three alternative organizational models (centralized, decentralized, and hybrid), in practice it is possible to identify many variations of each model, and pure forms may be the most rare. This analysis is meant to be a representative analysis of control factors in organizational design.

The benefits of each alternative organizational design must be investigated incrementally; that is, we make the assumption that we have an organization in place and that we desire to consider new ones. We consider each new one by evaluating its incremental effects upon efficiency and coordination. Efficiency is concerned with the input cost (or the stakeholder cost) of providing a unit of functional output. The optimum-size functional organization is one that operates at the minimum cost per unit of output. Of course, this is a theoretical ideal and is an extraordinarily difficult or impossible point to find in practice.

Coordination, on the other hand, is concerned with integrating diverse activities in a manner that will best serve customer needs (or the purpose of the organization). Factors of efficiency and coordination combine to produce effectiveness, which speaks to success in meeting organizational purpose. Effectiveness is concerned with balancing the key variables to achieve satisfactory performance with regard to goals. It is thus a more comprehensive criterion than efficiency or coordination.

Economies of scale (that is, reduced unit costs of output) occur in centralized organizations because

1. Size permits division of labor and specialization within a discipline, which enhances productivity whenever the task is complex. (Productivity is enhanced because specialization by task permits greater learning and often leads to the introduction of more specialized and productive capital equipment).
2. Functional resources are movable from one program to the next and can therefore be employed more fully than if functional resources are assigned directly to a given program only and are subject to the fluctuating demands for those resources by that particular program.
3. Uniform professional standards and constant interaction of members of a common discipline enhance learning and therefore productivity.

Once a functional organization surpasses the optimum size, however, it may be subdivided without loss of scale economies.

Problems of coordination and loss of effectiveness arise in centralized functional organizations when output is highly complex and nonroutine. The cognitive limits of general management are exceeded as the number of complex programs and different customers increases, and costly coordination problems develop. Coordination problems may lead to cost overruns, bottlenecks, and schedule slippages; program performance that falls short of requirements; and financial losses. These problems of program coordination represent potential costs associated with a highly centralized organization, and they are magnified when budget and time constraints are stringent. These problems, however, are being reduced at present by improvements in information technology and in set up methods.

We turn now to explore the net benefits of the matrix organization relative to the functional organization. Then we compare these net benefits with those of a decentralized organization relative to the functional organization. We use the functional organization as the basic model because, in practice, division of labor always requires that we establish functions, but division of labor in itself does not require either a matrix or a decentralized organization.

Matrix versus Functional

The matrix organization avoids the worst of the potential coordination problems in the management of complex programs, because it places total responsibility for the program in the hands of a manager whose exclusive task it is to plan, coordinate, and integrate the activities of multiple functions toward the achievement of a balance among performance, cost, and time variables. Therefore, improved coordination and motivation are the principal incremental benefits of the matrix organization over the functional organization.

The incremental cost of the matrix over the functional is twofold: (1) costs associated with the additional layer of management required to manage each program and (2) organizational difficulties created by separating responsibility for a program from the authority to direct the work necessary to carry out program goals. The first cost is quite easy to measure, but the second is variable, dependent upon other organizational considerations, and impossible to measure in a quantitative way.

We turn now to the potential organizational problems created by the matrix organization. To the extent that these problems occur, and they are not inevitable, only those considered incremental to the matrix should be counted.

Difference in Orientation Between Program and Functional Personnel

The predominant concern of the program managers is meeting and balancing performance, cost, and time requirements of the program. Often, however, functional personnel desire to pursue technical objectives without regard to the balance that is required to meet program goals, simply because functional goals often emphasize quality and norms of competence are established accordingly. Unless the reward structure and the financial controls established for both program and functional organizations are designed effectively, stress will develop. Program managers will pull in the direction necessary to achieve program goals, whereas functional personnel will pursue quality goals to an extreme and to the detriment of performance with regard to the time and cost variables of a program.

Clearly these tensions and the resultant negotiations are not all dysfunctional for the organization. It is in the long-run interest of an organization engaged in advanced-technology program work to develop and maintain functional personnel who are at the cutting edge of their discipline, and this is a major advantage of the matrix organization over a decentralized program organization. Yet such an organization is unlikely to survive the long run if it neglects cost and schedule control on current programs. The reward structure should attempt to balance short- and long-run goals and objectives by rewarding functional work that achieves program goals while simultaneously maintaining functional excellence. Program goals, on the other hand, should reflect both the short- and long-run interests of the organization of high-quality work. In other words, the reward structure for programs and functional organizations should reflect a balance between short- and long-run profits.

Diffuse Responsibility

Although program managers have ultimate program responsibility under the matrix structure, functional managers have technical responsibility for performing the work; as a result, it is often difficult to isolate responsibility for a given activity, especially when problems develop. Therefore, in practice, responsibility is distributed among program and functional personnel, thus making systems of account-ability difficult to administer and increasing potential conflict.

Although there are many potential conflict situations, the three most preva-lent are conflicts in the resolution of technical and cost problems and in priorities assigned to various programs by functional organizations.

Program Personnel in Temporary Assignments

A primary objective of a program manager and his or her office staff is to complete the program successfully and disband themselves. If no follow-on business exists to the program, the program manager and program staff are in organizational limbo, at least temporarily, until they can secure another assign-ment. Unlike the functional personnel assigned to a permanent organizational unit, the program office is a temporary organization unit. So long as the organi-zation as a whole is in a stable or growth phase of business, this potential inse-curity among program personnel will probably not become dysfunctional to program goals. In a no-growth situation, however, functional personnel will hesitate in moving to program responsibility, and program office personnel may attempt to increase artificially the duration of the program at the expense of program goals, thus increasing the cost of this organizational form. We should expect this problem to be especially severe for the organization during adverse economic periods.

The actual costs incurred as a result of these three potential organizational problems under the matrix depend upon the skill employed by program and func-tional managers in building effective informal relationships and designing goal-congruent reward structures to minimize these problems.

Although informal organizations and "grapevines" develop and are impor-tant in all organizations, the nature of informal relations that develop under the matrix structure is crucial for accomplishing program work and minimizing these organizational problems. The separation of responsibility for program work from authority to direct that work and differences in the orientation of program and functional personnel create the need to establish identification with program goals by functional personnel.

Communication, cooperation, and teamwork among functional personnel are essential in light of the complex interdependence of program activity. The interaction among functions required to accomplish the program work may be capitalized upon by the program manager to create strong identification of func-tional personnel with the goals of the program.

In addition to the need for informal organization relationships that rein-force formal organizational relationships, the reward structure should be designed to promote high-quality functional performance and effective program work. It must promote teamwork, problem-solving activity, and the resolution of conflicts within and among programs as well as good individual performance.

To summarize this section, there are clear incremental benefits of coordina-tion to be derived from the matrix organization over the functional organization for the management of complex programs. The incremental costs of the matrix include the addition of a new layer of management plus potential organizational problems. We have indicated that these organizational costs are to a large extent inversely related to the skill exhibited by program and functional managers in creating effective, informal organizational relationships between program and functional personnel.

Decentralized Organization versus Functional Organization

If programs are large enough and are of a very long duration, they may be made permanent organizational entities with their own program managers and functional groups. In this case, the functional groups report formally to the program manager. If these programs are very large, it may be possible to achieve the advantages of coordination that are inherent in decentralized program organizations, while not sacrificing any scale economies.

It is because most complex programs are of a relatively short duration and cannot provide enough work for functions to achieve full-scale economies that it is necessary to consider the matrix in the first place. If projects are very large and are of a long duration, they enjoy the best of both worlds, that is, all the advantages of both coordination and efficiency. In practice, however, this is rarely the case. It should be noted, however, that Peters and Waterman (1982, p. 201) found a strong preference for the decentralized structure over the functional organization among their excellent companies on grounds of improved motivation of management, innovation and entrepreneurship, and responsiveness to customer needs. In their judgment and in the judgment of many managers, these gains associated with decentralization swamp the loss in scale economies.

When decentralized program organizations are formed, they generally forgo some scale economies to achieve a higher degree of coordination in an effort to achieve a higher level of effectiveness. Therefore, an analysis of the decentralized versus the functional organization would involve a comparison of incremental gains in coordination versus the incremental managerial costs and lost scale economies. If net benefits are positive and relatively large, one would have reason to believe that a reorganization is in order.

THE MATRIX STRUCTURE AND STRATEGIC PLANNING

We saw earlier in this chapter that the divisional structure was partially a response by harried corporate executives to separate the responsibility for corporate strategic planning from the day-to-day operations of the enterprise. Another approach to resolve this tension between strategic planning and operations is to use a matrix structure: one dimension for strategic planning and one dimension for operations. This can be done in addition to a matrix structure for the operations side of a business.

This concept of a matrix organization within a larger matrix organization is employed by Texas Instruments (Lorange and Vancil, 1977, pp. 338–361) for the control of strategy. Exhibit 5-8 is a diagram of the matrix organization employed

Exhibit 5-8
Matrix for OST System at Texas Instruments

				Group 2					Group 1
			Division A			Division B			
O	S	T	PCC	PCC	PCC	PCC	PCC	PCC	PCC
		1	X						
		2	X						
	A	3		X					
		4					X		
1		5							X
		1			X				
	B	2			X				
		3	X						

Source: From Richard F. Vancil, *Texas Instruments Incorporated: Management Systems.* 1972, 9-172-054. Copyright © 1972 by the President and Fellows of Harvard College. Reprinted by permission of the Harvard Business School.

by Texas Instruments to control both the strategic and operations dimensions of the organization.

On the operations side (that is, the columns) of Exhibit 5-8, we see that the organization is decentralized into groups, divisions, and PCCs (product customer centers). On the strategy side (that is, the rows), the same organization is allocated responsibility for objectives, strategy, and tactics. The strategic planning system is thus called the OST (objectives, strategy, and tactics) system and is a matrix dimension of the organization.

Under the OST system, objectives, strategies, and tactics managers have a budget assigned to them for the pursuit of strategic long-term goals in addition to their responsibilities for operations. The OST managers are group, division, and PCC managers, which means that they wear two hats. Approximately seventy-five percent of these managers also have responsibilities in this strategic dimension of the business.

Personnel may be recruited by OST managers from anywhere in the company to staff OST programs. Performance is measured according to the time frame necessary for these programs to bear fruit. The reporting and reward systems of the company are designed to encourage both good short-term and long-term performance.

So we see that the matrix concept has broad applications for planning and control both at the strategy and the operations level of the enterprise. Major strategic thrusts of organizations can be conducted through this structure and may be made even more effective through the use of project management tools in the control process (see Chapters 15 and 16).

We are now at the point in our discussion of the topic of organizing for control to turn to the nature, purpose, and organization of the controller's function in a decentralized organization.

THE CONTROLLER'S ORGANIZATION

The controller plays a leading role in the design and operation of the control system itself. Moreover, the ambiguity in the reporting relationship of the controller can be understood only with the backdrop of the foregoing discussion concerning the divisional and matrix organization structures.

A corporate controller normally has responsibilities in the following areas:

1. Developing and maintaining the financial accounting system of the organization
2. Preparing annual and quarterly financial statements for purposes of external financial reporting
3. Evaluating the performance of the organization as an economic entity
4. Developing internal auditing systems for the control of the physical and monetary assets of the firm
5. Preparing the tax returns for the corporation
6. Designing and maintaining internal management control systems for planning and control
7. As staff to corporate management, providing advice to management on the financial implications of decisions under consideration
8. Providing functional supervision and training over the controller organizations at each of the divisions of the corporation

Division controllers have comparable responsibilities at the divisional level.

One of the key issues associated with the controller's function in a corporation is the proper reporting relationship of divisional controllers with respect to divisional general managers. The advisory and control systems design roles of divisional controllers favor a direct reporting relationship to general managers, since these are very important staff functions performed by the controller, whereas the remaining responsibilities call for a close if not direct (functional) reporting relationship to the corporate controller. As with functional units of the matrix organization, the controller's organization may be treated as a shared resource, since there are scale economies in this functional organization also. Unlike the functional units in a pure matrix, the controller's organization represents "permanent staff" to the divisional general manager.

The division controller is an example of a person serving under "two bosses" in the matrix organization structure, having functional accountability to the corporate controller and operating accountability to the division general manager. Where the division controller reports directly may not be as important as an acknowledgment by divisional management and the corporate controller of the need for this dual relationship. The corporate controller should exert functional control over division controllers, whereas division general managers should exercise operational control over divisional controllers. To say that this relationship is problem free, however, would be naive. It is subject to tensions of a similar kind to those found under the matrix organization. For the division controllers to function in all their capacities, these tensions must be resolved in a manner similar to those of the matrix organization. The evidence (Sathe, 1982, pp. 11–12) indicates that controllers in U.S. corporations do not perform the more managerial functions as effectively as both they and general management wish. There apparently exists substantial room for improvement on the operational side of the divisional controllers' function.

Sathe's empirical (questionnaire plus interview) study of the control function in large ($300 million plus), multidivisional, U.S. corporations revealed that the involvement of the typical controller in business decisions depended on seven variables (1982, p. 110). The variables, however, were not all of equal importance. The three most significant variables determining the degree of involvement of the divisional controller in the more managerial functions of the firm were

1. The extent to which the corporation has a financial orientation, emphasizes financial goals, and manages its businesses using a "portfolio" approach
2. The emphasis the company places upon formal tools for planning, programming, budgeting, and reporting, which is somewhat related to 1. above
3. The extent to which the corporation in general and the controller's organization in particular emphasize the development of controller personnel

The four less significant determinants of controller involvement in the management of the business were

1. The working capital intensity of a business
2. Corporate management's expectations regarding controller involvement in business decisions
3. The emphasis that the corporation places upon transfers from the line organization to the controller function as a part of the management development strategy
4. The emphasis the corporate controller organization places on the advisory role

Throughout this text we emphasize the importance of a "strong controller" organization for the design and operation of the control system. Sathe (1982, pp. 141–143) has enumerated the characteristics of strong controllers, and we reproduce these characteristics in Exhibit 5-9 (pp. 168–169). They clearly represent goals, very high goals indeed, for development of strong controllers.

THE ADAPTIVE ORGANIZATION

In the previous sections of this chapter we have discussed the relevant aspects of centralized, decentralized and matrix organizations. A number of environmental forces are creating the need for still more responsive organizations. These forces include the acceleration in the globalization of business, advances in information technology, and efficiency gains from TQM. Formal organization can impede change if it impedes communications across subunits and creates barriers for the reassignment of resources in response to external change.

We turn now to discuss newer organizational forms which attempt to design into the organization structure the adaptability necessary to meet the rapidly changing needs of the current environment. The structural changes described here represent a variety of modifications to formal structures to transform them into more informal structures. They seek to increase agility and adaptiveness by forming cross-functional teams within the organization and alliances with other organizations in order to quickly exploit an emerging opportunity.

Prior to describing the characteristics of the adaptive organization in terms of the adaptive control framework, let us review in some more detail the requirements imposed upon management by current environmental forces. These requirements can be grouped into three categories: gaining a global perspective, increasing the speed of decision making, and realigning resources rapidly.

GAINING A GLOBAL PERSPECTIVE

Global firms have some basic advantages over national or local firms. First, the global firm can take advantage of expertise that exists in many parts of the world. For example, a number of companies use very efficient and effective software engineering capability located in India. Labor rates in Mexico are approximately 30 percent of those in the United States and in Europe, thus creating opportunity for lower cost manufacturing.

The global firm can transfer learning efficiencies more rapidly. Motorola, for example, transferred TQM concepts from its co-owned subsidiary in Japan to other plants worldwide. Xerox developed its Leadership through Quality Program by examining the one in place at its Fuji–Xerox facility in Japan.

Strategic advantages also exist. Global firms can enter local markets by aggressively lowering prices, using profits from more profitable markets to subsidize those efforts. This permits the creation of long-term, strategic advantages in these newer markets.

The need for a global perspective is a reality in management. If a manager is associated with a local firm, he or she must be aware of threats posed by global firms. If the manager is associated with a global firm, he or she must be aware of the global environment. In either case, the manager must develop a global perspective.

INCREASING THE SPEED OF DECISION MAKING AND IMPLEMENTATION

In light of the rapid development of new threats and opportunities in the environment, speed of decision making is at a premium. To increase speed in decision making, an organization needs integrated information systems to gather and process large amounts of data continuously and to transport those data long distances in usable form. The requirement for speed also creates the demand for styles of management that favor rapid action. Moreover, after a strategic response is initiated, the time-to-market for implementation also must be accelerated.

QUICKLY REALIGNING RESOURCES

Realigning resources does not necessarily mean changing the formal organization, as Chandler suggested. It may require changing the formal organization, but it may also require the establishment of more informal, temporary arrangements.

Exhibit 5-9
Characteristics of Strong Controllers

Characteristic Number	Description of Characteristic	Specific Attributes and Behaviors
	Personal Qualities	
1.	Personal energy and motivation	Is a doer. Is aware of everything going on. Takes initiative.
2.	Personal integrity and professional commitment	Is unbiased source of information Doesn't try to bluff ("I don't know, but I'll find out"). Is the conscience of the division. Is not a "yes man." Is candid.
	Technical Competence	
3.	Accounting knowledge	Technical ability is not in question.
4.	Analytical skill	Determines not only what happened but also why something happened. Is good at arranging and rearranging numbers. Is able to spot trends before they become a reality. Is able to dig below the numbers.
	Business Judgment	
5.	Understanding of what management needs to run the business effectively	Is a businessperson. Has good business judgment. Is familiar with other parts of the division. Understands the division's business. Anticipates future business problems. Recommends action to deal with future business problems. Keeps an eye on the whole business. Is not always concerned about not spending.
	Communication Skills	
6.	Ability to judge what is important to management and make recommendations	Does not think only of financial control. Is able to summarize quickly and accurately. Mentally makes the same decisions as the division general manager. Provides management with information even before it realizes the need for it. Thinks the way the division manager thinks. Quickly grasps information of real concern to management. Is willing to estimate. Is able to judge the degree of accuracy needed.

Exhibit 5-9 (continued)

Characteristic Number	Description of Characteristic	Specific Attributes and Behaviors
		Does not emphasize accuracy as an end in itself.
		Does not get lost in allocating costs.
		Speaks the language used by management.
		Keeps the audience in mind.
		Is able to come to grips with facts and make recommendation.

Interpersonal Skills

Characteristic Number	Description of Characteristic	Specific Attributes and Behaviors
7.	Building relationships and developing influence	Gets along with everyone.
		Is accepted by all functional areas.
		Is part of the management team.
		Is management's trusted counselor.
		Is flexible in meeting management's demands.
		Is the general manager's alter ego.
		Is a sounding board for management when sensitive issues are discussed.
		Opens up communications.
		Is respected by management.
		Is trusted by management.
		Builds trust.
8.	Ability to challenge management constructively	Asks the right questions.
		Thinks about the impact of numbers.
		Continually challenges management's analysis and plans.
		Knows when to risk fights and when to give in.
		Is always asking questions.
		Does not hesitate to question management's action after it is taken.
		Does not hesitate to criticize management plans and actions.

Managing Dual Accountability

Characteristic Number	Description of Characteristic	Specific Attributes and Behaviors
9.	Recognizes important responsibility to both division and corporate management.	Understands corporate expectations.
		Recognizes responsibility to corporate management.
		Judgment is recognized by management.
		Is able to judge what is important and what is not.
		Has good rapport with corporate management.
		Is the eyes, ears, and sense of management.

Source: Reprinted by permission of Prentice Hall from Vijay Sathe, *Controller's Involvement in Management,* (Prentice Hall, Englewood Cliffs, New Jersey, 1982), pp. 110, 141–143.

The culture of the organization must permit the establishment of temporary teams and alliances. These teams may be formed with a former competitor, or they may be formed in a foreign country. The key is to mobilize combinations of skills and resources to solve specific problems both within and outside the company. This means that a significant portion of the formal structure, whether centralized, decentralized, or matrix, is cast into a fluid state. "Have skills, will travel" becomes the desirable attitude among managers and employees!

Managing the Adaptive Organization

In this section, we provide a set of guidelines for organizing and managing in this new environment. The guidelines are based upon the organizational design concepts that relate to *open systems*. These concepts assume that the organization is simultaneously attempting to adapt to its internal requirements of work, such as specialization of skills and coordination of effort, while at the same time trying to adapt to its changes in its external environment.

These external forces can be rapidly developing, such as the invasion into a market of a foreign product which changes the competitive balance and requires an organizational response. Or long-term trends might be present, such as the need for periodic innovations in products, which in turn create the need for a more decentralized structure placing engineering, manufacturing, and marketing closer to the customer.

First we examine the factors driving the need for the adaptive organization. Then we look at some of the opportunities provided by the newer developments in information technology (IT).

Environmental Factors

Environmental factors are contingency factors in the design of organizational structures (Mintzberg, 1979). When designing an adaptable control system, the designer must be aware that organizational structures may have to be adjusted to achieve control in light of various environmental circumstances. Several environmental factors affect organizational structure. We now consider four of these factors.

Environmental Uncertainty

Organizations tend to become more informal in response to environmental uncertainty. Management tends to increase verbal communications in order to better understand and respond to the environment. Management also tends to increase the use of ad hoc teams.

Environmental Complexity

Management may receive mixed or conflicting signals about a market or competition in that market. In light of this complexity in understanding markets, management might choose to decentralize into focused market segments to increase chances of fully understanding smaller market niches. The idea is to divide the market into small and focused segments so that a management team "can get their arms around the situation."

Environmental Diversity

In this situation, the market is divided into very different market segments because of different customers, products, or geographical locations. The typical organizational response is to form relatively autonomous business units for each market segment.

Environmental Hostility

When the management of an organization is threatened by severe hostility, such as adverse political changes, top management tends to centralize decision making. In this situation, top management must gather information very quickly and take rapid action in response to the hostility. This might also occur for commercial reasons. Let's say a competitor introduces a new series of products, thus fragmenting an existing market for a major new product line. In response, a company might centralize decision making for a time to develop a response to market changes. Management might centralize technical resources to accelerate product development, and decide to focus on certain product niches where the company has the best chance to regain market share.

The designer should be alert to these four environmental factors. When one or more are present, the organizational structure may have to be redesigned in order to achieve control.

INFORMATION TECHNOLOGY

Recent development of information technology permits an increase in the speed of decision making and may assist organizations in adapting to changes in the global market place. We turn now to discuss how this occurs and the resultant impact on the organization structure and measurement systems.

Information technology (IT) is impacting business on three levels. First, it is impacting business at the *industry level* by changing products and services and market structures. For example, when American Airlines introduced their computerized flight schedule and reservation system, they achieved a competitive advantage over other airlines who didn't take advantage of computerization. Travel agents could use the system to quickly book flights and improve the service they provided. Other airlines were eventually included in the system, but American listed its own flights first, thus giving them a competitive advantage in the industry.

The second level of impact of IT is at the level of the *firm*. By changing production economics and by restructuring competitive factors relating to buyers, suppliers, new entrants, and substitution of products, the firm's environment can dramatically change. For example, CAD/CAM can accelerate time-to-market for products, and materials requirements planning (MRP) systems can provide better control over the manufacturing of complex products.

The third level of impact of IT is at the level of the *strategy of the firm.* At the strategy level, IT can facilitate low-cost leadership and product differentiation, and it can help to provide a coordinated focus on market niches. For example, advances in telecommunications and reductions in the cost of information processing permit companies to focus advertising on specific interest television channels or tailor television broadcasts to specific regions on a cost effective basis, thus opening up new markets.

Internally, IT is impacting all organizational processes, the span of control, and company products. Computer-controlled manufacturing equipment can be linked with remote design sites. The result is faster time-to-market and the ability to tailor products to specific geographical locations. IT allows companies to network their global facilities into a coordinated global strategy by sharing data on a real-time basis and by holding strategy sessions via teleconferencing.

Information technology allows for linking dispersed facilities into a coordinated company, which can behave like a local company sensitive to the needs of the local market, while at the same time bringing the resources and scale economies of a global company to bear upon these local markets. Reporting status can be done on a real-time basis by using satellite links and teleconferencing. One of the authors (Kirby) participated recently in a design review held concurrently in California, Scotland, and Tucson, Arizona, using interactive telecommunications for the meeting as well as high-definition photographs of design drawings supplemented by immediate FAX communications.

Also, IT makes it possible for firms to seek out the highest value suppliers worldwide and share information with them as readily as with local suppliers. This opens up opportunities for firms to increase competitiveness by using the best suppliers worldwide.

ADAPTIVE CONTROLS THAT SUPPORT THE ADAPTIVE ORGANIZATION

Exhibit 5-10 summarizes many of the control system features of the adaptive organization. The culture of the adaptive organization should emphasize global awareness, change and opportunistic actions, lifelong learning, and agility in accepting and adjusting to new assignments. On the formal side, the infrastructure is characterized by organizational forms that are easily formed and dissolved, the use of ad hoc teams and projects, and the use of worldwide purchasing. The *planning* and *control processes* are characterized by a clear company vision and integrated strategy, integrated informations systems, rapid response times for information flows, accurate worldwide reporting, and relatively simple and rapid authorization procedures. The *reward system* should emphasize the ability to achieve excellence in an uncertain environment. *Coordination systems* should place a premium upon the use of management rotation on a global basis and on the use of multidisciplinary teams for accomplishing specific objectives.

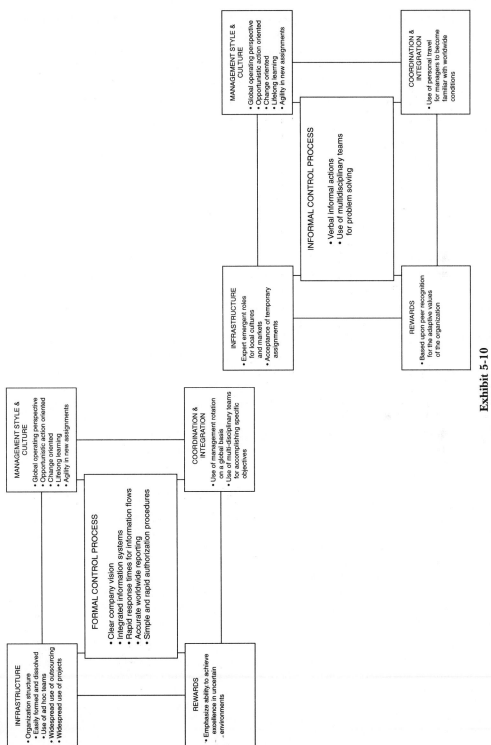

Exhibit 5-10
Controls for Adaptive Organizations

On the informal side, the *infrastructure* should emphasize the development of expert emergent roles for local cultures and markets and the acceptance of temporary assignments. The *planning* and *control processes* should emphasize verbal informal actions and the use of multidisciplinary teams to understand and solve problems. *Coordination mechanisms* should emphasize personal travel for the purpose of managers becoming accustomed to worldwide conditions. Informal *rewards* should be based upon peer recognition programs for the adaptive values of the organization.

CONCLUSION: THE ADAPTIVE ORGANIZATION

We have briefly examined the impact of today's dynamic global environment upon the organization and its measurement systems. Several modifications are needed to the classical formal organization structures to increase adaptability. First is the need to increase boundary spanning activity. Second is the need to set up temporary structures and coordination mechanisms. Finally, we discussed the impact of IT on control systems. IT results in industry, firm and strategic changes further increasing the need for boundary scanning procedures. An important change brought about by improved communications is the breakdown of geographical barriers, and the subsequent enhancement of the global firm. Global firms may now achieve significant improvements in competitiveness over local or national firms.

REFERENCES

BENIGER, JAMES R., *The Control Revolution: Technological and Economic Origins of the Information Society*. Cambridge, Mass.: Harvard University Press, 1986.

CHANDLER, ALFRED D., *Strategy and Structure: Chapters in the History of the American Industrial Enterprise*. Cambridge, Mass.: M.I.T. Press, 1962.

DAVIS, STANLEY M., *Matrix Organization and Behavior in Domestic and Multinational Enterprise*, 9-474-036. Boston: Intercollegiate Case Clearing House, 1973.

GALBRAITH, JAY, *Designing Complex Organizations*. Reading, Mass.: Addison-Wesley, 1973.

KEMP, ROBERT M., *Effective Management of High-Technology Projects*, Unpublished Ph.D. dissertation, Claremont Graduate School, Claremont, Calif., 1983.

LORANGE, PETER, AND RICHARD F. VANCIL, *Strategic Planning Systems*. Englewood Cliffs, N.J.: Prentice Hall, 1977.

MACIARIELLO, JOSEPH A., *Program-Management Control Systems*. New York: John Wiley, 1978.

MINTZBERG, HENRY, *Structuring of Organizations*. Englewood Cliffs, N.J.: Prentice Hall, 1979.

NAGEL, ROGER, DOVE RICK, AND OTHERS, *21st Century Manufacturing Strategy—An Industry Led View*, Volumes 1 and 2. Bethlehem, Pa.: Iacocca Institute, 1991.

NEWMAN, W. H., AND B. YAVITZ, *Strategy in Action*. New York: The Free Press, 1982.

PETERS, THOMAS J., AND ROBERT H. WATERMAN, *In Search of Excellence*. New York: Harper & Row, 1982.

PORTER, MICHAEL E., *Competitive Advantage: Creating and Sustaining Competitive Advantage*. New York: The Free Press, 1985.

SATHE, VIJAY, *Controller Involvement in Management*. Englewood Cliffs, N.J.: Prentice Hall, 1982.

SATHE, VIJAY, *Culture and Related Realities.* Homewood, Ill.: Richard D. Irwin, Inc., 1985, pp. 227–229.

THOMPSON, JAMES A., *Organizations in Action.* New York: McGraw-Hill, 1967.

TICHY, NOEL M., AND STAFFORD SHERMAN, *Control Your Own Destiny or Someone Else Will.* New York: Currency and Doubleday, 1993.

VANCIL, RICHARD F., *Decentralization: Ambiguity by Design.* Homewood, Ill.: Dow-Jones Irwin, 1979.

WATERMAN, R., T. PETERS, AND J. PHILLIPS, "Structure is Not Organization," *Business Horizons,* June 1980.

NOTES

1. Quoted by permission of CISR, The Sloan School of Management, M.I.T., Cambridge, Massachusetts.

Case 5-1 Electronic Division*

The electronics division of a Fortune 500 firm had a reputation in the industry for high-quality performance. It also had the dubious reputation of being unable to meet schedules and cost budgets. In 1991, project cost budgets were commonly overrun by 25 percent or more, and nearly 50 percent of the contracted projects were six months or more behind schedule. This case deals with some of the difficulties with the matrix organization structure that have contributed to the difficulties in controlling cost and schedule performance.

THE MATRIX ORGANIZATION

The organization chart for the electronics division is shown in Exhibit 5-11. The divi-

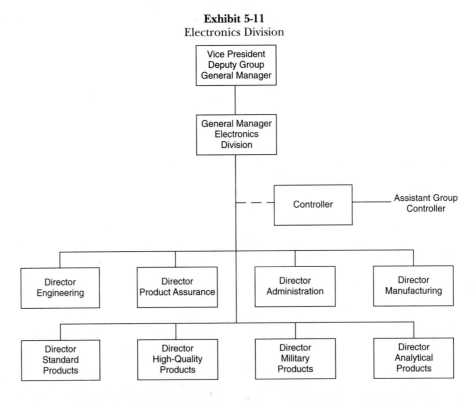

Exhibit 5-11
Electronics Division

*This case has been adapted by permission from a report prepared by James W. Coffman, Executive Management Program, Claremont Graduate School, Claremont, California.

Exhibit 5-12
Program Organization

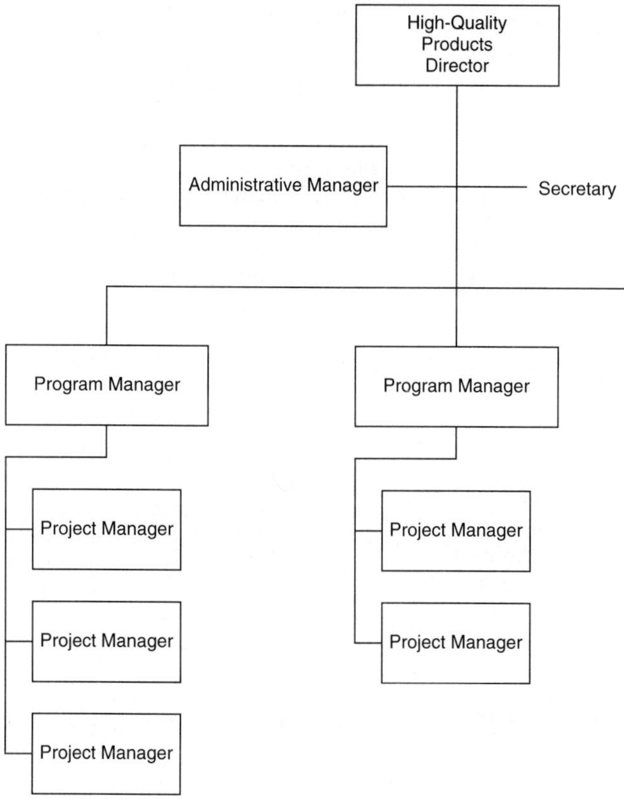

sional organization consists of three functional groups: engineering, manufacturing, and product assurance. There are also four program directors, one for each of the four main product groupings. Each of the four program directors is in turn organized as shown in Exhibit 5-12. Reporting to the program directors are program managers for major programs and, subordinate to the program managers, project managers for various subsystems. The programs then have a dashed-line relationship with the functional groups, sharing people with other programs. Typically, however, the engineering group will assign a project engineer whose responsibility is exclusive to a particular program.

PERCEPTIONS OF THE MATRIX

The perceptions of the way in which the matrix organization works or is supposed to work varies widely throughout the division. One product director views his program managers as integrators and expediters who simultaneously deal with customers as well as internal personnel to keep things moving on the inside. Keeping things moving by his definition includes checking drawings, hand-carrying parts, and running tests if necessary. A program manager in another product area sees his role and the role of the project managers under him as being responsible for overall cost, scheduling, and performance on the assigned projects. These responsibilities carry such duties as setting project priorities; making cost, schedule, and technical decisions based upon the advice, support, and help of the functional personnel; ironing out problems between functional groups employed on the project; dealing with customers; and representing the program and its priorities to the functional directors.

The following quotations from various functional personnel indicate still other perceptions of the role of program and project managers at the electronics division.

- Engineering manager to project engineer: "The only person you ever take direction from is the director of engineering."
- Shipping clerk to the project manager: "It's your job to get the parts to inspection, not mine."
- Engineering manager to program manager: "What do you mean you want a technical recommendation? On the old analyzer project, the engineer, director of engineering, and program manager would just sit down and engineer it."
- Material control clerk to project manager: "It's your job to see that all parts get or-

dered. I just order what you and Engineering tell me to buy."
- Test manager to project manager: "Your schedule doesn't mean anything to me. I test them when they get here."
- Publications manager to program manager: "Every test procedure I've got to type is hot. It's first-in, first-out unless my boss tells me differently."
- Facilities manager to program manager: "I don't care if the air-conditioning problem is keeping you from building electronics. I have to remodel these offices, and that has all my people tied up."

QUESTIONS

1. How do these differences in philosophy with regard to the matrix affect cost, schedule, and technical performance on projects?
2. Draw up a list of recommendations for making the matrix run smoothly in the electronics division. Concentrate on the roles of project managers, project engineers, functional directors, and functional personnel.

Case 5-2 Cable Technology Corporation*

Cable television is a method of bringing extended TV reception into a community by using coaxial cables. Cable Technology (CT) is a small manufacturer of these coaxial cables. It was founded in the late 1970s in Maryland. In 1986, the company moved its operations to a suburb of Denver, Colorado. This case concerns the problems that were encountered by the firm in reorganizing its operations in order to take into account the growth that was achieved as a result of the move.

WHY THE MOVE FROM MARYLAND TO COLORADO?

A principal strategy of CT is to serve rural cable operators by manufacturing and installing coaxial cable. The move to Colorado was in response to this strategy, since there is a greater rural demand in the West than in the densely populated eastern seaboard. As a result, the management of CT considered Denver the best location from which to establish its base of operations. The move to Colorado resulted in an initial doubling of the number of persons employed by the company, from 20 to 40 people.

THE TOP MANAGEMENT OF CT

The president, Dr. Brice W. St. John, founded the firm. St. John, trained as a physicist, has previously held a number of top-management positions in electronics firms. His role at CT is concerned with policy formulation, demand forecasting, technology scanning and assessment, and customer service. Mr. Fred Fritz, on the other hand, is a self-made businessman, with a number of years of managerial experience in technical companies. He is currently in charge of administration of all the departments of the corporation—procurement, assembly, and test. The two top positions have developed to suit the qualifications of these two key people.

ORGANIZATION OF THE COMPANY: BEFORE AND AFTER THE MOVE

The organization changed very little in response to the move. The organization chart before and after the move are shown in Exhibit 5-13. In the words of Mr. Fritz, "Looking over the basic organization structure, I don't find any difference in it now than when it was in Maryland, although there are more people working in different departments, and fewer hats are worn by any one individual. The biggest problem with growth is to know when you need additional hands and when you do not." Mr. Fritz recognizes that a change in management attitudes must occur if a firm wishes to grow beyond the limitations imposed by its present corporate structure. Fritz continues:

*This case was adapted from a document prepared by Carl Eric Johnson, Institute of Administration and Management, Union College, Schenectady, N.Y. It is included by his permission.

Exhibit 5-13
Cable Technology: Organization Before and After Move

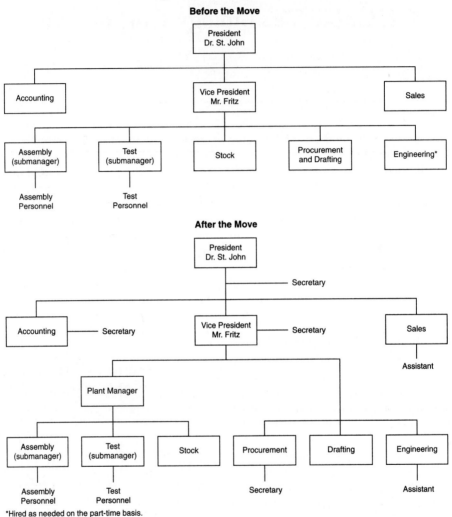

*Hired as needed on the part-time basis.

"All of the people in the company, and as always the management, including myself, are basically hands-on people. It is very difficult for us to assign jobs to others. After all, you can do a job many times faster than it takes to train somebody to do the job. But, of course, as the company grows, you can't do it all, and therefore assignments must be given and persons must be trained to do that particular job."

Matters are complicated, however, because of the attitude prevalent among to[p] management that no change should tak[e] place in the structure of the company, sin[ce] company success to date has been due t[o] the two principal managers in the compan[y.] Nevertheless, Mr. Fritz is committed to th[e] necessity of delegation of responsibility an[d] authority as the firm expands but cautio[ns] that delegation can only take place when su[...]

ordinates are receptive to their new responsibilities. Mr. Fritz describes the situation facing CT as follows: "The manager's ability to direct depends entirely upon the quality and quantity of work that his subordinates are willing to put out and how much they are willing to learn. If they are not willing to carry the load, and in effect force the manager to do more details than he need do, it severely cripples the entire company arrangement. He's got two choices: do the work himself or get new assistants. Of course, this is precisely the situation we are facing now." The company experienced two broad categories of problems in delegation of authority after the move to Colorado:

1. Top management was reluctant to yield the managerial autonomy that some of its new managers desired.
2. Managers were hired who were reluctant to assume the managerial and leadership roles that were desired by top management.

The appointments in the purchasing department illustrate the first class of problems. Miss Baker was hired in Colorado to manage the purchasing department (the former manager did not wish to make the move to Colorado). Many costly mistakes were made in purchasing, especially concerning the purchase of a year's supply of very expensive parts. Miss Baker resigned after a few months, and she was replaced by Mary J. Massar. Mrs. Massar had extensive experience in purchasing with an electronics supplier in Denver and seemed well suited to the position.

The top management was simply looking for a buyer to fill Miss Baker's position. In Mr. Fritz's words, "A buyer's job is simply to obtain the products and services required in the appropriate quantities at the best possible rate." Mr. Fritz wishes to retain the responsibility for authorizing the required parts, for forecasting appropriate quantities, and for determining desired inventory levels. While the company gave Mrs. Massar the title

of purchasing agent, management tried to make sure that she understood the limited nature of the position at the time she was interviewed for the job. Mrs. Massar misunderstood, and this created severe tension in the purchasing department. To make matters worse, Mrs. Massar was experiencing personal problems.

Although Mrs. Massar was exrtremely well liked in the company and received substantial encouragement from management, including limited increases in autonomy, a number of new costly mistakes were made in the purchasing department. Mrs. Massar's personal problems intensified, and she was forced by these problems to resign. Judy Fairley was hired to replace Mrs. Massar, but similar problems occurred. At first everything seemed to be working well, but then problems arose that forced her to resign also. She tried to expand her role in the company to include personnel relations. She established a suggestion box system that initially seemed to work well. Employees were given a vehicle whereby their views could be made known, but after some success, the employees began using the suggestion system for purposes of airing personal gripes. To make matters worse, Mrs. Fairley was not circumspect in the use of these gripes. Mr. Fritz explains: "Over and above all the other problems, Mrs. Fairley's credibility was severely damaged in the eyes of many people, but after presuming to take over the employee relations function, she left the company at a time when both St. John and I were out of town on a business trip. I find that difficult no matter what the provocation."

An illustration of the second problem occurred in the assembly department. Bill Foster was hired to manage this department but found it a bigger job than he had anticipated. Unlike the buyers, he wanted less, not more, responsibility. Mr. Foster had worked for larger corporations. He had become accustomed to having his position defined specifically. The requirements at CT were much broader. He was neither prepared nor willing to take the responsibility of multiple products with many individual variations. Foster was fired, and his position was filled by an Internal appointment.

To prevent the occurrence of problems like these in the future, top management has instituted weekly meetings with department heads to provide a forum for planning and discussion of any problems that occur. In addition, some formal policies and procedures are being instituted. Mr. Fritz states: "One of the major practices that has been dropped is the poor documentation of the product itself—especially parts lists, manuals, and the like. There is a great deal of concentration now on getting all the paperwork so that no one individual is depended upon for information. That includes myself. I could be run over by a railroad train quite easily. It is necessary that everything be documented, properly recorded, and kept up to date for smooth and efficient operations. The managers are to put their house in order paperwork-wise. They are to train someone to handle matters in their absence, whether due to illness, or whatever. In this way the company is being strengthened."

EMPLOYEE RELATIONS

In Maryland the employees knew each other intimately, and things were run on an informal basis. There were no quality control problems, and everyone seemed to work harmoniously together. When the company moved to Colorado, tension developed between the original employees and the new ones. The most serious difficulty concerned the technical aspects of the product. Mr. Fritz explains: "There was a distinct difference in the way things were done and in the training of the persons skilled in electronics in Colorado versus those on the east coast.

These differences are very subtle but significant in product manufacturing and testing. Technicians on the east coast primarily depended upon 'first pieces' and a minimum of paperwork, whereas those in Colorado seemed to require detailed drawings and written instructions."

Because of these differences, the two groups of employees had difficulty working together. These and other problems caused a great deal of discontent in the company. Employees thought the management to be distant. Management felt itself swamped by the problems of the move and of the resultant growth, and was unable to respond quickly to these personnel problems. The lack of rapport between the newer employees and management created an atmosphere of distrust and suspicion. In response, employees developed informal groups, which Mr. Fritz saw as a problem: "There was too much 'personality'—everyone was too friendly, from my point of view, in the sense that they were more interested in talking about and doing everything except what they should have been doing to pull the company through a very critical period. There was no sense of urgency on the part of these people—a necessity to get the job done."

PROSPECTS

Mr. Fritz offers the following comments about the future of Cable Technology: "Why has Cable Technology grown? The company has grown because we have offered our customers good service, always trying to maintain and update equipment in the field. All of this doesn't have the glory attached to it that selling new equipment at exorbitant expense does, but it has raised up a loyal following, and there does not seem to be an end in sight."

Mr. Fritz outlines two possible methods to finance expansion: "A firm can grow b going public or by using its own assets. We have chosen the latter method. The problem with going public is that we lose control of the company and have to report to a board of directors." Mr. Fritz is apparently willing to limit growth as the price of not relinquishing control over the business: "Our problems in the past year have been more than the problems associated with coping with growth. We've had to cope with a new location, which would set any company back. Our business grew significantly last year despite our many problems. We must be doing something right!"

QUESTIONS

1. Is CT doing something right?
2. Analyze the move and the resultant growth to isolate the problems that top management has had. What suggestions do you have for solving the current organization and staffing problems at CT?
3. What suggestions would you make to St. John and Fritz about their style of management and the formal organization structure? The informal organization?
4. To what extent does the firm's future growth depend upon solutions to these problems?

Case 5-3 21st Century Electronics: Metrology Department

Top management of 21st Century Electronics chartered a team of eight members from the metrology department and appointed the section head as leader. Management wanted the team to modify procedures and processes in order to reduce both the cost and the time involved in the calibration of electronic testing equipment.

The team had difficulty in establishing appropriate goals and team assignments. For example, an issue arose in the first meeting regarding technicians and the role they should play in the team. Disagreements resulted in blocking assignments for technicians.

Nevertheless, the team proceeded directly to formal planning and control activities while members were simultaneously exhibiting strong beliefs regarding the direction the solutions should take. Members debated who was best in documenting procedural changes (assuming the team would make some changes). This, in turn, led to planning and control activities, such as detailed discussions about the process of writing policies and procedures. These activities again led to the emphasis on beliefs, such as the belief that detailed procedures had limited value for technically trained people.

At this point, the team had a number of meetings where informal planning and control actions dominated, but then the team slipped into a discussion of appropriate measurements prior to determining the changes to be made.

The following pattern of activity characterized this team:

1. Organization issues remained unresolved and continued to reoccur, thereby blocking informal planning.

2. Formal planning and control activities seemed to dominate early meetings.
3. Conflicting individual beliefs and opinions tended to block attempts to initiate informal planning and control activities.

The team disbanded after the seventh meeting after having severe disagreements amongst themselves as to who would supervise the activity of one of the subteams. Top management ranked this team eight out of ten teams evaluated (during the relevant period) in terms of goal attainment. The team's activity had virtually no effect upon departmental performance.

The case writer interviewed three of the team members after the team had disbanded. One member stated:

> Team meetings were very stressful. We all had strong ideas on how to proceed. A number of members had their own agenda, which led to conflict.

A second member stated:

> The team had lots of potential, but discussions were limited to safe topics.

The third team member interviewed had the following reaction:

> This particular team leader needs more training in team leadership. He needs to be able to bring a team to consensus as opposed to isolating members with whom he disagrees.

QUESTION

- Why did team number eight fail to meet its improvement goals? (*Hint:* see the dynamics of the control process discussed in Chapter 3 and the material on organizing for control in Chapter 5.)

6

INFRASTRUCTURE II: AUTONOMY, RESPONSIBILITY CENTERS, AND PERFORMANCE MEASUREMENT

INTRODUCTION

A number of structural elements in an organization are used to exert influence over the behavior of managers. These factors are embodied in the organization itself and interact with the formal control process to influence behavior. We refer to the total of these factors as the *infrastructure of control systems*. Some of these factors are formal and some are informal.

These factors are among the most important elements of a control system. They influence the *autonomy* or the freedom of action of managers. They also influence the way managerial performance is measured and evaluated.

In this chapter we will first consider the determinants of autonomy at the divisional or profit center level. Next, we describe the nature and purpose of responsibility centers as structural control devices. Finally, we conclude the chapter with a discussion of overall divisional performance measurement systems including the measurement of transactions among semi-autonomous units. The emphasis throughout the chapter is upon the design of infrastructure elements that are both congruent with the goals of the organization and fair to individual managers within the organization.

DIVISIONAL AUTONOMY

A key issue for top management is the determination of the desired levels of autonomy to grant subordinate managers. The autonomy of a manager refers to the freedom that the manager has in decision making and the constraints on that decision making placed upon the manager by his or her superior. Autonomy is a dynamic concept; it ebbs and flows for an organization as a whole and for managers within an organization. The question facing top management is: How much decentralization of decision making should there be in the organization?

Corporate managers influence profit center managers through a network of relationships that establish the domain in which the manager has freedom of action to be creative as a change agent with regard to his or her environment. Profit center managers in turn establish control over their subordinate managers through a similar network of relationships.

This section describes a tool that management may use to set desired or intended levels of autonomy in the organization. Management must communicate desired levels of autonomy and attain congruence between the levels which management intends to give and the level which subordinate managers perceive. The design tool, originally developed by Vancil (1979, p. 128), is presented in Exhibit 6-1. This tool allows management to design certain structures and processes to achieve appropriate levels of autonomy.

The best way to understand Exhibit 6-1 is to relate it to Exhibit 1-1, which defines the mutually supportive subsystems that comprise a management control system. Autonomy is a part of the "infrastructure" subsystem defined in Exhibit 1-1. The variables that are determinants of autonomy (in Exhibit 6-1) are a major

Exhibit 6-1
A Theory of Decentralized Management

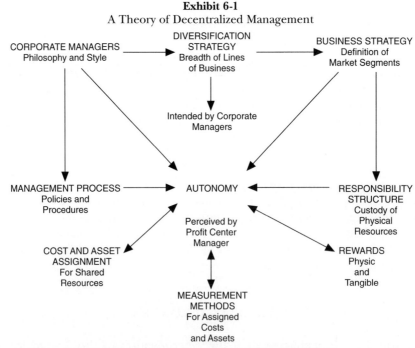

Source: Reproduced, by permission of Financial Executives Research Foundation, from R. F. Vancil, *Decentralization: Managerial Ambiguity by Design,* Dow Jones-Irwin, Homewood Illinois, 1979, p. 128.

subset of the elements that comprise the entire mutually supportive systems model of Exhibit 1-1. We shall proceed in this section to comment upon the eight variables of Exhibit 6-1 as each of these elements influences autonomy.

The eight separate variables may in turn be summarized into three groups: **management style and processes, responsibility structure, and measurement-reward systems**.

MANAGEMENT STYLE AND PROCESSES

Corporate Managers: Philosophy and Style

Chief executive officers (CEOs) have different concepts about how their organization is to be run. Will the organization be run as a holding company with loose control of profit centers? Will it be run in a centralized manner with most of the key decisions being made at the top? Will a balance be struck between central direction and decentralized action? These different concepts are often referred to as managerial styles.

As we saw in Chapter 4, managerial style consists of the many personal variables that influence the behavior of corporate management. These variables include (1) the desire of corporate managers to be involved in the details of the business or to delegate most of the decisions, (2) the day-to-day interactions of corporate managers with other managers, and (3) the level of trust and confidence top management has in the ability and experience of subordinate managers.

This matter of style and philosophy of management is illustrated by the following quotation from Alfred Sloan pertaining to the patterns of divisional autonomy established within General Motors (1964, p. 54):

> The basis upon which this study has been made is founded upon two principles, which are stated as follows:
>
> 1. The responsibility attached to the chief executive [of a General Motors Division] shall in no way be limited. Each such organization headed by its chief executive shall be complete in every necessary function and enable[d] to exercise its full initiative and logical development.
> 2. Certain central organization functions are absolutely essential to the logical development and proper control of the Corporation's activities.

Where corporate management draws the line between what Sloan referred to as the "full initiative" of the divisional chief executive and the proper centralized functions is in some respects a matter of economics (that is, economies of scale call for the centralization of certain corporate functions) and partly a matter of style and philosophy of management.

Management style influences the philosophy of decentralization with which upper management chooses to run decentralized operations. It is concerned with just how control over divisional operations is exerted by top management through personal interactions and policies and procedures, including planning systems. It has to do with the latitude that each divisional manager has over his or her operations. It has to do with who calls the shots in various decision-making situations. It is best summarized as a *continuum between highly directive or autocratic* management styles on the one hand and *highly participative* management styles on the other.

Style influences the design of the management systems for developing plans, budgets, performance reviews, and so on. Style influences the frequency of meetings held to explain and defend plans. It determines the detail that is necessary to explain and defend budgets. Style determines just how tightly the "screws" are on managers.

The prevailing style of top management and the culture of the organization has a profound effect both upon the perceived and actual autonomy of profit center managers. Each of the other seven variables of Exhibit 6-1 is in turn strongly influenced by style and culture.

Management Processes: Policies and Procedures

Policies and procedures are attempts by corporate managers to specify in advance the way in which certain major decisions are to be made under various recurring circumstances. They reduce the latitude of profit center managers in decision making. They are instituted so as to bring about uniform behavior among profit center managers with regard to certain decisions.

Technical and managerial staffs may be set up by corporate managers to carry out a broad range of managerial functions, thus restricting the latitude of division managers, or they may be set up as purely advisory groups. Management committees may be used to review divisional plans and budgets and thus to act as a check on divisional autonomy.

Diversification Strategy

The Vancil study found a fairly stable relationship between the diversification strategy chosen by management and the autonomy of profit center managers. Autonomy tended to be highest in firms that chose to grow by acquiring or developing unrelated businesses. On the other hand, autonomy of profit center managers tended to be most restricted in firms engaged in single businesses. The intuitive rationale for these findings is that when a firm expands in a single dominant or into a related business, the likelihood is higher that tangible or intangible relationships will exist with regard to certain of its operating functions. Pure economics leads to the centralization of these functions, compelling various profit centers to share these resources, thus restricting autonomy. On the other hand, when businesses are unrelated, it becomes more difficult to achieve these synergies, thus leading to fewer shared resources and to more autonomy.

Business Strategy

Business strategy is concerned with the market strategy to be followed for each division's business. Business responsibility is normally spelled out for each division in its divisional charter. The charter specifies the business and product domain that the division is to occupy. It spells out the broad business strategy including major product lines. The charter thus serves to limit or constrain the permissible operations of the division. It restricts the domain of divisional managers to those stipulated lines of business and market segments that may be pursued. As a result, constraints are placed upon the operation of the division by business strategy itself.

The particular business strategy chosen for a business by top management also influences the autonomy of the profit center manager. A cost strategy, for example, usually leads to the centralization of certain resources at the corporate level, which results in reduced autonomy for the managers of profit centers.

Vancil's empirical work suggests that the four variables discussed above: philosophy and style, management processes, diversification strategy, and business strategy have a dominant influence over the autonomy of profit center managers. They collectively represent the *first line of influence* top managers have over profit center managers.

RESPONSIBILITY STRUCTURE

Responsibility Structure: Custody of Physical Assets

The responsibility structure establishes the physical, human, and financial resources that are entrusted to the profit center manager. These resources represent the functional authority of the profit center manager, which should follow from the four variables discussed previously. *Functional Authority* is measured by the percentage of the resources needed to run the business of the profit center that is actually under the authority of the profit center manager. The balance consists of the corporate resources that must be shared by profit center managers who are under the authority of another manager. The custody of resources will influence the decision-making process for the profit center manager. It will, for example, determine the procedures that must be followed in approving capital investments as well as in appointing divisional executives.

Responsibility structure is thus the *second line of influence* top managers have over profit centers. Responsibility structure should be consistent with the variables in the first set.

MEASUREMENT–REWARD SYSTEMS

Cost and Asset Assignments

Cost and asset assignments convey to the division manager just what items of cost and investment the manager should be concerned about, regardless of whether they are local or assigned (for shared resources).

Vancil computed indices to assess cost (1979, p. 105) and asset (p. 107) assignments for the 300 firms in his study. Again the patterns of both local costs (that is, the portion of total resources under the control of the profit center manager) as well as assigned costs followed diversification strategies. Profit centers that were a part of corporations whose growth was through unrelated businesses had control over approximately 80 percent of the resources needed to run the business, whereas those in single-business firms had approximately 60 percent of the resources needed to carry out their responsibilities. When local plus assigned costs were taken into account, the unrelated business firms assigned approximately 97 percent of total costs to profit center managers. The total figure was approximately 94 percent for single-business firms.

For firms that do trace assets to divisions, similar patterns emerge. In divisions that are a part of single businesses, only approximately 50 percent of the total assets used are controlled locally. Another 25 percent are assigned by corporate managers. Divisions in unrelated businesses have local control over more than 80 percent of the assets they need to carry out their responsibilities and have another 15 percent assigned.

Measurement Methods: For Assigned Costs and Assets

Measurement methods convey just how concerned the division manager must be about the costs and assets assigned. Measurement methods stipulate the method of cost and asset assignment.

The three most common measurement methods are *proration, negotiation,* and *metering.* Proration involves allocation of shared resources based upon standard rules. Division managers have little to say about the results. Negotiation and metering give profit center managers more control over the amount and the quality of resources they use, thus increasing their autonomy over them. The important thing in measuring these shared costs and assets is that the methods used be perceived as fair.

Rewards: Tangible and Intangible

The reward system is normally based upon performance as determined by the measurement system. Financially, almost all profit center managers are compensated at least partly by performance as indicated by the measurement systems. The size and methods of awarding bonuses are related to the autonomy of the profit center manager.

The reward system for division managers consists of tangible and intangible rewards, both formal and informal. Intangible rewards include power, status, and feelings of accomplishment and are situational in their administration.

The measurement–reward systems should follow directly from the other two sets of variables. Vancil found these measurement and reward variables to be the *third line of influence* top managers have over profit centers.

These three measurement–reward variables have a two-way relationship with autonomy. On the one hand, autonomy that is intended by corporate management should be further reflected in the measurement–reward system. On the other hand, the measurement–reward system sends certain signals regarding autonomy to the profit center manager, so the arrows are two-directional.

We turn now to a discussion of responsibility centers, another aspect of the infrastructure of control.

RESPONSIBILITY STRUCTURE

The responsibility structure of an organization consists of responsibility centers and related performance measurement systems. A responsibility center is an organization subunit headed by a manager who is held responsible for achieving one or more goals. Responsibility centers form an organizational hierarchy or a means–end chain in pursuit of organizational goals. The responsibility center structure is a hierarchical structure of information processing channels, as illustrated in Chapter 2. The responsibility center hierarchy is the method the organization uses to "couple," however loosely, the decentralized decision-making structure so that decisions made in one part of the organization will be congruent with decisions made in other parts of the organization.

The responsibility structure includes a responsibility accounting system. A responsibility accounting system is a part of the information provided managers. It is a financial measurement system that records plans and performance according to the financial variables for which the manager is accountable. Other measures of performance discussed in Chapter 3 may also be included in the performance measurement system.

Exhibit 6-2 is a schematic representation of a responsibility center. As shown in Exhibit 6-2, a responsibility center is an organizational unit that uses inputs in the form of labor, materials, and capital and converts them into outputs consisting of products and services.

The coupling of the organization through responsibility centers is reinforced by measurement of performance vis-a-vis cost, quality, revenue, profit, and investment goals and by a system of rewards that seeks to blend the self-interest of organizational participants with objectives of the organization as a whole. Our discussion of rewards is deferred to Chapter 7.

Referring to Exhibit 6-2, we should note that there are at least three distinct methods of measuring the performance of a responsibility center. We may establish standards and measure performance with regard to the amount of inputs used over a specified period of time for a given level of output. This is an *efficiency* measure of performance. Examples are standards for labor and material that are established for a production operation.

Still another procedure for measuring the performance of a responsibility center is to emphasize the production process in the measure. This is a *process* measure of performance. Examples are requiring a review of lesson plans for teachers or sampling the quality of production during a production process to infer something about the quality of the final output before it is delivered or produced.

The third procedure for measuring performance in a responsibility center is to measure the output of the organization in terms of the overall goal of the organization. This is an *effectiveness* measure of performance. Examples are profit and return on investment for a period of time in relationship to a desired goal for these variables.

Exhibit 6-2
Schematic Representation of a Responsibility Center

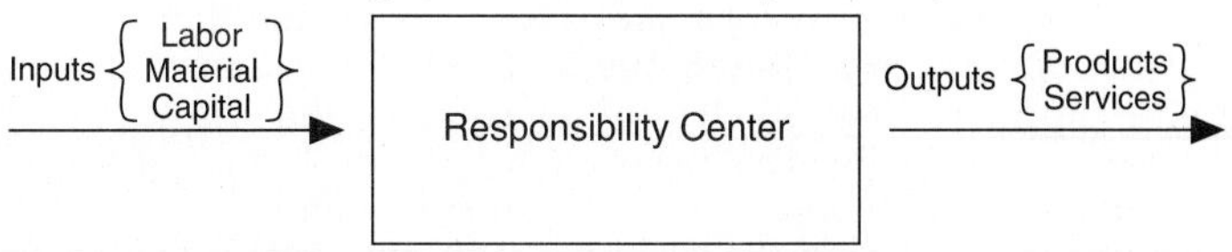

We use these three methods of performance evaluation to line up the overall objectives of the organization with the objectives of each responsibility center. We choose the efficiency, process, or effectiveness measure of performance to assess progress of a subunit in attaining its purpose and we do it in such a way that the manager of each subunit is held responsible for only those variables over which he or she has a reasonable amount of control. This results in a goal-congruent and fair system.

OVERALL EFFECTIVENESS MEASURES: RETURN ON INVESTMENT (ROI)

While we shall show later just how difficult it is to achieve optimal performance with regard to any one goal, we surely agree that as far as investors of capital are concerned, a most important objective of the firm is achieving a satisfactory return on investment.

Profit is too vague a goal form the point of view of the owners of the firm, for it does not consider the investment of the shareholder. Similarly, we cannot say that shareholders are better off if revenues are higher or if expenses are lower. All measures of performance must be related to shareholders' investment (that is, their input) if they are to be meaningful to owners.

The idea behind the hierarchy of responsibility centers and the responsibility accounting system is to distribute to the decentralized organizational subunits responsibility for various elements of ROI. Each responsibility center has assigned to it measures of performance that are appropriate to the elements of cost, quality, revenue, and investment that are assigned to that responsibility center. Rewards are then made in accordance with performance. The combination of responsibility centers, measures of performance, and rewards knits together decentralized centers of decision making so as to pursue effectively achievement of overall organizational goals that almost surely include profit and ROI.

Alfred P. Sloan put the challenge (1964, pp. 139–140) like this:

> . . . the general question remained: how could we exercise permanent control over the whole corporation in a way consistent with the decentralized scheme of organization? We never ceased to attack this paradox; indeed we could not avoid a solution of it without yielding both the actual decentralized structure of our business and our philosophy of approach to it . . .
>
> It was on the financial side that the last necessary key to decentralization with coordinated control was found. That key, in principle, was the concept that, if we had the means to review and judge the effectiveness of operations, we could safely leave the prosecution of those operations to the men in charge of them. The means as it turned out was a method of financial control which converted the broad principle of return on investment into one of the important working instruments for measuring the operations of the divisions. The basic elements of financial control in General Motors are cost, price, volume, and rate of return on investment.
>
> A word on rate of return as a strategic principle of business. I am not going to say that the rate of return is a magic wand for every occasion of business. There are times when you have to spend money just to stay in business, regardless of the rate of return. Competition is the final price determinant and competitive prices may result in profits which force you to accept a rate of return less than you hoped for, and for that matter to accept temporary losses. And, in times of inflation, the rate-of-return concept comes up against the problem of assets undervalued in terms of replacement. Nevertheless, no other financial principle with which I am acquainted serves better than rate of return as an objective aid to business judgment.

To understand the logic behind the concept of ROI, we next break it down into its elements. These were the elements used by Donaldson Brown of General Motors to subdivide the ROI calculation and build it into the divisional pricing policy of General Motors. (Brown came to General Motors from DuPont in 1921 and brought these concepts with him). These elements then became the basis for establishing performance measures for the various subunits of a division that are both goal congruent (in the sense that achieving predetermined standards with regard to these measures would contribute to the achievement of the desired divisional and corporate ROI) and fair, in the sense that each organizational unit would have control over the variables that influence the performance measure. Let us examine the elements of ROI. Then we will examine the performance measures used for responsibility centers to exert leverage over the variables influencing ROI.

First, let us define ROI as

$$\text{ROI} \quad = \quad \frac{\text{net profit}}{\text{invested capital}} \tag{1}$$

Equation (1) may be defined further in terms of profit margin and investment turnover as in Exhibit 6-3. In other words, ROI may be divided into two components, net profit as a percentage of sales revenue and turnover of investment in relation to sales revenue. Profit margin may be broken down into its elements as in Exhibit 6-4. Moreover, investment turnover may be broken into its elements as in Exhibit 6-5.

Beginning with this overall measure of economic performance, one can see the need for at least five different types of responsibility centers and related financial measures of performance to link together decentralized decision making. These responsibility centers are discussed below.

STANDARD COST CENTER

The first of these responsibility centers is the standard cost center within which performance is measured according to the ability of the organizational unit to achieve cost standards and future targets. Total standard costs are determined by multiplying the quantity of output by unit standard costs. The labor and material elements of costs of goods (that is, the direct costs) are under the control of cost center managers. Total actual costs are compared with total standard cost, and deviations are analyzed to ascertain responsibility for variances to seek corrective measures. The outputs of manufacturing departments are often measured this way.

The standard cost center is the responsibility center with the least potential for dysfunctionality. Standard input levels are determined from planned output levels by

Exhibit 6-3
Computation of ROI

ROI =	profit margin	=	net profit/sales revenue
	×		×
	investment turnover	=	sales revenue/invested capital

Exhibit 6-4
Computation of Profit Margin

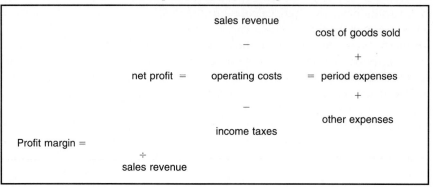

predetermined engineering standards. Performance in standard cost centers is measured primarily on the basis of efficiency and quality. Cost minimization, however, may occur at the expense of quality or volume, thus producing a lack of congruence with the goals of the firm. To minimize this tendency, it is reasonable to prescribe the type and amount of production desired as well as quality standards required.

REVENUE CENTER

A marketing organization is an example of a sales revenue center, the need for which is shown in Exhibits 6-3 and 6-4. Its output can be measured in terms of sales revenue. The cost of production and the size of its sales force are often outside the control of the marketing organization. Selling price and advertising expenses must be reviewed to avoid the possibility of increased sales volume at the expense of profits.

DISCRETIONARY EXPENSE CENTER

The discretionary expense center designation is appropriate for subunits in which the outputs cannot be related precisely to organization goals. For example, what

Exhibit 6-5
Computation of Investment Turnover

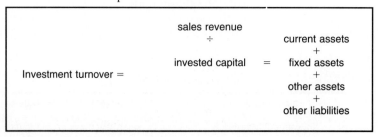

do public relations, personnel, and the legal departments contribute to profit? Because the contribution is quite indirect, it is difficult to establish appropriate input levels in any scientific manner. Costs are quantifiable, but contributions are not. Discretionary expense centers are overhead responsibility centers. Their costs are generally traced to products through overhead allocation and appear in cost of goods sold (see Exhibit 6-4). Some discretionary costs appear as period expenses (for example, selling and general and administrative expenses).

Since the value of output is not discernible with respect to the organization's objectives, input levels are decided primarily by managerial discretion and in accordance with industry procedure. Dysfunctionalities, including empire building, are therefore quite likely in this type of responsibility center.

The tendency for goal dysfunctionality is accentuated in some types of discretionary expense centers (for example, R&D and legal departments) because professional staff members have professional goals that sometimes conflict with the goals of the organization. Professional self-interest and not organizational goals may sometimes direct their behavior. The staff may want to develop the "ideal" system, program, or design because it is "good" to do so as far as furthering professional norms of competence. The ideal, however, is often more costly than the optimum as far as the organization is concerned. In profitable companies where increases in budget are routinely approved, this goal dysfunctionality is accentuated. In fact, this is one method of adding to organizational slack, where this type of slack represents inefficiency that is tolerated because organizational goals and objectives are being achieved.

In discretionary expense centers, efforts to establish plans and achieve control focus upon cost and quality variables. Costs must be watched carefully and programs evaluated fully to avoid dysfunctionalities.

PROFIT CENTER

A fourth type of responsibility center designation is that of the profit center. The subunit, to be held accountable for profits, must have traceable costs and sales revenue or have at least some indirect control over both cost and revenue variables. Ordinarily, it is involved in the manufacture and sale of outputs. Otherwise, profit, as a measure of performance, is undesirable.

Each profit center is a relatively independent operating unit, and its manager must have significant control over most operating decisions that affect profit (for example, volume of production, methods of operation, cost of goods sold, pricing, and product mix). It must be top management's belief that the basic goal of profit for the subunit is fair and congruent with the goals and objectives of the organization. Financial control systems for profit centers should measure inputs, outputs, and profit versus a standard of performance. However, because the profit center manager has little or no control over investment, the measurement of profit performance says nothing about return on investment, since the investment base is not included within the performance measure. Inherent in the measure, therefore, is potential dysfunctionality; profit may be earned by increasing investment. Attempting to maximize profit performance per se, therefore, may not be congruent with the goal of maximizing return on investment or other stakeholder goals.

When more than one profit center exists in an organization, transactions among profit centers require the establishment of a system of interprofit-center relations. There are two elements to such a system: sourcing decisions, that is, the rules governing the permissible sources of purchases and sales among profit centers, and transfer prices, the terms of those purchases and sales. Where interprofit-center transactions take place, the system of interprofit-center relations should be designed to ensure that a good decision from the division's point of view is a good decision from the entire organization's point of view. The subject of interprofit-center relations is elaborated later in this chapter.

INVESTMENT CENTER

A subunit is designated an investment center if it has control not only over sales revenues and operating costs but also over the assets employed in producing profit. The manager must to some extent be able to influence the size of the investment base as well as profit variables. The objective of any decentralized financial control system as it applies to investment in facilities is to provide an incentive for divisional management to purchase, retain, or retire facilities in accordance with the best interests of the organization.

The investment center is the broadest measure of economic performance for an entity in that it incorporates all elements of profit and investment. At first glance it appears very attractive, but upon closer examination it will be shown to be beset by many technical and conceptual measurement problems. We shall explore these and related problems later in this chapter. We will also consider the remedial steps that must be taken to develop a sound measure of investment performance.

Let us summarize this chapter to this point. Organizations have decentralized following their strategies for growth and diversification. Responsibility centers are necessary to couple, however loosely, the goals of individual subunits with the purposes the organization as a whole is pursuing. Broadly speaking, it is a problem of coordination and control, and again quoting Simon (1976, p. 274), "there is no guarantee that the decisions reached will be optimal with respect to any overall organizational goal."

If properly designed, the responsibility structure will motivate managers toward goal-congruent behavior. Given the complexities, it is difficult to define a "perfectly" goal-congruent responsibility structure. In practice, it is possible only to approximate goal-congruent behavior in profit, investment, and discretionary expense centers. Nevertheless, a well-designed responsibility structure will enhance the effectiveness with which the organization pursues its goals.

In this section of the chapter we have examined some of the key issues involved in decentralization: the determination of autonomy and the design of responsibility centers. We turn now to the related topics of measuring divisional performance and establishing interprofit-center relations.

MEASURING PERFORMANCE OF DECENTRALIZED OPERATIONS

This section is concerned with a number of fundamental issues that confront the control systems designer when he or she attempts to design a performance measurement system for a decentralized division of a multidivisional company. These issues include measuring both profit and investment performance and setting transfer prices for interdivisional transactions. These are the central issues in the design of performance measurement systems.

We should indicate before starting, however, that the techniques discussed below are *formal techniques* for the control of decentralized operations. They fit very well into market or bureaucratic-type governance systems. A clan-based control system would rely much more upon informal control (value based) mechanisms for performance measurement and evaluation. For example, the issues discussed in this section, ROI performance measurement, profit centers, and transfer pricing, are not as strongly emphasized among Japanese companies (Ouchi, p. 42). The emphasis there is upon teamwork and wherever teamwork is emphasized, individual organizational unit performance will be more ambiguous than described here. Nevertheless, even in these organizations, the informal, implicit performance measurement systems cannot stand alone.

MEASURING DIVISIONAL OPERATIONS

We have seen that the structure of control systems calls for measurement of decentralized operations. It is important to design measurement systems for decentralized operations that properly reflect the degree of intended autonomy given to division managers by corporate managers. The measurement methods for responsibility centers will depend upon the responsibility structure and the cost and asset assignments. The measurement systems for each responsibility center will reflect the measurement methods for the higher-level responsibility center.

Sloan set out the importance as well as the broad principle of design of measurement systems (see his quote pp. 192 and 193). He thought they should be financial and derived from the broad principles of return on investment, since return on investment is a dominant objective of the owners of a corporation[1]. The measurement system for each responsibility center should then reflect a portion of this return objective, how much depends upon the resources that have been placed under the custody of the responsibility center manager.

We shall in this chapter first look more deeply at return on investment as a measurement criterion for investment centers. Then we shall examine some alternative methods of measurement for investment responsibility centers. Next we consider measurement methods for profit centers. Measurement methods for standard cost and discretionary expense centers will be discussed in Chapters 12 and 13. We have chosen to delay a full discussion of cost centers until we have looked at cost accounting systems, since the topics are closely related.

Return on Investment as a Performance Measure

We recall that ROI is defined as

$$\text{ROI} = \frac{\text{revenue} - \text{expense}}{\text{investment}} \tag{1}$$

To apply ROI measurement to an investment center, the firm must define the revenue, expense, and investment base assigned to the responsibility center. Revenues are readily traced to the responsibility center. To assign expenses we must get into the question of cost assignment methods, which were discussed briefly earlier in this chapter and will be discussed in depth in Chapters 12 and 13. To assign an investment base, we must determine the assets to be assigned as well as the methods of measuring those assets assigned, as numerous measurement alternatives exist. The next section is primarily concerned with the asset measurement issue.

When a firm applies a budgeted ROI figure to a responsibility center to determine expected profit, (for example, 10 percent of the assigned investment base), the division manager uses that figure as a criterion for investing in assets. Depending upon divisional autonomy, this ROI target will influence investment proposals prepared for the approval of corporate managers as well as investments in assets over which the division manager has local control. In other words, the ROI budgeted figure, together with the measurement methods for determining the investment base, will significantly influence decisions as to the assets in which the division manager invests. The idea, therefore, is to set up the ROI measure so as to reflect the objectives of the corporation as accurately as possible, so that the division manager will be motivated by the measurement and the reward system to choose investment projects that corporate managers deem appropriate.

The cybernetic paradigm sheds much light on the use of ROI as a performance measure. If the firm seeks to attain a certain level of return on the total book value of the investment as reflected on the accounting statements, it becomes perfectly proper and goal congruent to hold managers of investment centers responsible for ROI as computed on the divisional income statement and balance sheet. This is seen as a very plausible goal, since the firm reports to its owners and the public at large through these financial statements. These return measures are used by financial analysts and investors to evaluate the performance of the company. The problem is that these financial statements do not always reflect the economic realities of the business.

If the firm and its owners believe that attaining a certain level of ROI is the same as achieving the equivalent economic rate of return (called the internal rate of return) on its investment, then it will be sadly disappointed. In other words, ROI is as legitimate a goal (that is, value premise) as is the internal rate of return (IRR) on investment, but these goals are far from the same thing, and designers of control systems and managers must recognize this.

Following an economic model of the firm, it would be ideal to have the performance measurement system on divisional books reflect "true" economic performance. This is an extremely difficult task to accomplish in practice, since the financial accounting system does not reflect completely the economic realities of investment projects, and the financial accounting system is the principal measurement system for the firm and its divisions. Let us turn to an examination of the differences between the ROI measure as traditionally applied and the requirements of a measurement system, based on IRR, which accurately reflects the economics of business investment.

Conceptual Differences in the Measures Themselves

We should first recall that under the IRR method of evaluating investment projects, the firm compares the IRR of a project with its cost of capital. If the IRR is equal to or greater than its cost of capital, the firm considers the project profitable. Let us consider an example that illustrates the conceptual differences between IRR and ROI[2].

We make the following assumptions.

1. The firm's cost of capital is 10 percent.
2. ROI is used as the performance measurement system for the divisions.
3. The firm has three divisions: A, B, and C. Division A is considered to have high profit potential, whereas division C is relatively new and is just developing its business. Division B, on the other hand, was the original business of the firm and is now mature. As a result, management sets a budgeted ROI of 20 percent for division A, a 5 percent ROI for division C, and a 12.5 percent ROI for division B, thinking that this reflects appropriate targets for the three divisions, given their potential.

The ROI performance measure will result in division A's applying a cutoff rate of 20 percent to all its investments, since it is being measured at the rate of 20 percent. Assuming equal risk, division A would reject investment proposals that yield 15 percent. These same investments would be accepted by both divisions B and C. Moreover, given the overall cutoff rate of 10 percent for the corporation, this project, which yields 15 percent, is indeed profitable for the company as a whole.

Division A, because of its ROI target, will reject projects that are profitable to the company. Division C, on the other hand, will accept investment projects that are clearly unprofitable to the corporation, since it has a cutoff rate of 5 percent, whereas the corporate rate is 10 percent. The general problem, therefore, is that ROI leads the divisions to apply different cutoff rates for similar investments without regard to the cutoff rate for the corporation as a whole.

The other side of this problem is equally severe. Although the average cutoff rate for the corporation is estimated at 10 percent, there are some types of investments that may have a higher or lower risk-adjusted cost of capital than others. For example, investments in inventory and accounts receivable may have average costs of capital that are only 6 percent to the corporation, perhaps because of lower risk or perhaps because some of these assets are financed by creditors on trade accounts at no cost.

Each division will apply its cutoff rate to investments in these assets. As a result, divisions A and B will underinvest in these local assets, whereas division C will overinvest, since division C will apply a rate of 5 percent. Therefore, the second difficulty with the ROI measure is that divisions will apply similar cutoff rates to investments that have different costs of capital to the corporation.

To summarize, the ROI performance measure leads division managers to make investment choices according to accounting measures of ROI that are different from true economic measures. This is not necessarily undesirable, since the firm may indeed be seeking goals in terms of reported accounting measurements. Yet different measures of profit and investment performance may improve *economic* profitability, and managers should be aware of this also, since these measures are crucial to owners. We turn now to a discussion of the second difference between ROI and IRR. We refer to this as a difference in the assumptions about the investment base.

Difference in the Investment Base

The IRR procedure has an implicit capital recovery scheme that is different from the explicit recovery scheme (that is, depreciation) contained in the expense assignments generally associated with the calculation of ROI. This means that depreciation expense assigned to the divisions under ROI calculation will be different from the economic depreciation—sometimes higher, sometimes lower, but not the same. We turn to another example to illustrate this difference.

Let us assume a potential investment project with an initial outlay (C_0) of $10,000, annual returns ($R_i$) of $2,500 for five years, received at the end of each period, with no salvage value. Depreciation is assumed to be in accordance with the straight-line method. Ignoring taxes, the IRR of the project is 7.93 percent.

If 7.93 percent is greater than the firm's cost of capital, this investment project would be desirable from the firm's point of view. If it is implemented, and assuming further that the actual savings turn out to be equal to estimated savings, we would like to compare the implicit capital recovery scheme and investment outstanding under IRR with accounting depreciation and the investment base under the ROI procedure.

The depreciation scheme affects expenses in the ROI calculation as well as the investment base. The investment base is the denominator of the fraction that forms the ROI calculation.

For our project to show an ROI on divisional books of 7.93 percent, the division must calculate depreciation according to the implicit capital recovery scheme assumed under IRR. Column 5 of Exhibit 6-6 displays the implicit recovery scheme assumed under the IRR method. The ROI calculation given in column 6 is based upon beginning investment outstanding, given in column 4.

Column 2 of Exhibit 6-6 gives the annual cash flows from the investment. Column 3 gives the annual returns on the outstanding investment, which itself is given in column 4. The capital recovery or depreciation scheme implicit in the IRR calculation is the difference between annual cash flows (column 2) and return on outstanding capital (column 3).

If the accounting records for the division were designed to produce the depreciation schedule shown in column 5 of Exhibit 6-6 and the investment base shown in column 4, then the ROI calculated in the investment center (column 6 of Exhibit 6-6) would be identical to the return on outstanding investment under the IRR procedure. The ROI calculations would then give divisional and corporate managers signals that were congruent with the economic realities of the project.

Exhibit 6-6
Implicit Cash Flows and Implicit Capital Structure

(1)	(2)	(3)	(4)	(5)	(6)
		7.93% Return on Investment	Investment Outstanding	Capital Recovery Implied	Return on Investment
Period	Cash Flow	Outstanding	(4)−[(2)−(3)]	(2)−(3)	Outstanding
0			$10,000		
1	$2,500	$793	8,293	$1,707	7.93%
2		658	6,451	1,842	
3		512	4,463	1,988	
4		354	2,317	2,146	
5		184	1*	2,316	

*Rounding error

   The depreciation schedule and investment base actually produced for this project according to generally accepted methods of financial accounting (that is, GAAP) are much different from those shown in Exhibit 6-6. Under GAAP, the depreciation schedule of an asset is dependent upon the depreciation method selected. The choice of the investment base reflects a conscious decision of management. Most companies use net book value (NBV) to calculate ROI, which is to be expected, since NBV is the value at which assets are reported on the balance sheet.
   We shall turn now to four examples of the calculation of ROI according to accounting records. Exhibit 6-7 provides an example of the calculation of ROI based upon the use of straight-line depreciation (SLD) (that is, the most common method) for both gross book value (GBV) and net book value (NBV) investment bases. Exhibit 6-8 shows the computation of ROI under sum-of-the-year's digits (SYD) depreciation for both the gross book and net book value investment bases.
   With SLD and GBV, the ROI is constant at 5 percent (column 6, Exhibit 6-8). This happens because capital recovery is constant (column 3) and investment base is constant (column 2), thus producing an earnings stream (column 4) that itself is constant. Using NBV, column 7 of Exhibit 6-7, the ROI varies from a low of 5.0 percent in period 1 to 25.0 percent in period 5, with an average return over the five-year period of 11.41 percent (column 8).

Exhibit 6-7
ROI Calculations Using Straight Line Depreciation

(1)	(2)	(3)	(4)	(5)	(6)	(7)	(8)
	Gross Book Value	Annual Depreciation		Accounting Income	ROI on		ROI on
Period	Value	(SLD)	Earnings	(4) − (3)	GBV	NBV	NBV
0	$10,000					$10,000	
1		$2,000	$2,500	$500	5%	8,000	5.0%
2						6,000	6.25
3						4,000	8.33
4						2,000	12.5
5						0	25.0

In both cases, the true economic return remains at 7.93 percent. The methods of computing depreciation and the investment base of Exhibit 6-7 thus give incorrect economic signals, leading to incorrect economic decisions.

Exhibit 6-8 produces even greater distortions to economic reality. With SYD depreciation, under GBV, ROI fluctuated between –8.33 in year 1 and +18.33 in year 5. Under NBV the results fluctuate from –8.33 in year 1 to an astronomical +275 percent in year 5. Clearly NBV produces the largest distortions under both straight-line and sum-of-the-year's-digits depreciation, yet these are the most commonly used methods of calculating the depreciation schedule and investment base.

The main point behind Exhibits 6-6 and 6-7 is that the investment base and capital recovery schemes ordinarily used in ROI calculations are much different from those assumed under the IRR method.

Since IRR captures the economic impact of investment projects more accurately, the use of ROI as a strong budgeting and evaluation tool will almost certainly lead to poor economic decisions and incentives.

The fact that ROI is widely used suggests one or more of the following explanations:

1. External reporting standards are strongly influencing internal performance measurement systems.
2. ROI is used along with other performance measures in evaluation and control systems.
3. Control systems designers are designing systems with major flaws in them.

If ROI is used as described in this chapter, it is potentially dangerous as a control tool unless modified appropriately. If modified or used along with other profit and asset selection criteria, it is very useful.

We now investigate possible improvements to ROI that will make it more useful as a control tool. This involves the introduction of the annuity method of depreciation. Since this is not an acceptable procedure for financial accounting, companies wishing to use it must keep two sets of books for depreciation and asset values.

Annuity Method of Depreciation

The annuity method of depreciation, also called the *present value method of depreciation,* is the capital recovery scheme implicit within the IRR method. They are *one*

Exhibit 6-8
ROI Calculations Assuming SYD Depreciation

(1) Period	(2) Gross Book Value	(3) Annual Depreciation (SYD)	(4) Earnings	(5) Accounting Income	(6) ROI on GBV	(7) NBV	(8) ROI on NBV
0	$10,000					$10,000	
1		$3,330	$2,500	$(833)	−8.33%	6,667	−8.33%
2		2,667		(167)	−1.67	4,000	−2.5
3		2,000		500	+5.00	2,000	20.0
4		1,333		1,167	+11.67	667	58.35
5		667		1,833	+18.33	0	275.0

and the same, and they are computed in an identical manner. Annuity depreciation is given in column 5 of Exhibit 6-6. The annuity method is a depreciation method that bases depreciation on the decline in the present value of the asset each year. The subsequent calculation of investment outstanding (column 4 of Exhibit 6-6) represents the present value of the asset, given the economic rate of return. Therefore, by using the capital recovery scheme and investment base of Exhibit 6-6 for ROI calculations on divisional books, the ROI calculations would be perfectly congruent with economic realities.

There are two practical problems with the annuity method of depreciation which tend to limit its use in practice. First, and perhaps most significant, if it is used, it must be used *in addition* to a generally accepted method of depreciation (that is, two sets of books). Second, the annuity method must be linked with the IRR method within the division to determine the schedule of depreciation for an asset. Very rarely do firms implement the entire capital budget as the result of IRR or NPV calculations. A sizable percentage of projects, both in numbers and dollar value, are implemented without IRR calculations, and on the basis of qualitative criteria. The use of these qualitative criteria for capital investment is discussed further in Chapter 10.

Without a rate-of-return calculation, it is difficult to develop an accurate depreciation schedule, although rough estimates may be made. When all these problems are considered, it is not surprising that annuity depreciation is so little used for measuring investment center performance. Nevertheless, it is useful to consider it, since it is feasible and it may find greater use in the future. It does solve the treacherous problem concerning the appropriate investment base and it does reinforce the need to carry out discounted cash flow analyses for the evaluation of investment projects.

If these were the only problems with ROI, it might be worth the effort to apply annuity depreciation. Because of the conceptual problems related to ROI, however, we are forced to consider an alternative; the residual income (RI) method is a reasonable alternative. We shall turn now to a discussion of the RI method of performance evaluation for decentralized profit and investment centers.

Residual Income as a Performance Measurement Concept

Under the residual income method of performance evaluation, divisions are charged with an opportunity cost of capital for the various categories of assets that they employ. Income after expenses, including these capital charges, is referred to as *residual income.* Different capital charges may be levied on various categories of assets if the firm wishes to incorporate a risk premium within the capital charge for various types of assets.

Bringing capital costs into the divisional income statements as an explicit expense yields a total cost calculation that is practically identical to "true cost" as defined by economic theory, since the accounting statement now includes a charge for the opportunity cost of capital. Residual income then becomes true profit after proper provision for capital costs adjusted for the riskiness of assets employed. Since divisions differ in profit potential, budgeted levels of residual income would differ from one responsibility center to another.

The RI measurement concept solves the conceptual problem associated with the ROI measure. Under RI, similar assets in different divisions are charged with identical capital costs and therefore identical cutoff rates in different divisions. Moreover, different assets have different cutoff rates in the same division.

Under RI, each division is assigned a budgeted RI. The divisional manager may then concentrate on decisions that maximize RI while pursuing goal-congruent behavior.

Although RI solves the conceptual measurement problem of ROI, the problem of the appropriate investment base remains. Residual income may be used along with annuity depreciation to solve the problem of the investment base also. We now examine the simultaneous use of annuity depreciation with RI. In Exhibit 6-9 we expand Exhibit 6-6 so as to include the calculation of RI along with annuity depreciation.

We assume that the firm incurs a 5 percent opportunity cost of capital for an investment of this risk class. Residual income (column 8) is then computed by subtracting from annual cash inflows (column 2) both annuity depreciation (column 5) and the opportunity cost of capital (column 7).

Notice from Exhibit 6-9 that RI is not constant, since the opportunity cost of capital varies depending upon the outstanding investment base. Notice also that it is possible to compute an ROI by using RI. In our case, the RI return on beginning investment is a constant 2.93 percent.

The fluctuations in RI in Exhibit 6-9 can be eliminated in a manner similar to that used in Exhibit 6-6 for ROI. To eliminate fluctuations in ROI that occur from one period to the next, we adopted annuity depreciation, which normalized the ROI at the correct level. Return on investment was made constant by varying the depreciation schedule. We did that by finding the internal rate of return on investment and subtracted that return from the investment outstanding at each point in time. Similarly, it is desirable for a project with a constant internal rate of return over its life to display a constant residual income, since a fluctuating residual income contains the seeds of potential dysfunctional decisions on the part of investment center managers. It causes the project to appear unequally profitable

Exhibit 6-9
Calculation of Residual Income Using Annuity Depreciation

(1)	(2)	(3) 7.93% Return on Investment Outstanding	(4) Investment Outstanding (4)−[(2)−(3)]	(5) Capital Recovery Implied (2)−(3)	(6) Return on Investment Outstanding	(7) Opportunity Cost of Capital (.05 × Beginning) Investment Outstanding)	(8) Residual Income (2)−(5)−(7)
Period	Cash Flow						
0			$10,000				
1	$2,500	$793	8,293	$1,707	7.93%	$500	$293
2		658	6,451	1,842		415	243
3		512	4,463	1,988		323	189
4		354	2,317	2,146		223	131
5		164	1*	2,316		116	68

*Rounding error.

in the various years of the project life, thus setting off potential dysfunctional decisions.

To achieve the same desirable result under the residual income method as achieved with annuity depreciation under the ROI method, we must adjust the depreciation schedule so that with the interest charge, residual income is constant, as ROI was. We begin this process by finding the annualized capital charge that will produce a 5 percent return on $10,000 and find that to be $2,310 per year. In other words, the NPV is zero at a 5 percent discount rate with a $10,000 initial outlay ($C_0$) and subsequent returns (R_i) of $2,310 in each of five years. Subtracting the $2,310 from the $2,500 cash flow, we find the residual income to be a constant $190 per year. Annuity depreciation is now found by taking 5 percent of outstanding book value and subtracting it from the $2,310. Therefore, the annualized 5 percent return is now divided between depreciation and a 5 percent opportunity cost (capital charge) on outstanding book value. The revised residual income calculation appears in Exhibit 6-10.

A comparison of column 5 of Exhibit 6-10 with column 5 of Exhibit 6-6 reveals that capital recovery begins somewhat faster under this procedure in which we smooth residual income. The project is planned to yield a constant level of residual income over its entire life. No incentives are created to ditch the project prematurely because of accounting results that differ from the economic analysis, as might be the case with a fluctuating residual income.

One of the most far-reaching benefits of utilizing annuity depreciation with residual income is that we may use the NPV criterion rather than the IRR criterion, since all we need to know is the opportunity cost of capital and not the IRR to compute the annuity depreciation schedule. Once the procedure is established correctly, dollars of residual income become an excellent measure of investment center performance.

The simultaneous use of residual income and annuity depreciation solves both problems we encountered previously with regard to the measurement of performance in investment centers.

To summarize, a firm that attempts to design the optimum performance measurement system to *maximize profits* should utilize discounted cash flow methods for project selection. Once a project is selected, the internal performance evaluation and measurement system should be designed to utilize residual income as

Exhibit 6-10
Calculation of Residual Income Using Annuity Depreciation

(1)	(2)	(3) 5% Return on Investment Outstanding	(4) Investment Outstanding	(5) Capital Recovery Implied	(6) Residual Income
Period	Cash Flow				
0			$10,000		
1	$2,500	$500	8,290	$1,810	$190
2		415	6,395	1,895	
3		320	4,405	1,990	
4		220	2,415	2,090	
5		121	121	2,215	

a measure of performance. The annuity method of depreciation, with all its problems, should be used in arriving at depreciation expenses. In doing so, we will encourage investment centers to undertake all investments that are deemed profitable from the firm's point of view and to reject those that the firm would reject. In essence, to this point at least, we have a goal-congruent system for monitoring and evaluating investment performance.

Again, however, we should note that annuity depreciation has its difficulties and is not likely to be used along with residual income. However, we should note the close similarity in the investment bases between column 4 of Exhibit 6-10 and NBV depreciation of Exhibit 6-7 (column 7). The use of net book value with residual income, while not perfectly goal congruent, may be second best and the best practical alternative for measuring investment center performance.

The major remaining difficulty in measuring divisional performance involves adjusting for inflation. See Appendix 6A if you wish to investigate the impact of inflation on performance measurement.

Conclusion: Performance Measurement of Decentralized Operations

The organization that finds itself using simple ROI with no adjustment for the investment base is likely to have a measurement system that does more harm than good, economically speaking. Yet you can also see that the solution to each of these problems is very demanding on the organization—especially annuity depreciation.

We have gone through this set of illustrations to show the direction that solutions must take to the problem of performance measurement in investment centers. These illustrations should help to inform our intuitions as to which proposals are likely to make some improvement in performance measurement of investment centers and which proposals are likely to make matters worse.

At a minimum, we should *abandon ROI* as a sole criterion of investment center performance. We should use *residual income* for measuring investment center performance, thus overcoming the practical problems inherent in ROI. This will definitely produce an improvement. We should not underestimate, however, the strong appeal of ROI to managers as attested to by its widespread use.

Net book value should be used as the investment base for those corporations that choose to assign asset responsibility to divisions. In periods of inflation, replacement costs should be used under the RI method. Under the requirements of FASB No. 33, large publicly held corporations were required to prepare supplementary information to financial statements, describing the impact of inflation upon their financial statements. Although this regulation is no longer in effect, these companies have sufficient experience with it so as to be able to make appropriate estimates of replacement costs of inventory, property, plant, and equipment at the present time.

These two recommendations (that is, residual income and replacement cost accounting) do not solve all the problems that were raised in this chapter, but combined with a policy that requires the use of discounted cash flow methods for the evaluation of new and replacement investments in all divisions, with exceptions made very carefully and in accordance with the principles discussed elsewhere in this book, the problems of performance evaluation in investment centers are resolved in a substantial way. Moreover, many other measures of performance should also be used, as indicated in Chapter 3.

It should not surprise us, however, especially in light of our knowledge of the cybernetic paradigm, to observe widespread use of ROI as a method of performance evaluation. It no doubt reflects the widespread presence of goals that reflect satisfactory performance on many indicators. Yet when looking for causes for the general decline in competitiveness of U.S. industry in international markets, we should not overlook the pervasive influence of these performance measurement systems (see Maciariello, Burke, and Tilley, 1989).

INTERPROFIT-CENTER RELATIONS

Decentralization results in the creation of divisional responsibility centers that are semi-autonomous entities. These divisions may be set up as investment centers or profit centers. This leads to considerable differentiation of the activities of the firm. One of the principal purposes of a control system in a decentralized organization is to "reintegrate" the differentiated firm to insure that the whole is more than merely the sum of its parts. The performance measurement system for divisional operations is a major structural device used by the firm to integrate its differentiated operations. The idea is to so design the measurement system that the divisional manager will be encouraged to act in the best interest of the overall corporation as he or she attempts to perform well, according to the prescribed "rules of the game."

Not only do we want to encourage our decentralized operations to make decisions that are in the best interest of the firm, but we also want to measure performance of each division so as to evaluate its performance as an economic entity to provide a basis for corporate decision making with regard to the decentralized operation. The very process of decentralization allows us to assess more accurately the various aspects of our business, since we are dealing with semi-autonomous units, so long as we devise measurement methods that are appropriate to the task. The remainder of this chapter focuses on the additional issues surrounding the measurement of divisional performance.

The measurement system is closely bound up with decisions related to cost, revenue, and asset assignments. One of the greatest difficulties in measuring divisional performance is concerned with the determination of prices for goods and services that are transferred between divisions. This is referred to as the problem of *transfer pricing*.

Of course, the problem of appropriate transfer prices arises only when divisions do business with one another. One way to eliminate the need to establish transfer prices is to eliminate all transactions among divisions. The problem with this solution is that it would forgo for the company and the divisions the very substantial tangible and intangible benefits, such as scale economies in manufacturing and management, that come as a result of being able to centralize certain corporate functions while simultaneously achieving the benefits of decentralization that have been stated in previous chapters. On the other hand, the greater the number of internal transfers relative to the volume of a division's operations, the less independent it becomes, and the more meaningless it is to establish separate divisions with profit and investment responsibilities.

We shall turn first in this section to an examination of the issues involved in setting transfer prices for those transactions that occur among profit centers. Then we shall look at some of the other issues involved in the measurement of divisional income.

SETTING TRANSFER PRICES

The establishment of transfer prices is governed by the two criteria that we have supported right along for the design of control systems: goal congruence and fairness. A goal-congruent transfer price would be one established in such a way that the buying and selling divisions involved in the transfer would make the same decisions regarding the price and quantity of transfers that would be made if these decisions were made by central management. On the other hand, a transfer price is fair if it leaves division managers with substantial autonomy to pursue and achieve their objectives. We should not, however, adopt a narrow view of fairness, since we would like profit center executives to focus on the welfare of the organization as a whole as well as the performance of the profit center. A transfer price system should also facilitate the implementation of strategy. Group incentives and rewards also should be employed to broaden the concept of equity or fairness in order to truly achieve goal-congruent performance.

The hallmark of a good transfer pricing system is that it will allow the corporation simultaneously to pursue decentralization of autonomy while not forgoing the benefits of centralization. It will allow divisional managers substantial freedom in the pursuit of the objectives and goals of their responsibility centers while simultaneously achieving the objectives and goals of the corporation as a whole. This is obviously a tall order, and rarely are we able to achieve it perfectly in practice.

Many transfer pricing schemes have been offered in the literature, although none is without difficulties. Nevertheless, many useful insights into practical solutions to the problem are made evident as a result of examining at least a few of these theoretical models. We turn now to such an examination.

Economics of Transfer Pricing

Jack Hirshleifer (1956) was first to apply the tools of microeconomics analysis to the problem of interdivisional transfer pricing for the very simple case of a two-division, single-product firm. It is instructive to review his analysis as a first step in our analysis of transfer pricing[3].

Let us assume a firm with two autonomous profit centers, a manufacturing division (selling division) and a distribution division (buying division), each striving to maximize its own profits. The manufacturing division seeks the highest possible price for its product, whereas the distribution division seeks to purchase manufactured goods at the lowest possible price. The firm as a whole also seeks to maximize its profits. The question is at what transfer price would the firm and each of the divisions maximize profits? That is, we are looking for a goal-congruent transfer price.

Let us first look at the problem from the point of view of central management and find the transfer price that will yield the optimum level of output for the firm as a whole. We begin by assuming that the manufacturing division has no outside market for its output and that the final product is sold in a competitive market. Moreover, we assume that the same unit of measure for output is appropriate for both the intermediate and final product so that it is legitimate to measure output on the same horizontal scale. Exhibit 6-11 shows the problem faced by central management.

As we can see from Exhibit 6-11, the firm's total marginal cost curve is divided into two parts: the marginal cost of manufacturing (*mmc*) and the marginal cost of distribution (*mdc*). Given the perfectly elastic demand schedule (*MQ*) faced by the distribution division (that is, the distribution division may sell all that it produces at the market price) and a price of *OM* for the final product, the total marginal cost curve (*mmc* + *mdc*) is equal to the marginal revenue curve *MQ* at a total output level *OL*. The marginal revenue curve is identical to the demand curve, *MQ* in this case, for the firm competing in a perfectly competitive market.

Exhibit 6-11
Optimal Transfer Price: Manufacturing Division Captive
and Competitive Market for Product of the Distribution Division

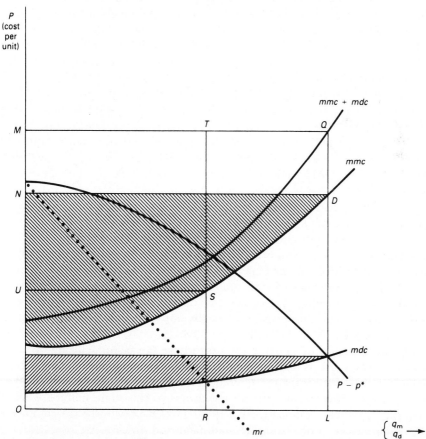

Source: This exhibit has been reproduced, by permission, from Jack Hirshleifer, "On the Economics of Transfer Pricing, *Journal of Business,* July 1958, p. 174.

Rather than force this optimum output level on either division, central management can achieve the same results through decentralization simply by asking the manufacturing division to supply the distribution division with a schedule of the quantities that it would provide the distribution division at various prices. Since it would be profitable for the manufacturing division to supply products to the distribution division as long as the price it received equaled its marginal costs, the schedule the manufacturing division submits would in fact be the *mmc* schedule! This result would be assured so long as the manufacturing division seeks to maximize profits.

The distribution division, in turn, will find a curve that gives the difference between the price it receives (P) for the final product and the transfer price (p^*) it must pay the manufacturing division for the intermediate good. We might refer to this curve ($P - p^*$) as the distribution division's net marginal revenue curve. Notice that the net marginal revenue curve ($P - p^*$) is the difference between the price the distribution division receives for the final product (OM) and the transfer price it must pay to the manufacturing division (p^*). The transfer price it must pay to the manufacturing division at a given volume is equal to the *mmc* schedule. To maximize its profits, the distribution division finds its output by setting its marginal cost curve (*mdc*) equal to its net marginal revenue curve ($P - p^*$). If both the buying and selling divisions are acting "rationally" in a profit-maximizing manner, the manufacturing and distribution divisions will produce the same output and establish the same transfer price (that is, ON) as would be established if the firm were centrally managed, thus producing goal-congruent results through the autonomous decision making of the two divisions.

Note that the shaded areas in Exhibit 6-11 represent the profit earned by the two divisions and are the difference between the price and the marginal costs incurred by each division. This simple example is a beautiful illustration of a goal-congruent system whereby the distribution division and the manufacturing division are motivated to behave as the central management would behave under a given set of circumstances. The system is not completely fair to the manufacturing division, however.

The manufacturing division sells only to the distribution division. It is, therefore, a captive of the distribution division and lacks control over the sales function, which affects its ability to influence revenue. Moreover, the distribution division must purchase its intermediate good from the manufacturing division, which forces it to bear any inefficiencies of the manufacturing division. In other words, these sourcing rules, which require the manufacturing division to sell to the distribution division and require the distribution to buy the intermediate good from the distribution division, limit the autonomy of each division to maximize its profits.

We proceed now to examine the case where the manufacturing division has access to outside markets and is permitted by management policy (that is, by management's policy with regard to sourcing) to sell to these outside markets. We also assume that the distribution division has access to this same market, where it is able to purchase the identical intermediate good it previously was compelled by management policy to buy from the manufacturing division. We now assume that both the market for the intermediate and the market for the final good are competitive (that is, the distribution and manufacturing divisions are price takers and can sell all they produce at the prevailing market price). Exhibit 6-12 displays the results of the analysis under these revised assumptions.

Now we are dealing with two market prices, P_d for the distribution division and P_m for the manufacturing division. The marginal cost curve for the manufacturing division is set equal to the marginal revenue curve, which in a perfectly competitive market is equal to price, and the optimum output of the manufacturing division is given as Q_m. The curve $P_d - MC_d$ is the price minus the marginal cost of processing for the distribution division, which is not the same construct as given by Hirshleifer's $P - p^*$ in Exhibit 6-11.

The distribution division maximizes its profits by setting its net revenue $(P_d - MC_d)$ equal to the market price of the intermediate good (P_m). Its optimum output is given as Q_d. We see from Exhibit 6-12 that Q_d is greater than Q_m, so the distribution division would purchase all the output that is produced by the manufacturing division and $Q_d - Q_m$ of the intermediate good on the open market. If the demands of the distribution division were less than the profit-maximizing output of the manufacturing division, the manufacturing division would sell the difference on the open market.

Given the assumptions of perfect competition in both markets, if both the manufacturing and distribution divisions act rationally so as to maximize profits, the market-based transfer price for the intermediate good will guide both the manufacturing and distribution divisions to produce the same output and establish the same transfer price (that is, pricing in a competitive market is marginal cost pricing) as would be established if the firm were centrally managed, thus producing goal-congruent results through the autonomous decision making of the two divisions.

The same conclusion follows even if the market for the product of the distribution division is not perfectly competitive and the distribution division is a price maker rather than purely passive as to pricing. This is illustrated in Exhibit 6-13.

Exhibit 6-12
Competitive Market for Intermediate and Final Product
and Complete Freedom of Sourcing for Both Divisions

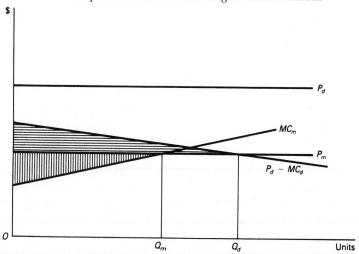

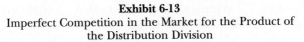

Exhibit 6-13
Imperfect Competition in the Market for the Product of
the Distribution Division

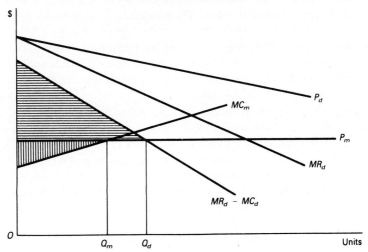

We may summarize the discussion to this point. So long as the market for the intermediate good is competitive, *a market-based transfer price system will permit goal-congruent behavior in a decentralized firm with autonomous divisions.* It does, however, require a sourcing policy whereby the manufacturing division is free to sell outside the firm and the distribution division is free to buy the intermediate good outside also. The result of this analysis is powerful in that it leads to some very helpful results in practice. We shall say more about the practical implications of this analysis later.

A more complex problem occurs when the market for the transferred intermediate good is also imperfectly competitive.

WORKABLE TRANSFER PRICING PROCEDURES

From the preceding analysis, we may come to a number of conclusions with regard to workable transfer pricing procedures, under various competitive conditions, regarding the goods transferred.

When divisions are not *captives of internal divisions,* and the divisions are free to do business both internally and externally, and when there are reasonably competitive external markets for the transferred products, the preceding analysis would indicate that a *market-based* transfer price is appropriate. This price would ordinarily be adjusted for any reduction in transportation and selling expenses realized by the selling division as a result of doing business internally.

If the external market for the transferred good is not reasonably competitive, we can be less certain of the correct transfer price. The only guidance economic analysis has to offer is that the transfer price should be somewhere between the *marginal cost* of the supplying division and the *external market price,* depending upon the extent to which the supplying division has *excess capacity* or not. The criterion of fairness would suggest that a reasonably objective procedure be used in these instances for determining transfer prices. One such procedure might be to arrive at the transfer price by estimating the *standard cost of the good* transferred and adding a return on the investment of the supplying division to standard cost in arriving at the transfer price. Still another possibility in this circumstance is to resort to a transfer price which is *negotiated* on a case-by-case basis.

TRANSFER PRICING IN PRACTICE

Vancil's 1979 study (p. 114) of large U.S. manufacturing corporations reported transfer pricing practices with regard to two broad categories of internal suppliers: among 129 firms that shipped goods from a centralized corporate manufacturing function to divisional profit centers and among 239 firms that shipped goods among divisional profit centers themselves.

Firms that shipped goods among divisional profit centers reported the following transfer pricing methods:

Method	As a Percentage of Total
1. Market	31%
2. Negotiation	22
3. Cost plus	17
4. Cost	30

Firms that transferred goods from the manufacturing function to divisional profit centers reported using the following methods of transfer pricing:

Method	As a Percentage of Total
1. Market	18%
2. Negotiation	16
3. Cost plus	16
4. Cost	66

The majority of firms reporting the use of cost-based transfer methods used "absorption" or "full cost" for computing cost. Fifty-three percent of the firms shipping among divisional profit centers used market or negotiated transfer pricing.

Case studies of transfer pricing practices in various countries (Eccles, 1985, and Carr, 1989) have highlighted the importance of strategy in the setting and administration of transfer pricing policies. That is, case studies indicate that top management views transfer pricing as a part of the decisions it makes in the formulation and implementation of strategy. So much so, that the subject of transfer pricing might be viewed as a special problem in the implementation of company strategy.

This completes our review of the problem of transfer pricing. We turn now to a brief discussion of some of the additional issues involved in the measurement of divisional performance.

DIVISIONAL INCOME STATEMENT: PERFORMANCE EVALUATION VERSUS ECONOMIC EVALUATION

As we discuss the remaining issues involved in the measurement of divisional income, we note that corporate management might find it desirable to allocate many expenses to divisions that are not controllable by divisional managers but are *traceable* to the division. These traceable expenses, although not controllable by the divisional manager, are avoidable in the intermediate and longer terms if the division is no longer part of the corporate entity. Therefore, although they are not controllable in the short term, they should be allocated to the divisions to arrive at a proper evaluation of the division as an *economic entity*.

The expenses that are traced to the divisions for the purpose of economic evaluation, however, are not the expenses that should be traced to the divisions for purposes of managerial evaluation. For purposes of managerial evaluation, we should concentrate upon the allocation of only those costs over which the divisional manager has at least some control. So long as divisional management has no control over the allocation of central corporate services, the concentration upon making the controllable margin as large as possible will also lead to the highest corporate contribution margin, thus yielding a goal-congruent performance measurement system while enhancing the autonomy of divisional management.

Three methods exist for allocating central expenses to divisional profit centers: metering, negotiating, and prorating. *Metering* involves user charges for the actual quantity of services employed. *Negotiation* involves bargaining over quantity of service as well as cost, whereas *prorating* involves the use of allocation rules. The first two methods provide the divisional manager at least some autonomy over central expenses. If the division is allowed to go outside for any of these services, such as for corporate consulting services, these services may be treated as purely controllable. If negotiation and metering involve only quantity determination, then controllable expenses include only the quantity and not the actual price. In this case, the divisions might be charged for their demanded quantity at a standard price, with the cost variances maintained in a separate corporate account. Expenses that are prorated and are only marginally influenced by the division manager are best left off the divisional income statement.

Solomons (1968, p. 72) has captured all these issues and put them very nicely in a sample income statement, which is reproduced in Exhibit 6-14. It is as valid today as it was when he produced it.

Exhibit 6-14 illustrates the principles involved in the design of divisional income statements that are fair and goal congruent *and* that give the firm a basis for evaluating the division as an economic entity. The technical issues surrounding the use of residual income were discussed above.

There is one last issue with regard to performance evaluation. Even if an income statement such as that shown in Exhibit 6-14 is constructed for a division, there are problems in using it as the sole basis for economic evaluation, since it is put together by using generally accepted accounting principles (GAAP), which only crudely reflect the economic realities of the business. Economic evaluation is better undertaken in special studies using the techniques of economic analysis discussed in Chapter 10.

Exhibit 6-14
Sample Divisional Income Statement for Economic Evaluation
and Performance Evaluation

Sales to outside customers
Transfers to other divisions at market value
Variable charges to other divisions for transfers not priced at market value

Less: Variable cost of goods sold and transferred
Variable divisional expenses
Variable profit

Add (deduct): Fixed charges made to (by) other divisions for transfers not priced at market value.

Less: Controllable divisional overhead
Depreciation on controllable fixed assets
Property taxes and insurance on controllable fixed assets
Controllable operating profit

Add (deduct): Nonoperating gains and losses
Less: Interest on controllable investment
Controllable residual income before taxes

Less: Noncontrollable divisional overhead
Incremental central expenses chargeable to division
Interest on noncontrollable investment
Net residual income before taxes

Less: Taxes on income
Net residual income after taxes

Source: Reproduced, by permission of Financial Executives Research Foundation, from David Solomons, *Divisional Performance: Measurement and Control,* Richard D. Irwin, Homewood, Illinois, 1968, p. 72.

ADAPTIVE CONTROL ELEMENTS WITH DECENTRALIZATION

Now that we have been through a discussion of all the elements associated with the issue of decentralization in the design of control systems, it is useful to summarize these issues in terms of our mutually supportive systems model. Exhibit 6-15 contains the summary.

APPENDIX 6A

ACCOUNTING FOR INFLATION IN PERFORMANCE MEASUREMENT SYSTEMS

Inflation has an effect upon the earnings of our investments as well as upon the market values of investment outstanding. It has an impact upon all entries of Exhibit 6-6. Therefore, during times of inflation we must come to grips with it and its effects in our performance measurement systems.

Referring to Exhibit 6-6, the cash flows of column 2 are stated in constant dollars, yet during a period of rising prices, we should expect the actual figures reported by the investment center to rise since they are stated in nominal (current) dollars.

If we continue to utilize historical costs for valuing our assets (i.e., column 4 of Exhibit 6-6) and for charging our opportunity cost of capital, then reported residual income (and, for that matter, ROI if used) will be inflated and distorted so that what looks like good performance by managers may be merely the result of inflationary processes at work in the economy.

If performance evaluation is distorted in investment centers through the use of nominal costs, the firm will not be able to judge accurately the relative profitability of its investment centers for the purpose of making resource allocation decisions even using the residual income method and annuity depreciation. Since assets change in price at specific rather than general rates, inflation will indeed change the relative profitability of investment centers. We must, therefore, devise an approach to handle this problem.

ILLUSTRATION OF THE EFFECTS OF INFLATION ON PERFORMANCE EVALUATION

Under generally accepted methods of financial accounting, items included in the investment base are recorded at original costs, and depreciation charges are based

Exhibit 6-15
MSSM for Decentralized Firm

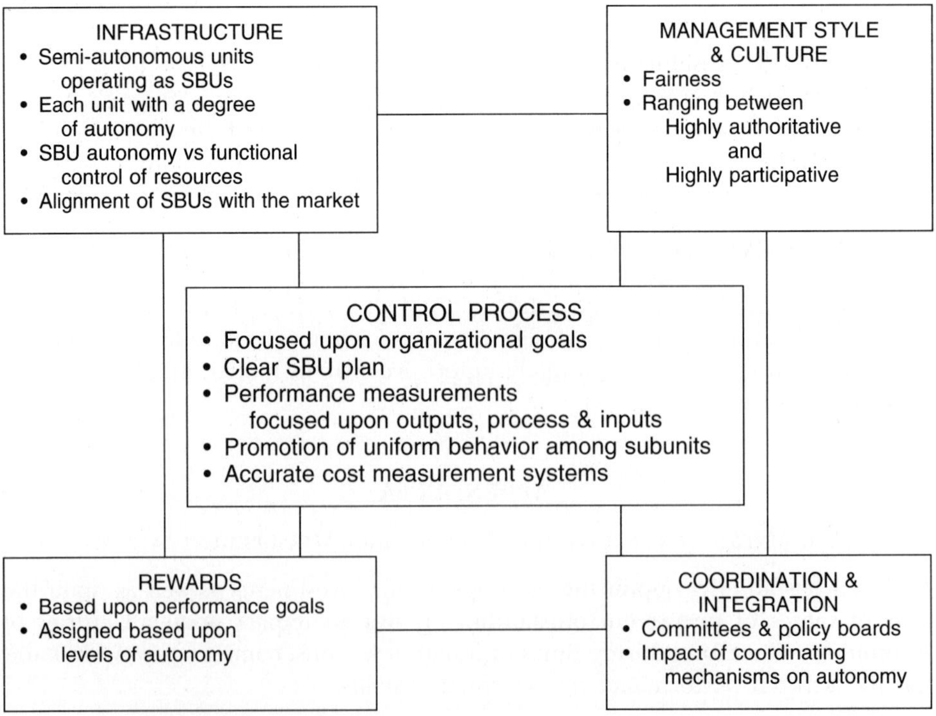

INFRASTRUCTURE
- Semi-autonomous units
  operating as SBUs
- Each unit with a degree
  of autonomy
- SBU autonomy vs functional
  control of resources
- Alignment of SBUs with the market

MANAGEMENT STYLE
& CULTURE
- Fairness
- Ranging between
  Highly authoritative
  and
  Highly participative

CONTROL PROCESS
- Focused upon organizational goals
- Clear SBU plan
- Performance measurements
  focused upon outputs, process & inputs
- Promotion of uniform behavior among subunits
- Accurate cost measurement systems

REWARDS
- Based upon performance goals
- Assigned based upon
  levels of autonomy

COORDINATION &
INTEGRATION
- Committees & policy boards
- Impact of coordinating
  mechanisms on autonomy

upon these original costs. As prices in the economy rise, net book values based upon historic costs understate the true market value of assets in the investment base. The manager then is no longer being evaluated based upon the true value (i.e., opportunity costs) of the assets under his or her stewardship but rather based upon understated (historic) values of assets. Three specific problems result, all of which tend to provide an optimistic appraisal of performance in investment centers:

1. Profitability, whether measured according to an ROI or an RI criterion, is overstated because it is measured with respect to an inaccurately small investment base.
2. Depreciation is understated because it is based upon historical costs so that profitability is again overstated.
3. Accumulated depreciation is inadequate as capital recovery to replace assets.

The use of replacement costs for assets is a solution to these problems, yet not without creating problems of its own.

Exhibit 6-16 provides a comparison of two measures of profit performance—net income and return on investment—on both an historic and a replacement cost basis. The cash flows (column 2) associated with the project are shown inflating at the rate of 10 percent, whereas replacement costs are shown (column 3) inflating at a rate of $200 per year.

A somewhat detailed explanation is necessary with regard to some of the other columns of Exhibit 6-16. Backlog depreciation (column 8) occurs because as the replacement costs increase, the new depreciation rate shown in column 7 must be applied **retroactively** to the preceding years. For example, the replacement cost for the equipment used in this example rises from $2,000 in period 1 to $2,200 in period 2. Annual depreciation on $2,200 for five years is $440. Yet we charged only $400 in year 1 for depreciation so we are **behind** by $40 in year 2. This results in charging $480 as depreciation to period 2. We subtract the accumulated depreciation for two years, $880, from the replacement cost at the beginning of year 2, $2,200, and arrive at a beginning replacement book value of $1,320 for year 3. But in year 3, replacement costs rise to $2,400 which means that annual depreciation rises to $480 and $80 must be added to year 3 depreciation expense so as to make up for the shortage in depreciation in previous years, and so on.

To reconcile the replacement value of a given year with beginning replacement book value plus accumulated depreciation, we must add the figure in column 10 for accumulated depreciation to the *beginning book value of the following period* to reconcile with the beginning replacement cost. For example, the replacement cost of the asset at the beginning of period 3 of $2,400 (column 3) is reconciled with the depreciated replacement value by adding the accumulated replacement depreciation at the end of period 3 of $1,440 (column 10) to the beginning fourth-period replacement book value of $960 (column 6).

These comparisons illustrate how depreciation expense is understated and net income is overstated, both by increasing amounts. Income should be $320 smaller in the fifth year (i.e., $155 versus $475 in columns 12 and 11) than it is under historic cost accounting. Due to this overly large income and to the understated net book value, ROI rises far faster under historic cost accounting than under replacement cost accounting (i.e., 118.8 percent versus 29.8 percent in year 5 in columns 13 and 14).

Exhibit 6-16
Comparison of ROI on Historic and Replacement Cost Basis

(1) Year	(2) Cash Flow (Increasing at 10%)	(3) Beginning Replacement Cost	(4) Beginning Book Value	(5)* Straight-Line Depreciation	(6) Beginning Book Value	(7)** Straight-Line Depreciation
1	$597	$2,000	$2,000	$400	$2,000	$400
2	657	2,200	1,600	400	1,600	440
3	722	2,400	1,200	400	1,320	480
4	795	2,600	800	400	960	520
5	875	2,800	400	400	520	560
6					0	

(8) Backlog	(9) Total Depreciation	(10) Accumulated Depreciation	(11) NI Original Cost	(12) NI Replacement Cost	(13)† ROI Original Cost	(14)‡ ROI Replacement Cost
—	$400	$ 400	$197	$197	9.9%	9.9%
$40	480	880	257	177	16.1	11.1
80	560	1,440	322	162	26.8	12.3
120	640	2,080	395	155	49.4	16.1
160	720	2,800	475	155	118.8	29.8

*   Column 4 + 5 years.
** Column 3 + 5 years.
†   Column 11 + column 4.
‡   Column 12 + column 6.

It also can be seen that depreciation based on historic costs does not recover the full cost of new equipment; a discrepancy of $800 exists at the end of five years, which must come from new sources of capital if and when the equipment is replaced. The fact that real capital is being steadily lost does not show up under conventional methods of depreciation.

The overall result of these imprecise and generally overstated profit signals is that managers are frequently led to make poor decisions. These include over distribution of profits in the form of dividends, inadequate price increases, and tolerance of lax operating management. Artificially high profit figures can lull decision makers into a complacent lack of awareness of real problems, preventing proper adjustment to operations of the investment center.

At this point it should be evident that we must incorporate replacement costs into our performance evaluation procedure during periods of significant inflation. We now proceed to make the inflation adjustment, and we begin with the example given in Exhibit 6-10 where we incorporated residual income and annuity depreciation into our evaluation procedure.

We are now going to assume that cash flows are estimated to increase at the rate of 10 percent because of inflation and that our assets replacement value will also increase by 10 percent each year. This is illustrated in Exhibit 6-17.

Exhibit 6-17
Comparison of Residual Income Based upon Annuity Depreciation and
Replacement Costs

(1)	(2)	(3)	(4) 5% on Investment Outstanding	(5) Capital Recovery Implied	(6) Residual Income
Period	Cash Flow	Replacement Cost			
0		$10,000			
1	$2,500	11,000	$[3,310]	$500	$2,810	$(710)
2	2,750	12,100	[3,410]	550	2,860	(660)
3	3,025	13,310	[3,520]	605	2,915	(495)
4	3,327	14,641	[3,641]	666	2,975	(314)
5	3,660	16,105	[3,774]	732	3,042	(114)

Note in Exhibit 6-17 that the annual cash flows required to produce a 5 percent IRR on this investment are given between columns 3 and 4 in brackets. Since we know from Exhibit 6-10 that $2,310 produces a 5 percent IRR on a $10,000 investment, we merely add the annual increments in asset replacement costs to $2,310 to produce the required 5 percent IRR on the $10,000 asset whose replacement cost is rising annually by 10 percent. There is no advantage in making this stream uniform, although it can be done easily, since cash flows are also non uniform. Even with uniform capital charges, residual income calculations would remain non uniform.

This method clearly shows that a previously profitable investment, one with a positive return of approximately 8 percent, now has a negative return. The true return is now –4.24 percent. Although cash and investment flows are rising at the same rate, investment is a relatively large absolute amount, and increases in replacement costs are significantly greater than increases in cash flows. Calculations of residual income do in fact show the correct pattern. This system provides management with a clear warning that the firm's profits are eroding, thus motivating investment center managers to take corrective action. Note, however, that because cash flows are variable, residual income also becomes variable.

REFERENCES

ABDEL-KHAIK, RASHAD A., AND EDWARD J. LUSK, "Transfer Pricing—A Synthesis." *The Accounting Review,* January 1974, pp. 8–23.

ANTHONY, ROBERT N., AND JOHN DEARDEN, *Management Control Systems,* 4th ed. Homewood, Ill.: Richard D. Irwin, 1980, pp. 94–101.

ANTHONY, ROBERT N., "Accounting for Capital Costs." In *Management Control Systems,* Robert N. Anthony, John Dearden, and Richard F. Vancil. Homewood, Ill.: Richard D. Irwin, 1965.

CARR, LAWRENCE P., *Multinational Transfer Pricing: A Management Systems Framework.*

Ph.D. dissertation, Union College, Schenectady, New York, 1989.

CORDINER, RALPH J., *New Frontiers for Professional Managers.* New York: McGraw-Hill, 1956.

CORDTZ, DAN, "How Auto Firms Figure Their Costs to Reckon the Price Dealers Pay," *Wall Street Journal,* December 10, 1957, p. 1.

ECCLES, ROBERT, *The Transfer Pricing Problem: A Theory for Practice.* Lexington, Mass.: Lexington Books, 1985.

HAYES, ROBERT H., AND WILLIAM J. ABERNATHY, "Managing Our Way to Economic De-

REFERENCES, *Continued*

cline," *Harvard Business Review,* May–June 1982, pp. 71–79.

HIRSHLEIFER, JACK, "On the Economics of Transfer Pricing," *Journal of Business,* July 1956, pp. 172–184.

HORNGREN, CHARLES T., AND GEORGE FOSTER, *Cost Accounting: A Managerial Emphasis,* 7th ed. Englewood Cliffs, N.J.: Prentice Hall, 1991.

MACIARIELLO, JOSEPH A., JEFFREY W. BURKE, AND DONALD TILLEY, "Improving American Competitiveness: A Management Systems Perspective." *Academy of Management Exec- utive,* Vol. III, no. 4, November 1989.

MANES, RENE P., "Birch Paper Company Revisited: An Exercise in Transfer Pricing." *The Accounting Review,* July 1970, pp. 565–572.

MANES, RENE P., "Birch Paper Company Revisited: An Exercise in Transfer Pricing," *The Accounting Review,* July 1970, pp. 565–572.

OUCHI, WILLIAM G., *Theory Z.* New York: Avon Books, 1981.

PORTER, MICHAEL E., *Competitive Advantage: Creating and Sustaining Superior Performance.* New York: The Free Press, 1985.

REECE, JAMES S., AND WILLIAM R. COOL, "Measuring Investment Center Performance," *Harvard Business Review,* May– June 1978, pp. 28–46, 174–177.

SIMON, HERBERT A., *Administrative Behavior,* 3rd ed. New York: The Free Press, 1976.

SLOAN, ALFRED P., *My Years with General Motors.* Garden City, N.Y.: Doubleday, 1964.

SOLOMONS, DAVID, *Divisional Performance: Measurement and Control.* Homewood, Ill.: Richard D. Irwin, 1968.

STAHL, DAVID R., "Evaluating the Costs of Regulating the Automobile Industry: An Econometric Systems Model," unpublished Ph.D. dissertation. Union College, Schenectady, N.Y., 1979.

VANCIL, RICHARD F., *Decentralization: Ambiguity by Design.* Homewood, Ill.: Dow-Jones Irwin, 1979.

____, "Managing the Decentralized Firm," *Financial Executive,* Vol. XLIII, no. 3, March, 1980, pp. 34–43.

NOTES

1. Some would argue that an excessive financial focus begun during Sloan's tenure was responsible for the recent significant loss of market share experienced by General Motors. The environment shifted and GM did not. That is hardly the fault of Sloan, since he was long gone from GM by the time the environment shifted.

2. This section assumes an elementary knowledge of discounted cash flow methods. If you are unfamiliar with these methods, it would be useful at this point to read the first section of chapter 10.

3. This section assumes an elementary knowledge of the tools of microeconomics.

Case 6-1 Citizens Hospital

I am searching for ways to meet the challenge of increased competition within the area served by our hospital. My investigation of management systems has introduced me to the concept of the strategic business unit (SBU). I can visualize how, by application of this concept, it would be possible to convert some of our departments from units with expense responsibility to units with strategic and profit responsibility. One department that appears to lend itself to this kind of conversion is the Department of Pathology. My expectation is that if the department can be freed from traditional expense controls, it can generate increased profits from new activities. It can then serve as a model for other hospital departments. As a result, I have assigned Madeline Fry, our Controller, the task of identifying the steps that must be taken to convert the department to a SBU. I now want to take steps to implement this proposal.

Phillip Roth,
CEO, Citizens Hospital
(in a discussion with the
case writer)

Background. Citizens Hospital is a 225-bed acute-care hospital located in an upper-income suburb of a large metropolitan area. The hospital was founded as a for-profit institution in 1946 by a group of investors. Services provided include general surgical/medical, ICU/CCU, obstetrics/gynecology, radiology, pharmacy, pathology/laboratory, and supportive services such as respiratory, physical, and speech therapies.

In addition, Citizens had recently added a 25-bed acute psychiatric unit that offered a variety of "in-patient" and "outpatient" mental health services. Plans were now under way for the construction of an outpatient surgery center as a joint venture. The new psychiatric unit and the new surgical center would also be candidates to become SBUs.

Corporate control of Citizens Hospital is in the hands of a 15-member board of directors, all of whom are investors in the corporation. Two of the original founders of the hospital remain on the board. The board has primary responsibility for policy and planning.

Overall operation of the hospital is the responsibility of the chief executive officer, an administrator with 22 years of service at Citizens. He recently hired a chief operations officer, who is designated as hospital administrator. Departments are organized along functional lines, and each has a director. Hospital departments, except for radiology and pathology, report to the chief operations officer. Medical departments heads report directly to the chief executive

---

This case is adapted by permission from the book *Executive Leadership in Health Care* by Lyal D. Asay and Joseph A. Maciariello, pp. 210–214. Copyright 1991 by Jossey-Bass Inc., Publishers, San Francisco.

officer and the board, thus giving medical matters top priority.

The formal budget and planning process is simple. Each department supervisor submits an annual budget to the chief executive officer, including requests for capital expenditures and staffing. The annual budget is approved by the board.

Pathology Department. This department provides traditional pathology services and has a full-service clinical laboratory. Emphasis is on completing tests quickly and accurately. Little regard is currently given to costs or profits. The department is headed by a chief pathologist (a medical doctor), and each service area within pathology is directed by a technical supervisor.

Proposal to Convert Pathology Department to an SBU. Madeline Fry's proposal to convert the Pathology Department to an SBU is contained below. Please read the proposal at this point.

**A PROPOSAL
TO
CONVERT THE PATHOLOGY DEPARTMENT
FROM AN EXPENSE RESPONSIBILITY CENTER
TO
AN SBU WITH PROFIT RESPONSIBILTY**
by
**Madeline Fry
Controller**

In response to your request, I have prepared an analysis of the steps we must take to convert the existing Pathology Department to SBU status. I have analyzed the changes that must be made in terms of the major management systems required for the operation of the department.

Mission. A clear statement of the "mission of pathology" as a strategic business unit (SBU) is essential and should be prepared by the CEO and the Board. While the mission statement might be more fully developed by the SBU manager, top management should insist that the mission include an emphasis on growth in both services and profitability.

The mission statement should emphasize that pathology use its laboratories, equipment, and resources to extend its services to individual physicians, clinics, extended care hospitals, industrial concerns, rehabilitation units, and so on. It should compete with other laboratories on the basis of accuracy and quality of testing and integrate this external business activity with the overall mission of the hospital.

Implementation of SBU Concept

Culture. Implementation of the SBU concept is consistent with the overall culture of Citizens since we are a "for-profit" hospital, but it may be at odds with the subculture of the pathology department. The subculture may require many behavioral changes.

Management's Style and Philosophy. A change will be required in the way the Department of Pathology is managed. The department can no longer operate in a passive manner, dependent upon the hospital for business, but must be active in pursuing new opportunities. For example, one of the new external programs that may be evaluated is large-volume drug testing for industrial clients. Volume drug testing is a specialty, and it requires separate equipment and training. A new unit would ultimately be necessary to handle this activity and the Chief Pathologist should take the initiative.

Organization Structure. Given the nature of the service it provides, the laboratory already has a quasi-independent aura that will allow the changeover to the SBU concept to be less stressful. No major changes will be required in the structure of the department. However, it will be necessary to add another pathologist, who will have the responsibility of coordinating outside sales and services. The existing pathologist will still coordinate overall operations. The chief technologist of each department will coordinate testing for all sources, while each department supervisor under the SBU structure will have responsibility for marketing and strategic planning. Training will be required, however, since this is a new activity for all concerned.

Communications. The chief pathologist now acts as the communication liaison between the department and the rest of the hospital, but that will have to change under the new SBU concept. To implement that change, a new committee consisting of the department supervisors and the pathologist should be formed. The chief pathologist will hold regularly scheduled meetings with department supervisors to discuss performance reports and plans. Supervisors will in turn meet with members of each department for similar discussions. The goal is to stimulate creative thinking and establish good relations among all departmental employees.

Planning and Resource Allocation. The department should develop a formal planning cycle to accommodate short-term as well as long-term planning. It should decentralize the planning process from the chief pathologist to include the supervisors and technicians, and it should institute a bottom-up and top-down goal formulation process. Each department supervisor should be asked to submit a budget that will focus on internal and external work for the coming year as well as for the more distant future.

Reporting. Reporting for the new SBU should focus on its contribution to overall hospital profitability. This is a change from the existing reporting system, which focuses exclusively on expenses.

Rewards. The most striking change that should take place involves rewards. The present salary level is linked to seniority, and the reward structure consists of an automatic step process that has only three levels of increase. Everyone with the same years of service earns the same amount of money. Under the SBU framework, however, rewards should be tied to productivity and performance. A bonus incentive program based on yearly outside sales and productivity should be established. Consideration should be given to a stock purchase program for staff members of the SBU as a long-term incentive to improved performance. The potential for personal development and rewards based on improved performance for the existing staff will provide strong motivation, and the director of the laboratory is enthusiastic about the challenge.

QUESTIONS

1. Diagram the changes that are necessary to the formal management systems of the Pathology Department (using the MSSM) in order to move from expense to profit responsibility.
2. How should Roth go about gaining acceptance for the changes required? What problems might he expect to encounter? How long do you think it will take to make these changes?
3. How should the Chief Pathologist go about gaining acceptance among department managers for the changes required?
4. What role should Roth ask Fry to play in implementation?
5. What does this case illustrate about the process of reorganizing from an expense center to a profit center?

Case 6-2 Mid-Atlantic University

The present budgetary system doesn't provide us with the incentives we need to grow and develop as a first-rate business school. The annual reports from the Controller's office on the finances of the School of Business are arcane, but because the Provost and the President read them, they make it difficult for us to make persuasive arguments for more staff. This has got to change.

Timothy Johnson, Dean

The Business School must understand that they are part of a larger university. As such, they have responsibilities to Mid-Atlantic and must not think only of their interests. We have to structure the new measurement system so that it provides them with the maximum possible autonomy and incentive to grow and develop, but within the context of the university. Also, we want to design a system that eliminates the nasty disputes that have occurred during the past 10 years.

Robert Williams, Assistant Controller

Mid-Atlantic University (MAU) has three main education divisions: the undergraduate division, the graduate and special programs division, and the semi-autonomous school of business administration. Each September the controller of MAU prepares and issues a college wide summary financial report for the preceding year, which includes a statement of income and expense for each division of the university.

Timothy Johnson, Dean of the School of Business, was quite upset about these annual reports, which for the last three years have shown the business school losing a significant amount of money. Dean Johnson had several fundamental objections to the income statements prepared for the business school. These are summarized as follows:

1. Course tuition for undergraduate students taking classes in the business school was not credited to the business school.

2. A share of the salaries of the business school faculty representing the proportion of their teaching loads spent in teaching undergraduate courses *was not* allocated to the undergraduate division.

3. The special grants from state government awarded to universities in the state for each degree conferred *were not* credited to the divisions conferring the degrees.

Dean Johnson was convinced that if these three items were taken into account appropriately, the year-ending report for the business school would show a profit and not a loss as the controller's statements have indicated. Moreover, Dean Johnson questioned the accuracy of many of the other items on the report prepared by the controller for the business school.

In response to the considerable unrest exhibited by Timothy Johnson, the provost of the university decided to commission a study to be carried out jointly by the assistant controller of the university, Robert Williams, and Dean Johnson of the business school. The purpose of the study was to set forth appropriate accounting procedures, including transfer prices, for computing revenue, expense, and income of the school of business. The provost charged these two gentlemen with the responsibility of arriving at a proposed procedure for computing income, which then would be submitted to the provost and president of Mid-Atlantic for approval prior to implementation. This, the provost expected, would solve the problems and conflict once and for all.

These two men worked amiably and persistently with the staff help of Geoffrey Barnes, a research assistant at the business school, toward the development of a proposal for the measurement of income of the school of business. Their proposal follows.

ACCOUNTING PROCEDURES FOR THE MEASUREMENT OF INCOME OF THE SCHOOL OF BUSINESS

The procedures for the accounting treatment of revenue and expense of the School of Business are designed to *credit* all "fair" revenue and *charge* all "fair" expense so as to provide consistent and appropriate measures of performance that are agreeable to all parties. All allocations and charges will be reflected on the books of the university. Moreover, it is assumed that the School of Business will be a contribution (that is, profit) center reporting to the provost of MAU.

REVENUE ACCOUNTING

Seven categories of revenue have been identified as potential sources of revenue for the business school. They are identified next along with proposed methods of measurement.

1. *The Systems Analysis Ph.D. Program.* Since this is a multidisciplinary Ph.D. program, sponsored by the university as a whole but located for administrative purposes within the School of Business, the tuition and fees paid by students *will not* be credited to the School of Business.
2. *The M.B.A. Program.* (a) All tuition and fees received by the university for graduate courses offered by the business school shall be credited to the School of Business *except* as noted in (b). (b) Tuition and fees for those courses offered by business school faculty *in the undergraduate* division as service courses *shall not* be credited to the business school. These include courses managed either by the business school or by the undergraduate departments.

The rationale for 2. above is that revenue for these courses is not *incremental* to the university. It would be received from full-time undergraduate students even if these service courses were not offered by the business school. A number of problems would be created if any attempt were made to allocate revenue for these courses to the business school.

Since undergraduate departments are not net contribution centers, their staff levels are derived, roughly at least, according to student-faculty ratios. If the business school attracts more students to its courses, we should expect pressure to be exerted upon undergraduate departments to reduce the size of their staffs. This would create a number of problems for MAU. First, we should not expect a department to reduce staff if, by doing so, it jeopardizes its ability to cover adequately all aspects of its discipline, even though it is experiencing a decline in student enrollments. Second, we should not expect a department to sit idly by as its course enrollments drop. While some competition among departments for enrollment is desirable, we are aware of some pernicious effects of a high level of competition. One is that students may be discouraged from following their interests when in fact we should be encouraging the opposite.

If departments do not reduce staff to reflect the loss of enrollments to the business school, the revenue allocated to the business school for undergraduate students is merely a paper transfer. These moneys do not represent incremental revenue from the point of view of MAU. To count them as revenue for the School of Business under these circumstances would be dysfunctional for the university, and we do not recommend it. The only circumstances under which it is desirable to count them is when undergraduate staff levels are adjusted to reflect shifts in enrollment towards the business school. If staff levels are adjusted, however, we should expect dysfunctional results from the ensuing competition between the business school and undergraduate departments.

3. *Development Revenues.* Revenues raised by the business school through gifts and grants from individuals, foundations, and corporations shall be credited to the School of Business. This should create maximum incentive for the business school to raise outside revenue, which we believe is quite desirable from the point of view of the university.
4. *State Funds.* The state in which MAU operates provides some assistance to private colleges and universities in the state in the form of modest incentive payments based upon the number of graduates. This figure is controlled by a series of elaborate regulations so as not to affect quality adversely in private colleges and universities. Because this incentive money is incremental to the university, it should be credited to the business school.
5. *Research Grants and Contracts of the School of Business.* All these revenues will be credited to the School of Business.
6. *Revenue from Restricted Endowment.* Revenue from endowment that has been specifically given to the university for the programs of the School of Business shall be credited to the School of Business. The endowment itself should be designated to the School of Business.
7. *Revenue from Unrestricted Endowment.* Revenue from endowment received by the university

with no restrictions as to its use *shall not* in any part be credited to the School of Business even if there is some connection between the donor and the business school.

EXPENSE ACCOUNTING

Ten categories of expense have been identified as incremental to the School of Business. They are as follows:

1. *General Expenses* (a) Salary is to be charged to the School of Business for all university faculty who teach courses in the School of Business at the rate of one-seventh of total compensation per course taught. The normal course load for a full-time member of the faculty at MAU is seven 10-week courses per year. (b) Fringe benefits are to be charged to the School of Business, pro rata to salary. (c) Supplies, services, and expendable equipment are to be charged to the business school according to the actual expenditures for these items. (d) Capital expenditures are charged as expenses to the business school according to actual expenditures for these items.
2. *Ph.D. Program.* Consistent with the treatment of revenue for this program, no charges will be made to the business school for *faculty* allocated to this program.

    Fellowships and assistantships paid by the university to Ph.D. candidates working with faculty members of the School of Business will be charged to the School of Business. This charge is made to the business school to create an incentive on the part of the business school to make the most efficient use of these fellows and assistants as well as in recognition of the benefits they provide to the business school by their availability.
3. *Business School—Managed Undergraduate Courses.* Some 10 undergraduate courses are currently offered by the business school. These courses are designed and staffed by the dean and business school faculty. All faculty expenses, including fringe, for these courses will be charged to an undergraduate service account, a de facto undergraduate department for accounting purposes.

4. *Business School—Staffed Undergraduate Managed Courses.* All faculty expenses associated with these courses, including fringe, will be charged to appropriate undergraduate departments.
5. *Development Program Expense.* Development program expenses will be charged to the business school at a specific overhead rate applied to all funds raised for the business school. This development "tax" is set at 20 percent and is to be reviewed biannually by the controller and the Dean of the School of Business.
6. *Research Grants and Contract Expense.* All these expenses incurred by the business school will be charged to the business school. In addition, the controller will negotiate with the dean a contract-specific university overhead rate that will reflect traceable overhead costs incurred by the university as a result of the grant or contract.
7. *Faculty Travel Expense.* Faculty expenses associated with the attendance of scholarly meetings for the purpose of presenting research papers will be shared equally by the business school and the university because the benefit of faculty enrichment benefits the entire university. Faculty travel for purposes of recruiting new faculty members, however, is to be charged fully to the School of Business.
8. *Services Provided the Business School.* The Graduate School of MAU provides administrative support for the Business School in the areas of publicity, admission, and registrar functions. Costs for these services will be allocated to the business school based upon proration of the administrative staff time to the various university programs. It is necessary to make these prorations since both the School of Business and the Graduate School as a whole are contribution centers.
9. *General Administrative Expense Associated Directly with the School of Business.* These expenses include the dean's office and all administrative support at *the business school.* It excludes any allocations for university administration.
10. *General University Overhead Charge.* The university will assess the School of Business an overhead charge of 15 percent of the costs determined in factors 1-9. This charge will be offset in part or wholly by the contribution the School of Business makes to the university as a whole by including undergraduates students in graduate courses and by providing other consulting services to the university from time to time. Undergraduate credits are to be computed at the graduate tuition rate per course. The credit shall not exceed the overhead charge in a given year.

Consulting credits are to be negotiated on a case basis. A specific record of the Business School contribution to the university will be made at the time of the preparation of the annual statement of income and expense.

RESIDUAL

Any excess of revenue over expense for the business school, as computed, will be set aside by the university for the business school as funds functioning as endowment for the School of Business. This endowed fund will be available to make up for the shortfalls that might occur in any given year.

The provost and president are reviewing the proposed measurement system prior to implementation.

QUESTIONS

1. What are the strengths and weaknesses of the proposed measurement system from the point of view of the Business School? From the point of view of MAU?
2. In reviewing the proposal, the primary interest of the president and provost is to bring unity between the interests of MAU and the Business School? Advise them as to how they should proceed.

Case 6-3 Tate Brothers Ice Cream

Tate Brothers Ice Cream was founded in 1920 by the father of the current president, Mr. Phillip Tate. The company began its activities as a small producer of ice cream, selling ice cream to major supermarkets and dairies in upstate New York. In 1930, it began marketing ice cream directly to consumers through a network of Tate Ice Cream Stores. In the early 1950s Tate integrated backward into milk production. Its growth stagnated in the late 1950s, at which time it expanded its ice cream stores into Bread and Butter shops.

Each of the 95 Bread and Butter shops is a profit center that reports to one of eight regional managers who cover New York state, excluding New York City. The regional managers report to the director of store operations at company headquarters. Sales in 1990 were approximately $80 million. Tate's average annual growth rate of sales has been approximately 15 percent annually. Mr. Tate believes that he has saturated the market in New York state with Bread and Butter Shops and, being a farm boy at heart, has no desire to enter the New York City market on a retail basis. He believes his next most productive area of growth lies in *milk and ice cream production*. He has, therefore, made these two departments profit centers, and he has instructed them to deal with each other and with the director of store operations on an arm's-length basis as though they were separate companies. This has resulted in the formation of small marketing organizations in both the milk and ice cream departments with the retail organizations being only one customer, although by far the largest, accounting in 1990 for over 50 percent of the sales of the other two departments. Mr. Tate imposed only one major sourcing constraint upon the Ice Cream Department: it must purchase all its milk from the Milk Department. In return, the Milk Department would price internally somewhat below the going market price for milk. Mr. Tate thought this was fair to both departments, since the Milk Department avoided transportation costs on internal sales, and these cost savings on internal sales more than covered the price reductions. The Ice Cream Department, on the other hand, was able to purchase milk somewhat below market.

A partial organization chart for Tate Brothers is given in Exhibit 6-18.

Although Mr. Tate's primary motive for the creation of three major profit centers was to encourage further growth in sales and profits and to prevent stagnation that otherwise seemed imminent, he also believed that it would encourage the development of general managers because of the emphasis at the department level on profit and loss. Mr. Tate was approximately five years from retirement himself, and his two sons were quite young, which meant that Tate had to be concerned about management succession. He felt that the profit center concept would provide a good training ground from which he could groom a successor.

To ensure that there was maximum incentive for growth and profitability, Tate estab-

Exhibit 6-18
Partial Organization Chart for Tate Brothers

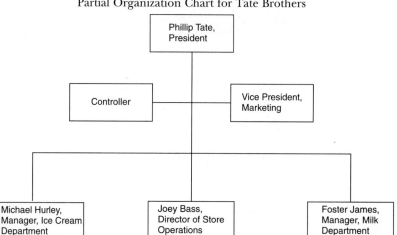

lished a reward structure that was based upon profit. The remuneration of all store managers, the director of store operations and the managers of the Milk and Ice Cream Departments was based primarily upon profits.

At first, all things appeared to be going smoothly. Then in 1991, during a very severe recession, Michael Hurley, manager of the Ice Cream Department, began to take a very aggressive posture. He began to emphasize quality and higher margins on his ice cream, not only to his marketing organization but also to the public through the use of promotional campaigns.

At about this time, Joey Bass, director of store operations, was seeking to contract for the delivery of 100,000 gallons of ice cream. He received the following three bids:

Hurley (Tate)	$186,000
Sealfast	168,000
Dairylea	167,000

Ordinarily, Bass would go with the lowest bidder, which in this case would be Dairylea, but he thought that Hurley's bid was very high considering the excess capacity he knew Hurley and Foster James, the manager of the Milk Department, were experi-

encing as a result of the recession that was hitting the Northeast particularly hard. Moreover, there were other complications. Sealfast's bid included the purchase of packaging and printing for the 100,000 gallons from Tate (Hurley) at an expected purchase price of $27 per thousand.

Bass decided to take the matter to Mr. Tate himself. In extensive discussions with Tate, Hurley reiterated: "I've established a marketing strategy and I've given my salespeople orders to maintain margins over full cost. They have done it very well, and despite the recession my sales and profits are holding up well. If I cut my price to Bass, I would be undoing my strategy.

"There is one possibility, however. If you can convince James to lower his price on milk to me, I could pass on the cost reduction to Bass without undoing my strategy."

Mr. Tate was somewhat perplexed and wanted his controller to advise him as to what should be done. Tate told Bass not to place the order until the investigation was completed.

Controller Stewart proceeded by collecting cost data in both the Ice Cream and Milk departments. Both Hurley and James were uncomfortable with Stewart since he was an accountant, and in their judgment he never appreciated the problems of the business. Moreover, this profit center and transfer business was new to Stewart also. Stewart estimated the following cost relationships for this order (per thousand gallons):

Ice Cream Department

- $186 bid: $147 incremental cost plus transfers from Milk Department
  39 contribution to overhead and profit
- $147 incremental cost plus transfers:
  $106 transfers from Milk Department
  41 incremental cost

- $27 packaging and printing for Sealfast:
  $ 22 incremental cost
  5 contribution margin

Milk Department

- $106 transfers:
  $ 64 incremental costs
  42 contribution to overhead and profit

Stewart delivered this analysis to Mr. Tate, but he was unsure where it led.

QUESTIONS

1. Prepare an analysis of this problem for Mr. Tate. From whom should Bass buy the 100,000 gallons? Would you advise Mr. Tate to impose a solution in this case?
2. Is there anything wrong with the transfer price system at Tate Brothers? If so, how can it be remedied?

Case 6-4 Warren Ford

Warren Carmen, the new owner of Warren Ford, an automobile dealership in the Adirondack region of New York State, had seen his career blossom while employed as a member of a four-man executive team that was put together at the insistence of creditors of a large-capital district (New York) dealership that had encountered deep financial trouble during the early 1990s. Prior to that appointment, Carmen was used-car manager in the same dealership. He had been employed there for a total of 15 years.

The management team was successful and restored liquidity and profitability to the dealership by a series of moves including reductions in the work force, tight cost control of the service center, the institution of stronger rewards for sales and service activity, reductions in its inventory, sale of many used cars at the local wholesale auction, and increases in its sales of new automobiles. These moves were taken during a two-year period in which the automobile industry was experiencing a major depression brought about by a deep recession in the economy, escalating car prices, and intense foreign competition. These moves so impressed the creditors of the dealership that they renegotiated the debt outstanding. Moreover, these dramatic moves allowed the dealership to qualify for a relatively large low-interest loan from the Small Business Administration, which resulted in a sounder capital structure and ensured the survival of the firm.

Warren was widely recognized and praised for the part he played in the rescue operation. This experience convinced Warren that he was ready to take on his own dealership. His application to become a dealer was approved by the company, and Warren proceeded to buy his own dealership. The dealership he purchased had previously served as a stepping stone for one of the giant dealers in upstate New York. For the last 17 years, under the second owner, Walter, it had been profitable but only modestly so. The second owner was not as aggressive as the first in advertising and promotion. He did not offer leasing services. The income statement for the business during the last year under the previous owner appears in Exhibit 6-19.

Carmen intended to be much more aggressive since, at the time, he had the only Ford dealership in that region, which included one city with a population of 50,000 and summer resorts that attracted people from all over the eastern coast of the United States during the months of July and August. The summer people created a large potential market for leased cars, which he was determined to capitalize upon.

Carmen was pondering a number of questions as to the strategy he should pursue for the dealership and as to the organization structure he should implement. He was aware of the powerful positive effects that the initiation of the profit center concept and associated reward system had in his previous

Exhibit 6-19
Warren Ford Income Statement 1991–1992

Sales revenue		
New cars	$653,761	
Used cars	254,978	
Service to outside	187,943	
Total sales		$1,096,682
Cost of sales		
Cost of new cars sold	$473,547	
Allowance on trades	161,319	
Sales commissions, new	51,456	
Sales commissions, used	23,785	
Service expenses		
Reconditioning	$ 51,110	
Outside customers	$145,973	
Product expenses		$ 907,090
Contributions margin		$ 189,492
Period expenses		
Interest expense	$ 24,765	
Advertising expense	2,432	
Depreciation expense	9,976	
Other expenses	4,893	
General and administrative expenses	38,400	
Total period and general and administrative expenses		$ 80,466
Profit before taxes		$ 109,026

position in preventing bankruptcy and in returning the first dealership to profitability.

He very much wanted to capitalize on these same incentives. Yet that had been an emergency situation.

ORGANIZATION AND RESPONSIBILITY-CENTER STRUCTURE

Carmen inherited Walter's organization and personnel. The organization consisted of a new car manager, Chuck Farley; a used car manager, Ralph Sawchuck, and a service manager, Chuck Watt. The organization chart for Warren Ford appears in Exhibit 6-20.

Each of these departments was treated as a profit center by the previous owner with rewards tied very closely to profits in each department. Carmen had heard rumors that the reward system had caused much tension

in the organization, and he was determined to investigate and resolve the problem quickly.

TROUBLE AT WARREN FORD

Carmen didn't have to wait long before he was presented with a crisis. In his first week, the new car manager, Chuck Farley, was dealing with a customer who was interested in purchasing a 1993 Mercury that carried a list price of $16,400.

The customer wished to trade a 1989 popular-model car, in very good condition, for the new Mercury. Chuck Farley asked the used car manager, Ralph Sawchuck, for advice as to an appropriate trade-in value for the used car. Sawchuck examined the car quickly and told Farley that the mean Blue Book buying price for the car was approximately $6,200.

Exhibit 6-20
Warren Ford Organization Chart

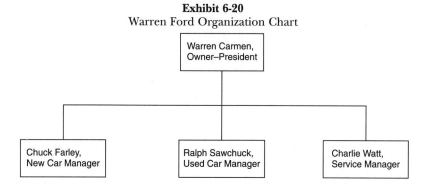

Realizing that the customer had a wildly inflated notion of what the used car was worth and knowing that a good cash price, from the dealer's point of view, without a trade for the new car would be $15,600, Farley offered the customer $7,200 for the used car under the condition that the customer pay $16,400 for the new car. The customer haggled some more with Farley and they agreed on a price of $9,000 plus the trade, meaning that Farley allowed the customer $7,400 on the trade. Warren's cost for the 1993 Mercury was $13,600. The deal was completed, the papers were signed, and the customer drove off with the new Mercury. The used car went directly to the shop for reconditioning under the assumption that it would be delivered to the used car manager for sale at retail.

A few days later Charley Watt, service manager, and Sawchuck, the used car manager, burst into Carmen's office. Sawchuck began the discussion: "I am always getting stuck with lemons as a result of Farley's generous deals. He allowed $7,400 for that junk that Chuck has just discovered needs a new transmission. Farley didn't even drive the car! Nor did he ask Chuck to examine it first. To make matters worse, your accountant charged the entire $7,400 to my departmental expense accounts. I can't go on this way. If you don't solve this problem, I am leaving

this dealership. I can't make any money here with this guy [Farley] here."

Carmen asked Watt if this were true, but Watt was more interested in talking about his problem with the deal: "I feel like I am being used in this place. I get this car from Farley; it's a mess. I'm expected to fix it at cost when my bonus, which is a big part of my annual compensation, depends to a great extent on my department's profit. It is an unfair system we got here, and I hope you are going to straighten it out quickly."

CARMEN'S INVESTIGATION

Carmen thought that this would be a good case to use to investigate the workings of the system that Walter used to run the business. He asked the accountant to hold up on the charge for the used car. He told Farley, Sawchuck, and Watt that he was investigating immediately and to "hold their fire."

As he began his investigation, he learned that the system for running the business was not very formal. Walter had an agreement with his three managers that they would be compensated partly on the basis of salary and partly on the profits of their respective departments. This resulted in a compensation pattern in which the new car manager was earning, on average, approximately 30 percent more than the used car and service managers.

As far as doing business with one another, Walter had established the following informal rules, which were followed closely in practice:

1. The new car manager had the option of selling trade-ins to the used car manager or wholesale at the weekly auction.
2. The used car manager had the option of purchasing the trade-ins from the new car manager or could purchase used cars at the auction or from any other source.
3. The service manager was obliged to give first priority to service the new and used cars of the dealership and was free to service outside customers as he had both the opportunity and the slack capacity.

The pattern that was followed in setting transfer prices was also informal, but as far as Carmen could tell, it worked like this:

1. The used car manager negotiated the price for trade-ins with the new car manager. Sawchuck used the mean Blue Book buying price as a guide in the negotiations. Farley knew what his opportunities were for any used car, since he had access to a listing of mean wholesale prices for used cars. Although negotiated market price was the basis for transfer of used cars between the new and used car departments, it was not always clear just when title passed. In other words, it was a very informal process.
2. The service manager priced outside jobs as follows:
   a. Materials were charged to the customer at cost plus 30 percent overhead.
   b. Labor was charged to the customer based upon the standard Blue Book rate for the job. This rate included the cost of labor plus profit.
3. It was customary for the service manager to price inside jobs as follows:
   a. Material was charged at cost plus 15 percent overhead. The feeling was that 15 percent of material cost was sufficient to cover the overhead of the service department.
   b. Labor was charged to internal jobs at its variable cost for the job.

Carmen thought he could use this trade for the new 1993 Mercury as a test case to work out a transfer price system that was fair to Farley, Sawchuck, and Watt and would lead each manager to make the decisions that Carmen would make if he had all the information. He was not sure just how to proceed, but he did collect the following facts from Farley, Sawchuck, and Watt concerning the deal that had been consummated for the Mercury.

1. Watt estimated that it would take approximately $300 at internal costs to recondition the used car and another $900 to put in a new transmission, although the current transmission might last for another four months. Similar work done for outside customers would be priced at 33 percent more or $400 and $1200, respectively.
2. Sawchuck believed that the wholesale price for a good condition car of the model traded was approximately $5,600, assuming the transmission did not flare up before the sale.
3. The Blue Book buying price for a model like the one traded that was in good condition was approximately $6,200, as reported.
4. Commissions of 9 percent and 7.5 percent respectively are paid on cash receipts for the sale of used and new cars.

QUESTIONS

1. Analyze the problem of the trade-in from the point of view of the new car manager (Farley) and from the point of view of the entire dealership. Will Farley make the same deal in disposing of the used car as would be optimal from the point of view of the dealership? Assume that Farley will have to negotiate with Sawchuck over the matter of the transmission repair. Assume further that the present informal transfer rules are still in effect. Illustrate just how your solution would work.

2. Once you arrive at a decision from Farley's point of view, compute the resultant contribution margin of Warren Ford and the new, used, and service departments. State your assumptions clearly.
3. Advise Carmen as to an appropriate responsibility center structure for the dealership, including responsibility centers for each department, sourcing policies, transfer pric-

ing rules, and rewards. Assume that Warren would like to be a "balanced" dealership, while maintaining or creating (he isn't sure of the current image of the business in the community) a high-quality image. Moreover, assume that Warren wants to achieve rapid growth in sales and profits.
4. What are the ethical dimensions of this business as far as this situation is concerned?

7

REWARD SYSTEMS

PURPOSE

Reward systems are necessary in organizations in order to blend the interests of stakeholders with the interests of managers. For example, the interests of stockholders, who are by and large not managers, must be blended with the interests of managers, who by and large are not major stockholders. It is the *separation of ownership from control* that creates a need for effective and efficient managerial reward systems.

Shareholders are interested primarily in the profitability and growth of the enterprise. This goal is often stated as "wealth maximization." The design of the firm's reward system is a major tool that shareholders use to ensure that the interests of managers are blended with the interests of shareholders. We should simultaneously attempt to use the performance measurement system to blend the interests of managers with all stakeholders.

Reward systems are instrumental for recruiting and retaining participants in the organization. They thus serve as a major motivational tool for securing the participation of individuals in the pursuits of the organization's goal. We normally think of rewards as being directed toward employees and managers, but we may broaden the concept of rewards to include all stakeholders of an organization, including customers, stockholders, creditors, and the public. The concept of stakeholders who all make contributions in return for rewards is the proper conceptual scheme to employ in the analysis of rewards.

Rewards are an important source of communication and feedback. They communicate just what the firm values and just how valued an individual is to the firm.

The feedback or rewards may be positive, seeking to reinforce and encourage certain behavior, or negative, seeking to alter behavior to a more desirable pattern.

GOAL CONGRUENCE

An effective reward system will lead managers to make the same decisions as the relevant stakeholder when confronted with a decision situation. An effective reward system thus requires the establishment of *goals, performance measurements,* and *reward criteria.*

Congruence is a goal of reward systems, but it is one that is impossible to attain perfectly in practice. The motivational and measurement problems are immense, so we strive in practice for fairness, simplicity, and efficiency in the design of our reward systems.

Motivation of managers is complex; many factors enter into the equation, and they vary significantly from one person to the next. Performance measurement problems are also complex. For these two reasons, goal congruence is an elusive goal, but it is the proper one to seek in the design of reward systems.

Reward systems should not be thought to be independent of the entire control system. Many aspects of the design of the entire control system are related to rewards. We therefore should think about reward systems in light of the overall MSSM. Moreover, rewards should be designed to be consistent with and supportive of the remainder of the control system, following our mutually supportive systems model.

PERFORMANCE VARIABLES

The choice of performance variables determines what the managers are to pay attention to in their environment, and the importance assigned to them by the firm determines the extent to which managers are to pay attention to them. Performance variables should be established to produce goal congruence between the interests of the stakeholders and the interests of managers.

CONTROLLABLE

A reward system is considered "fair" if managers are rewarded based upon variables whose values are primarily under their control and influence. When managers are held accountable for variables that are outside of their control, the reward system becomes more arbitrary and less motivating.

NONCONTROLLABLE

Corporate managers often hold subordinates responsible for variables that are at least partially out of their control, thus introducing a source of unfairness into the reward system. The rationale for this is that doing so may cause subordinates to become interested in these variables and attempt to compensate for any undesirable values these variables take. This results in sacrificing some fairness in the reward system in order to gain behavioral responses that management considers desirable. Managers held accountable for variables that are not under their control may seek to influence the people who do control these variables, thus creating desirable responses from the organization's point of view.

FINANCIAL

Performance variables are both financial and nonfinancial. The financial variables are derived from the accounting system and are widely understood and comparable to other organizations. They are prepared on a regular basis as a part of the financial accounting process. Examples of financial performance measures are sales, operating profit, profit after taxes, earnings per share, return on equity, operating margin, and cash flow.

NONFINANCIAL

Key success factors are often quantitative but nonfinancial, such as productivity measures, yield, cycle time, direct measures of quality, on-time delivery, supplier defects, customer complaints, customer satisfaction, and new product introductions versus competitors.

THE BALANCED SCORECARD

Organizations tend, over the long run, to reap what they measure and reward. The key issue in the design of performance measures for the purpose of granting formal rewards is to achieve a proper balance among performance measures involved in the position to be evaluated. Kaplan and Norton (1991) have attempted to define a balanced performance measurement system to drive performance. They define four groups of performance measures: financial, customer, internal, and innovation and learning. Clearly, it is also desirable to develop performance measures for other stakeholders, such as suppliers.

Exhibit 7-1 is an example of a balance scorecard for one of the 12 companies Kaplan and Norton studied. Adaptation and expansion of these four measures for each managerial position in an organization are a sound basis for individual and group rewards.

FEEDBACK

Rewards and penalties associated with behaviors and performance send strong signals as to what the organization desires and what it values even though manage-

Exhibit 7-1
Balanced Business Scorecard

Financial Perspective	
Goals	**Measures**
Survive	Cash flow
Succeed	Quarterly sales growth and operating income by division
Prosper	Increase market share and ROE

Customer Perspective	
Goals	**Measures**
New products	Percent of sales from new products
	Percent of sales from proprietary products
Responsive supply	On-time delivery (defined by customer)
Preferred supplier	Share of key accounts' purchases
	Ranking by key accounts
Customer partnership	Number of cooperative engineering efforts

Internal Business Perspective	
Goals	**Measures**
Technology capability	Manufacturing geometry vs. competition
Manufacturing excellence	Cycle time
	Unit cost
	Yield
Design productivity	Silicon efficiency
	Engineering efficiency
New product introduction	Actual introduction schedule vs. plan

Innovation and Learning Perspective	
Goals	**Measures**
Technology leadership	Time to develop next generation
Manufacturing learning	Process time to maturity
Product focus	Percent of products that equal 80% sales
Time to market	New product introduction vs. competition

ment philosophies and policies state otherwise. *The most powerful feedback to individuals from an organization is provided by what the organization measures and rewards.* Especially prominent are people decisions: hiring, firing, and promotion. The criteria that are used to make these people decisions send loud signals as to what the organization really rewards and what it penalizes. These criteria, whether formal or informal, are powerful motivators of people.

DESIGN CONSIDERATIONS

REWARDS INTEGRATED WITH MSSM

Rewards are both tangible and intangible, monetary and nonmonetary. Some of the most effective rewards for individuals are the values of the organization themselves. Many of the variables within the MSSM have the ability to produce incentives or disincentives depending upon how they are designed.

For example, autonomy is an incentive in itself. The feeling of having discretion over resources is a very powerful incentive for managers. The organization structure, including reporting relationships and status, is a very powerful motivator.

The values of the organization and the style of management are powerful forces generating incentives and disincentives for individuals. Barnard thought values were the most stable incentives an organization had to offer (1938, p. 146).

Communication and integration structures are important motivators. For example, extensive employee involvement and participation in decision making and problem solving may be highly valued by employees of the organization.

As a result of these interactions with other elements of the MSSM, one should not think of rewards in isolation from the rest of the control system.

ATTAINABILITY

Performance targets should be challenging but attainable. Easily attainable targets are not motivating and do not cause individuals to extend themselves and grow. Highly motivated individuals respond best to challenging but attainable targets. On the other hand, targets that are truly impossible to achieve are demotivating.

FORMAL

Formal rewards are specified by the definition of goals, responsibilities, performance measures, standards expected, methods and frequency of measurement, and rewards expected.

A number of criteria should be followed when setting formal rewards:

1. Performance measures should be congruent with the organization's objectives and goals.
2. Managers should be evaluated based upon variables over which they have a significant amount of control.
3. Performance measures should be objectively measured.
4. Standards of performance should be challenging but attainable.
5. Rewards should be competitive with those offered in comparable organizations.
6. The reward system should be simple to understand and to administer.

INFORMAL

Informal rewards are implicit and have to do with peer recognition and approval. Informal rewards stem from informal relationships between employees of an organization. As such, informal rewards are part of the broader formal organization. Informal rewards are intrinsic, stature oriented, and related to performance. Usually, they involve recognition of performance by personal contact on the part of management.

INDIVIDUAL REWARDS

Organizations are cooperative systems. Most of the work of real significance takes place as a result of cooperative effort. Nevertheless, it is important to motivate and reward individual performance.

Individual goals and rewards have the tendency to encourage individuals to do their best because somebody *cares* and because it *counts*. They also encourage productivity, creativity, individual autonomy, and accountability.

On the negative side, excessive emphasis upon individual rewards may restrict the kind of cooperative behavior that is right at the heart of the workings of effective organizations.

Formal individual rewards, including compensation, should reflect individual contributions. They should also be at market rates, since other organizations are competing for the services of the same people.

Many organizations hand out bonuses based upon current or long-term performance and do so by the use of a ranking process. The ranking process may work like this: managers rank their people in terms of individual performance and the ranking is passed up the line with the top 20–30 percent of the people receiving performance bonuses. The people so identified on a continuing basis eventually become candidates for promotion.

GROUP REWARDS

Group goals and rewards encourage cooperative effort and are very important for the integration of the parts of the organization into a workable whole. They also encourage peer pressure for the achievement of organizational goals. As a result, some of the most effective rewards are those tied to overall organizational performance.

On the negative side, group goals may encourage "free riders" and may be demotivating for high-performing individuals working in underperforming groups.

LONG-TERM REWARDS

Vesting of stock options is a very common long-term performance reward and is made conditional upon the performance of the individual or upon the organization's meeting a specified earnings per share target a number of years hence. Of course, promotions are among the strongest rewards for effective long-term performance.

SHORT-TERM REWARDS

Short-term measures, both financial and nonfinancial, are often used as the basis for short-term rewards. Bonuses may also be tied to this period's performance measures such as the earnings per share goal.

MSSM INTERACTIONS AND DYNAMICS OF REWARDS

Reward systems should be designed to motivate behavior on a continuous basis in support of the goals of the organization. In addition, the reward system should be mutually supportive to other subsystems of the control system. As a result the reward system may require redesign over time as changes occur in market conditions, strategies, and in the number and type of personnel.

Rewards have subtle ongoing effects on behavior, and this should be understood. These subtle, dynamic impacts of rewards are not always understood by management. For example, certain rewards may be provided by a firm to obtain a certain contract. The employee perceives that in order to obtain the contract, he or she must engage in unethical conduct that violates the formal code of ethics of the organization but is "winked at" by management in this particular case. The rewards may indeed be valued and unethical conduct may result, but the secondary effect of putting employees in this situation is to create a lack of respect for the management of the firm. This lack of respect could result in reduced motivation in the future.

Still other subtle aspects of relationships between various aspects of the control system influence the effectiveness of rewards. There are strong relationships among style, culture, and past experience and the manner in which rewards and recognition are interpreted. Take the case of a production worker who joins an empowered quality improvement team after working all of his or her life in a more authoritarian supervisory environment. The incentives and recognition systems in an empowered team are different from those the worker experienced previously. While other team members feel rewarded by their ability to set work schedules and by the recognition of being valued contributors, the new worker may merely perceive the job as "more work."

If the new worker becomes demoralized because of the extra work and begins to increase the use of sick days, the rest of the team may become demoralized by the behavior of the new worker. These subtle relationships exist at all levels of the organization from policy boards to worker teams. It is important, therefore, to recognize the strong interrelationships among style, culture, and past experiences and the manner in which rewards and recognitions are perceived by employees and managers.

In Chapter 3, a dynamic model of the control process was developed. We saw there that the reward and recognition system of the organization should be used to facilitate the "learning organization" by creating positive reinforcing loops. In order to be positively reinforcing, rewards and recognition must foster trust,

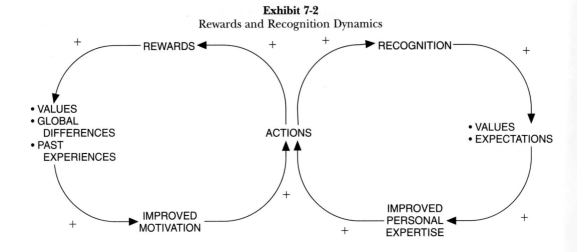

Exhibit 7-2
Rewards and Recognition Dynamics

inspire confidence in management, promote self-respect, reinforce the values of the organization, and encourage self-learning.

Exhibit 7-2 describes the dynamic reinforcing loops that should be considered for an appropriately constructed reward and recognition system. The model also considers some of the subtle issues that can arise between rewards and other aspects of the MSSM.

The left side of Exhibit 7-2 refers to commonly used formal rewards, such as merit increases and bonus programs, which are used to motivate personnel to achieve organizational objectives. The left loop shows that before formal rewards actually impact motivation positively, they pass through a "screen" of cultural values, global differences, and past training; if they are consistent with this screen, they become effective in motivation. If conflicts arise, the strength of the reinforcement diminishes.

The right side of Exhibit 7-2 represents informal activities. Before recognition leads to improvement in personal expertise, it too must pass through a screen of cultural values and expectations. When both the left and right loops are positively reinforcing, employees are powerfully motivated toward actions that help achieve organizational objectives.

By using the dynamic model represented in Exhibit 7-2 and by carefully addressing the interrelations among all aspects of the MSSM as far as they affect rewards, management will encourage the maximum development of the individual in the organization.

CASE STUDY: REWARDS INTEGRATED INTO MSSM—USML[1]

Let's turn to an example of a company with a well-integrated reward system. We use this example to illustrate the need to think about reward systems as integrated with the entire control system rather than as an isolated part of the control system. This is fundamental to our approach to control systems design.

U. S. Medical Laboratories (USML)   U. S. Medical Laboratories, a subsidiary of a Fortune 500 company, is the fourth largest provider of clinical laboratory services in the country. USML consists of 70 facilities throughout the United States, supplying laboratory testing for hospitals, medical groups, and private physicians. The parent company acquired a group of small eastern laboratories in 1969, all operating under different names. Through expansion and a series of acquisitions, this small decentralized company reached $30 million in sales by 1974.

By 1978, USML had been established as one of the largest private laboratories in the country, showing a profit margin significantly above industry standards. That year it acquired a group of financially troubled laboratories. The acquisitions resulted in a doubling of sales while significantly diluting profits. Absorbing these acquisitions took a good part of two years, during which time a number of internal problems caused by philosophical differences with these acquired laboratories were being addressed.

USML recovered (mostly) from the pains of acquisition by 1980 and began a trend of annual 15 percent growth in sales with corresponding profit improvement. USML now represents 15.6 percent of total sales of the top six laboratories in the United States.

CULTURE AND MANAGEMENT STYLE

USML is a corporation trying, so far successfully, to maintain an ongoing 15 percent compounded growth rate in sales while encouraging a small-company, almost family atmosphere. Top managers are treated in a very personal manner and all know the president and his wife. The company holds two or three management meetings annually where social interaction is not forced but made available in a relaxed setting. All managers above a certain level and their spouses are invited along with a number of lower-level managers who show consistent high-level performance.

The atmosphere in the company, particularly among top and middle managers, is one of loyalty and dedication. The company is regarded as a living entity, largely because of the personalities of the president and the CEO. The president is a very personable man in his mid-40s who demonstrates an honest caring for employees that is recognized by the lowest-level employee 3000 miles away. He is held somewhat in awe and has created a very successful company while demonstrating high ethical principles and advocating dedicated attention to detail from his people.

If the president is the family father, the CEO is the respected uncle who runs the company on a day-to-day basis. He is very pleasant personally but mentally tough regarding business issues. He demands absolute attention to detail and expects commitments to be met. He is intolerant of USML's not "meeting budget" in all areas. He limits the circle of people he deals with directly and creates a situation where all major projects must be presented in a united form from this circle. Disagreement among the executives is encouraged, but it is expected that the best decision will prevail. He will referee conflicts, however, if necessary.

This combination of personalities creates an atmosphere of loyalty, respect, and an overwhelming drive to do what is right for the entity as a whole. In the past six years, only one top manager has left the company voluntarily.

A strong degree of financial control exists at USML. Top management uses staffs extensively to oversee operations and to pursue tight budgets. Although all levels of management participate in the decision-making process, the style of management tends to be somewhat autocratic. That style is backed up by a very detailed performance measurement system that allows management to retain a tight hold on all parts of the organization.

Performance review meetings are frequent, and accountability is high and detailed. A heavy measurement orientation exists in the company. On the other hand, business departments are headed by general managers who are treated as profit centers and have a fair amount of latitude in operations. They are measured and rewarded according to performance.

ORGANIZATION STRUCTURE

The 14 general managers are responsible for profit and are in charge of USML's 14 major product lines. They are further organized into four major divisions, each headed by a vice president. Sales managers are, in turn, responsible for revenue. Their departments are correspondingly treated as revenue centers. The director of operations is held responsible for standard cost performance. All other departments are treated as discretionary cost centers.

As a rule, large medical laboratories are run at the top by a medical or scientific person. The general attitude is that they are laboratories first and just happen to be in business. USML is run at the top by people who are in a business that happens to be a laboratory. In the early history of the company this was a problem, because USML did not have a very good reputation for quality; prior to the late 1970s this reputation was probably deserved. The current president of the parent company was instrumental in leading USML toward shedding this reputation. A new scientific affairs group was established, and a number of pathologists, Ph.D.s, and technical staff personnel were added.

Each general manager has access to people possessing scientific, financial, and management skills to ensure that the best business decisions are being made while not sacrificing quality. USML turns out to be ahead of its time in this kind of thinking. Until recently, economic efficiency and optimum quality were thought of as mutually exclusive by the medical community.

Because USML has operated under the "good medicine–good business" philosophy for a number of years, they are a leader in sales growth and total profits.

COMMUNICATIONS

A number of communication mechanisms are mentioned in the previous section, such as management meetings, family atmosphere, and so on. In addition, there are executive meetings each month lasting approximately four hours. Participants in these meetings include the CEO, the four decision vice presidents, VP Finance, VP Operations, VP Marketing, Director of Finance, and Director of Operations. Other staff and line personnel are brought in as needed to address topics as they come up.

All divisions are evaluated as follows: (1) last month's forecast versus actual performance, (2) last month's budget versus actual performance, (3) current month's forecast versus budget, and (4) three-month rolling forecast versus budget.

Details of problems in various locations are discussed. Potential action plans are also discussed. Decisions are made as to the plan of attack for problems, or additional information and analysis is requested. Assignments are then made to solve the problems.

A second meeting of about two hours is held to review information, plans, and progress on problem areas only. Field action plans are developed, and a short-term improvement plan is requested from general managers in these problem areas. A long-term improvement plan is requested from joint staff and line managers. Progress on the action plan is reviewed at subsequent monthly review meetings.

PLANNING AND RESOURCE ALLOCATION

1. Plans prepared by general managers are compared to plans prepared by the various staff groups, and the differences between the two plans are resolved. Capital budgets are then evaluated by the financial and operations staff for major projected needs.
2. Capital and personnel requests are initiated by line management and approved or rejected by general and division management. Requests above $20,000 are submitted to headquarters staff for evaluation. The staff can return the requests for additional information or rewrite the proposals. The staff also makes rejection recommendations to division managers. If the staff concurs, the proposals are sent to the CEO and president for approval. Proposals above $100,000 require the approval of the parent company.
3. The budget is prepared by line management in the field and reviewed by division management. It is then reviewed by the corporate staff for accuracy, assumptions, and past performance. The budget package is then reviewed by the executive staff for credibility and correspondence to corporate goals. The final divisions and consolidated budgets are then presented to the CEO and the president. The budget for USML is presented to the parent company at the annual corporate budget meeting in November.
4. Each month, general managers submit three-month forecasts. These forecasts are checked by corporate staff for performance, accuracy, assumptions and against previous forecasts for month-to-month changes. A summary of the monthly forecasts is reviewed by the executive staff. The summary is presented to the CEO at the monthly "numbers" meeting.

Improvements Planned for the Resource Allocation Process

Even though USML is a very effective, high-performing organization, and this is a great source of pride for its managers and employees, management is currently addressing some problems. First, extensive staff involvement in business decisions has encouraged field managers to pass on many of the tasks that involve preparing capital and staff requests. The result has been a reduction in line accountability. Second, extensive staff involvement has slowed down the approval process to as long as two months for routine proposals. As a result of these two problems, management has taken the following actions that hold promise for further improvement.

1. Headquarters staff has been pared down. Their focus has shifted from analysis and review to adding value to line projects and decisions and to enforcing a uniform corporate review of proposals.
2. Accountability through the division vice presidents has been increased for all proposals submitted. Automatic rewrite of proposals by staff has been eliminated. All proposals not containing enough information and analysis are simply rejected.

REPORTING

A profit and loss meeting is held at each of the field locations each month. Participants at these meetings are the staff accountant for the field location, technical operations director, and the sales manager. Variances by line item are explained and assignments are made to gather further information, do additional analysis, and initiate changes in practices to close undesirable variances. A summary of the analysis and corrective actions are available for presentation at the monthly management meetings.

Productivity

USML has an extensive system for managing the productivity of its personnel. There has been a dramatic increase in productivity, as shown in Table 7-1 during the last five years.

Table 7-1
Statistics on Productivity

Year	Personnel Head count	Sales per Employee
1986	1972	54
1987	1916	60
1988	1970	69
1989	2070	82
1990	2157	87
	Sales per employee up	57%
	Head count up	9%

Personnel Control Mechanisms

Numerous reporting mechanisms have been established for personnel at USML. Table 7-2 gives the various mechanisms that are in place and the date when each was put into place.

Formal rewards are different for the various managers of USML.

Top Managers

The top management of the company, vice presidents and up, are rewarded on the basis of performance both in their areas of responsibility and in the company as a whole. An annual bonus is awarded commensurate with individual achievement, and stock options are vested according to the achievement of overall earnings per share targets five years out.

Top executives are invited to two to three management meetings each year in vacation-like places that are designed to show appreciation for a collective job well done. The timing and the location of the meetings are usually based on how well the company has done in comparison to budget.

General Managers

General managers are rewarded on the basis of a combination of profit performance of their departments and achievement of other goals agreed upon at the beginning of the year. Rewards include stock options and bonuses. The evaluations are subjective but are based upon performance.

Table 7-2

Reporting and Control Mechanisms	Date Established
USML workload productivity standards	1973
Personnel saving equipment additions	ongoing
Position number control system	1982
Monthly headcount meeting	1984
Tight personnel requesting system	1986
Standardized methodology	1986
Temporary help approval system	1988
Forecast of authorized labor	1989
Temporary help forecast	1990

Sales Managers

Sales managers and sales staff are rewarded by a very generous commission structure. Numerous sales contests are run throughout the year. Moreover, a prestigious Sales Masters meeting is held each year for the top performers of the company.

Staff and Line Managers

These managers are rewarded by a bonus plan based upon individual performance in relation to predetermined goals. Evaluations are based upon quantitative and qualitative factors.

All Employees

Each employee has received a Christmas bonus in each of the last six years. The amount is related to how well the company has done during the year but has historically been established at about two weeks' salary. Some employees receive more and some less. In 1990, the president was so pleased with the performance of the company that he raised the bonus per employee by $500.

SUMMARY

United States Medical Laboratories has been presented as an example of a well-run medical organization. It demonstrates many of the characteristics in each of the six subsystems of control that we have advocated. In this company the philosophy of top management is well understood. It contributes to a culture that is accepted and highly valued by the entire staff. The structure of the organization is clearly defined and well designed to enhance participation and communication. Communication systems are excellent in both directions. Planning is thorough, and resource allocation is carefully controlled. Reporting systems are well developed, providing appropriate and timely information. Reward systems are based upon demonstrated efficiency and effectiveness.

In conclusion, this case study illustrates how each of the subsystems of the MSSM contribute to the overall performance of the company and well-being of each of the executives and employees. The formal reward system supports the overall control system and contributes to the fulfillment of the needs of the people in the organization. This case study gives some insight into methods of providing the rewards that make people want to continue to serve a company and contribute to achieving the goals of the organization. It also illustrates the fallacy of thinking too narrowly about rewards.

REWARDS: A STILL BROADER VIEW

Personnel make up one critical group of stakeholders. We have been discussing rewards for personnel. But, as we have seen in Chapter 1, all of the participants must be induced to participate in the organization, including personnel, customers, stockholders, bondholders, suppliers, and government. An organization induces these stakeholders to participate in the organization by offering inducements or rewards that are equal to or exceed those offered by competing organizations.

To achieve control of any organization, management must gain the cooperation and the contributions of the key constituents of the organization. Three of the most critical constituents are customers, personnel, and providers of capital.

Griesinger (1984, p. 4) noted, ". . . it is beneficial to brainstorm the larger set of stakeholders who affect or are affected by the actions of the firm, classifying them roughly in terms of power to affect the organization and the degree to which they are affected." It is worthwhile to list each stakeholder's contribution to the organization and relate it to the cost of eliciting that contribution.

Monetary rewards play only a part in satisfying the broader set of stakeholders. For example, the role of advertising and promotion is to influence the perceptions of the customer but also those of the other constituents.

REFERENCES

ASAY, L. A., AND J. A. MACIARIELLO, *Executive Leadership in Health Care.* San Francisco: Jossey-Bass Publishers, 1991.

BARNARD, CHESTER I., *The Functions of the Executive.* Cambridge, Mass.: Harvard University Press, 1938, p. 146.

ECCLES, R. G., "The Performance Measurement Manifesto," *Harvard Business Review,* January–February 1991, pp. 131–137.

GRIESINGER, DONALD W., *Innovation for Stakeholder Advantage: A Stakeholder Approach.* Graduate Management Center, GMC 8401, Claremont Graduate School, Claremont, California, 1984.

KAPLAN, R. S., AND A. A. ATKINSON, "Executive Contracts and Bonus Plans," Chapter 16 in *Advanced Management Account-*ing, 2nd ed. Englewood Cliffs, N.J.: Prentice Hall, pp. 719–746.

KAPLAN, R. S., AND DAVID P. NORTON, "The Balanced Scorecard—Measures That Drive Performance," *Harvard Business Review,* January–February 1992, pp. 71–79.

Merchant, K. A., *Rewarding Results: Motivating Profit Center Managers.* Cambridge, Mass.: Harvard Business School Press, 1989.

OUCHI, WILLIAM G., *Theory Z.* New York: Avon Books, 1981.

SLOAN, ALFRED P., JR., *My Years with General Motors,* Garden City, New York: Doubleday & Company, 1964.

VANCIL, R. F., *Decentralization: Managerial Ambiguity by Design.* Homewood, Ill.: Dow-Jones Irwin, 1979.

NOTE

1. This case is adapted by permission from Lyal D. Asay and Joseph A. Maciariello, *Executive Leadership in Health Care,* pp. 116–122; copyright 1991 by Jossey-Bass Inc., publishers.

Case 7-1 USML

QUESTIONS

1. Refer back to the USML case described in this chapter. Identify possible sources of rewards besides the stipulated formal rewards. The list may include both informal and formal rewards.

2. Comment on the following statement made in the text: "Reward systems should not be thought to be independent of the entire control system. Many aspects of the design of entire control systems are related to rewards."

Case 7-2 Lincoln Electric Company, 1989

The Lincoln Electric Company was the world's largest manufacturer of arc-welding products and a leading producer of industrial electric motors. The firm employed 2,400 workers in 2 U.S. factories near Cleveland and an equal number in 11 factories located in other countries. This does not include the field sales force of more than 200. The company's U.S. market share (for arc-welding products) is estimated at more than 40 percent.

James F. Lincoln, head of the firm since 1914, died in 1965 and there was some concern, even among employees, that the management system would fall into disarray, that profits would decline, and that year-end bonuses might be discontinued. Quite the contrary, in 1989 the company appears as strong as ever. Each year, except the recession years 1982 and 1983, has seen high profits and bonuses. Employee morale and productivity remain very good. Employee turnover is almost nonexistent, except for retirements. Lincoln's market share is stable. The historically high stock dividends continue.

A HISTORICAL SKETCH

Lincoln Electric Company was founded in 1905 by John C. Lincoln. In 1907, after a bout with typhoid fever forced him from Ohio State University in his senior year, James F. Lincoln, John's younger brother, joined the fledgling company. In 1914 he became active head of the firm. One of his early actions was to ask the employees to elect representatives to a committee that would advise him on company operations. This "Advisory Board" has met with the chief executive officer every two weeks since that time.

The first year the Advisory Board was in existence, working hours were reduced from 55 hours per week, then standard, to 50 hours a week. In 1923, a piecework pay system was in effect, employees got two weeks paid vacation each year, and wages were adjusted for changes in the consumer price index. Approximately 30 percent of the common stock was set aside for key employees in 1914. A stock purchase plan for all employees was begun in 1925.

The board of directors voted to start a suggestion system in 1929. The program is still in effect, but cash awards, a part of the early program, were discontinued several years ago. Now, suggestions are rewarded by additional "points," which affect year-end bonuses.

The legendary Lincoln bonus plan was proposed by the Advisory Board and accepted on a trial basis in 1934. The bonus plan has been a cornerstone of the Lincoln management system, and recent bonuses have approximated annual wages.

By 1944, Lincoln employees enjoyed a pension plan, a policy of promotion from within, and continuous employment. Base pay

*This case was prepared by Arthur Sharplin, McNeese State University, Lake Charles, La. 70601. It is reproduced here by permission.

rates were determined by formal job evaluation and a merit rating system was in effect.

In the prologue of James F. Lincoln's
last book, Charles G. Herbruck writes regarding the foregoing personnel innovations:

> They were not to buy good behavior. They
> were not efforts to increase profits. They were
> not antidotes to labor difficulties. They did
> not constitute a "do-gooder" program. They
> were expressions of mutual respect for each
> person's importance to the job to be done.
> All of them reflect the leadership of James
> Lincoln, under whom they were nurtured
> and propagated.

Certainly since 1935 and probably for
several years before that, Lincoln productivity has been well above the average for similar companies. The company claims levels of
productivity more than twice those for other
manufacturers from 1945 onward.

COMPANY PHILOSOPHY

James F. Lincoln was the son of a Congre-
gational minister, and Christian principles
were at the center of his business philosophy.

There is no indication that Lincoln attempted to evangelize his employees or customers—or the general public, for that
matter. Neither the chairman of the board
and chief executive, George Willis, nor the
president, Donald F. Hastings, mention the
Christian gospel in their recent speeches and
interviews. The company motto, "The actual
is limited, the possible is immense," is prominently displayed; but there is no display of
religious slogans, and there is no company
chapel.

ATTITUDE TOWARD THE CUSTOMER

James Lincoln saw the customer's needs as
the *raison d'être* for every company. "When
any company has achieved success so that it is

attractive as an investment," he wrote, "all
money usually needed for expansion is supplied by the customer in retained earnings. It
is obvious that the customer's interests, not
the stockholder's, should come first." This is
reflected in Lincoln's policy to "at all times
price on the basis of cost and at all times
keep pressure on our cost...." Lincoln's
goal, often stated, is "to build a better and
better product at a lower and lower price."

ATTITUDE TOWARD STOCKHOLDERS

Stockholders are given last priority at Lincoln. This is a continuation of James Lincoln's
philosophy: "The last group to be considered
is the stockholders who own stock because
they think it will be more profitable than
investing money in any other way." Concerning division of the largess produced by
incentive management, he wrote, "The absen-
tee stockholder also will get his share, even
if undeserved, out of the greatly increased
profit that the efficiency produces."

ATTITUDE TOWARD UNIONISM

There has never been a serious effort to organize Lincoln employees. While James Lincoln criticized the labor movement for
"selfishly attempting to better its position at
the expense of the people it must serve," he
still had kind words for union members.
Lincoln's idea of the correct relationship
between workers and managers is shown by
this comment: "Labor and management are
properly not warring camps; they are parts of
one organization in which they must and
should cooperate fully and happily."

BELIEFS AND ASSUMPTIONS ABOUT EMPLOYEES

If fulfilling customer needs is the desired
goal of business, then employee performance

and productivity are the means by which this goal can best be achieved. It is the Lincoln attitude toward employees, reflected in the following comments by James Lincoln, which is credited by many with creating the success the company has experienced:

> The greatest fear of the worker, which is the same as the greatest fear of the industrialist in operating a company, is the lack of income. . . . The industrial manager is very conscious of his company's need of uninterrupted income. He is completely oblivious, evidently, of the fact that the worker has the same need.
>
> If money is to be used as an incentive, the program must provide that what is paid to the worker is what he has earned. The earnings of each must be in accordance with accomplishment.

LINCOLN'S BUSINESS

Arc-welding has been the standard joining method in shipbuilding for decades. It is the predominant way of connecting steel in the construction industry. Most industrial plants have their own welding shops for maintenance and construction. While advances in welding technology have been frequent, arc-welding products, in the main, have hardly changed. Lincoln's Innershield process is a notable exception. This process lowers welding cost and improves quality and speed in many applications. The most widely used Lincoln electrode, the Fleetweld 5P, has been virtually the same since the 1930s. The most popular engine-driven welder in the world, the Lincoln SA-200, has been in production for at least four decades. A 1989 model SA-200 even weighs almost the same as the 1950 model, and it is little changed in appearance.

The company's share of the U.S. arc-welding products market appears to have been about 40 percent for many years. The welding products market has grown some-

what faster than the level of industry in general. The market is highly price-competitive, with variations in prices of standard items normally amounting to only a percent or two. Lincoln's products are sold directly by its engineering-oriented sales force and indirectly through its distributor organization. Advertising expenditures amount to less than three-fourths of a percent of sales. Research and development expenditures typically range from $10 million to $12 million, considerably more than competitors.

The other major welding process, flame-welding, has not been competitive with arc-welding since the 1930s. However, plasma-arc-welding, a relatively new process, which uses a conducting stream of superheated gas (plasma) to confine the welding current to a small area, has made some inroads, especially in metal tubing manufacturing, in recent years. Major advances in technology that will produce an alternative superior to arc-welding within the next decade or so appear unlikely. Also, it seems likely that changes in the machines and techniques used in arc-welding will be evolutionary, rather than revolutionary.

PRODUCTS

In addition to arc-welding products, Lincoln also produces electric motors ranging from one-half horsepower to 200 horsepower. Motors constitute about 8 to 10 percent of total sales. Several million dollars has recently been invested in automated equipment that will double Lincoln's manufacturing capacity for one-half to 20 horsepower electric motors.

Lincoln and its competitors now market a wide range of general-purpose and specialty electrodes for welding mild steel, aluminum, cast iron, and stainless and special steels. Most of these electrodes are designed to meet the standards of the American Welding Society, a trade association. They, thus, are essentially the same in size and composition from one manufacturer to another. Every electrode manufacturer has a limited number of unique products, but these typically constitute only a small percentage of total sales.

MANUFACTURING PROCESSES

The main plant is in Euclid, Ohio, a suburb on Cleveland's east side. There are no warehouses. Materials flow from the half-mile-long dock on the north side of the plant through the production lines to a very limited storage and loading area on the south side. Materials used on each work station are stored as close as possible to the work station. The administrative offices, near the center of the factory, are entirely functional. A corridor below the main level provides access to the factory floor from the main entrance near the center of the plant. *Fortune* magazine recently declared the Euclid facility one of America's 10 best-managed factories, and compared it with a General Electric plant, also on the list:

> Stepping into GE's spanking new dishwasher plant, an awed supplier said, is like stepping "into the Hyatt Regency." By comparison, stepping into Lincoln Electric's 33-year-old, cavernous, dimly lit factory is like stumbling into a dingy big-city YMCA. It's only when one starts looking at how these factories do things that similarities become apparent. They have found ways to merge design with manufacturing, build in quality, make wise choices about automation, get close to customers, and handle their work forces.

THE LINCOLN ELECTRIC COMPANY, 1989

A new Lincoln plant, in Mentor, Ohio, houses some of the electrode production operations, which were moved from the main plant. Electrode manufacturing is highly capital intensive.

Lincoln welding machines and electric motors are made on a series of assembly lines. Gasoline and diesel engines are purchased partially assembled, but practically all other components are made from basic industrial products (e.g., steel bars and sheets and bar copper conductor wire).

Individual components, such as gasoline tanks for engine-driven welders and steel shafts for motors and generators, are made by numerous small "factories within a factory." The shaft for a certain generator, for example, is made from raw steel bar by one operator, who uses five large machines, all running continuously. A saw cuts the bar to length, a digital lathe machines different sections to varying diameters, a special milling machine cuts a slot for the keyway and so forth, until a finished shaft is produced. The operator moves the shafts from machine to machine and makes necessary adjustments.

Another operator punches, shapes, and paints sheetmetal cowling parts. One assembles steel laminations onto a rotor shaft, then winds, insulates, and tests the rotors. Finished components are moved by crane operators to the nearby assembly lines.

WORKER PERFORMANCE AND ATTITUDES

The typical Lincoln employee earns about twice as much as other factory workers in the Cleveland area. Yet the company's labor cost per sales dollar in 1989, 26 cents, is well below industry averages. Worker turnover is practically nonexistent, except for retirements and departures by new employees.

Sales per Lincoln factory employee currently exceed $150,000. An observer at the factory quickly sees why this figure is so high. Each worker is proceeding busily and thoughtfully about the task at hand. There is no idle chatter. Most workers take no coffee breaks. Many operate several machines and make a substantial component unaided. The supervisors are busy with planning and recordkeeping duties and hardly glance at the people they "supervise." The manufacturing procedures appear efficient—no unnecessary steps, no wasted motions, no wasted materials. Finished components move smoothly to subsequent work stations.

Appendix A includes summaries of interviews with employees.

ORGANIZATION STRUCTURE

Lincoln has never allowed development of a formal organization chart. The objective of this policy is to insure maximum flexibility. An open-door policy is practiced throughout the company and personnel are encouraged to take problems to the persons most capable of resolving them. Once, Harvard Business School researchers prepared an organization chart reflecting the implied relationships at Lincoln. The chart became available within the company, and present management feels that [it] had a disruptive effect. Therefore, no organizational chart appears in this case.

Perhaps because of the quality and enthusiasm of the Lincoln work force, routine supervision is almost nonexistent. A typical production foreman, for example, supervises as many as 100 workers, a span of control that does not allow more than infrequent worker-supervisor interaction.

Position titles and traditional flows of authority do imply something of an organizational structure, however. For example, the vice president of sales and the vice president of Electrode Division report to the president, as do various staff assistants, such as the personnel director and the director of purchasing. Using such implied relationships, it has been determined that production workers have two or, at most, three levels of supervision between themselves and the President.

PERSONNEL POLICIES

RECRUITMENT AND SELECTION

Every job opening is advertised internally on company bulletin boards, and any employee can apply for any job so advertised. External hiring is permitted only for entry-level positions. Selection for these jobs is done on the basis of personal interviews—there is no aptitude or psychological testing. Not even a high school diploma is required—except for engineering and sales positions, which are filled by graduate engineers. A committee consisting of vice presidents and supervisors interviews candidates initially cleared by the personnel department. Final selection is made by the supervisor who has a job opening. Out of over 3,500 applicants interviewed by the personnel department during a recent period, fewer than 300 were hired.

JOB SECURITY

In 1958, Lincoln formalized its guaranteed continuous employment policy, which had already been in effect for many years. There have been no layoffs since World War II. Since 1958, every worker with over two year's longevity has been guaranteed at least 30 hours per week, 49 weeks per year.

The policy has never been so severely tested as during the 1981–1983 recession. As a manufacturer of capital goods, Lincoln's business is highly cyclical. In previous recessions, the company was able to avoid major sales declines. However, sales plummeted 32 percent in 1982 and another 16 percent the next year. Lincoln not only earned profits, but no employee was laid off and year-end incentive bonuses continued. To weather the storm, management cut most of the nonsalaried workers back to 30 hours a week for varying periods of time. Many employees were reassigned and the total work force was slightly reduced through normal attrition and restricted hiring.

PERFORMANCE EVALUATIONS

Each supervisor formally evaluates subordinates twice a year using the card shown in Exhibit 7-3. The employee performance criteria, "quality," "dependability," "ideas and cooperation," and "output," are considered to be independent of each other. Marks on the cards are converted to numerical scores, which are forced to average 100 for each evaluating supervisor. Individual merit rating scores normally range from 80 to 110. Any score over 110 requires a special letter to top management. These scores (over 110) are not considered in computing the required 100 point average for each evaluating supervisor. Suggestions for improvements often result in recommendations for exceptionally high performance scores. Supervisors discuss individual performance marks with the employees concerned. Each warranty claim is traced to the individual employee whose work caused the defect. The employee's performance score may be reduced, or the worker may be required to repay the cost of servicing the warranty claim by working without pay.

COMPENSATION

Basic wage levels for jobs at Lincoln are determined by a wage survey of similar jobs in the Cleveland area. These rates are adjusted quarterly in accordance with changes in the Cleveland area wage index. Insofar as possible, base wage rates are translated into piece rates. Practically all production workers and many others—for example, some forklift operators—are paid by piece rate. Once established, piece rates are never changed, unless a substantive change in the way a job is

done results from a source other than the worker doing the job.

In December of each year, a portion of annual profits is distributed to employees as bonuses. Incentive bonuses since 1934 have averaged about 90 percent of annual wages and somewhat more than after-tax profits. The average bonus for 1988 was $21,258. Even for the recession years 1982 and 1983, bonuses had averaged $13,998 and $8,557 respectively. Individual bonuses are proportional to merit-rating scores. For example, assume the amount set aside for bonuses is 80 percent of total wages paid to eligible employees. A person whose performance score is 95 will receive a bonus of 76 percent (0.80 x 0.95) of annual wages. Bonuses totaled $54 million in 1988.

WORK ASSIGNMENT

Management has authority to transfer workers and to switch between overtime and short-time as required. Supervisors have undisputed authority to assign specific parts to individual workmen, who may have their own preferences due to variations in piece rates. During the 1982–1983 recession, 50 factory workers volunteered to join sales teams and fanned out across the country to sell a new welder designed for automobile body shops and small machine shops. The result—$10 million in sales and a hot new product.

EMPLOYEE PARTICIPATION IN DECISION MAKING

Thinking of participative management usually evokes a vision of a relaxed, nonauthoritarian atmosphere. This is not the case at Lincoln. Formal authority is quite strong. "We're very authoritarian around here," says Willis. James F. Lincoln placed a good deal of stress on protecting management's authority. "Management in all successful departments of industry must have complete power," he

Exhibit 7-3
Merit Rating Cards

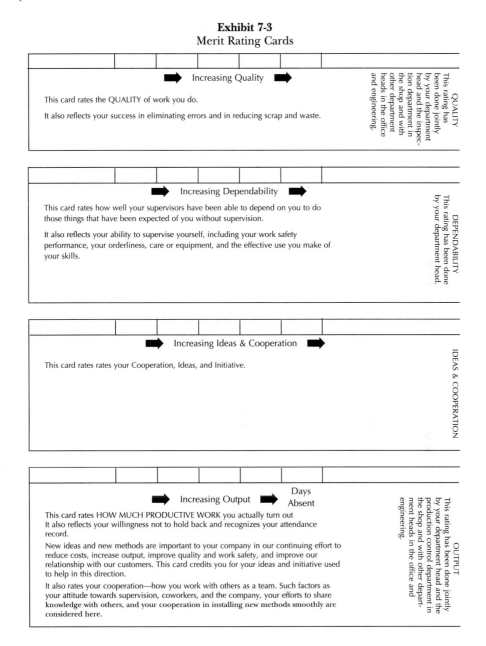

Increasing Quality ➡

This card rates the QUALITY of work you do.

It also reflects your success in eliminating errors and in reducing scrap and waste.

QUALITY
This rating has been done jointly by your department head and the inspection department in the shop and with other department heads in the office and engineering.

Increasing Dependability ➡

This card rates how well your supervisors have been able to depend on you to do those things that have been expected of you without supervision.

It also reflects your ability to supervise yourself, including your work safety performance, your orderliness, care or equipment, and the effective use you make of your skills.

DEPENDABILITY
This rating has been done by your department head.

Increasing Ideas & Cooperation ➡

This card rates rates your Cooperation, Ideas, and Initiative.

IDEAS & COOPERATION

Increasing Output ➡ Days Absent

This card rates HOW MUCH PRODUCTIVE WORK you actually turn out It also reflects your willingness not to hold back and recognizes your attendance record.

New ideas and new methods are important to your company in our continuing effort to reduce costs, increase output, improve quality and work safety, and improve our relationship with our customers. This card credits you for your ideas and initiative used to help in this direction.

It also rates your cooperation—how you work with others as a team. Such factors as your attitude towards supervision, coworkers, and the company, your efforts to share knowledge with others, and your cooperation in installing new methods smoothly are considered here.

OUTPUT
This rating has been done jointly by your department head and the production control department in the shop and with other department heads in the office and engineering.

said. "Management is the coach who must be obeyed. The men, however, are the players who alone can win the game." Despite this attitude, there are several ways in which employees participate in management at Lincoln.

Richard Sabo, assistant to the chief executive officer, relates job enlargement/ enrichment to participation. He said, "The most important participative technique that we use is giving more responsibility to employees. We give a high school graduate more responsibility than other companies give their foremen." Management puts limits on the degree of participation which is allowed, however. In Sabo's words:

> When you use "participation," put quotes around it. Because we believe that each person should participate only in those decisions he is most knowledgeable about. I don't think production employees should control the decisions of the chairman. They don't know as much as he does about the decisions he is involved in.

The Advisory Board, elected by the workers, meets with the chairman and the president every two weeks to discuss ways of improving operations. Every employee has access to Advisory Board members, and answers to all Advisory Board suggestions are promised by the following meeting. Both Willis and Hastings are quick to point out, though, that the Advisory Board only recommends actions. "They do not have direct authority," Willis says. "And when they bring up something that management thinks is not to the benefit of the company, it will be rejected."

Under the early suggestion program, employees were awarded one-half of the first year's savings attributable to their suggestions. Now, however, the value of suggestions is reflected in performance evaluation scores, which determine individual incentive bonus amounts.

FRINGE BENEFITS AND EXECUTIVE PERQUISITES

A medical plan and a company-paid retirement program have been in effect for many years. A plant cafeteria, operated on a break-even basis, serves meals at about 60 percent of usual costs. The Employee Association, to which the company does not contribute, provides disability insurance and social and athletic activities. The employee stock ownership program has resulted in employee ownership of about 50 percent of the common stock. Under this program, each employee with more than two years of service may purchase stock in the corporation. The price of these shares is established at book value. Stock purchased through this plan may be held by employees only. Dividends and voting rights are the same as for stock that is owned outside the plan. Approximately 75 percent of the employees own Lincoln stock.

As to executive perquisites, there are none—crowded, austere offices, no executive washrooms or lunchrooms, and no reserved parking spaces. Even the top executives pay for their own meals and eat in the employee cafeteria. On one recent day, Willis arrived at work late due to a breakfast speaking engagement and had to park far away from the factory entrance.

FINANCIAL POLICIES

James F. Lincoln felt strongly that financing for company growth should come from within the company—through initial cash investment by the founders, through retention of earnings, and through stock purchases by those who work in the business. He saw the following advantages of this approach:

1. Ownership of stock by employees strengthens team spirit. "If they are mutually anxious to make it succeed, the future of the company is bright."
2. Ownership of stock provides individual incentive because employees feel that they will benefit from company profitability.
3. "Ownership is educational." Owners-employees "will know how profits are made and lost, how success is won and lost. . . . There are few socialists in the list of stockholders of the nation's industries."
4. "Capital available from within controls expansion." Unwarranted expansion would not occur, Lincoln believed, under his financing plan.
5. "The greatest advantage would be the development of the individual worker. Under the

incentive of ownership, he would become a greater man."

6. "Stock ownership is one of the steps that can be taken that will make the worker feel that there is less of a gulf between him and the boss. . . . Stock ownership will help the worker to recognize his responsibility in the game and the importance of victory.

Until 1980, Lincoln Electric borrowed no money. Even now, the company's liabilities consist mainly of accounts payable and short-term accruals.

The unusual pricing policy at Lincoln is succinctly stated by Willis: "At all times price on the basis of cost and at all times keep pressure on our cost." This policy resulted in the price for the most popular welding electrode then in use going from 16 cents a pound in 1929 to 4.7 cents in 1938. Lincoln's prices increased only one-fifth as fast as the consumer price index from 1934 to about 1970. This resulted in a welding products market in which Lincoln became the undisputed price leader for the products it manufactures. Not even the major Japanese manufacturers, such as Nippon Steel for welding electrodes and Osaka Transformer for welding machines, were able to penetrate this market.

RELATION TO STAKEHOLDERS

Lincoln electric differs from most other companies in the importance it assigns to each of the groups it serves. Willis identifies these groups, in the order of priority ascribed to them, as (1) customers, (2) employees, and (3) stockholders.

Certainly the firm's customers have fared well over the years. Lincoln prices for welding machines and welding electrodes are acknowledged to be the lowest in the marketplace. Quality has consistently been high. The cost of field failures for Lincoln products was recently determined to be a remarkable 0.04 percent of revenues. The Fleetweld

electrodes and SA-200 welders have been the standard in the pipeline and refinery construction industry, where price is hardly a criterion, for decades.

Perhaps best-served of all management constituencies have been the employees. Not the least of their benefits, of course, are the year-end bonuses, which effectively double an already average compensation level.

While stockholders were relegated to third place by James F. Lincoln, they have done very well indeed. Recent dividends have exceeded $11 a share and earnings per share have approached $30. In January 1980, the price of restricted stock, committed to employees, was $117 a share. By 1989, the stated value, at which the company will repurchase the stock if tendered, was $201. Risk associated with Lincoln stock, a major determinant of stock value, is minimal, because of the small amount of debt in the capital structure, because of an extremely stable earnings record, and because of Lincoln's practice of purchasing the restricted stock whenever employees offer it for sale.

CONCLUDING COMMENT

It is easy to believe that the reason for Lincoln's success is the excellent attitude of the employees and their willingness to work harder, faster, and more intelligently than other industrial workers. However, Sabo suggests that appropriate credit be given to Lincoln executives, whom he credits with carrying out the following policies:

1. Management has limited research, development, and manufacturing to a standard product line designed to meet the major needs of the welding industry.
2. New products must be reviewed by manufacturing and all producing costs verified before being approved by management.
3. Purchasing is challenged to not only procure materials at the lowest cost, but also to

work closely with engineering and manufacturing to assure that the latest innovations are implemented.

4. Manufacturing supervision and all personnel are held accountable for reduction of scrap, energy conservation, and maintenance of product quality.
5. Production control, material handling, and methods engineering are closely supervised by top management.
6. Management has made cost reduction a way of life at Lincoln, and definite programs are established in many areas, including traffic and shipping, where tremendous savings can result.
7. Management has established a sales department that is technically trained to reduce customer welding costs. This sales approach and other real customer services have eliminated nonessential frills and resulted in long-term benefits to all concerned.
8. Management has encouraged education, technical publishing, and long-range programs that have resulted in industry growth, thereby assuring market potential for the Lincoln Electric Company.

APPENDIX A: EMPLOYEE INTERVIEWS

During the late summer of 1980, the author conducted numerous interviews with Lincoln employees.

Interview with Roger Lewis, 23-year-old Purdue graduate in mechanical engineering who had been in the Lincoln sales program for 15 months and who was working in the Cleveland sales office at the time of the interview.

Q. How did you get your job at Lincoln?
A. I saw that Lincoln was interviewing on campus at Purdue, and I went by. I came to Cleveland for a plant tour and was offered the job.
Q. Do you know any of the senior executives? Would they know you by name?
A. Yes, I know all of them—Mr. Irrgang, Mr. Willis, Mr. Manross.
Q. Do you think Lincoln salesmen work harder than those in other companies?

A. Yes. I don't think there are many salesmen for other companies who are putting in 50- to 60-hour weeks. Everybody here works harder. You can go out in the plant or you can go upstairs, and there's nobody sitting around.
Q. Do you see any real disadvantage of working at Lincoln?
A. I don't know if it's a disadvantage but Lincoln is a Spartan company, a very thrifty company. I like that. The sales offices are functional, not fancy.
Q. Why do you think Lincoln employees have such high productivity?
A. Piecework has a lot to do with it. Lincoln is smaller than many plants, too. You can stand in one place and see the materials come in one side and the product go out the other. You feel a part of the company. The chance to get ahead is important, too. They have a strict policy of promoting from within, so you know you have a chance. I think in a lot of other places you may not get as fair a shake as you do here. The sales offices are on a smaller scale, too. I like that. I tell someone that we have two people in the Baltimore office, and they say, "You've got to be kidding." It's smaller and more personal. Pay is the most important thing. I have heard that this is the highest-paying factory in the world.

Interview with Joe Trahan, 58-year-old high school graduate, who had been with Lincoln 39 years and who was employed as a working supervisor in the toolroom at the time of the interview.

Q. Roughly what was your pay last year?
A. Over $50,000—salary, bonus, stock dividends.
Q. How much was your bonus?
A. About $23,000.
Q. Have you ever gotten a special award of any kind?
A. Not really.
Q. What have you done with your money?
A. My house is paid for—and my two cars. I also have some bonds and the Lincoln stock.
Q. What do you think of the executives at Lincoln?
A. They're really top notch.
Q. What is the major disadvantage of working at Lincoln Electric?

A. I don't know of any disadvantage at all.

Q. Do you think you produce more than most people in similar jobs with other companies?

A. I do believe that.

Q. Why is that? Why do you believe that?

A. We are on the incentive system. Everything we do, we try to improve to make a better product with a minimum of outlay. We try to improve the bonus.

Q. Would you be just as happy making a little less money and not working quite so hard?

A. I don't think so.

Q. You know that Lincoln productivity is higher than at most other plants. Why is that?

A. Money.

Q. Do you think Lincoln employees would ever join a union?

A. I don't think they would ever consider it.

Q. What is the most important advantage of working at Lincoln?

A. Compensation.

Q. Tell me something about Mr. James Lincoln, who died in 1965.

A. You are talking about Jimmy, Sr. He always strolled through the shop in his shirtsleeves. Big fellow. Always looked distinguished. Gray hair. Friendly sort of guy. I was a member of the Advisory Board one year. He was there each time.

Q. Did he strike you as really caring?

A. I think he always cared for people.

Q. Do you get any sensation of a religious nature from him?

A. No, not really.

Q. And religion is not part of the program now?

A. No.

Q. Do you think Mr. Lincoln was a very intelligent man, or was he just a nice guy?

A. I would say he was pretty well educated. A great talker—always right off the top of his head. He knew what he was talking about all the time.

Q. When were bonuses for beneficial suggestions done away with?

A. About 15 years ago.

Q. Did that hurt very much?

A. I don't think so, because suggestions are still rewarded through the merit rating system.

Q. Is there anything you would like to add?

A. It's a good place to work. The union kind of ties other places down. At other places, electricians only do electrical work, carpenters only do carpenter work. At Lincoln Electric we all pitch in and do whatever needs to be done.

Q. So a major advantage is not having a union?

A. That's right.

QUESTIONS

1. Diagram the formal and informal systems of control at Lincoln from the data in the case.
2. What challenges would another company face if it were to implement the Lincoln control system?

Case 7-3 *The J. Walter Thompson Advertising Agency**

There were plenty of anxious faces among the top officials of JWT Group, Inc., the parent company of the J. Walter Thompson advertising agency, on January 27, 1982. They knew that they had a big problem and the impression was fortified when who should arrive at the midtown Manhattan offices but Ivan Fisher, briefcase in hand.

Mr. Fisher, a tall, combative criminal lawyer, had recently earned a degree of fame as the chief defense counsel in the murder trial of Jack Henry Abbott, the convict–author protégé of Norman Mailer. This time, though, his client was no notorious felon but a member of JWT's own inner circle—dark-haired, vivacious Marie Luisi, age 46, a JWT senior vice president.

At the agency, Mrs. Luisi was known affectionately, and sometimes not so affectionately, as the "Godmother." She had started there at age 17 as a secretary fresh out of a Brooklyn high school and had worked her way up the ranks to one of the most powerful positions on Madison Avenue. Her main job was the placement and purchase of ads, or "spots," on individual television and radio stations throughout the United States, an activity that Thompson, the second largest ad agency, does more than any other firm in the ad business.

"She was a media success story," says Alan Buckman, the sales manager at WBZ-TV, Boston. "If you're in the business, you have heard of Marie Luisi."

A BLOW TO STOCKHOLDERS

The public was not to know of the implications of Mr. Fisher's visit until eight days later, on February 4, when JWT issued the first of several announcements that were to stun the advertising and broadcast worlds. The company said that it had suspended Mrs. Luisi from her duties without pay, citing "improper handling" of the internal records in a unit she headed that was part of her spot buying operations.

Such an announcement rarely heralds good news for a company, but JWT's stockholders did not feel its full effect until February 16, when the company said it would charge $18 million against the JWT's pretax earnings for the period 1978 through September 30, 1981. Two days later, the company said that its 1981 fourth quarter earnings would be reduced by a further charge of $6.5 million before taxes. JWT explained that the revenue of Mrs. Luisi's unit, which had been reported as totaling $29.3 million during the 1978–1981 period, included $24.5 million that consisted of "fictitious entries" in the unit's computer.

---

*Reproduced from *The Wall Street Journal,* March 30, 1982, by permission, and with some deletions made for brevity.

JWT officials haven't accused Mrs. Luisi herself of wrongdoing. But Stephen Salorio, JWT's general counsel, says pointedly, "We wanted to discuss the matter with her. When we had questions that were a bit difficult, she left the office, hired a lawyer, and began talking to us through him."

STARTING SMALL

The bookkeeping scheme—whoever perpetuated it—started small in 1978, when Mrs. Luisi's unit evidently fell a bit short of its revenue and profit targets, JWT officials say. Phony computer entries made it appear that the unit had met its goals, but this, in turn led to the unit's target's being set higher for 1979. When the 1979 targets weren't met, more bogus revenue was booked, leading to a rise in next year's targets—and the cycle continued on a vastly increased scale in 1980 and 1981, according to company officials. JWT executives have said that the money apparently wasn't stolen and that clients were not improperly billed for services rendered. But they have been conducting an intensive investigation into the finances of Mrs. Luisi's unit. So far, they say, this much is certain: the company will never recover most of the $30 million it poured into the unit during the period when it was posting constantly rising performance figures.

ALLEGED CONFLICT OF INTEREST

More painful than the financial damage may well be the injury to JWT's image. Mr. Fisher has maintained, in the advertising trade and elsewhere, that Mrs. Luisi is being blamed for JWT's own sins. His assertion of Mrs. Luisi's innocence—any computer shenanigans, he says, were the fault of a Luisi lieutenant—gets a sympathetic response from her numerous admirers in the industry, who describe her as a shrewd, tough negotiator but also as fair and extremely likeable. In particular, Mr. Fisher's charges that JWT is making Mrs. Luisi a scapegoat for unethical business practices involving, as he puts it, "conflicts of interest up and down the entire system."

JWT officials angrily dismiss Mr. Fisher's charges as "smoke" designed to draw attention away from what they see as the main issue—that revenues in Mrs. Luisi's unit were faked over a period of four years.

However, there seems little doubt that JWT's financial and internal controls left a lot to be desired. Former employees of Mrs. Luisi's unit say that its computerized accounting system was riddled with what appeared to be erroneous entries, so much so that employees had to resort to keeping their own records. "A basic problem," says Herbert H. Eames, Jr., JWT's executive vice president and chief financial officer, "was that accounting was done in the individual operating units of the company rather than centrally." Mr. Eames went to JWT in July 1980 from F. W. Woolworth Co., where he had been controller, and he has spent much of his time reorganizing and centralizing JWT's financial reporting system.

Moreover, former JWT employees tell of long-standing pressure to improve the company's profit performance—pressure that Mrs. Luisi passed down the line to her subordinates, who got to see another part of her personality. Particularly, they remember her sometimes blunt language.

For all the pressures to perform, JWT top management apparently made few efforts to probe into what Mrs. Luisi and her associates were doing. "Marie had been there over 20 years and was a bright light in the company and the industry," says one former JWT middle-level executive. "She was handling an area that management didn't understand very well, and everything seemed to be going smoothly. She was a very forceful presenter. Management placed tremendous pressure on her and other people, but they had no one knowledgeable enough to question her."

The main activity that Mrs. Luisi supervised, buying spots, is straightforward enough and involves the simple payment of cash for commercial advertising time on broadcast stations. But the unit in which the bogus revenue was reported, JWT Syndication, is concerned with the more complex business of barter syndication.

It worked like this: At any one time, JWT would have a collection of TV programs—one-hour musical specials, half-hour adventure series, health shows, cartoons, interview shows—that it had acquired from independent producers or distribution companies and that, in turn, it would swap with local TV stations in exchange for a certain amount of commercial advertising time on broadcast stations. This would build up a "bank" of time. JWT would then sell spots from the bank (usually at discount prices) to such blue-chip clients as Ford, Eastman Kodak, and Burger King.

In theory, everyone is supposed to be happy. The station gets something of value—ready-made programming—for time it might not otherwise sell. The ad agency's client gets its spots at perhaps a 20 percent discount. (This is because a station generally reserves the right to "bump" a barter spot in favor of one paid for cash.) And the agency gets its standard 15 percent commission on each spot used, plus a chance for an extra margin of profit provided it can bring in more revenue from its off-the-shelf programming than it pays in costs of syndication.

But, in practice, critics say, JWT and a number of other ad agencies have tried in recent years to squeeze too big a profit margin for themselves—possibly at the expense of clients—from their barter wheelings and dealings. "There was underlying pressure, never stated outright," says Bill Maddox, the national sales manager at KAMC in Lubbock, Texas, "that if you helped them (JWT) out by taking their syndicated programs, you would

probably get better budgets"—that is, a heftier portion of the JWT client ad schedules for which JWT planned to pay cash.

MRS. LUISI'S OFFER REFUSED

These unspoken promises allegedly were being delivered by Mrs. Luisi's spot buyers in JWT's regional offices around the country. "Marie set the tone," says one former buyer. Mr. Fisher concedes as much, but he also maintains that Mrs. Luisi told top management "time and time again: 'This stinks.'" "She pushed hard," Mr. Fisher notes, "for the creation of a new subsidiary—which she was to head—to market syndicated TV programs for cash, separate from the operations of the spot buying department."

In fact, Mr. Fisher says, the whole flap over Mrs. Luisi and the supposedly phony revenue stems from JWT's belated sensitivity to the conflict-of-interest problem inherent in barter syndication. Most of the disputed computer entries, he contends, represent genuine barter deals, but old ones with time banks that expired partly unused. Mrs. Luisi and her subordinates, Mr. Fisher says, obtained "oral agreements" from station representatives that the time banks would continue to be available past the original expiration dates. Mrs. Luisi could easily prove the authenticity of the computer entries by getting station executives to acknowledge these oral agreements, according to Mr. Fisher, but JWT refused an offer to have her try.

"Why, I guess they suddenly got to be concerned with a practice [using JWT's influence with stations] that they had been content with for years," Mr. Fisher replies.

JWT officials dismiss Mr. Fisher's claims and assert that as part of its investigation it recently received over 200 mailed responses from stations, the majority of which disclosed substantial discrepancies between station records and time bank numbers stored in the JWT Syndication computer.

Moreover, a sampling of opinion at TV stations indicates that virtually all such agreements are routinely put in writing. As one station manager puts it, "Oral agreements are worth exactly what they're printed on."

PROBLEMS IN THE RANKS

In any event, says JWT's general counsel, Mr. Salorio, the issues raised by Mr. Fisher "are very much side issues. The point is that transactions were entered into the computer as if they had been done when in fact they hadn't been done."

Former buyers remember having strange problems with the unit's computer system. Time banks would mysteriously appear in printouts as having been earned, several former buyers recall. "You tried to call and tell New York that you didn't have the time bank," one says, "but it was like fighting City Hall." This former buyer says that her superiors in New York sometimes shrugged off the discrepancies as computer failure and sometimes took the position that the shortfalls could easily be made up in the future with a little extra effort.

Meanwhile, on the basis of the unit's apparent glowing sales record, JWT was pouring millions of dollars into it to acquire new programming to barter with the stations' one-hour musical specials such as "The Osmonds at the Ohio State Fair," a 22-episode half-hour mystery series "Tales of the Unexpected," and a five-times-a-week series of "Cartoon-a-Torials," to name just a few.

This added to the pressure on buyers to do more and more barter deals. But the buyers often couldn't meet the objectives that New York had set. "Some of the shows they had were 'Vic Damone on Campus'—now who wants to see that?" asks Nancy Baldwin, who used to work as a buyer in JWT's San Francisco office and now works for another ad agency. "You would take it to a station manager and he would laugh." Conse-

quently, there was a heavy turnover among the spot buyers, which compounded the unit's troubles and exacerbated the bookkeeping confusion caused by the New York computer's bizarre behavior.

"WHAT IF" GAMES

According to JWT's officials, the computer was being manipulated to indicate that the barter syndication unit was throwing off a high level of revenue. Theoretically, this required that real clients were making use of real time banks, because JWT recognizes revenue at the time the spots go on the air. Some real business was taking place, of course, but, in addition, JWT officials say, fictitious time banks were created, and, in effect, fictitious clients used the fictitious spots. The tricky part was preventing unexplained paperwork—bills, receipts, checks—from being sent to clients of TV stations.

All this was made easier, says JWT's Mr. Eames, because the unit's computer system employed a device called a "test estimate," which involved the use of make-believe client codes. "It was there," he says, "for a totally legitimate purpose: to play 'what-if' games. For example, What rate will a client have to pay for a spot buy in this market? Or, What are the demographics?" By entering hypothetical spot buys into the computer, JWT personnel could get answers to such questions.

"What they did," says Mr. Eames, referring to perpetrators whom he declined to identify, "is simply leave the test estimates in the computer and roll them forward month after month." Through a series of complicated steps, he adds, "they" were able to produce a printout, which was delivered each month to JWT's central accounting office, which counted the test spots as having been drawn from the time bank and used. The printout was used to total the level of revenue and return on investment that Mrs. Luisi's barter syndication unit had earned.

LACK OF PAPERWORK

A real spot for a real client would, of course, set off a flurry of paperwork involving JWT, the station, and the client. The station would send an affidavit that the spot had run, along with a bill—in the case of a barter spot, a "no-charge,"—since the spot had already been "paid for" in advance with programming. Receipt of an affidavit and a "no charge" would trigger JWT's barter syndication unit to send a bill to the client.

If the spot were phony, however, there would be no documentation sent by the station, and hence no bill would be sent to the client. Nor would any checks be sent by JWT to the station, since the barter spots supposedly had been prepaid.

The scheme involved additional entries, Mr. Eames says, to suppress the billing mechanism of the unit's computer.

Mr. Fisher concedes: "Entries were made into the computer misleading people into thinking that the time bank had been utilized, when it hadn't." It was done, he says for two reasons: "Negligence and a desire to conceal poor performance" of the unit. Mr. Fisher puts the blame for it on JWT senior vice president Michael Tremper, age 42, Mrs. Luisi's second in command.

In January, Mr. Tremper agreed with the company that he would cooperate with JWT in straightening out the barter syndication fiasco in exchange for indemnity from any company lawsuits and a guarantee of at least six months' severance pay. "He was an assistant and had nowhere the level of responsibility Luisi had," declares JWT's Mr. Salorio.

Regardless of who is to blame, did Mrs. Luisi know about the misleading computer entries? "Yes," Mr. Fisher replies. Starting when? "I don't want to comment on that," he says. "Mrs. Luisi didn't realize that JWT was taking these recorded entries of time bank use and booking them as revenue. She knew

that cash wasn't going to come in from clients to pay for much of the recorded use, but JWT, motivated by a desire to find revenue, chose to ignore the obvious and booked the revenue anyway," Mr. Fisher asserts.

But if Mrs. Luisi didn't understand what counted as revenue, how was she able to discuss her unit's revenue and profit targets intelligently? "Because they would talk about them (targets) in terms of percentages," Mr. Fisher replies. For example, she would say, "We'll do 20 percent better this year," he says.

JWT officials say Mr. Fisher's whole line of reasoning is ridiculous. "How could someone not know—whether they're working with percentages or anything else—that their targets are being missed by a mile?" demands Mr. Salorio.

"This was our only unit that resorted to dishonest means to meet its objectives," he continues. "We sure wish we had known they were cheating. This was a tower that was going over sooner or later, and in the meantime we were pouring money into the operation."

The bogus revenue was discovered, JWT officials say, as the result of a program begun last May by the new chief financial executive, Mr. Eames, to improve the company's cash flow. Mr. Eames's staff came across some peculiar balances in the barter syndication unit, which led to questions, answers, more questions, and finally, starting in January, a full-scale investigation. "We sort of backed into this," Mr. Eames says.

QUESTION

- Diagnose the problems at JWT that created this fiasco. Your analysis should include consideration of:

  1. The performance measurement system
  2. The reward system
  3. Pressures created by these systems that might lead to unethical behavior.

Case 7-4 Integrated Securities Group and the Drysdale Fiasco*

The Institutional Banking Division of the Chase Manhattan Bank is responsible for the dealings of the Chase Bank with securities firms. The division decided in late 1979 to expand its securities lending business as a part of management's efforts to increase earnings and return on assets. This decision was made in response to a declining pattern of divisional earnings that had resulted from the withdrawal of balances left by small banks at Chase in return for the services provided the banks by the Institutional Banking Division.

To implement this decision, division management formed a separate unit, the Integrated Securities Services Group, and put Peter Demmer, a bank vice president with a background in operations, in charge of the unit. The purpose of the Integrated Securities Services (ISS) unit is to participate in the government securities lending business. In 1982, the new unit employed nine professionals.

THE GOVERNMENT SECURITIES LENDING MARKET

The government securities lending market is currently (1982) a $150-billion-a-day business where securities firms and trading operations of big banks lend and borrow government securities from each other as a source of cash. The lender earns interest above the rate earned on the security lent, and the borrower pays this rate so as to obtain a source of ready cash by selling these securities. At the end of the term of the loan, the borrower repurchases the same government security and returns it to the lender. These agreements are often referred to as repurchase agreements (or repos).

In recent times, trust divisions of large banks have lent government securities that they were holding in trust for customers. Customers of the trust department earn interest on these securities while the bank earns a lending fee from the borrower.

THE RESPONSIBILITY AND REWARD SYSTEM FOR ISS

To reverse a trend of slow growth in earnings, Chase altered its control structure in the mid-1970s and moved to increase decentralization of its operations and to establish more profit centers at the divisional level to motivate improved profitability among its managers. Under its new president, Thomas Labrecque, a decentralization strategy was implemented whereby each division of Chase became a profit center with responsibility for its own marketing, operations, and accounting. These moves have been a key to the significant improvement in Chase's profitability over the last five years. Return on assets has

*This case was prepared based upon published information from *The Wall Street Journal*, June 11, 1982. It is included here by permission.

increased from .24 percent in 1977 to .59 percent in 1981, a relatively high rate of return for banks.

As a by-product of this philosophy of decentralization, and the increased pressure for profit performance, the Institutional Banking Division instituted an incentive plan for the Integrated Securities group whereby bonuses for the six salespersons and three officers were linked to the fees earned by the group, thus providing maximum incentive for high volume. This particular kind of incentive plan had not been used extensively in the bank.

DRYSDALE GOVERNMENT SECURITIES, INC.

Drysdale Government Securities, Inc., was a major borrower of government securities from ISS. Drysdale is a securities firm that was formed in February 1981. It was turned down by many other banks in its borrowings because of its small net worth and its untested ability. Chase itself refused to do busi-

ness with Drysdale in other parts of the bank, including other parts of the Institutionals Banking Division. But the ISS unit chose to deal with Drysdale, and the size of the dealings was staggering, amounting to as much as $4 billion of securities at one time. ISS charged a .25 percent annual fee, based on the dollar value of the transaction, for this service.

In May 1982, Drysdale defaulted on the repayment of $270 million of government securities to ISS, which meant that Chase incurred a loss of approximately $135 million after taxes less what it salvaged from the liquidation of the Drysdale portfolio following its bankruptcy petition. This sum resulted in the elimination of approximately all of one quarter's earnings of the bank.

QUESTION

- What difficulties in the responsibility and reward systems at Chase and in the Institutional Banking Division contributed to the Drysdale fiasco?

8

COMMUNICATIONS AND INTEGRATION

INTRODUCTION

We now consider a number of devices and behavioral attitudes that are fundamental to the work of integration and coordination in complex organizations. They are right at the heart of the design of effective control systems and are at the center of many of the innovations currently taking place in the design of control systems.

A number of factors are responsible for the paradigm shift away from the so-called hierarchial "command and control" organization to the "knowledge-based, value-driven, team-oriented" organization. First is the shift in the nature of work away from manual work to knowledge-based work. Second is the dramatic improvement in information processing. Third is the emphasis on control by values and informal mechanisms rather than formal mechanisms. Fourth is the widespread use of teams rather than formal organization for the accomplishment of critical improvement tasks.

This chapter deals with both the traditional, formal communication and integration mechanisms and with the newer informal communication and integration mechanisms. Many of the changes in the design of control systems relate to the issues raised in this chapter.

COMMUNICATIONS AND INFORMATION PROCESSING

Communications must be adapted to the specific needs of management in order to be effective. Top management must deal with a vast amount of complex information, including market information, competitor status, environmental data, and political communications. They must use this information to set objectives, prepare long-term strategies, and establish policies for the organization.

To make these decisions, top management relies on factual and statistical data, personal contacts, and face-to-face discussions. They usually operate in a highly uncertain environment. As a result, they use informal contacts and discussions to gather as much information as possible. Because of time constraints, they attempt to gather as much information as possible in as little time as possible.

On the other hand, lower-level managers usually do not have to cope with confusing data. They receive objectives and goals from top management and they engage in communications in order to coordinate and integrate their tasks. Communications at this level support the formation of relationships with other interdependent subunits and the coordination of various goal-seeking activities. Uncertainty is much lower at this level, and periodic written reports are usually adequate for carrying out the coordination and integration functions.

Uncertainty may increase at lower levels of management if the technological complexity of the product changes. Then, more personal contacts and discussions are required at this level also.

From these examples, we see that different communication methods are required in different situations in order to convey and gather information that is appropriate for the decision. Draft and Lingel (1984, pp. 191–233) have coined a concept called "richness" to convey the amount of information that is carried in a given communication method. They contend that face-to-face communication has the highest richness, whereas written memos and formal numeric data such as computer output has the lowest level of richness. A "wink," for example, can be a rich communication method. They also contend that as uncertainty and complexity increase, management must use very rich communication methods.

Therefore, when management designs communication mechanisms to improve coordination and integration, they should be sensitive to the level of uncertainty the method is supposed to address. Management must today establish networks of coordinating mechanisms that differ in the level of personal contact and informality depending on their specific situation. Global firms have still additional challenges for establishing appropriate communication methods for coordination and integration. They have to be sensitive to language and cultural differences. This is especially true in personal communications that are high in socially oriented cues or "richness."

Bartlett and Ghoshal (1988) identify three elements that are necessary to achieve successful integration of global firms:

1. A clearly defined and tightly controlled set of operating systems
2. A people-linking process employing such devices as temporary assignments and joint teams
3. Interunit decision forums, particularly subsidiary boards, where views can be exchanged and differences resolved

When developing effective communication and integration devices, management must start by examining the particular level of the firm they are concerned with, the degree of global dispersion with which they must deal, the amount of uncertainty or complexity they are facing, their specific role in the firm, and the specific objectives the communication system must facilitate. Management must also be aware that when one of these key variables changes, the type of coordination required or the emphasis placed upon a given communication method can also change.

We turn now to discuss various communication and integration devices.

FORMAL COMMUNICATION AND INTEGRATION DEVICES

COMMITTEES

Although one decries the inefficiency of committees, and it has been suggested that the surest way to kill an idea is to appoint a committee to study it, committees serve a very useful purpose. They are a means of facilitating communication and coordination and bringing expert opinion to bear upon problems. Individuals with a variety of points of view and special skills can deliberate together, and be assured that all sides of a question are studied. In order for good decisions to be made about important problems, alternative points of view should be encouraged. Although this may promote conflict, ultimately, if managed properly, it can help to promote a consensus. By so doing, the likelihood of not only rational but acceptable action is increased.

Management must be careful not to allow committees to operate in a vague unchartered manner. Each committee should have a clear charter, in the case of a standing committee, or a clear objective or purpose, in the case of ad hoc teams or special focus groups. For example, if a committee is to set policy, it must know in which functional areas the policy is to cover, what business strategy it is to support, and what organizational units are subject to its policy.

Management should not ask lower-level committees to set policies that could have an adverse impact on members of the committee. In this case, the committee may sidestep difficult issues to the detriment of the organization as a whole.

Committee membership is also crucial. Members should know how to operate in a team environment. If they do not, they may have to be trained, or the firm may have to use a facilitator. Interdisciplinary membership is also very important to the successful operation of the committee. Selection of members with an appropriate mix of skills and geographical or organizational affiliation can be critical to the committee's achieving its purpose.

Committees, teams, or other communication groups should periodically report progress and accomplishments toward achieving their purposes to a higher formal authority. The discipline of reporting helps the group to remain focused on their purpose.

Although organizations have a multitude of committees, the most important committees from the point of view of control systems design are those made up of top management. The primary control issues that must be addressed by top management are those associated with strategy and operations. The primary goal of these committees is to manage resource allocation. Inevitably, there are differences of opinion on how resources should be allocated. The major differences often revolve around which resources should be allocated for present operations and which resources should be allocated to advance the future of the business. For example, how much of available resources should be applied to salaries, and how much to capital investment? The latter is often difficult to justify, because salary demands frequently put great pressure on management to use resources now rather than applying them to the future. Although capital expenditures may sometimes be difficult to justify, they may create future growth and they may make the existing staff more productive.

Committee on Strategy

This committee should consist of the top officers and managers of an organization as well as a number of top-level staff people. The committee has the responsibility for long-term planning and interperiod resource allocation. It must provide the guiding light to lead the organization down the path to success. However, its strategy cannot be a rigid, unchanging program. Rather, it must be fluid and responsive to changes both inside and outside the organization. Its function is to determine where the organization is today, and what strengths are available to cope with changes in the environment. It must determine how capital expenditures will affect the future. It can then identify the strategic thrusts needed to move forward.

Operating Management Committee

The second committee is the operating management committee. It might have nearly the same composition as the committee on strategy, but it has a distinctly different function. It is involved in decisions concerning the allocation of resources among operating programs (intraperiod allocations).

Although these two committees form an integral part of the formal communication system, they are only a part of the methods an organization uses to coordinate and integrate its activities.

Planning Meetings

Formal meetings of key managers are held periodically. The purpose is to formalize the results of the planning process, integrate the acitivities of the whole organization, and enhance communication and identification with the plans. The intent of these larger meetings is to knit the organization together and to have each manager make a public commitment of what he or she proposes to achieve during the next period and beyond. These meetings build commitment to plans among managers, allow managers to share problems and ideas, and provide a forum whereby solutions can be advanced.

JOB ROTATION

Job rotation is a tool management has at its disposal to improve coordination, communication, and integration within the organization. Periodic job rotation may seem to be inefficient, because employees have to learn skills of the new position and that has the initial effect of reducing productivity, but it has long-term payoffs of improved motivation and increased knowledge of and commitment to the work of the organization. This is especially true if it is performed at the executive level.

INFORMATION TECHNOLOGY

The explosive growth of information technology provides unprecedented opportunity for more effective and efficient methods of communication and integration both within and across organizations. The number of management levels as well as the number of managers can be sharply cut as a result of advances in communications and coordination brought about by information technology (Drucker, 1988, p. 46). Many management layers simply act as "relays," to convey information from one level of the organization to another. Improvements in information processing have resulted in a reduction of the need for many of these relays. Therefore, information technology is a major driver of the move to organizations with fewer levels.

INFORMAL COMMUNICATION AND INTEGRATION DEVICES

Many of the most dramatic innovations in the area of communication and integration involve the informal control system. Two wide-scale developments involve the use of teams and the reliance on values to improve communications and integration.

PERFORMANCE IMPROVEMENT TEAMS

The shift to knowledge work makes the coordination of specialists a necessary part of the solution to many business problems. Employee improvement teams are small groups formed for the purpose of identifying and solving business problems. Temporary cross-unit teams are formed at all levels of the organization for the purpose of identifying and solving quality, cost, and productivity problems. These teams are chartered by management and are often given extensive training in leadership, visioning, and problem-solving techniques. The teams are then given a problem to solve. When run effectively, teams contribute immensely to motivation, integration, productivity, and quality.

Exhibit 8-1 depicts the relationship between performance improvement teams and the formal organization.

CANDOR, OPENNESS, HONESTY, AND TRUST

Openness, candor, honesty, and trust go a long way toward facilitating the work of organizations. They lead to more participation and cooperation, and result in less

Exhibit 8-1
Relationship of Teams to Formal Organization

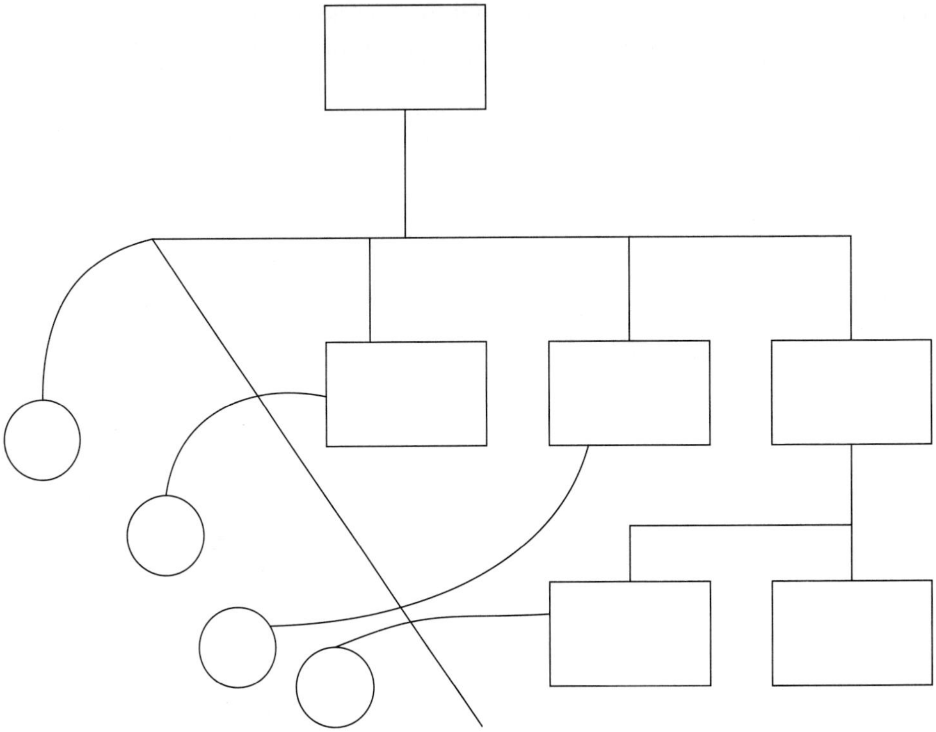

self-protecting behavior, thereby enhancing problem-solving activity and performance (Ouchi, 1981, p. 86). In that way they facilitate communication and coordination and in general make the work of organizations more effective and satisfying. Trust is encouraged by honesty in relationships. It is further enhanced by an open sharing of ideas and problems and by an atmosphere wherein candid evaluations of all problems can take place. These attributes work together to produce a more satisfying and productive organization.

An atmosphere characterized by openness, candor, honesty, and trust is particularly effective in resolving conflict which occurs continuously in organizations.

EXAMPLE OF THE USE OF COMMUNICATION AND INTEGRATION TECHNIQUES: THE DESIGN AND IMPLEMENTATION OF JUST-IN-TIME SYSTEMS

Just-in-Time (JIT) is a system which relies on each input to a process arriving at each process step just in time for processing. JIT relies very extensively upon the communication and integration methods discussed in this chapter; along with other aspects of the MSSM. We use it as an example in this section because it is a widely used system and because it so nicely illustrates the material described in this chapter.

Exhibit 8-2 illustrates JIT as a system of management requiring the integration of all of the functions of an organization.

Casual Connection between Inventory Levels and Quality

Just-in-time proponents believe, and experience confirms, that there is a causal connection between reduction in inventory and improvements in quality. Reducing buffer stocks forces management to improve quality in order to eliminate work stoppages. Improving quality, on the other hand, eliminates the need to hold buffer stocks. This bi-directional process requires continuous communications between engineering and manufacturing.

The reduction in inventory buffers also requires close communication and cooperation with the customer to stay on top of changing customer needs. The absence of inventories and changing customer needs create pressure to reduce setup time and improve response time.

JIT Controls

JIT pushes controls down to the lowest level. Controls emphasize informal methods and self-adjustment. The work cells under JIT are engaged in self-adjustment as information and feedback are received directly from the process so that corrections

Exhibit 8-2
JIT Communications

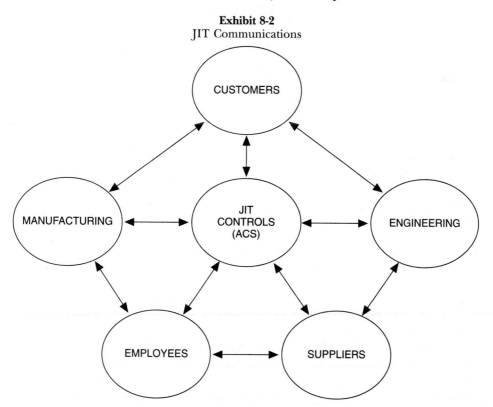

can be made before problems occur in large numbers. Controls are simplified and rely more upon employee involvement, team interaction, and peer pressure. Variance information is often collected for the work cell rather than for the job.

A strong focus of the measurements under JIT is on *time:* time in engineering for design; time for suppliers to fill an order; time in production for manufacturing; time in sales for responding to customers; and time for the service organization to provide customer service. In product development, it is the time from conception of the product to introduction on the market. In production, it is cycle time. In customer service, it is response time. As time is reduced, so is cost.

As a result of the focus on time, a crucial aspect of the JIT controls is the need for real-time communications on material releases, advanced shipment notices, and location and control of an order as it moves from the supplier's loading docks to the manufacturing plant.

Responsibility centers under JIT focus upon the cell. As a result, more elements of cost are traced directly to the cell. Measuring throughput time is central to a JIT process. *Throughput time* is defined as:

$$\text{Throughput time} = \text{processing time} + \text{inspection time} \\ + \text{conveyance time} + \text{waiting time}$$

The basic measure of manufacturing efficiency is

$$\frac{\text{Processing time}}{\text{Throughput time}}$$

In an ideal process, throughput time would equal processing time, and there would be no nonvalue-added time.

JIT SUPPLIERS: INVOLVEMENT

Suppliers are a vital part of the system that makes JIT work smoothly, ensuring quality inputs and timely delivery. If either the timeliness of delivery or the quality of parts is deficient, the entire production process is threatened. To ensure rapid response from suppliers, the firm must qualify a few vendors and design its products in cooperation with suppliers. As a result strong and trusting relationships are needed with a relatively small group of suppliers. Suppliers become an extension of the organization. Care must also be taken to insure sufficient compliance pressure exists to maintain and improve vendor efficiency. Regular communications, including electronic linkages and electronic data exchanges, and performance reviews with suppliers tend to guide future performance and future relationships.

Electronic data exchange with suppliers is appropriate for mail, price lists, quotes, orders, delivery status reports, invoices, inventory information, funds transfer, and shared CAD–CAM graphics. This results in strong interorganizational linkages. These same linkages, however, can become barriers to changing vendors if it becomes necessary.

JIT Customers: Involvement

JIT is a demand pull system; involvement of the customer in the operations of the firm is therefore mandatory. The ability to meet customer needs in a high-quality way brings an increase in customers. Quality products delivered in a timely manner allow the customer to decrease carrying costs. This promotes goodwill.

As retailers increase their use of point of sales (POS) terminals, an opportunity is created to link retail sales directly to the manufacturing process by electronic data exchanges (EDE) thus moving retailing into a JIT philosophy.

JIT: Engineering

Engineers must have close ties to customers, suppliers, and manufacturing. Information from the customer must be the primary input to the research and engineering process, not only to inform engineering about products that are in demand but to inform them about the details of product features that customers are looking for in the products. Current and future suppliers must be involved at the time a new product is being developed to ensure that raw materials will be available for the new product. Manufacturing must be involved in new product development to ensure that the manufacturing process can be developed for the new product.

JIT Employees: Involvement

JIT focuses employee effort within teams and encourages employee involvement. When it works properly, employees feel that they are vital contributors, not cogs in the system. They feel challenged; by contributing to solutions to problems, they gain self-respect. Common topics for performance improvement teams are reduced lead and set-up time, vendor ratings, scrap losses and other areas that in total lead to continuous improvement.

As time becomes crucial, there is a push to integrate computer aided design (CAD) systems with computer aided manufacturing (CAM) systems into an integrated computer integrated manufacturing (CIM) system. Strong integration should also exist between the sales force in the field and the manufacturing organization. Cellular communications technology now allows this. Order terminals, with voice capability, can be placed at remote customer locations to permit customer order placement around the clock.

CASE STUDY: PRODUCTIVITY AND QUALITY IMPROVEMENT AT HUGHES AIRCRAFT USING TEAMS

Improving productivity and quality can follow many courses of actions, but all improvement methods are forms of continuous adaptation. This example illustrates the results that can be achieved through the application of adaptive control systems. The focus of management in this example was upon the acceleration of significant quality and productivity improvements. These improvements were themselves the result of changes in informal control systems, with a particular emphasis upon changes in informal methods of communication and integration.

Management utilized informal processes to communicate improvement values, to establish both management and output goals, and to encourage the use of informal controls.

THE PROGRAM

The AN/BSY-1 Combat and Control System is produced for the Los Angeles-class nuclear submarines used by the U.S. Navy. As a major subcontractor, Hughes Aircraft is responsible for a number of complex subsystems produced by other major contractors and integrated at their facilities.

As a major subcontractor to the AN/BSY-1 program, Division 1E of the Ground Support Group of Hughes Aircraft Company supplies a large suite of command and control electronics. The system, when installed on the Navy vessels, provides a complex stream of data to the operators in charge. The electronic systems consist of multiple electronic control units, modules, appropriate interfaces, and housings. The control units are built from an array of electronic modules that are contained in drawers. Without timely completion of the appropriate mix and quantity of modules, the system cannot be assembled and the total program suffers a delay.

MANAGEMENT CONTROL SYSTEM

The program was organized in a formal matrix structure. A program manager, along with manufacturing, quality, engineering, and material managers all reported to the division manager. Formal program reviews were held, with each functional area reporting on its specific activities. Formal cost information, material requisitions, and quality systems were used to control operational status. Project plans, including cost, schedule, and quality, had been developed early in the program and monitored at program reviews.

The program struggled to meet objectives over a period of months. During this time, each manager had a good rationale for his particular problems. In general, the individual managers felt they were performing their specific functions adequately. A growing amount of internal pressure was being placed upon each functional group at program reviews to meet current goals. Interpersonal communications were sporadic, but largely directed at identifying causes for schedule slippage.

The essential formal control system was in place, but the informal "teamwork" was not being utilized by management to support the program purpose or adapt to current needs. Productivity and quality did not meet management expectations.

After a lengthy and complicated design phase, production was initiated in early 1986; product flow progressed slowly. In July of 1987, module production stopped due to yield and productivity issues. Multiple internal inspections were implemented, and 7700 complex module assemblies were being reviewed at various stages of assembly. The program was in danger of falling behind schedule. These problems were all internal issues. Management was determined to ship excellent hardware on time and on schedule to the customer.

The challenge facing management was to improve quality, increase productivity, and regain schedule integrity concurrently, and quickly. The situation was not unlike many that are found in U.S. industry today. The customer desired strict compliance to contract specification as well as improved timeliness of delivery and increased productivity. The challenge was to dramatically improve all three parameters.

The Improvement Effort

During the following 18-month period, no major capital investments were made, management personnel remained basically stable, customer pressure was intense but steady, and no major changes in the functional scope of the product were initiated. The major change was an extensive effort to improve productivity and quality, which led to the development of appropriate informal adaptive controls.

The improvement effort really began on July 10, 1987. A multidisciplinary ad hoc team chaired by the division manager was formed. Membership consisted of various individuals from all levels of both organizations. The team concept was supported both by the customer and by Hughes management, which had agreed to "work together" to meet the challenge that faced both organizations. As a result, both Hughes and customer were called upon, as needed, to resolve issues immediately. At first, the *purpose* of the improvement team and the program was clearly established. Specifically, the program purpose was restated as "to produce high-quality products at low cost, on time to meet the customer's complete satisfaction." The team was to assist in achieving the purpose. The following operative values were explicitly established in direct support of the purpose:

1 Each individual will respond to meet their customer's needs.
2. Each individual will be responsible for the quality of his or her output.
3. Each individual will support other members.
4. Each individual will continue to improve his or her performance.
5. Ad-hoc process improvement teams will be utilized.
6. If problems arise, individuals will seek expert advice.

Over the next few months, the multidisciplinary team met daily. Individuals began surfacing needs, quality reports were clarified, process plans were clarified, and "skills" training was instituted. A great demand began to be placed upon the "experts" from both companies who were actually able to solve problems regardless of reporting level or subunit assignment.

Management demonstrated support for the establishment of appropriate interpersonal relationships by actually establishing more ad hoc management teams. Management utilized appropriate personnel regardless of organizational structure. By communicating the new dominant values the functioning of networks at all levels was encouraged. Additionally, past values and norms that were perceived as barriers were changed. For example, previously, if an individual raised a concern it was considered "complaining" about problems. The new values encouraged everyone to not only "complain" but to "suggest changes."

At the same time, informal adaptive controls were being strengthened by implementing appropriate informal rewards. Management presented certificates, team awards, and held informal cake and coffee celebrations to reinforce the new culture that supported adaptive controls.

In December 1987, the original division level ad hoc team was disbanded, and local management teams began to track progress. Informal networks were reasonably well established, and changes had been made in the formal quality and production systems.

In September 1988, work cells (clans) were introduced. Workers were cross-training each other as they informally managed the product through their respective areas. Members began searching for new improvement efforts. As an example, Just-in-Time production was introduced into the work flow.

By July 1989 over 1000 improvement suggestions had been received and implemented. The informal control processes were being utilized. The program was able to adapt quickly to schedule changes and to new quality requirements. Changes were also made to the formal control systems.

Additionally, management style had changed to be more participative in support of the team concept. Consensus decision making was used, as management more often assumed a facilitative role.

RESULTS

Within the period from July 1987 to November 1989, quality defects were reduced from 23 defects/module to 0.04 defect/module or only *two-thousandth* of the previous defect total. The program schedule went from six months behind schedule to completely on schedule. The module cycle time decreased from approximately 39 weeks to 5 weeks. Costs were reduced significantly. The local customer representatives stated that the assemblers were extremely enthusiastic and conscientious and that the modules were the best quality that they had ever seen. Exhibits 8-3 and 8-4 summarize these results.

The improvements were the result of management cooperation, increased teamwork, a clear sense of purpose and "hard work." Management did not just implement improvement teams or new techniques such as JIT or SQC, nor did they implement a set of improvement projects. Instead management established the appropriate informal controls by addressing issues in all five subsystems plus defining a clear purpose complete with supporting values and beliefs. They created the appropriate informal control system. The result was tremendous improvement in both quality and productivity. Virtually no changes could be detected in the formal management control system (Exhibit 8-5) except in style and culture.

When the adaptive control framework is used to explain and evaluate the changes, a major improvement in management controls is noted in the informal

Exhibit 8-3
BSY-1 Circuit Card Assembly Measurements
CYCLE TIME REDUCTION

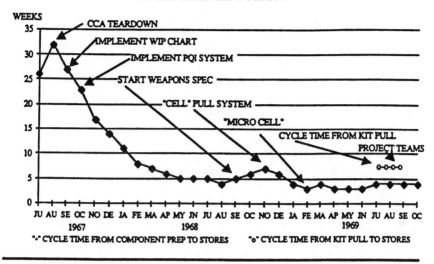

% DEFECTS PER UNIT: CIRCUIT CARD ASSEMBLIES

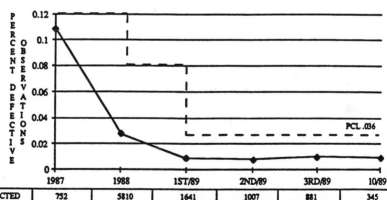

	1987	1988	1ST/89	2ND/89	3RD/89	10/89
QUANTITY INSPECTED	752	5810	1641	1007	881	345
QUANTITY DEFECTS	845	1951	124	77	79	35
NO. OF OBSERVATIONS	772487	7093269	1400123	936060	769668	368687
DEFECTIVE	0.109	0.028	0.009	0.008	0.010	0.009
DEFECTS PER UNIT	1.12	0.34	0.08	0.08	0.09	0.10

controls (Exhibit 8-6). Each of the five subsystems was strengthened, and a clear purpose with appropriate supportive values was described and accepted by the organization.

The organization now is able to adapt to change much more quickly. The organization implemented statistical controls, work cells, team activities, cycle-time reduction techniques, and Just-in-Time production while constantly resetting its goals. Continuous Improvement as a new value is now supported by management

Exhibit 8-4
BSY-1 Circuit Card Assemble Measurements

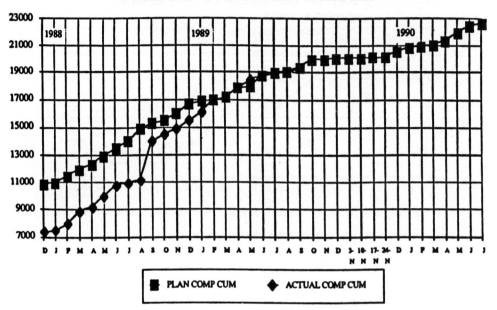

SCHEDULE - OUTPUT PLAN VS ACTUAL

and is increasing the commitment of individual contributors. The use of informal, adaptive controls contributed substantially to the dramatic improvement in performance.

REFERENCES

BARTLETT, CHRISTOPHER, A., and SUMANTRA GHOSHAL, "Organizing for Worldwide Effectiveness: The Transnational Solution," *California Management Review,* Fall 1988.

DAFT, RICHARD L., and ROBERT H. LENGEL, *Research in Organizational Behavior,* Greenwich, Conn.: JAI Press Inc., 1984, Vol. 6, pp. 191–233.

DRUCKER, PETER F., "The Emerging Theory of Manufacturing," *Harvard Business Review,* May–June, 1990, pp. 94–102.

DRUCKER, PETER F., "The Coming of the New Organization," *Harvard Business Review,* January–February, 1990, pp. 45–53.

DUFFIE, DWIGHT, "The Technology of Just-In-

Time," unpublished paper, Claremont Graduate School, Spring 1991.

OUCHI, WILLIAM G., *Theory Z.* New York, Avon Books, 1981.

PIPP, FRANK J., "Management Commitment to Quality: XEROX Corp.," *Quality Progress,* 1983, pp. 12–17.

REIDMAN, FRED A., "Analysis of Just-In-Time Control Methods," unpublished paper, Claremont Graduate School, Fall 1991.

TICHY, NOEL M., and STAFFORD SHERMAN, *Control Your Own Destiny or Someone Else Will,* New York: Currency and Double-day, 1993.

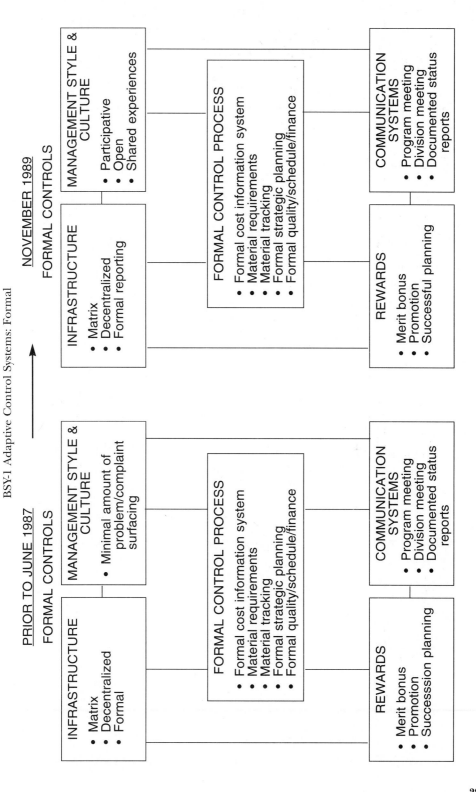

Exhibit 8-5
BSY-1 Adaptive Control Systems: Formal

PRIOR TO JUNE 1987
FORMAL CONTROLS

NOVEMBER 1989
FORMAL CONTROLS

INFRASTRUCTURE
• Matrix
• Decentralized
• Formal

MANAGEMENT STYLE &
CULTURE
• Minimal amount of
  problem/complaint
  surfacing

FORMAL CONTROL PROCESS
• Formal cost information system
• Material requirements
• Material tracking
• Formal strategic planning
• Formal quality/schedule/finance

COMMUNICATION
SYSTEMS
• Program meeting
• Division meeting
• Documented status
  reports

REWARDS
• Merit bonus
• Promotion
• Successsion planning

INFRASTRUCTURE
• Matrix
• Decentralized
• Formal reporting

MANAGEMENT STYLE &
CULTURE
• Participative
• Open
• Shared experiences

FORMAL CONTROL PROCESS
• Formal cost information system
• Material requirements
• Material tracking
• Formal strategic planning
• Formal quality/schedule/finance

COMMUNICATION
SYSTEMS
• Program meeting
• Division meeting
• Documented status
  reports

REWARDS
• Merit bonus
• Promotion
• Successful planning

285

Exhibit 8-6

BSY-1 Adaptive Control Systems: Informal

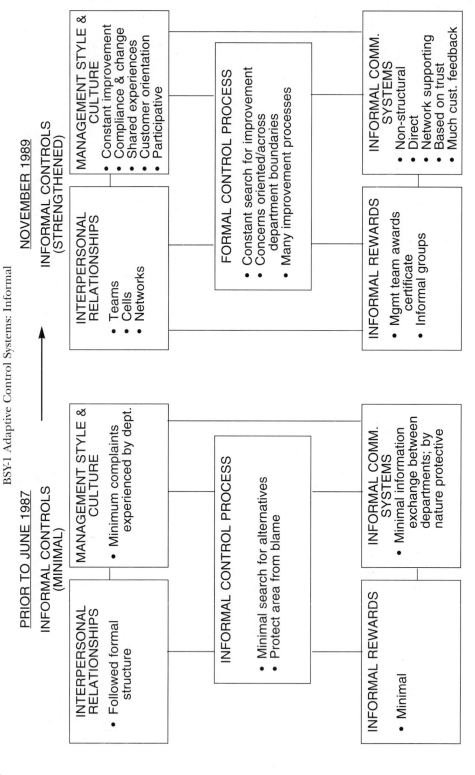

PRIOR TO JUNE 1987

INFORMAL CONTROLS
(MINIMAL)

NOVEMBER 1989

INFORMAL CONTROLS
(STRENGTHENED)

MANAGEMENT STYLE & CULTURE
- Minimum complaints experienced by dept.

INTERPERSONAL RELATIONSHIPS
- Followed formal structure

INFORMAL CONTROL PROCESS
- Minimal search for alternatives
- Protect area from blame

INFORMAL COMM. SYSTEMS
- Minimal information exchange between departments; by nature protective

INFORMAL REWARDS
- Minimal

MANAGEMENT STYLE & CULTURE
- Constant improvement
- Compliance & change
- Shared experiences
- Customer orientation
- Participative

INTERPERSONAL RELATIONSHIPS
- Teams
- Cells
- Networks

FORMAL CONTROL PROCESS
- Constant search for improvement
- Concerns oriented/across department boundaries
- Many improvement processes

INFORMAL COMM. SYSTEMS
- Non-structural
- Direct
- Network supporting
- Based on trust
- Much cust. feedback

INFORMAL REWARDS
- Mgmt team awards certificate
- Informal groups

Case 8-1 VeriFone*

In November 1989, Hatim Tyabji reflected on the developments over the past three years since he took over as President and CEO of VeriFone, a leader in the rapidly emerging Transactions Automation industry. Much had been accomplished during this period to put the company in its commanding marketing position, but the 43-year-old CEO was far from satisfied.

With the active involvement of this top management team (see Exhibit 8-7), Hatim envisioned VeriFone "... to become recognized as the creator *and* leader of the 'Fourth Wave of Computers'; placing computers into the hands of people who don't know they are using computers." The following passage was excerpted from a published corporate document. "Wherever transactions can be automated, there exist potential applications and markets for VeriFone products. With the proper economies of scale and cost structures, the company's base technology has virtually unlimited applicability. This is the essence of the Fourth Wave of Computing and its global applications."

In its Centennial Edition (June 23, 1989), *The Wall Street Journal* selected VeriFone as one of 56 "Corporate Stars of the Future . . . for their potential to bring vision and innovation to the marketplace of tomorrow." Also *Business Week* numbered VeriFone as one of 25 "High-Tech Startups to Watch"

in its special June 1989 issue, "Innovation in America."

VeriFone's transaction systems could be found in most retail stores which accepted customer payment via credit cards. The Point-of-Sale (POS) "terminal" served as the vehicle by which transactions could be delivered, whether the transaction was a simple credit card authorization or an actual transfer of funds from the customer's bank account to the retailer's bank account. This "fourth wave computer" could be programmed to run many different transaction applications. In addition to the "CPU," a transaction system would include peripherals (printer, pin pad, bar code reader). The appropriate telecommunication capability was built into the CPU; in fact the ability to be certified on as many as 50 different networks was a major "perimeter of defense," largely responsible for the company's success.

VeriFone's original core market had been financial institutions, which provided electronic payment processing services to retailers. A bank would buy (in bulk) VeriFone's transaction systems, including the application software specific to its needs and then sell these systems to each of its retail accounts. As of 1989, 78 of the 100 largest banks in the U.S. were VeriFone customers. Transaction systems were also sold to oil and gas companies, and VeriFone now also domi-

*This case has been abridged and reproduced by permission from a case prepared by Wendy Wanderman, under the direction of Professor Vijay Sathe, in collaboration with Dean Sidney Harris, all of the Claremont Graduate School, as a basis for class discussion rather than to illustrate effective or ineffective handling of an administrative situation. Copyright 1990 by Vijay Sathe.

Exhibit 8-7
Backgrounds of Corporate Officers

William Melton—Founder and chairman of the Board, 47 years old. Bachelor of Arts (psychology—Westmar College), Master of Science (Asian Studies and Chinese Language and Philosophy—University of Hawaii). Founded the company in 1981. Prior to VeriFone, he founded Real Share Inc.

Hatim Tyabji—President, Chief Executive Officer, and Director, 43 years old. Bachelor of Science (Poona, India), Master of Science (SUNY), MBA (Syracuse), AMP (Stanford). Joined the company in his present position in November 1986. Prior experience included 13 years in management positions at Sperry Corporation. In his last position at Sperry, he was responsible for all research and development, product engineering, and manufacturing for commercial information systems.

F. Thomas Aden—Vice President and General Manager, International, 39 years old. Bachelor of Science (MIT). Joined the company in present position in October 1987. Prior experience included extensive experience in both domestic and international business, including sales management and product management positions with NBI, a major international supplier of office automation products.

Thomas Hubbs—Vice President, Finance, Chief Financial Officer, 45 years old. Bachelor of Science (business administration—Lehigh), MBA (Santa Clara). Joined VeriFone in present position January 1987. Prior experience included senior finance positions with several high-technology corporations.

Gregory Lewis—Vice President and General Manager, North America, 44 years old. Joined VeriFone in October 1984 to organize a sales function, promoted to current position in October 1987. Prior experience included 13 years in customer service, product management, sales and operations at National Data Corporation.

Ashok Narasimhan—Vice President, Market and Product Development, 41 years old. Bachelor of Science in physics (Madras, India), MBA (Indian Inst. of Mgmt.). Joined the company in December 1988 in present position. Prior experience included 18 years of financial and general management experience in the computer and automotive industries, and founder and president of Wipro Systems Limited, India's largest producer of commercial software.

Nason (Tuck) Newport—Vice President, New Business Development, 40 years old. Bachelor of Arts (Occidental), Master of Science (management—Stanford). Joined the company in November 1984, and headed the marketing effort before assuming his current position at the end of 1988. Prior experience in the areas of marketing, publishing, computer software development and politics, included six years as editor and publisher of the *Hawaii Observer*.

James Palmer—Vice President, Operations, 53 years old. Bachelor of Science (EE—Drexel). Joined the company in mid-1987, and headed both manufacturing and product development before assuming current position in December 1988. Prior experience included 25 years of technical, manufacturing and engineering management positions at Sperry Corporation.

William Pape—Vice President, Information Systems and Controls, Chief Information Officer, 37 years old. Bachelor of Arts (psychology—Stanford), Master of Arts (psychology & communications—Hawaii). Joined VeriFone in

1983 and was responsible for product development, software development, product marketing, prior to assuming his current duties in May 1988.
Clive Taylor—Vice President, Worldwide Marketing, 49 years old. Joined VeriFone in 1988 and is responsible for product management, product marketing, systems marketing, training and education, technical publications and corporate communications. Prior experience included 25 years of international marketing, sales, support and general management with Sperry Corporation and Unisys Corporation.

nated this market segment. Regardless of the distribution chain, the end users were the retail clerks and gas station attendants, people who were usually not computer literate.

GENESIS

VeriFone was founded in Honolulu, Hawaii in 1981 by William (Bill) Melton, an entrepreneur who had previously founded Real Share, Inc., a network service provided for TeleCheck check guarantee franchises throughout the United States and Puerto Rico. His original intention for VeriFone was to design and market a low cost, intelligent terminal system for the retail end of the credit card and check authorization pipeline.

Based upon his previous experience in Real Share and his educational background in psychology, Bill wanted to create VeriFone's culture in accordance with his belief that "a corporation's culture should reflect its type of product." Since VeriFone's transaction devices "forward deploy the intelligence from the mainframe to the point of transaction," a compatible culture would further deploy the corporate intelligence to offices located close to the customer. This decentralized structure continued to the present time and was a fundamental part of the Company's operations (modus operandi).

Bill felt that the technical specialist often knew more than his non-technical manager, but just as often the specialist's communication skills were inversely propor-

tional to his or her technical abilities. These specialists were generally more comfortable "talking" to a computer screen than having a face to face (or phone) conversation with another employee or with a customer. Bill saw the manager's role as that of a translator between the customer and the specialist; he or she could translate the customer's needs to the specialist who would then be able to provide the technical solution to meet those needs. In order to motivate the specialists, Bill determined that he must encourage trust and respect by aiding and supplementing their lack of communication skills and providing "ownership" over projects. Since the technical specialist comprised a large proportion of VeriFone employees, Bill was determined to develop an open, consultative culture. One early employee stated that there were literally no rules and policies at VeriFone because, "Bill had this habitual distaste for bureaucracy and structure."

In order to accommodate the dispersed nature of the organization and the communication skills (or lack thereof) of the technical specialists, electronic mail (E-mail) was installed at the company's formation and had continued to serve as the main communications tool.

THE EARLY YEARS (1981–1984)

The company's first product was designed to perform only one function—obtain credit card authorization. It had limited intelligence, functionality and flexibility. The first systems, which were shipped in 1982, had a DOA (Dead on Arrival) rate of 50%! Fortunately, the competition's products were just as limited in functionality, and cost twice as much. The market for transaction devices looked promising, but was still in its infancy and had not yet attracted many entrants. These two factors allowed VeriFone to "hobble along" while it tried to resolve some of its design problems.

A major change in the design philosophy occurred in 1983 when William R. Pape joined the organization. Will had just returned to Hawaii following his successful formation of a software company which had produced Spellguard, the first spelling checker for microcomputers. VeriFone's terminal was one of the few high-tech projects in Honolulu at that time; that, combined with Bill's charisma, attracted a small group of bright entrepreneurial engineers and programmers to try and make the product viable. In 1983, Will described VeriFone as a "loose confederation of people working towards a goal."

Will's strong programming background and previous work with microcomputers convinced him that the intelligent and versatile attributes of the computer should be introduced into VeriFone's product. Prior to this time, the entire functionality of the terminal was "hard wired"; even small modifications entailed significant engineering and manufacturing changes. (This type of device was referred to as a dedicated controller.) The mass marketing of the microprocessor and memory chips (ROMs and RAMs) in the early 1980s dramatically altered the architecture of many products, including VeriFone terminals. The philosophy of general purpose computers could be applied to the design of these terminals—build a general purpose microcomputer and then develop specific applications (credit card authorization, electronic funds transfer, inventory man-

agement, etc.) as software programs to run on these computers. The ability to add to or modify existing functionality, as well as to fix "bugs," would then require a software rather than a hardware change. This significant shift in design philosophy proved to be one major factor in VeriFone's eventual success.

In an effort to provide quicker response to customer needs and in keeping with Bill Melton's philosophy of forward deployment of intelligence, the application programmers were separated from the operating system designers and moved into the sales offices, enabling them to work directly with their customers on specific applications. This also ensured that a specific need of one customer did not alter the "general purpose" nature of the unit's operating system, but rather would be solved within that customer's application software. Subsequent development of proprietary transaction automation software languages enabled even faster turnaround time on new and/or modified applications; these language tools were also available to customers who wished to develop their own software.

Another key contributor during the company's early years was Gregory (Greg) A. Lewis, currently Vice President and General Manager, North American Division. After working informally with Bill for several months, Greg formally joined VeriFone in early 1985, bringing with him 18 years of marketing and sales experience in the credit card and financial transaction industries. Greg had long been convinced of the viability of transaction automation devices; his particular dream was to have the ability to ". . . down-line load the application software to terminals at the customer site, via telephone lines."

At this point in time, software changes could only be made by physical interaction with each terminal; either by replacing a memory chip or reprogramming the unit at the customer site. With banks (or service providers) having thousands of retail customer locations, physical interaction was obviously undesirable, and a major impediment to market growth. Greg was convinced that VeriFone had the ability to achieve his dream: "I really believed from what Will had told me that the software was going to be available to change the industry. The platform was already there." (Downline loading ability was accomplished in early 1986.)

When Greg first joined VeriFone, it was one million dollars in debt, had negative cash flow, had borrowed fifty thousand dollars against a VISA order for two hundred terminals and was several months behind in that delivery. Terminals were being manufactured (on credit) in Taiwan, but there was no money to send a VeriFone engineer to Taiwan to oversee the production. With the critical need to obtain orders, the company attended at ATM (Automated Teller Machine) show in New Orleans; this visibility, combined with Greg's extensive industry contacts, served as the catalyst for new orders. In just the last 60 days of 1984, close to one million dollars worth of orders were booked. Revenues that year were $3 million.

NEW PRODUCTS AND VENTURE CAPITAL

During 1985 VeriFone introduced their "Junior Terminal"; this smaller, cheaper and "smarter" device helped VeriFone in its quest for greater marketshare. Omron, a Japanese company, and GTE were then the industry leaders. While at the end of 1984 VeriFone was either #12 or #13 in a field of 13 competitors, by the end of 1986 it had become the industry leader.

In early 1985, desperate for cash, Bill Melton realized that he had to seek financing with venture capitalists (VCs). He compared this to: "... taking that first drug needle; there is no turning back." Bill was grateful that he had been able to run the company without outside financing for its first four years. Because the company was "born and bred" in Hawaii, it had developed an informal, familiar culture very much in tune with the Hawaiian culture. Without interference from VCs and other outside investors, Bill was able to mold VeriFone in accordance with his own "social experimentation concepts." Bill felt that if the company had been started in the Silicon Valley, there would have been considerable pressure for VeriFone to fit the prescribed "formulas" of a typical high-tech, Silicon Valley company with respect to geographical dispersion, number of employees, travel budgets, etc.

The first external funds were provided by a British investor, John Porter, in early 1985. John was introduced to VeriFone by Tuck Newport (Exhibit 8-7), a fellow Sloan Program alumnus. John took an equity position and active managerial interest in VeriFone, and assumed some of Bill Melton's management responsibilities (Co-Chairman of the Board, and direct responsibilities for marketing and finance. Bill continued running development and manufacturing). John also used his extensive contacts to pursue larger and more long-term financing. He was able to persuade several blue chip Venture Capital firms to invest in late 1985— Kleiner, Perkins, Caufield and Byer, Technology Venture Investors, Sigma Associates, and Morganthaler.

To the experienced VCs (as well as Bill Melton, John Porter, and the key company staff), it was apparent that a successful product alone would not guarantee a successful company; thinly managed VeriFone required structured leadership and business controls to guide it toward a dominant position in the Transaction Automation industry. Thus began a search for a leader who could move VeriFone from a start-up firm (which had never made a profit) to a successful, profitable company. The investments in late 1985 were made with the understanding that a search for a

President and CEO would be the first order of business. The investors also insisted that VeriFone move its headquarters from Hawaii to the San Francisco area in order to be closer to the Venture Capitalists, and the majority of its customers. Exhibit 8-8 presents financial information from 1982 to 1989.

HATIM TYABJI TAKES CHARGE

The CEO search began in early 1986. Several specialized search firms were asked to present viable candidates, with the proven ability to take a profitless start-up company (approximately 30 million dollars in revenue) and grow it to a profitable giant. Bill Melton recalled that he felt like a young bachelor knowing that it is the right time to marry, being presented with a list of suitable brides (many with excellent credentials), but none generating an emotional reaction. Nevertheless, Bill was determined to choose a "good bride" for his company.

While Bill and VeriFone's Board of Directors were looking for its CEO, TVI (one of VeriFone's investors), which also held equity positions in several other companies, was trying to interest Hatim Tyabji, a high-ranking executive at Sperry Corporation, to take a leadership position at one of these firms. Hatim's name had not appeared on VeriFone's list of "potential brides" because

the nature of the two businesses (VeriFone and Sperry) were completely different (small, low-cost terminals vs. large, expensive mainframe computers; decentralized, loose management vs. centralized, bureaucratic management; etc.) One day in mid-1986, both Bill Melton and Hatim Tyabji were visiting the TVI offices. Bill (with the Board's approval) had just made his "bridal" selection; Hatim was there to discuss his future involvement with TVI. Bill and Hatim were introduced by Burton McMurtry, TVI's Managing Partner. Casual conversation between the two turned into more serious discussions; it was like "love at first sight," Bill recalled. He told Burt McMurtry to cancel the just agreed-upon "bride." Bill was determined that Hatim would become the next President and CEO of VeriFone. Although Hatim had an excellent position with Sperry, and was promoted again after the merger with Burroughs, he felt the bite of the "entrepreneurial bug" and wanted to take on the challenge. He joined VeriFone in November 1986.

DIGGING IN

Hatim's background in product development, manufacturing, finance and general management proved to be invaluable as VeriFone's financial weaknesses and lack of systems and controls became apparent. Although, by the

Exhibit 8-8
Summary Financial Data: 1982–1989

| | Actuals—$ millions | | | | | | | Est. |
	1982	1983	1984	1985	1986	1987	1988	1989
Revenue	0.3	1.6	3.3	15.3	31.2	44.5	73.2	119.6
Operating Income	(0.1)	0.0	(0.8)	1.4	0.5	1.2	10.5	17.0
Net Income	(0.1)	0.0	(1.1)	0.9	0.1	0.1	6.4	10.0
Headcount	12	25	41	127	265	307	402	745
ROE	NA	NA	NA	19.5%	0.6%	0.7%	12.2%	16.6%
Total Assets				7.6	23.0	32.6	70.7	93.6

end of 1986, VeriFone's products had gained a reputation for quality and reliability, with almost 200,000 systems in the financial/retail marketplace, the financial picture was bleak. The Company's plan projected profit before tax (PBT) and revenue for 1986 to be 3 million dollars and 30 million dollars respectively. Detailed analysis revealed an actual loss of 2 million dollars, due to overvalued, obsolete inventory and a host of other financial control losses. One of the investors, who had to inject more capital into the company said that VeriFone suffered in those years from "profitless prosperity."

Hatim took action to correct the lack of accountability and controls. The Board had a CFO search underway since Fall 1986. Tom Hubbs was hired in January 1987 as Vice President of Finance and CFO. He had extensive start-up experience, and began to assemble a financial team, including a controller, systems specialist and planner. James (Jim) A. Palmer, Vice President of Operations, joined VeriFone in February 1987. Jim had been associated with Hatim during his 25 years of manufacturing management experience at Sperry Corporation. His most recent assignment, as Executive V.P., Manufacturing, Japan, provided VeriFone with the critically important understanding of how to manage a manufacturing operation in the Far East.

Despite the strengths of both Tom and Jim, revenues and profits in the first half of 1987 proved to be abysmal (2.7 million dollar loss by July). Hatim believed that there were two main reasons for this disastrous performance: mismatched and underutilized strengths of the management team; and fratricidal warfare among the organizational groups. The newly hired (by Hatim) Vice President of Sales was not a team player; the Engineering and Manufacturing groups were not "in sync" with each other; there was virtually no Product Marketing. Hatim was also

being tested and challenged by the troops: "On top of all the in-fighting we were rapidly running out of money." Hatim felt that 1987 was the lowest point in his professional life. If ever there was a time for him to use his management and leadership skills, it was now!

One of Hatim's strongest allies was, in fact, Bill Melton. Contrary to what many entrepreneurs found very hard to do ("allow their baby to be raised by another") Bill was determined that Hatim's leadership position should be unchallenged. Hatim could then use Bill's considerable talents in the product and customer parts of the business. In mid-1987, Bill moved from Hawaii to one of the sales offices located in the Washington, D.C. area. "If I had stayed in Honolulu, many VeriFone employees and customers might have assumed that the corporate headquarters hadn't really moved. If I had moved to the new San Francisco headquarters, many would have interpreted this as a sign that I was still in charge. I purposely moved to the Washington area to demonstrate my original concept of "forward deployment of intelligence" and at the same time, to make clear to all concerned that Hatim was the one and only CEO of VeriFone." In addition, the VeriFone organization chart at the time clearly showed Bill Melton (Chairman) reporting to Hatim Tyabji (CEO).

HATIM'S SECOND YEAR AS CEO

During his second year at the helm, Hatim orchestrated four major events, two involving personnel and functional reorganizations and two involving outside financing. In October, 1987, he proposed his first major organization, which included: transferring Will Pape from Vice President of Software Development in Hawaii to Vice President of Product Marketing at headquarters in Redwood City; firing the recently hired Vice President of

Sales and promoting Greg Lewis into that position; placing product development (both hardware and software) onto Jim Palmer's broad shoulders (he still had manufacturing) and also moving Jim from Taiwan to the Honolulu development center. Placing engineering and manufacturing under the same vice president was intended to produce a more coordinated and cooperative effort. The Board of Directors had reservations about the reorganization ("Was Hatim just playing musical chairs?"); however, they went along and the changes were implemented. The end of 1987 did, in fact, show a slight profit.

With a pressing need to obtain more financing, Hatim prepared to meet with some VCs in New York during mid-October, 1987. The latest financing, done in August 1986, had been at $1.10 per share. VeriFone's board told Hatim that, given the poor financial profile of the company, he would be lucky to get $1.20, but Hatim wanted $1.75 per share. His presentation to the financiers, scheduled for October 20, one day after Black Monday, was postponed to mid-November. Hatim recalled the details of the all-day meeting:

> I presented for six hours, during which time they asked a lot of tough questions. Their decision to do the deal came down to the Management Team's credibility; we were able to obtain a sliding scale deal, based on future results, something unusual in the venture capitalist world. We raised 6.9 million dollars; the number of shares, and therefore, the price per share would depend on the 1988 PBT (profits before taxes). The price would be $1.10 for PBT less than 5 million, 1.45 for 7 million PBT, and 1.85 for PBT greater than 9 million. We actually ended up with 10.3 million PBT. We started moving forward in the 4th quarter of 1987 and have never looked back since!

The Management Team's credibility with the Board of Directors naturally soared. Asked what he thought was responsible for the turnaround starting in late 1987, Hatim said: "I had my team in place, my guys responded, and the Board was behind me."

The second reorganization, which was finalized in May 1988, was the direct result of Hatim's extreme frustration at the inability of the financial group to report revenue and profit actuals in a timely manner. Hatim could not get the actual numbers for almost two weeks following any month end. Will Pape described the situation: "It's like trying to navigate a ship from the back instead of from up front; how can you see where you're going?" At a staff meeting in mid-April 1988, Will proposed the development of an information system which could extract the daily projected sales, invoices, etc. from the present accounting system and then report and predict revenue and PBT estimates on a *daily* basis. Tom Hubbs, CFO, (who had line responsibility over MIS), strongly supported Will's proposal and further suggested that due to Will's strong background in software and information science, the MIS function should be transferred to Will. By the end of May, Hatim had promoted Will to Vice President of Information Systems and Control and CIO, with line responsibility over MIS, Human Resources and Administration. According to Hatim: "This was the single best move I've made. I organize around people; I recognize their strengths, and then restructure and capitalize on those strengths." REVWatch and PBT Flash began in July, 1988 and proved to be accurate within 2 to 3%.

The reorganized management team combined with the 6.9 million dollar financing was contributing towards continued profitability in 1988. Although Hatim was not actively pursuing more financing, he was then presented with an unusual opportunity. One of VeriFone's major oil customers wanted to have a service contract on all of the terminals located at its gas stations, but VeriFone did not have a nationwide field service organization. At their customer's suggestion, VeriFone approached DataCard, with an eye to potentially subcontracting the field service work to them. In the course of these discussions, DataCard (who also owned Datatrol—one of VeriFone's competitors), became interested in forming an alliance with VeriFone. In June, 1988, a deal was negotiated whereby VeriFone subcontracted its service business to DataCard and DataCard agreed that VeriFone would develop and manufacture the terminals to be sold by its Datatrol division.

DataCard was also interested in obtaining an equity position in VeriFone. Based on the first six months PBT, Hatim was confident that his previous financing would come in at $1.85 per share; furthermore the company did not need cash per se. At a negotiating meeting in Minneapolis in late June, 1988, DataCard, a privately held company, and its owners, agreed to purchase 6 million shares at $5 per share. The transaction was consummated in mid-August.

REASSIGNMENTS AND NEW PLAYERS

During 1988, Hatim continued to restructure his management team in order to use each person's talents most effectively. Clive Taylor, an associate from Sperry Corporation, with over 25 years of international management experience joined VeriFone in mid-1988, helped administer the joint venture agreement with DataCard, and became Vice President of Worldwide Marketing in January 1989. At the end of 1988, Ashok Narasimhan joined VeriFone as Vice President of Market and Product Development, thus relieving Jim Palmer of his "double duty." Ashok had 18 years of financial and management experience, including the founding and developing of Wipro, the second largest computer company in India. (See Exhibit 8-9)

Nineteen eighty-eight was the first truly profitable year for VeriFone; it ended with a 10 million dollar profit on 73 million dollars of revenue. Hatim felt that the management restructuring which he began in 1987 had been successfully accomplished by the end of 1988.

DEVELOPING A NEW VISION

Bill Melton's motto, "Twice the functionality at half the cost" of the early days was transformed to, "low cost, high value," i.e., holding costs and prices down while bringing quality up, so as to deliver the highest value to the customer. Since this was the strategy that many Japanese firms used with great success, and because VeriFone had already surpassed its chief rival, Omron (an independent billion dollar Japanese conglomerate), Hatim was fond of saying, "We have out-Japanesed the Japanese!"

Earlier in the fall of 1987, while in the midst of addressing tactical issues, Hatim had decided that it was also necessary to develop long-range strategic plans. The point-of-sale financial market was still growing rapidly, but that growth would slow in 1990-91. At the time, VeriFone held a 55% market share. What new markets would be compatible with VeriFone's products and expertise? Where could small, powerful, low-cost, user-friendly terminals with embedded telecommunications be used? These terminals were not only small, but their memories were designed to retain information (non-volatile) even when power was removed. This battery-backed feature would be useful in markets where portability was important.

The informal structure of the management team (Hatim, Bill and the vice presidents) encouraged each team member to candidly state his views on the subject under discussion. After full discussion, one member would synthesize the various opinions and try to achieve consensus. Bill Melton used to lead these discussions in the early days, and Tuck Newport later assumed the responsibility for putting this down on paper.

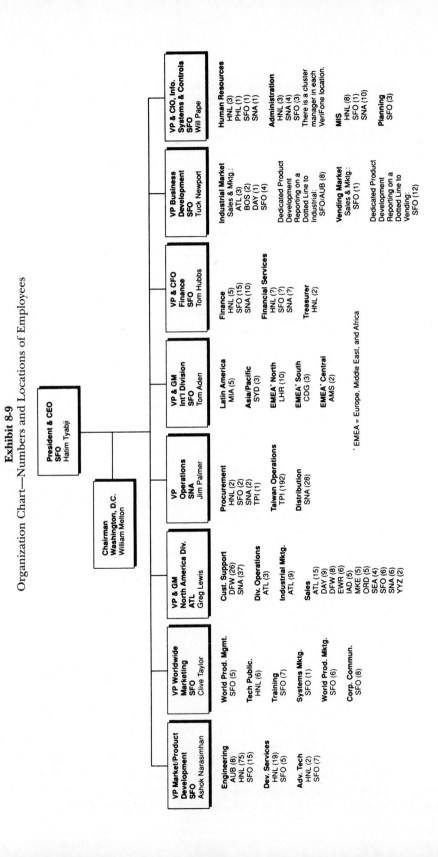

Exhibit 8-9
Organization Chart—Numbers and Locations of Employees

President & CEO
SFO
Hatim Tyabji

Chairman
Washington, D.C.
William Melton

VP Market/Product Development
SFO
Ashok Narasimhan

Engineering
AUB (8)
HNL (75)
SFO (15)

Dev. Services
HNL (19)
SFO (5)

Adv. Tech
HNL (2)
SFO (7)

VP Worldwide Marketing
SFO
Clive Taylor

World Prod. Mgmt.
SFO (5)

Tech Public.
HNL (6)

Training
SFO (7)

Systems Mktg.
SFO (1)

World Prod. Mktg.
SFO (6)

Corp. Commun.
SFO (8)

VP & GM North America Div.
ATL
Greg Lewis

Cust. Support
DFW (26)
SNA (37)

Div. Operations
ATL (3)

Industrial Mktg.
ATL (9)

Sales
ATL (15)
DAY (9)
DFW (8)
EWR (6)
IAD (5)
MKE (5)
ORD (5)
SEA (4)
SFO (6)
SNA (6)
YYZ (2)

VP Operations
SNA
Jim Palmer

Procurement
HNL (2)
SFO (2)
SNA (2)
TPI (1)

Taiwan Operations
TPI (192)

Distribution
SNA (28)

VP & GM Int'l Division
SFO
Tom Aden

Latin America
MIA (5)

Asia/Pacific
SYD (3)

EMEA˙ North
LHR (10)

EMEA˙ South
CDG (3)

EMEA˙ Central
AMS (2)

˙ EMEA = Europe, Middle East, and Africa

VP & CFO Finance
SFO
Tom Hubbs

Finance
HNL (5)
SFO (15)
SNA (10)

Financial Services
HNL (?)
SFO (?)
SNA (?)

Treasurer
HNL (2)

VP Business Development
SFO
Tuck Newport

Industrial Market
Sales & Mktg.:
ATL (3)
BOS (2)
DAY (1)
SFO (4)

Dedicated Product
Development
Reporting on a
Dotted Line to
Industrial:
SFO/AUB (8)

Vending Market
Sales & Mktg.:
SFO (1)

Dedicated Product
Development
Reporting on a
Dotted Line to
Vending:
SFO (12)

VP & CIO, Info. Systems & Controls
SFO
Will Pape

Human Resources
HNL (3)
PHL (1)
SFO (1)
SNA (1)

Administration
HNL (3)
SNA (4)
SFO (3)

There is a cluster
manager in each
VeriFone location.

MIS
HNL (8)
SFO (1)
SNA (10)

Planning
SFO (3)

It was at one such meeting, in December 1987, that the vision of "Fourth Wave of Computing" was created. VeriFone's terminals were, in fact, microcomputers; they were presently being used by thousands of (often) computer-illiterate retail clerks. This product line could be modified (mostly through software) to take any type of transaction, automate it and deliver it, via phone lines, dedicated networks, or other telecommunications methods, to any front-end processor or large mainframe computer. The transaction could just as easily be hourly employee attendance records as electronic funds transfer (EFT). According to Hatim: "We are tying to create mass markets, where none now exist, by revolutionizing price points."

NEW STARS ON THE HORIZON

The Electronic Benefits Transfer (EBT) market was very similar to VeriFone's credit card bank (bank and oil company) transaction (core) market. Washington State had automated their unemployment benefits distribution process with the use of VeriFone terminals. When an individual became eligible for unemployment benefits, he or she would be issued a plastic "unemployment payment" card, with identification information embedded within a magnetic strip (similar to most credit cards). In order to receive his or her unemployment payment, the individual would go to a participating supermarket, where the VeriFone systems would be located at the customer service counter. These systems communicated (via telephone lines) to a mainframe computer which housed all pertinent unemployment information. If the individual was eligible for a payment, the amount would be transmitted back to the VeriFone terminal and a credit slip would automatically be printed on VeriFone's printer. The individual would then be able to cash in this credit slip at the same supermar-

ket. (The supermarkets were quite happy to participate because usually the unemployed individual used part of his or her benefit to buy groceries.) In 1989, New Jersey was looking at such a system; the competitive bidders (VeriFone's customers) were the large system integrators (EDS, etc.) and *all* were specifying VeriFone's terminal systems for the user-end of the system.

The potential size of the EBT market was enormous; welfare benefits could be distributed in the same manner as unemployment benefits. (Ramsy County, Minnesota already had such a system.) The verification and transfer of medical benefits was another large and lucrative market for VeriFone systems. Private or government medical plans could issue each eligible subscriber a plastic "benefit card" and install a VeriFone system in each participating pharmacy or doctor's office. Assignment of benefits would be automatically transacted at the time of the visit, eliminating the need for expensive and time consuming paperwork.

During 1988, VeriFone also began to experiment in two new markets which bore less resemblance to the core market than EBT. Tuck Newport, who had joined VeriFone in 1984, became the Vice President of New Business Development to oversee initiatives in the industrial and vending markets. The industrial market included data collection applications, such as time and attendance reporting and inventory management. The vending market was concerned with unattended POS (point-of-sale) transactions using prepaid cards in vending machine purchases as well as turning parking lots and movie ticket sales into unattended POS transactions by accepting prepaid cards.

The International Division, which was formed in October 1987 when F. Thomas (Tom) Aden joined VeriFone, introduced VeriFone's transactional systems into the financial communities in Europe, Asia, and Latin America. Although the basic process of transaction automation delivery and credit card verification was similar, the telecommunications protocols and hardware safety regulations varied from one country to another. Therefore, VeriFone was developing a modular design concept, including modular telcom boards, so that products could be tailored to each country's standards without any hardware modifications. The market potential was enormous and International's revenue growth reflected that potential.

PROBLEMS OF SUCCESS

Hatim, and his management team of eight vice presidents, started 1989 with a goal of consolidating VeriFone's position as the creator and leader of "The Fourth Wave." However, they were now faced with the types of business issues which many successful companies, especially rapidly growing ones, had to deal with.

STRESS

PBT Flash, the daily "state of the company," was sent via E-mail to all involved home office and field personnel. Since this "memo" gave a daily picture of how well the current month's projections were being met, all employees clearly knew when actual revenues fell behind forecasts. Each month-end at the Costa Mesa Distribution Center was particularly stressful, because extra efforts were made to ship every possible order to meet the monthly forecasts. What was unusual about this "end-of-the-month crunch," commonly found in companies trying to meet their monthly targets, was the absence of game playing to meet the numbers. For example, in August 1989, a major shipment was held up because no signed purchase order had been received from the customer, only verbal authorization. Other companies trying to make the monthly numbers might have shipped the order in antici-

pation of receiving it (the purchase order), or on the customer's assurance that it was forthcoming.

Although Taiwan and Costa Mesa both reported to Jim Palmer, providing smooth product flow and communication, the Costa Mesa employees had no control of when products bulk-shipped by sea from Taiwan would reach the distribution center in Costa Mesa. Although there was four weeks of finished goods inventory on hand in Costa Mesa, a typhoon in Asia could disrupt product flow, and exacerbate the end-of-the-month crunch. In that case, the stress on the Costa Mesa employees was enormous.

E-MAIL

Electronic mail (E-mail) had been a major form of communication at VeriFone since the company was founded in 1981. Due to the vastly dispersed work force, it had always been essential to have a communication tool which eliminated time and distance considerations. The first culture shock for most new employees was the fact that VeriFone did not have secretaries and circulated no hard copy memos. Each employee had either a terminal or a PC and an E-mail account. Few companies had such a policy, which represented a major capital investment. With new employee orientation consisting of a series of computerized tutorials, a very strong message was sent to each new employee about the importance of computers and E-mail. Everyone was expected to manage his or her own E-mail messages with no exceptions. Each account was by first name, last initial (i.e., HATIM__T); even the phone book was alphabetized by first name, with the three-letter designation of the home-base airport in parentheses! Thus, everyone from janitor to CEO was on a first name basis, and each employee's travel schedule (flights, hotels, etc.) were accessible to other employees via E-mail.

The familial culture was thus reinforced by the E-mail system.

Most managers were comfortable with E-mail and used it extensively. Although unaccustomed to this operating mode when he joined VeriFone, Hatim had no difficulty fitting into this part of VeriFone's culture and learned to type up to 45 words per minute within the first year. As a matter of fact, he had become one of E-mail's strongest proponents. A few managers expressed concern about the amount of time they each spent on E-mail. One manager asked: "Why send an E-mail message to someone at my own facility? Isn't it easier just to walk down the hall and get an answer?"

Since E-mail was the major communication tool, employees who did not stay on top of their mail found themselves outside the loop of decision making. Operational decisions were often put in the form of a default message, for example: "Should I first run report X or report Y? If I don't hear from you within two hours, I'll run report X." Most of the mid-level managers estimated receiving almost 60 messages per day, while the top executives dealt with over one hundred daily messages. As the company grew from 300 employees in 1987 to 400 in 1988 to over 650 employees in 1989, the amount of E-mail traffic also grew. Would this communication mode continue to be effective as the company grew even larger?

All employees were encouraged to purchase PCs and modems for their homes, and an allowance of up to $3,000 per employee was given for this purpose. Most employees appreciated this as a terrific company benefit, but there was some concern that this tied them to the company on a 24-hour basis. As one senior executive stated: "I think a man's home is his castle, a place for privacy. E-mail can tie you to the company 24 hours per day; you are never free."

E-mail also proved to be a very fast and convenient method for requisition approvals.

Tom Hubbs described one such incident: "A capital expenditure request went from the engineering originator in Redwood City, to the Chief Engineer in Hawaii, to the Vice President for Market and Product Development in Taiwan, to myself in Costa Mesa, to Hatim somewhere on the East Coast. The entire approval process was completed within an eight-hour day; this probably would have taken much longer if formal requisition paperwork had to follow the same path." Hatim added:

> We accept electronic signature approvals, something most companies have not come to grips with, not only for capital expenditures but also for personal requisitions, salary increases, and stock options. I approved the 4.5 million dollar new facility investment in southern Taiwan by pressing a button on my PC. Other mangers also have approval levels, which can be pulled up on the computer and reviewed on-line in case there is any question about what the limit for a particular managerial level is. We can do electronic signature approvals because we have a different mind-set. We do not accept truisms; we challenge conventional wisdom. As another example, we do not have personal secretaries. I have insisted on not having one ever since I first came to VeriFone because I believe in leadership by example—do as I do, not as I say: "Please get one, Hatim," my staff often kid me; they can't very well ask for a personal secretary when I don't have one!

TRAVEL

Although E-mail bridged the time and distance gap for internal memoranda and certain operational decisions, it did not, and could not, take the place of face-to-face meetings. Hatim felt strongly that there was no substitute for face-to-face contact and communication, and this was one of the reasons why he and his management team traveled constantly, to visit customers, facilities, or one another. The management team held regular two-day meetings at various VeriFone offices each quarter; the meeting calendar was established a year in advance in order to avoid any scheduling conflicts, and enabled people to plan their time. The schedule, once established, was religiously adhered to.

VeriFone's internal travel office had a direct computer hook-up to an airline's computer reservation system. Each employee's travel schedule was available to all other employees via computer terminal, so that he or she could always be contacted.

COMPANY CULTURE

While the E-mail system, the constant travel, the first-name informality, and the absence of secretaries and paper were the most visible manifestations of the VeriFone culture, Hatim had personally crafted a "VeriFone Philosophy" statement to clearly communicate the beliefs and practices which he deeply felt were fundamental to the company's success. According to Hatim: "We are trying to create and perpetuate a familiar and *honest* environment; a distinctly different place to work. The VeriFone philosophy is our guiding document. Its principles are practiced."

However, due to the company's youth, percentage of newcomers, and the widely dispersed operations, it was not clear to what extent VeriFone managers and employees had understood and "bought into" this statement of philosophy. According to one senior manager: "Hatim is clearly passionate about this philosophy, and so are a few of the managers on his team, but some elements of the philosophy (e.g., 'dedicated to meeting our customers' needs') are clearly more evident than are others (e.g., 'accountability and teamwork'). Exhibit 8-10 contains VeriFone's philosophy statement.

Exhibit 8-10
VeriFone's Philosophy Statement

VeriFone Philosophy

Philosophy:
> A system of motivating concepts or principles; the system of values by which one lives.

We are committed to:

- Building an excellent company.
- Meeting the needs of our customers.
- Recognizing the importance of each individual.
- Promoting a team spirit.
- Focusing accountability in everything we do.
- Fostering open communications.
- Strengthening international ties.
- Living and working ethically.

Commitment:
> A pledge to do a specific act or thing; the state of being bound emotionally or intellectually to a course of action.

We Are Committed to Excellence

Excellence:
> The state, quality or condition of excelling; superiority.

As a way of life, excellence is reflected in how we design our products, provide service to our customers and behave toward each other.

At VeriFone, "Quality By Design" means:

- We design excellence into our products, projects and processes.
- We do things right the first time, conforming to the specifications of our products or services.
- We correct the root causes of problems.
- We analyze the processes by which we carry out our jobs, constantly seeking ways to improve.
- We pay close attention to detail.
- We take pride in the products and services we provide.

Providing excellent products and services leads to credibility in the marketplace. VeriFone's growth and success will be a natural by-product of the respect and loyalty we earn from our customers.

We Are Dedicated to Meeting Our Customers' Needs

Customer:
One who buys goods or services.

Our motto is:

- We shall satisfy our customer requirements with on-time delivery of defect-free systems and services.
- Our products are tools for helping customers solve business problems. We provide complete system solutions by working closely with our customers to satisfy their specific requirements. We balance cost, quality and innovation to maintain fair and competitive prices.
- Service is an essential element of product quality. We are committed to providing the best customer service in the industry. We go the extra mile to bring solutions to our customers.
- Excellence begins at home. We provide the same level of support to both internal and external customers.

Each Individual in Our Organization is Important

Importance:
Having great value, significance or consequence.

An excellent company needs excellent employees—people who bring productivity, enthusiasm, and excellence to their jobs.

To draw on the strengths of our employees, we provide a challenging and exciting environment that nurtures individual growth. To encourage outstanding performance, we:

- Help identify opportunities for personal growth.
- Encourage continuing education.
- Offer competitive compensation.
- Reward, retain and promote those individuals who contribute to the achievement of our corporate goals.

Management is dedicated to providing equal opportunities for employment, development and advancement to all qualified employees. VeriFone employees earn recognition through high productivity and a commitment to excellence in all things they do.

We Are an International Company

International:
 Extending across the boundaries of two or more nations.

VeriFone is not just another multinational company. Our decentralized operations and extensive communications network link customers and employees worldwide; we are truly an international company.

At VeriFone, an international perspective means:

- We design our products to satisfy international requirements.
- We decentralize our development, manufacturing, sales and service centers.
- We endeavor to understand and adapt to cultural norms wherever we operate.
- We encourage open dialogue between employees, regardless of geographical distribution.
- We consider the impact a decision will have on employees in all of our offices.

We Live and Work Ethically

Ethics:
 The accepted principles of right and wrong that govern the conduct of an individual in relationship with others.

The goal of any business is to make a sound profit. Our dedication to quality will help us realize that goal. We do not compromise our integrity in the name of profits.

VeriFone is changing the way people do business. Because we truly have an impact on people's lives, we must set a positive example of leadership and credibility in all things we do.

- We fulfill our commitments.
- We treat others with dignity and respect.
- We are honest and fair in all transactions with our customers, suppliers, shareholders and each other.
- We obey the laws of the countries in which we operate.

It is our duty to make a positive contribution to the communities in which we operate. Excellence in everything we do will ratify VeriFone's world citizenship.

We Work as a Team in a Spirit of Trust and Cooperation

Teamwork:
 Cooperative effort by group members to achieve a common goal.

Teamwork is synergistic—together we can do more than we could as individuals working alone. Teamwork creates a productive environment where ideas and initiatives flourish.

At VeriFone, we respect each other's abilities and contributions to the team. That respect is the cornerstone of trust and cooperation. We depend on each other to get the job done. We assist and support each other; we share the rewards together.

We Focus Accountability for Every Assignment

Accountable:
 Answerable; capable of being explained.

VeriFone is a "Buck Stops Here" company.

By defining responsibility and accountability for each product or task, we:

- Provide a clear local point for both internal and external customers to channel questions or requests for support.
- Eliminate duplication of effort.
- Ensure that all employees are working toward a common goal.

The people who know best how the job should be done are the ones doing it. We involve employees directly in the management of their own areas of responsibility.

We Believe in Open Communication

Communication:
The exchange of thoughts, messages or information.

An open communications policy at VeriFone means:

- We promote informal and open dialogue throughout the company.
- We respect the right to be heard. Every employee is encouraged to offer suggestions, express concerns and voice opinions.
- We communicate responsibly. We direct our comments to the appropriate decision makers and focus on solving problems.
- We answer questions honestly and as fully as possible. We admit when we cannot discuss sensitive or confidential issues rather than give vague or misleading responses.

VeriFone's electronic mail (E-mail) system provides both vertical and horizontal communication links—internationally. Through E-mail, any employee may reach the entire company instantaneously (anonymously, if desired).

The use of electronic tools models the larger application of our products in the marketplace. We invite our customers to communicate with us through E-mail.

TAKING THE COMPANY PUBLIC

By Fall 1989, both revenues and profits were continuing to climb; VeriFone projected over 17% pretax profit on 120 million dollars of revenue in 1989. It was anticipated that an initial public offering (IPO) would begin by the mid-1990 time frame. There was some concern about how the proposed IPO would impact both VeriFone employees as well as potential investors.

As was common with IPOs, concern about its impact on employees was expressed at several levels within the company. What would happen to the organization if those with large equity stakes sold their stock and left VeriFone? If this small group decided to stay, would they steer the company differently in order to protect their investments?

What about the natural resentments felt by those employees who had either small or no equity? Given the pressure felt by almost all in the product chain, several people wondered why they should be placed under so much stress when they would get no direct benefits from a public sale.

Hatim had worked hard to move Veri-Fone to a dominant market position. Was it possible that, with all of that hard work, he had neglected to nurture and develop successor talent? He felt that he had an excellent management team, but was there "CEO material" in that group? Hatim knew that he was a very strong and highly visible leader: "Some of my staff are confident enough to frankly state their opinions, but some of the others are not so outspoken. What if I got hit by the proverbial truck tomorrow? I feel strongly that a CEO should be responsible for developing leadership talent around him, so that he can be replaceable. This was my one failing at Sperry. I sure as heck don't want a repeat of that here."

For his part, Bill Melton had withdrawn from day-to-day management responsibilities. He had, in fact, recently announced to the VeriFone senior management team that he would henceforth play the role of an "outside" board member, rather than an "inside" member. He now wanted to see how his "baby" would fare under public scrutiny that awaited the company.

LOOKING AHEAD

Looking beyond the planned IPO, Hatim and his management team were taking steps to position the company for global competitive advantage in the 1990s. A 9-million-dollar capital investment had already been made to upgrade the company's information systems, develop its CAD capability, and improve its manufacturing productivity. In addition, a new 4.5-million-dollar manufacturing facility had been opened in southern Taiwan, and ten million dollars in cash had been invested in the ICOT acquisition. Specific tactical position steps now being planned included the following:

1. Continue to build upon VeriFone's dominant position in the domestic financial marketplace.
2. Open VeriFone offices in London, Paris, and The Hague by the end of 1989. (The market conditions in Europe were viewed as similar to what the U.S. market was in 1985, and VeriFone was hoping to create and capitalize on the expected explosive growth.)
3. Continue installations in the financial marketplace throughout the rest of the world, where the growth prospects were seen as promising. (VeriFone units had already been installed in 40 countries.)

4. Create a fully staffed business unit in 1990 to attack the multi-lane retail, supermarket and fast food markets. (ICOT, acquired by VeriFone in 1989, had a presence in these market segments.)
5. Make major inroads into the international petroleum market. (Shell, Mobil, Exxon, BP, Amoco, Unocal, Citgo, and Total were already customers in the domestic market, and major orders from Shell, Canada were received in 1989.)
6. Invest in the embryonic EBT market. Because of the dependence on state and local government and the long sales cycles, patience would be needed to succeed in this market.
7. Plan for slower penetration into the Industrial marketplace. (Results for 1988 were on plan, but 1989 results were disappointing. With continued investments in 1989 and 1990, major payoff was now expected in 1991.)
8. Plan for payoff in the Vending marketplace during the second half of 1991, with continued investments in 1989 and 1990.

In the manufacturing and development areas, several tactical positioning actions were also being planned:

1. Establish a factory in the EEC in the first quarter of 1991.
2. Open a second distribution center on the east coast of the U.S. in late 1990.
3. Open customer support/repair depot in India for Southeast Asia/Australia in mid-1991.
4. Maintain and grow the product development centers in Hawaii, Auburn and Taipei, with common CAD tools and networking for instantaneous communication.
5. Establish a fully-functioning development center in Bangalore, India by early 1990.

Other tactical positioning steps already in motion included the following:

1. Continue to emphasize *integrated system solutions* (including the telecommunication interface) in contrast to the competition' "box oriented" approach, which require the customer to be the integrator of the system.

2. Perpetuate the "lean and mean" headquarter staff (VeriFone's productivity in terms of revenues per employee was among the highest in the industry).

3. Continue to vertically integrate the firm by developing and manufacturing peripheral products presently being purchased. (The printer, which was at one time supplied by Epson, was already being manufactured in-house, but Epson still supplied the internal assembly. Such components could be developed and manufactured by VeriFone; other components, such as ICs, could be *designed* internally and farmed out for manufacture.) The rationale for vertical integration was not only to reduce dependence on external suppliers, but also to take advantage of VeriFone's superior development and manufacturing capability. (For example, the margins on printers increased from 32% when supplied by Epson, to 47% currently, to a projected 55%.)

4. Verticalize the sales organization into true lines of businesses in order to achieve the proper focus on the different market segments. (Hatim stated: "This reorganization will not occur until the end of November 1989, when I know that we have met our year-end numbers. I'll announce the changes in early December; then everyone will be ready and energized for the new year.")

These specific positioning steps and a strong balance sheet and cash position gave Hatim and his team some confidence that VeriFone could indeed accomplish its mission. Equally important was the loyalty that both VeriFone's customers and employees had exhibited. For example, strong support was displayed by customers at the Advisory Council meeting in Denver on October 18, 1989, and all VeriFone managers based in San Francisco scheduled to attend that meeting had done so despite the great difficulties in getting out of the area the morning after the San Francisco earthquake. Employee loyalty was also demonstrated by VeriFone's employee turnover statistics. A 1987 turnover rate of 26% (compared to 23% and 17% respectively in the computer and telecommunications industries), dropped to 13.5% in 1988 and was 11% in 1989 (compared to industry turnover rates that remained unchanged from 1987 levels).

With the benefit of all these assets, there was a good chance that VeriFone could realize its dream of achieving world dominance in the industry it was trying to create, and thus reach its objective of becoming the recognized creator and leader of the "Fourth Wave." Hatim wondered what else he could do, or do differently, to ensure this success.

QUESTION

- Analyze the informal control systems at VeriFone, using the MSSM diagram. Are they mutually supportive? Are they adaptive? What aspects of their communication and integration methods seem innovative and usable by other companies?

Case 8-2 The Role of the Chiefs*

The medical director of a large Health Maintenance Organization (HMO) was searching for ways to increase the effectiveness of his chiefs of service. Chiefs are physicians who also serve as the head of their departments such as the Chief of Surgery, Radiology, Internal Medicine, and so on.

Heretofore, chiefs had been selected primarily because they were excellent clinicians and had the support of their departments. Unfortunately, this system had not always worked well. The chiefs of service did not have well-defined rules; consequently, each had carved out his own territory, sometimes at the expense of other departments. Some had fully staffed departments that functioned well. Others were struggling. Some were very good at strategic planning and using resources. Others had little concept of planning. Not surprisingly, the medical director had concluded that both a better selection process and a training program were required.

The medical director decided that he could either bring in a group of consultants to design a training program or involve the chiefs in the process of working out their own programs. Past experience had taught him that staff participation in the design of a program always resulted in much more effective implementation; therefore, he chose the latter approach.

A preliminary questionnaire was sent out to the chiefs asking them to designate those qualities that they thought it important for a chief of service to have. These qualities were then collated under such titles as personal characteristics, communication skills, planning skills, and the structure to be understood and managed. The lists were made available to the chiefs for reference. They were then invited to a weekend retreat where they could collaborate on the definition of their role and begin the planning process for the selection and orientation of new chiefs.

Two sessions were held each morning. The first session, which was conducted in small study groups was devoted to listing the functional areas of responsibility. In the second session the whole group discussed these areas and came up with a ranking of the top five. The next morning, each of these five functional areas of responsibility—physician recruitment, physician retention, quality of care, quality of service, and envisioning and planning—was assigned to a small group for further study. Each area was then analyzed for the outcomes desired, the skills and resources needed, and the recommended methods of assessment. After they were presented to the whole group, it became possible to reach a consensus. The medical director was then ready to proceed with the

*This case is adapted by permission from Lyal D. Asay and Joseph A. Maciariello, *Executive Leadership in Health Care*, pp. 10-71, by Jassey-Bass Inc., publishers.

design of a system for selecting new chiefs of service, as well as the development of an orientation program for all chiefs.

QUESTION

- What characteristics of good committee/team performance are illustrated by this case?

9

STRATEGIC PLANNING AND PROGRAMMING

INTRODUCTION TO PART III:
OVERVIEW OF THE MANAGEMENT CONTROL PROCESS

Part III of this text is concerned with identifying and explaining the various elements of the management control process. The entire management control process is concerned with *decision making*. Within it, objectives and goals are set for each organization unit, measures are defined that are indicative of performance toward objectives and goals, standards are established for these performance measures, decisions are made as to what constitutes significant deviations from standard, corrective action is decided upon and implemented, and decisions are followed up to determine whether the corrective action that was applied actually brought about the desired change in performance.

Information flows and information tools[1] must be designed to support this management control process. It is customary to refer to decisions, information flows, and information tools as the control process, although there is an important distinction among them. The information systems, once set, are altered infrequently. They are, therefore, more like structural elements of the MCS, whereas the control process is repetitive decision making and goes on continuously within the organization. Another way to think about these connections is to envision the information flows as links between the control structure and the control process. That is, the information systems are tailored to the organization structure to facilitate the control process.

This text follows the tradition established in the control systems literature and merges the discussion of information flows with the discussion of the control process. Accordingly, we consider five elements of the control process.

The control process supports both strategic and operational decision making. The elements of the control process include environmental scanning and strategic planning, programming and capital budgeting, operational budgeting, accounting and measurement, and reporting and analysis.

These elements are often formal activities in large, diversified, multi-divisional organizations and more informal in organizations of smaller size and reduced complexity. Moreover, the sequencing of relationships among these elements is not always the same from one organization to another. The need for formal systems arises from the enormous complexity and detail that must be managed in the modern organization.

The accompanying chart in Exhibit 9-1 illustrates many of the elements of the process in chronological order and in the context of the various management levels of a complex, multidivision organization. We shall use this chart to provide an overview of the various formal planning processes and their interrelationships with each other and with the organization structure. This chart merely represents a typical formal control process, and while it may be adapted to many organizations, it does not represent the actual process found in any organization. Moreover, even if an elaborate formal process is in place, many decisions may be made in more informal processes.

The typical formal process involves four levels of responsibility centers in an organization: corporate, divisional, product, and functional. Top management is generally responsible for activities leading to the formulation of goals and objectives, strategies, policies for the acquisition of resources, and the allocation of resources among the company's "portfolio" of businesses.

Divisional management, on the other hand, is involved in the formulation of divisional goals and objectives and establishing strategies, policies, and plans to achieve these goals. Product and functional managements have the responsibility to contribute to these plans and to develop a set of feasible action programs that would implement divisional policies from which the division, in light of its goals, would select a subset to be executed.

The process itself is initiated with the collection and evaluation of economic, political, technological, and social data with regard to the domestic and international environment. The formal process of scanning the environment precedes the planning process and takes place at corporate and divisional (that is, business unit) levels. The corporate scanning process is concerned with forecasting variables and deriving uniform planning assumptions for the divisions. The divisions, on the other hand, attempt to forecast more detailed environmental variables affecting specific markets and products. Each responsibility center scans its own environment, yet the lower the level in the organization, the more a unit is influenced by the internal organizational environment as opposed to the environment of the outside world. Therefore, the lower the level, the more internal and informal is the environmental scanning.

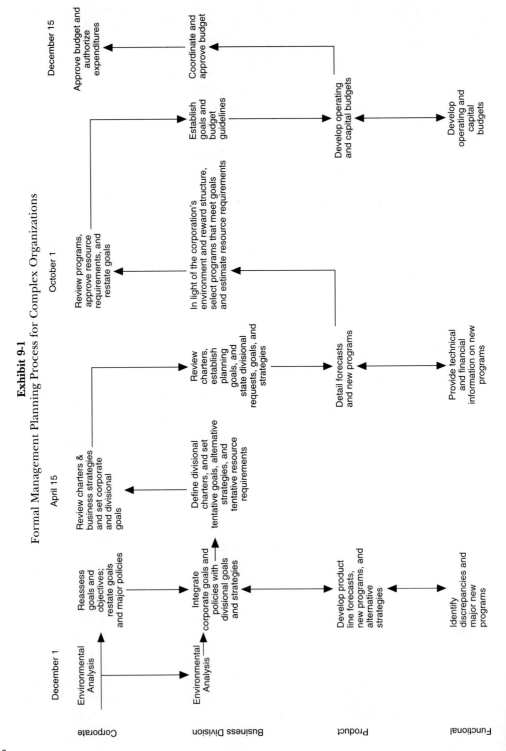

Exhibit 9-1

Formal Management Planning Process for Complex Organizations

Next, corporate managers proceed to revise and restate corporate objectives, goals, strategies, and policies. In parallel, divisions begin the programming and capital budgeting process. This involves forecasting sales for existing product lines and investigating new products and programs, along with resource implications. The programming process involves divisional, product, and functional management and may take place, at least initially, without contact or comment from corporate management. Once preliminary forecasts are made by divisions and objectives and goals are tentatively set at the corporate level, a preliminary negotiation process takes place between corporate and divisional management. Out of this comes tentative agreements on divisional and corporate goals and objectives. This negotiation process takes place in March or April of the planning year.

As a result of this negotiation process, divisions may redefine their charters and market strategy, and may estimate their resource requirements in a tentative manner. At the end of this step, divisions have set firm objectives, and goals, strategies, and policies and are then in a position to request detailed product line forecasts and detailed program proposals, including technical and economic analyses of new products and programs. These detailed forecasts become the basis of negotiation within the division, from which comes a more refined estimate of new programs and capital resource requirements. These are reviewed and approved or modified at the corporate level by October 1.

Once programs and resource requirements are approved, the corporation restates the divisional goals and objectives and calls for the operating, capital, and cash budgets. The divisions prepare budget guidelines, and the product and functional groups submit detailed budget requests. These budgets are coordinated and approved at the divisional level and are then submitted to corporate headquarters by December 15 for approval.

The budget is put into effect on January 1, at which time the control process turns to measurement, reporting and analysis, and corrective action with regard to the budgets and plans implemented on January 1 and to environmental scanning, planning, and programming with regard to the budgets and plans that will be put into effect in the subsequent year.

We conclude this brief overview of the formal control process by reviewing each of the elements that will be taken up in succession in this part of the text.

ELEMENTS OF THE CONTROL PROCESS

Environmental Analysis

Environmental analysis is the process of scanning the external environment and drawing up certain assumptions for the environment over the planning horizon. It is performed primarily by the corporate staff and by top management. During this process, forecasts are made of macroeconomic variables, such as GNP, interest rates, consumer expenditures, and inflation rates; political and social trends; of markets that the company is either currently serving or wishes to serve; and of company-relevant technologies. These forecasts are used to provide a uniform basis of planning for the company and its divisions.

Strategic Planning

Environmental analysis is closely related to strategic planning. Strategic planning is concerned with the analysis and choice of appropriate responses in light of environmental threats and opportunities as well as internal strengths and weaknesses.

The strategic planning process provides the framework within which an organization works out its goals and objectives and makes major resource allocation decisions. Decisions made in this process are intended to guide future growth and capital expenditures over the next two to ten years.

Strategic planning is based upon the mission statement of the organization. The mission statement should contain the following three elements: (1) the opportunities that the organization can exploit or the needs that it can meet, (2) the strengths of the organization, and (3) what members of the organization believe in (Drucker, 1989). It should state what the organization intends to do. The strategic plan then amplifies and seeks to implement that mission.

Strategic planning includes planning for each of the major businesses of the organization as well as the overall mix of businesses. Business planning normally goes on at two or more levels of the organization. At the corporate level, it is concerned with balancing the returns and risks of a portfolio of company businesses. In this process, the corporation attempts to answer such questions as:

1. Which business units should be included within the portfolio of businesses to provide a "balanced" portfolio or to achieve other risk–return goals?
2. How much of our total capital should be allocated to each business?
3. Which business units should be expanded, contracted, or eliminated?

Business units themselves engage in business planning when they repeat these questions for their portfolio of products.

Programming and Capital Budgeting

With the backdrop of goals, objectives, and strategies, divisions, product, and functional organizations engage in forecasting expected performance of existing products and programs together with new products and programs. Top management is involved to the extent that a planning gap exists, that is, a discrepancy between corporate goals and objectives and projected results from divisional operations. If a planning gap exists, management may distribute a portion of this gap to each division. The division in turn addresses the gap in the programming process.

Budgeting

Operating budgets are used for planning and coordinating overall activities of an organization as well as for each of its responsibility centers. The end output of a budgeting process is a plan for achieving the short-run objectives of an organization. Budgets are set for each responsibility center in terms of the performance measures for which each center is held accountable. For organizations without a formal planning system, the budget becomes the principal formal planning document. For organizations with a formal planning system, the budget becomes the first year of the long-range plan.

Budgeting is a form of simulation whereby managers run an organization on paper without actually implementing it. The budget provides a forum for creative analysis of existing activities. Managers may test alternative products and programs together with alternative spending levels to ascertain their effects on short-run plans before deciding on a plan of action.

Given cognitive limitations, managers tend to be "firefighters," solving one pressing problem after another. The budget process forces managers to drop back, gain perspective, and plan for the next year. As managers plan for the next period, they are forced to anticipate problems as well as develop alternative solutions to these problems. This will tend to improve performance and control. Moreover, the collective assumptions of various responsibility centers are coordinated, one with another, and any inconsistencies are made plain and adjusted.

On the behavioral side, budgeting allows the organization an opportunity to gain goal congruence throughout the organization as a result of a process of participation in goal formulation whereby functional, divisional, and executive management participate in goal setting, priority determination, and decision making. If properly done, this should improve motivation and more closely knit the organization together.

Once approved, the budget becomes a detailed blueprint of what has been agreed to for the next period, thus providing a guide for performance that may be consulted periodically. Moreover, it provides detailed standards against which performance may be compared, thus setting the stage for performance evaluation.

Accounting and Measurement

A control system requires a formal mechanism to regulate performance of the various responsibility centers. The standards, plans, and objectives set during the budgetary process become the reference point for the control system. A measurement system is necessary for assessing progress toward objectives in each responsibility center.

Three broad types of accounting measurements are useful in control systems. First are the financial accounting measurements that measure costs and revenues according to an *object* classification that corresponds to the accounting ledger accounts. Second are the cost and revenue measurements for each responsibility center according to the measure of performance used (that is, costs, revenue, profit, return on investment). In management accounting terminology, this is referred to as *responsibility accounting*. The last accounting measure is by *product* or *program*, whereby we measure costs and revenues across responsibility centers so far as they pertain to a program or product. This last measurement is sometimes referred to as *activity costing*.

We shall not be concerned with object measures in this text, since they are not as central to the control process as are responsibility and activity measures. Cost accounting is the body of knowledge within which activity costing and responsibility accounting fall. Of all the methods of cost accounting, activity-based costing is the most useful for purposes of planning and control, since it provides appropriate cost data for responsibility centers and for programs.

Reporting and Analysis of Performance

Once standards are derived for indicator variables and measurements are made, it is a straightforward process to calculate variances between targets and actuals. Techniques of variance analysis allow managers to manage by exception. Variances between actual and targets may be calculated and the differences ascribed to various cost and revenue items, either by responsibility center or by product.

Investigating the cause of a variance always involves an opportunity cost, and management must assess these costs and weight them against the benefits of investigation. One benefit of investigation is the costs saved in the future if a legitimate problem is detected and corrective action is taken.

THE MANAGEMENT CONTROL PROCESS: A DECISION-MAKING PROCESS

Decisions are made continuously in the control process. Managers learn ways in which to make decisions based upon past experience with similar problems. Once a problem is identified, the manager begins a search and evaluation effort that is directed toward finding a solution. Search is motivated by a failure to reach an objective by the control process.

Because of cognitive limitations, search tends to proceed, at least at first, with simple models of causality. We tend to look first in the neighborhood of a problem for a solution. The manner in which the problem is viewed and the direction of the search almost always reflect the position, past experience, and training of the manager making the decision.

When simple causal models do not succeed in solving the problem, we tend to expand our search toward newer alternatives. Ultimately, the search procedure will lead to a satisfactory solution, although it may require a shift to performance indicators against which the organization performs well.

This completes our overview of the control process. The entire process is a decision-making process and decisions occur in each phase. It is a process that involves scanning the environment; setting strategic and operational objectives; measuring performance; and taking corrective action. It is a cybernetic process, and it can be analyzed in terms of the cybernetic paradigm.

Each of the chapters in this part of the text deals with one aspect of the control process in detail.

CRITERIA FOR EVALUATING MANAGEMENT SYSTEMS

As we move through the text, it will be helpful to keep in mind certain criteria for evaluating the effectiveness of a formal control system.

There are two very important *output* criteria. The first is the extent to which the formal systems are actually used by management to make decisions in the control process. If the systems are not used, they cannot be effective no matter how sophisticated they are. Conversely, we should never expect formal management systems to be relied upon exclusively for decision making. Informal systems are also widely used in practice.

The second criterion is more difficult to apply, but it is of no less importance. It has to do with the quality of the decisions made in the control process and the influence of the systems on this quality. The most objective measure here is the extent to which the organization has been achieving its objectives and goals over a reasonable period of time.

In addition there are four *input*-related criteria against which management systems should be evaluated. The first has to do with the extent that each part of the formal management system is linked with the other. There should be a reasonably tight connection among the subprocesses of environmental analysis, business planning, programming, budgeting, and reporting and analysis. If not, the formal systems may not be having much influence upon the control process.

The second input criterion has to do with the role of staff. There should be enough staff support to line management so as to facilitate or provide a catalyst for the control process. On the other hand, these formal systems should be integrated into the management process of an organization rather than being the special "tools" of the staff.

The third input criterion has to do with the extent to which the systems focus upon building commitment to organizational goals and objectives. To build commitment, organizations should encourage participation in the planning and control process. Emphasis should also be placed on gaining explicit commitments during the control process that are voluntarily subscribed to by managers and are made public within the organization.

The fourth important criterion is that the system should encourage strategic and operational thinking on the part of all managers in the organization. It should not encourage premature and excessive quantitative manipulations, which crowd out thinking about fundamental business variables. The philosophy of the formal control system should be to focus upon strategic and operational issues and to do so by using good data.

We shall return to these evaluation criteria from time to time in this part of the text. They will be important to us in evaluating the various control processes of complex organizations. We turn now, however, to examine the first two elements of the control process in more detail: Strategic Planning and Programming.

The formal planning process in complex organizations tends to focus the limited time of managers upon issues and data that are important for strategic and operational decision making. It is a process within which decisions are made that match the human, physical, and technological resources of the firm with the demands or potential demands of the environment within which the firm operates. The limited resources of the firm are allocated under time pressures, in the face of uncertainty about the environment, and within policy and structural constraints placed upon organizational units.

The cybernetic paradigm indicates the crucial importance of environmental scanning to achieve control. Control is possible only to the extent that environmental disturbances are predicted far enough in advance to allow adequate reaction time.

We shall be concerned in the remainder of this chapter with the interrelated subprocesses of environmental scanning and strategic planning and programming. We first examine the need for environmental scanning. We then look at the relationship between environmental scanning and strategic planning. Finally, we look at the programming process.

ENVIRONMENTAL ANALYSIS

The control process usually includes, or should include, some mechanism to scan and analyze the corporate environment, and it takes place at various levels of the organization. The analysis of the environment affects the premises upon which decisions are made throughout the organization. It provides a consistent basis for planning and focuses attention upon the environmental factors that are crucial to the success of the organization and its subdivisions (that is, the key success factors). Each subdivision of the organization then evaluates additional environmental variables peculiar to the particular market within which it operates.

Peters and Waterman (1982) found that excellent firms make a point of staying very close to their customers. Environmental analysis should incorporate a large dose of just plain listening to customers, including their problems and their needs. Listening to customers provides the "factual premises" upon which decisions are made. It improves perceptions of the market and therefore of decision making.

An analysis of the environment is difficult and laden with uncertainty. Yet one thing is certain: *managers cannot assume that the environment will stand still while it optimizes its operating and strategic plans,* even though this latter approach does simplify the way in which we think about problem solving.

The values of economic, political, social, and technological variables over which management has little or no control are often crucial to the success of a firm. From the cybernetic paradigm of control, we learn of the importance of being able to predict the movement of these environmental variables. A procedure that allows the firm and its divisions to scan its environment systematically and thoroughly is important.

To summarize to this point, environmental analysis includes, but certainly is not limited to, economic forecasting for the firm and its divisions. In addition, firms are influenced significantly by the political process, the international environment, competition, technological changes, and social conditions. Political regulation in the form of environmental, fuel economy, and health and safety standards has enormous impact upon operations and especially upon business investment. And these investments are made *by necessity,* not as a result of an analysis of profitability. Often these investments are made at the expense of productivity-improving investments.

As George Steiner reminds us, "The total possible number of forces, both internal and external, that can be exploited to the advantage of a business or can wreck it, boggles the mind."[2] Therefore, it is important to assess systematically all the forces in the environment that are likely to have a significant influence upon the values of variables that are crucial to success. Some of these forces are better analyzed at the corporate level because of their pervasive impact upon the organization, whereas others may be assessed more effectively at the division level, where external forces have their major impact upon one division alone. Moreover, many technological changes are best evaluated at the functional level.

Exhibit 9-2 summarizes the major categories of environmental forces that may have significant impact upon a firm and the microvariables upon which changes in the environmental variables are likely to be felt. The chart is to be studied from the outside in. Desired reactions of the organization are given in Exhibit 9-2 in response to various changes in environmental variables. Of course, this chart does not indicate the crucial role of *prediction* and of the importance of *timing* as far as the company reaction is concerned. All moves to take advantage of environmental opportunities and avoid damage from environmental threats take time to implement. For them to be effective, the future environmental condition must be predicted enough in advance to provide sufficient time for reaction. This is at the heart of the requirements for achieving control.

Some of these environmental forces are national and international, whereas others pertain only to the operation of the specific industry. During the environmental analysis process, an organization should enumerate all the environmental forces that could have a major impact upon the firm and assess values or projections for these variables over the planning horizon. Contingent decisions should be evaluated for major potential changes in these environmental key variables. These variables should be monitored more or less continuously according to their importance.

STRATEGIC PLANNING: WHAT STRATEGY IS AND IS NOT

To understand strategic planning it is useful to consider both what strategy is and is not. Strategy formation requires a careful analysis of the organization's present situation, its strengths and weaknesses, followed by a determination of where it should go together with the steps proposed to get there. It is, as Yavitz and Newman (1982, p. 4–5) say,

> . . . not a response to short-term fluctuations in operations of the environment . . . not a set of numbers merely projected out three to five years . . . not a rationalization of what was done last year . . . not a functional plan, not even a long run one . . . not a statement of pious intentions or optimistic wishes. . . . Instead, a strategy must be feasible in terms of resources that will be mobilized, and must identify ways by which at least some form of superiority over competitors is to be achieved . . . is not a cluster of ideas in the minds of a few select leaders of the company . . . Rather, the concepts are disseminated and understood by all managers to at least the middle levels of the organization and perhaps below.

Strategy is not a fixed concept but must be constantly revised. While it is projected into the future, usually two or more years, it must constantly be modified according to environmental changes. A different but integrated strategy is indicated for different levels of the organization.

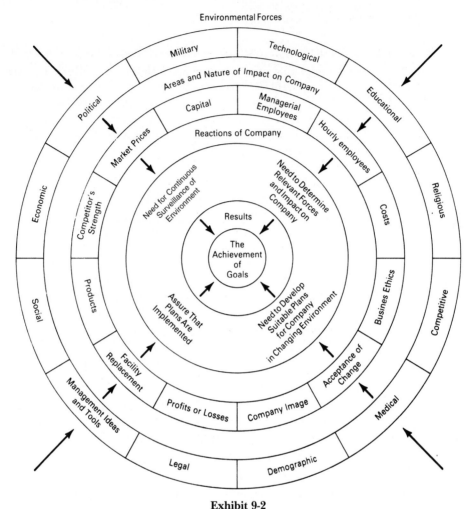

Exhibit 9-2
Environmental Impacts and Organizational Reactions.
Source: Adapted and reproduced by permission from George A. Steiner,
Top Management Planning, Macmillan Publishing Co., New York, 1968. p. 204.

FOUR ELEMENTS OF STRATEGY

The four elements of strategy, as described by Yavitz and Newman, (1982) are domain sought, differential advantage, strategic thrusts, and targeted results expected.

DOMAIN SOUGHT

Each business entity should analyze the environment in which it is working or contemplates working in the future. It should determine what is happening in the environment. Is it stable, deteriorating, or improving? What is happening to business activity in general? Are there changing needs that should be addressed? Are customers expecting different kinds of products or services than they have expected in the past? Do customers have sufficient resources to pay for the product and services of our organization? What are the best practices of competitors? These and many more questions need to be asked about the domain in which the organization plans to operate.

The process of *benchmarking*, which consists of comparing products and operations against those of the strongest competitors is a tool of the strategic planning process. Benchmarked goals are often implemented in the strategic planning process. Benchmarking is discussed extensively in Chapter 14, but you should be aware of its relationship to the strategic planning process.

DIFFERENTIAL ADVANTAGE

One must look first at the competitive advantages that set the organization or the individual business apart such as superior capability, new technology, location, low cost, or low prices. Each business has different strengths and weaknesses. Executives must identify the differential advantages for each business and strengthen them further while shoring up weaknesses.

STRATEGIC THRUSTS NECESSARY AND THEIR APPROPRIATE TIMING

After reviewing the domain and differential advantage, the manager should then plan the strategic thrusts required to implement the strategy: Are costs to be kept low so that prices may be modest? What will be done to attract the customer group that is targeted? How does one plan to market new products or services? How does one indoctrinate the staff so that they reflect the values that one wishes to impart? All these and more need to be considered.

TARGET RESULTS EXPECTED

Finally, one should anticipate and measure at periodic intervals actual results against targeted results. Is there a reasonable return on investment? Is the rate of growth of the sales as planned? Are customers happy with your products and services? Is our staff satisfied?

In large and complex organizations the strategic planning process must be more formal and complex, because of the need to involve the managerial staff at the lowest level. Since these managers must be involved in implementing the plan, most should understand and agree with the plan.

THE PROGRAMMING PROCESS

The programming process is an organizational process for making long-term resource allocation choices. Chapter 10 deals extensively with some tools that are useful for evaluating capital investment decisions in the programming process.

The analytical tools described in the next chapter are used within broader organizational processes described in this chapter; these processes must be designed and redesigned to meet managerial objectives.

Although terminology differs and is somewhat a matter of taste, it is useful to treat programming as one subprocess of the management control process. Programming is a process that involves all responsibility centers of the organization as they attempt to plan for the achievement of the strategic goals of the organization.

On the basis of environmental information and on information pertaining to goals and internal strengths, the divisions, business units, and corporate executives forecast financial variables for the intermediate term, say, from 5 to 10 periods in advance, for existing product lines and for new products and programs. Forecasting is done as a part of the planning to meet the long-term goals assigned to various responsibility centers. Also as a part of this process, division and corporate executives compare their long-term goals with the forecasts of performance and identify a planning gap. It is not unusual for aspiring corporations to have a positive planning gap. This planning gap becomes the basis for additional search and pressure to identify new programs internally that will result in closing the planning gap. It is reasonable at this time for organizations also to look externally for potential acquisitions and mergers so as to close the gap.

Any new programs developed as a part of this long-term planning process can be expected to involve product and functional management in the "detailing" that is required to develop new programs. New programs include any of the following changes:

1. New products or alterations to existing products so as to increase their marketability
2. Pursuit of new technology with regard to manufacture and distribution of goods and services
3. The design of new systems, including control systems, to improve efficiency and productivity
4. The acquisition of new fixed assets, such as machinery and equipment, so as to improve operations
5. Programs to upgrade the performance level of the human resources of the organization
6. New and improved policies for doing business that improve effectiveness and efficiency. An example might include new pricing, advertising, packaging, or product research policies
7. Improved management techniques, including reorganizations that raise productivity and effectiveness

Programming, therefore, is the process of decision making whereby an organization commits itself to resource allocation decisions that involve expenditures in the present in anticipation of returns in the future. Programming is a process that is directed toward the attainment of the long-term goals of the organization.

Programming results in the development of a set of feasible programs stemming from an organizational process directed toward the achievement of long-term goals. It includes formal or informal procedures for the definition, evaluation, and implementation of new programs. It is carried out in conjunction with the long-term planning process. All businesses engage in programming, if only in an informal manner. The need to formalize the programming process depends upon the size, functional interdependence, and diversity of the organization.

Programming as a formal process is relatively common in the United States today. When it is formalized as a part of the management control process, the intent is to do a better job in matching programs to goals and in the planning and control of these programs. When the programming process is formalized, the capital budget results as a by-product of the process.

The expenditure decisions arrived at in the programming process are crucial to the success of the organization. In order to remain competitive, a firm must replace worn-out equipment. To grow, it must extend its capacity to provide goods and services. It must also adapt its capabilities to changing environmental conditions. All these types of difficult decisions are made in the programming process. The quality of these decisions has a significant influence over the ability of the firm to survive and to achieve its goals and objectives. The past performance of U.S. firms in this area has been criticized by Hayes and Abernathy (1980), Hayes and Garvin (1982), and many others (see Maciariello, Burke, and Tilley, 1989).

We shall in this chapter elaborate a model of the decision-making process concerning these long-term programmatic decisions that corresponds to the precepts of the cybernetic paradigm. We start by reviewing the widely cited and extensive clinical study by Bower (1972) of the investment decision-making process in a large multinational firm. We begin with a short summary of Bower's model of the investment decision-making (that is, the programming) process.

BOWER'S MODEL OF THE INVESTMENT DECISION-MAKING PROCESS[3]

Bower found that the investment process is typically initiated by a discrepancy between desired results and actual results with regard to a performance variable (as the cybernetic paradigm indicates). For example, information from the production planning and control system might indicate that orders exceed or will soon exceed plant capacity, or perhaps, from the cost accounting system, information that unfavorable labor variances are appearing that seem to have their origin in an uneconomic-size plant for existing volume.

Another discrepancy might be from the profit planning system, which might indicate an unfavorable price variance on an existing product line, which could reflect a deterioration in the competitive posture of the company. Still another discrepancy is the planning gap, which is identified as a result of long-term planning.

A discrepancy produced by the information systems of an organization initiates a search for a solution that may result in the definition of a capital expenditure project. Such a project requires both technical and economic analysis. The technical and economic analysis is carried out in the initiating phase of the resource allocation process.

The focus in the initiating phase is on a discrepancy between the actual versus desired value of a key variable, such as size of market, profit margin, price, operating cost, quality, and technological competitiveness. The discrepancy is often first noted at a low level of management, and the type of discrepancy depends both on the key success factors that have been communicated through the organization as well as the information systems present in the organization. Definition of a project, then, often begins at a fairly low level within the organization, where technical expertise is most likely to be found. Once a project is defined, it is then subjected to economic analysis.

The next subprocess of the resource allocation decision-making process involves selling the project; it is in this second subprocess where the greatest discrepancy exists between the projects actually selected and those that would be selected if a formal selection procedure alone led to the choice. Normally, approval for major investment decisions lies at top levels of a firm; that is, it is vested in corporate managers and managers of investment centers. Projects, defined at low levels of the organization, usually are proposed for approval by upper-level division managers.

It is at the division manager level, therefore, where projects must find support, or what Bower calls *impetus.* This is a subprocess where division managers evaluate the division goals and objectives and decide whether to "promote" a project for approval. Often, in the process, the division manager attempts to influence the definition of the project to bring it more closely into line with division and corporate objectives and strategies.

In deciding whether to support a project, a division manager considers both corporate objectives and the responsibility and reward structure of the firm. The division manager must be convinced that the organizational benefits of a project exceed the costs, and the manager arrives at his or her subjective measure of benefits and costs by observing the reward structure of the organization.

If the rewards of an organization are so structured that managers are promoted based upon their "batting average," then division managers will seek projects to promote that are most likely to be winners when postaudits of projects are conducted rather than those that offer a moderate probability of an extremely large return but also a moderate probability of being labeled "losers." With this reward structure, a manager would be more likely to choose and promote a project with a short payback period (and presumably low risk) than one with an extremely high, but risky, net present value. With this kind of reward structure in an organization, one can immediately see the relevance of the payback method, wherein projects are ranked according to the speed in which capital outlays are expected to be recovered, even though the payback method is inferior to the net present value method as an economic resource allocation tool.

On the other hand, if managers who take the firm into new and exotic, but marginally profitable, businesses are rewarded, the promoter will find those projects attractive and might be led to define and support such "imaginative" projects on the basis of criteria such as payback.

Only if the reward structure leads to the promotion of managers with high-yield projects or with high "slugging averages" (that is, a number of big successes among sponsored projects) will the net present value (that is, profit-maximizing) criterion be completely relevant to the division manager. If corporate management wishes to produce such results, it has to bring its reward structure into congruence with profit-maximizing criteria, such as the NPV method. It can do that by using the approval phase of resource allocation to screen out proposals without this justification and by promoting managers to corporate ranks who have good track records in promoting highly profitable projects.

In summary, Bower's model of the programming process suggests that project ideas often come from the lower levels of an organization as a result of the identification of gaps identified in the control process; middle management plays an important role in the resource allocation process in that it rationalizes and matches the desires of lower levels with the criteria of upper levels; upper management sets the ground rules (the context), approves major projects, and establishes rewards.

To get a major capital investment project approved, the initiator must build confidence in the project at middle levels of the organization (especially with managers who have a good track record of getting projects approved), and middle managers must reconfigure the project so that it meets top management approval. Top management must design the context of the programming process, which includes strategy, criteria for acceptance, approval levels, the process itself, and rewards.

We may say that a division manager will normally choose to support and sponsor investment projects that, based upon corporate goals and the reward structure, advance his or her position in the organization. We should expect the NPV method to be the rational selection tool only when the reward structure emphasizes profitable projects in its definition of a good track record for managers. It is not surprising, therefore, to see the widespread adoption of multiple criteria and criteria other than NPV in formal capital budget procedures.

Extension of Bower's Model to Incorporate Additional Influences on the Investment Approval Process

Kovar (1986) has proposed and tested a model of the capital investment approval process that incorporates a number of enhancements to Bower's model. In particuliar, Kovar's model illustrates those aspects of the overall programming process that influence behavior during the early stages of investment decision making. It is reproduced in Exhibit 9-3.

Exhibit 9-3 illustrates three phases of the investment process that take place at different levels of the organization. The three phases are the initiating phase, the middle or integrating phase, and finally the corporate phase. In the early going on an investment proposal, the initiating and integrating levels are active in sifting and evaluating new possibilities, while the corporate level is active in defining the overall organization context wherein the criteria to be applied to proposals are determined.

The process that a proposal moves through, on the other hand, is shown horizontally on Exhibit 9-3 as definition, impetus, and approval. The horizontal investment pipeline through which an investment project moves consists of the generation of ideas, the selection of candidates for proposals, and the rejection of

Exhibit 9-3
Capital Investment Approval Process

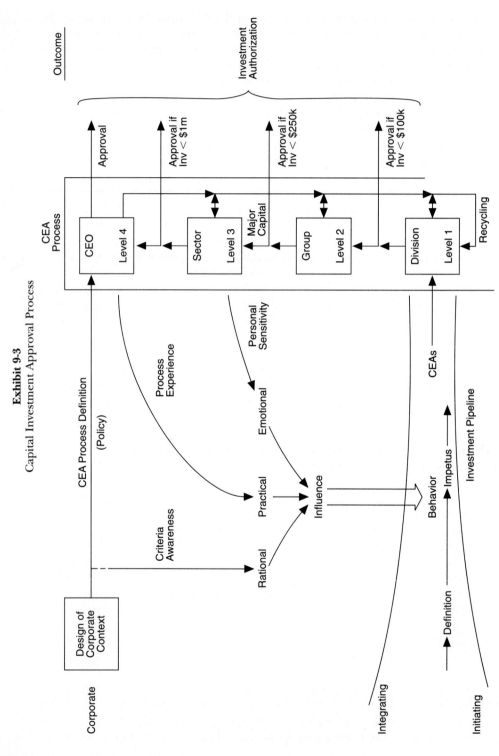

Adapted by permission Donald G. Kovar, *The Decision Making Environment of the Capital Investment Approval Process.* Figure 3.3 Ph.D. dissertation, Claremont Graduate Schol, Claremont, Calif., 1986.

unfavored alternatives, building support for proposed projects and ultimately formal submission of a capital expenditure authorization request. The pipeline narrows as the process moves from broad project alternatives to specific investment projects.

The approval levels required depend upon the dollar amount of the investment proposal. Major proposals requiring capital expenditures over $250,000 require the approval of sector management in this example, and those over $1 million require the approval of the chief executive officer.

Organization behavior in the programming process is complex, consisting of rational, practical, and emotional factors. These factors are induced by the design of the approval process (that is, the design of corporate context). In designing the approval process, certain criteria such as rate of return, linkage to strategy, and legal constraints have been defined. The awareness of these rational factors has an influence over the definition of alternatives early in the investment pipeline, because these factors involve explicit acceptance criteria. Practical factors include forms to fill out, the calendar for approval and authorization, approval sequences, and authorization limits. These practical considerations also influence investment planning. Emotional factors include the personal sensitivities of the preparers of project proposals to those who approve the proposals and the degree of accountability built into the investment process. Proposals that require management approval expose preparers to close scrutiny by those who have a great influence over their future, and this affects behavior in the investment pipeline.

The control systems designer should be aware of the influences of these rational, practical, and emotional factors on investment proposals and seek to design a process that results in the best mix of investments being selected for submission and approval without discouraging innovative and opportunistic projects.

Excessive attention to the rational factors may lead to behavior that results in fitting the proposal to the criteria, or what has been called "reverse engineering." As individuals gain familiarity with the practical aspects of the system, the designer should expect attempts to "beat the system" and should guard against them. On the other hand, if personal sensitivity to investment proposals is too low, the quality of proposals is likely to be affected.

We turn now to describe the major process parameters of the programming process that are subject to design and redesign so as to improve the rationality of the programming process.

PROCESS PARAMETERS OF THE PROGRAMMING PROCESS

The programming process has a number of specific process parameters associated with it that are themselves subject to design and redesign so as to improve the capital resource allocation process of an organization. Kovar (1986) identifies nine such parameters. We examine them below.

1. Linkage to the strategic plan.   Major investment projects should be consistent with and implement the strategic plan of an organization. This linkage should be demonstrated in the evaluation of the project and in the capital authorization document. We should allow for cases where opportunistic investments generate new strategies.

2. Approval limits.   Enough autonomy should be given over capital authorizations so that division and corporate management are not overwhelmed with numerous capital appropriation requests. The idea is to establish approval limits throughout the hierarchy at levels whereby top management acts upon relatively few requests but upon a large proportion of the dollar amount spent.

3. Number of approval steps and signatures.   The greater the number of steps and signatures required in the approval process, the slower the process and the lower the accountability for results. This is a problem in motivation.

4. Line management involvement and accountability.   The programming process should be the responsibility of line management with staff people acting as catalyst. The potential danger is that the process will be taken over by staff people and that line managers will not feel accountable for the results, which in turn will negatively influence decision making.

5. Financial analysis and supporting detail.   The programming process ought to emphasize strategic considerations. Programming processes that excessively emphasize financial analysis are prone to ignore significant strategic elements in the environment and therefore sacrifice strategic thinking for the "illusion of exactness" created by quantitative analysis. Balance is the key here.

6. Discount rate.   It is important for an organization to know its opportunity cost of funds. Yet one can overdo it. Many strategic projects that are successful are likely to be quite insensitive to large movements in the discount rate. Those that are unsuccessful are likely to be unsuccessful regardless of the discount rate. The large investments are unlikely to be so sensitive to the discount rate that we should worry if our estimates are off by a few percentage points.

7. External environmental analysis.   One of the keys to making the right investment choices is to make an accurate assessment of the environment facing the firm. On this, the success of the entire programming process rises and falls. Formal processes should be in place to supplement the informal mechanisms for gaining an accurate understanding of the external environments.

8. Identification and analysis of alternatives.   Following the cybernetic paradigm, there are often multiple investment projects and multiple configurations of a project that may be evaluated to solve a problem. The process should emphasize identification and analysis of multiple alternatives.

9. Education and training.   The objectives of the programming process as well as methods for carrying it out should be the subject of extensive education and training for all participants.

MUTUALLY SUPPORTIVE MANAGEMENT SYSTEMS FOR THE IMPLEMENTATION OF STRATEGY THROUGH PROGRAMMING DECISIONS

The control systems designer requires a model or framework for examining and redesigning *all* of the management systems associated with long-term resource allocation decision making. The MSSM is such a framework. It was described extensively in Chapter 1. We are using the model here for the purpose of assisting us in designing the elements of the programming process.

We reproduce a version of the model in Exhibit 9-4 to help guide us through a discussion of the design issues.

The model provides the framework for auditing the management systems supporting resource allocation decisions in complex organizations. It allows us to ask the following questions:

1. Is the organization structure consistent with strategy? Does the organization structure assist in the implementation of strategy?
2. Are assignments made to managers throughout the organization for the accomplishment of strategic objectives?
3. Do the performance measurement and reward systems lead managers to focus upon both long-term goals and short- term objectives in the resource allocation process?
4. How do the style of management and organization culture influence the resource allocation process?
5. Do the planning and reporting systems for resource allocation decision making support the implementation of strategy?
6. Do the communication mechanisms established by the organization facilitate the resource allocation process?

Organization Structure and Strategy

There are two sets of questions here. The first, raised extensively in Chapter 5, is does the organization structure reflect the strategy of the firm? If a cost leadership strategy is being pursued, for example, does the organization structure lead to scale economies in manufacturing? If a product innovation strategy is being followed, does the organization structure facilitate that?

Exhibit 9-4
Mutually Supportive Subsystems Model

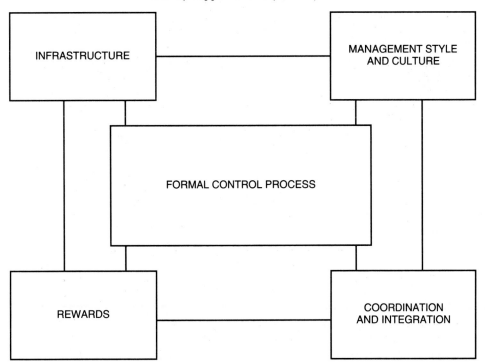

The second question is, has the firm distributed responsibility within the organization for design and implementation of strategy? At Texas Instruments this is done by overlaying responsibilities for objectives, strategies, and tactics on top of the operating organizations. At General Electric, it is done by identifying strategic business units (SBU's) and managers who are responsible for strategy development in their SBUs. Other companies incorporate strategic responsibility into the charters and responsibilities of divisions and business units. This question is important because organizations have difficulty managing the tension between the demands of current operations and the creativity required for innovations and future growth. In the absence of explicit organizational attention, the long-term planning usually gets neglected.

Performance Measurement and Rewards

Here the designer is interested in whether the performance measurement system captures progress and problems toward the achievement of long-term strategies and goals as well as short-term objectives. In addition, these long-term pursuits should be reflected prominently in the reward system. Bonuses, for example, should be tied to both short-term and long-term success. The measurement system also should be carefully tailored to the structure of short- and long-term responsibilities in the organizations.

Management Style and Organization Culture

Management style and culture affect the way the firm organizes itself and makes decisions. The resource allocation process and management systems of an organization must support the style of decision making if they are to be effective. Style influences managerial autonomy in decision making. Culture, by establishing "the way things are done," is very influential in capital investment decision making both in terms of the actual decisions made and in terms of the process used in making them. Peters and Waterman (1982) found that the managements of excellent companies allow significant managerial autonomy and encourage internal competition, which in turn stimulates innovation and entrepreneurship.

Planning and Reporting

The long-term planning processes of an organization should support the resource allocation decisions by providing the information and the forum for discussions and analysis. It should also include financial planning systems that roll out the financial implications of various programs and join them to short-term operating budgets. The reporting systems should report expenditures by program category and not confuse operating expenditures with strategic expenditures.

Communication Mechanisms

A number of communication mechanisms are required to manage the tension between short-term and long-term resource allocation decision making. Conflict at a certain level must be encouraged in order to generate fertile innovation. The maverick must have a hearing. Committees and meeting schedules must be established for short-term and long-term resource decision making and for resolving conflict over program alternatives.

In describing and evaluating these management systems in terms of their impact upon resource allocation decision making, we should recognize that there is no one best configuration of systems. Many alternative designs have produced excellent results. It is important, however, that these systems be mutually consistent and reinforcing. Exhibit 9-4 illustrates the interdependence of these systems. We should seek congruent systems as far as resource allocation systems are concerned.

FORMAL PROGRAMMING PROCEDURES

Formal programming procedures support and provide tools for the organization processes of initiation, selling, and impetus that characterize the programming process. Organizations, in other words, develop formal programming procedures for defining, evaluating, and implementing investment projects. These steps are normally institutionalized within the control process of the firm. We turn now to examine these procedures in detail. We should not forget, however, that these procedures often take on a supportive or secondary role to the previously identified organizational processes, especially for the larger investment decisions.

Project Definition

Project definition is instigated by deviations from goals reported through information systems in various responsibility centers of the organization. For example, if cost variances are reported in the cost accounting system, a search may be instigated to determine the cause. After investigation, management may conclude that variances are due to equipment inefficiencies in a standard cost center, thus instigating a search for a solution that may lead to the definition of an investment project. Another plant investment project may be defined as a result of sales forecasts that exceed plant capacity. Still another may be defined as a result of a softening of profit margins, posted prices, or sales.

A manager uses the information systems that are in place to compare performance (for example, on quality, cost, or profit) with goals of the responsibility center. Discrepancies or variances set off a search process to close these gaps from which a project may be defined. Because a manager's rationality is bounded, the alternatives considered and their evaluation will be a direct result of the information reaching him or her.

Given the cognitive limits of managers, only a limited number of alternatives may be considered. It is, therefore, important that the information provided a decision maker focus upon the key success factors of the responsibility center. The success factors are those variables (for example, quality and cost) to which short-term objectives and long-term goals are most sensitive. Project definition and evaluation ordinarily should be done with reference to these key success factors.

In complex organizations, most capital proposals originate at the operational level of the enterprise. The controller normally manages the proposal process and prescribes just how the definition is to progress. The detailing of a proposed project requires a description of the objectives and purposes of the project, together with an explanation of the proposed technology. Companies often prescribe a detailed checklist that should be adhered to in the preparation of proposals, including legal, contractual, and regulatory implications. For example, in preparing a proposal to introduce a new product, demand forecasts and pricing assumptions should be checked against past experience with similar products.

A crucial aspect of project definition concerns the review of the specific purpose of each project. Again, recalling our discussion of key success variables of Chapter 3, it should be clear that not all proposals should be regarded as equally advancing the goals and objectives of the responsibility center and of the firm. It is natural, therefore, to consider systematically in the programming process the manner in which a capital project influences key success factors. In other words, questions should be answered regarding the variables that are influenced by a project. Is the project one that improves our cost, quality, or market share position in relation to competitors? How will the project improve our chances of success in the business? How does the technology represented in the project relate to the technological change taking place in the industry? The proposal and review process should direct attention to the business purpose served by the project so that attention is constantly directed to key success factors.

Project Evaluation

Since project proposals may originate at any level in the organization, it is necessary to provide detailed instructions so as to direct properly proposal preparation and facilitate analysis and review.

Organizations normally prescribe in "capital appropriation manuals" the procedures and paperwork to follow in processing capital appropriation requests. The procedures usually differentiate between various categories of projects and apply different evaluation criteria and techniques to each category. The most stringent criteria are applied to the projects perceived as possessing the greatest uncertainty.

Although procedures can be expected to vary greatly depending upon industry peculiarities and management style, it is normally desirable in practice to differentiate among project categories. Each project category has its own characteristics and, in most cases, selection criterion. This is necessary because of the wide variation in the degree of discretion the firm has among categories and because of the variation in uncertainty present among categories. We turn now to examine some typical project categories.

Health and Safety

Projects that by law, labor agreement, or managerial judgment are necessary to maintain or improve health and safety standards cannot or should not be subjected to benefit–cost analysis. These projects are usually justified on the basis of degree of necessity.

The degree of necessity method of capital allocation is one that selects and ranks projects on the basis of the urgency that they command, with the "most urgent" accorded higher priority than the "least urgent." It is almost purely a qualitative criterion. Projects that are absolutely necessary for survival are given first priority. Secondary and tertiary priorities are then allocated to those projects that "simply shouldn't" be postponed for the health and well-being of the organization.

This method, although widely used in practice, has several serious deficiencies. First, there is always the alternative of doing nothing and the possibility that such an alternative is indeed the best course for the owners of a firm. Second, it totally ignores the productivity of capital and the opportunities forgone by employing capital in a given project. Third, and related to the first two, it almost invariably leads to the rejection of some projects that are more profitable than those undertaken. Finally, it places a premium upon the persuasive skills and influence of the promoter of a project and removes the objectivity that a systematic selection procedure should bring to the resource allocation process.

Theoretically, if an investment in this category is required by law, there is always the alternative of discontinuing operations, and these alternatives may be examined in a benefit–cost framework. Practically speaking, however, this alternative is rarely acceptable to the managers of an enterprise. It is possible and desirable, however, to subject alternative methods of accomplishing identical health and safety objectives to an analysis of differential costs using discounted cash flow methods.

Equipment Replacement with Identical Equipment

Many capital projects merely involve replacing existing equipment with identical equipment with no savings. While it may be desirable to evaluate optimal replacement time in a benefit–cost framework, these projects are customarily approved by the necessity criterion once existing equipment has reached the end of its economic life. Again, there is always the possibility of ceasing a particular operation, thus creating an alternative choice problem, but we should not consider the alternative of ceasing operations a realistic one.

Quality

Projects designed to improve the quality of present product lines are normally difficult to evaluate in a benefit–cost framework. While it is relatively easy to arrive at the incremental cost of projects to improve quality, it is difficult to specify the expected benefits in quantitative terms.

Mandatory Projects

Mandatory capital expenditures are those that must be made to fulfill obligations that the firm has taken on contractually, such as the provision of products to a specified customer over a period of time. Practically speaking, these expenditures must be made; the only question might concern the least costly alternative. The project itself is decided on the basis of necessity.

Profit

Projects intended to increase profits may be classified into three subgroups:

Cost-Reduction Projects. Projects justified primarily on the basis of reduction in existing costs can normally be evaluated quite conclusively within the benefit–cost framework. There is often no change in products, prices, or volume.

Cost reductions associated with new equipment, for example, can be quantified since we are simply comparing one known (the new equipment) with another (the existing equipment). These incremental reductions, including tax effects, are the incremental benefits of the project. Incremental costs of the new equipment are readily estimated.

Cost-reduction projects are ready made for the discounted cash flow methods. Uncertainty usually is limited to economic life of the new equipment. Unless there is rapid technological change, this is usually manageable.

Projects Designed to Increase Production Capacity for Existing Products. For proven existing product lines following a somewhat predictable growth trend, the benefit–cost framework is useful since benefits may be estimated, usually, however, with much more uncertainty than that existing for cost-reduction projects. The uncertainty is greater for this category of project, since demand forecasts are notoriously inaccurate over the longer term. In Chapter 10, we will discuss methods for dealing with this uncertainty.

Projects Designed to Support New Products. These are loaded with uncertainty, there being no firm knowledge concerning demand. Since these products face extreme uncertainty, management often decides to proceed sequentially. First, it may seek to test the market to obtain more information about consumer reaction to the new product. It may seek to piggyback new product production on the backs of existing production facilities until market demand becomes clearer. It may simply require a very high discount rate or short payback period to compensate for the uncertainty.

Strategic Investments. Strategic investments such as acquisitions, diversification into major new product lines, and vertical integration are characterized by very large capital outlays over long periods of time and by much uncertainty. They are rarely selected by quantitative techniques alone. They may "fall out" as the result of strategic decisions without much subsequent analysis. The primary method of dealing with uncertainty is by progressive revisions, as the result of feedback, whereby we reconsider periodically (for example, annually) the predictions upon which the strategy and investment were based and take appropriate action.

Therefore, strategic investments cannot be forced into a simple category but must follow different patterns consistent with the importance of these investments to the firm. We should also expect the degree-of-necessity technique to be used here (Dean, 1951, pp. 140–148).

Once we admit that survival is a dominant goal of the management of a firm and that benefits of certain projects are virtually impossible to measure, we can see how management can rationalize certain strategic investments, such as vertical integration, to ensure a steady source of supply of raw materials (for example, coal or oil for utilities) or investments in research and development to produce a steady stream of new and higher-quality products on the basis of the necessity criterion.

Given the uncertainty surrounding strategic investments, it is not surprising that the track record of the promoter should play an important role in decision making. If a promoter of a project has an excellent record of successful projects (by some criterion), then his or her credibility is enhanced in the eyes of the superiors who ultimately choose among project proposals. This would appear to be especially important for strategic investments, although also important for other investment decisions as well.

The Use of Multiple Criteria for Project Evaluation

Although we shall see in the next chapter that the net present value method is the correct procedure for evaluating capital projects, many organizations use multiple selection criteria with perhaps each particular selection criterion being utilized to illustrate a different characteristic of a project. For example, although we shall show that the accounting rate of return (or what might be called the return on funds employed) is economically speaking absurd, since it double-counts depreciation and since it fails to take into account the time pattern of earnings, it does provide a measure of return on assets in an accounting sense, according to the accounting methods utilized to measure return on assets. Investors and potential investors do pay attention to these accounting calculations, and because they do, management might like to obtain a sense of the impact of a given project on this measure. Irrational? It depends upon your point of view.

If the project is considered from the point of view of the manager of the investment center, who is evaluated based upon return on assets as measured by the accounting system, it is very "rational" from his or her point of view to use the accounting rate of return. While this definitely leads to suboptimal economic behavior from the point of view of the firm, some suboptimum behavior is inevitable in loosely coupled, complex organizations for reasons discussed elsewhere in this book.

To avoid the worst of suboptimum results, the firm should establish a policy requiring all investments in certain categories to be subject to discounted cash flow analysis. Moreover, the firm might also want a quantitative assessment of uncertainty and, therefore, require calculations of payback for certain categories of projects. Thus, it is understandable that firms would indeed employ multiple selection criteria for project selection.

Project Implementation and Control

The system of control over capital expenditures begins in the definition and evaluation phases. Once investment programs have been defined, evaluated, and approved, they must be implemented. Implementation requires planning capital outlays, monitoring capital expenditures, and controlling expenditures against project specifications.

Major capital projects, such as product introductions, plant expansion, and acquisitions, together with many others, have major effects upon the organization as well as upon the organizations of suppliers and subcontractors. Contracts are issued to outside organizations that generally fix the legal commitments of all parties. The portion of the project performed internally, however, has no such fixed contractual commitments, but requires close surveillance and control to ensure that performance is according to the proposal and that costs are within the budget. Many of the performance control techniques of project management are relevant during this control phase,[4] performance, cost, and schedule parameters are far from fixed at budgeted levels.

They must be monitored constantly and evaluated and controlled. The sophistication in controls should be related to the magnitude and complexity of the capital project. In light of this, it is interesting to note, although not surprising, that practitioners find the most crucial and difficult phases of project analysis to be project definition and project implementation, not project evaluation.

The Capital Projects Manual

The formal institutional details concerning the policies related to project definition, evaluation, and implementation are normally reduced to a standard operating procedure that is to be followed throughout the organization. The informal organization processes of initiating, providing impetus, and selling projects must be discovered by experience in each organization. One cannot generalize about these.

The capital projects manual usually contains the following instructions:

1. An investment authorization schedule stipulating the levels of the organization at which various projects must be approved. Generally, the higher the dollar amount, the higher in the organization the authorization level.
2. Forms for carrying out the financial evaluation and criteria to be used in project evaluation.
3. Forms for time phasing the capital expenditures of the project.
4. Financial and schedule status reports for each project and for all capital projects of an organization, giving authorizations, expenditures to date, including outstanding financial commitments, by category of expenditures, and estimates of cost at completion.
5. Procedures for periodic project audit reports to ascertain the extent to which actual results (financial and otherwise) conform to expected or predicted results.

FORMAL AND INFORMAL PROCESSES FOR STRATEGIC AND PROGRAMMATIC DECISION MAKING

One danger of the preceding analysis is that you may be led to the conclusion that strategic and programmatic decision making is a neater and more formal a process than it really is.

Organizations rarely make strategic allocation decisions according to the timetable of the repetitive formal planning process. Rather, much analysis, thought, and interaction regarding these decisions take place outside the formal planning process. The greatest value of the formal planning and programming process is to collect, analyze, and communicate information about strategic and program alternatives under consideration by the organization.

Quinn (1981) summarizes the strategic decision process as follows:

> Typically you start with a general concern, vaguely felt. Next, you roll an issue around in your mind until you think you have a conclusion that makes sense for the company. Then you go out and post the idea without being too wedded to its details. You then start hearing the arguments pro and con, and some very good refinements of the idea usually emerge. Then you pull the idea in and put some resources together to study it so that it can be put forward as more of a formal presentation. You wait for "stimuli occurrences" or "crises," and launch pieces of the idea in these situations. But they lead toward your ultimate aim. You know where you want to get. You'd like to get there in six months. But it may take three years, or you may not get there at all. And when you do get there, you don't know whether it was originally your own idea—or somebody else had reached the same conclusion before you and just got you on board for it. You never know. The president would follow the same basic process, but he could drive it much faster than an executive lower in the organization.

Strategic and programmatic decision making tends to be incremental, opportunistic, and organizational. Formal systems should be designed to facilitate this process.

REFERENCES

BOWER, JOSEPH L., *Managing the Resource Allocation Process.* Homewood, Ill.: Richard D. Irwin, 1972.

DEAN, JOEL, *Capital Budgeting: The Management Policy on Plant, Equipment, and Product Development.* New York: Columbia University Press, 1951.

DRUCKER, PETER F., *Managing in Turbulent Times.* New York: Harper and Row, 1980.

HAYES, ROBERT H., and WILLIAM J. ABERNATHY, "Managing Our Way to Economic Decline," *Harvard Business Review*, July–August 1980, pp. 67–77.

———, and D.A. GARVIN, "Managing as if Tommorrow Mattered," *Harvard Business Review*, May–June, 1982, pp. 71–79.

KOVAR, DONALD G., *The Decision-Making Environment of the Capital Investment Approval Process.* Ph.D. dissertation, Claremont Graduate School, Claremont Calif., 1986.

MACIARIELLO, JOSEPH A., JEFFREY W. BURKE, and DONALD TILLEY, "Improving American Competitiveness: A Management Systems Perspective," *Academy of Management Executive*, Vol. III, no. 4, November 1989.

PETERS, THOMAS J., and ROBERT H. WATERMAN, JR., *In Search of Excellence.* New York: Harper and Row, 1982.

STEINER, GEORGE A., *Top Management Planning.* New York: Macmillan, 1969.

QUINN, JAMES B., "Formulating Strategy One Step at a Time," *Journal of Business Strategy*, Winter 1981, pp. 42–63.

VANCIL, RICHARD F. and PETER LORANGE, *Strategic Planning Systems.* Englewood Cliffs, N.J.: Prentice Hall, 1977.

VANCIL, RICHARD F., *Implementing Strategy: The Role of Top Management.* Boston: Division of Research, Harvard Business School, 1982.

———, *Implementing Strategy: The Role of Top Management, Teacher's Manual.* Boston: Division of Research, Harvard Business School, 1982.

YAVITZ, BORIS, and WILLIAM H. NEWMAN, *Strategy in Action: The Execution, Politics and Payoff of Business Planning*, New York: The Free Press, 1982.

NOTES

1. We shall use the terms *information flows, information tools,* and *information systems* interchangeably in this section of the text to highlight different aspects of the management systems that support the control process.
2. George A. Steiner, *Top Management Planning.* New York: Macmillan Publishing Company, 1968, p. 205.
3. This section assumes an elementary knowledge of financial evaluation techniques, including discounted cash flow methods.
4. For a detailed exposition of these project implementation techniques, see Chapters 15 and 16.

Diversified Electronics*

In this section, we present three short capital investment cases from Diversified Electronics, a diversified, high-technology company with a worldwide presence. These capital decision-making processes are typical of those found in large organizations. Their purpose is to provide a set of realistic cases so that you can gain experience with the climate of actual capital investment decision-making processes found in practice.

The Company and Its Practices

Diversified is one of the top 200 firms on the Fortune list of 500 U.S. industrial corporations. The company is organized into three sectors; these cases are based upon one of those sectors. The sector under study produces electronic information and services. In carrying out these businesses, the sector is organized into six major groups, and these are further subdivided into divisions. For strategic planning, a division usually constitutes a strategic business unit (SBU). The sector has 15 SBUs.

Planning is done annually. Beginning early in the year and continuing for about six months, each business unit considers its five-year strategic plan. Each strategic plan contains a mission statement, strategic/competitive position assessments, evironmental evaluations, strategic alternatives, market and product ap-proaches, resource requirements (including capital), and a five-year financial projection.

Financial projections include sales, profits, assets, various efficiency ratios, and capital appropriations and expenditures. In addition, strategic action programs are identified. Action programs are actions and investments that must be implemented during the coming year in order to achieve the strategic results expressed in the plan. Projected results of the strategic action programs are merged with operating forecasts to insure that managers are accountable for their implementation. A totally new strategic plan is usually not required each year for well established business units unless there are major shifts in the competitive environment. Each year's plan usually extends or refines that of the prior year.

Following the completion and review of the strategic plan (in the May–June period), SBUs begin the preparation of the operating plan for the next calendar year. The operating plan is a more detailed expression of the first year of the strategic plan. The operating plans become the basis of the month-to-month control. Performance to the operating plans is an important factor in management compensation.

The operating plan is reviewed by top management in the September–November period. The operating plan is reviewed and revised if necessary once in the February–March period and again in the June–July period.

*The three cases in this chapter have been adapted by permission from a series of ten cases which appear in Donald G. Kovar, *The Decision Making Environment of the Capital Investment Approval Process*, Ph.D. Dissertation, Claremont Graduate School, Claremont, CA, 1986.

Toward the end of a calendar year, the operating and capital forecasts from each business unit are aggregated to produce group, sector, and ultimately company-level plans. If financing is inadequate compared to the need for funds, then adjustments must be made to the plans.

The actual capital commitments as opposed to planned capital commitments are facilitated in the implementation phase by a document called a capital expenditure appropriation (CEA). The CEA requires a technical description of the project and a check of the consistency of the project with the most recent strategic plan. It also requires a calculation of the internal rate of return of the project. At the time of the cases, the real cutoff internal rate of return was 12 percent throughout the company.

In the event that the proposal is no consistent with the strategic plan, a strategi investment proposal is prepared. These pro posals contain the same elements of th strategic plan and must be approved by a appropriate level of management: the ap proval level depends upon the amount of th investment.

When a CEA is initiated, it is firs reviewed by appropriate managers and sta within the SBU that generated it. If the CE exceeds the approval authority of the divisio manager of the SBU, it must be approved b group, sector, or top management. The ove all capital budgeting process used withi Diversified is similar to the process used i many large, diversified firms.

Case 9-1 New Semiconductor Product

The SBU in this case was engaged in the design and manufacturing of special-purpose semiconductor assemblies called *hybrids*. This product involved mounting and interconnecting active and passive microelectronic components within a single, small package.

At the time of the preparation of the 1990 strategic plan, a decision was made to transfer responsibilities for these hybrids to this SBU. The SBU then assumed responsibility for maintaining and expanding hybrid products.

At mid-year, contacts with a major existing customer indicated possible interest in a very large quantity of hybrids for controlling small electric motors. The product manager became very interested in capitalizing on this opportunity to expand sales, consistent with the new business unit responsibility.

After exploratory conversations with the customer, it became apparent to the product manager that capital investment of over $1 million would be required to procure the production equipment to meet these new production requirements. Since this opportunity was not foreseen when the previous strategic plan was revised, a strategic investment proposal was normally required.

The product manager used a series of informal channels to alert upper management to the possibility of this investment. She also prepared a preliminary version of the CEA for review, subject to refining the final details based upon continuing conversations with the customer. In preparing this preliminary version of the CEA, the product manager took care to ensure that the financial analysis was well supported and of high quality. In turn, upper management began to alert the CEO as opportunity presented itself. The proposal was considered highly attractive in informal discussions at this stage because of the general reputation of the customer. Also, expansion of this product line was consistent with the new strategic charter of the business unit. Moreover, economic returns were promising.

On the basis of this preliminary atmosphere of approval, the investment was included in the capital plan even though it was not included in the strategic plan prepared only a few months earlier. The actual investment was subject to the preparation and approval of the CEA. With all of this pre-warning, coupled with very favorable investment characteristics, the CEA worked its way up the approval latter very quickly. It was signed by the president of the company one month after its preparation.

QUESTIONS

1. What actual role did the formal approval process play in the actual approval of this project?
2. Who provided the impetus for this project?

Case 9-2 Computer-Aided Design System

In the 1980s, Diversified had developed a dominant position in the technology for designing and manufacturing high-performance, large-scale integrated circuits. The business grew very rapidly and by 1990 had reached $40 million in sales; it was then recognized as a profit center of the company.

Large-scale integrated circuit products involve many thousands of interconnected, equivalent transistors, densely packed onto a semiconductor surface smaller than the size of a fingernail. Designing such products requires the use of computer-based systems, which allow the engineer to work at graphics terminals that display the chip layout at many times its actual size. The rapid growth of the division led to the recommendation in the strategic plan of further investments in design automation systems to improve designs.

In late 1990, a CEA was initiated for the graphics work station needed to expand the design automation equipment. The amount of the investment was $500,000. No IRR was calculated since the investment was for general capability. The CEA was approved at the division level but was held up at the group level because the investment was dependent upon another investment, namely, the computer system to drive the graphics display. The division then prepared the CEA for the computer. The computer also involved an investment of about $500,000. Again, no IRR was calculated. The integrated investment proposal of $1 million was then submitted to the CEO. Even though there was no financial justification, the strategic linkage was quite clear, and the CEAs were approved. Total processing time for the CEAs was two months.

QUESTION

- What role did the formal capital budgeting system play in this decision? What value did the formal system have in this case?

Case 9-3 Facility Expansion

One of the divisions of Diversified was a contractor to the U. S. Department of Defense. It specialized in the design, development, and installation of complex computer systems for the Air Force. In the preparation of the 1990 strategic plan, special attention was given to expansion opportunities involving long-term contracts with the Air Force. In order to qualify for these contracts, the strategic plan contained provision for a new facility.

In the fall of 1990, the business unit was successful in winning two of these contracts. Shortly after the first of these was received, a CEA was prepared for computer equipment and associated peripherals, amounting to more than $1 million. Following the receipt of the second contract, another CEA was prepared for word-processing equipment amounting to several hundred thousand dollars. The IRR for both of these CEAs was well in excess of the company's hurdle rate.

The CEAs were not approved when they were submitted to the staff at the group level. The reason given was that the CEAs for computer hardware and software should be considered as part of an integrated group when the CEAs for the land and the new building were submitted. The initial IRR of the total investment indicated a rather low IRR of 11 percent, which was less than the company's hurdle rate.

At this point the group staff began a series of working sessions involving division and sector staffs and management. The financial analysis was rather complex, involving a variety of depreciation schedules. Government contracting rules on the treatment of taxes and financing had to be carefully checked. As it turned out, the initial financial analysis had not treated some of these areas properly, since once the proper methodologies were applied, the IRR was determined to be above the hurdle rate.

Managers involved with this project felt that they would have submitted this investment proposal even if there were no improvement in IRR. They further believed that it would have been approved by the CEO. Naturally, they were pleased with the favorable shift in the IRR. Now the approval process would be smoother.

QUESTIONS

1. What role did the formal approval process have in this case?
2. What does the case illustrate about the relationship between strategic plans and capital investment?

OVERALL QUESTION ON DIVERSIFIED ELECTRONICS

- What do these three cases illustrate about the formal and informal nature of the programming process in complex organizations?

10

CAPITAL BUDGETING METHODS

INTRODUCTION TO CAPITAL BUDGETING

A number of quantitative methods have proved very helpful in the financial evaluation phase of the capital budgeting process. Some of these are quite elementary, but others are more complex. This chapter deals with some of the more important methods.

Capital budgeting methods may be classified into two groups: nondiscounted cash flow methods and discounted cash methods.

NONDISCOUNTED CASH FLOW METHODS

We shall discuss two of the most widely used nondiscounted cash flow methods: payback and accounting rate of return.

Payback Method

The payback method enjoys widespread use, especially among Japanese managers, as a criterion for project selection. It results in the calculation of a payback period for a number of projects and selects those projects that result in recovering the initial investment in the shortest period of time.

The payback period is calculated as follows:

$$\text{Payback period} = \frac{\text{total investment}}{\text{average annual net cash inflow}} \qquad (1)$$

where total investment represents the sum of all capital outlays and average net annual cash inflow represents average annual cash inflows less average annual cash expenses.

The payback period, then, is the number of years it takes to recover the total outlay of an investment. As a criterion for project selection, it places a premium on the "liquidity" of a project and ignores completely an evaluation of the time value of earnings. Because it ignores the time value of earnings, it evaluates the projects with identical investments and identical average annual cash flows equally, even though one may have relatively low initial and high long-term returns and the other high initial and low long-term returns. In its crudest form, it also ignores the effects of taxes and depreciation on the profitability of projects. As a result, the selection criterion often leads to choices that are less profitable (that is, have shorter payback periods yet lower total profits) than do others available.

The payback method has a first cousin, the discounted payback method, which is actually a discounted cash flow method and will be discussed with these methods.

ACCOUNTING RATE-OF-RETURN METHOD

This method comes in many variations, and the results one arrives at may fluctuate dramatically depending upon the variation utilized. A general representation of the accounting rate-of-return method might begin simply as a ratio of average annual income to investment.

Each term, however, has been defined in two or more ways. Income is defined as annual income as estimated by the financial accounting process. But annual income might be total income or income net of taxes and depreciation. Furthermore, investment might be total investment or average investment, where average investment is defined as the average net book value (original cost minus accumulated depreciation) of the asset over its accounting (not economic) life.

Unlike the payback method, the accounting method yields a rate of return, yet this rate of return is (1) far from unambiguous, since its size is dependent upon the particular definitions of income and investment chosen, and is (2) insensitive to the effects of the time pattern of income and investment. Furthermore, the rate of return so computed usually double-counts the capital charge, once in the denominator (that is, investment) and once in the numerator (that is, by subtracting depreciation from gross income in arriving at net income), which leads to an erroneous rate of return.

DISCOUNTED CASH FLOW METHODS

The distinguishing characteristic of these selection criteria is that they seek to identify the incremental time pattern of revenues and expenditures associated with a project and subsequently reduce this time pattern to a common point in time.

THE NET PRESENT VALUE METHOD

The NPV is considered by economists to be the premier selection criterion, superior to all others for producing project recommendations that lead the firm to profit-maximizing choices. Let us now examine this method in detail.

The NPV criterion advises us to accept a project only if the discounted value (that is, the net present value) of its receipts equals or exceeds the discounted value of its outlays.

It recognizes explicitly that capital is productive and that it, therefore, has an opportunity cost. If the outlay associated with a given project were to be employed elsewhere, say, by investing it in a government security, it would earn interest annually. This interest is forgone when an investment is undertaken and, thus, represents an opportunity loss (or cost) that becomes the absolute minimum return that the internal project should earn to be considered economically viable. Since capital may be put to productive uses outside the firm, it has an opportunity cost associated with its use, a cost that must be reflected in the project selection criteria.

Furthermore, because capital may be invested at a positive annual return, it has a time value. That is, one dollar in hand is worth more than the same one dollar scheduled to be received one year from now, simply because one dollar in the present may be invested to yield one dollar plus interest one year from now. In two years, one dollar will earn the first year's interest and the interest upon the combined original one dollar and the first year's interest. Thus is demonstrated the well-known power of compound interest. This return on investment is forgone by internal investment and (approximately) represents the minimum a project should earn to justify the capital allocated to it.

The NPV method captures the time value and opportunity cost of money by employing the following formula:

$$\text{NPV} = -C_0 + \frac{R_1}{(1+i)} + \frac{R_2}{(1+i)^2} + \frac{R_3}{(1+i)^3} + \frac{R_n + S_n}{(1+i)^n} \tag{2}$$

where

$$C_0 = \text{the initial investment outlay at time zero or the present value of investment outlays}$$

$$R_1 = \text{the net return (earnings less expenses) associated with the project and received at the end of year 1}$$

$$R_2, \ldots, R_n = \text{the net return received in years 2 through } n \text{ (} n \text{ represents the last year of the project's life)}$$

$$S_n = \text{the scrap or market value of the asset at the end of its economic life}$$

$$i = \text{the discount rate approximating the annual opportunity cost of capital employed on this project}$$

$$(1+i), \ldots, (1+i)^n = \text{the present value factor applied to each annual net return so as to reduce distant returns to equivalent present values}$$

Now that we have defined the equation for finding the NPV, let us examine how one arrives at estimates for each of the terms (parameters) of the equation.[1]

Initial Investment Outlay (C_0) Most projects have large initial outlays followed by subsequent annual returns. The investment outlay should include only the capital costs that are incremental to the project under evaluation, not any so-called "sunk costs." In other words, if a new project utilizes capital facilities that are owned by the organization but are currently unemployed, no charge should be made to the project for these facilities at the outset of a new project.

On the other hand, if a new project utilizes facilities that are currently unemployed or underemployed but that are expected to be used, say, for an existing product line that is expanding in sales, the incremental capital costs associated with finding adequate capacity to accommodate the expanding product must be added to the project that displaced the expanding product, but *in the year* when new capacity is to be added, not in the present.

Similarly, new projects or products often are accommodated with the existing staff of representatives, managers, finance personnel, and other overhead personnel, at least initially. When, however, the new project or product expands and takes on a life of its own in the organization, it often requires the addition of overhead personnel. Therefore, estimates must be made of the personnel additions to a firm's overhead that a new project will require, and these charges must be subtracted from returns at the point at which these personnel are expected to be added to the project.

The lesson here is this: in the short run it is often possible for a project to be staffed by existing overhead personnel. As the project matures, it requires the addition of new overhead personnel as a direct result of its volume. Therefore, when a project results in the addition of new people, the charges so incurred must be included in estimating the NPV, but care must be taken to ensure that these charges are placed in the appropriate years and not simply included in C_0.

Another common problem occurs in estimating the additions of working capital required as a direct result of the introduction of a new product.[2] Since working capital must be financed by the use of permanent capital, any addition to it caused by a new product is indeed a part of the investment required by the new product and must be included as such in the analysis. On the other hand, when the level of working capital required by a new product is reduced, the reduction is considered to be a positive return of capital and is added to the revenue stream generated by the project in the year of its return.

Since addition and subtraction of working capital causes so many problems in project evaluation, it might be worthwhile to consider an example.

Let us assume that a firm is evaluating the economic feasibility of adding a new product (with a six-year life) to its product lines in 1993 and that the following levels of working capital are required to finance existing operations and inventories and accounts receivable for the new product.

Year	1993	1994	1995	1996	1997	1998	1999
Working capital (000s)	$300	$350	$410	$420	$390	$350	$300

We see quickly that the new product requires an addition to working capital of $50,000 in 1994, $60,000 in 1995, and $10,000 in 1996. Then the product reaches a phase in its life cycle where working capital is reduced by $30,000 in 1997, $40,000 in 1998, and by the remaining $50,000 in 1999. As far as the NPV method is concerned, the incremental additions to working capital are treated as investments and the incremental reductions returns of the project as they occur.

Another difficulty that often crops up when defining C_0 is the treatment of old assets that will be replaced if the new project is chosen. The only consideration relevant is: What economic value does the old asset have at the time of project evaluation? This value may take two forms.

Resale Value of the Old Equipment. If the equipment that is to be replaced has resale value, the value is used to reduce the initial capital outlay of the new project. Since we consider only incremental capital costs of the new project, we must be sure to subtract from the outlay of the new equipment the value of the old. This net value is truly the incremental effect of undertaking a project, since the old asset will be sold only if the new is acquired (that is, the prospect of the new allows us to sell the old).

Book Value of the Old Equipment. If the equipment that is to be replaced has an undepreciated book value but zero resale value, the undepreciated book value provides a tax deduction from the ordinary income of the firm.[3] Therefore, it reduces the incremental capital costs by the amount of the tax deduction, an amount that is found by multiplying the book value by the tax rate. If the old asset has a resale value lower than its undepreciated book value, only the difference between book and resale value is treated as a deduction from income taxes. The resale value is treated as recovery of capital.

Incremental Returns $(R_1, \ldots, R_n)$. The annual returns of a project consist of the incremental income produced during the project's life. Income is determined net of taxes. Taxes are reduced by the deduction from taxes provided by depreciation of the new equipment. This tax reduction provided by depreciation is called the *depreciation tax shield*. Let us turn now to a discussion of each of these points.

Incremental Income Net of Taxes. Taxes must be subtracted from each year's incremental return to provide the true effects of a new project on net income. The problem is complicated somewhat, because the new project will result in a stream of depreciation allowances that *shield* a portion (and in many cases a major portion) of the incremental returns from income taxes. Depreciation is subtracted from incremental income in arriving at taxable income but is then added back to income after taxes to arrive at the net incremental return (R) that appears in the NPV equation. To not add back depreciation in arriving at the net incremental return would result in counting capital costs twice and is a common error committed in reality. Let us illustrate the role of taxes and depreciation by a simple example.

Assume that we are considering a project that provides incremental returns of $2,000 per year for 10 years and has an initial capital cost of $10,000. Assume further that the rate of taxation is 50 percent and that depreciation is accomplished by the straight-line method.

We should note immediately that $C_0 = \$10,000$. Now let us compute $R_1, \ldots, R_{10}$. The straight-line method of depreciation requires us simply to divide the capital charge (in this example $10,000) by the economic life (10 years) to arrive at the annual depreciation charge. In this case, depreciation is at an annual rate of 10 percent, resulting in a charge of $1,000 per year. Now, to compute income taxes, we subtract depreciation from income (that is, $2,000 − $1,000 = $1,000) and subject the difference to taxes ($1,000 at 50% = $500). Therefore, our tax of $500 reduces our incremental income by $500 and results in an annual net return (R) of $1,500.

Therefore, to arrive at our net annual return, we add depreciation ($1,000) back to our income after taxes ($500) because not to do so results in double-counting our incremental capital costs.[4] This because our capital charges ($10,000) are already included in C_0 and should not be included in $R_1, \ldots, R_{10}$ other than to offset taxes paid on the project.

The problem is complicated further if an accelerated method of depreciation is employed on the new equipment, since the size of the tax shield will vary from year to year and will decrease progressively during the life of the equipment. Fortunately, tables are available that facilitate the calculation of the tax shield when accelerated methods of depreciation are employed. Such a table, calculated for the sum-of-years'-digits method of depreciation, is reproduced in Appendix C of this chapter.

Although tax rules change frequently in the United States and they differ from country to country, we will use the sum-of-years'-digits (SYD) method of depreciation to illustrate the impact of accelerated depreciation on investment proposals. Then we will compare the results with what we would have achieved using the straight-line method of depreciation. We assume a discount rate of 10 percent.

The NPV using the straight-line method of depreciation simply requires us to find the present value of $1,500 received each year for 10 years at a discount rate of 10 percent. Appendix B of this chapter contains a table for finding the present value factor for a constant stream of earnings. The table gives the present value of $1 received annually for a given number of years at a specified discount rate. One dollar received for 10 years at 10 percent produces a present value factor of 6.145. Therefore, $1,500 received for 10 years at 10 percent yields a present value of $9,217.50 (that is, $1,500 × 6.145). When subtracted from the initial investment (C_0) of $10,000, we find the project should be rejected on the NPV criterion.

If we substitute SYD depreciation for straight-line depreciation, the NPV will change in a material way. To find the NPV using the SYD method, we first find the present value of the depreciation tax shield from Appendix C. At a 10 percent discount rate and a useful life of 10 years, the present value factor is 0.701, which yields a present value for the depreciation tax shield of $7,010 (that is, 0.701 ×

$10,000). The present value of the depreciation tax shield using straight-line depreciation is found in Appendix A to be $6,145 (that is, $10,000 for 10 years at 10 percent). Therefore, the net effect of SYD depreciation is to raise the present value of the depreciation tax shield by $865.

We now proceed to solve the problem. The tax shield of $7,010 reduces taxes by $3,505 (the tax rate of 50 percent multiplied by $7,010). Therefore, if we assume that the entire proceeds of $2,000 per year are taxed at 50 percent, the present value of what remains is $6,145 ($1,000 × 10% for 10 years). Now we must add back the tax savings that result from the depreciation tax shield, which produces an NPV of $9,651 ($6,145 + $3,505).[5] Therefore, the effect of using the accelerated depreciation procedure increases the present value of the revenue stream by $433.50 and yields an NPV of –$349. Although the switch to SYD does not make this project acceptable, it does make it much less unacceptable. It is not difficult to think of examples where a switch to SYD would make an unacceptable project acceptable.

Scrap or Residual Value of New Project (S_n).   The new project under evaluation may have, at the conclusion of its economic life, equipment remaining that continues to have residual value. This residual value, often referred to as scrap value, must be estimated and included as a refund of capital costs in the period (that is, period n) when it is expected.

The Rate of Discounting (i).   The rate of discounting (or the discount rate) is perhaps the most controversial aspect of the net present value method. It should represent an estimate of the opportunity cost of employing funds on a given project. The difficulty involves estimating this opportunity cost. In a profitable organization, it is always greater than the cost of borrowing funds, but the real question is: How much greater? We proceed now to answer this question.

There are two main sources of funds: debt and equity. Debt consists of funds provided by creditors who have legal claims on the firm for the payment of interest and for the repayment of their original capital. The two most common types of debt are corporate bonds and bank loans (or notes).

Equity funds are provided by the stockholders or owners of a firm and provide holders of equity with what is customarily referred to as a *residual claim on income.* That is, stockholders have no legal claim to dividends or a return of their original capital. Rather, they share the income remaining after all legal claims of government, employees, and creditors are met. Equity financing may generally take three forms: earnings retained by the firm, sale of common stock, and sale of preferred stock. We turn now to compute the cost of each source of funds.

Cost of Debt

When computing the cost of debt capital, we must choose a perspective. That is, from whose point of view are we evaluating the problem? In all theoretical models, it is assumed that cost of capital calculations are made from the point of view of the owners of the firm. Owners or stockholders are interested in after-tax returns.

Therefore, our calculation of the cost of capital should be in terms of after-tax costs to the stockholders of a firm.

The sources of funds are not treated equally by the tax system. Interest expense, arising out of debt claims, is deductible from federal income taxes. As a result, interest expense shelters income from taxation by an amount equal to the tax rate multiplied by interest expense. Therefore, the after-tax cost of debt is reduced by the tax deduction provided by interest expense. The after-tax cost of debt (K_d) is defined formally as

$$K_d = K_b(1 - t) \tag{3}$$

where K_b = the cost of debt before taxes
t = the tax rate

To see the effect of the tax treatment of debt, let us consider the after-tax cost of a bond at an interest rate of 9 percent and a tax rate of 50 percent. Such a bond results in an after-tax cost of 4.5 percent: $0.09(1 - 0.50)$. Of course, this calculation is valid only if the firm expects a positive value of income subject to taxes. For if the firm is incurring losses, the tax rate is zero and the after-tax cost of debt is equal to the before-tax cost of debt. The formula for computing the cost of debt capital applies to all forms of long-term debt.

Cost of Equity

Unlike sources of funds provided by creditors, there are differences in the computation of after-tax costs of alternative source of equity. In addition, for reasons that will soon become apparent, the cost of equity capital is slightly more ambiguous than is the cost of debt capital. Let us now consider each source of equity funds in turn.

Preferred Stock

Preferred stock is a hybrid security with characteristics similar to those of bonds on one hand and those of common stock on the other. As with bonds, dividends on preferred stock represent a commitment by the firm to pay a fixed sum regularly to preferred stockholders. Unlike bond interest, however, dividends on preferred stock are not deductible from income taxes. Like common stock, dividends are paid only insofar as the firm has income after taxes, but preferred stockholders have the first claim on the income that remains after taxes.

Since dividends on preferred stock are paid after taxes, the true after-tax cost of preferred stock (K_p) is given by

$$K_p = \frac{D_p}{P_n} \tag{4}$$

where D_p = the dividend paid on preferred shares and P_n = net proceeds per share of preferred stock.

Therefore, if the firm sells preferred stock yielding $100 per share and pays a dividend of $9, the after-tax cost of preferred stock simply becomes 9 percent.

That is, the firm must earn $9 per share after taxes to cover its preferred dividends without invading income available for common shareholders. We quickly see that issues of debt and preferred stock that carry identical nominal costs have vastly different real costs after the effects of taxes are considered.

Before leaving our discussion of preferred stock, it is important to note that the net proceeds from the sale of preferred stock are found by subtracting the costs associated with floating an issue of preferred stock from the sales price. The proceeds of an issue are always lower than the market price of the shares.

Earnings Retained by the Firm

To estimate the cost of retained earnings, we have to begin with questions similar to those just considered. In the case of debt and preferred stock, we first began by finding the rate of interest or dividends required by creditors and investors to market the securities; then we had to consider the effect of taxes upon the after-tax cost of capital to the firm.

Similarly, when we consider the cost of retained earnings, we must ask what return the common stockholders require, for these earnings are the property of shareholders, retained for reinvestment by the firm. What rate of return do the shareholders require to allow the firm to retain a portion of its earnings? The answer is that stockholders purchase a stock both for its current dividend yield plus expectation of future growth in earnings and dividends. If actual earnings fall below expected earnings, the market price of the firm's stock will almost certainly fall. Therefore, shareholders require the firm to earn at least enough to prevent the share price from falling, which implies that the firm must earn, on the funds reinvested, a rate equal to the sum of the current dividend yield plus anticipated growth in that yield. In other words, the cost of retained earnings (K_r) is approximated by

$$K_r = \frac{D_0}{P_0} + g \tag{5}$$

where D_0/P_0 = the current dividend yield and g = the rate of growth in earnings and dividends.

If the firm earns more than K_r on funds retained in the business, we should expect the share price to rise. If it earns less, we should expect the share price to fall. If K_r is earned on the new project, the share price will not move, at least not as an effect of the investment and financing decision.

Cost of Common Stock Financing

The cost of common stock (K_c) financing to existing shareholders is similar to the cost of retained earnings. The only difference is in the additional transaction costs incurred. Transaction costs include the cost of preparing and distributing a prospectus for the offering and the brokerage costs involved in marketing the securities. These flotation costs tend to raise the cost of capital above the cost of retained earnings (the other form of equity capital).

The cost of common stock financing may be found by modifying the preceding formula for retained earnings as follows:

$$K_c = \frac{D_0}{P_0 \, (1 - FC)} + g \qquad (6)$$

where FC = the flotation costs associated with the common stock financing as a percentage of total proceeds.

This formula produces a cost of capital that is slightly higher than that found for retained earnings, since it reduces the proceeds from the sale by the per share flotation costs. The higher cost of capital ensures that no project using common stock financing will pass the NPV criterion unless it returns enough to cover the current dividend yield plus growth as well as the flotation costs associated with the issue.

Now that we have provided formulas for estimating the cost of capital for each source, we may add a few general comments regarding the composition of an optimal capital structure. As we noticed from the preceding analysis, the after-tax cost of debt is likely to be considerably lower than any other source of capital. This occurs for two reasons: (1) a smaller inducement is necessary to attract bondholders than stockholders, since bondholders (and all creditors, for that matter) have a claim to earnings that precedes the claim of all equity owners, and (2) interest paid to bondholders is deductible from the firm's income taxes.

Since the sale of bonds seems to be the least costly method of financing investment, one might think a firm would be wise to finance all its investments using debt. There is a problem, however, with this strategy, since a rise in interest expenses becomes very risky to bondholders, and especially to stockholders.

As the level of interest expense rises, the risk of insolvency increases, because the level of gross income necessary to meet interest expense rises. To default on interest or principal payments is cause for bankruptcy. Therefore, the greater the proportion of debt (or leverage) in a firm's capital structure, relative to the normal level for that particular industry (or risk class), the higher the interest charges required on future debt, and the higher the dividend (plus growth) required on equity to induce investors to purchase the equity offerings of such a firm. The dividend yield is raised to the required level by a drop in the price of the stock, a real additional cost of debt borne by existing stockholders as a result of the decision to raise a firm's ratio of debt to total capital.

Consider the effect of increasing leverage on a firm with an all-equity capital structure, as indicated in Exhibit 10-1.

Let us take the same earnings stream but assume that the firm's capital structure consists of 50 percent debt and 50 percent equity, with that same equity represented by 50,000 shares. Furthermore, let us assume that the firm incurs a fixed interest expense on the debt of $100,000. The results for various earnings are given in Exhibit 10-2. Comparing earnings per share given on line 3 of Exhibits 10-1 and 10-2, we find that leverage increases the variability of stockholders' earnings. The range of earnings in Exhibit 10-1 is $0.50 to $2.50, as contrasted to a range of $0 to $4.00 in Exhibit 10-2. Increased variability occurs because the fixed interest

Exhibit 10-1
All Equity Capital Structure

		1	2	3	4	5
1.	Alternative levels of earnings before taxes	$100,000	$200,000	$300,000	$400,000	$500,000
2.	Earnings per share before taxes, 100,000 shares	$1.00	$2.00	$3.00	$4.00	$5.00
3.	Earnings per share after taxes, 50% tax rate	$0.50	$1.00	$1.50	$2.00	$2.50

expense reduces income before taxes at lower levels of income, whereas the smaller number of shares results in higher earnings per share at income levels above some point, in our case at and above earnings level 3.

Therefore, the effect of leverage is to magnify both the losses and the gains to shareholders. The greater the leverage, the greater the variability (or variance) and consequently the greater the risk of returns to shareholders. The greater the risk, the greater the expected return must be to induce investors to purchase and hold the shares of the firm. Thus, as leverage increases, the expected return and cost of equity capital increase.

Therefore, the real cost of debt to the firm may be expected to rise gradually as its proportion of total capital rises, because both bondholders and stockholders must be compensated for the increased risk they bear. It gradually takes on a cost that is equal to or greater than that of equity, but the cost of debt and equity are so interrelated that it is difficult to arrive at a pure measure of either. Furthermore, the market for a firm's debt and equity is affected by general forces that themselves cause a fluctuation in the market price (and therefore cost) of each. Because financial managers may be expected to adapt to market conditions, they are often involved in *marketing* both debt and equity issues simultaneously, and it is also extremely difficult to determine where precisely the capital for "project X" was obtained.

To summarize this section, we may say that while it is practically impossible to determine the precise opportunity cost of capital for a given project, an operational second or third best procedure does exist, and in reality we must settle for

Exhibit 10-2
Mixed Capital Structure

		1	2	3	4	5
1.	Alternative levels of earnings before taxes	$0	$100,000	$200,000	$300,000	$400,000
2.	Earnings per share before taxes, 50,000 shares	—	$2.00	$4.00	$6.00	$8.00
3.	Earnings per share after taxes, 50% tax rate	—	$1.00	$2.00	$3.00	$4.00

this kind of approximation to the true cost of capital. Roughly, it requires that we find a weighted average cost of capital by determining the after-tax cost of debt and the after-tax cost of equity and assign weights to each source of capital equal to the proportion they represent in the total capital structure. For example, consider a firm with the structure of capital given in Exhibit 10-3.

Therefore, the cost of capital is 8.8 percent in this example and becomes an estimate of the rate of discounting (i) in our NPV formulation of the problem. The weighted average cost of capital does approximate the true opportunity cost of capital for the potential projects of an organization, since paying off lenders and owners is a distinct choice that the firm has in the investment process. The firm acts in the welfare of owners by choosing projects that have proceeds that exceed the riskless opportunity of paying back debt and equity sources.

The preceding computation may be used to estimate the cost of various sources of debt and equity, and a weighted average cost of capital in our NPV criterion is a compromise solution that is justified on the grounds that in practice (1) the cost of debt and equity are highly interrelated and (2) it is difficult to isolate the precise source of financing for a given project. Thus, a weighted average cost of capital provides a good second- or third-best estimate of the true opportunity cost of funds for a firm.

Economic Life (n) of a Project. One of the most difficult parameters of the NPV method to choose is the economic life of a project. The economic life represents the time period during which each project under evaluation is expected to be productive. In the case of equipment, it is likely to be shorter than the physical life simply because technological advance often makes the economic life shorter than the physical life. That is, once a more advanced piece of equipment enters the market, it becomes necessary to consider it, for if it truly represents a technological breakthrough, it may not only pass the NPV criterion, but force the firm to invest to remain competitive in its market. In this case, the physical life of the old equipment may exceed its economic life by a number of years.

Although there are few guidelines for estimating the economic life of a new product, we are fortunate in the case of equipment investment, since the U.S.

Exhibit 10-3
Computation of Weighted Average Cost of Capital

Source of Capital	After-Tax Cost	Proposition of Total Capital	Weighted Cost of Capital
Debt (40%			
Bonds	4.5%	0.20%	0.90%
Long-term bank notes	4.0	0.20	0.80
Equity (60%)			
Preferred stock	11.0	0.10	1.10
Common stock	12.0	0.50	6.00
Total		1.00%	8.80%

Treasury Department's *Depreciation Guidelines* provides some help. These guidelines are formulated for various categories of assets with explicit consideration given to the history of obsolescence for each category. Since these depreciation guidelines consider technological obsolescence from actual surveys of asset replacement, they often provide good estimates of economic life of assets, including buildings and equipment.

This completes our discussion of the NPV method. As stated earlier, it is the criterion of evaluation most acceptable to economists, because it considers all the relevant components of a study (the time value of money, incremental cost and revenues over time, project life, taxes, and depreciation) without encountering any serious theoretical difficulties. Such theoretical difficulties beset all other techniques, including the internal rate-of-return criterion, which is a variation of the NPV criterion. We turn now to a discussion of this criterion.

INTERNAL RATE OF RETURN METHOD (IRR)

We restate the NPV model as

$$\text{NPV} = C_0 + \frac{R_1}{(1+i)} + \frac{R_2}{(1+i)^2} + \frac{R_3}{(1+i)^2} + \frac{R_n + S_n}{(1+r)^n} \tag{2a}$$

In the IRR method we move C_0 to the left side of the equation and replace the discount rate i with the internal rate r as follows:

$$C_0 = \frac{R_1}{(1+r)} + \frac{R_2}{(1+r)^2} + \dots + \frac{R_n + S_n}{(1+r)^n} \tag{2b}$$

Under the IRR method, we solve for the internal rate of return r that sets the discounted benefit stream (that is, the right side of the equation) equal to initial outlay or to the present value of the outlays of the project (that is, C_0). A project is considered acceptable if the internal rate is greater than or equal to the discount rate.

While the IRR method does have the advantage over the NPV method of providing a single measure of the profitability of a project, which is very useful for ranking projects and choosing among mutually exclusive projects, it is not without its problems. We turn now to a discussion of its two most serious problems.

Multiple Rates of Return.   Under certain conditions, the IRR method may produce multiple rates of return for a given outlay and income stream, thus providing an ambiguous evaluation of the merits of a project. We will illustrate this potential problem by presenting an example of its occurrence.

Let us assume that we are considering replacing a pump for removing oil from a well with a larger pump. The larger pump has an initial cost of $1,600 and is expected to yield proceeds of $20,000 at the end of year 1, and nothing thereafter, since the well will be depleted. The old pump is slower, and with it we will not remove all the oil until the end of the second year, thus spreading the total proceeds of $20,000 evenly into two annual payments of $10,000. We assume further that taxes, depreciation, and salvage value are to be ignored in this problem.[6]

The incremental stream of outlays and income generated by this investment consists of an outlay of $1,600 now, a subsequent incremental income of $10,000 (that is, the $20,000 received minus the $10,000 that would be earned using the old pump) at the end of year 1, and a negative income flow of $10,000 in year 2 (that is, the firm receives nothing with the new pump in year 2 as opposed to the $10,000 it would receive if it retained the old pump).

Exhibit 10-4 contains the net present value of this prospective project at various rates of discount. Exhibit 10-5 is merely a diagrammatic representation of these data. As we quickly see from examining Exhibits 10-4 and 10-5, there are two rates of discount that equate the outlays with the revenue stream and thus produce a net present value of zero. Therefore, there are two internal rates of return, one at 25 percent and the second of 400 percent. Which is the true rate of return for the project? Is it 25 percent or 400 percent? Surely something has gone wrong!

Let us examine how these queer results occur. At a zero rate of discount, the project has an NPV of −$1,600 (simply the algebraic sum of the the three incremental cash flows). At rates of discount up to 24 percent the NPV is negative. The reason this occurs is that at low rates of discount, the large negative flow in year 2 is having an impact significant enough to produce a negative NPV; that is, the discount rate has not yet reached a level that completely offsets the −$1,600 algebraic sum of three flows. It does reach that level at 25 percent. At 25 percent the NPV of −$10,000 in year 2 is exactly $1,600 less than the NPV of $10,000 received in year 1 so as to equal the initial outlay of $1,600.

At rates higher than 25 percent, the NPV becomes positive because rates above 25 percent result in discounted values of the negative return of the second year that are smaller than the discounted value of the first-year return by amounts progressively greater than the initial outlay of $1,600. In other words, the higher the interest rate, the less the influence the larger negative outlay in period 2 has

Exhibit 10-4
Dual Rates of Return

ate of discounting	0%	10%	15%	20%	25%	30%	40%	50%	60%	70%	80%
et present value	−$1,600	−$774	−$466	−$211	$0	+$175	+$441	+$622	+$744	+$822	+$869

ate of discounting	90%	100%	125%	150%	175%	200%	225%	250%	275%	300%	325%
t present value	+$893	+$900	+$869	+$800	+$714	+$622	+$530	+$440	+$356	+$275	+$193

te of discounting	350%	375%	400%	500%	600%	700%	800%				
t present value	+$128	+$62	0	−$211	−$376	−$506	−$612				

Exhibit 10-5
Dual Rates of Return Under IRR Method

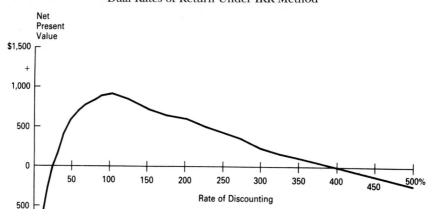

on net present values. The NPV hits a peak at a discount rate of 100 percent and then begins a slow decline, because at discount rates above 100 percent the initial outlay begins to have a very large influence on net present values and year 1 and 2 relatively less, thus slowly dropping the NPV. Finally, at 400 percent the NPV becomes zero and then progressively negative thereafter because of the enormous discounting of period one and two values.

Mathematically speaking, the equation for the internal rate of return is a polynomial of degree *n*, which means that *n* different solutions are possible to the polynomial equation. For the normal project where we have relatively large outflows at the beginning and positive inflows throughout the project life, all the solutions or roots of the equation will be either imaginary or negative except one, which will be positive. Therefore, for normal projects, only one positive IRR occurs. The possibility of multiple positive solutions arises when there are relatively large reversals in the signs of cash flows, predominately and simultaneously at the beginning and end of the project life. The theoretical maximum number of real IRRs for a project is determined by the number of sign reversals, yet multiple rates are most likely to occur in situations similar to our new pump project.

To see how these results follow, let us assume in our pump example that the new pump has a salvage value at the end of year 3 of $1,000. The investment flows in the IRR model become

$$\$1,600 = \frac{\$10,000}{(1 + r)} - \frac{\$10,000}{(1 + r)^2} + \frac{\$1,000}{(1 + r)^3}$$

Exhibit 10-6 gives the NPVs for these new cash flows. Notice that the NPV becomes zero at two points (10.5 percent and approximately 395 percent), which means two positive IRRs. At rates beyond 395 percent, the NPV becomes increasingly negative and *never* will become positive again. This is true despite another sign reversal (that is, the $1,000 positive salvage value in year 3). Now, if we make the last flow (somehow!) in year 3 a positive $10,000 so that we have a relatively large flow change the last year, rather than having three real rates of return, we have only one IRR of 429 percent, because the relatively large positive flow of year 3 prevents the NPV from falling to zero at discount rates below 429 percent. In fact, as discount rates rise even higher, all terms but the $1,600 outflow at time zero will gain less dominance in the NPV calculation. As discount rates rise even higher, all terms but the $1,600 will have smaller and smaller effects upon the NPV, and it will approach −$1,600.

Both these examples illustrate the prerequisite for relatively large outflows at the end of a project for the occurrence of multiple rates of return. Yet practice suggests that multiple rates of return do occur frequently enough to call attention to the problem; it is definitely another limitation of the IRR method. The problem is not so widespread as to destroy the usefulness of the IRR method, but it occurs enough to require the attention of users.

Multiple rates of return are most likely to occur whenever a project possesses relatively large incremental negative returns *both* at the beginning and end of project life. These situations are very common in mining where heavy costs are incurred in either closing a mine or restoring a coal field to its previous natural state to meet environmental standards.

Conflicting Evaluations of Mutually Exclusive Investment Projects

A more serious problem besetting the IRR criterion concerns the possibility of accepting the *wrong* project when selecting among mutually exclusive investment opportunities. Mutually exclusive projects are two or more projects that accomplish almost identical objectives, such as two similar warehouses, so that only the

Exhibit 10-6
Dual Rates of Return

te of discounting	0%	10%	10.5%	15%	20%	25%	30%	40%	50%	60%	70%	80%
t present value	−$600	−$22	$0	$191	$368	$512	$630	$805	$919	$988	$1,026	$1,040

te of discounting	90%	100%	125%	150%	175%	200%	225%	250%	275%	300%	325%	350%
present value	$1,038	$1,025	$957	$864	$762	$659	$559	$464	$374	$290	$212	$139

e of discounting	375%	400%	500%	600%	700%	800%	1,000%	1,500%	2,000%	3,000%	4,000%	5,000%
present value	$71	$8	−$206	−$373	−$504	−$611	−$773	−$1,104	−$1,146	−$1,287	−$1,362	−$1,408

most profitable one is to be chosen. As an illustration, we assume the data for two mutually exclusive projects given in Exhibit 10-7.[7]

The internal rate of return of project A is 78.5 percent, whereas the internal rate of return on project B is 73 percent. On an IRR criterion, project A is superior to project B. But note the results shown on Exhibit 10-8 and Exhibit 10-9.

From Exhibits 10-8 and 10-9 we see that project B has a higher NPV at discount rates between 0 and 30 percent, but at higher rates (from 40 to 80 percent) project A is preferable. Therefore, if we selected 20 percent as a discount rate (a reasonable rate), project B would be preferable to project A by the NPV criterion. On the basis of the IRR criterion, however, project A is the best choice. Thus we have contradictory evaluation of the two projects by the two criteria.

The resolution of this problem simultaneously identifies the weakness of the IRR method. The crucial assumption contained by both the NPV and IRR criteria is that the proceeds received throughout the life of a project may be reinvested at the discount rate chosen, in the case of the NPV criterion, or at the rate of return calculated, in the case of the IRR method.

Let us illustrate the impact of this assumption by using an example drawn from personal finance. When an individual purchases a $1,000 bond with a 10 percent or $100 coupon and a life of 10 years, he or she receives $100 a year for 10 years plus his original capital of $1,000 at the end of year 10. If he or she were to simply put the annual interest checks in a safe spot at home, at the end of 10 years the total sum would be $2,000.

If we now ask the rate of return this investor earns employing this strategy, we would have to find the discount rate which equates $2,000 received at the end of year 10 with a present sum of $1,000, a rate approximately equal to 7 percent. Therefore, the investor's strategy yields a return of not 10 percent but 7 percent!

Why does this happen? It happens because the investor failed to reinvest the coupon checks as they were received. To truly achieve a 10 percent return over the life of the bond, he or she would have had to reinvest each check at 10 percent over the life of the bond.

Exhibit 10-7
Mutually Exclusive Projects

Time	A	B
0	$-85	$-90
1	17	21
2	35	33
3	68	57
4	131	94
5	216	155
6	357	255
7	546	420
8	555	695
9	345	1,150

Exhibit 10-8
Conflicting Evaluations of Mutually Exclusive Projects
Using NPV and IRR Methods

Rate of discounting	0%	10%	20%	30%	40%	50%	60%	70%	80%
Net present value, project A	$2,185	$1,121	$611	$345	$198	$110	$56	$21	−$3
Net present value, project B	$2,790	$1,331	$678	$360	$192	$99	$43	$8	−$15

From this simple example we see that the NPV method contains the implicit assumption that funds will be reinvested at the discount rate as they are received. If they can be reinvested only at a lower rate, then the true rate of return earned on the project will be somewhat less than the discount rate. Similarly, the IRR method contains the implicit assumption that the proceeds from the project will be reinvested at the calculated internal rate of return.

Now to return to our original example of the mutually exclusive investment projects. Project A has an IRR of 78.5 percent, and project B has an IRR of 73 per-

Exhibit 10-9
Conflicting Evaluations of Mutually Exclusive Projects
Using NPV and IRR Methods

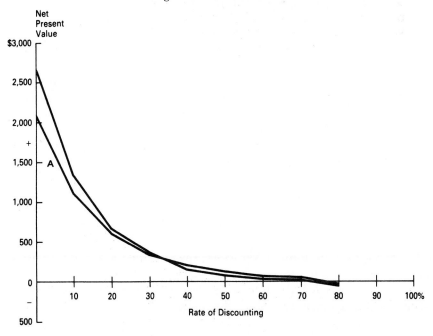

cent. Project A is the choice of the IRR criterion simply because its proceeds are realized at a faster rate than are those of project B and are implicitly assumed to be immediately reinvested at the higher calculated rate of return. On the NPV criterion, however, a lower discount rate (than 78.5 percent) is applied to annual net cash flows, and it is that rate that becomes the rate of reinvestment assumed. At a reasonable cost of capital, for example, one between 10 and 20 percent, project B has a higher NPV because such a low rate allows the relatively large flows of years 8 and 9 to have a significant impact on the NPV of project B, a project that has a much larger undiscounted net cash flow ($2,880 versus $2,195).

CORRECT PROCEDURE: NET PRESENT VALUE CRITERION

We may conclude from the foregoing discussion that the IRR criterion has some very serious difficulties and contains an implicit assumption concerning reinvestment that does not square well with reality. We may be confident that reinvestment opportunities more closely resemble our chosen opportunity cost of capital, which is chosen to represent known opportunities that the firm has to employ funds rather than some calculated rate of return on a particular project. Clearly, if reinvestment rates are to be treated implicitly, they are best reflected within the NPV model.

To summarize, the IRR method is beset with two technical difficulties and contains a reinvestment assumption that does not square with reality. The NPV criterion suffers no such problem and is therefore the theoretically preferred procedure. The IRR method may be used only when its potential problems are not likely to occur. It should be said that there are likely to be many applications where the IRR method is quite useful.

DISCOUNTED PAYBACK PERIOD METHOD

The discounted payback period method may be used to supplement the NPV method and may be calculated at the same time. It simply uses all the data of an NPV calculation to calculate a payback period from the incremental time stream of outlays and earnings, but now using discounted data rather than absolute data. The resultant discounted payback period then represents the amount of time a particular project is expected both to return its initial capital *and* to earn just the requisite rate of return given by the discount rate.

Using alternatives A and B of the previous example, and a discount rate of 10 percent, we calculate payback period of four years for project B and three years for project A. At this reduced discount rate, the relatively larger early positive flows of project A yield a quicker recovery of the initial outlay than is the case for project B. To the extent that a decision maker judges the uncertainty of a project evaluation to be inversely related to its discounted payback period, the decision maker would prefer project A over B at 10 percent, become neutral at 20 percent and 30 percent, and prefer A over B at or above 40 percent.

Because the future is so difficult to predict, a decision maker might very well rank those projects that are likely to recover the initial investment plus normal return most quickly ahead of slightly more profitable, but, because of distant returns, more risky alternatives. In any event, the discounted payback method provides further information to the decision maker, which along with the NPV data may allow a decision to be made according to his or her own preferences.

To conclude this discussion, we may say that the net present value selection criterion is superior to all others on theoretical grounds for a firm seeking the most profitable projects for investment. It does not, however, come with a set of instructions for dealing with the leading character in the resource allocation process: *uncertainty*. Provision for uncertainty must be discussed further, but even then we will have no perfect solution. A few of the other methods discussed, especially the discounted payback method, have the virtue that they attempt to deal with this character, albeit rather crudely. Let us now turn to examine common procedures for making provision for uncertainty within the framework of the NPV criterion.

PROVISION FOR UNCERTAINTY

Virtually every investment project that is to be evaluated requires that we provide *estimates* for the various parameters to arrive at a decision. Because it is extremely rare to know these values with certainty, our procedures for project selection must allow us to make provision for uncertainty. We should not expect different projects to possess equal amounts of uncertainty, for we know that a project that involves replacing a piece of existing equipment has revenue estimates (that is, cost savings) that are likely to be far more certain than the revenue estimates associated with a completely new product. Since uncertainty should be expected to vary depending upon the nature of the project under evaluation, we may expect the methods of providing for uncertainty to vary also.

Numerous procedures have been proposed for dealing with the uncertainty that exists regarding estimates of outlays, revenues, project life, and discount rate. In this section we review four such methods.

ADDITION OF RISK FACTOR TO DISCOUNT RATE

This widely used technique provides for the addition of a risk adjustment to the cost of capital in arriving at an estimate of the rate of discount. It has the effect of further reducing the influence of future returns on present values to compensate for the uncertain nature of estimates of outlays and proceeds. This procedure, however, is quite arbitrary and comes with no set of instructions for choosing the size of the risk factor.

A slight variation of this procedure makes the value of the risk factor a positive function of time. This modification results in progressively higher rates of discount for the more distant cash flows of a project. It suffers from the same limitations that the simpler risk factor procedure does.

TRUNCATING THE ESTIMATED LIFE OF A PROJECT

This procedure simply truncates the estimated life of a project somewhat short of its expected economic life to provide a conservative assessment of the NPV. The truncation procedure is very arbitrary and has no redeeming virtue, except, perhaps, that it is easy to apply.

SENSITIVITY ANALYSIS

Sensitivity analysis is a procedure that requires us to identify the parameters of an NPV calculation to which the NPV is most sensitive and then choose alternate values, including worst-case ones, for those sensitive parameters whose values are clearly uncertain. If the NPV remains positive or becomes zero when worst-case values are used in the NPV procedure, then we can have more confidence in our original positive evaluation.

Similarly, if optimistic values of sensitive but uncertain parameters do not alter a negative NPV, we may have more confidence in our original negative evaluation. For those projects whose evaluation is altered by this procedure, we can say little except that the most crucial parameters ought to be estimated more closely and accurately if we are to avoid serious error.

Sensitivity analysis also may be carried out in conjunction with any particular method of evaluating investment projects. Moreover, its use is greatly facilitated by the widespread availability of computer programs that allow us to carry out complete sensitivity analyses in a matter of minutes. As a result, most firms use sensitivity analysis to assess uncertainty in project evaluation.

RISK ANALYSIS USING PROBABILITIES AND MONTE CARLO SIMULATION

David Hertz (1964), in what has become a classic *Harvard Business Review* article, proposed a probabilistic method of analyzing risk in capital investment decisions. The method requires us to:

1. Identify the key elements of the investment project.
2. Establish probability distributions for each element.
3. Calculate a large number of solutions, using random numbers in providing values for each of the distributions.
4. Infer the nature of the risk associated with a prospective investment project from a distribution of solutions using statistical techniques.

We will now illustrate the technique, using the capabilities of the Interactive Financial Planning System (IFPS) to solve the example Hertz used in the article.[8]

A chemical firm is evaluating a $10 million addition to its processing plant, which would give it the opportunity to enter a product market in which it does not currently now compete. After extensive study and deliberations, management identifies the following key elements in the decision and a range of values for each:

Element	Most Likely Value	Range of Values
1. Market size	250,000 tons	100,000–340,000 tons
2. Market growth	3%	0–6%
3. Selling price	$510/ton	$385–$575/ton
4. Market share	12%	3–17%
5. Investment	$9.5 million	$7.0–$10.5 million
6. Operating cost	$435 per unit	$370–$545 per unit
7. Fixed cost	$300,000	$250,000–$375,000
8. Residual value	$4.5 million	$3.5–$5.0 million
9. Useful life	10 years	5–15 years

Hertz does not complicate the problem further by introducing depreciation and taxes. We shall follow his example here also in order to keep the example relatively simple. Let's look at how this problem is solved and the IRR is found using IFPS. The IFPS model is given in Exhibit 10-10.

Let's go through the model line by line. Statement 10 simply identifies the model. The asterisk after line number 10 simply instructs IFPS that what follows is merely descriptive information, not calculational data. Line 20 defines the life of the project. We have set the project life at 10 years, the most likely value, and stipulated 10 years' or columns' worth of information for the remaining variables of the model. (We could later run the model, varying this assumption, but we will not in order to simplify matters).

Line 30 defines the size of the entire market for the investment in probabilistic terms. Recall that the entire market was estimated at 250,000 tons but that the possible size was estimated at between 100,000 and 340,000 tons per year. We have used the IFPS function TRIRAND to model the distribution of

Exhibit 10-10
IFPS Risk Analysis Model

```
10 * HERTZ MODEL OF CHEMICAL COMPANY
20 COLUMNS 1,10
30 MARKET = TRIRAND (100000,250000,340000), PREVIOUS*TRIRAND(1,1.03,1.06)
40 SELLING PRICE=TRIRAND(385,510,575)
50 MARKET SHARE=UNIRAND(.12,.17)
60 SALES VOLUME=MARKET*MARKET SHARE
70 INVESTMENT=TRIRAND(7,9.5,10.5)*1000000,0
80 LIFE=10
90 OPERATING COST=TRIRAND(370,435,545)
100 FIXED COST = TRIRAND(250,300,375)*1000
110 *
120 REVENUE=MAXIMUM(0,(SELLING PRICE – OPERATING COST)*SALES VOLUME)
130 NET INCOME=REVENUE-FIXED COST
140 SALVAGE VALUE=0 FOR 9, TRIRAND(3.5,4.5,5)*1000000
150 *
160 RATE OF RETURN=IRR(NET INCOME+SALVAGE VALUE, INVESTMENT)
END OF MODEL
```

values for market size. This is a very useful distribution because while the estimator(s) may be unable to provide a complete distribution for these key parameters, he or she will usually be able to provide a most likely value, a lower limit, and an upper limit.

Line 30 thus specifies the market to be triangularly distributed with a most probable value of 250,000 tons, a lower value of 100,000 and an upper value of 340,000 tons. These are the values for the first period; subsequent values will grow because the market is expected to grow at a rate somewhere between 0 and 6 percent per annum. This is incorporated into line 30 using the PREVIOUS function of IFPS which results in using last period's value and increasing it by the appropriate market growth rate, which itself is triangularly distributed between 0 and 6 percent (that is, by the factors 1.0, 1.03, and 1.06 in line 30).

Line 40 gives the selling price data, also assumed to follow the TRIRAND function. Line 50 uses the UNIRAND function to estimate market share, UNIRAND being an IFPS function for the uniform distribution. All values between 12 and 17 percent are assumed to be equally likely. Line 60 calculates sales volume by multiplying market share and market size. Line 70 is the equation for investment using TRIRAND. Line 80 is the equation for the life of the investment.

Operating costs and fixed costs (Lines 90 and 100) are assumed to follow the triangular distribution. The equation for revenue is designed to prevent negative profits by choosing the maximum of incremental revenue over incremental costs times sales volume or zero, which simply means that the company will choose not to sell below its variable cost. Line 130 subtracts fixed costs from revenues to arrive at the net profit or loss of the project for each year of its life. Salvage value, line 140, is zero for nine periods and triangularly distributed in the tenth year, which is the end of project life.

The internal rate of return (IRR) is calculated in line 160 using the IRR function of IFPS, which has two arguments: CASH INFLOWS (net income + salvage value in line 160) and INVESTMENT (investment in line 160) and that completes the model.

When issuing the command SOLVE, IFPS uses the mean value for each variable when probabilistic distributions are specified. By the solving the model in this way we find that the IRR of the project is 9.92 percent, as shown in Exhibit 10-11.

We next solve the model 200 times, using the monte carlo simulation option, whereby IFPS selects values at random for each variable following the probabilities of the distributions specified for each variable for each of the 200 solutions. The frequency distribution and the sample statistics for these 200 runs are given in Exhibit 10-12.

The monte carlo option gives management a much richer set of information upon which to base this decision. From the frequency table in Exhibit 10-12, we see that the probability of the return's being greater than zero is between 60 and 70 percent. The probability of the return's being greater than 10 percent is 50 percent. The possible rates of return range from -12.7 percent to $+39.7$ percent. So although the mean return is 9.9 percent, there is some chance that the project will earn a negative return.

Exhibit 10-11
IFPS Risk Analysis Model Solution

	1	2	3	4	5	6
Hertz Model of Chemical Company						
Market	230000	236900	244007	251327	258867	266633
Selling Price	490	490	490	490	490	490
Market Share	0.1450	0.1450	0.1450	0.1450	0.1450	0.1450
Sales Volume	33350	34351	35381	36442	37536	38662
Investment	9000000	0	0	0	0	0
Life	10	10	10	10	10	10
Operating Cost	450	450	450	450	450	450
Fixed Cost	308333	308333	308333	308333	308333	308333
Revenue	1334000	1374020	1415241	1457698	1501429	1546472
Net Income	1025667	1065687	1106907	1149364	1193095	1238138
Salvage Value	0	0	0	0	0	0
Rate of Return						

	7	8	9	10
Hertz Model of Chemical Company				
Market	274632	282871	291357	300098
Selling Price	490	490	490	490
Market Share	0.1450	0.1450	0.1450	0.1450
Sales Volume	39822	41016	42247	43514
Investment	0	0	0	0
Life	10	10	10	10
Operating Cost	450	450	450	450
Fixed Cost	308333	308333	308333	308333
Revenue	1592866	1640652	1689871	1740567
Net Income	1284532	1332318	1381538	1432234
Salvage Value	0	0	0	4333333
Rate of Return		0.0093	0.0357	0.0992

There is still more useful information to be gleaned from Exhibit 10-12. Notice that the 10 percent and 90 percent confidence intervals are also given in the sample statistics. This information tells us that there is an 80 percent chance that the true return of the project will be between 9.11 percent and 12.96 percent.

The discipline of thinking through the uncertainties of the problem in this way should help management understand the uncertainty associated with an investment project and in doing so, it should sharpen management's investment intuition and improve decisions.

Exhibit 10-12
Solution Monte Carlo Simulation of Risk Analysis Model

Frequency Table

PROBABILITY OF VALUE BEING GREATER THAN INDICATED

	90	80	70	60	50	40	30	20	10
Net Income									
10	−320	−287	90	712	1427	2078	2630	3407	4749 *1000
Rate of Return									
10	−0.127	−0.118	−0.066	0.016	0.100	0.162	0.234	0.280	0.397

Sample Statistics

	Mean	Std Dev	Skewness	Kurtosis	10 PC Conf	Mean 90 PC
Net Income						
10	1761740	2040064	1.0	3.0	1577094	1946385
Rate of Return						
10	0.1104	0.2127	.7	3.0	0.0911	.1296

ADJUSTMENTS FOR INFLATION

There is another complication to the NPV model that is necessary to consider. It has to do with incorporating the effects of inflation.

Inflation normally has different effects on costs than on benefits. If its effects are ignored in the NPV model, serious errors are possible. To illustrate, we repeat the NPV model below, using summation notation.

$$\text{NPV} = -C_0 + \sum_{j=1}^{z} \frac{R}{(1 + i)^t} \tag{7}$$

If it is assumed the investment outlay C_0 is made in the present, if all incremental revenues and incremental costs of a project increase at the same rate of inflation, the NPV will be the same if inflation is incorporated explicitly into the R's and i or if it is incorporated implicitly by excluding it from the R's and i so long as both the numerator and denominator include identical adjustments for the estimated rate of inflation over the life of the project.

The discount rate i ordinarily includes an estimate of future inflation, for in a period of inflation lenders of capital will not ordinarily loan money in one period in order to receive less in terms of purchasing power in the next. They will seek to ensure that the purchasing power is maintained and that some premium accrues to them for foregoing claims to those resources in the present.

In light of this tendency to incorporate rates of inflation into loan and equity agreements, the discount rate must be reduced for the inflation adjustment assumed in the discount rate i if incremental returns (R's) are to be estimated in terms of current prices (that is, in constant dollars).

The point here is that so long as inflation affects the incremental costs and benefits in an identical manner, we may choose to incorporate the effects of inflation into both our numerator (R's) and our denominator (i) or we may choose to ignore inflation in the numerator and to use a real cost of capital in the denominator, thus also ignoring the impact of inflation in the denominator.

In practice, however, inflation does not usually affect the incremental revenue stream in the same way as it affects the incremental cost stream. This because incremental cost elements inflate at rates different from incremental revenues and because some elements of cost (for example, depreciation) are absolutely fixed and don't inflate. We turn to a detailed model to illustrate the detailed effects of inflation on investment proposals.

Exhibit 10-13 presents an analysis of a project with an initial investment of $100,000.[9] This analysis adjusts for inflation implicitly. The investment analysis in Exhibit 10-13 is presented in terms of constant dollars during a period of time in which the general rate of inflation is expected to average approximately 10 percent. The discount rate excludes any amount for inflation so both the numerator and denominator of equation (7) are presented in constant terms and are therefore consistent. The project results in an NPV of $5,919 at a real discount rate of 12 percent.

Exhibit 10-14 presents the same project flows, but now both revenues and expenses are adjusted explicitly by the general rate of inflation except for depreciation which is both fixed and limited to the historical cost of the asset by generally accepted accounting principles and by U. S. tax laws. The second step in the procedure to incorporate inflation explicitly into the project evaluation requires us to convert inflation-adjusted cash (computed in step 1) flows to constant dollars, which we do by dividing the nominal flows by the general price level index for each year as illustrated in step 2 of Exhibit 10-14. The constant dollar cash flows then must be discounted by the real discount rate of 12 percent to arrive at the NPV of the project. Notice that the NPV is now a negative $1,554.50. The NPV falls when we adjust this project explicitly for inflation because the tax saving or shield provided by depreciation does not inflate. It is a fixed amount.

The implicit procedure followed in Exhibit 10-13 is less damaging during periods of inflation when one of the following three conditions is present:

1. The firm has a zero tax rate because of losses in overall business.
2. The organization is exempt from taxes because it is a not-for-profit organization.
3. The rate of inflation is positive but negligible, so distortions created by inflation are not likely to be significant.

Otherwise, the firm should make explicit adjustments for inflation according to the procedure followed in Exhibit 10-14.

INCORPORATING MACROECONOMIC
AND INDUSTRY VARIABLES EXPLICITLY

Macroeconomic and industry variables affect project evaluations. Most project evaluations incorporate these environomental effects implicitly through estimates

Exhibit 10-13
NPV with Implicit Inflation Adjustment

	Year 1	Year 2	Year 3	Year 4
Revenues	$60,000	$75,000	$75,000	$45,000
Expenses				
Labor	10,000	10,000	10,000	8,000
Materials	8,000	12,000	12,000	8,000
Depreciation	25,000	25,000	25,000	25,000
Total expenses	(43,000)	(47,000)	(47,000)	(41,000)
Before-tax profit	17,000	28,000	28,000	4,000
Taxes (50%)	(8,500)	(14,000)	(14,000)	(2,000)
After-tax profit	8,500	14,000	14,000	2,000
Add back				
Depreciation	25,000	25,000	25,000	25,000
After-tax cash flows	$33,500	$39,000	$39,000	$27,000

Conversion of nominal cash flows to real cash flows

After-tax cash flows	Discount factor (12%)	Present value of cash flows
$33,500	.89286	29,910.81
$39,000	.79719	31,090.41
$39,000	.71178	27,759.42
$27,000	.63552	17,159.04
		105,919.68
Less cost of project		(100,000.00)
Net present value		$ 5,919.68

of revenues and costs. Yet in many strategic capital investments (for example, new products and additional capacity) these variables are crucial. Environmental variables such as gross national product, interest rates, inflation, and industry volume have a variable time path of their own, and to treat them as constant is likely to cause serious strategic error. The widespread availability of time-share computer services providing macroeconomic and industry forecasts now allows firms to incorporate these variables explicitly when it is deemed important to do so. It is then a relatively simple matter to construct "satellite models" of demand for the firm and for various products of the firm under alternate economic scenarios. Access to these economic information systems can be attained at modest expense.

SURVEY OF CURRENT PRACTICES

There has been a dramatic increase over the last four decades in the use of discounted cash flow methods by large U. S. firms. Moore and Reichert (1983) report the result of five surveys between 1955 and 1981 which show the percentage of these firms employing discounted cash flow techniques rising from 9 per-

Exhibit 10-14
NPV with Explicit Inflation Adjustment

Assumption: General price level increase of 10 pertcent each of the next four years

	Year 1	Year 2	Year 3	Year 4
GPL index	1.10	1.21	1.331	1.464
Revenues	$66,000*	$90,750	$99,285	$65,880
Expenses				
Labor	11,000	12,100	13,310	11,712
Materials	8,800	14,520	15,972	11,712
Depreciation	25,000	25,000	25,000	25,000
Total expenses	(44,800)	(51,620)	(54,282)	(48,424)
Before-tax profit	21,200	39,130	45,543	17,456
Taxes	(10,600)	(19,565)	(22,771)	(8,728)
After-tax profit	10,600	19,565	22,772	8,728
Add back:				
Depreciation	25,000	25,000	25,000	25,000
Nominal after-tax				
cash flows	$35,600	$44,565	$47,772	$33,728

Conversion of nominal cash flows to real cash flows

Nominal after- tax cash flows	General price level index	Real after-tax cash flows
35,600	1.10	35,600/1.10 = 32,363.64
44,565	1.21	44,565/1.12 = 36,830.58
47,772	1.331	47,772/1.464 = 35,891.81
33,728	1.464	33,728/1.464 = 23,038.25

Conversion to present value of real cash flows

Real after-tax cash flows	Discount factor (12%)	Present value of cash flows
32,363.64	0.89286	28,896.20
36,830.58	0.79719	29,360.97
35,891.81	0.71178	25,547.07
23,038.25	0.63552	14,641.26
		98,445.50
Less cost of project		(100,000.00)
Net present value		(1,554.50)

*Revenue and cash expenses were converted to purchasing power equivalents of each year, for example, Year 1 revenues of $60,000 × 1.1 = $66,000.

cent to 86 percent. Klammer (1984) also indicates that the trend is continuing. In a study reported by Horngren and Foster (1991, pp. 685–686) and reproduced in Exhibit 10-15, Klammer, Koch, and Wilner report on the following trends in the use of discounted cash flow methods (that is, NPV and IRR) as primary capital evaluation methods.

Moreover, a number of studies, including those of Fremgen (1973), Neuhauser and Viscone (1973), Petty, Scott, and Bird (1975), Moore and Reichert (1983),

Exhibit 10-15
Firms Using DCF as the Primary Evaluation Method

Capital Budgeting Project Category	1970	1975	1980	1988
Replacement projects	28%	45%	56%	60%
Expansion–existing operations	44	62	75	86
Expansion–new operations	41	58	71	87
Foreign operations	45	59	72	79
Abandonment	36	47	55	62
General and administrative	21	29	36	41
Social expenditures	10	14	14	16

Horngren/Foster, *Cost Accounting: A Managerial Approach*, 7e, © 1991, p. 686. Adapted by permission of
  Prentice Hall, Englewood Cliffs; New Jersey.

and Hendricks (1983), report a consistent preference for the IRR method over the NPV method as the primary selection tool. These studies also report widespread use of multiple methods of project evaluation, sensitivity analysis and capital rationing by these same firms.

Hendricks (1983) in his survey of Fortune 500 firms found 66.3 percent of respondents favoring the IRR method as the primary selection tool, whereas only 9.8 percent used the NPV method as primary. The payback method was used by 64.8 percent and the NPV method by 41.5 percent of the firms as the secondary selection method.

Given the superior qualities of the NPV method, it is discouraging to find the IRR method favored in practice. It does illustrate the appeal of a procedure that produces an index of return on investment.

Two of these surveys probed the methods used by management to establish discount rates. Petty, Scott, and Bird (1975) found that only 25 percent of the respondents calculated the weighted average cost of capital, while most set discount rates based upon management targets. In a study by Hendricks (1983), however, 45 percent of the firms studied based their discount rates on the weighted average cost of capital.

In light of this U. S. data, it is interesting to note that in studies of Japanese companies Gultekin and Taga (reported in Horngren, 1991, p. 686), report that the preferred method (47 percent) of capital evaluation is the *payback method*! The accounting rate of return (23 percent) follows, with IRR (18 percent) and NPV (12 percent) trailing badly. Apparently, the Japanese are less concerned with precise quantitative evaluations of capital projects than are U. S. firms!

Finally, a recent survey of the risk analysis practices of 146 large UK firms by Ho and Pike (1991, p. 231) indicates a preference among executives for the use of intuitive techniques of risk assessment (i.e., low, medium, high, risk) followed by the relatively high use of sensitivity analysis of investments to changes in estimates of variables comprising NPV calculations.

CRITICISMS OF DISCOUNTED CASH FLOW METHODS

We have shown the superiority of discounted cash flow for decision making on theoretical grounds. While the IRR method seems to be preferred to the NPV method, the dramatic increase in the use of discounted methods hides the fact that major resource allocation decisions are seldom made on the basis of the results of these techniques alone. There is a general distrust of the use of these techniques as the basis for strategic resource decisions. Practitioners complain that excessive attention to quantitative techniques masks the real challenge of resource allocation decision making. Hastie (1974) believes more progress could be made in improving investment decision making by seeking ways to ask more appropriate strategic questions and by improving assumptions that form the basis for these decisions rather than by refining financial evaluation techniques.

Gold, Roesseger, and Boylon (1980) point to the "illusion of exactness" that exists in the quantitative investment models and to the scant attention paid in the literature to potential errors in estimates. We must admit that it is possible that errors in assumptions behind estimates of costs, benefits, and discount rates will swamp the errors in less sophisticated and judgmental decision models.

Others (Hayes and Abernathy, 1980; Hayes and Garvin, 1982) have expressed concern about the trends in decision making that might have been induced by these quantitative techniques. They refer to overly analytical and risk-adverse managerial behavior, which they see diluting the entrepreneurial responsibilities of management. The value of options created by investments and their strategic value together with potential competitive responses are rarely considered explicitly in these quantitative models. Moreover, researchers have not as yet been able to show a positive relationship between the financial performance of organizations and the use of these techniques (Klammer, 1972; Haka, Gordon, and Pinches, 1985).

REFERENCES

BAUMOL, WILLIAM J., *Economic Theory and Operations Analysis*, 4th ed. Englewood Cliffs, N.J.: Prentice Hall, 1978.

BOWER, JOSEPH L, *Managing the Resource Allocation Process.* Homewood, Ill.: Richard D. Irwin, 1972.

DEAN, JOEL, *Capital Budgeting: The Management Policy on Plant, Equipment, and Product Development.* New York: Columbia University Press, 1951.

FREMGEN, JAMES M., "Capital Budgeting Practices: A Survey." *Management Accounting*, May 1973, pp. 19–25.

GOLD, BELA, "Shaky Foundations of Capital Budgeting," *California Management Review*, Winter 1976, pp. 51–59.

GOLD, BELA, G. ROESEGGER, AND M. G. BOYLON, JR., *Evaluating Technological Innovations.* Lexington,

Mass.: D. C. Heath and Company, 1980.

HAKA, SUSAN F., LAWRENCE A. GORDON, AND GEORGE E. PINCHES, "Sophisticated Capital Budgeting Selection Techniques and Firm Performance," *The Accounting Review*, October 1985, pp. 651–669.

HASTIE, LARRY K., "One Businessman's View of Capital Budgeting," *Financial Management*, Winter 1974, pp. 36–44.

HAYES, ROBERT H., AND WILLIAM J. ABERNATHY, "Managing Our Way to Economic Decline," *Harvard Business Review*, July–August 1980, pp. 67–77.

HAYES, ROBERT H., AND D. A. GARVIN, "Managing as if Tomorrow Mattered," *Harvard Business Review*, May–June 1982, pp. 71–79.

HENDRICKS, JAMES A., "Capital Budgeting Practice Including Inflation Adjustments: A Survey,"

Managerial Planning, Vol. 31, no. 4, January–February 1983, pp. 22–28.

HERTZ, DAVID B., "Risk Analysis in Capital Investment," *Harvard Business Review*, January–February 1964, pp. 95–106.

HO, SIMON S. M., AND RICHARD H. PIKE, "Risk Analysis in Capital Budgeting Contexts: Simple or Sophisticated? *Accounting and Business Research*, Vol. 21, No. 83, pp. 227–238, 1991.

HORNGREN, CHARLES T., AND GEORGE FOSTER, *Cost Accounting: A Managerial Approach*, 7th ed., Englewood Cliffs, N.J.: Prentice Hall, 1991.

KLAMMER, THOMAS, "Empirical Evidence of the Adoption of Sophisticated Capital Budgeting Techniques," *The Journal of Business*, July 1972, pp. 387–394.

KLAMMER, THOMAS, "The Continuing Increase in the Use of Sophisticated Capital Budgeting Techniques," *California Management Review*, Fall 1984, pp. 137–147.

LORIE, J., AND L. J. SAVAGE, "Three Problems in Capital Rationing," *Journal of Business*, October 1955, pp. 229–239.

MAGEE, JOHN F., "Decision Trees for Decision Making," *Harvard Business Review*, September–October 1964, pp. 79–96.

MOORE, JAMES S., AND ALAN K. REICHERT, "An Analysis of the Financial Management Techniques Current Employed by Large U. S. Corporations," *Journal of Finance and Accounting* (U.K.), Winter 1983, pp. 623–645.

NEUHAUSER, JOHN N., AND JERRY A. VISCONE, "How Managers Feel About Advanced Capital Budgeting Methods," *Management Review*, November 1973, pp. 16–22.

PETTY, J. WILLIAM, DAVID F. SCOTT, AND MONROE M. BIRD, "The Capital Expenditure Decision Making Process," *Engineering Economist*, Vol. 20, no. 3, Spring 1975, pp. 159–172.

SCHLAIFER, ROBERT, *Analysis of Decisions Under Uncertainty*. New York: McGraw-Hill, 1969.

SOLOMON, EZRA, ed., *The Management of Corporate Capital*. New York: Free Press, 1959.

WESTON, FRED J., AND EUGENE F. BRIGHAM, *Managerial Finance*. Hinsdale, Ill.: Dryden Press, 1975.

NOTES

1. It should be noted that the present value of the net return so calculated with present value factors is the value that, if compounded at the same rate of interest, would in fact yield the net return found in the equation for any particular year. Therefore, discounting is a process that is simply the reverse of compounding. The longer away the net return, the higher the discount factor and the lower the present value equivalent per dollar of net return. This is so because the farther removed the receipt of a given sum, the lower its value in the present.

2. Working capital may be defined as current assets minus current liabilities. That is, working capital is that part of current assets (that is, cash, government securities, accounts receivable, inventories) that is not financed by current liabilities (that is, accounts payable, notes payable, taxes payable) but rather must be financed by the permanent capital of the firm (that is, long-term debt and equity).

3. Assuming, of course, that the principles of tax accounting used by the firm treat book loss in this customary manner; many regulated companies do not treat book losses in this way for purposes of tax accounting. Rather, they revise future depreciation schedules to reflect past experiences and, in a sense, postpone the tax deduction until some time in the future.

4. Precisely this double-counting occurs when the accounting rate of return is used as a selection criterion, because depreciation typically is not added back to net income. Since depreciation is a capital charge,

and since the capital investment appears in the denominator also, this criterion results in double-counting.

5. But note: if the old equipment has undepreciated book value remaining, the tax shield forgone on the old equipment should be subtracted from the tax shield of the new equipment in arriving at the net tax shield of the new project.

6. This classic example was originally provided by Ezra Solomon. It is reprinted here with permission of Macmillan Publishing Company from *The Management of Corporate Capital*, p. 78, edited by Ezra Solomon, 1959. Copyright © by the Graduate School of Business, University of Chicago. The solution to the problem, however, appears here in much more expository detail than that accompanying the original statement of the problem by Solomon.

7. This example is drawn from a well-known article by James H. Lorie and Leonard J. Savage, which first appeared in the *Journal of Business*, October 1955 and is reprinted in Ezra Solomon, ed., *The Management of Corporate Capital*. The solution appears here in a much expanded form. It is used by permission of the University of Chicago Press.

8. This example is adapted from David Hertz, "Risk Analysis in Capital Investment," *Harvard Business Review*, May–June, 1982, pp. 71–79.

9. Exhibits 10-13 and 10-14 are reproduced by permission from Raiborn and Ratcliffe, "Are You Accounting for Inflation in Your Capital Budgeting Process?" *Management Accounting*, September 1979.

Appendix 10-A
Present Value of $1

Years Hence	1%	2%	4%	6%	8%	10%	12%	14%	15%	16%	18%	20%	22%	24%	25%	26%	28%	30%	35%	40%	45%	50%
1	0.990	0.980	0.962	0.943	0.926	0.909	0.893	0.877	0.870	0.862	0.847	0.833	0.820	0.806	0.800	0.794	0.781	0.769	0.741	0.714	0.690	0.657
2	0.980	0.961	0.925	0.890	0.857	0.826	0.797	0.769	0.756	0.743	0.718	0.694	0.672	0.650	0.640	0.630	0.610	0.592	0.542	0.510	0.476	0.414
3	0.971	0.942	0.889	0.840	0.794	0.751	0.712	0.675	0.658	0.641	0.609	0.579	0.551	0.524	0.512	0.500	0.477	0.455	0.406	0.364	0.328	0.296
4	0.961	0.924	0.855	0.792	0.735	0.683	0.636	0.592	0.572	0.552	0.516	0.482	0.451	0.423	0.410	0.397	0.373	0.350	0.301	0.260	0.226	0.198
5	0.951	0.906	0.822	0.747	0.681	0.621	0.567	0.519	0.497	0.476	0.437	0.402	0.370	0.341	0.328	0.315	0.291	0.269	0.223	0.186	0.156	0.132
6	0.942	0.888	0.790	0.705	0.630	0.564	0.507	0.456	0.432	0.410	0.370	0.335	0.303	0.275	0.262	0.250	0.227	0.207	0.165	0.133	0.108	0.088
7	0.933	0.871	0.760	0.665	0.583	0.513	0.452	0.400	0.376	0.354	0.314	0.279	0.249	0.222	0.210	0.198	0.178	0.159	0.122	0.095	0.074	0.059
8	0.923	0.853	0.731	0.627	0.540	0.467	0.404	0.351	0.327	0.305	0.266	0.233	0.204	0.179	0.168	0.157	0.139	0.123	0.091	0.068	0.051	0.039
9	0.914	0.837	0.703	0.592	0.500	0.424	0.361	0.308	0.284	0.263	0.225	0.194	0.167	0.144	0.134	0.125	0.108	0.094	0.067	0.048	0.035	0.026
10	0.905	0.820	0.676	0.538	0.463	0.386	0.322	0.270	0.247	0.227	0.191	0.162	0.137	0.116	0.107	0.099	0.085	0.073	0.050	0.035	0.024	0.017
11	0.896	0.804	0.650	0.527	0.429	0.350	0.287	0.237	0.215	0.195	0.162	0.135	0.112	0.094	0.086	0.079	0.066	0.056	0.037	0.025	0.017	0.012
12	0.887	0.788	0.625	0.497	0.397	0.319	0.257	0.208	0.187	0.168	0.137	0.112	0.092	0.076	0.069	0.062	0.052	0.043	0.027	0.018	0.012	0.008
13	0.879	0.773	0.601	0.469	0.368	0.290	0.229	0.182	0.163	0.145	0.116	0.093	0.075	0.061	0.055	0.050	0.040	0.033	0.020	0.013	0.008	0.005
14	0.870	0.758	0.577	0.442	0.340	0.263	0.205	0.160	0.141	0.125	0.099	0.078	0.062	0.049	0.044	0.039	0.032	0.025	0.015	0.009	0.006	0.003
15	0.861	0.743	0.555	0.417	0.315	0.239	0.183	0.140	0.123	0.108	0.084	0.065	0.051	0.040	0.035	0.031	0.025	0.020	0.011	0.006	0.004	0.002
16	0.853	0.728	0.534	0.391	0.292	0.218	0.163	0.123	0.107	0.093	0.071	0.054	0.042	0.032	0.028	0.025	0.019	0.015	0.008	0.005	0.003	0.002
17	0.844	0.714	0.513	0.371	0.270	0.198	0.146	0.108	0.093	0.080	0.060	0.045	0.034	0.026	0.023	0.020	0.015	0.012	0.006	0.003	0.002	0.001
18	0.836	0.700	0.494	0.350	0.250	0.180	0.130	0.095	0.081	0.069	0.051	0.038	0.028	0.021	0.018	0.016	0.012	0.009	0.005	0.002	0.001	0.001
19	0.828	0.686	0.475	0.331	0.232	0.164	0.116	0.083	0.070	0.060	0.043	0.031	0.023	0.017	0.014	0.012	0.009	0.007	0.003	0.002	0.001	
20	0.820	0.673	0.456	0.312	0.215	0.149	0.104	0.073	0.061	0.051	0.037	0.026	0.019	0.014	0.012	0.010	0.007	0.005	0.002	0.001	0.001	
21	0.811	0.660	0.439	0.294	0.199	0.135	0.093	0.064	0.053	0.044	0.031	0.022	0.015	0.011	0.009	0.008	0.006	0.004	0.002	0.001		
22	0.803	0.647	0.422	0.278	0.184	0.123	0.083	0.056	0.045	0.038	0.026	0.018	0.013	0.009	0.007	0.006	0.004	0.003	0.001	0.001		
23	0.795	0.634	0.406	0.262	0.170	0.112	0.074	0.049	0.040	0.033	0.022	0.015	0.010	0.007	0.006	0.005	0.003	0.002	0.001			
24	0.788	0.622	0.390	0.247	0.153	0.102	0.066	0.043	0.035	0.028	0.019	0.013	0.008	0.006	0.005	0.004	0.003	0.002	0.001			
25	0.780	0.610	0.375	0.233	0.146	0.092	0.059	0.038	0.030	0.024	0.016	0.010	0.007	0.005	0.004	0.003	0.002	0.001	0.001			
26	0.772	0.598	0.361	0.220	0.135	0.084	0.053	0.033	0.026	0.021	0.014	0.009	0.006	0.004	0.003	0.002	0.002	0.001				
27	0.764	0.586	0.347	0.207	0.125	0.076	0.047	0.029	0.023	0.018	0.011	0.007	0.005	0.003	0.002	0.002	0.001	0.001				
28	0.757	0.574	0.333	0.196	0.116	0.069	0.042	0.026	0.020	0.016	0.010	0.006	0.004	0.002	0.002	0.002	0.001	0.001				
29	0.749	0.563	0.321	0.185	0.107	0.063	0.037	0.022	0.017	0.014	0.008	0.005	0.003	0.002	0.002	0.001	0.001	0.001				
30	0.742	0.552	0.308	0.174	0.099	0.057	0.033	0.020	0.015	0.012	0.007	0.004	0.003	0.002	0.001	0.001	0.001					
40	0.672	0.453	0.208	0.097	0.046	0.022	0.011	0.005	0.004	0.003	0.001	0.001										
50	0.608	0.372	0.141	0.054	0.021	0.009	0.003	0.001	0.001	0.001												

Present Value of $1 Received Annually for N Years

Years (N)	1%	2%	4%	6%	8%	10%	12%	14%	15%	16%	18%	20%	22%	24%	25%	26%	28%	30%	35%	40%	45%	50%
1	0.990	0.980	0.962	0.941	0.926	0.909	0.893	0.877	0.870	0.862	0.847	0.833	0.820	0.806	0.800	0.794	0.781	0.762	0.741	0.714	0.690	0.66
2	1.970	1.942	1.886	1.833	1.783	1.736	1.690	1.647	1.626	1.605	1.566	1.528	1.492	1.457	1.440	1.424	1.392	1.361	1.289	1.224	1.165	1.11
3	2.942	2.884	2.775	2.673	2.477	2.487	2.402	2.322	2.283	2.246	2.174	2.106	2.042	1.981	1.952	1.923	1.868	1.816	1.696	1.589	1.493	1.40
4	3.902	3.808	3.630	3.465	3.342	3.170	3.037	2.914	2.855	2.798	2.690	2.589	2.494	2.404	2.362	2.320	2.241	2.166	1.997	1.849	1.730	1.60
5	4.853	4.713	4.452	4.242	3.993	3.791	3.605	3.433	3.352	3.274	3.127	2.991	2.864	2.745	2.689	2.635	2.532	2.436	2.220	2.035	1.876	1.73
6	5.795	5.601	5.242	4.917	4.623	4.355	4.111	3.889	3.784	3.635	3.498	3.326	3.167	3.020	2.951	2.885	2.759	2.643	2.385	2.168	1.983	1.82
7	6.728	6.472	6.002	5.582	5.206	4.868	4.564	4.288	4.160	4.039	3.812	3.605	3.416	3.242	3.161	3.083	2.937	2.802	2.508	2.261	2.057	1.88
8	7.652	7.325	6.733	6.210	5.747	5.335	4.968	4.639	4.487	4.344	4.078	3.837	3.619	3.421	3.329	3.241	3.076	2.925	2.598	2.331	2.108	1.92
9	8.566	8.162	7.435	6.802	6.247	5.759	5.328	4.946	4.772	4.607	4.303	4.031	3.786	3.566	3.463	3.366	3.184	3.019	2.665	2.379	2.144	1.94
10	9.471	8.983	8.111	7.360	6.710	6.145	5.650	5.216	5.019	4.833	4.494	4.192	3.923	3.682	3.571	3.465	3.269	3.092	2.716	2.414	2.168	1.96
11	10.368	9.787	8.760	7.887	7.139	6.495	5.937	5.453	5.234	5.029	4.656	4.327	4.035	3.776	3.656	3.544	3.335	3.147	2.757	2.438	2.185	1.97
12	11.255	10.575	9.385	8.334	7.536	6.814	6.194	5.660	5.421	5.197	4.793	4.439	4.127	3.851	3.725	3.606	3.387	3.190	2.779	2.456	2.196	1.98
13	12.134	11.343	9.986	8.853	7.904	7.103	6.424	5.842	5.583	5.342	4.910	4.533	4.203	3.912	3.780	3.656	3.427	3.223	2.799	2.468	2.204	1.99
14	13.004	12.106	10.563	9.295	8.244	7.367	6.628	6.002	5.724	5.468	5.008	4.611	4.265	3.962	3.821	3.695	3.459	3.249	2.814	2.477	2.210	1.99
15	13.865	12.849	11.118	9.711	8.669	7.606	6.811	6.142	5.847	5.575	5.092	4.675	4.315	4.001	3.859	3.726	3.483	3.268	2.825	2.484	2.214	1.99
16	14.718	13.578	11.652	10.106	8.851	7.824	6.974	6.265	5.954	5.669	5.162	4.730	4.357	4.033	3.887	3.751	3.503	3.283	2.834	2.489	2.216	1.99
17	15.562	14.292	12.166	10.477	9.122	8.022	7.120	6.373	6.047	5.749	5.222	4.775	4.391	4.059	3.910	3.771	3.518	3.295	2.840	2.492	2.218	1.99
18	16.398	14.992	12.659	10.828	9.372	8.201	7.250	6.467	6.128	5.818	5.273	4.812	4.419	4.080	3.928	3.765	3.529	3.304	2.844	2.494	2.219	1.99
19	17.226	15.678	13.134	11.158	9.604	8.365	7.366	6.550	6.198	5.877	5.316	4.844	4.442	4.097	3.942	3.799	3.539	3.311	2.848	2.496	2.220	1.99
20	18.046	16.351	13.590	11.470	9.818	8.514	7.469	6.623	6.259	5.929	5.353	4.870	4.460	4.110	3.954	3.808	3.546	3.316	2.850	2.497	2.221	1.99
21	18.857	17.011	14.029	11.764	10.017	8.649	7.562	6.687	6.312	5.973	5.384	4.891	4.476	4.121	3.963	3.816	3.551	3.320	2.852	2.498	2.221	2.00
22	19.660	17.658	14.451	12.042	10.201	8.772	7.645	6.743	6.359	6.011	5.410	4.909	4.488	4.130	3.970	3.822	3.556	3.323	2.853	2.498	2.222	2.00
23	20.456	18.292	14.857	12.303	10.371	8.883	7.718	6.792	6.399	6.044	5.432	4.925	4.499	4.137	3.976	3.827	3.559	3.325	2.854	2.499	2.222	2.00
24	21.243	18.914	15.247	12.550	10.529	8.985	7.784	6.835	6.434	6.073	5.451	4.937	4.507	4.143	3.981	3.834	3.562	3.327	2.855	2.499	2.222	2.00
25	22.023	19.523	15.622	12.783	10.675	9.077	7.843	6.873	6.464	6.097	5.467	4.948	4.514	4.147	3.985	3.834	3.564	3.329	2.856	2.499	2.222	2.00
26	22.795	20.121	15.983	13.003	10.810	9.161	7.896	6.906	6.491	6.118	5.480	4.956	4.520	4.151	3.988	3.837	3.566	3.330	2.856	2.500	2.222	2.00
27	23.560	20.707	16.330	13.211	10.935	9.237	7.943	6.935	6.514	6.136	5.492	4.964	4.524	4.154	3.990	3.839	3.567	3.331	2.856	2.500	2.222	2.00
28	24.316	21.281	16.663	13.406	11.051	9.307	7.984	6.961	6.534	6.152	5.502	4.970	4.528	4.157	3.992	3.840	3.568	3.331	2.857	2.500	2.222	2.00
29	25.066	21.844	16.984	13.591	11.158	9.370	8.022	6.983	6.551	6.166	5.510	4.975	4.531	4.159	3.994	3.841	3.569	3.332	2.857	2.500	2.222	2.00
30	25.809	22.396	17.292	13.765	11.258	9.427	8.055	7.003	6.566	6.177	5.517	4.979	4.534	4.160	3.995	3.842	3.569	3.332	2.857	2.500	2.222	2.00
40	32.835	27.355	19.793	15.046	11.925	9.779	8.244	7.105	6.642	6.234	5.548	4.997	4.544	4.166	3.999	3.846	3.571	3.333	2.857	2.500	2.222	2.00
50	39.196	31.424	21.482	15.762	12.234	9.915	8.304	7.133	6.661	6.246	5.554	4.999	4.545	4.167	4.000	3.846	3.571	3.333	2.857	2.500	2.222	2.00

Appendix 10-C
Present Value of Sum-of-Years' Digits Depreciation

Years of Useful Life	2%	4%	6%	8%	10%	12%	14%	15%	16%	18%	20%	22%	24%	26%	28%	30%	35%	40%	45%	50%
3	0.968	0.937	0.908	0.881	0.855	0.831	0.808	0.796	0.786	0.764	0.745	0.726	0.707	0.690	0.674	0.658	0.621	0.588	0.558	0.011
4	0.961	0.925	0.891	0.860	0.830	0.802	0.776	0.763	0.751	0.728	0.706	0.685	0.665	0.646	0.628	0.611	0.572	0.538	0.567	0.479
5	0.955	0.914	0.875	0.839	0.806	0.775	0.746	0.732	0.719	0.694	0.670	0.647	0.626	0.606	0.588	0.570	0.530	0.494	0.463	0.435
6	0.949	0.902	0.859	0.820	0.783	0.749	0.718	0.703	0.689	0.662	0.637	0.613	0.591	0.570	0.551	0.533	0.492	0.456	0.425	0.328
7	0.943	0.891	0.844	0.801	0.761	0.725	0.692	0.676	0.661	0.633	0.606	0.582	0.559	0.538	0.518	0.500	0.458	0.423	0.392	0.366
8	0.937	0.880	0.829	0.782	0.740	0.702	0.667	0.650	0.635	0.605	0.578	0.553	0.530	0.508	0.488	0.470	0.420	0.394	0.364	0.338
9	0.931	0.869	0.814	0.765	0.720	0.680	0.643	0.626	0.610	0.580	0.552	0.527	0.503	0.482	0.462	0.443	0.402	0.368	0.338	0.313
10	0.925	0.859	0.800	0.748	0.701	0.659	0.621	0.604	0.587	0.556	0.528	0.502	0.479	0.457	0.437	0.419	0.378	0.345	0.316	0.292
11	0.919	0.848	0.786	0.731	0.682	0.639	0.600	0.582	0.565	0.534	0.506	0.480	0.456	0.434	0.415	0.397	0.357	0.324	0.297	0.273
12	0.913	0.838	0.773	0.715	0.665	0.620	0.580	0.562	0.545	0.513	0.485	0.459	0.435	0.414	0.394	0.376	0.338	0.306	0.279	0.257
13	0.907	0.828	0.760	0.700	0.648	0.602	0.562	0.543	0.526	0.494	0.465	0.439	0.416	0.395	0.376	0.358	0.320	0.289	0.264	0.242
14	0.902	0.818	0.747	0.685	0.632	0.585	0.544	0.525	0.508	0.476	0.447	0.421	0.398	0.377	0.358	0.341	0.304	0.274	0.250	0.229
15	0.896	0.809	0.734	0.671	0.616	0.569	0.527	0.508	0.491	0.459	0.430	0.405	0.382	0.361	0.343	0.326	0.290	0.261	0.237	0.217
16	0.890	0.799	0.722	0.657	0.601	0.555	0.514	0.492	0.475	0.443	0.414	0.389	0.367	0.346	0.328	0.312	0.277	0.248	0.225	0.206
17	0.885	0.790	0.710	0.644	0.587	0.538	0.496	0.477	0.460	0.428	0.400	0.375	0.352	0.332	0.315	0.298	0.264	0.237	0.215	0.196
18	0.880	0.781	0.699	0.631	0.573	0.524	0.482	0.463	0.445	0.413	0.386	0.361	0.339	0.320	0.302	0.286	0.253	0.227	0.205	0.187
19	0.874	0.772	0.688	0.618	0.560	0.510	0.468	0.449	0.432	0.400	0.372	0.348	0.327	0.308	0.291	0.275	0.243	0.217	0.136	0.179
20	0.869	0.763	0.677	0.606	0.547	0.497	0.455	0.436	0.419	0.387	0.360	0.336	0.315	0.296	0.280	0.265	0.233	0.208	0.188	0.171
21	0.863	0.754	0.666	0.594	0.535	0.485	0.442	0.424	0.406	0.376	0.349	0.325	0.304	0.286	0.270	0.255	0.224	0.200	0.181	0.164
22	0.858	0.746	0.656	0.583	0.523	0.473	0.631	0.412	0.395	0.364	0.338	0.315	0.294	0.276	0.260	0.246	0.216	0.193	0.174	0.158
23	0.853	0.738	0.646	0.572	0.511	0.461	0.419	0.401	0.385	0.354	0.327	0.305	0.285	0.267	0.252	0.238	0.208	0.186	0.167	0.152
24	0.848	0.729	0.636	0.561	0.500	0.450	0.409	0.390	0.373	0.344	0.318	0.295	0.276	0.258	0.243	0.230	0.201	0.179	0.161	0.147
25	0.842	0.721	0.626	0.551	0.490	0.440	0.398	0.380	0.364	0.334	0.308	0.286	0.267	0.250	0.236	0.222	0.195	0.173	0.156	0.142
30	0.818	0.683	0.582	0.504	0.442	0.393	0.353	0.336	0.320	0.292	0.269	0.249	0.232	0.216	0.203	0.191	0.167	0.148	0.131	0.120
35	0.794	0.648	0.542	0.463	0.402	0.355	0.317	0.300	0.286	0.260	0.238	0.220	0.204	0.190	0.178	0.168	0.146	0.129	0.116	0.105
40	0.771	0.616	0.507	0.428	0.368	0.323	0.286	0.271	0.257	0.233	0.213	0.196	0.182	0.170	0.159	0.149	0.129	0.114	0.102	0.093
45	0.749	0.586	0.476	0.397	0.339	0.296	0.261	0.247	0.234	0.212	0.193	0.178	0.164	0.153	0.143	0.134	0.116	0.103	0.092	0.083
50	0.728	0.559	0.418	0.370	0.314	0.272	0.240	0.227	0.214	0.174	0.176	0.162	0.150	0.139	0.130	0.122	0.106	0.093	0.083	0.083

Case 10-1   Downtown Parking Authority

In January, a meeting was held in the office of the mayor of Oakmont to discuss a proposed municipal parking facility. The participants included the mayor, the traffic commissioner, the administrator of Oakmont's Downtown Parking Authority, the city planner, and the finance director. The purpose of the meeting was to consider a report by Richard Stockton, executive assistant to the Parking Authority's administrator, concerning estimated costs and revenues for the proposed facility.

Mr. Stockton's opening statement was as follows:

> As you know, the mayor proposed two months ago that we construct a multilevel parking garage on Elm Street. At that time, he asked the Parking Authority to assemble pertinent information for consideration at our meeting today. I would like to summarize our findings.
>
> The Elm Street site is owned by the city. It is presently occupied by the remains of the old Embassy Cinema, which was gutted by fire last June. The proprietors of the Embassy have since used the insurance proceeds to open a new theater in the suburbs; their lease of the city-owned land on which the Embassy was built expired last month.
>
> We estimate that it would cost approximately $80,000 to demolish the old Embassy. A building contractor has estimated that a multilevel structure, with space for 800 cars, could be built on the site at a cost of about $4 million. The useful life of the garage would be around 40 years.
>
> The city could finance construction of the garage through the sale of bonds. The finance director has informed me that we

could probably float an issue of 20-year tax-exempts at 5 percent interest. Redemption would commence after three years, with one-seventeenth of the original number of bonds being called in each succeeding year.

> A parking management firm has already contacted us with a proposal to operate the garage for the city. They would require a management fee of $60,000 per year. Their proposal involves attendant parking, and they estimate that their costs, exclusive of the fee, would amount to $480,000 per year. Of this amount, $350,000 would be personnel costs; the remainder would include utilities, mechanical maintenance, insurance, and so forth. Any gross revenues in excess of $540,000 per year would be shared 90 percent by the city and 10 percent by the management firm. If total annual revenues are less than $540,000, the city would have to pay the difference.
>
> I suggest we offer a management contract for bid, with renegotiations for every three years. The city would derive additional income of around $100,000 per year by renting the ground floor of the structure as retail space. It's rather difficult for the Parking Authority to estimate revenues from the garage because, as you know, our operations to date have been confined to fringe-area parking lots. However, we conducted a survey at a private parking garage only three blocks from the Elm Street site; perhaps that information will be helpful.
>
> This private garage is open every day from 7 a.m. until midnight. Their rate schedule is as follows: $1.50 for the first hour, $1 for the second hour, and 50 cents for each subsequent hour, with a maximum rate of $4 per day. Their capacity is 400 spaces. Our survey indicated that during business hours 75 percent of their spaces were occupied by "all-day parkers"—cars

whose drivers and passengers work downtown. In addition, roughly 400 cars use the garage each weekday with an average stay of three hours. We did not take a survey on Saturday or Sunday, but the proprietor indicated that the garage is usually about 75 percent utilized by short-term parkers on Saturdays until 6 p.m., when the department stores close; the average stay is about two hours. There's a lull until about 7 p.m., when the moviegoers start coming in; he says the garage is almost full from 8 p.m. until closing time at midnight. Sundays are usually very quiet until the evening, when he estimates that his garage is 60 percent utilized from 6 p.m. until midnight.

In addition to this survey, we studied a report issued by the city college economics department last year. This report estimated that we now have approximately 50,000 cars entering the central business district (CBD) every day from Monday through Saturday. Based on correlations with other cities of comparable size, the economists calculated that we need 30,000 parking spaces in CBD. This agrees quite well with a block-by-block estimate made by the Traffic Commissioner's office last year, which indicated a total parking need in the CBD of 29,000 spaces. Right now we have 22,000 spaces in the CBD. Of these, 5 percent are curb spaces (half of which are metered, with a two-hour maximum limit of 50 cents), 65 percent are in open lots, and 30 percent are in privately owned and operated garages.

Another study indicated that 60 percent of all auto passengers entering the CBD on a weekday were on their way to work; 20 percent were shoppers; and 20 percent were businesspersons making calls. The average number of people per car was 1.75. Unfortunately, we have not yet had time to use the data mentioned so far to work up estimates of the revenues to be expected from the proposed garage.

The Elm Street site is strategically located in the heart of the CBD, near the major department stores and office buildings. It is five blocks from one of the access ramps to the new crosstown freeway that we expect will be open to traffic next year, and only three blocks from the Music Center that the mayor dedicated last week. As we all know, the parking situation in that section of town has steadily worsened over the last few years, with no immediate prospect of improvement. The demand for parking is clearly there, and the Parking Authority therefore recommends that we go ahead and build the garage.

The mayor thanked Mr. Stockton for his report and asked for comments. The following discussion took place:

Finance director: I'm all in favor of relieving parking congestion downtown, but I think we have to consider alternative uses of the Elm Street site. For example, the city could sell that site to a private developer for at least $2 million. The site could support an office building from which the city would derive property taxes of around $400,000 per year at present rates. The office building would almost certainly incorporate an underground parking garage for the use of the tenants, and therefore we would not only improve our tax base and increase revenues but also increase the availability of parking at no cost to the city. Besides, an office building on that site would serve to improve the amenity of downtown. A multilevel garage building above ground, on the other hand, would reduce the amenity of the area.

Planning director: I'm not sure I agree completely with the finance director. Within a certain range we can increase the value of downtown land by judicious provision of parking. Adequate, efficient parking facilities will encourage more intensive use of downtown traffic generators such as shops, offices, and places of entertainment, thus enhancing land values. A garage contained within an office building might, as the finance director suggests, provide more spaces, but I suspect these would be occupied almost exclusively by workers in the building and thus would not increase the total available supply. I think long-term parking downtown should be discouraged by the city. We should attempt to encourage short-term parking—particularly among shoppers—in an effort to counteract the growth of business in the suburbs and the consequent stagnation of retail outlets downtown. The rate structure in effect at the privately operated garage quoted by Mr.

Stockton clearly favors the long-term parker. I believe that if the city constructs a garage on the Elm Street site, we should devise a rate structure that favors the short-term parker. People who work downtown should be encouraged to use our mass transit system.

Finance director: I'm glad you mentioned mass transit, because this raises another issue. As you know, our subways are presently not used to capacity and are running at a substantial annual deficit that is borne by the city. We have just spent millions of dollars on the new subway station under the Music Center. Why build a city garage only three blocks away that will still further increase the subway system's deficit? Each person who drives downtown instead of taking the subway represents a loss of one dollar (the average round trip fare) to the subway system. I have read a report stating that approximately two-thirds of all persons entering the CBD by car would still have made the trip by subway if they had not been able to use their cars.

Mayor: On the other hand, I think shoppers prefer to drive rather than take the subway, particularly if they intend to make substantial purchases. No one likes to take the subway burdened down by packages and shopping bags. You know, the Downtown Merchants Association has informed me that they estimate that each new parking space in the CBD generates on average an additional $20,000 in annual retail sales. That represents substantial extra profits to retailers; I think retailing after-tax profits average about 3 percent of gross sales. Besides, the city treasury benefits directly from our 3 percent sales tax.

Traffic commissioner: But what about some of the other costs of increasing parking downtown and therefore, presumably, the number of cars entering the CBD? I'm thinking of such costs as the increased wear and tear on city streets, the additional congestion produced with consequent delays and frustration for the drivers, impeding the movement of city vehicles, noise, air pollution, and so on. How do we weigh these costs in coming to a decision?

Parking administrator: I don't think we can make a decision at this meeting. I suggest that Dick Stockton be asked to prepare an analysis for the proposed garage along the lines of the following questions:

QUESTIONS

1. What is the present value of the multi-level garage?
2. How sensitive is the NPV to changes in key estimates?
3. How should Mr. Stockton respond to the three questions raised by the parking administrator?

Case 10-2   Cycle World, Inc.*

(*Note:* This is an integrative case for Chapters 10 and 11.)

Dave Burke, president of Cycle World, Inc., has been working on next year's budget for the past several weeks. The company, a retailer of bicycles and motorcycles, has managed to pay dividends to its shareholders ever since it was incorporated 10 years ago. At that time it moved into its present quarters, a one-story, concrete block structure with a showroom in front and a parts storeroom and repair shop in the rear. Sales volume increased rapidly at first, but the growth rate has been very small for the past five years. Rising operating costs have kept net income at about the same level it reached five years ago. The cash flow from operations has been about equal to the sum of net income and depreciation.

This pattern seems likely to continue for the next few years, and Mr. Burke sees little chance of increasing the size of the cash dividend on the company's stock, now running at $24,000 a year, unless he can come up with some new money-making ideas. "If we just go on as we have," he said, "we'll make about $28,000 a year. That will cover the dividend, but without much to spare."

A tentative profit budget drawn up on this basis is summarized in Exhibit 10-16. Three items need some explanation: (1) product warranty reimbursements, (2) salaries, and (3) depreciation. Product warranty reimbursements are the amounts recovered from the manufacturers to cover Cycle World's costs of repairing defective merchandise under the terms of the manufacturers' warranties to purchasers of their bicycles and motorcycles. The amount shown for salaries includes Mr. Burke's $60,000 a year, together with the salaries of a salesperson and a bookkeeper-typist. Depreciation covers the building, various pieces of repair equipment, a typewriter, and storage cabinets for the company's inventories of spare parts. (A zero income tax rate has been assumed to eliminate unnecessary complexity in the case.)

Mr. Burke has always viewed budget preparation as an occasion for reviewing operations and discussing the firm's financial position with his banker. He has not hesitated to make major decisions at other times, as he did when he added a line of light motorcycles shortly after the firm moved into its present location, but many of the innovations he has effected have emerged from his annual wrestling match with the budget.

"Maybe I'd better see what would happen if I took on that Ivrea line of motor scooters," he continued. "I've never sold scooters, but I've been servicing the Ivreas for years and I know they're a good product. Dom Bosco (Ivrea's regional manager) has been pushing me to take on an exclusive dealership for this area. He started

*This case has been adapted and revised by permission of Gordon Shillinglaw, *Managerial Cost Accounting*, 5th ed., Homewood, Ill.: Richard D. Irwin, 1982, pp. 248–251.

Exhibit 10-16
Preliminary Projection of Net Income
from Present Operations

Revenues		
Product sales		$300,000
Repair services		200,000
Less: Uncollectible accounts		(6,000)
Net revenues		$494,000
Expenses		
Cost of goods sold		$170,000
Mechanics' wages		86,000
Salaries		110,000
Repair supplies		40,000
Heat and light		11,000
Advertising	$20,000	
Less: Reimbursements from Sussex	10,000	
Depreciation		12,000
Property taxes		18,000
Interest		4,000
Other		12,000
Total expenses		473,000
Less: Product warranty reimbursements		7,000
Total expenses		466,000
Net income		$ 28,000

working on me two years ago, and his terms have gotten better and better. Now he says it's time to fish or cut bait; they'll set up their own sales branch if we don't accept this final offer."

Taking on the Ivrea line would require Cycle World to invest $40,000 in an inventory of scooters and repair parts. Adequate space is available to carry these added inventories. Ivrea would finance one-half this requirement with a permanent credit line of $20,000 and with no interest charge, but Cycle World would have to finance the remainder from other sources. Cycle World would also have to hire an additional full-time mechanic, who would be trained at Ivrea's expense before being transferred to the Cycle World payroll.

Judging from data provided by Mr. Bosco, combined with his own experience in introducing new lines in the past, and with

some help from the bank, Mr. Burke has drawn up the forecasts for the Ivrea line summarized in Exhibit 10-17. All these figures represent increments to the figures arising from Cycle World's present business. According to Mr. Burke, the figures given for the second year seem likely to be representative of what later years would bring.

If the Ivrea line is taken on, Mr. Burke expects net accounts receivable (after deducting the allowance for uncollectible amounts) to go up by $60,000 during the first year and by another $40,000 in the second.

While he was thinking about this proposition, Mr. Burke had a call from the Sussex Bicycle Company, one of Cycle World's major suppliers. Sussex has been reimbursing Cycle World for the full cost of local advertising of Sussex bicycles, up to a $10,000 annual limit. Sussex has now offered to pay half the cost of

Exhibit 10-17
Projection of Income from Introduction of Ivrea Motor Scooters

	First Year	Second Year
Revenues		
Product sales	$100,000	$150,000
Repair services	22,000	26,000
Less: Uncollectible accounts	(2,000)	(3,000)
Net revenues	$120,000	$173,000
Expenses		
Cost of goods sold	66,000	99,500
Mechanics' wages	29,000	29,600
Repair supplies	2,000	4,200
Advertising	8,000	8,000
Other	1,000	1,000
Total	106,000	142,300
Less: Product warranty reimbursements	3,000	4,000
Total expenses	103,000	138,300
Incremental income	$ 17,000	$34,700

local advertising, with a $5,000 limit on its contribution. "We could cut this advertising out completely," Mr. Burke said, "but I know it has brought in quite a few customers in the past. Sussex is a good name, and it brings people into the store. We're selling about $60,000 worth of Sussex bikes now, at a 45 percent gross margin. I'd hate to take a chance of losing any of that."

Whether he takes on the Ivrea line or cuts back on Sussex advertising, Mr. Burke had a number of other projects under consideration for next year. For one thing, his chief mechanic has put in a request for $4,000 to buy several pieces of shop equipment to replace equipment that no longer functions reliably. The annual depreciation expense will go up by $200 if the replacements are made. If the replacements are not made, depreciation charges will remain at $12,000 a year, but other shop expenses will exceed the amounts in Exhibit 10-16 by about $600 next year, mainly in increased equipment maintenance costs. During the past five years, replacement expenditures

have ranged from $2,000 to $4,000, averaging about $3,600 a year.

Another possible expenditure is $6,400 to modernize the showroom with better lighting, a new front window, and new interior decoration. This would be accounted for as a current expense.

A third proposal is to spend $3,800 to renovate the lavatory. It is difficult to keep clean, one of the units is permanently out of service, and the mechanics have been grumbling that they'd rather use the facilities in the gasoline station across the street. This expenditure would also be treated as an expense.

Finally, Mr. Burke is considering a request from the local Chamber of Commerce for $6,000 for the chamber's municipal improvement fund, to be used to attract more business to stores and shops in the downtown area. Mr. Burke is one of the chamber's directors this year. Cycle World itself is not located in the downtown area, but Mr. Burke is convinced that a decaying business center would eventually affect business in the outlying districts as well.

Cycle World has little access to capital other than the amounts it can generate by its own operations. When the business was incorporated 10 years ago, Mr. Burke and eight other people bought shares of stock in the new corporation: "I'm related to most of them in one way or another," Mr. Burke commented. "None of them has any extra money to invest, and they wouldn't give it to me if they did. We've paid their dividends regularly, but they all expected more than we've been able to cough up so far. I still own a controlling interest, but I'd sure get a lot of flack if I got the board to cut the dividend next year."

"The picture on borrowed money is a little brighter. We've got all the bank loans we can get on the basis of our present operations. I play golf with the president of the bank, and he's really laid it on the line. I showed him our projections on the Ivrea line, though, and he and his chief loan officer have agreed to a new $40,000 term loan at 8 percent interest if we go through with the deal. But that's it; they won't go any farther." This loan would be made at the beginning of the year.

QUESTIONS

1. Prepare a discounted cash flow analysis for the addition of the Ivrea line. Make all your assumptions explicit. Assume a discount rate of 10%.
2. Is it desirable for Mr. Burke to add the Ivrea line?
3. What assumptions are most important to your conclusions? How valid are they?

11

OPERATIONAL PLANNING

BUDGET PLANNING

It is very difficult, if not impossible, to separate short-term and long-term planning. Organizations that have a formal planning system usually link their long-term plans to their budgets; that is, the first year of the long-term plan is the operating budget. Some organizations have both a budgeting and long-term planning system with little interaction between them. In this case, the long-term planning system is focused on the conceptual, strategic, and qualitative and the budgeting system on the quantitative. Still others have only a budgeting cycle, and any long-term planning done is incorporated as part of the budget cycle.

We shall proceed in this chapter to illustrate the budget process by providing a detailed example of its operation as an integral part of the management control system. We shall illustrate an integrated planning and budgeting system for a new and rapidly growing division of a large corporation. Although it is an integrated planning and budgeting system, its focus is upon financial data. It is essentially a three-year budgeting and profit planning process. The first year of the business plan becomes the operating budget.

Once we have completed our example, we will provide some generalizations about the budgeting process. This will be followed by a discussion of some of the difficulties of budgeting for discretionary expense centers. Finally, we shall take up the subject of computer budgeting.

The case described in this chapter represents the budget system of an actual division of a U. S. corporation. It has been disguised, however, and is used only for instructional purposes.

WATER FILTRATION SYSTEM (WFS)

WFS, a newly created division of the Scope-Johnson Company, is a supplier of high-quality prepackaged filter systems and pumps to selected segments of business. Previously, WFS operated within the Aqua Division of the company. Aqua manufactures commercial and residential swimming pool equipment and accessories.

WFS's products include standard lines of packaged filter systems and standard products specifically aimed to solve the needs of each identified market segment. Sales in 1993 were approximately $9.7 million. One of the main products of WFS is filter systems for water cooling towers. Most of the sales to date have been for the repair and overhaul of cooling tower filtration systems in industrial plants and in commercial buildings. In the majority of instances, the units have been sold to contractors who have been hired by institutions to rebuild and repair existing cooling towers.

During its four years of operation WFS has developed the following strengths:

1. Acceptable gross margins have been achieved on its products.
2. Customers now include many companies that are themselves identified as leaders in their field, such as National Lead, General Foods, Coca-Cola, IBM, Gould, Hughes Aircraft, Getty Oil, Occidental Oil, and the Wilson Company.
3. WFS has penetrated markets that have been, are presently, or are expected to be growth markets. These markets include electronics, pharmaceuticals, hospitals, commercial banking, as well as recreational and cultural water users.
4. WFS has achieved interchangeability of key components, which allows it to achieve low manufacturing costs. This allows for a relatively low investment in raw material inventory.
5. WFS has developed a strong staff of sales engineers and of manufacturer's representatives.

GOALS AND OBJECTIVES

The goals of WFS are

1. To continue to be a high-quality supplier of prepackaged filter systems and pumps.
2. To achieve operating income of 15 percent of sales while growing to be a significant (that is, greater than 1 percent) contributor to overall corporate growth.

Specific measurable objectives are

1. To reach an operating income of 15 percent of sales within four years.
2. To reach a sales level of at least 1 percent of corporate sales within five years, assuming a growth rate in corporate sales of 10 percent per year.
3. To attain an ROI of 20 percent within three years.

A summary of the financial objectives through 1998 is presented in Exhibit 11-1.

ORGANIZATION AND RESPONSIBILITY CENTERS

WFS is organized along functional lines, including the functions of engineering, marketing, manufacturing, finance, and administration. The performance of the

Exhibit 11-1
Performance Measurement Objectives (In Thousands)

	1993	1994	1995	1996	1997	1998
Sales	$9,770	$23,970	$35,560	$54,000	$81,000	$115,000
Cost of goods sold	5,380	13,210	19,570	29,700	44,550	63,250
Expenses	5,400	8,410	11,260	16,930	24,300	34,500
Earnings before income taxes	$(1,010)	$ 2,350	$ 4,330	$ 7,370	$12,150	$17,250
Asset base	20,000	25,000	29,000	36,850	60,750	86,250
Marley-Wylain sales base	$6,978,571	$7,990,000	$8,466,666	$9,473,684	$10,384,615	$11,500,000
Objectives:						
1. Operating income (15% of sales)	(10.3)%	9.8%	12.2%	13.7%	15.0%*	15.0%
2. Corporate† sales ratio	.0014	.0030	.0042	.0057	.0078	.0100
3. ROI	—	9.4%	14.9%	20%*	20%	20%

*Point at which WFS meets its objectives and goals.
†Divisional Sales divided by Marley-Wylain sales base.

division is measured by return on investment. Corporate allocations are made to each division for taxes, interest, and other corporate expenses. Nonfinancial objectives are also included in the measurement system, although they do not have great weights attached to them under the current reward system.

Each department within the division is designated as a responsibility center. Manufacturing is an engineered expense center: it is held responsible for meeting cost and quality standards. Purchasing and production control report to the manufacturing department and are both discretionary expense centers; their performance is assessed based upon meeting expense budgets. Marketing is a profit center, being held accountable for contribution margin, which itself is determined by using standard variable costs. Finance, engineering, and administrative departments are all discretionary expense centers. The controller reports directly to the division manager and indirectly to the corporate controller. Exhibit 11-2 gives the organization structure for WFS.

PERFORMANCE EVALUATION AND REWARDS

The system of performance evaluation used in WFS blends short-term performance measures such as ROI with long-term performance measures such as growth in sales. The division does not seek to maximize ROI; financial incentives for the division manager are associated with set upper limits of ROI that, when achieved, do not yield additional financial incentive. Accordingly, goals and objectives are set that combine short-term profit and return-on-investment objectives together with longer-term growth objectives. Therefore, instead of striving to reach an incremental increase in ROI, the division is motivated by the system of performance evaluation to invest in new equipment, tooling, and marketing pro-

Exhibit 11-2
WFS Division Organization

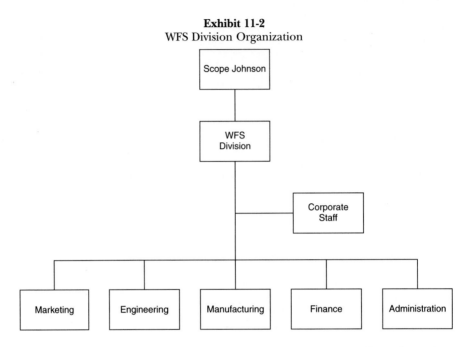

grams that are expected to bear fruit only in the longer term. These latter investments may deteriorate ROI performance in the short term. Since the reward system does not encourage incremental increases in short-term ROI, it guards against some of the worst problems associated with ROI.

TRANSFER PRICING

WFS purchases many of its components from its sister division, Aqua. Since the components used by WFS are uniquely manufactured by Aqua, this places a strong sourcing constraint on WFS. WFS is a captive, so to speak, of Aqua. The corporate guidelines for transfer pricing make provisions for transfers at "full cost." Full cost is computed by adding period manufacturing expenses to standard variable cost. Period manufacturing expenses are computed as 10.2 percent of the sales of the manufacturing division. Approximately 20 percent of all material purchases of WFS are from the Aqua Division.

CONTROL PROCESS

Programming

The annual profit plan is intended to serve as both a programming and a budgeting tool. The plan covers a period of three years, with the first year serving as the budget for performance evaluation and objective setting. New and proposed programs are included within the three-year business plan, and they are ranked by priority, including proposed capital requirements. Significant attention is given to defining and developing new product lines during the profit-planning process.

BUDGETING

1. The controller is responsible for administering the business plan. The controller provides the budget instructions and guidelines, the timetable for the various steps in the business plan, as well as the forms that must be completed at each step in the process. He collects proposals from the various responsibility centers, reviews them, and puts them together into a coordinated package. He advises all functional managers as well as the division manager on the financial dimensions of business decisions.
2. The business planning process begins each year with the marketing plan whereby the marketing manager estimates the variable cost and contribution margin of each standard product. The marketing manager then asks the sales engineers to estimate sales and selling expenses. The marketing manager next compares the estimates with divisional profit and sales objectives and goals. The consolidated marketing plan is then tested against manufacturing capacity for its feasibility, and appropriate adjustments are made to fit within anticipated manufacturing capacity.

Estimating Product Costs

3. WFS utilizes a standard cost system for product costing whereby a standard unit cost is established for every type of material and labor going into a prepackaged filter system and pump. The standards are adjusted annually for anticipated price increases during the next year.
4. Standard rates for variable overhead are also established annually. Fixed overhead of manufacturing and all other service departments is traced and allocated to the divisional income statement as period expenses. Exhibit 11-3 contains an estimate of variable costs and variable margin for a standard water treatment system (that is, pump and automatic filter) for a recirculating water cooling system.

Estimate of Standard Contribution Margin

5. To estimate standard contribution margin, the marketing manager subtracts variable product costs from the selling price of each prepackaged system and multiplies the per unit contribution margin by the number of products sold for each system. Then the contribution margins are summed across all products to arrive at a total marketing contribution margin for the division.

Estimating Period Expenses for Marketing

6. The marketing manager next asks the sales engineer to estimate period marketing expenses, assuming the same market strategy and the same size sales force. This estimate is then reviewed by the marketing manager and is adjusted accordingly. Exhibit 11-4 presents a detailed schedule of discretionary period expenses for the marketing organization. Once approved, this amount is subtracted from contribution margin to

Exhibit 11-3
Standard Variable Cost and Standard Variable Margin

Net selling price			$3,450.00
Standard variable product costs			
Material	$958.00		
Labor	74.00		
Overhead	70.00		
Variable product costs		$1,102.00	
Other direct charges			
Shipping	$ 24.00		
Warranty	518.00		
Commissions	59.00		
		$ 603.00	
Unit variable and direct costs			$1,705.00
Variable margin at standard			$1,745.00

Exhibit 11-4
Detailed Marketing Expenses (In Thousands)

	1993 Amount	1994 Amount	1995 Amount
Indirect labor	—	—	—
Salaries	$1,444.4	$1,666.5	$1,916.5
Commissions and awards	452.8	522.4	600.8
Overtime premium	—	—	—
Fringe benefits	300.3	364.5	398.5
Outside services and fees	41.2	47.5	54.6
Advertising	347.2	400.6	460.7
Travel and entertainment	465.4	537.0	617.6
Supplies and materials	17.5	20.2	23.2
Telephone and telegraph	10.3	11.9	13.7
Occupancy	12.1	14.0	16.0
Insurance, general liabilities	3.1	3.6	4.1
General and miscellaneous	25.7	29.7	34.2
Total	$3,120.0	$3,599.9	$4,129.9

arrive at the net marketing contribution margin. Exhibit 11-5 presents the tentative net contribution margin budget for the marketing function for 1993.

The Manufacturing Plan

7. Once the tentative marketing plan is prepared, the manufacturing manager is then able to put the production plan together. The production plan consists of material and labor requirements, overhead requirements, and production schedules. From

Exhibit 11-5
Net Marketing Plan (In Thousands)

	1993 Amount	1994 Amount	1995 Amount
Gross sales	$9,770	$23,970	$35,560
Less: freight	20	100	180
cash discount	—	—	—
Net sales	$9,750	$23,870	$35,380
Standard variable cost			
Material	3,220		
Labor	440		
Overhead	410		
	4,070	10,070	14,860
Variable margin at standard	$5,680	$13,800	$20,520
Direct charges			
Shipping	60	140	210
Commissions	780	1,800	2,680
Warranty	160	380	570
	$1,000	$2,320	$3,460
Period expenses			
Marketing	3,120	3,600	4,140
Net marketing margin	$1,560	$7,880	$12,920

the labor requirements, the personnel department completes the personnel plan, which specifies the quantity, quality, and mix of personnel required to carry out the manufacturing plan.

Discretionary Expense Center Budgets

8. Once the marketing and manufacturing plans are in place and the planned volume of business is established, discretionary budgets are established for engineering, finance, and the administrative staff. Since engineering is involved in direct, measurable support of standard, packaged, product lines, a part of the engineering budget is considered an "engineered" or "standard cost" expense budget. The balance of the engineering budget includes product development, cost reduction, and other outputs, which are by their very nature more discretionary. The finance and administrative staff budgets are considered purely discretionary.

Business Plan

9. The proposed budgets from marketing, manufacturing, finance, engineering, and the administrative staff are reviewed and consolidated by the controller. The controller then incorporates allocations from the corporation, other income, interest expense, and taxes into the plan. The result is the profit plan of the division. The profit plan is given in Exhibit 11-6.

   If the controller is satisfied that this plan achieves corporate and divisional objectives and goals, he forwards the plan to top management. If the plan does not seem to be based on realistic assumptions and expectations, or if the plan does not meet goals and objectives, the controller has the option of sending it back to WFS for review and revision. Top management, of course, also has the option of rejecting the plan and sending it back for revision.

Capital and Cash Budgets

While preparing the business plan, each of the WFS executives prepares capital request proposals that are directed toward meeting the long-term goals of growth in sales and earnings. Each project is processed through a capital appropriation procedure and, if approved, finds its way, along with all other operating items, into the capital budget. The entire operating and capital budgets are tested for their feasibility in the cash budget. Exhibit 11-7 is a cash budget for WFS over the time period encompassing the business plan. Exhibit 11-7 indicates that WFS is budgeted at the end of the third year to be generating almost enough cash from operations to finance both working capital additions and additions to capital assets.

Asset Base

At the end of the business planning process, the controller calculates the net book value of the asset base projected to be employed within the WFS division. These numbers are shown in Exhibit 11-1 and become the denominator for ROI calculations.

Monthly Statements

The annual operating budget and cash flow statements are broken out into monthly segments, and these totals serve as standards against which actual data will be compared as the year progresses. These statements are shown for 1993 in

Exhibit 11-6
Tentative Profit Plan for WFS Division (In Thousands)

	1993 Amount	1994 Amount	1995 Amount
Gross sales	$9,770	$23,970	$35,560
Less: freight	20	100	180
cash discount	—	—	—
Net sales	$9,750	$23,870	$35,380
Standard variable cost			
Material	3,220	7,966	11,757
Labor	440	1,089	1,606
Overhead	410	1,015	1,497
	4,070	10,070	14,860
Variable margin at standard	$5,680	$13,800	$20,520
Direct charges			
Shipping	60	140	210
Commissions	780	1,800	2,680
Warranty	160	380	578
	$1,000	$ 2,320	$ 3,460
Variances (favorable)			
Material			
Labor			
Overhead			
Inventory adjustment			
Other			
	290	720	1,070
Variable margin at actual	$4,390	$10,760	$15,990
Period expenses			
Manufacturing	$1,000	$2,440	$3,630
Engineering	600	690	1,000
Marketing	3,120	3,600	4,140
Administrative	680	1,680	2,490
	$5,400	$ 8,410	$11,260
Operating income	$(1,010)	$ 2,350	$ 4,330

Exhibit 11-8 and 11-9. Each responsibility center has its corresponding profit, revenue, and cost budgets broken out into detail by product (if appropriate) and by expense classification by month.

PURPOSE AND CHARACTERISTICS OF THE BUDGETING PROCESS

Now that we have considered a complete illustration of the budget process in a realistic setting, we are in a position to describe the purpose and characteristics of the budgetary process. It truly is a process that is right at the heart of management control.

In Chapter 1, we defined a management control system as a set of interrelated communication structures that facilitates the processing of information for the purpose of assisting managers in coordinating the parts and attaining the purpose of an organization on a continuous basis. Communication structures are established in the managerial control process to plan what an organization and its subunits are to accomplish during a specified period of time, coordinate the plans and activities of all parts of the organization so as to ensure that all are working towards the same purpose, process information within each subunit and between subunits for purposes of decision making, and evaluate information and decide what, if any, action should be taken to bring correction to a situation.

It turns out that all these steps are involved in the budgetary process. WFS uses its budgeting process to plan the activities of each responsibility center and to coordinate the functions of marketing, engineering, manufacturing, finance, and administration so as to achieve its goals and objectives. The budget process is used to process information among functions for purposes of decision making. Once the operating and cash budgets are put together, imbalances are corrected by the

Exhibit 11-7
WFS Cash Flow Budget (In Thousands)

	1993	1994	1995
Cash provided from operations			
Net income	(537)	1,250	2,304
Depreciation	884	2,072	2,554
Amortization	—	—	—
Cash used for working capital	$ 307	$3,322	$4,858
Cash	—	—	—
Accounts receivable	(987)	(2,423)	(2,550)
Inventories	(1,302)	(3,196)	(1,133)
Accounts payable and accrued expenses	839	2,060	1,247
Cash available for other purposes	$(1,143)	$(237)	$2,422
Property additions	(1,103)	(2,706)	(2,834)
Net book value of disposals	—	—	—
Change in other assets	—	—	—
Prepaid expenses	—	—	—
Contribution to working capital	—	—	—
	$(2,246)	$(2,943)	$(412)
Add: Credits to control account			
Intercompany purchases	644	1,593	2,351
Payroll taxes	2,134	5,237	5,384
Income taxes	(473)	1,100	2,026
Other	—	1,267	747
Deduct: Debit to control account			
Intercompany sales	—	—	—
Other	—	—	—
Total cash transfer to (from) corporate division	$59	$6,254	$10,096

Exhibit 11-8
WFS Monthly Profit Plan (In Thousands)

	Jan.	Feb.	Mar.	Apr.	May	June	July	Aug.	Sept.	Oct.	Nov.	Dec.	Total
Gross sales	$755	$793	$710	$819	$1,034	$960	$835	$819	$801	$728	$691	$625	$9,770
Less: freight cash discounts	1.5	1.6	1.4	1.6	2.2	2.0	2.0	2.0	1.6	1.4	1.4	1.3	(20)
Net sales	$754	$791	$709	$817	$1,032	$958	$933	$917	$799	$727	$689	$624	$9,750
Standard variable cost													
Material	260	273	251	282	350	324	310	287	250	231	210	192	3,220
Labor	35	37	33	39	49	40	43	40	36	32	29	27	440
Overhead	33	35	31	35	44	41	39	37	32	30	27	26	410
	328	345	315	356	443	403	392	364	318	293	266	245	4,070
Variable margin at standard	$426	$446	$394	$461	$589	$553	$541	$553	$481	$434	$423	$379	$5,650
Direct charges													
Shipping	5	5	5	5	5	6	6	5	5	4	4	5	60
Commissions	20	30	40	40	50	60	70	80	90	90	100	110	780
Warranty	12	12	11	10	13	12	19	18	17	12	12	12	160
	$ 37	$ 47	$ 56	$ 55	$ 68	$ 78	$ 95	$103	$112	$106	$116	$127	$1,000
Variances (favorable)													
Material	—	—	—	—	—	—	—	—	—	—	—	—	—
Labor	—	—	—	—	—	—	—	—	—	—	—	—	—
Overhead	—	—	—	—	—	—	—	—	—	—	—	—	—
Inventory adjustments	—	—	—	—	—	—	—	—	—	—	—	—	—
Other	9	10	10	12	15	29	29	35	35	33	35	33	290
Variable margin at actual	$380	$389	$328	$389	$506	$446	$417	$415	$334	$295	$272	$219	$4,390
Period expenses													
Manufacturing	83.3	83.3	83.3	83.3	83.3	83.3	83.3	83.3	83.3	83.3	83.3	83.7	1,000
Engineering	50	50	50	50	50	50	50	50	50	50	50	50	600
Marketing	260	260	260	260	260	260	260	260	260	260	260	260	3120
Administrative	57	57	57	57	57	57	57	57	57	57	57	53	680
	$450.3	$450.3	$450.3	$450.3	$450.3	$450.3	$450.3	$450.3	$450.3	$450.3	$450.3	$446.7	$5,400
Operating income	$(70.3)	$(61.3)	$(122.3)	$(61.3)	$55.7	$(4.3)	$(33.3)	$(35.3)	$(116.3)	$(155.3)	$(178.3)	$(22.7)	$(1,010)
Other income (expense)	—	—	—	—	—	—	—	—	—	—	—	—	—
Interest	—	—	—	—	—	—	—	—	—	—	—	—	—
Overhead adjustment	—	—	—	—	—	—	—	—	—	—	—	—	—
Income before income taxes	—	—	—	—	—	—	—	—	—	—	—	—	—
Income taxes	—	—	—	—	—	—	—	—	—	—	—	—	—
Net income	—	—	—	—	—	—	—	—	—	—	—	—	—
Intercompany sales	—	—	—	—	—	—	—	—	—	—	—	—	—
Special sales	—	—	—	—	—	—	—	—	—	—	—	—	—

Exhibit 11-9
WFS Monthly Cash Flow Statement (In Thousands)

	Jan.	Feb.	Mar.	Apr.	May	June	July	Aug.	Sept.	Oct.	Nov.	Dec.	Total
Cash provided from operations													
Net income	(26)	(37)	(21)	23	(102)	(84)	(74)	(69)	(83)	(62)	(54)	52	(537)
Add: Depreciation	50	50	50	63	63	63	75	75	75	93	93	94	844
Amortization	—	—	—	—	—	—	—	—	—	—	—	—	—
	$24	$13	$29	$55	$(39)	$(21)	$1	$8	$(8)	$31	$39	$146	$307
Cash used for working capital													
Cash													
Accounts receivable	(1,162)	(2,492)	(1,810)	2,825	(1,505)	805	427	303	464	474	474	210	(987)
Inventories	(103)	(125)	(53)	(127)	(165)	(120)	(212)	(443)	(208)	(167)	327	94	(1,307)
Accounts payable and accrued expenses	875	96	(150)	428	236	(142)	(127)	(466)	219	(253)	449	(328)	839
Contribution to working capital	$(390)	$(2,519)	$(2,013)	$3,126	$(1,434)	$543	$88	$(606)	$475	$54	$1,250	$(24)	$(1,450)
Other cash transactions													
Property additions	(78)	(78)	(78)	(194)	(70)	(62)	(47)	(47)	(178)	(78)	(93)	(100)	(1,103)
Net book value of disposals	—	—	—	—	—	—	—	—	—	—	—	—	—
Change in other assetss	—	—	—	—	—	—	—	—	—	—	—	—	—
Prepaid expenses	—	—	—	—	—	—	—	—	—	—	—	—	—
Contribution to working capital	(444)	(2,584)	(2,062)	3,018	(1,543)	460	42	(647)	289	7	1,196	22	(2,246)
Add: Credits to control account													
Intercompany purchases	54	54	54	53	54	54	54	53	54	54	53	53	644
Payroll taxes	179	179	179	187	187	187	178	178	170	170	170	170	2,134
Income taxes	—	(43)	(25)	38	(118)	(98)	(85)	(81)	(47)	(21)	(13)	20	(473)
Other	233	190	208	278	123	143	147	150	177	203	210	243	2,305
Deduct: Debits to control account													
Intercompany sales	—	—	—	—	—	—	—	—	—	—	—	—	—
Other	—	—	—	—	—	—	—	—	—	—	—	—	—
Total cash transfer to (from) corporate division	$(211)	$(2,394)	$(1,854)	$3,296	$(1,420)	$603	$189	$(497)	$466	$210	$1,406	$265	$59

decisions of management. The budget process is a goal-seeking process. It serves as one of the major communication tools of the firm. Thus we see that the budgeting process is at the heart of the managerial control process and crucial to the successful management of an organization.

An effective budget process requires the contribution of all the managers of an organization. This is illustrated in Exhibit 11-10. The first step in the budget process is the preparation of action plans. The action plans of the various functional groups are highly interrelated and require close coordination amongst themselves. Marketing starts the process by preparing its forecast of business activity. Production determines the extent to which the marketing forecast is feasible and recommends appropriate adjustments. Once a feasible forecast is negotiated between marketing and production, the human resource department may make its plans for acquiring or releasing human resources. Purchasing may make plans for acquiring the necessary supplies of outside services and materials. Finally, the facilities department may make plans to acquire or release facilities to support the marketing and production plans of the organization.

Next the action plans are converted to revenue and expense budgets. Once the action plans are developed, revenue and expense budgets are formulated leading to the development of the profit plan, which is the operating budget. In turn, the action plan and profit plan lead to the formulation of capital and cash budgets, which in turn lead to the formulation of the financing plan. All projected assets and liabilities are then arranged in the budgeted balance sheet for the organization. Exhibit 11-10 contains a schematic description of the way the action plans of functional groups typically interact in the preparation of the operating and financial budgets.

The WFS case illustrates the use of the strong controller concept, whereby the controller is not only responsible for administering the business plan but is also involved in reviewing the substantive issues surrounding the budget and making recommendations to general management regarding its general acceptability. It also illustrates the use of feasibility tests in making budget decisions. The marketing plan is tested against manufacturing capacity for its feasibility, and appropriate adjustments are made to fit the plan within anticipated manufacturing capacity. The operating and capital budgets are tested for their feasibility in the cash budget.

It is instructive to look at the mutually supportive dimensions of the budgeting process. We do this next.

MUTUALLY SUPPORTIVE DIMENSIONS OF THE BUDGETING PROCESS

Many aspects of the MSSM are involved in the budgeting process and should be designed to be supportive of it. We review them one by one.

Style and Culture

The style of top management determines whether the budgetary process is primarily top down, as it would be in the more centralized and autocratic organiza-

Exhibit 11-10

A Model of The Budget Process

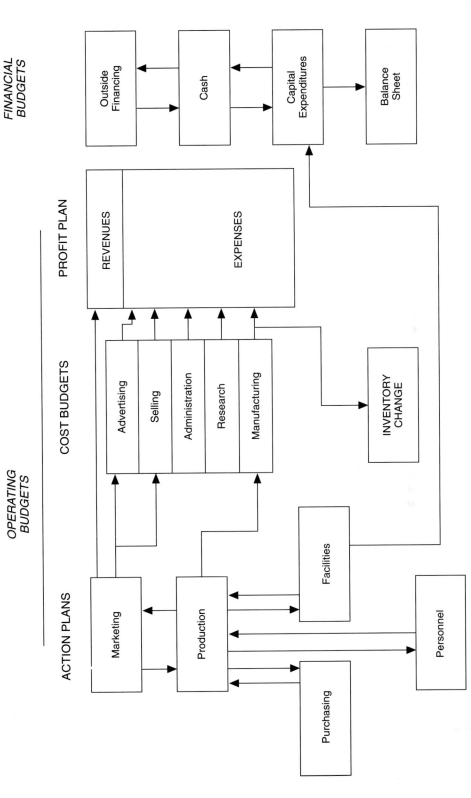

Reproduced and adapted by permission from Figure 8-1, p. 210 of Gordon Shillinglaw, *Managerial Cost Accounting*, 5th ed. Homewood, Ill.: Richard D. Irwin, 1982.

tions, or bottom up, as it would be in the more decentralized and participative organizations. It also determines how frequently performance is reviewed and at what level of detail. It also determines the extent to which the staff participates in reviewing and challenging various budgets.

Infrastructure

The level of autonomy of division management has a major influence over how much decision authority the division manager has in the budget process.

The budget is prepared according to the responsibility designations of each unit of the organization structure. Profit budgets are prepared for profit centers; expense budgets are prepared for discretionary expense centers, and so on. The budget process is thereby tied directly to the organization structure and to responsibility designations.

The controller is responsible for designing and operating the budget process, although decision making within the budgetary process belongs to operating management. The controller may report to divisional management and serve as an advisor to operating management and thereby play a larger role in the decisions that are involved in the budget process. Or the controller may report to the corporate controller and serve in more of a fiduciary role with respect to the divisional manager. The controller may have a separate staff dedicated to the work of budgeting. That staff may be headed by a budget director.

Rewards

Reward systems of the organization are tied closely to budgetary performance. Moreover, management must decide which accounts are to be used in measuring performance for the purpose of granting rewards. If leading indicators of performance (for example, quality, market share, growth in sales) are to be used to assess short-term performance toward long-term goals, these too must be specified (Merchant, 1989, pp. 68 and 91).

Coordination and Integration

As we indicated earlier, the budgetary process is a major tool to integrate the plans and performances of the parts of the organization into a more cohesive whole.

Also, organizations often form budget committees to guide and oversee the operations of the budget process and to make resource allocation decisions. The budgetary committee is responsible for establishing budgetary guidelines and budgetary forms and procedures and for guiding operating personnel in the preparation of the budget.

Control Process

The budget is in fact a part of the control process, but it must be designed. Items such as the budget timetable must be established; guidelines must be published; and forms to be completed must be distributed. Guidelines should include statements from top management about the likely economic climate and key economic assumptions to use, together with performance goals that should be sought.

Managers in turn must hold various meetings to enumerate assumptions and train personnel in how they are to prepare budget estimates and explore alternative scenarios for the future.

Budgets once prepared must go through both a technical review by the controller's staff and a management review—both a local unit and superior unit review.

The reporting process on previously approved budgets goes on throughout the year and variances from plans are investigated by both the controllers staff and by operating management. Budgetary revisions are submitted if warranted.

Exhibit 11-11 summarizes a number of issues involving the MSSM which influence and must be synchronized with the budgeting process.

Now that we have described the nature and purpose of budgeting, we are in a position to examine some of the difficult issues surrounding the establishment of budgets for discretionary expense centers.

Exhibit 11-11
Mutually Supportive Dimensions of the Budget Process

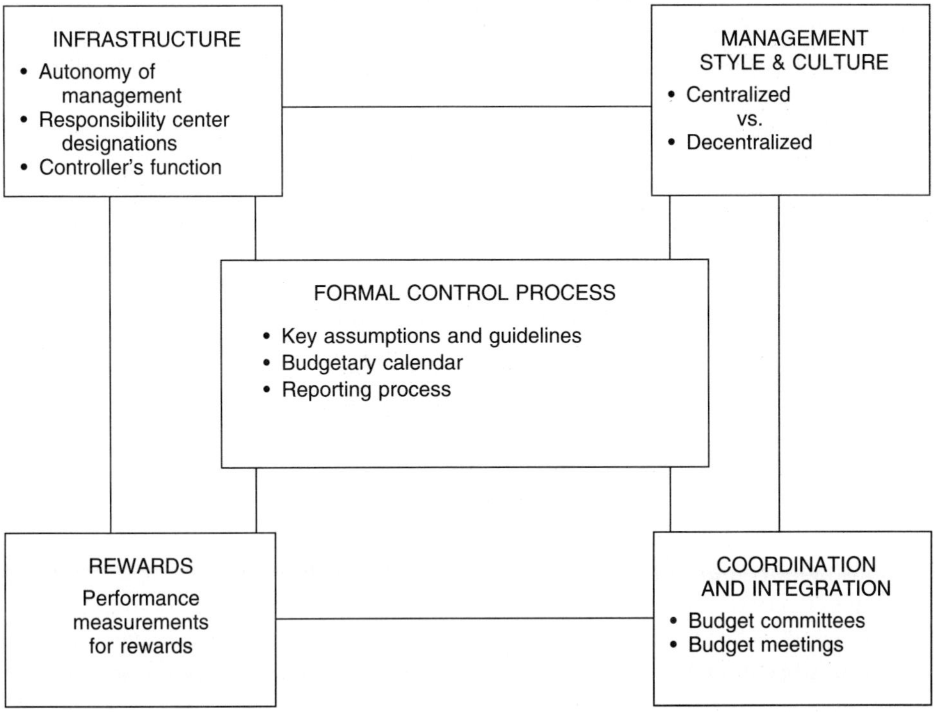

INFRASTRUCTURE
- Autonomy of management
- Responsibility center designations
- Controller's function

MANAGEMENT STYLE & CULTURE
- Centralized
  vs.
- Decentralized

FORMAL CONTROL PROCESS
- Key assumptions and guidelines
- Budgetary calendar
- Reporting process

REWARDS
Performance measurements for rewards

COORDINATION AND INTEGRATION
- Budget committees
- Budget meetings

BUDGETING IN SERVICE CENTERS

Most responsibility centers in organizations are not concerned directly with manufacturing; rather, they are service centers. The budgets for most of these centers are determined by managerial discretion, since the engineering relationships between inputs and outputs are only partially known, at best.

Exhibit 11-12 gives the relationships between inputs and outputs in responsibility centers. In a manufacturing responsibility center, there is a technological relationship between the variable inputs of labor, material, and capital and product outputs. For a given level of production, we know from our standard cost sheets on a product what level of inputs is required to produce the product. It is then quite straightforward to set a budget for these variable inputs of the manufacturing operations. Variances from these standards are also somewhat reliable measures of performance.

This is not the case for many other responsibility centers, such as marketing, research and development, engineering, public relations, maintenance, personnel, legal, administration, computer operations, production control, purchasing, and other service organizations. Although it is usually possible to construct engineering relationships for at least a portion of the activities of these service centers, these relationships cannot be stated for the entire function in the case of these service centers. For example, to achieve a certain image in the community, a large merchandising store might employ a public relations staff. How large should that staff be to achieve company objectives? How large a legal staff should be maintained to protect the interests of the company? How large a staff of systems analysts and computer programmers should be maintained? What is the appropriate level of advertising? How about the level of health care benefits for employees?

Since it is very difficult to specify exactly the level of input required in each of these centers to achieve organizational goals, management must use a fair amount of discretion in establishing budgets for these responsibility centers. It is for this reason that practically all of these responsibility centers are established as discretionary expense centers with marketing almost always serving as the exception. It turns out that, although there is no perfect solution to the problem of establishing budgets for discretionary expense centers, many helpful techniques are available to aid management in this important decision process. We turn now to examine some of the more useful of these techniques.

TOOLS FOR BUDGETING IN DISCRETIONARY EXPENSE CENTERS (DECs)

Standard costing provides a system for planning and performance evaluation in responsibility centers in which engineering relationships can be established for activities. Because engineering standards cannot be established for most discretionary expense center activities, variances from budget are not reliable as indicators of performance for DECs as they are for standard cost centers. Therefore, we

Exhibit 11-12
Inputs and Outputs in Responsibility Centers

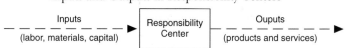

need to utilize tools that will allow managers to establish budgets properly and that will provide effective tools of performance evaluation.

We now examine six tools, each having some potential to aid in the solution of this problem. A combination of any of these may be employed by management in the solution of the planning and control problems raised by DECs.

AN EFFECTIVE BUDGET PROCEDURE

There are a number of characteristics of the budgeting process which, if present, are helpful in developing effective budgets for DECs. We turn now to examine these characteristics.

Participation in the Planning of the Budget

Budget making for DECs should involve all participants in the budget process. This is especially important with regard to the planning of the job that is to be done in the DECs. Participation in planning the scope of the job and personnel requirement levels is a key control tool for management in that it provides management with an opportunity to review and influence the direction of the work itself in the DECs. Participation will also enhance the motivation of employees to fulfill the objectives and the scope of the job.

Task-Oriented Budgets

Budgets for DECs should be prepared in terms of major and minor tasks to be performed. Budgets that are prepared solely in terms of expense classifications (that is, in terms of inputs) have the weakness of not revealing the purposes of the budget expenditures to the manager reviewing them. Expense budgets cannot be easily related to output, thus making it difficult to judge the effectiveness of budget allocations. A task-oriented format makes it easier for management to understand requests for budget increases, since increases can be related to their cause, thus establishing causal relationships.

This is essentially budgeting by purpose. Requests for budget increases should contain explanations of changes in terms of activity increases, products added, new personnel added for given tasks, and so on. This makes the budget process more rational for DECs. We shall return to this issue in Chapters 12 and 13 when we discuss cost accounting systems.

Strong Work Force Control

The major expense for most DECs is personnel expense, since service centers are by their very nature labor intensive. Stringent controls over addition of personnel will end up creating stringent controls over the entire budget of the DEC.

Variance Analysis for Costs and Personnel

Although variance analysis is not as helpful for control in DECs as it is in standard cost centers, it is important that DEC managers be asked to explain deviations from expense budgets on a task basis to management. This serves to create a check on DEC managers so that they might not ignore cost control while pursuing their objectives.

A STRONG CONTROLLER ORGANIZATION

There are many behavioral and economic reasons why forces are created in DECs for budget expansion. Salaries, prestige, and power tend to be a positive function of organizational size. Moreover, many highly educated employees in DECs (for example, scientists in R&D organizations) look toward their profession for their rewards and are sometimes motivated to put professional interests ahead of employer interests.

Strong countermeasures, including careful checking and screening of budget requests, are necessary to offset these tendencies for DEC budgets to grow over time. This kind of control is possible only when a controller's organization exists with the charter, authority, and resources to carry out these functions for management. It takes the proper financial resources, high-quality staff, and management support for a controller's organization to head off the inefficiencies that are otherwise likely to occur in DECs.

From our model of the control process paradigm, we can see the likelihood of expenditures growing in DECs in organizations that have not been encountering any difficulty in achieving profit and growth goals. Under these circumstances, budget requests from DECs are unlikely to undergo the same kind of scrutiny that they would in tougher times, even with a vigilant controller organization. These "excess" resources together form a pool of resources that might be referred to as *organizational slack*. They are more than what is necessary to do the job and represent a fund of resources that serves as a cushion in periods of downturn in business activity or any other kind of environmental turbulence, since they may be reduced with little effect on the principal operations of the business. In other words, in growth periods, the organization may not want to fight hard against the growth of slack in DECs. But, if it does, it should establish a strong controller concept.

IDENTIFY ENGINEERED COST RELATIONSHIPS WHEREVER POSSIBLE

Although input–output relationships are difficult to define for most DECs, at least some of the activity in all DECs may be reduced to engineering relationships. For example, the order-filling function associated with marketing involves some well-defined tasks that are quite repetitive for different orders. It is usually possible to establish a flexible budget relating order-getting expense to the volume of sales. This is also true for the drafting function of engineering and for the bookkeeping aspects of financial accounting.

Where it is possible to establish expenses for a DEC as reliably dependent upon a cost driver (for example, sales, volume of activities, parts), it becomes possible to establish flexible budgets for the task. While DECs will differ, some of the activities of virtually all DECs are amenable to this kind of analysis.

TRACK RECORD OF DEC MANAGERS

A number of factors relating to the track record of managers might be used in budgeting for DECs. Track record refers to the impressions formed in the organization about managers with regard to their budget requests. Are they considered "empire builders?" Do they have the reputation of promoting the interests of their subunit to the detriment of the organization as a whole? How do their expenditures for items that are easy to understand, such as entertainment, dues, and subscriptions, compare with those in other organizational units? What have been the past internal appraisals of the DEC manager?

COMPARATIVE INDUSTRY DATA

This approach seeks to compare staffing and budget levels of DEC units with comparative organizations. The data are usually collected by a trade association or by a company survey and are normalized for size and for some of the differences that come about as a result of classification differences between organizations.

While this approach never produces conclusive results as to over- or under-staffing, it can be used to shift the burden of proof to the DEC manager for any staffing levels above the industry average. Used properly, the data can form the basis for discussions as to proper staffing levels. They should not be used as a club to gain cost or personnel reductions.

Comparative industry data may be used to set up a creative tension between the controller and the controllee in place of a market mechanism that is lacking in these situations. Of course, these data, to be credible, must be adjusted for major non-comparabilities among the organizations in the study. If the data are not credible, they will not serve any useful purpose for control and quite likely will worsen the control problem. The firms in the data base should be comparable, and careful attention should be paid to data collection methods to take into account differences among organizations and differences in budget classifications used by these organizations.

ZERO-BASE REVIEWS

Much has been written about zero-base budgeting since it was first implemented by Peter Pyhrr at Texas Instruments during the 1960s. The discussion about ZBB appears to have been useful. However, the really new part of ZBB—having DEC managers justify their *entire operation* on an annual basis—is not workable. The workable part of ZBB—budgeting by tasks and ranking tasks as to their priority— is not really new. Nevertheless, it is possible to ferret out of the ZBB system a very powerful set of procedures for budgeting DEC expenses. Moreover, it is desirable and realistic to review each DEC from scratch periodically, that is, a zero-base review, on a rotating basis (for example, each responsibility center every two or three years). Both parts (that is, the task-oriented and periodic comprehensive reviews) take patience to implement and are fraught with potential difficulty. Improvements in information processing, however, do help here, given the need under ZBB for enormous information processing.

Zero-base budgeting is a misnomer. Budgeting is inherently an incremental process. The limits of human information processing make it extremely difficult, if not impossible, to evaluate all activities from scratch each period. Moreover, there is the pressure of time; the budget process normally takes place within a three- or four-month period of time. Whenever ZBB has been used, a large portion of activities has been exempted from zero-base review. So rather than zero-base review, it has more often been 80 percent-base review, with only 20 percent of the budget subject to complete review on an annual basis. This is merely another example of incremental budgeting, although we should expect continual progress towards zero-base reviews in the future as information-processing technology and software programs permit improvements in the budgetary process.

The effective part of ZBB has been its rational approach to the budget process in DECs. ZBB efforts begin by structuring the activities of responsibility centers, often called *decision units* in ZBB, into task-oriented budgets, which are called *decision packages*. Approximately 20 percent of the dollar value of the packages is subjected to close scrutiny each year. These packages are ranked within each decision unit, and the rankings are used at successively higher levels of the organization to arrive at still new rankings. These rankings are used in budget decision making. We turn now to itemize each step required in the ZBB process.

1. Define basic budgetary units called decision units (our responsibility centers).
2. Subdivide the work of each decision unit into decision packages.
3. Prepare for each decision package a statement of purpose and objectives, alternative methods of carrying out objectives, benefits and costs of each alternative, and the budget required to achieve the minimum objective of the task. Guidelines usually stipulate that the minimum level is approximately 70 percent of the current level and that other alternatives are, say, at 90, 100, 110, 120, and 130 percent of current levels.
4. Each decision unit manager decides which of all packages should fall into the lowest 20 percent category, in terms of dollar amount. The packages in the lowest 20 percent category are then ranked in descending order of priority. Each increment of a package above its minimum level is assigned a priority in the structure of priorities. For example, a manager may decide that all minimum packages should be ranked ahead of increments to any decision package. Only the packages and increments within the marginal 20 percent category are at risk in the budgetary process.
5. Rankings are consolidated, and new rankings are established at each level of the organization. This results in a uniform ranking of department, division, or corporation, depending upon the scope of the program. Again, only DEC budgets are included in the process.

6. Engineered expenses and planned profit before taxes are subtracted from forecasts of sales revenue. Remaining resources are applied to the DEC packages with the highest priority, including those representing new tasks.

Care must be taken in implementing this procedure for DECs. It should be implemented on a piecemeal basis, using the experiences of a pilot study in subsequent applications. In a full-blown system, it is usually necessary to establish ranking committees at various levels of the organizational hierarchy to deal with the ranking issues.

The primary benefits of a budget procedure established along the lines of ZBB is that it allows new packages to compete equally for priority with existing packages. Without a procedure such as this, new programs are forced to compete with themselves for limited new funds, even if they are more important to the organization than an existing program that under pure incremental budgeting is considered justified simply because it has been done before. It eliminates one of the most severe limitations of 100 percent-base budgeting, namely, the need for new resources to fund new programs, thus inhibiting improvement unless more resources are added to previous-period levels.

Once this procedure is in place, it becomes possible to carry out an effective zero-base review in each DEC on a rotating basis, perhaps once every five years. This will permit capturing some of the benefits of an annual zero-base review (that is, the original concept behind ZBB) while not suffering the cathartic defensive behavior that would accompany zero-base budgeting.

COMPUTER BUDGETING

From our cybernetic model of the control process, we see that if the preliminary budget does not meet the objectives of management, forces are set into motion to bring about changes in order to bring plans into line with objectives. The gap cannot persist for long. If a gap exists, it is necessary to devise new programs, cut planned expenses, or seek measures to improve revenues on existing programs. If the gap still persists, the only alternative is to change the objectives.

The need to revise plans may come about as a result of cash needs. The combination of capital requirements created by planned investments, together with cash flow requirements of current operations, may exceed planned cash inflows of the period(s) in question. While it is possible on a manual basis to consider alternative modifications to the budget to solve problems such as this one, the time required to do it systematically may exceed the time available. Many budget processes are quite intricate, requiring massive coordination among participants and numerous internal agreements. To change a plan in a systematic manner if it fails to meet objectives may be painful indeed; hence the use of "across-the-board" measures such as across-the-board cost cuts.

The problem given creates the need for asking "what-if" questions. This lends itself to the technique of computer simulation, using a computer model of the financial variables affecting the budget process. Typically the model should include at least three parts:

1. A line-by-line format of the income statement and cash flow statement coupled with the time periods involved in the planning horizon (that is, months or quarters).
2. Formulas that provide instructions as to how each line is to be calculated.
3. The input data for the first period of the planning horizon.

To illustrate computer budgeting we will construct a model of Exhibit 11-8 (WPS Monthly Profit Plan) using EXCEL. Then we will assume an alternative scenario affecting sales to examine its impact upon monthly operating income. The sample EXCEL model is reproduced in Exhibit 11-13 and the new scenario is reproduced in Exhibit 11-14.

COMPUTER-BASED PLANNING AND CONTROL IN THE CORPORATE HIERARCHY

Computer programs, like EXCEL, now allow us to create a financial model for the entire corporate hierarchy within which we may integrate the financial planning for a corporation, even a complex one with many foreign subsidiaries. These programs are now sufficiently advanced to allow us to model the financial variables of each responsibility center and then to integrate each appropriately into the control structure. Case 11-2 provides an exercise in modeling the corporate hierarchy for a representative multinational firm.

REFERENCES

COOK, ARTHUR, "Preparation and Use of Budgets," in PAUL J. WENDELL, ed., *Corporate Controller's Manual*, Vols. 1 and 2, Boston, Mass.: Warren Gorham, 1993.

HOFSTEDE, G. H., *The Game of Budget Control.* London: Tavistock, 1968.

HORNGREN, CHARLES, and GEORGE FOSTER, *Cost Accounting: A Managerial Approach*, 7th Ed. Englewood Cliffs, N.J.: Prentice Hall, 1991.

LAWLER, E. E., and J. G. RHODE, *Information and Control in Organizations.* Santa Monica, Calif.: Goodyear, 1976.

MERCHANT, KENNETH A., *Rewarding Results: Motivating Profit Center Managers.* Boston, Mass.: Harvard Business School Press, 1989.

SCHIFF, M., and A. Y. LEWIN, "The Impact of People on Budgets," *Accounting Review*, Vol. 45 (1970), pp. 259–268.

SHILLINGLAW, GORDON, *Managerial Cost Accounting*, 5th ed. Homewood, Ill.: Richard D. Irwin, 1982.

SWEENY, ALLEN H.W., and ROBERT RACHLIN, eds., *Handbook of Budgeting.* New York: John Wiley, 1981.

Exhibit 11-13
Sample WFS Profit Plan

	Jan.	Feb.	Mar.	Apr.	May	June	July	Aug.	Sept.	Oct.	Nov.	Dec.	Total
Gross sales	$755	$793	$710	$819	$1,034	$960	$935	$919	$801	$728	$691	$625	$9,770
Less: Freight	1	2	1	2	2	2	2	2	2	1	1	1	20
Net sales	$754	$791	$709	$817	$1,032	$958	$933	$917	$799	$727	$690	$624	$9,750
Standard variable cost													
Material	249	262	234	270	341	317	309	304	265	240	228	206	3227
Labor	34	36	32	37	47	43	42	41	36	33	31	28	440
Variable overhead	32	33	30	34	43	40	39	39	34	31	29	26	411
Variable margin at standard	$439	$460	$413	$475	$600	$557	$543	$533	$465	$423	$402	$363	$5,673
Direct overhead													
Shipping	5	5	5	5	5	6	6	5	5	4	4	5	60
Commissions	20	30	40	40	50	60	70	80	90	90	100	110	780
Warranty	12	12	11	10	13	12	19	18	17	12	12	12	160
Total direct charges	37	47	56	55	68	78	95	103	112	106	116	127	1000
Period expenses													
Manufacturing	83.3	83.3	83.3	83.3	83.3	83.3	83.3	83.3	83.3	83.3	83.3	83.3	999.6
Engineering	50	50	50	50	50	50	50	50	50	50	50	50	600
Marketing	260	260	260	260	260	260	260	260	260	260	260	260	3120
Administrative	57	57	57	57	57	57	57	57	57	57	57	57	684
Total administrative	450.3	450.3	450.3	450.3	450.3	450.3	450.3	450.3	450.3	450.3	450.3	450.3	5403.6
Operating income	($48)	($37)	($94)	($30)	$82	$29	($3)	($20)	($98)	($133)	($165)	($214)	($731)

Exhibit 11-14
Sample WFS Profit Plan 10% Increase in Net Sales

	Jan.	Feb.	Mar.	Apr.	May	June	July	Aug.	Sept.	Oct.	Nov.	Dec.	Total
Gross sales	$830	$872	$781	$901	$1,137	$1,056	$1,028	$1,011	$881	$801	$760	$687	$10,745
Less: Freight	1	2	1	2	2	2	2	2	2	1	1	1	20
Net sales	$829	$870	$780	$899	$1,135	$1,054	$1,026	$1,009	$879	$800	$759	$686	$10,725
Standard variable cost													
Material	249	262	234	270	341	317	309	304	265	240	228	206	3227
Labor	34	36	32	37	47	43	42	41	36	33	31	28	440
Variable overhead	32	33	30	34	43	40	39	39	34	31	29	26	411
Variable margin at standard	$514	$539	$484	$557	$704	$653	$636	$625	$545	$496	$471	$426	$6,648
Direct overhead													
Shipping	5	5	5	5	5	6	6	5	5	4	4	5	60
Commissions	20	30	40	40	50	60	70	80	90	90	100	110	780
Warranty	12	12	11	10	13	12	19	18	17	12	12	12	160
Total direct charges	37	47	56	55	68	78	95	103	112	106	116	127	1000
Period expenses													
Manufacturing	83.3	83.3	83.3	83.3	83.3	83.3	83.3	83.3	83.3	83.3	83.3	83.3	999.6
Engineering	50	50	50	50	50	50	50	50	50	50	50	50	600
Marketing	260	260	260	260	260	260	260	260	260	260	260	260	3120
Administrative	57	57	57	57	57	57	57	57	57	57	57	57	684
Total administrative	450.3	450.3	450.3	450.3	450.3	450.3	450.3	450.3	450.3	450.3	450.3	450.3	5403.6
Operating income	$27	$42	($23)	$52	$185	$125	$91	$72	($18)	($60)	($96)	($152)	$244

Case 11-1 Cycle World

Refer back to Case 10-2.

QUESTIONS

1. Prepare a three-year operating budget and cash flow budget for Cycle World under the assumption that the Ivrea line *will not* be undertaken. These two statements should be prepared on spreadsheets.
2. Prepare a three-year operating budget and cash flow budget for the Ivrea line alone. These two statements also should be prepared on spreadsheets.
3. Consolidate the operating and cash budgets for Cycle World and for Ivrea.
4. Assume that Mr. Burke wants to undertake the Ivrea Project; how can he finance it? Assume that he must have at least $500 of positive net cash flow each year to protect against uncertainties. What options does he have? Defend your choices.
5. It has often been said that the budget process is a decision-making process. Explain on the basis of the analysis done for Cases 10-2 and 11-1.

Case 11-2   Medco, Inc.*

Medco is a multinational pharmaceutical company that markets three products: aspirin, vitamins, and Valium. The company is organized into a domestic division and an international division. Medco's domestic division consists of two branches: the Atlanta branch and the Boston branch. Both branches in the domestic division produce and sell all three products.

Medco's international division is composed of two branches: the Switzerland branch and the Canadian branch. The Switzerland branch manufactures and sells Valium, while the Canadian branch manufactures and sells only aspirin. The Swiss branch is 75 percent owned by Medco. The Canadian branch is 100 percent owned by Medco.

The controller of Medco wants to create a hierarchical budgeting model for 1994 for the entire corporation arranged by division and branch and consolidated at the corporate level in U.S. dollars. In addition, operating budgets should be constructed for each of the products in each branch. Exhibit 11-15 is a schematic of the proposed budgeting system prepared by the corporate controller.

Exhibit 11-16 gives the revenue and expense data for each of the domestic branches by quarter. Exhibit 11-17 gives the revenue and expense data for each of the international branches. Projected exchange rates converting international operations into U.S. dollars are given in Exhibit 11-17.

QUESTIONS

Prepare a spreadsheet, by quarter, for Medco containing the following:

1. Projected income statements for each product of each branch.
2. Projected income statements for each branch in local currencies.
3. Projected income statements by division in U.S. dollars.
4. Projected consolidated income statements for Medco as a whole in U.S. dollars.

*This problem is adapted by permission from page 2-1 of CRMS™ (formerly IFPS) *Consolidation Techniques*, Comshare, Inc., 1984.

Exhibit 11-15
Medco Budget Planning Structure

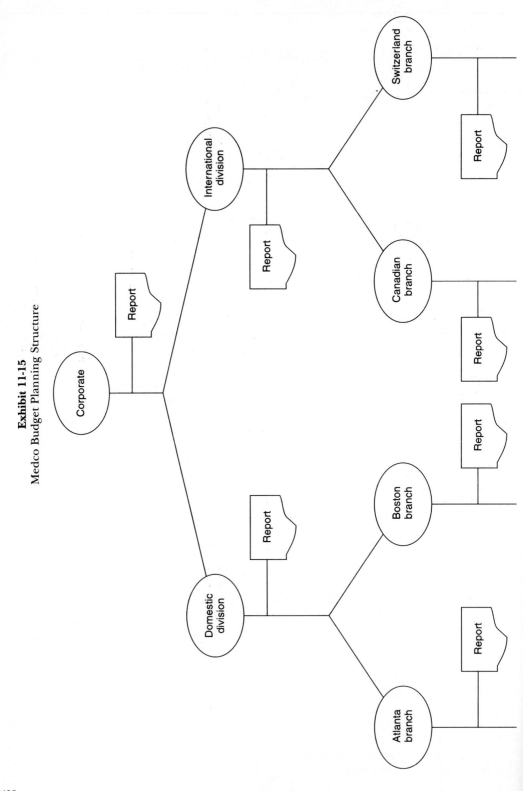

Exhibit 11-16
Domestic Division Product Data

Location: Atlanta					**Location: Boston**				
Aspirin	Q1	Q2	Q3	Q4	Aspirin	Q1	Q2	Q3	Q4
Units	100,000	100,000	100,000	100,000	Units	85,000	85,000	85,000	85,000
Price	$2.54	$2.54	$2.54	$2.54	Price	$2.54	$2.54	$2.54	$2.54
Costs	$200,000	200,000	200,000	200,000	Costs	$200,000	200,000	200,000	200,000

Location: Atlanta					**Location: Boston**				
Vitamins	Q1	Q2	Q3	Q4	Vitamins	Q1	Q2	Q3	Q4
Units	60,000	40,000	40,000	60,000	Units	60,000	40,000	40,000	60,000
Price	$3.75	$3.75	$3.75	$3.75	Price	$3.75	$3.75	$3.75	$3.75
Costs	$125,000	115,000	120,000	130,000	Costs	$125,000	115,000	120,000	130,000

Location: Atlanta					**Location: Boston**				
Valium	Q1	Q2	Q3	Q4	Valium	Q1	Q2	Q3	Q4
Units	37,500	37,500	37,500	37,500	Units	30,000	30,000	30,000	30,000
Price	$13.52	$13.52	$13.52	$13.52	Price	$13.22	$13.22	$13.22	$13.22
Costs	$110,000	110,000	105,000	130,000	Costs	$85,000	95,000	80,000	80,000

Exhibit 11-17
International Division Product Data

Location: Canada				
Aspirin	Q1	Q2	Q3	Q4
Units	120,000	125,000	115,000	120,000
Price				
(Can. $)	$3.00	$3.00	$3.05	$3.10
Costs				
(Can. $)	$250,000	275,000	290,000	300,000
Exchange				
Rate	0.86	0.88	0.87	0.85
Medco Ownership	100%			

Location: Switzerland				
Valium	Q1	Q2	Q3	Q4
Units	20,000	15,000	17,000	23,000
Price	SF 7.6	9.29	7.50	7.96
Costs	SF550,000	490,000	510,000	600,000
Exchange				
Rate	0.46	0.42	0.52	0.49
Medco Ownership	75%			

Case 11-3 McDonough Corporation*

Allan Spivey, president and chief executive officer of McDonough Corporation, had just come back from an extended business trip, during which time he came across an old but prominent article on zero-based budgeting. Although the article was over ten years old, he was intrigued with it because it reported success with the technique as it was applied by a competitor. He was especially puzzled as to why the technique seemed to work in some organizations and not in others.

Years ago he had applied mild pressure on the corporate controller of McDonough to implement such a system for the discretionary expenditures of the organization, expenditures that he was convinced were now out of control. Spivey remembered that the controller had then said that the technique was "not really very good." Moreover, he had said, "What's good about ZBB is not new and what's new is not very good." After reading the article, he was pondering just what his next step might be. He decided to give the new controller a copy of the article and asked him why the results could not be duplicated at McDonough. The article is reproduced below.

BUDGET PLANNING

Proponents of zero-base budgeting argue that the method stands an excellent chance of yielding great benefits in the form of budgetary control. It fails to work only when it is applied incorrectly. Yet it is difficult for any organization that is accustomed to less demanding budgetary processes to discipline itself in the ways that ZBB requires.

This article is a history of an exemplary case in which ZBB actually delivered greater benefits than had been expected. The care and planning that were devoted from start to finish suggest that ZBB may live up to its promise in most instances when skilled people invest enough time and effort.

The authors were involved together in applying ZBB in a particularly challenging situation. They began their work in June 1978 during a period of unrest at Alcan Aluminum Corporation, the Cleveland-based U.S. subsidiary of Alcan Aluminum Ltd. of Montreal. Recent sales growth had boosted sales of the U.S. company above $1 billion and had generated a corresponding growth in expenses. In particular, sales, research, and administrative expenses had become difficult to manage as their total cost had jumped to $50 million.

THE REASON FOR USING ZBB

The traditional budgeting approach did not provide corporate and divisional management with the required detailed information to improve "before-the-fact" spending for sales, research, and administration. The method provided a systematic, constructive

*Reproduced and abridged by permission from James E. Connell, John D. Schoonover, and Paul F. Corty, "ZBB at Its Best," in *Management Focus*, Peat, Marwick and Mitchell & Co., November–December 1979.

determination of funding levels. It was a logical tool for discriminating among expenses that should be reduced. It meshed well with other phases of planning by providing funding for both short-term and long-term objectives and enhancing the company's MBO program. The detailed activity analysis, effort-level identification, and decision package preparation provided the environment in which to allow managers to focus more directly on the various spending opportunities.

Alcan has benefited in other ways. More division personnel became involved in the budgeting process. These people attained a deeper insight into the relationship of activity levels and costs. In addition, all who prepared their decision packages expressed what they could accomplish as a result of the approved spending levels. The level of managerial accountability increased.

As a result of ZBB, Alcan established spending priorities for sales, research, and administrative expenses in three of six divisions. In the event of an economic slowdown, these priorities can assist management in selecting funding reductions. If additional resources become available, this organized list of spending opportunities can help to identify the activities to be funded more liberally.

PREPARING PEOPLE IS VITAL

The most important ingredient in the success of the ZBB program was training and educating personnel in the techniques to be used. Alcan's top management is convinced that the time and effort spent initiating personnel was essential to the project's ultimate success.

To set up an effective budgeting structure, an assistant to the controller, Kory, was appointed corporate ZBB manager. Each division provided two categories of personnel to the project participants: cost center managers responsible for preparing the budget requests and "coaches" who supervised 4 to 10 participants each. This internal structure helped

personnel to more readily understand the program and appreciate their roles in it.

In-depth instruction in ZBB concepts and techniques was a major section of the program, especially for the coaches who led the participants. As a result of this training effort, Alcan personnel came to appreciate ZBB as a process that coordinates a variety of sound management techniques for maximum resource utilization.

The logic of ZBB requires managers to analyze the operating activities by degree of requirements and to build the budget accordingly. For each activity, the manager must budget expenditures according to effort levels appropriate for that activity. The minimum level should represent the budget required to attain the absolute minimum goal for the activity. Additional spending requests (incremental increases) are then justified in terms of the benefits that would probably be derived from the additional resources applied. All budget requests are then ranked in order of importance and are funded to the extent that resources are available. Obviously, the required activities would be funded before other discretionary activities.

GETTING DOWN TO DETAILS

Three divisions were selected for the initial implementation of ZBB. The unique characteristics of each provided an excellent challenge to ZBB as an effective management tool. One division was expanding its sales and marketing efforts, including a very strong advertising program. Corporate management wanted a better understanding of the nature of the expenditures to support this increased effort.

A second division underwent a major reorganization of the sales and marketing function simultaneously with the implementation of this program. ZBB was expected to help these managers to understand more quickly their new functions and responsibilities. The third division was needed to prepare a traditional budget before the ZBB effort began. This provided a comparison of the two budgetary approaches, and, in this situation, the ZBB results generated a smaller level of funding than the traditional approach.

STEP BY STEP TO SUCCESS

Implementation of Alcan's ZBB project was divided into three phases to help management control the various tasks.

Phase I was an analytical review of the organizational structure and the activities conducted. Exhibit 11-18 is an example of the organization analysis form. Its purpose is to verify the reporting relationships and functional responsibilities and, most impor-

tant, to identify the major activities that fulfill the functional responsibilities.

The primary purpose of ZBB is to budget in response to the activities needed to operate the business, and it is within this framework that activities are identified. An activity was defined as an identifiable work process or collection of closely related tasks intended to accomplish or provide a specific result. For example, the process of entering a customer's order includes reviewing stock availability, shipping schedules, credit status, and creation of necessary documents. For ZBB purposes, all these tasks would be grouped into one activity (i.e., order entry). The form for the second step to phase I is shown in Exhibit 11-19. It assists the partici-

Exhibit 11-18
Organization Analysis

Division _____ Aluminum Sales _____

Organization Analysis
(Form ZBB #1)

Participant's Name _____ Mr. T. Carson _____ Date _____ 7/2/78 _____

Title _____ Manager _____ Department _____ Customer Service _____

Reports to _____ Mr. P. Smith, Vice President — Administration _____

Person(s) Supervised — Status Quo __ J. Parson, T. Small, M. Jatcy,
D. Gould, P. Olson, L. Jackets, M. O'Neill

Purpose of the function The Customer Service Department is to provide
any assistance which customers need so as to enhance consumer
satisfaction. Primarily, this assistance is in the form of furnishing
information or processing necessary paperwork.

Activities of the function (Budget year) __ A. Order Entry: the processing
of customer orders as quickly as possible.

B. Formal Quotations: the preparation and mailing of written
    quotations in response to requests.

C. Expediting and Customer Returns: the process of expediting orders,
    answering questions and processing for returned merchandise.

Approval:
    Local — Manager _____ P. Smith _____ Date __ 7/5/78 __

Review:
    Local — Coach _____ M. School _____ Date __ 7/5/78 __

    Corporate ZBB Manager _____ P. Kory _____ Date __ 7/5/78 __

Exhibit 11-19
Activity Analysis

Division _____Aluminum Sales_____

ACTIVITY ANALYSIS
(Form ZBB #2)

Participant's Name _____Mr. T. Carson_____ Date ___7/2/78___

Department _Customer Service_ Activity name/Ref. letter _Order Entry — A_

Description of Activity	Order entry includes all the tasks to accept and process a customer order, both taken over the telephone or received in the mail. The availability of merchandise must be obtained from the stock status records, and price quotes developed (telephone orders). Delivery schedules also need to be reviewed to advise customers of probable delivery dates.
Requirement classification (Roman numeral)	**II**
Reason for Requirement Classification	Corporate and Division management has directed that customers' orders and inquiries must be processed as quickly as possible. This service is considered critical to the overall marketing program.

Objective Conformity	Corporate	Division	Department
	Meet customer service objective related to sales goals.	Meet customer service objective related to sales goals.	Meet customer service objective related to sales goals.

Questionable Tasks Data Generated	Manually prepared statistical data which appears to be duplicated in sales system reports.
Effects of Activity Elimination: THIS Dept.	The four persons performing this activity would be eliminated.
OTHER Depts. or Divisions	Some other department would have to assume the responsibility for order entry because it is an integral part of the business.
Alternatives for Activity	Automate the order entry process in such a way that it integrates with the inventory stock status system.

What will be accomplished at each level?

Effort Levels to be Zero Base Budgeted	1. Provide a level of service which allows processing all orders within 72 hours of receipt. 2. Provide a level of service which allows processing all orders within 48 hours of receipt. 3. Provide a level of service which allows processing all orders within 24 hours of receipt. 4. N/A

Approval:
Local — Manager _____P. Smith_____ Date ___7/5/78___

Review:
Local — Coach _____M. School_____ Date ___7/5/78___

Corporate ZBB Manager _____P. Kory_____ Date ___7/8/78___

413

pant in critically reviewing the activity, investigating any viable alternatives, and identifying reasonable levels of effort.

Directly related to the activity analysis was an activity time analysis shown in Exhibit 11-20. This tool helped the participant to review with each employee the time allotted to each activity and, thereby, confirmed that all major departmental activities had been identified.

THE SECOND PHASE: REQUESTS FOR FUNDING

Phase II of the project, the development of the activity budget request, was divided into two sections: development of the financial

and personnel requirements for each effort level within an activity and preparation of decision packages to communicate the funding request to ranking committee members.

Exhibit 11-21 demonstrates the work paper used to identify the financial and personnel requirements for the various effort levels of an activity. The elements of expense are the accounts used in the corporate financial statements. Divisions whose chart of accounts provided a subaccount structure were free to develop a more detailed budget, but the expenses eventually had to be summarized into the format shown in this exhibit. All fixed expenses had to be included in the minimum effort level, leaving

Exhibit 11-20
Activity Time Analysis

Division _____ Aluminum / Sales _____

Activity Time Analysis
(Form ZBB #3)

Participant's Name _____ T. Carson _____ Date _____ 7/2/76 _____

Employee Name	% OF TIME				Act. J	Act. K	Act. L	OPEN TIME	Consumed Time TOTAL%
	Act. A	Act. B	Act. C	Act. D					
T. Carson	40	30	30						100
J. Parson	90	10	—						100
T. Small	80	10	10						100
M. Jatcy	90	10	—						100
D. Gould	90	10	—						100
P. Olson	5	90	5						100
L. Jackets	—	95	5						100
M. O'Neill	5	15	80						100
Total of Percentages	400	270	130						800
Full Time Employee Equivalent	4.0	2.7	1.3						8.0

Approval:
  Local — Manager _____ P. Smith _____ Date _____ 7/5/76 _____
Review:
  Local — Coach _____ M. School _____ Date _____ 7/5/76 _____

  Corporate ZBB Manager _____ P. Kory _____ Date _____ 7/8/76 _____

Exhibit 11-21
Cost Analysis for Activity Incremental Effort Levels

Cost Analysis for Activity Increment Effort Levels (Form ZBB #4)

Division __Aluminum Sales__

Participant's Name _____Mr. T. Carson_____

Approval:
Local — Manager _____P. Smith_____ Date __7/29/78__

Activity Name ____Order Entry____ Reference Letter __A__

Review:
Local — Coach _____M. School_____ Date __7/29/78__
_____P. Kory_____ Date __8/2/78__

Elements of Expense	1978 Budget	1978 Projected	1 of 3	2 of 3	3 of 3	4 of	5 of	6 of	Total
Memberships and subscriptions	300	200	200	—	—				200
Office expense	9,000	9,500	7,000	3,000	5,000				15,000
Rent	3,500	4,000	5,000	—	—				4,000
Retirement income and life insurance	3,500	5,500	4,000	1,100	3,200				8,800
Other employee benefits	5,500	5,500	4,000	1,100	3,200				8,800
Salaries	53,000	55,000	38,000	16,000	32,000				86,000
Special services and supplies	2,000	2,000	1,500	500	1,000				3,000
Subsidies and samples									
Taxes other than income									
Telephone, telegraph and cable	12,000	14,000	11,000	4,000	5,000				20,000
Traveling	3,000	2,000	1,500	500	1,000				3,000
Miscellaneous	500	500	500	—	—				500
Total — selling, research, and administrative expenses before allocation	92,800	97,700	71,700	27,200	50,400				—
Total — cumulative effort levels	—	—	—	98,900	149,300				149,300
Cumulative as percent of prior year	—	—	73%	101%	153%				153%
Number of employees — increment/cumulative	4	4	3/3	1/4	2/6				

The "1979 Budget Year Decision Packages (Effort Levels)" spans columns 1 of 3, 2 of 3, 3 of 3, 4 of, 5 of, 6 of.

Explanation of Expense Increases: (use additional paper, if necessary)
1. Employee expenses increase with staff increase which is explained in decision package 3/3.
2. Office expenses include Special Services and Supplies and Traveling increase because of additional people at level 3 of 3.
3. Telephone is approximately $3,500 per person at levels 1 of 2 and less ($2,500) at level 3; 1978 projected is $3,500 per person.

subsequent effort levels to reflect incremental costs. The resulting personnel and financial requirements flow directly from this work paper into the decision package form.

Having developed the resource requirements for the various effort levels, each participant constructed the presentation necessary to justify the budget request to top management. The decision package, shown in Exhibit 11-22 is the form used for this communication. One decision package is developed for each effort level. Therefore, if an activity has been identified as having three possible effort levels, three decision packages are prepared and are referred to as a decision package series.

A decision package overview prepared for each decision package series is shown in Exhibit 11-23. This form has two primary purposes. First, it explains the extent to which an activity relates to the corporate planning process both long term and short term. Second, it discusses alternative means of conducting an activity, especially noting reasons for not utilizing these alternatives.

FINALLY, THE CHOICE OF ACTIVITY LEVELS

Exhibits 11-21, 22, and 23 are submitted to the respective decision-ranking committees, responsible for reviewing the documents, discussing the budget requests among them-

Exhibit 11-22
Decision Package

Decision Package %(Form ZBB #5)	Activity Name Ref. Letter	Level	Requirement	Ojb. Conformity		
	Order Entry — A	1 of 3	Classification 11	Corp.	Div.	Dept.

Division	Dept.	Prepared By:	Rank	
Aluminum Sales	Customer Services	T. Carson Date: 8/1/78	Division	Corporate

Resources expenses Required	1978 Budget	1978 Projected	1979 request	
			This package	Cumulative
Personnel number	4	4	3	3
Personnel (Inc. fringe)	$ 63,500	65,500	46,000	46,000
Office expenses	$ 9,000	9,500	7,000	7,000
Traveling	$ 3,000	2,000	1,500	1,500
Other expenses	$ 18,300	20,700	17,200	17,200
Total expenses	$ 93,800	97,000	71,700	71,700

List results expected at this effort level

Process telephone and written customer orders as quickly as possible with the ultimate goal of confirming the order to the customer within 24 hours of receipt. At this level we can guarantee confirmation within 60 hours to 72 hours.

List the work required to accomplish the results expected

All orders received must be checked as to inventory availability or production scheduling, pricing, delivery method and date of delivery; the order must be confirmed to the customer by mail.

Detriments compared to status quo

Orders are currently confirmed within 48 hours; however, with a 38% increase in tonnage it will be difficult to meet this performance.

Performance — Measures Standards

Orders confirmed within 60 to 72 hours/Plan of 24 hours.

Consequences of not funding

Customers would not be aware of our receipt of orders, nor our scheduled date of shipment. Result in lost business because of poor performance.

Summary of incremental effort — Levels in this decision package series

LEVEL	No. of Personnel		Operating Expenses		Reviewed:	
	Incr.	Cum.	Increment	Cumulative		
1/3	3	3	71,700	71,700	Approval Manager P. Smith	8/2/78
*2/3	1	4	27,200	98,900	Local Coach	
3/3	2	6	50,400	149,300	M. School	8/3/78
4					ZBB Manager	
5					P. Kory	8/5/78

*Place an asterisk in front of the level which is the status quo.

Exhibit 11-23
Decision Package Overview

Decision Package Overview
(form ZBB #6)

Activity name/ref. letter   Department   Division

  Order Entry/A   Customer Service   Aluminum Sales

Prepared by: T. Carson   Date: 8/1/78

Strategic plan

This activity supports the sales and marketing directions outlined in the
Strategic Plan.

Short-term plan

Order entry processing and confirmation had been operating at 48-hour
turnaround. The plan calls for reducing turnaround time to 24 hours in
support of increased production and sales.

Alternative means of performing the activity

1. Develop a computerized order entry system which would be integrated
   with the inventory stock status system.

Reasons for not utilizing alternative means of performing the activity

A special study is required to identify the specific system requirements and
probable cost. A decision package requesting spending for this study is being
prepared by the division's systems department.

Approved by: Local Manager   P. Smith   Date   8/2/78

Reviewed:
Coach   M. School   Date   8/3/78

ZBB Manager   P. Kory   Date   8/5/78

---

selves and with participants if necessary, and ultimately placing the decision packages in priority.

A 10-point mechanism was used in the ranking process. Decision packages to which rankers assigned high spending priorities received relatively many points, while low-priority decision packages received few points. After each ballot was taken, the ranking committee members discussed the results and any factors that they believed should be considered before an ultimate listing of activities in order of priority was established.

Members of the corporate policy committee constituted the corporate ranking committee. Their function was to review all decision packages not funded within the division's preset cutoff limits and ultimately to decide which budget requests should be approved. During the ranking meetings, division presidents were provided with sufficient time to explain each decision package that their division had forwarded to the corporate ranking committee.

WHY ZBB SUCCEEDED

A ZBB project can succeed only if internal personnel actively support the effort. Alcan's personnel became enthusiastic about the project and committed to its success. Most important was the support provided by top management at both corporate and division levels.

Alcan chose persons from its most competent and creative managers to serve as coaches for their respective divisions. These individuals injected the necessary dedication and leadership to ensure the project's successful and timely completion. The objective was strongly communicated to the participants, that is, that ZBB was being used to determine the proper funding level, not just to cut costs. If it had not been so thoroughly explained, the participants' efforts might easily have been dissipated.

The division ranking committees significantly assisted the corporate ranking process by eliminating inappropriate decision packages at the division level and then submitting to the corporate ranking committee only serious funding requests. Finally, each participant was able to evaluate the ZBB project at three stages (training, activity analysis, and final budget) as part of the critique process. Comments were highly constructive and provided insights for the future changes to the system—especially concerning the forms that had been used.

WEAK SPOTS CAN BE ERASED

Not all aspects of Alcan's ZBB experience were positive or favorable. The most significant drawback was the serious time constraint placed on the project, a shortcoming that had been anticipated from the start. Its impact was to subdue the participants' creative thinking about alternative ways of conducting activities. In addition, this time limitation obviously put a great amount of pressure on the participants, who had ongoing responsibilities during this period. In some cases corporate or division objectives were not communicated thoroughly or on a

timely basis. Some managers prepared decision packages without knowing whether those activities were to respond directly to some stated objective. But the identification of activities and appropriate effort levels for the activities were generally very good, although in some cases, functions were fragmented into too many activities or too many effort levels. More time and experience with ZBB will help managers to improve definitions of activities and effort levels.

After review and revision, virtually all the decision packages expressed very well exactly what would be accomplished at each effort level. These descriptions, however, frequently were in general and rather nonquantifiable terms. Specific performance measurement standards were not strongly addressed, even though such precision is an inherent advantage of ZBB. Without using performance measurement standards, ZBB cannot assist in evaluating efficiency. A careful identification of performance measurement standards, which are subsequently monitored or reviewed, can significantly assist in tying the budgeting process to a sound management by objectives program.

LOOKING AHEAD

Alcan is continuing to use ZBB for the preparation of 1980 sales, research, and administrative expense budget. The corporate office and the divisions that did not use ZBB in preparing the 1979 budget will use the ZBB program in its full composition. The three divisions that have already experienced the process will use the following guidelines.

1. Only those departments that have experienced major changes in activities (such as from reorganization or changes in management personnel) or that identify viable activity alternatives will use the full-blown ZBB process, resulting in the preparation

of decision packages for a minimum level, status quo, and any incremental increases considered appropriate.

2. Those departments without major changes in activities or viable alternatives will proceed directly to the preparation of decision packages at the status quo level and any incremental increases considered appropriate.

Alcan managers have not only implemented a sound management tool; they have successfully adopted it for their particular environment.

QUESTION

- As the controller of McDonough, take a position either for or against the use of ZBB to control the discretionary expense budgets of the corporation. If you should decide for ZBB, back up your recommendations with the procedures you suggest following at McDonough. If you decide to recommend against ZBB, support your recommendation with another procedure for the control of discretionary expense center budgets which is as good or better for McDonough than the ZBB system illustrated in the article.

12

MANAGERIAL COSTING I: TRADITIONAL SYSTEMS[1]

The primary managerial goal of cost systems is to provide information for decision making. These decisions include: pricing products, managing costs, selecting market segments and distribution channels, evaluating make–buy and outsourcing decisions, establishing transfer prices, evaluating plant closings, and making capital investment and abandonment decisions.

At first glance, the problems dealt with by cost systems seem quite straightforward: simply add up the costs associated with each of these decisions. The problem is that many of the costs of doing business cannot be traced directly to a given product or a given cost objective. These costs must be allocated, and this is where the difficulties of cost measurement begin.

Several cost systems have been developed to handle this problem of assigning costs to various cost objectives. The purpose of this and the next chapter is to give you a working knowledge of these systems. This chapter describes traditional costing systems and the next, activity-based costing systems.

THE TWO-STAGE MODEL

Most cost systems can be understood in terms of a two-stage model of cost allocation. Direct costs, usually labor and material, are traced directly to the cost object, as shown in Exhibit 12-1. Overhead is allocated to products through what may be described as a *two-stage process*.

In the first stage of the overhead allocation procedure, overhead costs are allocated to cost pools (for example, machines, departments, and so on), using

Exhibit 12-1
The Two-Stage Procedure

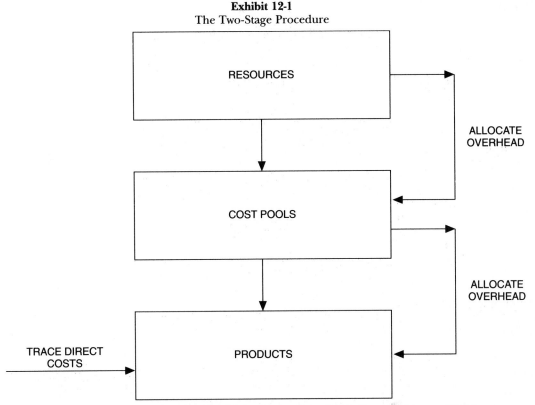

The formulation of the two-stage model is adapted by permission from Robin Cooper. It is generalized from Chapter 2 of Cooper and Kaplan, *The Design of Cost Management Systems,* Englewood Cliffs, N.J.: Prentice Hall, 1991, Chapter 2.

predetermined allocation criteria or cost drivers. The costs allocated to cost pools in the first stage are then allocated to cost objects (for example, products) in the second stage using cost drivers, which are chosen to capture a products consumption of overhead costs.

Traditional costing methods have had little trouble in tracing direct labor and direct material to cost objects. But overhead allocations, both in the first stage and in the second, have been problematic, leading to very inaccurate measurements of product costs as well as costs associated with other decisions.

This chapter describes the major cost system options available to the designer. Which option is chosen depends upon the circumstances facing the organization.

COST SYSTEM OPTIONS

Exhibit 12-2 contains an overview of the options that exist for cost system design.

The rows of Exhibit 12-2 describe the nature of the production process used by the firm for producing goods and services. The columns describe the alterna-

Exhibit 12-2
Cost System Design Options

Type of system used for costing products or services / Nature of process whereby goods and services are produced	ACTUAL COSTING SYSTEMS	STANDARD COSTING SYSTEMS	ACTIVITY-BASED COSTING SYSTEMS
Job-order production	• Unique products or services • Actual direct labor and material charges • Standard overhead rates • Relatively few first- and second-stage drivers for overhead	• Unique products or services • Standard direct labor and material charges • Standard overhead rates • Relatively few first- and second-stage drivers for overhead • Variances computed for jobs	• Unique products or services • Actual or standard direct labor and material charges • Actual or standard overhead rates • Multiple first- and second-stage drivers for overhead
Process production	• Homogenous products or services • Actual direct labor and material charges • Actual overhead charges • Relatively few first- and second-stage drivers for overhead	• Homogenous products or services • Standard direct labor and material charges • Standard overhead rates • Relatively few first- and second-stage drivers for overhead • Variances computed for processes	• Homogenous products or services • Actual or standard direct labor and material charges • Actual or standard overhead rates • Multiple first- and second-stage drivers for overhead
Mixed Job-order/Process production	Combines elements of job-order and process production and uses all three costing systems		

tive costing systems that are available for costing products and services produced under the alternative production processes.

Job-order production processes are suitable for firms that produce many unique products, each requiring different amounts of labor, material, and overhead per unit. In these processes, both direct labor and direct material costs are traced directly to products. Overhead costs are allocated to products through the use of cost pools and a number of first- and second-stage cost drivers for the allocation of these overhead costs. Variances are calculated for each job. Job-order processes are used widely in the service sector.

Process production processes are used in firms that are engaged in the production of a large number of relatively homogeneous products. Under process costing systems, direct labor, direct material, and overhead are all allocated to products through the use of a number of cost pools and a number of first- and second-stage cost drivers. The result is the computation of an *average unit cost* for the products produced. Variances are calculated for each process under process production.

Mixed job-order and process production processes are used when the production process has attributes of both job order and process. For example, in the manufacture of certain types of clothing, the items differ in terms of the quality of materials used, but the other operations are the same. In this case, direct material costs are traced to each article of clothing as under job-order methods, but direct labor and overhead costs are allocated as under process methods.

Three alternative costing systems are in use for both job-order and process production. These systems differ in the type of data that are used in cost measurement, and they differ in the number of cost drivers that are used in the first- and the second-stage allocations of overhead. Actual costing systems use actual costs for measuring direct labor and direct material, but (normally) standard costs for overhead. Standard costing systems use standard costs for measuring labor, material, and overhead. Activity-based systems may use either standard or actual costs for all three elements of cost. Activity-based costing systems differ from actual and standard systems in that they use multiple first- and second-stage drivers for overhead attribution and allocation.

The best way to explore these alternative production processes and cost measurement systems is by a few examples. We will first illustrate the use of actual costing systems in both job-order and process production environments. We start with an example of job-order production because it tends to be the simplest to describe and illustrate.

JOB-ORDER PRODUCTION

Under job-order production, we attempt to allocate costs to specific products or batches of products; each product or batch is identified as a "job." Each job is costed separately, and work is scheduled as orders are received. Job-order production is used in industries as diverse as printing, construction, airframe manufacturing, consulting, auto repair, and heavy machinery.

Under job-order production, we compute the costs of each of job by tracing direct labor and direct material to the job and by allocating overhead to the job.

In an actual costing system, we trace actual material and labor costs and allocate overhead. In a standard costing system, we establish standard rates for labor, material, and overhead. In an activity-based system, we trace labor and material directly to products, and we allocate overhead to products by the use of multiple drivers in the first and second stage of the production process.

Case Example: Tipografia Stanca, S.P.A.[2]

Mr. Giulio Cattani, founder and president of Tipografia Stanca, S.P.A., was worried. The company was doing more business than ever before—sales were at an annual rate of about $1,250,000 a year—but net income had decreased slightly during recent months, and the ratio of income to sales had dropped sharply. Mr. Cattani wondered what had gone wrong and what he could do about it. He called in his chief (and only) accountant, Mr. Gaetano Pareto, and asked him to find out what was happening.

Tipografia Stanca was an Italian corporation located in Milan and doing a general printing business on a customer order basis. Mr. Cattani set the price to be charged for each job. When possible, he waited until the work was done and then quoted a price equal to 140 percent of the cost of the paper stock used, plus $25 for each labor hour. Straight-time wage rates in the past, adjusted for recent wage rate increases, had averaged about $8 an hour, and this formula seemed to provide an adequate margin to cover overhead costs and provide a good profit.

Most of Tipografia Stanca's work was done on the basis of predetermined contract prices. In bidding on these jobs, Mr. Cattani applied his standard pricing formula to his own estimates of the amount of labor and paper stock the job would require. He prided himself on his ability to make these estimates, but he sometimes quoted a price that was higher or lower than the formula price, depending on his judgment of the market situation.

Stanca's production procedures were fairly simple. When a customer's order was received, it was assigned a production order number and a production order was issued. The material to be printed, known as the customer's copy, was given to a copy editor, who indicated on the copy the sizes and styles of type that should be used. The editor sometimes made changes in the copy, usually after telephoning the customer to discuss the changes.

Once the customer's material had been copy-edited, it was sent to the composing room, where it was set in type. A proof copy was printed by hand and returned to the copy editor, who checked the printed copy against the original. Any errors in the proof were indicated in the margin, and the marked proof was sent to the customer for approval. At this point the customer might decide to make changes in the copy, and these changes, as well as the corrections of typesetting errors, were made as soon as the corrected proof was returned to the composing room.

In some cases a second proof was sent to the customer for his approval, but at Tipografia Stanca most orders were sent to the pressroom as soon as the customer's corrections had been made and the second proof had been approved by the copy editor.

At this point, the order was ready for production on one of the presses in the pressroom. Printing instructions were contained in the production order, which specified the particular press to be used, the number of copies to be printed, the color, size, style, weight, and finish of the stock or paper to be used, and similar details. Copies were then printed, bound, and packaged for delivery to the customer.

An order could take as little as one day in the copy-editing and composing-room stages or as long as several weeks. Printing, binding, and packaging seldom took more than two days except on very large production runs of multipage booklets.

For many years the shop had had enough work to keep it busy steadily throughout the year, without serious seasonal slack. As a result, Tipografia Stanca's before-tax profit had fluctuated between 13 and 15 percent of net sales. The interim profit report for the first half of 1992, therefore, came as a great shock to Mr. Cattani. Although volume was slightly greater than in the first half of 1991, profit was down to 8.8 percent of sales, an all-time low. The comparison, with all figures expressed as percentages of net sales, was as follows:

	1992	1991
Net sales	100.0%	100.0%
Production costs	77.6	72.3
Selling and administrative costs	13.6	13.9
Profit	8.8	13.8

Mr. Pareto knew that the company's problem must be either low prices or excessive costs. Unfortunately, the cost data already available told him little about the cost–price relationship for individual jobs. Tipografia Stanca's operating costs were classified routinely into 20 categories, such as salaries, pressroom wages, production materials, depreciation, and so forth. Individual job-cost sheets were not used, and the cost of goods in process was estimated only once a year, at the end of the fiscal year.

Detailed data were available on only two kinds of items: paper stock issued and labor time. When stock was issued, a requisition form was filled out, showing the kind of stock issued, the quantity, the unit cost, and the production order number. Similar details were reported when unused stock was returned to the stockroom.

As for labor, all employees directly engaged in working on production orders filled in time sheets each day, on which they recorded the time they started on a given task, the time they finished it or moved on to other work, and (in the case of time spent directly on a specific production order) the order number. Department numbers and individual pay grades were recorded on the time sheets by the payroll clerk.

Mr. Pareto's first step was to establish some overall cost relationships. Employees, for example, fell into three different pay grades, with the following regular hourly wage rates:

Grade	Rate
1	12
2	8
3	6

These rates applied to a regular work week of 44 hours a week. For work in excess of this number of hours, employees were paid their hourly wage plus an overtime premium of 50 percent of their hourly wage. Overtime premiums were negligible when the work load was light, but in a normal year they averaged about 5 percent of the total amount of hourly wages computed at the regular hourly wage rate. In a normal year this was approximately 40 cents a direct labor hour.

In addition to their wages, the employees also received various kinds of benefits, including vacation pay, health insurance, and old-age pensions. The cost of these benefits to Tipografia Stanca amounted to about 70 percent of direct labor cost, measured at regular straight-time hourly rates. The overtime premiums didn't affect the amount of fringe benefits paid or accrued. Mr. Pareto estimated that all other shop overhead costs—that is, all copy department, composing room and pressroom costs other than direct materials, direct labor, overtime premiums, and employee benefits on direct labor payrolls—would average $4 a direct labor hour in a normal year.

Armed with these estimates of general relationships, Mr. Pareto then proceeded to determine the costs of several recent production orders. One of these was order A-467. This was received for copy editing on Monday, October 5 and delivered to the customer on Friday, October 9. Mr. Cattani had quoted a price of $1800 on this job in advance, on the basis of an estimate of $480 for paper stock costs and 45 direct labor hours. All requisitions and time records relating to order A-467 are included in the lists in Exhibits 12-3 and 12-4. (To save space, some of the details shown on the requisitions and time tickets have been omitted from these tables.)

QUESTIONS

1. Why are the profit margins falling at Tipografia Stanca?
2. Develop a costing rate or rates for labor costs, to be used to charge a job cost sheet or factory overhead account for an hour of labor time. You must decide whether to

Exhibit 12-3
Partial List of materials requisitions (for the week of October 5–9)

Requisition No.	Job. No.	Amount*
4058	A-467	$300
R162	A-469	(20)
4059	A-467	60
4060	A-442	6
R163	A-455	(10)
R164	A-472	(8)
4060	A-467	36
R165	A-465	(12)
4062	A-467	96
4063	A-471	320
4064	A-473	264
4065	A-458	22
R166	A-467	(32)
4066	A-481	176

*Amounts in parentheses are returned materials.

Exhibit 12-4
Partial summary of labor time sheets (for the week of October 5–9)

Employee No.	Pay Grade	Dept.	Job No.*	Hours
14	2	Copy	A-463	6.6
14	2	Copy	A-467	1.4
15	1	Copy	A-467	3.3
15	1	Copy	—	2.7
15	1	Copy	A-467	8.8
18	3	Press	A-467	4.0
18	3	Press	A-472	4.6
22	1	Composing	A-455	3.8
22	1	Composing	A-467	8.4†
22	1	Composing	—	1.5
23	2	Press	A-458	3.4
23	2	Press	A-467	4.7
23	2	Press	—	1.1
23	2	Press	A-459	2.5†
24	2	Copy	A-470	7.4
28	1	Press	A-467	7.0
28	1	Press	A-458	1.0
31	3	Press	—	8.0
33	1	Composing	A-471	7.6
33	1	Composing	A-472	4.2
40	2	Press	A-469	3.6
40	2	Press	A-467	4.9
40	2	Press	—	0.2
43	1	Press	A-467	3.5
43	1	Press	A-481	5.8

*A dash indicates time spent on general work in the department and not on any one job.
†Employee No. 22 worked six hours overtime during the week, none of them on the job A-467, while employee No. 23 worked eight hours of overtime, including four hours spent on job A-467.

include various kinds of fringe benefit costs in the labor costing rates or to regard these as overhead. Also, develop an overhead rate for use in charging shop overhead costs to individual job orders.

3. Prepare a job-order cost sheet for production order A-467, and enter the costs that would be assigned to this order, using the costing rates you developed in the answer to (2) above.

Analysis of Tipografia Stanca

To understand the reason why his profit margins are falling, it is necessary to examine the formula that Mr. Cattani used to establish selling prices.

Pricing Formula

His formula is one that is very common in job-shop operations: time and materials pricing, in which the price is arrived at by estimating labor and material charges and adding overhead, period expenses, and profit to estimates of labor and materials. The formula may be written as:

$$Y = (1.4 * \text{direct materials dollars}) + (\$25 * \text{direct labor hours})$$

This led him to quote a price of $1800 for job A-467 since he estimated that the job would take 45 labor hours and that $480 of paper stock would be required. The $1800 is found by rounding-up the calculation as follows:

$$Y = (1.4 * \text{direct materials dollars}) + (\$25 * \text{direct labor hours})$$
$$= (1.4 * \$480) + (\$25 * 45 \text{ hours})$$
$$= \$672 + \$1125$$
$$= \$1797 \text{ or } \$1800$$

The pricing formula that Mr. Cattani used was not entirely arbitrary. The $25 per labor hour charged for labor was found by starting with the average pay grade for the past year of $8 per labor hour. To that was added the cost of fringe benefits, which averaged 70 percent of the average wage. The labor rate with fringe was then 1.7 * $8, or $13.60. Overtime premium added 5 percent of the average wage (0.05 * $8), or $0.40, thus bringing the labor charge per hour to $14.00. In addition, the remaining overhead averaging $4.00 per labor hour was added, thus giving a labor charge of $18 an hour ($4 + $14). To get to $25 per hour from $18 Mr. Cantini divided $18 by 1 minus the sum of the average selling and administrative and profit percentages desired (from the exhibit in the case, each approximately 14 percent of sales) as follows:

$$L = \$18/(1-0.28)$$

or

$$L = \$18 * (1/1-0.28)$$
$$= \$18 * 1.4$$
$$= \$25$$

The reason he divided by 1 minus the sum of these two percentages is that he wanted to price in such a way as to earn 14 percent of sales for selling and administrative expenses and 14 percent of sales for profit. Neither of these two variables is included in the estimates of overhead, yet they are "costs" that Mr. Cattani seeks to cover in the price he charges.

Now, you should understand why he also multiplied material costs by 1.4. It allows him to recover selling and administrative expenses, and to profit on his material costs just as he recovered selling and administrative costs and profited on his labor and overhead estimates in the $25 per labor hour charge. He has thus included in the selling price all of his costs (direct labor, direct material, overhead, selling and administrative and profit).

Costing Rates and Job Cost Sheet for Tipografia Stanca

We have developed three different direct labor-charging rates for each pay grade: direct labor; direct labor and fringe benefit; and direct labor, fringe benefits, and overtime. They are presented in Exhibit 12-5. We need to determine

Exhibit 12-5
Charging Rates and Job Cost Sheet for Job A-467

Charging Rates:	(1) Direct Labor	(2) (1) Plus Fringe	(3) (2) Plus O/T Prem
Direct labor			
Grade 1	12.00	20.40	21.00
2	8.00	13.60	14.00
3	6.00	10.20	10.50
Overhead			
Fringe benefits	5.60	—	—
Overtime premium	0.40	0.40	—
Other overhead	4.00	4.00	4.00
Total overhead	10.00	4.40	4.00

Charging Rates:	(1) Direct Labor	(2) (1) Plus Fringe	(3) (2) Plus O/T Prem
Direct labor			
Grade 1 (31 Hrs)	372.00	632.40	651.00
2 (11 Hrs)	88.00	149.60	154.00
3 (4 Hrs)	24.00	40.80	42.00
Total labor	$484.00	$822.80	$847.00
Overhead	460.00	202.40	184.00
Direct material	460.00	460.00	460.00
Total cost	$1,404	$1,485.20	$1,533.00
Price based on actual cost	$1,950	$2,063	$2,130

which of the three sets of labor-charging rates to use to cost A-467. Of course, it would be more accurate if overtime and fringe benefits had their own cost pools, but at the moment our choices lie with either pricing them in the direct labor cost pool or in "other" overhead costs.

The major question to ask is whether fringe benefits and overtime pay for workers of different wage grades correlate with the wage of these workers. If these costs are correlated with wages, they should be included in the labor charging rate (that is, in the direct labor cost pool). If they do not correlate with wages, they should be included in the overhead cost pool.

In other words, when a worker of wage grade X works Y hours on a job, should we attach his or her standard allocated amount of overtime and/or fringe benefits proportionately to the direct labor cost of that job (direct labor cost pool), or should we include fringe benefits and overtime costs for the firm in the overhead cost pool and allocate them to jobs by the amount of the application base (direct labor hours) used on the job, without relating them to the specific wage costs on the specific job?

If we choose to use the first set of charging rates (direct labor only), we choose to allocate fringe benefits and overtime premium on the same basis as other overhead (that is, the number of direct labor hours used). If we choose to use the second set of labor charging rates, we choose to allocate fringe benefits to each job as a function of the total labor cost of that job. In this case, the jobs with higher-costing labor will be charged more fringe benefits. In the second case, overtime premium is still included in the overhead cost pool and applied to each labor hour.

If we choose the third set of charging rates, both fringe and overtime premiums are charged to the job in proportion to their labor costs (that is, included in the direct labor cost pool). As a result, the jobs with the higher cost of labor will have more overtime premium and fringe. Under case three, only "other overhead" will be allocated and the number of hours worked will be used.

The question is: which of the three sets of rates is more accurate? It's really hard to tell. Most cost accountants would choose set two, but it is not clear that it is any more accurate than set three or set one. The problem is that although direct labor and direct materials are charged to products based upon the amount consumed by each product, it is not clear that any of the rates accurately mirror the way fringe, overtime premium, and other overhead are consumed by each of the products.

What is clear from examining the second part of Exhibit 12-5 is that each of the three sets of rates produces different costs for job A-467. And each produces a price considerably higher than the original $1800 estimate. For example, the price under the first set of rates is $1950 ($1404/0.72) and the price under set three is $2130. Each of these three sets of rates would help Tipografia Stanca improve its falling profit margins. But they are not necessarily a more accurate reflection of the true costs of A-467.

PROCESS PRODUCTION

Process costing systems are most appropriate in circumstances where multiphase mass production is the underlying process of production. Process costing production is used in industries as diverse as oil refining, glass, steel, banking, fast-food restaurants, and cement.

Under process production, products often go through multiple phases of production. The production process is continuous, and resources are brought in on an ongoing basis, keeping pace with the production process. By the end of the accounting period in one department, a large amount of the product has gone on to the next phase in the next department. But, because production is continuous, and it takes time to assemble a product, there usually remains a portion of the product in a given department to be completed in the next period. These incomplete products are at varying stages of completion and will be moving into later phases of production in the next period.

As a result, management cannot allocate all of its current period costs to products completed this period because that would ignore the portion of costs incurred in the current period that were incurred by products in progress but not completed in the current period. Management must allocate costs of the current period to units completed in this period and transferred out in this period and to units worked on in this period but to be completed and transferred out in the next period.

The central problem in process production environments is determining the cost of goods transferred and the cost of goods remaining in process in a department. To accomplish this task, process systems use a concept known as "equivalent units of production."

Equivalent Units

Process costing systems proceed to cost units complete and units in progress by calculating the cost per equivalent unit completed during the period. Then it applies the cost per equivalent unit completed to units complete and to units in progress. Units in progress are costed according to their degree of completion (that is, according to equivalent units complete).

Equivalent units measure output in terms of the quantities of each production factor that has been applied. In other words, equivalent units measure how much it would take to make one whole unit of output, based on the amount of resources required.

Under process production, costs are divided into two categories: materials and conversion. Conversion costs include both labor and overhead costs. Because process production is used for mass-produced products, direct labor is usually a relatively small part of total cost and is for that reason included with overhead costs in the conversion category.

To calculate unit costs in process systems, the following five-step process is followed[3]:

1. Summarize the flow of physical units
2. Compute output in terms of equivalent units
3. Summarize the total costs to account for
4. Compute equivalent unit costs
5. Apply costs to units completed and to units ending in WIP

Method for Calculating Costs

Many of the units completed under process costing involve costs incurred in two periods, thus creating a need to integrate costs of two periods in calculating unit costs. Various methods are used to calculate costs. Among them are the Weighted Average Method and the First-In, First-Out (FIFO) method. The major difference between these two methods is in the way they calculate the equivalent number of units produced in a period.

The Weighted Average Method averages the costs and the units of both periods in order to calculate an equivalent cost per unit. The FIFO method, on the other hand, uses only the costs and the number of units produced in the current period to determine unit costs. The easiest way to understand these two methods is by the use of an example.

CASE EXAMPLE: DASHING DASHOUND DIPPERS[4]

Dashing Dashound Dippers are made in two sequential processes, bristle toning and assembly. The bristle toning department manufacturers bristle sets, while the assembly department assembles the final product. The data are

Bristle toning department

- Opening inventory: 400 units, 100 percent complete as to materials ($1900) and 50 pecent complete as to conversion costs ($1860).
- Units started during month: 3150.
- Bristle sets completed and transferred to assembly: 3000.
- Units spoiled: 50. This is considered normal; scrap recovery of $75 is credited against current period materials cost.
- Closing inventory: 100 percent as to materials, 40 percent complete as to conversion costs.
- Costs for the current period: materials, $9375 (before credit for scrap recovery); labor, $6000; other conversion costs (variable), $4500; other conversion costs (fixed), $3000.
- Unit costs are determined by the moving average method.

Assembly department

- Opening inventory: 200 units, 100 percent complete as to materials ($5300) and 25 percent complete as to conversion costs ($975).
- Materials required in this process (per finished unit): two bristle sets from bristle toning; one bristle holder, at $3 (required at start of process).
- Units started: 1500.
- Units transferred to finished goods: 1500.
- Units spoiled: none.
- Closing inventory: 100 percent complete as to materials, 75 percent complete as to conversion costs.
- Costs for the current period: materials, to be computed from data given above; labor, $8000; other conversion costs (variable), $6400; other conversion costs (fixed), $4800.
- Ending inventories and transfers to finished goods are costed on a FIFO basis.

Required

- Prepare a production cost summary and distribution sheet, distributing the full costs of each department by the method specified.

In solving this problem we will organize the solution according to the five-step procedure we outlined above. We begin with the bristle toning department, since bristle toning is the first process employed in the manufacture of dippers.

1. Summarize the flow of physical units.

Physical Flows: Bristle Toning

Units in beginning inventory	400
(100 percent complete as to materials; 50 percent complete as to conversion)	
Units completed and transferred	3000
Units in ending inventory	500
(100 percent complete as to materials; 40 percent complete as to conversion)	

2. Compute output in terms of equivalent units (doses of input).

The moving average cost flow assumption is used in the bristle toning department to compute equivalent units of output.

Equivalent Units: Moving Average Method

	Materials	Conversion
Goods completed and transferred	3000	3000
Ending inventory	500	200
Moving average divisor	3500	3200

The moving average division is found by adding the number of units completed to the number of equivalent units in ending inventory in terms of doses of materials and conversion.

3. Summarize the total costs to account for and
4. Compute equivalent unit costs.

Financial Flows: Bristle Toning

	Materials	Unit Cost
Beginning inventory	$1,900	
Materials (net of scrap)	9,300	
Total materials	$11,200	$3.20

	Conversion	Unit Cost
Beginning inventory	$1,860	
Labor	6,000	
Other variable expenses	4,500	
Fixed expenses	3,000	
	$15,360	$4.80
	$11,200	$3.20
	$26,560	$8.00

To arrive at financial flows we sum the costs for each dose in inventory to those costs that were added during the period. To compute unit costs, we divide the sum of the costs for each resource by its equivalent units, calculated in step 2.

For example, total material costs were \$11,200 and equivalent units for the material resource are 3500; therefore, unit cost for each unit as to materials is \$3.20. Similarly, total conversion costs are \$15,360 and equivalent units as to conversion are 3200. Unit cost as to conversion is therefore \$4.80. Total unit cost is \$8.00.

5. Apply costs to units completed and to units ending in WIP.

Cost Distribution: Bristle Toning

	Units		Cost	Transferred to Assembly
Completed bristle sets:	3,000	*	\$8.00	\$24,000
Ending inventory: 500 units				
100% complete as to materials	500		3.20	1,600
40% complete as to conversion	200		4.80	960
Total cost distributed				\$26,560

This last step results in the distribution of beginning inventory costs plus this period's costs to goods completed and transferred to the next department, and to those costs left in inventory, thus completing the exercise so far as the Bristle toning department is concerned. Bristle sets are now sent to the assembly department for assembly, where it takes two sets of bristles to make one brush. Therefore, the 3000 bristle sets become 1500 brushes to the assembly department.

The five steps are then repeated for the assembly department but now using the FIFO cost flow assumption. We turn to the assembly department.

1. Summarize the flow of physical units

Physical Flows: Bristle Toning

Units in beginning inventory	200
(100% complete as to materials;	
25% complete as to conversion)	
Units completed and transferred	1,500
Units in ending inventory	200
(100% complete as to materials;	
75% complete as to conversion)	

2. Compute output in terms of equivalent units (doses of input)

The FIFO cost flow assumption is used in the assembly department to compute equivalent units of output.

Equivalent Units: FIFO

	Materials	Conversion
Goods completed and transferred	1500	1500
Ending inventory	200	150
Moving average divisor	1700	1650
Minus		
Beginning inventory (equiv. units)	200	50
FIFO divisor	1500	1600

The FIFO divisor is found by first finding the moving average divisor and subtracting the equivalent units of beginning inventory.

3. Summarize the total costs and
4. Compute equivalent unit costs.

Financial Flows: Assembly

	Materials	Unit Cost
Beginning inventory	$ 5,300	
Transfers: Bristle dept.	24,000	16.00
Materials added	4,500	3.00
Total materials	$33,800	$19.00

	Conversion	Unit Cost
Beginning inventory	$ 975	
Labor	8,000	$5.00
Other variable expenses	6,400	4.00
Fixed expenses	4,800	3.00
	$20,175	$12.00
	$53,975	$31.00

To arrive at financial flows we sum the costs for each dose in inventory to those costs that were added during the period. To compute unit costs, we divide the sum of the costs for each resource by its equivalent units calculated in step 2. But unlike moving average, under FIFO, we compute unit costs only for this period's cost, so we omit beginning inventory in the unit cost calculation. For example, total material costs this period were $28,500 and equivalent units for the material resource are 1500; unit costs for each unit as to the materials resource are $19.00. Similarly, total conversion costs this period are $19,200 ($20,175−$975) and equivalent units as to conversion are 1600. Unit cost as to the conversion resource is therefore $12.00. Total unit costs are $31.00.

5. Apply costs to units completed and to units ending in WIP.

Cost Distribution: Bristle Toning

			Equiv. Unit Costs	Units Cost Dist.
Ending inventory: 200 units				
100% complete as to materials	200	*	19.00 = $ 3,800	
75% complete as to conversion	150	*	12.80 = $ 1,800	
Total ending inventory				$ 5,600
Completed dippers:				
$53,975 − $5,600 = $48,375				$48,375
Per unit $48,375 /1500 = $32.25				
Total cost distributed				$53,975

Because the FIFO cost flow assumption results in the calculation of current period unit costs, ending inventory should be priced at these current costs because last periods costs are the first to go out (first-costs-in-first-costs-out) which means that ending inventory has associated with it most recent costs (that is, current period unit costs). Since we know the total costs (including beginning inventory) and the total cost of ending inventory, we can compute the cost of goods transferred by subtracting the latter from the former. Notice that the unit cost of the goods transferred is $32.25 (a combination of this period and last period costs), while the current period unit cost is $31.

Fluctuations in costs under the two cost-flow methods are usually due to fluctuations in material costs more than conversion costs. If the company experiences a cost increase in the current accounting period, the cost per unit calculated under FIFO would be higher than those calculated under the weighted average, because the costs in the latter would be mitigated by the lower costs of the beginning inventory from the previous period. Changes in the number of units produced would also lead to a difference in costs under the two methods, because the relative weight of the allocation bases shifts, affecting costs under the weighted average less than costs under FIFO.

The advantage of using FIFO is that management can compare performance from one accounting period to another more accurately, because unit costs of each period are separate and not the result of averaging. Total costs under both methods are the same, because all costs are accounted for. The difference lies in costs of goods transferred out and the costs of goods in the ending inventory under each system.

Neither method is very precise in the way it allocates overhead to products; they are both massive exercises in averaging. Labor and overhead are allocated to departmental cost pools by using various first-stage allocation methods. Overhead cost pools are then allocated to products with units of production as the second-stage cost driver.

STANDARD COSTING SYSTEMS

We will illustrate standard costing for the overhead cost element by building on one of our previous examples: Tipografia Stanca. An extensive case study using a complete standard costing system is provided in Case 12-1 at the end of this chapter. Standard costing is widely used in practice in both job-order and process production environments. Moreover, it will provide a basis of comparison with activity-based costing systems, since standard costing and activity-based costing are based upon different philosophies of cost measurment.

Exhibit 12-6 illustrates the details of the second stage of a typical job-order production system. Standards may be established for direct labor and direct material, or these cost pools may be traced to products on the basis of actual charges (as in the case of Tipografia Stanca). Overhead is almost always charged to jobs based on a predetermined, standard rate; Exhibit 12-6 illustrates this procedure for developing such an overhead rate.

The procedure for developing the second-stage overhead rate is to first estimate the overhead cost pool for the next period, usually a year. The overhead cost pool may itself be estimated as a result of a procedure that uses very elaborate first-stage drivers to estimate the overhead pool from departmental accounts.

Exhibit 12-6
Developments of Standard Overhead Rates in Job Order System

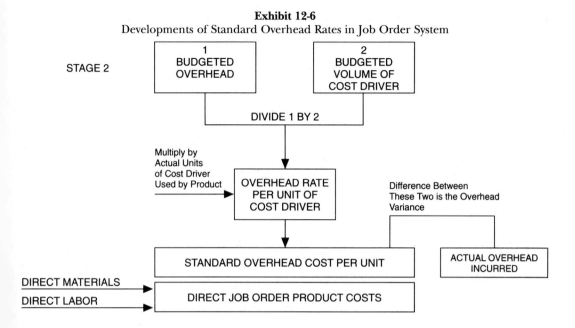

Next, we estimate the volume that is expected for the second-stage overhead driver. Then we divide the total expected volume of the driver into budgeted overhead in order to arrive at an application rate for overhead in the second stage. As actual data are collected for the application driver, overhead is applied to jobs based on the budgeted overhead rate times actual driver usage for a job during a given period of time. This is very similar to the process followed in the Tipografia Stanca case example, although we did not develop the budgeted overhead rate, it was given in the problem.

At the end of the period, a comparison is made between the actual overhead incurred during the period, and the overhad applied to jobs by using actual driver usage and the budgeted overhead rate. The difference (that is, the overhead variance) is either closed directly to cost of goods sold or prorated among the inventory accounts and cost of goods sold.

Elaborate systems of variance analysis may be constructed under standard costing. They are usually constructed at the department level in process production and at the job level for job-order production. To illustrate, let us look at a variance analysis of the Tipografia Stanca case. Exhibit 12-7 illustrates this analysis.

The first column of Exhibit 12-7 is Mr. Cattani's original estimate of job A-467 in standard costing format. Forty-five labor hours were expected to be used. A direct labor charging rate including fringe overhead is applied to direct labor hours. Material costs are as originally estimated, and overhead is applied at the overhead rate times the estimated volume of the application rate (that is, 45 hours).

The second column contains actual data for job A-467 according to the same job costing format. The third column displays the variances. We see from an *analysis of variance* that labor hours were estimated very well, but the labor rate was way off. Job A-467 used much higher-cost labor than the estimate assumed. Material costs were actually below estimate by $20. Other overhead costs were also below estimate.

The variance analysis isolates the problem: *the labor rate.* Management may now use this information to revise its estimating procedure in the future and/or to make changes in its operations to make sure that the right labor is used on each job.

Exhibit 12-7 illustrates variance analysis of overhead costs in a job-order production process. Case 12-1 at the end of the chapter illustrates a variance analysis at the departmental level for a company that uses standard costs for estimating labor, material, and overhead costs. The variance analysis demonstrated there is much more extensive than the variance analysis illustrated in Exhibit 12-7.

PROCESS PRODUCTION USING STANDARD COSTING

Most companies using process production tend to use standard costs. In process production using standard costing systems, standard unit costs are developed for both direct materials and conversion costs. These costs are then applied in a constant fashion to both completed units and to units in progress. Standard costs are therefore the cost per equivalent unit. Units in both beginning and ending inventory are simply valued at standard cost per equivalent unit for material and conversion costs.

Variances between standard and actual costs are derived each period for both material and conversion at the department level. The variances can then be analyzed to determine their approximate causes.

SUMMARY: THE MAIN COSTING OPTIONS

Alternative costing systems have two basic choices associated with them. The first is fairly well directed by the nature of the product produced and the production process used (see Exhibit 12-1). Job-order and process are the extreme cases. Job-order is used when there is a large number of diverse products. It represents a *divergent* process, in that it typically uses similar resources to produce a great variation of products. Process costing is used where a few products are mass produced;

Exhibit 12-7
Comparing Estimated vs Actual Costs of Job A-467

	Estimate	Actual	Variance	% Var
Labor hours	45	46	+1	2%
Labor cost	612	822.80	+210.80	+34%
Material cost	480	460	−20	−4%
Overhead	198	202.40	+4.40	+2%
Total cost	$1,290	$1,485.20	+195.20	+15%

it is a *convergent* process: different production processes converge to produce a product. The nature of the production process (that is, job order or process) to be used is more or less forced upon the organization by the nature of the product.

The second dimension is concerned with the type of costing system used. Here there are three alternatives: actual costing, standard costing and activity-based costing. These three systems differ along two dimensions: whether actual or standard costs are used and how many cost drivers are used in both the first and second stage to allocate overhead. Both actual and standard costing systems tend to use relatively few cost drivers in the first and second stage to allocate overhead. Activity-based systems tend to use multiple cost drivers to allocate overhead in the first and second stages. These drivers correspond to the different types of over-head in the organization, an analysis of which leads to a deeper understanding of the nature of costs in an organization. Unlike the type of production process that may be used, organizations can choose the level of accuracy they want reflected in overhead cost allocations.

Standard costing systems were adequate in the early twentieth century when product variety was minimal and product direct labor cost was high. However, in today's competitive environment with companies producing a multitude of products and with information-gathering technology becoming less expensive, companies need a system that provides more accurate cost data. They also need to extract more information from the costing system, such as resource consumption, department interaction, and methods to control costs at their sources. Out of these necessities activity-based costing was born. We examine activity-based costing in detail in the next chapter.

REFERENCES

1. BRINKER, BARRY J., ed., *Handbook of Cost Management*, Boston, Mass.: Warren, Gorham & Lambert, 1992.

2. COOPER, ROBIN, AND ROBERT S. KAPLAN, *The Design of Cost Management Systems: Text, Cases and Readings*, Englewood Cliffs, N.J.: Prentice Hall, 1991.

3. COOPER, ROBIN, AND ROBERT S. KAPLAN, *Solutions Manual and Teaching Notes, The Design of Cost Management Systems*, Englewood Cliffs, N.J.: Prentice Hall, 1991.

4. HORNGREN, CHARLES T., AND GEORGE FOSTER, *Cost Accounting: A Managerial Emphasis*, 7th ed. Englewood Cliffs, N.J.: Prentice Hall, 1991.

5. SHILLINGLAW, GORDON, *Managerial Cost Accounting*, 5th ed. Homewood, Ill.: Richard D. Irwin, 1982.

NOTES

1. We are grateful to our graduate research assistant, Nadir Kabani, for his help with the material in this chapter.

2. Copyright 1967 by IMEDE, Lausanne, Switzerland. The International Institute for Management Development (IMD), resulting from the merger between IMEDE, Lausanne, and IMI, Geneva, acquires and retains all rights. Not be be used or reproduced without written permission from IMD, Lausanne, Switzerland. This case was prepared by Gordon Shillinglaw as a basis for class discussion rather than to illustrate either effective or ineffective handling of an administrative situation. Revised and updated in 1976 and 1992.

3. Charles T. Horngren and George Foster, *Cost Accounting: A Managerial Emphasis*. Englewood Cliffs, N.J.: Prentice Hall, 1991, p. 146.

4. This example is adapted by permission from a case written by John C. Burton.

Case 12-1
Paramount Cycle Company*

Paramount Cycle began operations as a small job shop in Dayton, Ohio in 1940. The firm grew rapidly during World War II by manufacturing specialty items for the military. At the end of the war, with 125 employees and $1 million in sales, the firm began searching for commercial products. Because of his interest in physical fitness, Scott Meadow, the firm's founder, decided to manufacture single-speed bicycles for adults. The firm changed its name to Paramount Cycle in 1954, when the firm became exclusively a manufacturer of bicycles. By 1969, annual unit sales were approximately 125,000 for sales of over $6 million. At that time Paramount produced four lines of children's bicycles, two single-speed adult models, and two three-speed adult models.

Paramount cycles were sold primarily through independently owned bicycle shops which carried bicycles from several manufacturers, usually Paramount and two or three foreign manufacturers. Murray and Huffy, the two largest selling U.S. bicycle lines, were sold primarily through mass merchandisers, while Schwinn was sold through an exclusive dealer network. Paramount had been able to maintain a pretax profit margin of 9% to 11% of sales, greater than those of either Huffy or Murray, but probably below that of Schwinn. Since Mr. Meadow felt that Paramount bicycles were of higher quality than

either Murray of Huffy, but somewhat below that of Schwinn, he planned to continue the existing distribution system.

RAPID GROWTH

In 1968, responding to an increasing national concern for physical fitness among Americans, Mr. Meadow began developing an engineering department capable of supporting the manufacture of 10-speed bicycles. He also began contracting supply sources for 10-speed components (then located primarily in England, France, and Italy). In 1970, when Paramount produced its first 10-speed, total bicycle sales in the U.S. were 6.6 million units, approximately the same as the 1967 to 1969 annual average. Unit sales in the U.S. increased to 8.7 million units in 1971, to 13.4 million in 1972, and a record high of 15.2 million in 1973 before declining to 13.6 million in 1974.

This growth came almost entirely in the lightweight segment of the market. By maintaining high quality, Paramount was able to triple unit sales from 1969 to 1974, for a slight increase in market share. Mr. Meadow felt that Paramount had increased market share by offering higher quality components than comparably priced bicycles. Although Paramount had been unable to maintain its historic profit margins, profits had increased each year. Mr. Meadow felt that when sales leveled off the firm would regain its normal 10% pretax margin. However, when U.S. sales fell to 7.3 million units in 1975, Paramount suffered its first loss. By 1977, U.S. unit sales had increased to 9.3 million; however, Paramount's pretax margin had increased to only 5%.

ACCOUNTING

Paramount had estimated the cost per bicycle prior to the beginning of each year. Industrial engineering provided parts and component lists for material in each bicycle. By multiplying material quantity by estimated cost obtained from the purchasing manager, the finance department was able to calculate estimated material cost. The manufacturing department maintained a record of labor hours per bicycle. By multiplying hours per bicycle times the estimated labor cost per hour (from personnel), finance was able to calculate estimated labor cost per bicycle. Using the annual budget, finance divided budgeted overhead by budgeted direct labor dollars to obtain an overhead cost per labor dollar. The total of material, labor, and overhead was used throughout the year as the cost of a bicycle for both inventory costing and for product pricing.

Although Mr. Meadow realized that these costs were only rough estimates, they had proved satisfactory until 1970. The inventory had been increased by purchases of material, labor, and overhead and reduced by unit sales multiplied by cost per bicycle. Accounting inventory at year-end had been within 5% of the priced physical inventory taken by Paramount's CPA firm. In addition, Paramount had maintained its 10% pretax margins.

In 1970, when margins had decreased, Paramount began experiencing larger differences between accounting inventory and the physical inventory at year-end. In 1974, the physical inventory had been 12% less than accounting inventory, and in 1975 and 1976 the difference had grown to 15%. Because of the inability to control costs, Mr. Meadow decided to have a standard cost system installed. In early 1977, a controller was hired and told to design a standard cost system which paralleled the manufacturing system as closely as possible.

Although Mr. Meadow desired a system which would be capable of accurately valuing inventory, he was more concerned that the system provide a means of controlling costs. In addition, he felt that the system should provide information which would permit analysis of cost by product group and by product series, if possible.

MANUFACTURING

Paramount had originally divided bicycle production into three manufacturing departments, each supervised by one or more foremen. A parts department produced components which were not purchased externally, such as seats, handlebars, fenders, and other items. A frame assembly department cut tubing to length, brazed the frame, and then painted the finished frame. An assembly department assembled the bicycle, using the manufactured frame and purchased and manufactured components. The assembly department also boxed bicycles for shipment.

When Paramount expanded into 10-speed bicycles, Mr. Meadow had insisted that additional departments be created. To maintain different levels of quality, he felt that it was necessary to maintain separate production lines. Paramount's bicycles were divided into three product groups, based on overall quality. Each product group was further divided into four or more series. Standard cost and selling price for different models within a series were the same since differences were minor. In the children's series, for example, slightly different seats and handlebars were provided as well as different color and trim. In the adult series, differences were limited to frame size, men's or women's frame, and, in some cases, choice of color. The current products are as follows:

Product Group	No. of Series	Series
100	4 Children's single-speed	AA-AD
	1 Children's 5-speed	AE
	2 Adult single-speed	BA-BB
	1 Adult 3-speed	CA
200	1 Adult 3-speed	CB
	4 Medium-priced 10-speed touring	DA-DD
300	2 High-priced 10-speed touring	EA-EB
	2 High-priced 10-speed racing	FA-FB

Separate production facilities are maintained for each of the product groups with the exception that parts for product groups 100 and 200 are produced on the same production line. The production lines are as follows:

Production Departments

001   Parts department — 100 and 200 series
102   Frame assembly — 100 series (children's, single-speed adult, 3-speed adult)
103   Final assembly — 100 series
202   Frame assembly — 200 series (adult's 3-speed, medium-priced 10-speed models)
301   Parts department — 300 series (high-priced 10-speed models)
302   Frame assembly — 300 series
303   Final assembly — 300 series

The payroll department records direct labor by department so that each foreman can be held responsible for his or her operations. Materials are issued to each line when a production order is issued. If additional material is required to complete an order, the issue is charged to the department rather than the job. Each line keeps a small supply of parts so that additional material issues will not be required each time more parts are used than had been issued. Thus, whenever a request for additional material is made, it is for enough material to cover at least two to three weeks of production.

STANDARD COST SYSTEM

During 1977 and 1978, a standard cost system was developed and tested. The full system was installed in January of 1979. To verify that the system was operating properly, a special inventory was taken on June 30, 1979. That physical inventory differed from accounting inventory by less than 2%. Based on that inventory, Mr. Meadow decided that extensive use should be made of the cost information. The basic system is described next.

Engineering Standards. Engineering standards had been developed both for material quantity and labor hours for each piece part and for each operation. Dollar standards were developed for material by obtaining an estimate of material cost per unit from the purchasing department, and then reviewing any major price changes with the vice-president of manufacturing. An estimate of a plant-wide labor rate was obtained from the vice-president of industrial relations, and then reviewed with the vice-president of manufacturing. Final standards for material and labor were developed by October 31 of each year to apply to the following year.

Standard Overhead Rates. During the budgeting process, the finance department estimated total manufacturing overhead for 1979 using a form similar to Schedule 5. Total budgeted overhead was then divided by budgeted direct labor dollars (standard labor cost per unit multiplied by estimated units produced) to obtain a 1979 overhead rate of $1.50 per direct labor dollar. While it would have been more accurate to calculate separate overhead rates for each department, rates were expected to be similar enough so that a single plant-wide rate was preferred because of simplicity.

Cost of Goods Sold. Cost of goods sold shown on the income statement (Schedule 10) is the sum of cost of goods sold at standard (Schedule 7) plus all manufacturing variances. Those variances are summarized in Schedule 8.

Purchase Price Variance. The purchase price variance is simply the difference between the standard cost of a purchase order (units × standard price) and the amount shown on an invoice. Since there is considerable overlap between series within a product group, but very little overlap between product groups, the purchase price variance report is summarized by product groups. A portion of the monthly report is shown in Schedule 1.

Material Usage Variance (Material Scrapped). A primary feature of the cost system is that it is designed to utilize paperwork used by the manufacturing department. When a production order is scheduled on one of the manufacturing lines, a pick list is prepared for that order. The pick list is a schedule of raw material and parts required to produce an order. As an example, a pick list for seats would list a standard quantity of rivets, nuts, and bolts and a standard amount of bar steel, steel wire, and leather. If an order were placed for 100 seats to be produced on line 301, the raw material and parts inventory clerk would issue enough material to the line 301 foreman to manufacture 100 seats.

At any one time between 50 and 100 orders are in process on lines 001 and 301, while between 5 and 25 orders are in process on most other lines. To minimize paperwork, a foreman can produce either fewer or more parts than an order called for. In addition, foremen are permitted to request additional material without reference to a specific production order. This permits lines to carry a small supply of parts so that manufacturing operations are not disrupted by shortages. It is also common for foremen to split orders so that the final part of an order might be turned in several weeks after the initial turn in of finished parts, frames, or bicycles. Because of these and other complications, the controller decided to produce one material usage variance for each line, rather than a variance by product or by production order. The basic technique is that beginning inventory on a line plus material issued to that line is the material available. Of the total available, some is transferred to stock, some is lost, and some remains on the line as ending inventory. Because of the large number of parts in process at any one time and because of the complexity of the operation, it was not considered feasible to count in-process inventory on a line without stopping operations. As a reasonable approximation, all orders in process are valued at 100% of standard material. While some material issued will have been lost through scrap, a small supply of additional material is kept on each line to avoid disrupting manufacturing operations. These offsetting factors tend to make the 100% valuation of material on a line a reasonable estimate.

The material usage variance is calculated as the balance after subtracting ending inventory and material to stock from the material available. Schedule 2 shows production orders open as of June 30 (beginning inventory) and as of July 31 (ending inventory) for line 303. Those are summarized by product at the bottom of the schedule, as are total units to stock. Schedule 3 calculates the value of material in beginning and ending inventory and in goods to stock. Schedule 4, panel A, shows the calculation of the material usage variance, by production line, based on data from Schedule 3 and from total material issued to each production line.

Scrapped Labor Variance. Since some of the material scrapped also includes labor from previous operations (previous hours), labor is also scrapped. That calculation is identical to the material usage variance except that previous hours are used rather than material. Labor hours scrapped are removed from standard inventory at the standard labor rate of $6.50 per hour (Schedule 4, panel B). Since overhead is in inventory as a fixed percent of labor dollars (150%), overhead is also scrapped.

Labor Rate Variance. Direct payroll is maintained by production line. Since a plant-wide standard labor rate of $6.50 per hour is used, calculating a labor rate variance by line is straightforward. As shown in panel C of Schedule 4, labor hours paid to a line are multiplied by $6.50 to obtain standard labor dollars. Actual wages paid are subtracted from standard to obtain a labor rate variance.

Labor Efficiency Variance. Although each direct labor employee fills out a time card listing hours worked by production order, the controller questioned the validity of those time reports. Since employees were not on a bonus system, he felt that the time cards were probably not that accurate. He was also concerned because in many cases items could be produced on one of several machines. Newer machines were generally more efficient, so that depending on the current machine loading, an order might take more or less labor than standard simply because of availability of a machine. Rather than look at variances by either operator or production order, he decided to accumulate labor efficiency variances by line, as was done for material usage.

The calculation was similar to the process used to calculate material usage variance, except rather than valuing units in process at 100% of standard, units were valued at 50% of standard labor required to complete a unit on a line. The 50% figure was based on a sample inventory of three lines which showed that, on average, 50% of total standard labor had been expended on parts and units in process (on average, units were half completed). See Exhibit 12-8.

Using units in inventory and to stock from Schedule 2, labor hours are calculated for line 303 inventory and for goods to stock on Schedule 3. Both beginning and ending inventory of total standard hours on line 303 are multiplied by 50%. Those hours are then used in panel D of Schedule 4 to calculate a labor efficiency variance. Since the hours are lost (removed) from inventory at a standard cost of $6.50 per labor hour, overhead must also be removed at $1.50 per labor dollar.

Inventory. Inventory is maintained at standard cost. Schedule 9 lists journal entries which affected the inventory account during July. Purchases of material, labor, and overhead are initially recorded in purchases accounts (material purchases, direct labor, and manufacturing overhead), and then transferred to inventory at standard cost. Any manufacturing variances are recorded to maintain the inventory at standard cost. Finally, all shipments are removed from inventory as cost of goods sold at standard.

Exhibit 12-8

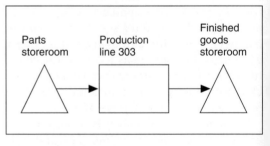

Material for a		
production order	100%	100%
Average	100%	
Labor for a		
production order	0%	100%
Average	50%	

Schedule 1
Purchase Price Variance Report
July 1979

Product Group 300

Part No.	Description	Voucher No.	Quantity	Standard Cost Per Unit	Standard Cost Total	Invoice Amount	Variance
A021-22	Tires	36058	100	$ 2.52	$ 252.00	$ 304.84	$ 52.84
A021-23	Tires	36035	100	2.61	261.00	321.39	60.39
A021-24	Tires	36104	100	2.80	280.00	336.84	56.84
A022-21	Chains	36072	50	4.12	206.00	281.14	75.14
A022-23	Chains	36023	50	4.83	241.50	306.94	65.44
A023-20	Brakes	36127	60	8.14	488.40	522.84	34.44
A023-23	Brakes	36041	40	9.52	380.80	415.61	34.81
A024-19	Crankset	36084	25	8.63	215.75	284.14	68.39
A024-21	Crankset	36014	40	9.12	364.80	486.12	121.32
A024-22	Crankset	36117	60	10.14	608.40	709.31	100.91
A025-21	Derailleur	36091	50	18.29	914.50	1421.16	506.66
A025-23	Derailleur	36042	60	21.17	1270.20	1846.31	576.11
A026-19	Hubs	36063	100	2.56	256.00	316.21	60.21
A026-22	Hubs	36029	120	3.19	382.80	489.14	106.34
	Total, Group 300				$141,316.35	$160,336.48	$19,020.13
	Total				$682,419.48	$701,941.48	$19,522.00

Variance by product group

	100						$ 283
	200						219
	300						19,020
	Total						$19,522

Schedule 2
Manufacturing Work in Process (WIP) Summary Report
July 1979

Dept. 303—Final Assembly
   Racing/Touring

Production Order #	Series	Model	Units Started	Units in Process June 30	Units in Process July 31	Units to Stock July	
6-18	FA	2209	100	100	0	100	
6-33	EA	1012	200	150	0	150	
6-42	EB	1209	150	100	0	100	
6-47	EB	1205	100	60	0	60	
6-61	FB	2214	150	150	0	150	
6-66	EA	1018	150	150	0	150	
6-70	FA	2216	100	100	0	100	
7-4	EB	1205	150	0	0	150	
7-11	EA	1013	200	0	0	200	
7-19	FA	2216	100	0	0	100	
7-32	EA	1013	200	0	0	200	
7-43	EB	1209	100	0	0	100	
7-47	EA	1012	150	0	50	100	
7-52	FB	2214	100	0	70	30	
7-58	FA	2209	100	0	40	60	
7-60	EB	1209	200	0	120	80	
7-63	EA	1018	100	0	0	100	
7-72	EA	1012	150	0	150	0	
7-78	FA	2209	100	0	100	0	
7-85	FB	2214	100	0	100	0	
7-88	FA	2209	200	0	200	0	
Totals	EA			300	200	900	To
	EB			160	120	490	Schedule 3
	FA			200	340	360	
	FB			150	170	180	

Schedule 3
Extension of Work in Process Report
July 1979

Dept. 303—Final Assembly
Racing/Touring

		Standard Cost Per Unit			Total Standard Cost		
	Units	Material	Previous Labor Hours	Labor Hours Line 303	Material	Hours From Previous Departments	Hours Line 303
Beginning Inventory							
EA	300	$57.57	5.12	2.14	$ 17,271	1536	642
EB	160	69.43	6.27	2.68	11,109	1003	429
FA	200	63.86	5.45	2.41	12,772	1090	482
FB	150	73.64	6.64	2.67	11,046	996	400
					$ 52,198	4625	1953
				× 50%			976
Ending Inventory							
EA	200	$57.57	5.12	2.14	$ 11,514	1024	428
EB	120	69.43	6.27	2.68	8,332	752	322
FA	340	63.86	5.45	2.41	21,712	1853	819
FB	170	73.64	6.64	2.67	12,519	1129	454
					$ 54,077	4758	2023
				× 50%			1012
To Stock							
EA	900	$57.57	5.12	2.14	$ 51,813	4608	1926
EB	490	69.43	6.27	2.68	34,021	3072	1313
FA	360	63.86	5.45	2.41	22,990	1962	868
FB	180	73.64	6.64	2.67	13,255	1195	481
Totals to Schedule 4					$122,079	10837	4588

Schedule 4
Calculation of Manufacturing Variances—Work in Process
July 1979

Department	001	102	103	202	203	301	302	303	Total
A									
Beginning inv., matl.	$41,216	$23,684	$120,364	$24,618	$132,816	$18,362	$23,425	$52,198	$436,686
+ Material issues*	86,219	49,302	263,879	42,619	271,319	39,814	47,286	127,042	927,480
Goods available	127,435	72,989	384,243	67,237	404,135	58,176	70,711	179,240	1,364,166
− Goods to stock	85,326	51,206	251,312	42,106	267,108	31,612	32,725	122,079	883,474
− Ending inventory	42,778	20,833	131,618	25,218	134,318	17,017	21,812	54,077	447,601
Material usage var.	$ 669	$ −950	$ −1313	$ 87	$ −2,709	$ −9,547	$ −16,174	$ −3154	$ −33,091 (u)
B									
Beg. inv., previous hrs.		623	13,104	718	12,378		856	4,625	32,304
+ Hours in matl. issued*		1314	26,518	1268	25,318		1932	11,363	67,713
Hours available		1937	39,622	1986	37,696		2788	15,988	100,017
− Previous hours to stock		1361	25,733	1210	25,023		1760	10,837	65,924
− Ending inv., previous hours		542	13,612	780	12,604		741	4,758	33,037
Labor hours scrapped		−34	−277	4	−69		−287	−393	−1,056
Labor $ scrapped (× $6.50)									$ −6,864 (u)
Overhead scrapped (× $1.50)									$ −10,296 (u)
C									
Labor hours worked (paid)†	23,625	11,628	10,794	12,418	13,206	4,210	7,486	4,612	87,979
× $6.50 standard	$153,562	$75,582	$70,161	$80,717	$85,839	$27,365	$48,659	$29,978	$571,863
− Wages paid†	152,807	76,347	71,231	80,653	86,107	27,518	48,587	30,315	573,565
Labor rate var. ($)	$ 755	$ −765	$ −1070	$ 64	$ −268	$ −153	$ 72	$ −337	$ −1,702 (u)
D									
Beginning inv., in process hours (50% of std.)	6806	3107	2823	2916	4384	1481	1618	976	24,111
+ Labor hours paid†	23,625	11,628	10,794	12,418	13,206	4210	7486	4612	87,979
Hours available	30,431	14,735	13,617	15,334	17,590	5691	9104	5588	112,090
− Hrs., to stock (100%)	23,216	11,014	10,874	12,273	13,407	3912	6314	4588	85,598
− Ending inv., in process Hours (50% of std.)	6683	3612	2796	3023	4326	1217	1527	1012	24,196
Labor eff. var. hours	−532	−109	53	−38	143	−562	−1263	12	−2,296
Labor efficiency var. (× $6.50)									$ −14,924 (u)
Excess overhead (× $1.50)									$ −22,386 (u)

* From computerized listing of material issued by department.
† From computerized payroll by department.
(u) Unfavorable

Schedule 5
Manufacturing Overhead Budget Comparison

Account No.	Direct Labor $	1979 Budget		July			Year to Date		
		Budget Per Direct Labor $	Fixed Budget	Flexible Budget	Actual Expense	Spending Variance	Flexible Budget	Actual Expense	Spending Variance
	Direct Labor $			$571,863			$3,659,344		
014	Foremen's salaries		$35,200	35,200	$36,430	$— 1,230	246,400	$ 253,210	$— 6,810
015	Indirect labor	$0.5643		322,702	327,324	— 4,622	2,064,968	2,097,326	— 32,358
017	Mfg. engineers		17,200	17,200	16,832	368	120,400	114,279	6,121
020	Clerical		7,850	7,850	8,727	— 877	54,950	59,324	— 4,374
101	Payroll tax	0.1051		60,103	61,394	— 1,291	384,597	391,622	— 7,025
102	Overtime & shift premium	0.1122		64,163	74,362	—10,199	410,578	443,117	— 32,539
103	Holiday & vacation	0.1444		82,577	85,118	— 2,541	528,409	539,723	— 11,314
104	Employee benefits		85,600	85,600	86,321	— 721	599,200	602,831	— 3,631
105	Workmen's comp. ins.	0.0161		9,207	9,731	— 524	58,915	57,986	929
202	General insurance		5,600	5,600	5,520	80	39,200	38,230	970
204	Outside services		5,000	5,000	4,650	350	35,000	34,650	350
201	Office supplies		1,800	1,800	1,603	197	12,600	13,619	— 1,019
304	Factory supplies	0.0232		13,267	14,003	— 736	84,897	93,910	— 9,013
305	Repair & maint.—bld.		25,000	25,000	23,285	1,715	175,000	193,214	— 18,214
306	Repair & maint.—equip.	0.0301		17,213	16,683	530	110,146	114,369	— 4,223
308	Depreciation		33,150	33,150	32,120	1,030	232,050	238,628	— 6,578
311	Heat, light, & power	0.0231		13,210	12,380	830	84,531	92,612	— 8,081
312	Tax—sales & use	0.0251		14,354	12,394	1,960	91,850	103,229	— 11,379
401	Shipping supplies	0.0273		15,612	16,318	— 706	99,900	105,392	— 5,492
	Total	$1.0709	$216,400	$828,808	$845,195	$— 16,387	$5,433,591	$5,587,271	$— 153,680

449

Schedule 6
Calculation of Overhead Volume Variance July 1979

Labor hours worked (Sch. 4)	87,979 hrs.	
× std. labor rate ($6.50)		
Standard labor to inventory	$571,863	
× std. overhead rate ($1.50)		
Standard overhead absorbed in inventory		$857,795
Less: budgeted overhead (from Sch. 5)		828,808
Variance due to volume:		$ 28,987

Journal Entry

Inventory	857,795	
Spending variance	16,387	
Volume variance		28,987
Manufacturing overhead		845,195

Schedule 7
Cost of Goods Sold at Standard July 1979

Product Group	Series	Units Sold	Standard Cost Per Unit Material $	Standard Cost Per Unit Labor Hours	Total Standard Cost Material $	Total Standard Cost Labor ($6.50/hr)
100	AA	2040	$13.60	1.59	$ 27,744.00	$ 21,083.40
	AB	2480	15.92	1.88	39,481.60	30,305.60
	AC	3010	16.01	1.84	48,190.10	35,999.60
	AD	2580	18.23	2.16	47,033.40	36,223.20
	AE	2040	21.47	2.43	43,798.80	32,221.80
	CA	1840	27.14	3.03	49,937.60	36,238.80
	Total 100				256,185.50	192,072.40
200	CB	1950	30.14	2.58	58,773.00	32,701.50
	DA	1010	32.07	3.89	32,390.70	25,537.85
	DB	1600	37.16	4.63	59,456.00	48,152.00
	DC	1620	42.94	5.14	69,562.80	54,124.20
	DD	1230	47.07	5.83	57,896.10	46,610.85
	Total 200				278,078.60	207,126.40
300	EA	820	57.57	7.26	47,207.40	38,695.80
	EB	420	69.43	8.95	29,160.60	24,433.50
	FA	430	63.86	7.86	27,459.80	21,968.70
	FB	210	73.64	9.31	15,464.40	12,708.15
	Total 300				119,292.20	97,806.15
	Totals				$653,556.30	$ 497,004.95
	Overhead ($1.50 × labor $)					$ 745,507.42
	Total COGS at standard					$1,896,068.67

Schedule 8
Cost of Goods Sold Summary July 1979

	From Schedule		
Material			
COGS—standard	7	$653,556.30	
Purchase price var.	1	19,522.00	
Material usage var.	4	33,091.00	
			$ 706,169.30
Labor			
COGS—standard	7	$497,004.95	
Scrapped labor	4	6,864.00	
Labor rate var.	4	1,702.00	
Labor efficiency var.	4	14,924.00	
			$ 520,494.95
Overhead			
COGS—standard	7	$745,507.42	
Scrapped overhead	4	10,296.00	
Overhead on excess labor	4	22,386.00	
Spending var.	5	16,387.00	
Volume var.	6	(28,987.00)	
			$ 765,589.42
Total COGS			$1,992,253.67

Schedule 9
Inventory Journal Entries July 1979

1. Inventory at standard	$ 682,419.48	
Purchase price variance	19,522.00	
Material purchases		701,941.48
Inventory at standard	571,863.00	
Labor rate variance	1,702.00	
Direct labor		573,565.00
Inventory at standard	857,795.00	
Spending variance	16,387.00	
Volume variance		28,987.00
Manufacturing overhead		845,195.00
To transfer material, labor, and overhead to inventory at standard cost		
2. Material usage variance	33,091.00	
Scrapped labor	6,864.00	
Scrapped overhead	10,296.00	
Inventory at standard		50,251.00
To record material usage variance		
3. Labor efficiency variance	14,924.00	
Overhead on excess labor	22,386.00	
Inventory at standard		37,310.00
To record labor efficiency variance		
4. Cost of goods sold at standard	1,896,068.67	
Inventory at standard		1,896,068.67
To record COGS at standard		

Schedule 10
Income Statement
July 1979

Sales	$2,689,103
Cost of goods sold	1,992,254
Gross margin	$ 696,849
Manufacturing	122,841
Engineering	121,495
Marketing	105,217
Sales	83,418
Finance	67,502
Administration	79,283
Total	579,756
Net income before tax	$117,093
Income tax	58,000
Net income	$ 59,093

QUESTIONS

1. Explain how cost of goods sold is determined.
2. Explain how the overhead spending and volume variances are calculated. How does Paramount develop its standard overhead rates?
3. How is the material usage variance calculated?
4. Explain how the labor efficiency variance is calculated.
5. Where were the major variances incurred in July?
6. How can the Paramount system be used to estimate the cost of a bicycle? Use series FB as an example.
7. What are the strengths of the Paramount cost system? What functions does it do well?
8. What are the weaknesses of the Paramount cost system? What functions are missing?
9. How would you describe the production process at Paramount?

13

MANAGERIAL COSTING II: ACTIVITY-BASED COSTING*

EMERGENCE OF ACTIVITY-BASED COSTING (ABC)

The decade of the 1980s was one of increasing industrial competition for firms in the United States. Young and eager companies from abroad were producing goods of better quality at lower cost. As the market share of major American firms declined, management looked for ways to increase their competitiveness. In the process, many American companies began to understand the inadequacies of their costing systems, which led to inaccurate pricing and which provided little information on how to reduce costs.

For broad financial purposes, such as reporting financial results to stockholders and calculating overall profits on sales, traditional costing systems were quite adequate. But with increased competition, management needed reliable information on product and unit costs, as well as information on how resources could be employed more efficiently. Traditional methods could not adequately address those concerns, and as a result, activity-based costing methods emerged as a strong alternative.

THE NATURE OF ABC

The major weakness of traditional managerial costing systems is their inability to allocate indirect costs (that is, overhead) to products in a way that accurately reflects the manner in which these products consume resources. When traditional

*We are grateful to Professor Robin Cooper for his help with the material in this chapter.

costing is used, direct costs such as direct materials and direct labor are easily and accurately traced to products. Indirect costs, however, are typically grouped into one or two first-stage cost pools and allocated to products using second-stage drivers (such as direct labor hours or dollars) that have little relation to a product's actual consumption of indirect costs.

This method of allocating indirect costs was adequate in the early twentieth century, when product variety was minimal, product direct labor cost was high, indirect costs were relatively small, and technology was relatively simple. But in the 1980s, overhead became the dominant cost in most manufacturing firms, amounting to as much as 400 percent of direct labor costs. Furthermore, the demands of increased competition called for lower prices, higher quality, and more product variety.

These demands call for a costing system that can provide accurate costs and give an indication of which activities of the firm cause costs to be what they are. The new costing system has to provide much more than traditional cost reporting. If companies want accurate product or service costs, they can no longer casually link overhead costs to arbitrary cost drivers that have little relationship to the true amount of overhead consumed by products and services.

An accurate costing system for a firm would be one that reflects the relationship between all overhead costs and products, and assigns these costs to products in proportion to the resources consumed by the products. ABC provides one method of doing this. ABC assumes that costs are generated by the activities performed by an organization and that each activity carried out by the firm is a process which consumes resources in order to produce outputs. Thus, ABC links *activities* to *overhead costs* because *activities consume overhead resources and products to activities because products use activities.*

Activity-based costing organizes overhead costs into resource centers (stage one), such as departments or pools (for example, energy costs). Overhead costs from these centers are then allocated to activity centers (such as maintenance, material handling, setups, and the like) using first-stage drivers. Overhead accumulated in these activity centers is then allocated to products, using second-stage drivers, based on the proportional usage products make of these activities.

Activity-based costing, like traditional systems, uses the two-stage model but unlike traditional systems, ABC uses activity centers and drivers in the second stage, not arbitrary allocation bases. Moreover, ABC typically has many more activity centers (and drivers for each) than traditional systems have cost centers. Exhibit 13-1 illustrates the two-stage model applied to activity-based costing.

Drivers and Costs

The second-stage driver rate for activity X is calculated by dividing the budgeted amount of overhead costs in X's corresponding activity center by the budgeted volume of the driver for the activity.

The driver for the first stage is usually calculated by finding out how much time or resources each "resource center" puts into each activity. The overhead in resource centers is then allocated to activity centers proportionately to the time or

Exhibit 13-1
Two-Stage Assignment Process: Activity-Based Costing

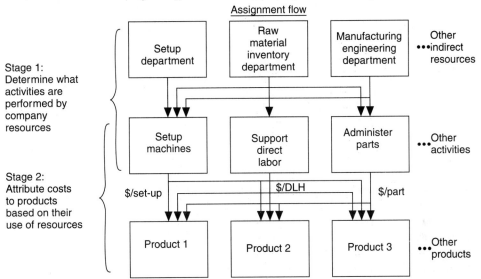

Robin Cooper/Robert S. Kaplan, *The Design of Cost Management Systems: Text, Cases, and Readings,* ©
1991, p. 270. Reprinted by permission of Prentice Hall, Englewood Cliffs, New Jersey.

resource driver. For example, an engineering department might spend 30 percent
of its time on maintenance activities, 30 percent on setups, 20 percent on quality
control and 20 percent on process improvement. The budget for that department
would be divided in these proportions to the various activity centers (for example,
maintenance, setups, quality control, and process improvement).

In the second stage a driver is found for each activity center which best represents the relationship between the activities and consumption of these activities
by products. It is necessary to take care in selecting both the activities and their
respective drivers. The activities should represent value-added activities that best
reflect resource consumption. They should also be dominant activities. Activity drivers should reflect a causal relationship between the activity center and products.

Resource and activity centers together with first- and second-stage drivers
may be established by using either budgeted or actual data. If budgeted data are
used, they should be updated periodically (in most cases annually).

Comparing the Results of Traditional versus Activity-Based Systems

Before getting into a detailed example of an ABC application, it is useful to compare the ABC model with the traditional model of costing. Exhibit 13-2 is a diagrammatic comparison. Let's examine it carefully.

Under ABC, product costs are subdivided into four categories: *unit, batch,
product,* and *facility.* Unit-level costs are those that vary proportionately with the
number of units produced. Batch-level costs are those that vary with the number of

batches of a product produced. Product-level costs are those that vary with the number of different products produced. And facility-sustaining costs are those incurred to keep the facility operating.

Activity-based costing seeks to develop in the first and second stage different drivers for each of these costs, since they behave differently in terms of how they affect products. Traditional costing systems treat all of these costs as unit-level costs. In other words, these costs are allocated to products on a unit-level basis, even though they are not all caused by unit-level activity. This is the source of distortion in product costs and in estimates of product profitability in traditional systems.

A General Approach to the Design of Activity-Based Costing Systems[1]

Signals of Malfunction of Existing Cost Systems

There are a number of signals which may alert management that all is not well with its costing system. Assume management considered their machinery and production process to be highly efficient for high volume production. If the company regularly provides competitive bids for business to customers and finds itself the low bidder primarily on low volume products and the high bidder on high volume products, it might become suspicious that the costing system is over costing high volume products and under costing low volume products. This outcome often happens in practice.

Exhibit 13-2

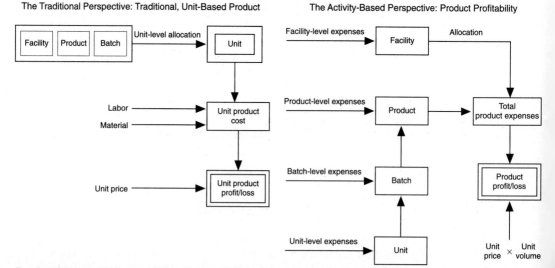

Reprinted by permission from Robin Cooper, "Activity-Based Costing for Improved Product Costing," in Brinker, ed., *Handbook of Cost Management.* Warren, Gorham and Lamont, 31 St. James Ave., Boston, MA 02116. 1992. pp. B-1-6 and B-1-7. All rights reserved.

Another common signal is emitted in the make versus buy decision. The firm may be making more of its intermediate parts than its competitors because the costing system is under representing the true costs of making or over representing the true costs of purchasing these parts.

Still another signal may come from the failure of management to penetrate a desirable market segment. It may be seeking to penetrate the high quality, relatively high price segment of its market and find that it is actually more competitive in the moderate quality and relatively low price segment. Its costing system may be distorting cost estimates and prices. The result may also be accompanied by a decline in profit margins against expectations.

Evaluating the Existing Costing System and Diagnosing Potential Problems

Once management becomes suspicious of the existing costing system it should proceed to identify the sources of error. The two-stage model can be a helpful tool in diagnosing problems.

Let us assume the firm is typical and is using a traditional costing system. We would proceed to identify all the overhead cost accounts at Level 0 of the two-stage model. Then we would look to see how the existing cost system groups these accounts into overhead cost pools at Level 1 (i.e., what first-stage drivers are used?). Next, we would examine the methods that are used to allocate these overhead pools to products. Are the overhead costs grouped into a small number of consolidated resource cost pools or are they simply allocated to products? Exhibit 13-3 shows an example in which five overhead cost accounts are grouped into three overhead cost pools. These overhead cost pools are defined by grouping the Level 0 cost accounts into those which are related to direct labor costs, direct material costs and machine hour costs.

Finally, we should identify the second-stage drivers which are used to allocate the costs in these overhead cost pools to products in Level 2 of the two-stage model. On Exhibit 13-3, we note the direct material related overhead cost pool is allocated to products based upon the direct material dollars contained in a given product. The direct labor cost pool is allocated to products based upon the number of direct labor hours in products. Finally, the machine hour cost pool is allocated to products based upon the number of machine hours used in products.

Exhibit 13-3 is actually more sophisticated than many traditional cost systems in that it uses three second-stage overhead cost pools and three second-stage drivers while many systems use only one of each. Yet, the two-stage diagram of the system suggests a number of potential cost distortions. First, all three of the drivers are *unit-level drivers*, costs are allocated from each pool to products in the second-stage in proportion to the number of units of product; for example, the more units of a product produced, the more material dollars used which leads to proportionately more of the direct material overhead cost pool allocated to products. The same is true for the other two second-stage drivers. As a result, the amount of overhead allocated is proportional to the number of units of products produced.

The potential difficulty with this costing system can be seen in moving from the five overhead cost accounts (i.e., Level 0) to the product level (i.e., Level 2).

Exhibit 13-3

A Two-Stage Model Representing a Traditional Standard Costing System

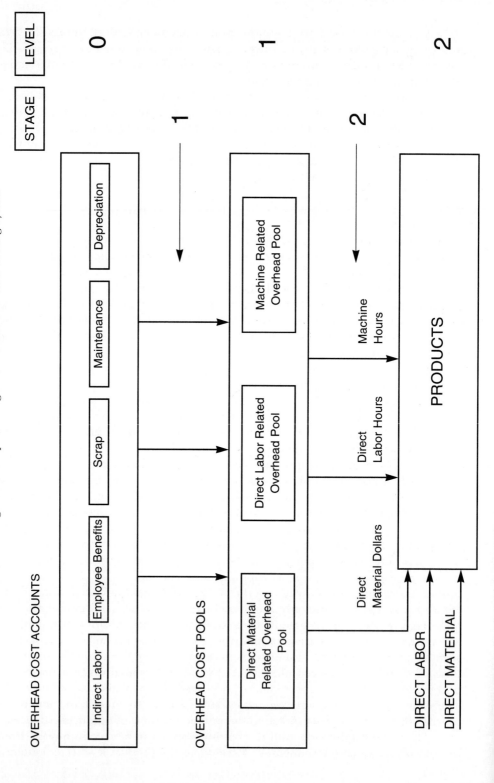

458

Some of these overhead cost accounts are clearly related to the number of units produced. But some, especially indirect labor, and scrap may be more closely related to the number of different products produced rather than to the number of total product units produced. If that is so, the existing system spreads these product level costs evenly across all products and under represents the costs of products which are produced in small volumes. These low volume products should absorb the bulk of the costs which are related to the **range of products** produced by the company.

Still more potential difficulty can be observed regarding those costs among the five categories of overhead which are devoted to set-up related activity. These overhead costs are caused by the number of batches of products produced. Set-up related costs may be found in the indirect labor, employee benefits and scrap overhead accounts. The proper allocation of these costs requires that they be *proportional* to the number of *batches of products* produced not *proportional* to the *volume of products* produced.

Finally, some of the costs in the five overhead cost accounts are clearly not related to individual products but are necessary to operate the entire plant (i.e., they are *facility-sustaining costs*). Certainly, some of the depreciation and maintenance costs are necessary simply to maintain the operation of the plant facility. Any attempt to allocate these costs to products produces arbitrary results and distorts product costs.

Designing an Activity-Based Costing System

Once we have diagnosed the potential distortions in our existing cost system, we can turn to a revised version of the two-stage model to address most of these distortions. Our task is to re-examine the overhead cost accounts (in Level 0) by interviewing personnel in the departments who expend these resources and attempt to determine the major activities that are performed in these departments. These major activities with cost budgets will then comprise activity center pools at Level 1 of the two-stage model. In order to arrive at these activity center cost pools we must allocate a portion of the five overhead cost accounts to each activity center. The allocations might be made based upon the percentage of the overhead cost account which is related to each activity center (i.e., or by one or more other first-stage driver).

Exhibit 13-4 defines eight different activity center cost pools. Each has its own second-stage driver defined to best represent the way the products of the firm consume resources from the activity center cost pools. Moreover, the eight pools are identified as being associated with either *unit-level, batch-level, product sustaining-level,* or *facility-level activities*.

Three unit-level drivers are identified for the activity center cost pools which are related to material, labor and machine usage. These unit-level drivers have a similar form to those used in the traditional system. The second-stage drivers for these activities are *direct material dollars, direct labor hours,* and *machine hours.* Driver rates are then established respectively as *percentage of direct material dollars, dollars per direct labor hour,* and *dollars per machine hour.*

Exhibit 13-4*

A Two-Stage Model Representing an Activity-Based Costing System

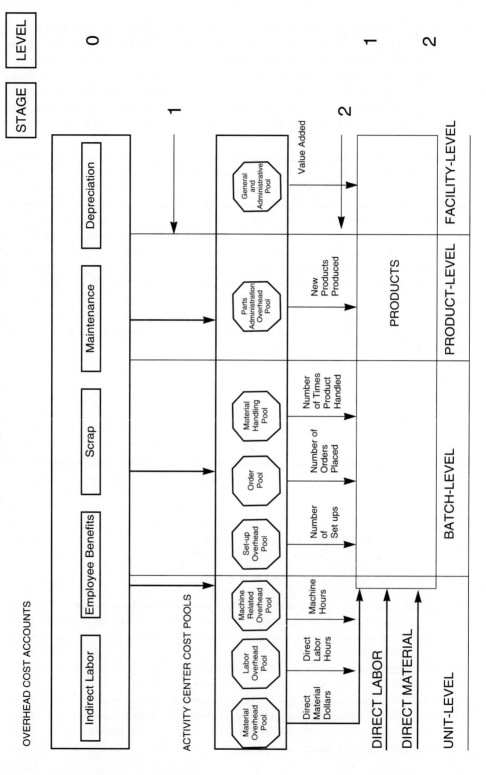

Three batch-level activity center cost pools and drivers are identified next. The three batch-level activity centers are set-up costs, order costs, and material handling costs. These activities are all related to the number of batches of various products which are produced. Set-up costs are then allocated to products based upon *number of set-ups*, ordering costs are then allocated based upon *number of orders placed* for a given product, and material handling costs are allocated according to dollars per *number of times the product is handled* during a specific time period. Driver rates for batch activities are then established respectively as *dollars per set-up*, *dollars per order placed*, and *dollars per each handling activity*.

Product-level activity costs are allocated to products based upon *new products* produced. *The driver rate is dollars per product.*

Facility overhead costs are simply assigned to one *general and administration* activity pool. They are allocated according to products based upon the *value added by the firm to products*. The driver rate is *dollars times value added*. Although this driver is as reasonable as any for allocating facility sustaining expenses, it is still arbitrary.

Once we cost our products under the new activity-based system, we will immediately observe some significant differences. Exhibit 13-5 depicts the general categories of product costs under both the old and new system.

As can readily be seen there are eight drivers in the second-stage under the new system and only three under the old system. This manifests itself in more detailed and accurate costing under the new system. Moreover, the cost structure of the product is more fully revealed under the new system permitting a better understanding of the causes of product costs; thereby permitting a better understanding of the steps that may be taken to reduce product costs in the future.

Exhibit 13-5
General Categories of Product Costs

Old System: Cost per Unit	New System: Cost per Unit
Direct Labor	Direct Labor
Direct Material	Direct Material
Overhead	Overhead
Allocated as % Direct Material $	*Unit-level*
Allocated as $ amt per Direct Labor Hour	Allocated as % Direct Material $
Allocated as $ amt per Machine Hour	Allocated $ amt per Direct Labor Hour
Total Cost per Unit of Product	Allocated as $ amt per Machine Hour
	Batch-level
	Allocated as $ amt per setup
	Allocated as $ amt per product order placed
	Allocated as $ amt per product handled
	Product-level
	Allocated as $ amt per product produced
	Facility-level
	Allocated as $ amt per product value added
	Total Cost per Unit of Product

Still another notable advantage of the new system is that it permits a closer analysis of the appropriate costs that should be attached to the different kinds of decisions that may have to be made regarding this product. Typical decisions that call upon cost data are enumerated in the next two sections of this chapter.

Given the increased accuracy of the new costing system over the old, it is not unusual for major differences in product cost and product profitability to result. Products that were thought to be profitable at current prices often turn out to incur losses (i.e., typically the low volume products); products that were thought to be unprofitable or modestly profitable under the old system are often found to be very profitable under the new system (i.e., typically the high volume products).

BENEFITS OF ABC

Because ABC results in a better identification of the resources consumed by products, it can be used for a variety of analytical studies.

Activity-based costing results in the identification of activities that need to be cut in order to reduce costs. These activities might include set ups, material handling, and transportation. Transportation costs may be reduced by making fewer deliveries to and from the factory. Set-up overhead may be reduced by reducing the time it takes to set up, by producing larger batches with fewer resultant set ups and by using factory workers rather than more expensive indirect labor to perform set ups. Material handling costs may be reduced by reducing the number of parts in a product.

Many improvements may be made based upon the ABC analysis. There is one danger, however. Management might become defensive if the new cost data require many changes in perception as to product profitability and as to product emphasis. This defensive behavior may lead management to reject the conclusions of the ABC study and do nothing to improve cost and profitability performance. Clear expectations about the possibility of change should be established by top management before embarking on the ABC study to prevent dysfunctional behavior from developing afterwards.

With a constructive attitude towards the findings of an ABC study, management might initiate a number of improvements and reap a number of benefits such as:

1. An ABC study may convince management that they must take a number of steps to become more competitive. As a result they could attempt to increase quality while simultaneously focusing on reducing costs. The cost analysis could highlight just how expensive the manufacturing process is. This in turn could spur activities to reorganize the process, improve quality, and reduce costs.
2. Management will be in a position to make more sound competitive bids.
3. Activity-based costing can help with the make-buy decisions management must make. The nine drivers help to identify more accurately the costs management will shed if it purchases parts and services.
4. With the improved cost analysis, management could conduct more accurate analyses of the volume required to break-even on low volume products.
5. Through an analysis of the cost data and resource consumption patterns, management can begin to re-engineer the manufacturing process to achieve more efficient and higher quality output patterns.

6. Because the ABC system contains numerous activity cost centers and second-stage drivers, the budgeted costs that are used to conduct an ABC study should be expected to be far closer to actual costs than under traditional systems. This advantage drastically reduces the necessity to conduct variance analysis between budget and actual costing. The role of variance analysis under ABC is therefore likely to diminish in importance.

7. The key challenge to decision making in regards to overhead costs has to do with identifying the overhead costs that matter for a particular decision. Not all, or even most, overhead costs vary with many types of decisions. The new system, because it separates overhead into four categories; unit-level, batch-level, product-level, and facility sustaining-level, improves management's ability to make informed decisions. Traditional cost systems do not separate overhead into those that are related to production batches of products from those that are product sustaining, such as set ups and material handling activities. Batch and product sustaining costs decrease only if the number of batches or products are reduced by a prospective decision. These costs are not affected if only the number of units of production are expected to decrease as a result of the decision.

Traditional systems measure resources consumed in proportion to the number of units of the individual product, but some resources are not caused by the number of units produced but are a function of batch, product, and facility-sustaining activities. The chief advantage of using ABC is its ability to measure consumption of overhead by batch and product sustaining activities and allocate them accurately to products. The advantage is especialy important when we understand that a large proportion of overhead is often caused by non-unit-level activities. Only facility sustaining overhead suffers from inaccurate allocation measures under ABC, because it does not consist of many activities that can be related *directly* to products.

SUMMARY OF DIFFERENCES BETWEEN ABC AND TRADITIONAL COSTING SYSTEMS

1. Activity-based costing uses activities as drivers to determine how much indirect overhead each product consumes. Traditional systems allocate overhead arbitrarily based on one or two nonrepresentative allocation bases, thus failing to capture true overhead consumption by individual products.

2. Activity-based costing divides consumption of overhead into four categories: unit, batch, product and facility sustaining. Traditional systems divide overhead costs into unit and "other."

3. As a result, ABC calculates resource consumption, not merely organizational spending. It focuses on the source of costs, not only where they are incurred. This makes results more useful for decision making. Management can track how costs are generated and find ways to lower them.

4. The focus of ABC is on costs, quality, and time factors. Traditional systems focus mostly on short-term financial performance, such as profit, for which they are quite accurate. When traditional systems are used for pricing and to identify products that are profitable, the numbers are unreliable.

5. Activity-based costing requires input from all departments. This requirement leads to better integration of the organization and gives a cross-functional view of operations.

6. Activity-based costing has much less need for variance analysis than traditional systems, because cost pools and drivers are far more accurate and distinct, and because ABC can use historical costs at the end of a period to compute actual costs if the need arises.

CAVEATS ON THE USE OF ABC

1. When a company drops a product, resources are freed. Management might expect that this would lead to a decrease in spending. However, this is usually not the case.

Management often does not act to remove the resources freed (such as workers or managers) when a product is dropped, leading to excess capacity and waste. Also, the resources released might not be sufficient to allow spending to decrease. For example, if the work of one-fourth of an engineer is freed, this does not effect the engineer's salary or compensation. We conclude that the relationship between resources and costs look more like step functions than linear relationships. This should be taken into account when decisions are made.

2. It takes many activities to run the factory; it would be impossible to monitor all of them and impractical to monitor more than a few. The solution is to aggregate them. This could be done by combining activities that lead to other activities because of the strong relationship involved. Of course, management should use cost–benefit analysis to determine how many activities to include in the ABC system, keeping in mind that as the number of activities in the cost system decreases, so does the accuracy of the system.

3. There are several conditions that might lead management to switch to an ABC system; they include:
   • Decreasing cost of data gathering and processing
   • Increasing cost of errors for the company
   • Increasing competition
   • A changing overhead structure
   • A changing product mix

4. The optimal use of ABC is for improving cost performance by improving activities. If activities generate costs, then the key to reducing costs, improving quality, and increasing efficiency is reducing activities, improving their impact and quality, and making them more efficient.

5. Activities can be classified as value added or nonvalue added. The nonvalue-added activities represent waste and are indicated by activities that do not add value to products, value as perceived by the consumer. Some examples include maintaining inventories, quality testing, and transportation time to and from various functions. Nonvalue-added activities are the activities that should be targeted for elimination. For example, reducing inventory through introducing a successful JIT system reduces the costs of handling inventory; "building" quality into the process saves time, effort, and costs in the rework area; placing consecutive manufacturing processes closer together reduces transportation time and costs.

USE OF ABC INFORMATION IN DECISION MAKING

Activity-based costing systems provide cost information to assist in some of the most fundamental decisions managers are called to make. In this section, we review the nature of these decisions and the cost implications of each.

PRICING

Inaccurate costing may lead to inaccurate pricing, which in turn may lead to poor strategy. If the cost system of the firm results in understating product costs and prices are based upon these costs, prices will be set in such a way as to attract volume but at very low profit margins. This is the problem we saw in the Tipografia Stanca case in Chapter 12. Prices were set below full costs plus markup and as a result, the firm backed into a strategy of being a low-cost producer, but the result was falling profit margins.

Conversely, if the costing system overcosts products, the firm could end up being a high-price, low-volume producer and not know it. Accurate costing is essential for pricing decisions. With accurate costs in hand, management can then choose its strategy and pricing policy intelligently.

A long-run pricing strategy of covering all the costs in the ABC model (that is, unit, batch, product sustaining and facility sustaining) is a sound one. Short-run pricing then can be adjusted to the special decisions that confront management and their assessment of which costs in the four categories are relevant for each decision.

MARKET SEGMENTS AND DISTRIBUTION CHANNELS

There are numerous market and distribution classifications whose profitability is of interest to management. Marketing segments include customer groups, regions, product lines, and order size. Distribution channels include retail, wholesale, and direct mail.

Some customer groups and distribution channels are more expensive to serve than others. Managers need to know the true costs of serving various market segments and distribution channels so as to set prices and allocate resources appropriately. Many of the costs of marketing and distribution are buried in "selling and administrative expenses" and need to be traced or allocated to segments and channels in order to arrive at accurate costs.

MAKE–BUY DECISIONS AND OUTSOURCING

A good decision regarding the choice as to make or buy a product or part, or to focus on core competencies and purchase others, requires an accurate analysis of costs under each alternative. If overhead is allocated capriciously, products that should be made may be bought and vice versa.

TRANSFER PRICING

Decentralization requires internal pricing. In all those cases in which cost-based transfer pricing is appropriate, cost estimates must be provided. It is important for these prices to reflect true incremental short-run and long-run costs if correct signals are to be provided to managers. Otherwise, a major misallocation of resources will be possible, because decisions to buy internally versus externally will be based upon inaccurate data.

PLANT CLOSINGS

Low-cost foreign competition causes management to evaluate offshore production. In these cases, it is important for management to assess accurately the costs under each alternative, including a proper allocation of overhead and selling and administrative expenses under each alternative.

CAPITAL INVESTMENT

Investment in new technology depends upon a proper evaluation of costs and benefits. New technology often improves cycle time, raises productivity, and reduces costs. Capturing the full impact of capital investment requires a proper assessment of the impact of the new technology upon overhead costs and upon quality and quality costs.

IMPLEMENTING AN ACTUAL ACTIVITY-BASED SYSTEM

We turn now to review the detailed steps that are necessary to implement an ABC system in practice. To do this, we review the results of an actual implementation of ABC in the etch circuitry department at Hughes Aircraft, Ground Support Group. This facility produced over 1000 parts, grouped into 54 individual product families, mostly for other divisions of Hughes Aircraft.

This department was selected for a pilot ABC project by the division manager because of the product diversity in the department, a stable production process, and a desire on the part of department management to improve productivity. An overview of the pilot program in the etch circuitry department is given in Exhibit 13-6.

Exhibit 13-6 is a simplification of the actual process. The pilot site actually had 35 activity centers in the production process. Ten of these activity centers are listed in Exhibit 13-7. Thirteen of the product groups are listed in Exhibit 13-8.

Exhibit 13-6
A Simplified Representation of the Pilot ABC Program at Hughes Aircraft

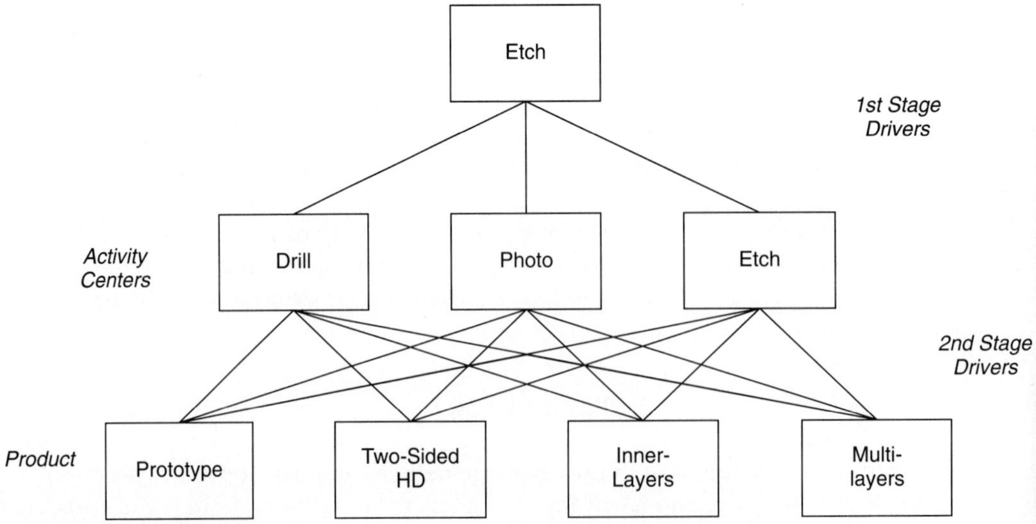

Reproduced by permission from Haedicke and Kirby, "Hughes Aircraft Pilots Successful Activity-Based Costing Program," *Corporate Controller*, July/August, 1990, p. 15.

Exhibit 13-7*
Partial Activity Center Listing the Pilot ABC Program at Hughes Aircraft

A/C	A/C Name	Activity Center Description	A/C Cost Pool	%
1	Sched.	Scheduling/material requirements	460,374.50	4.7
2	Buy	Procure parts/raw material	260,118.47	2.6
3	Dispatch	Material handling	488,418.15	5.0
4	Plan	Develop planning/tooling	490,114.15	5.0
5	Prod. control	Stores/kit/track/pack/ship w/o	896,739.03	9.1
6	Admin.	Administration	1,413,545.71	14.4
7	Quality	Total quality/defect analysis	1,045,631.76	10.6
8	Oxide	Oxide treat/oxide remove	66,761.88	0.7
9	Lam.	Laminate	85,731.62	0.9
10	Inspect	In-process/final inspection	502,262.98	5.1

*Reproduced by permnission from Haedicke and Kirby, "Hughes Aircraft Pilots Successful Activity-Based Costing Program," *Corporate Controller,* July/August, 1990, p. 15.

Exhibits 13-6–13-8 were put together by a multidisciplinary team of personnel consisting of those performing the activities, systems analysts, controller personnel, industrial engineers, and the department manager. The ABC team required expertise in product characteristics, supervision, process flows, ABC software, and the existing financial system.

The ABC team took the following steps:

1. Overhead costs were allocated to activity centers using first-stage drivers. Activity centers were chosen by aligning major product families with their specific flow through

Exhibit 13-8*
Partial Listing of Products, the Pilot ABC Program at Hughes Aircraft

Product ID	Product Description	P/Ns
HD-01UP	Two-sided PWB (HD)	18
HD-02UP	Two-sided PWB (HD)	6
HD-03UP	Two-sided PWB (HD)	216
HD-04UP	Two-sided PWB (HD)	161
HD-06UP	Two-sided PWB (HD)	6
HD-012UP	Two-sided PWB (HD)	1
IL-01PANEL-STD	Inner-layer (std)	457
IL-01PANEL-VIA	Inner-layer (via)	9
MECH ASSY	PC54 mech assy	—
ML-01-92-5728246-3	Multi-layer (adcap)	1
ML-01UP	Multi-layer PWB	56
ML-01UP-1-3205143	Multi-layer (413)	1
ML-01UP-1682265	Multi-layer (BSY-1)	1

*Reproduced by permission from Haedicke and Kirby, "Hughes Aircraft Pilots Successful Activity-Based Costing Program," *Corporate Controller,* July/August, 1990, p. 16.

the production process. The selection of activity centers must take into account specifically how each part is processed uniquely through the production flow.

Service groups such as department supervision, process engineering, coordination and dispatch, and quality inspection, previously allocated by direct labor dollars, were distributed to activity centers by carefully interviewing each employee in these functions in order to apportion their specific efforts to each activity center. The allocations were validated by having employees log their efforts in each activity center for a certain period of time.

Other costs, such as building usage costs, depreciation, materials, and supplies, were allocated to activity centers by more traditional cost accounting methods.

2. Once all the costs had been allocated to the activity centers, the team proceeded to identify the best causal relationship between the activity being performed and the way in which the material being processed absorbs the costs of the activity being performed. This results in the identification of second-stage cost drivers. There is no precise formula for developing the second-stage cost drivers. It must be the result of a multidisciplinary team effort. Key members of the team developing second-stage drivers at Hughes were department supervision, industrial and process engineers, quality experts, machine operators, and finance personnel. This effort was constrained by the need to collect new data once drivers were established.

For example, Exhibit 13-9 shows the 15 second-stage drivers used to attribute costs from the activity centers to the 54 product families. The costs of the drill activity center are allocated to products by the number of holes being drilled in that center (cost driver 13B). The use of this driver resulted in a separate collection effort to determine the number of holes drilled.

3. With the ABC elements sufficiently defined, the ABC team was able to input the data into the data systems computer model. To facilitate the process, the ABCs software package developed by Robin Cooper and Robert Kaplan and marketed by Peat Marwick was used. The team proceeded to calculate product costs under ABC and to compare these costs to the costs determined by the traditional cost accounting system.

Exhibit 13-10 shows the results of this costing process. The "0" line represents no difference in costs when either system is used. Only one product fits that description. In general, highly complex, multilayer boards are shown to be costed higher under the ABC system than under the traditional system, and the simpler high-density boards are costed lower under the ABC system. As a result, the traditional system overcosted the simpler products and underestimated the costs of more complex products.

The reasons for the difference in costs between the two systems are as follows:

1. *Activity center participation.*   Not all part numbers go through the same number of activity centers, nor do they absorb the costs identically in each activity center. The traditional system distorted costs in that it assumed a linear relationship between the use of direct labor and participation in an activity center's costs.

2. *Variability in support costs requirements.*   Different part numbers require different levels of support that are not necessarily in proportion to the direct labor expended to produce the product. For example, highly complex products might require attention from process and quality engineering, more planning support for equipment setup, and closer supervision. These cost distortions can have serious effects upon the pricing strategy of a manufacturing firm. Management might under price development orders and overprice the resultant production orders. The result is that the firm might win small development proposals and lose big production orders.

3. *Volume of production relationships.*   Setup time for various products can vary because of the complexity of the production process. If setup time is performed by more highly priced engineers, and allocated to specific products using direct labor, rather than board complexity, the more complex products will be under costed.

Exhibit 13-9*
Second-Stage Drivers Used to Allocate Activity Center Costs

Cost per Unit of Second-Stage Cost Drivers in Hughes Aircraft's Activity-Based Costing Pilot Program

C/D	C/D Name	Cost Driver Description	Total Cost Pool	%	Qty of C/D	Unit Cost
1B	Roll rqmts.	No. of rolldown rqmt. line items (A/C 1)	460,374.50	4.7	10,168.00	45.2768
2B	Purch. orders	No. of purchase orders (A/C 2)	260,118.47	2.6	934.00	278.4994
3B	Test	No. of card tests (A/C 28)	280,137.70	2.8	80,295.00	3.4889
4B	Plan pkg.	No. of new/replan planning/tooling pkgs. (A/C 4)	490,114.15	5.0	4,765.00	102.8571
5B	Work order	No. of work orders/batches (A/C 5, 8, 14, 16, 26)	1,104,052.80	11.2	12,757.00	86.5449
6B	Setup hrs.	No. of setup hours (A/C 35)	224,897.99	2.3	11,753.30	19.1349
7B	Panel vol.	Panel volume (A/C 9, 12, 12, 17, 19, 21, 22, 25, 27)	1,118,229.40	11.4	199,550.00	5.6038
8B	Move	No. of batches handled (A/C 3)	488,418.15	5.0	110,939.00	4.4026
9B	Defects	No. of defects (A/C 7)	1,045,631.76	10.6	42,923.00	24.3606
10B	Check hrs.	No. of production check hours (A/C 29)	341,491.59	3.5	10,504.68	32.5085
11B	Inspect hr.	No. of inspection hours (A/C 10)	502,262.98	5.1	14,161.86	35.4659
12B	Sq. ft. area	Sq. ft. area of panel (A/C 15, 18, 20, 23, 24)	761,680.45	7.7	107,024.50	7.1169
13B	Holes	No. of holes drilled (A/C 11)	243,204.83	2.5	80,674,032.00	0.0030
14B	Prod. volume	Production volume (A/C 30-34)	1,104,202.30	11.2	241,975.00	4.5633
15B	Man-hours	No. of actual man-hours (A/C 6)	1,413,545.71	14.4	167,755.00	8.4263
		Allocation total	9,838,363.00	100		

*Reproduced by permission from Haedicke and Kirby, "Hughes Aircraft Pilots Successful Activity-Based Costing Program," *Corporate Controller,* July/August, 1990, p. 17.

USING ABC DATA IN THE MANUFACTURING FIRM

The operational uses of the improved cost information provided by ABC was very significant for Hughes. Some of the key applications were as follows:

Shop-Mix Analysis

At Hughes, internal manufacturing capability is expected to be cost competitive with vendor facilities. A program manager may purchase goods inside or outside. In the past these make-versus-buy decisions were made on the basis of distorted cost information. The ABC analysis did alter significantly what was made and what was purchased externally.

Exhibit 13-10
Results of Activity-Based Costing Study

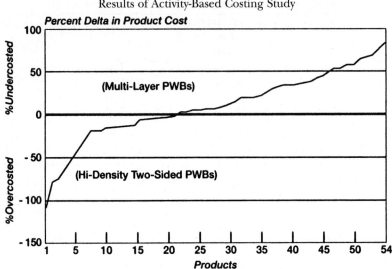

Reproduced by permission from Haedicke and Kirby, "Hughes Aircraft Pilots Successful Activity-Based Costing Program," *Corporate Controller,* July/August, 1990, p. 18.

Investment Opportunities

If shop-mix analysis indicates that the product is not competitive with outside sources, yet it represents a critical core competence, process improvements and related investment may be indicated.

Comparison Across Facilities

When a firm has multiple facilities, ABC can provide a method for benchmarking costs between facilities. Since each facility will have been built at different times, each will have its own dimension of excellence for performing certain types of work. The findings may be used to create "centers of excellence" whereby inefficient facilities are eliminated and other centers will concentrate on those items they can most efficiently perform.

Estimating

The estimating process under ABC will be much more accurate and better understood by all parties, because the buildup of cost objectives follows the production process.

Design to Cost

An ABC system focuses on the drivers of production and as a result allows a design engineer to predict more accurately the impact of design changes.

Empowering Work Cells

A well-designed ABC system will make the link between activity centers and work cells. The data provided by ABC can be used by work cells to improve productivity just as quality yields, statistical analyses, self-checks, and cycle time data are used. ABC provides another source of improvement data such that very specific contributions to cost can be identified and analyzed.

PROCESS OF IMPLEMENTATION

Practical experience with ABC yields a few guidelines to facilitate the implementation process. They are

1. Inform the management team, internal customers, and members of the department that you intend to use a new costing method.
2. Carefully describe why the cost system must change and get visible support for this change from senior management of the department, division, or company.
3. Educate all members who will be involved in the use of the output from the system. The concept of ABC is not complex, but implementation may be complex.
4. Involve in the ABC study everyone who you think will benefit from the system. This will enhance continuing management support.

REFERENCES

BRINKER, BARRY J., ed., *Handbook of Cost Management*, Boston, Mass.: Warren, Gorham and Lambert, 1992.

COOPER, ROBIN, AND ROBERT S. KAPLAN, *The Design of Cost Management Systems: Text, Cases and Readings.* Englewood Cliffs, N.J.: Prentice Hall, 1991.

COOPER, ROBIN, AND ROBERT S. KAPLAN, *Solutions Manual and Teaching Notes, The Design of Cost Management Systems.* Englewood Cliffs, N.J.: Prentice Hall, 1991.

HAEDICKE, JACK, AND CALVIN KIRBY, "Hughes Aircraft Pilots Successful Activity-Based Costing Program," *Corporate Controller,* July/August 1991.

HORNGREN, CHARLES T., AND GEORGE FOSTER, *Cost Accounting: A Managerial Emphasis,* Englewood Cliffs, N.J.: Prentice Hall, 7th ed., 1991.

NOTES

1. The general approach to the design of Activity-Based Costing Systems described in this section is developed based upon the overall approach to the subject contained in Robin Cooper and Robert Kaplan, *Design of Cost Management Systems: Text, Cases, and Readings,* Prentice Hall, 1991.

Case 13-1 Quality Machine Products*

BACKGROUND

Quality Machine Products (QMP, the Company) is a discrete automotive component supplier. The Company was founded in 1934, and has expanded from producing axles for Model T Fords to providing a full line of components. As the global automotive industry has become more competitive during the past decade, so has the automotive component supplier industry. The U.S. automotive manufacturers realized that in order to compete effectively in a world market it was necessary to develop long-term mutually beneficial relationships with fewer suppliers. This process required selecting those suppliers that could provide quality, competitively priced components.

While QMP has consistently won recognition for its quality service and products, the changing environment of the industry has placed downward pressure on margins. The management of QMP has decided to focus only on those products in which the company has a competitive cost advantage. The plant managers and accounting staff of QMP realized that the Company's traditional cost accounting system had not significantly changed in over 25 years. The management of QMP realized that making strategic product decisions in today's environment with a 25-year-old costing system was foolish. In the past, several of the senior executives of QMP

have had discussions with other automotive component suppliers on the effectiveness of activity-based costing (ABC). Although QMP never implemented an ABC program, these discussions caused several of the managers of QMP to think about their existing costing system.

While management was deciding what to do with its existing costing system, the Company was approached by one of the domestic automotive manufacturers to consider expanding its production of two products. At this time, Product A was produced by two automotive component suppliers, with each company producing approximately 50 percent of the volume. The existing standard cost systems indicated that Product A was a marginal profit generator and if the additional volume was to be assumed, the sales price should be raised in order to increase the gross margin. The domestic automotive manufacturer felt that allowing one company to produce all of Product A should allow for some additional economies of scale and a price reduction. Product B was a low-volume product with a high margin. QMP's customer wanted them to bid on an additional ten service run jobs that were similar in characteristics to Product B. The management of QMP saw this quoting situation as an excellent opportunity to examine the effectiveness of their traditional costing system versus an activity-based costing system.

---

*This case was prepared by John F. Hoffecker, KPMG Peat Marwick. It is reproduced by permission.

EXISTING REPORTING SYSTEM DEFICIENCIES

Traditional costing systems allocate overhead based on a standard unit-based measure that all products have in common (e.g., machine hours, processing time, or direct labor hours) but these allocation measures assume all overhead costs are directly related to units produced. QMP uses a standard allocation method for overhead of 400% of direct labor costs. To produce 100,000 units of Product A requires $250,000 of direct material and $50,000 in direct labor costs. To produce 2,000 units of Product B requires $5,000 in direct materials and $1,000 in direct labor costs. Product A sells for $6.00 and Product B. for $7.50.

ABC PROCESS

The implementation of an ABC system requires an organization to change its way of analyzing the costing of a product. The people involved must change their focus to what specific overhead activities are involved in the production of the product and the costs of these activities. ABC links all the costs of activities (e.g. order processing, setup, material handling) to a product, based on the consumption of that resource by the product.

The activity centers chosen by the team and their associated annual costs were

Activity Center	$ Per Activity Center
100 Quality	$800,000
110 Production Scheduling	50,000
120 Set-Up	600,000
130 Shipping	300,000
140 Shipping Administration	50,000
150 Production	1,500,000

The cost drivers and their total quantity for each activity center were

Number of shipments: shipping administration	1,000
Number of machine hours: production	10,000
Number of containers shipped: shipping	60,000
Number of setups: production scheduling and setup	500
Number of pieces scrapped: quality	10,000

The accounting department and production management of QMP analyzed the activities for a one-year period of all of QMP.

Cost Driver	Product A Cost Driver Consumption	Product B Cost Driver Consumption
Number of pieces scrapped	1,000	120
Number of setups	12	4
Number of containers shipped	500	10
Number of shipments	100	14
Number of machine hours	500	15

QUESTIONS

1. Prepare a schedule calculating the unit cost and gross margin of Product A and B, using QMP's traditional costing system.
2. Prepare a schedule calculating the unit cost and gross margin of Product A and B, using an activity-based costing approach.
3. If QMP were able to win the bid for Product A, another 100,000 units, discuss how this would affect the unit cost of Product A (assume that no new production equipment is required).
4. Which key factors have contributed to the change in gross margins? Which product should the Company more aggressively pursue in the future and why?

Case 13-2   Destin Brass Products Company*

Every month it becomes clearer to me that our competitors either know something that we do not know or they are crazy. I realize that pumps are a major product in a big market for all of us, but with the price cutting that is going on it is likely that no one will be able to sell pumps profitably if they keep forcing us to match their lower prices. I guess we should be grateful that competitors seem to be overlooking the opportunities for profit in flow controllers. Even with the 12½% price increase we made there, our sales representatives report no new competition.

Roland Guidry, President of Destin Brass Products, was discussing product profitability in the latest month with his controller, Peggy Alford, and his manufacturing manager, John Scott. The meeting among the three was taking place in an atmosphere tinged with apprehension because competitors had been reducing prices on pumps, Destin Brass Products' major product line. With no unique design advantage, managers at Destin had seen no alternative except to match the reduced prices while trying to maintain volumes. And the company's profits in the latest month had slipped again to be lower than those in the prior month.

The purpose of the meeting was to try to understand the competitive trends and to develop new strategies for dealing with them if new strategies were appropriate. The three managers, along with Steve Abbott, Sales and Marketing Manager (who could not attend because he was away), were very concerned because they held significant shares of ownership in Destin Brass Products. Locally they were a success story; the company had grown to be a significant business in Destin, Florida,

better known for its white sand beaches and as "The Luckiest Fishing Village in the World."

THE COMPANY

Destin Brass Products Co. was established by Abbott, Guidry, and Scott, who purchased a moribund commercial machine shop in 1984. Steve Abbott had sensed an opportunity in a conversation with the president of a large manufacturer of water purification equipment who was dissatisfied with the quality of brass valves available. John Scott was a local legend for the brass boat fittings he had always manufactured for the fishing fleet along the Florida Gulf Coast. Roland Guidry had recently retired from the United States Air Force, where he had a long record of administrative successes. The three then selected Peggy Alford, an accountant with manufacturing experience, to join them.

John Scott was quick to analyze the nature of problems other manufacturers were having with water purification valves. The tol-

*This case was prepared by Professor William Bruns, Jr. of the Harvard Business School. It is reprinted by permission of the President and Fellows of Harvard College, Harvard Business School Case 190-089.

erances needed were small, and to maintain them required great labor skill or expensive machine controls, or both. Within weeks of forming the company, Scott and his shop crew were manufacturing valves that met or exceeded the needed specifications. Abbott negotiated a contract with the purification equipment manufacturer, and revenues soon were earned.

The company had grown quickly because the demand for water purification equipment increased and Destin Brass Products became the sole supplier of valves to its customer. But Abbott and Guidry both had greater ambitions. Knowing that the same manufacturing skills used in machining valves could also be used in manufacturing brass pumps and flow controllers, they created an engineering department and designed new products for those markets. Pumps were known to be an even larger market than valves, and flow controllers were often used in the same fluid distribution systems as valves and pumps. By specializing in brass, the company could exploit Scott's special knowledge about working with the material.

Destin did no foundry work. Instead, components were purchased from brass foundries and then were precisely machined and assembled in the company's new modern manufacturing facility. The same equipment and labor were used for all three product lines, and runs were scheduled to match customer shipping requirements. The foundries had agreed to just-in-time deliveries, and products were packed and shipped as completed. Guidry described the factory to his friends as "a very modern job shop in specialized products made from brass."

THE PRODUCTS

Valves (24% of company revenues) were created from four brass components. Scott had designed machines which held each compo-

nent in jigs while they were machined automatically. Each machinist could operate two machines and assemble the valves as machining was taking place. The expense of precise machining made the cost of Destin's valves too high to compete in the nonspecialized valve market, so all monthly production of valves took place in a single production run which was immediately shipped to their single customer on completion. Although Scott felt several competitors could match their quality in valves, none had tried to gain market share by cutting price, and gross margins had been maintained at a standard 35%.

Pumps (55% of revenues) were created by a manufacturing process which was practically the same as that for valves. Five components required machining and assembly. The pumps were then shipped to each of seven industrial product distributors on a monthly basis. To supply the distributors, whose orders were fairly stable so long as Destin would meet competitive prices, the company scheduled five production runs each month.

Pump prices to distributors had been under considerable pressure. The pump market was large, and specifications were less precise than those for valves. Recently, it seemed as if each month brought new reports of reduced prices for pumps. Steve Abbott felt Destin had no choice but to match the lower prices or give up its place as a supplier of pumps. As a result, gross margins on pump sales in the latest month had fallen to 22%, well below the company's planned gross margin of 35%. Guidry and Alford could not see how the competitors could be making profits at current prices unless pumps were being subsidized by other products.

Flow controllers (21% of revenues) were used to control the rate and direction of flow of liquids. As with pumps, the manufacturing operations required for flow controllers were similar to those for valves. More components were needed for each finished unit, and more labor was required. In recent months, Destin had manufactured 4,000 flow controllers in 10 production runs, and the finished flow controllers had been distributed in 22 shipments to distributors and other customers.

Steve Abbott was trying to understand the market for flow controllers better because it seemed to him that Destin had almost no competition in the flow controller market. He had recently raised flow controller prices by 12½% with no apparent effect on demand.

THE MEETING

After the latest month's results had been summarized and reported, Roland Guidry had called Peggy Alford and John Scott into his office to discuss what changes they could or should make in their course of actions. The meeting began with Guidry's statement, at the opening of the case. Guidry had a copy of the product profitability analysis (Exhibit 13-11) on his desk.

JOHN SCOTT (MANUFACTURING MANAGER): It really is amazing to me as well that our competitors keep reducing prices on pumps. Even though our manufacturing process is better than theirs, I truly do not believe we are less efficient or cost effective. Furthermore, I can't see

what their motives can be. There are many manufacturers of pumps. Even if we, or even several competitors, were to drop out of the market, there would still be so many competitors that no monopoly or oligopoly pricing could be maintained. Maybe the competitors just don't realize what their costs are. Could that be, Peggy?

PEGGY ALFORD (CONTROLLER): That does not seem likely to me! Cost accounting is a well-developed art, and most competent managers and cost accountants have some understanding of how product costs can be measured. In manufacturing businesses like ours, material and labor costs are pretty easily related to products produced, whether in the product design stage or after the fact. So, if anything, our competitors must be making some different assumptions about overhead costs or allocating them to products in some other way. Or, as you said, Roland, maybe they have stupidly forgotten that in the long run prices have to be high enough to provide product margins that cover corporate costs and produce return to owners.

ROLAND GUIDRY (PRESIDENT): Peggy, I know you have explained to me several times already the choices we could make in allocating overhead to products. In fact, last month you almost sold me on what you called a "modern costing approach,"

Exhibit 13-11
Destin Brass Products Co.
Product Profitability Analysis

	Valves	**Pumps**	**Flow Controllers**
Standard unit costs	$37.56	$63.12	$56.50
Target selling price	57.78	97.10	86.96
Planned gross margin (%)	35	35	35
Last Month			
Actual selling price	$57.78	$81.26	$97.07
Actual gross margin (%)	35	22	42

which I rejected because of the work and cost of the changeover. I also was worried about the discontinuity it might cause in our historical data. But I feel that I might need another lesson to help me understand what is happening to us. Could you try once more to explain what we do?

PEGGY ALFORD: I would be happy to try again. We have a very traditional cost accounting system that meets all of our needs for preparing financial reports and tax returns. It is built on measurements of direct and indirect costs and assumptions about our production and sales activity [Exhibit 13-12]. Each unit of product is charged for material cost and labor cost; material cost is based on the prices we pay for components, and labor cost is based on the standard times for run labor multiplied by the labor pay rate of $16 per hour. Overhead cost is assigned to products in a two-stage process. First, the overhead costs are assigned to production—in our case we have only one producing department so

Exhibit 13-12
Destin Brass Products Co.
Monthly Product and Cost Summary

Product Lines	Valves	Pumps	Flow Controllers	
Monthly production	7,500 units (1 run)	12,500 units (5 runs)	4,000 units (10 runs)	
Monthly shipments	7,500 units (1 shipment)	12,500 units (7 shipments)	4,000 units (22 shipments)	
Manufacturing Costs				**Monthly Total**
Material	4 components 2 @ $2 = $ 4 2 @ 6 = 12	5 components 3 @ $2 = $ 6 2 @ 7 = 14	10 components 4 @ $1 = $ 4 5 @ 2 = 10 1 @ 8 = 8	
Total material	$16	$20	$22	$458,000
Labor ($16 per hour including employee benefits)				
Setup labor	8 hours per production run	8 hours per production run	12 hours per production run	168 hours
Run labor	.25 hours per unit	.50 hours per unit	.40 hours per unit	9,725 hours
Machine usage	.50 hours per unit	.50 hours per unit	.20 hours per unit	10,800 hours
Manufacturing Overhead				
Receiving	$20,000			
Materials handling	200,000			
Engineering	100,000			
Packing and shipping	60,000			
Maintenance	30,000			
Total	$410,000			
Machine depreciation (units-of-production method) $25 per hour of use				$270,000

we know all overhead costs are assigned correctly at the first stage. Then we allocate the total overhead cost assigned to production on the basis of production-run labor cost. Every dollar of run-labor cost causes $4.39 of overhead to be allocated to the product to which the labor was applied. You can see how this works in our Standard Unit Costs sheet, which I brought with me [Exhibit 13-13]. This is a fairly inexpensive way to allocate overhead cost because we have to accumulate direct labor cost to prepare factory payroll, and we just use the same measurement in product costing.

ROLAND GUIDRY: All this looks familiar to me. But remind me again what the choices we discussed earlier were.

PEGGY ALFORD: Well, one choice advocated by some would be to forego the overhead cost allocation altogether. Overhead costs could be charged each month as period expenses. Product profitability would then be measured at the contribution margin level, or price less all variable costs, which in our situation are direct material costs. We would still have to make some adjustments at the end of any period we held inventory to satisfy reporting and tax return requirements, but the effort to do that would be fairly trivial. The bigger danger would be that we would forget that all overhead costs have to be covered somehow, and we might allow our prices to slip.

JOHN SCOTT: Yeah, the salesman's mentality in Steve Abbott would make that kind of direct cost accounting dangerous. He would be looking for marginal customers willing to pay marginal prices based on marginal costs. From the outset we have succeeded in part because we insisted on trying to maintain a 35% gross margin on costs *including* allocated overhead.

Exhibit 13-13
Destin Brass Products Co.
Standard Unit Costs

	Valves	**Pumps**	**Flow Controllers**
Material	$16.00	$20.00	$22.00
Direct labor	4.00	8.00	6.40
Overhead @439% of direct labor $	17.56	35.12	28.10
Standard unit cost	$37.56	$63.12	$56.50
Overhead			
Machine depreciation		$270,000	
Setup labor		2,688	
Receiving		20,000	
Materials handling		200,000	
Engineering		100,000	
Packing and shipping		60,000	
Maintenance		30,000	
		$682,688	

Total run labor = 9,725 hours x $16 = $155,600

$$\text{Overhead rate} = \frac{682,688}{155,600} = \$439\%$$

Exhibit 13-14
Destin Brass Products Co.
Revised Unit Costs

	Valves	Pumps	Flow Controllers
Material	$16.00	$20.00	$22.00
Material overhead (48%)	7.68	9.60	10.56
Setup labor	0.02	0.05	0.48
Direct labor	4.00	8.00	6.40
Other overhead (machine hour basis)	21.30	21.30	8.52
Revised standard cost	$49.00	$58.95	$47.96
Material-related Overhead			
Receiving		$ 20,000	
Materials handling		200,000	
Total		$220,000	

Overhead Absorption Rate

$$\frac{\$220,000}{\$458,000} = 48\% \text{ (materials cost basis)}$$

Other Overhead			
Machine depreciation		$270,000	
Engineering		100,000	
Packing and shipping		60,000	
Maintenance		30,000	
Total		$460,000	

Overhead Absorption Rate

$$\frac{\$460,000}{10,800 \text{ hours}} = \$42.59 \text{ per machine hour}$$

ROLAND GUIDRY: John, the competitors are real and so are their prices. If we want to stay in pumps we probably have to meet them head-on. Peggy, please go on.

PEGGY ALFORD: The last time we discussed this, Roland, I showed you these revised standard unit costs [Exhibit 13-14]. These are based on a more modern view of the proper way to allocate costs. I put these together in an attempt to better allocate overhead based on activities. First, I identified material-related overhead, the cost of receiving and handling material, and allocated that to each product line based on the cost of material. The justification for this change is that material handling does not have any relationship to the labor cost of machining. Second, I took setup labor cost out of the total overhead and allocated it to each product line. This is a small amount, but the cost of setups also had no relationship whatever to the total labor cost of a production run. Finally, I substituted machine hours for labor dollars as a basis for allocating the remaining factory overhead. John [Scott] has really done wonders with our machines, but our expenses for machines are probably more than double the cost of labor. Therefore, it seems to me that machine hours better reflect use of an expensive resource and should be used to allocate overhead costs.

The results of this proposal made sense to me and may contain a clue about why competitors are chasing lower prices in the pump market. The revised standard cost for pumps is more than $4 below our present standard and would show a gross margin percentage of 27% compared to our current 22%. Maybe our competitors just have more modern cost accounting!

ROLAND GUIDRY: And you said this modern approach would not cost much more to maintain once we adopted it?

PEGGY ALFORD: No, it wouldn't. All I really did was to divide the overhead costs into two pools, each of which is allocated on a different measure of activity.

ROLAND GUIDRY: And we could use the same numbers for financial reports and tax returns?

PEGGY ALFORD: Absolutely.

(John Scott had been examining the revised unit costs and suddenly spoke up.)

JOHN SCOTT: Peggy! This new method makes valves look more costly and flow controllers even more profitable than we know they are.

PEGGY ALFORD: . . . or thought they were! The profit for each product line will change if we change the way we allocate overhead costs to products.

JOHN SCOTT: I realize that. But it seems to me that product costs should have more to do with the costs caused by producing and selling the product. That's usually true for material, and maybe direct labor, but it is not true for most of these overhead costs. For example, we probably spend one-half of our engineering effort on flow controllers, but whether you use direct labor dollars or machine hours to allocate engineering costs to products, flow controllers don't get much of the engineering costs.

I've been thinking about this a lot since last week when I attended an Excellence in Manufacturing conference in Tallahassee. One presentation was about cost accounting for the new manufacturing environment. I couldn't follow all of the arguments of the speaker, but the key seemed to be that activity, rather than production volume, causes costs. In our operations it is receiving and handling material, packing and shipping, and engineering orders that cause us to incur costs and not the length of any production run.

If I understood what this speaker was advocating, it was that whenever possible overhead costs that cannot be traced directly to product lines should be allocated on the basis of transactions—since transactions cause costs to be incurred. A product that required three times as many transactions to be incurred than another product would be allocated three times as much of the overhead cost related to those transactions than the other product would be allocated. Or said another way, a product which causes 3% of the total transactions for receiving components would be allocated 3% of the total cost of receiving components. At a basic level, this seems to make sense to me.

PEGGY ALFORD: Recently I've been reading a lot in my professional magazines about this activity-based-costing (ABC) . . .

ROLAND GUIDRY: But to cost products that way has got to be more expensive. It's more complex; also, who keeps count of transactions?

PEGGY ALFORD: It can't be too hard. All overhead allocation is somewhat arbitrary. We could experiment with estimates to see how the product costs might be affected. The product costs for material, direct labor, and setup labor will be the same as for my revised unit costs, and to allocate other overhead costs we just need to estimate how many transactions occur in total and are caused by each product.

JOHN SCOTT: I'd like to ask Peggy to put together an analysis for us. The managers at the conference from companies that have used these transaction-based costing systems really seemed excited about what they said they learned.

ROLAND GUIDRY: OK. Peggy, you and John get together this afternoon to put together the activity estimates you need. Get back to me as quickly as you can. Maybe we can figure out why the competitors think they should sell pumps regardless of price.

After lunch, Peggy Alford and John Scott met in Peggy's office. They discussed transactions and effort related to each type of overhead cost. The result was the overhead cost activity analysis shown in Exhibit 13-15.

QUESTIONS

1. Estimate product costs for valves, pumps, and flow controllers, using the overhead analysis in Exhibit 13-15 and other manufacturing costs.
2. Compare the estimates with product costs that are derived from standard unit costs. What causes the different results?
3. What are the strategic implications of your analysis? Could the production process for flow controllers be changed in such a way to allow the company to reduce the cost of flow controllers? How?
4. How would you evaluate the costs and benefits of the new activity-based costing system?

Exhibit 13-15
Destin Brass Products Co.
Monthly Overhead Cost Activity Analysis

	Valves	Pumps	Flow Controllers
Receiving and Materials Handling			
Receive each component once per run	4 transactions (3%)	25 transactions (19%)	100 transactions (78%)
Handle each component once per run	4 transactions (3%)	25 transactions (19%)	100 transactions (78%)
Packing and Shipping			
One packing order per shipment	1 transaction (3%)	7 transactions (23%)	22 transactions (73%)
Engineering			
Estimated engineering work-order percentage (subjective)	20%	30%	50%
Maintenance			
Machine hour basis	3,750 hours (35%)	6,250 hours (58%)	800 hours (7%)

Case 13-3   Prism Printing Company*

Prism Printing Company was a large printer of high-quality color printed materials. Representative of the company's products were annual reports and small advertising brochures, using mostly four or more colors and premium-quality papers and inks. In February of 1988, Mike Rollins, Prism's president, was faced with the decision of whether to pursue a potential major growth opportunity in a new segment of the printing industry: printing high-volume, quality catalogs for mail-order businesses.

Prism's revenues in 1987 were $25 million. Sales had risen steadily, but not spectacularly, since the company's incorporation 20 years earlier. In recent years, sales growth had just kept pace with GNP growth and Prism's financial performance had been average for the industry. In 1987 Prism's return on sales stood at 4% and its return on investment (after taxes) was 11.5%. Mike Rollins, the president, owned 25% of the company. The rest was owned by family members who were not active or interested in the operation of the company. To keep the company going as an independent company, Tim Rollins had identified his strategic objectives as:

- Protect the profitable part of existing business.
- Increase profitability ROS from 4% to 5%.
- Increase ROI from 11.5% to 15% to make it attractive to invest or reinvest in the business.

- To achieve those objectives, Prism probably has to enter some attractive faster-growing markets than some of the ones we now serve.

(See Exhibits 13-16, 13-17, and 13-18 for Prism's cost/profit structure, balance sheet, and a breakdown of fixed assets, respectively.)

A substantial portion of the sales in the industry was with large customers who required a mix of long-, medium-, and short-run printing. It was Prism's strategy to focus on these customers and service all of their needs. Sales were made nationally, through nine sales districts across the United States. Sales Manager Tim Johnson was always alert for opportunities the competition might be missing.

THE INDUSTRY

The printing industry was characterized by many small firms which tended to be focused both geographically and by product. The small companies competed vigorously for the higher-margin small- and medium-sized orders, considered to be those under $50,000. (Local quick printing shops were not capable of producing the type of printing that Prism did.)

Prism's segment of the printing industry focused on full color reproduction of

*This case was prepared as the basis for class discussion by Ralph F. Baxter with the assistance of research assistant Michael Kraft, and Associate Professor Richard R. Ellsworth of the Claremont Graduate School. It is reproduced by permission.

Exhibit 13-16
Prism Printing Company

	Cost Structure (1987)			
	Overall Company	**Average Large**	**Average Medium**	**Average Small**
Total Sales in $000s	25,000	10,000	9,000	6,000
Direct material (largely paper, ink, pkg.)	46%	60%	45%	25%
Direct labor	10%	6%	10%	15%
Total direct cost	56%	66%	55%	40%
Contribution margin	44%	34%	45%	60%
Variable and Semi-Variable Costs				
Factory indirect	3%			
Overtime premium	1%			
Energy, waste disposal	1%			
Supplies	2%			
Maintenance and repair	2%			
Idle time	1%			
Total variable indirect costs	10%			
Fixed and Relatively Fixed Costs				
Depreciation	2%			
Real estate taxes, insurance, fees	1%			
Other	1%			
Total fixed costs	4%			
Total mfg. cost	70%			
Gross profit	30%			
Sales and marketing	11%			
General and Administrative	8%			
Other—allowance, bad debts, discounts	4%			
Total S G & A	23%			
Profit before tax	7%			
Taxes	3%			
Net after tax	4%			

photographs with good (but not art level) fidelity. Competitors in this segment had to be able to turn around jobs rapidly to meet customer deadlines. The larger presses could print multiple pages per imprint which then had to be cut, collated and assembled. By comparison with art book publishers, the printing was less demanding and there were far fewer pages per run. High quality magazine printing was usually done on even faster presses. Mass market catalogs, such as Sears, were also produced on much faster presses with more limited color capabilities.

One major competitor, Atlas Printing Company, served the same mix of large, medium and small orders as did Prism. Atlas was somewhat larger, at $40 million sales in 1987. Atlas was a publicly held company. Its history and performance had been quite parallel to Prism until three years ago when it had entered the business of printing high

Exhibit 13-17
Prism Printing Company
Balance Sheet
(December 31, 1987)

	(in $000s)
Cash	$ 500
Receivables—net	3,500
Inventories	2,000
Fixed assets (net of depreciation)	5,800
	$11,800
Accounts payable	$ 2,300
Accrued liabilities and expenses	300
Short-term debt	500
Long-term debt	1,000
Equity	7,700
	$11,800

volume, quality mail order catalogs, which now took over 20% of their capacity.

The equipment used by Prism and by Atlas for their high volume work was not unique. As many as thirty other printers had it—but they used it for many other purposes such as packaging, premiums and promotional materials. Among those with this equipment, only Atlas and Prism had the proven support capabilities in art, plate making and assembly to provide the service in their market segment for a mixture of large, medium and smaller jobs.

Prism's management considered cost, reliability in meeting customer deadlines, performance to the specified level of quality, and full-line service to be critical to success in its segment of the industry.

THE SITUATION

On March 8, Tom Johnson, Sales Manager, sent a memo to Prism's President, Mike Rollins, discussing the possibility of entering what could be a promising new market. In

Exhibit 13-18
Prism Printing Company
Summary of Fixed Assets
(December 31, 1987)
($000s)

	Cost	Net Book	Replacement Value
Building and land	$1,000	$ 800	$2,000
3 lg. presses, 2–8 yr old	5,000	2,500	7,000
5 med. presses, 3–12 yr old	3,000	1,000	5,000
7 sm. presses, 2–10 yr old	1,500	700	2,000
Art, plate making, inspection	400	300	500
Factory improvement, equipment, tools, etc.	800	300	1,500
Office and administration (furniture, phones, fixtures, computers)	300	200	400
Total fixed assets	$12,000	$5,800	$18,400

the memo, Johnson described the situation. He had received an inquiry from one of the nation's leading, premium-quality mail-order businesses, V. J. Greenleaf, which sold men's and women's clothing. Greenleaf was interested in very high volume catalogs which differed from PPC's existing business by being printed on somewhat lower-cost papers, using good but less demanding art and printing, and having much higher volumes per run and much lower prices. The initial order would be for $1 million, with reorders likely at the customer's option. It would provide entry into a market with a potential future business of $2–10 million per year and expected growth of 15% per year over the next five years. This represented a major growth opportunity for Prism.

The mail order business had been growing rapidly, and it was moving into servicing customers who had traditionally bought goods from high-end department stores. Before this mail-order retailing had been generally confined to low-end or low-volume goods. The current trend, Johnson thought, could provide an opportunity to use Prism's abilities in producing high-quality catalogs in an area that was inadequately serviced by the competition.

At the expected selling price, the initial order would have a contribution margin of only 20%. To stay and grow in that business segment, not much improvement in price or contribution margin could be expected.

The new order would run on Prism's existing large presses, but it would squeeze the capacity of the indirect staff and the facility, forcing considerable overtime and preempting capacity for other opportunities. If the new business grew, the next increment of capacity would serve an additional $4 million of sales and would cost $1.5 million for equipment and another $300,000 for building and installation. Because of improvements in equipment, direct costs would be reduced and the contribution margin would increase to 24%.

COMPETITION

Prism's major competitor in the new area, Atlas Printing, was headquartered in Chicago. Atlas had long printed catalogs for several major middle-market department stores. They were now making inroads into the higher-quality high-volume catalogs. Johnson believed that Atlas was pricing its competing catalogs at a level that produced a contribution margin of not more than 24%. Johnson also believed that Atlas did not currently have a significant competitive advantage in high volume, quality mail-order publishing, although he thought that they might gain an advantage in that area if they went unchallenged for very long. Therefore, he concluded that Atlas was buying market share, and trying to preempt entrants into the new market, although he could not rule out the possibility that Atlas had a lower total cost structure. He knew Atlas was running a lot of overtime—which almost surely meant they were pushing their capacity. But it also meant they were spreading their overhead over more volume, which should make their costs look good.

THE MEETING

Mike Rollins called a meeting with Fred Hamilton, Operations Manager, Tim Johnson, Sales Manager, and Linda James, Controller, on March 11. Mike Rollins opened the meeting by summarizing the opportunity presented by the new potential customer that Tim Johnson had been working with. He emphasized the need for everyone's input and help in figuring out whether this is a good opportunity for Prism. The conversation began with a discussion of the existing large order business. (See Exhibit 13-19 for the staffing of the factory in February 1988 and Exhibit 13-20 for the order mix and capacity utilization by press size in 1987.)

Exhibit 13-19
Prism Printing Company
Factory Staffing
(February, 1988)

Factory Press Room (Operates 2 shifts)	Employees Per Shift*
Direct—pressmen and helpers	27
Direct—packaging, material handling	6
Indirect—inspection, supervision, mechanics, ink technicians	8

Other Factory (Operates single shift)	
Indirect—art and plate making	4
Indirect—factory administration, production control	6

*Total factory employment, including both shifts in the factory press room, equals 92 people.

TIM JOHNSON: At a 34% contribution margin, the existing large order business represents $3.4 million of our $4.2 million gross profit after sales and marketing expenses. We'd be dead without it. And unless we want to stand still, we need to grow it.

LINDA JAMES: This business is obviously important, but its profitability depends on how you allocate the indirect and fixed costs. Traditionally we have done this on a sales dollar basis—it's the simplest way. For the large volume business that shows we are losing money before tax. Now I'll admit these allocations are inexact and the large order businesses may do a bit better than that. But if we want to improve our profit margins and meet our company goal of improving return on sales from 4% to 5%, I can't get very enthusiastic about more low-margin businesses.

TIM JOHNSON: Well, in reality we all know that our sales and marketing expenses

Exhibit 13-20
Prism Printing Company
Order Mix and Capacity Utilization
(1987)

	Press Size		
	Large	**Medium**	**Small**
Order size	$50,000 up	$5–70,000	$1–10,000
Order size average	$100,000	$15,000	$3,000
Number of orders/yr	100	600	2,000
$ volume/yr	$10 million	$9 million	$6 million
Contribution margin/press/hr	$378	$270	$171
Sales $/press hr	$1,110	$600	$286
Capacity utilization rate	88%	90%	70%
Sales $	40%	36%	24%
Usable press hr—2 shifts	9,000	15,000	21,000
Direct labor (people)	10/shift	10/shift	7/shift

for the large order businesses are lower per sales dollar than the company average.

FRED HAMILTON: I don't think our indirect and fixed costs can be considered as an average percentage of sales, either. In the plant, some of the major variable costs move with press hours, with man-hours, and with capacity. Let me give you a few examples.

First, with only three presses out of fifteen producing 40% of the dollar volume, the supervision and support people spend closer to 20% of their time rather than the 40% the formula allocates.

Second, the art and plate making is a fixed team, with widely varying workload. Overflow is subcontracted. We really ought to charge that to the job as a setup cost, not allocate it as an average. Large runs use far fewer plates, even though they require top quality. Consequently, I think long runs are being overcharged by our formula.

Lastly, overtime and idle time are characteristics of the order size and the level of utilization. Larger orders book a lot of overtime and then have gaps. But the small press group costs us more than its share of idle time.

MIKE ROLLINS: Don't you have to start off by agreeing whether our present large order business is profitable or not before you can judge any new business?

Next, Johnson took up the topic of pursuing the $1 million Greenleaf order, which represented incremental business.

TIM JOHNSON: You all know that I think this is an important proposition. Our growth, in my view, depends on finding opportunities like this one. But we shouldn't look at this as just a one-shot bid. If we develop this business, we should be willing to add capacity to service the customers. I figure that even at 20% contribution margin we will have more profit at the bottom line with this business than without it, and the low price doesn't contaminate our other business.

LINDA JAMES: What I want to know is how can Atlas sell at that kind of price? If they can keep it up, do we really want to be in this business—unless we can make a breakthrough on costs? In addition there's the possibility that this low margin business might take capacity and service away from our other businesses, eventually changing the character of our business.

FRED HAMILTON: My guess is that we can handle the incremental volume and only slightly affect the service we give to our regular customers.

LINDA JAMES: Well, that's encouraging. Another bright spot is that of the 23% of the expenses that we generally use as a fixed percentage in our pricing (sales expenses, G & A, etc.), only some would be variable with this volume. Maybe a quarter to a third.

FRED HAMILTON: And not all of the variable indirect costs are variable. I can't prove it, but my feeling is that only two thirds are close to variable.

LINDA JAMES: We also know that many of our so-called variable costs are really fixed, at least from quarter to quarter—even much of direct labor. That means this extra business would absorb idle time and open capacity. I'm for taking this order as long as we don't have to expand capacity to hold it and grow it.

FRED HAMILTON: I still can't see how Atlas can live at those prices. What are they doing?

MIKE ROLLINS: All of this sounds very vague. But somehow we need to figure it out rapidly. If Atlas is really close to capacity as Tim says they are, we have a chance to add business and not push them into adding capacity. That is worth doing if we want the business. But we have to decide fast. I'd like your basis for deciding whether or not we want this incremental business.

Finally, the discussion turned to the subject of adding capacity costing $1.8 million to pursue future high volume, low margin business.

TIM JOHNSON: You have heard my reasoning already, but I want to add these thoughts. First, we must find a way of matching Atlas' price. Otherwise, they will eventually squeeze us out. Second, I can cut sales and marketing costs to 5% on this kind of very large order business, but other departments must adjust their costs. This type of business just cannot carry 11% G & A and other charges.

LINDA JAMES: I'm trying to look at the return on investment if we expand. What volume can we expect to sell of the potential $4 million capacity? Will all of it be at about 24% contribution margin or can we expect margins to get better or worse over time as we try to fill the capacity? Aren't we running a risk of lousing up a sound business by expanding it? Show me how we can get an attractive ROI on this business if we add $1.8 million in expansion.

FRED HAMILTON: I tell you, I'd like to get my hands on one of those new presses. We then would be evenly matched with the best Atlas could have and be sure

they have no advantage over us in direct costs.

TIM JOHNSON: I'll throw in one more set of reasons why I think we need to expand. We think that with new modern capacity we can go after this growing segment of what is now Atlas business. Well, equally, if Atlas should get a surplus of that kind of capacity in their hands, couldn't they come after our large order customers more aggressively than they do now? If we make most of our money on large order business now, as I believe we do, then we must expand and modernize to protect existing good business.

This was one of the few opportunities Mike Rollins had seen in recent years for significant new business growth for Prism. Yet he had questions about the true profitability of the venture. He also had questions about Atlas and its intent. Did they have appreciably lower costs than Prism or were they buying market share? He knew these were critical factors that would determine Atlas' competitive response to a bid on the Greenleaf business and on future business opportunities. How could he get a better handle on Atlas' intent?

As the meeting drew to a close, he wondered how he could resolve the paradox he faced.

QUESTIONS

1. Should Prism enter the high-volume, low-cost printing business represented by Greenleaf's order?
2. How should it evaluate the competition for this business?
3. Should Prism expand capacity?

14

CONTINUOUS PROCESS IMPROVEMENT METHODS

INTRODUCTION

The concept of continuous process improvement (CPI) became popular in industry concurrent with the rise in the popularity of total quality management (TQM). Continuous improvement is the *philosophy of doing business which encourages every member of the organization to continuously strive to serve his or her customer more efficiently.* The customer can be either external, such as a major purchaser of the product, or internal, such as the next operator on an assembly line. *The objective of continuous process improvement is to sustain the improvement momentum within an organization over time and to align improvement activities in support of strategic objectives.*

The challenge of CPI is to promote activities that continuously modify processes, procedures, task content, and process interfaces to better achieve complete customer satisfaction as well as to reduce costs and increase product quality while achieving schedules.

Continuous process improvement also has some limitations as a methodology for achieving long-term business objectives. For example, most businesses are subject to innovations causing changes in the business market. Products are periodically outdated due to new, more advanced entrants into the market. CPI usually does not lead to major technical breakthroughs or innovations.

Therefore, a company which relies exclusively on CPI will be subject to the threat of innovative products capturing large shares of company markets. Conversely, companies that rely exclusively on technical innovation soon lose the advantage to other companies that catch up to the innovation and then continue to refine products and reduce costs through continuous improvement.

In today's markets a company's interests are usually best served by striving to innovate in a market environment where the company is also practicing continuous improvement.

Innovation and continuous improvement require somewhat different approaches. Innovation usually requires a technical staff, business plans, and investment plans. Continuous improvement, on the other hand, usually requires the establishment of a supportive culture, provision of extensive member training in the use of appropriate techniques, and the continuous support of management.

In order to facilitate the implementation of continuous improvement, management must introduce various tools and techniques into all company functions. In Chapter 4, we discussed several individual total quality tools. Management has found that the most efficient way to implement CPI is to combine sets of various tools into improvement methods. Techniques that are appropriate for TQM and for improving manufacturing processes, such as statistical process controls, might not be appropriate for CPI and engineering design. The latter might rely more heavily upon the use of tools that aid in the design of experiments.

In this chapter we focus on how various tools are integrated into the operating philosophy of continuous improvement for the purpose of improving the operating results of a company.

Specifically, we will focus upon improvements in the quality of processes, the cost of operations, and the strategic planning process. To do so, we will concentrate on three improvement methods that are of enduring value to organizations: *benchtrending* (and related *benchmarking*), a technique that facilitates determination of relative strengths and weaknesses of the firm vis-à-vis the competition; *target costing*, a technique for reducing product costs over a product's life cycle, especially design related costs; and *process quality teaming*, a technique for continuously reducing process costs while concurrently increasing output quality.

In practice, management has found that successful implementation of these methods requires a reasonable understanding of the philosophy, focus, and techniques of total quality management. The investment of time is a necessary prerequisite for successful implementation of these methods. Course work, seminars, and practical applications are all necessary for successful implementation.

TARGET COSTING[1]

INTRODUCTION TO TARGET COSTING

When a company wants to introduce a new product, it might test the market to determine the price it can charge in order to be competitive with products already on the market of similar function and quality. A target cost is the maximum manufactured cost for a product. It is calculated by subtracting its expected market price from the required margin on sales.

Target costing is a market-driven design methodology. It involves estimating a cost for a product and then designing the product to meet that cost. It is used to encourage the various departments involved in design and production to find less expensive ways of achieving similar or better product features and quality.

Target costing is a cost management tool for reducing a product's costs over its entire life cycle. This means that there could be several target costs developed during different stages of a product's life. Target costs thus become an important reference point for cost management. Target costing includes actions management must take to: establish reasonable target costs, develop methods for achieving those targets, and develop means by which to test the cost effectiveness of different cost-cutting scenarios.

There are several stages to the methodology.

Conception (Planning) Phase

A company must first establish what type of product it wishes to manufacture based upon its strategic business plans. Here is a typical scenario under traditional, design, costing and manufacturing methods.

Traditionally (before target costing), once the type of product was determined, its development was assigned to the product design department. There, engineers used their endowed knowledge and produced a product that they believed would meet the technical requirements of the market. The product was then sent to the costing department, which assessed the cost of the design and frequently found it more expensive to produce than the market would tolerate.

The design was then returned to the design department with instructions to reduce its costs, usually by compromising its quality. The product design was sent back and forth between the two departments until a consensus was reached. The product was then sent to the manufacturing department, which often concluded that it was impossible to manufacture it in its proposed state. It was then sent back to the design department, and so on. Much time, money and effort were spent before the product reached the production stage. As a result, profit suffered.

Under target costing, a product's design begins at the opposite end. It establishes a price at which the product can be competitive and then assigns a team to develop cost scenarios and search for ways to design and manufacture the product to meet those cost constraints. Several steps must be taken in order to establish a reasonable target cost.

1. Market research should be done to determine several factors. First, it is necessary to establish what the competition is doing. Competitors' products should be analyzed with regard to price, quality, service and support, delivery, and technology. Much of this information can be gathered through public records, by surveying consumers, and by testing competitors' products. After a preliminary test of competitors' products, it is necessary to establish the features consumers value in this type of product, and the important features that are lacking. Such studies are mostly made by surveying consumers and asking them what features they would like to see the product provide. Consumers should also be asked to identify how important the various features are.
2. After preliminary testing, a company should be able to pinpoint a market niche it believes is undersupplied, and in which it believes it might have some competitive advantage. Only then can a company set a target cost close to competitors' products of similar functions and value. The target cost is bound to change in the development and design stages. However, the new target costs should only be allowed to decrease, unless the company can provide added features that add value to the product.

Development Phase

It is unrealistic to expect that a company can simply go out and produce a product at its target cost. In fact, establishing a competitive cost is only a necessary first step in the target costing process. The company must find ways to attain the target cost. This involves a number of steps.

1. First, an in-depth study of the most competitive product on the market must be conducted. The design department should subject these sample products to reverse engineering analysis. This study will show what materials were used and what features are provided, and it will give an indication of the manufacturing process needed to complete the product. From these notions and preliminary data, the design department can start to piece together the competitor's cost structure. By gaining increased information on the different parts that make up the product, the company can also begin conducting a make–buy analysis.

    Once a better understanding of the design has been achieved, the organization can target the costs against this "best" design. But its competition will probably be engaged in similar analysis and will further improve its product toward this "best" design. For this reason, the company is aiming at a moving target. It is necessary when performing comparative cost analysis, and trying to establish the competitor's cost structure, that adequate attention be paid to the competitive advantages of the competitor, such as technology, location, and vertical integration.

2. After trying to identify the cost structure of the competitor, the company should develop estimates for the internal cost structure of its own products. This is most effectively done by analyzing internal costs of similar products already being produced by the company. It should take into account the different needs of the new product in assessing these costs. QFD (see p. 496) is often used to transform customer requirements into internal product and process requirements thus facilitating cost estimation.

3. After preliminary analysis of the cost structures of both the competition and itself, the company should further define these cost structures in terms of *cost drivers*. Using multiple cost drivers to calculate costs gives a better picture of the dynamics of the company's costs, and how they change as the consumption of resources changes. The focus on cost drivers also gives the company a better idea of the manufacturing process involved and helps pinpoint problems. Focusing on cost drivers can help reduce waste, improve quality, minimize nonvalue-added activities, and identify ineffective product design. The use of multiple drivers leads both to a better understanding of the inputs and resources required to produce products, and a better cost analysis through more detailed cost information.

    If the multiple drivers used to generate the internal cost structure are activity-based drivers, this will illustrate the underlying roots of costs, and analysis of these activities can be a major factor in reducing costs to meet the target. Furthermore, target costing can be made more specific, and can be related not only to total costs, but also to individual activities. In other words, the company could target activities as well as costs.

    When enough cost information is available, the product development team is able to generate cost estimates under different scenarios. After this, the designers, manufacturers, marketers, and engineers on the team should conduct a session of brainstorming to generate ideas on how to substantially reduce costs (by smoothing the process, using different materials, and so on) or add a number of different features to the product without increasing target costs. In these brainstorming sessions, no idea is rejected, and the best ideas are integrated into the development of the product.

    In brainstorming sessions, target costs become a motivator that induces the product development teams to find ways to reduce costs and improve the product. Options to reduce costs always exist; it is up to the team to find some of them.

Production Phase

Target costing is most effective in the development and design phases of new products, but it is also useful in the later stages of the product life cycle. In these stages, target costing becomes a tool for reducing costs of existing products. It is highly unlikely that the design, manufacturing, and engineering groups will develop the optimal, cost-efficient process at the beginning of production. The search for better, less expensive products should continue in the framework of continuous improvement.

1. The use of ABC can be enormously beneficial as a tool for target costing of existing products. ABC can assist in identifying nonvalue-added activities and can be used to develop scenarios on how to minimize them. Using ABC, a company can attack the root causes of costs (through cost driver analysis). Target costing at the activity level makes opportunities for cost reduction highly visible.
2. Target costing is also strongly linked to consumer requirements, and tries to identify the features consumers want products to provide. These features could include performance specifications, services, warranties, and delivery. Consumers may also be questioned about which features they prefer in products, and how much they are worth to them. These surveys help management do cost–benefit analysis on different features of a product, and then try to reduce costs on features that are not ranked highly. Using consumers as a benchmark to determine what is important in a product increases a product's competitiveness and provides a guide as to desirable features.
3. Target costing also provides incentives to move toward less expensive means of production, as well as production techniques that provide a more even flow of goods. Just-in-time becomes especially helpful. JIT provides an environment where there is better monitoring of costs and product quality as well as access to ideas for continuous improvement and better production strategies.

BENEFITS OF TARGET COSTING

1. The target costing process provides detailed information on the costs involved in producing a new product, as well as a better way of testing different cost scenarios through the use of ABC. These benefits lead companies to make better selections as to the use of materials, product design, and manufacturing processes.
2. Target costing reduces the development cycle of a product. Costs can be targeted at the same time the product is being designed, bringing in the resources of the manufacturing and finance departments to ensure that all avenues of cost reduction are being explored and that the product is designed for manufacturability at an early stage of development. Traditional methods, as we have seen, address the costs and manufacturability of a product only after the design stage, wasting time and leading to a more expensive, less functional product. In addition, target costing reduces the need to rely on a traditional experience curve to reduce costs.
3. The internal costing model, using ABC, can provide an excellent understanding of the dynamics of production costs and can detail ways to eliminate waste, reduce nonvalue-added activities, improve quality, simplify the process, and attack the root causes of costs (cost drivers). It can also be used for measuring different cost scenarios to ensure that the best ideas available are incorporated from the outset into the production design.
4. Target costing greatly increases the profitability of new products, through promoting reduction in costs while maintaining or improving quality. Target costing also promotes the requirements of consumers, which leads to products that better reflect consumer needs and find better acceptance than existing products.

5. Target costing is also used to forecast future costs and to provide motivation to meet future cost goals. Thus, it provides an attitude of continuous improvement that promotes competitiveness over the long run.

6. Target costing is very attractive because it is used to control costs before the company even incurs any production costs, which save a great deal of time and money (from having to control these costs after the production process is in place). More leverage exists before design and production than after production! Furthermore, target costing may be used continually to control costs throughout the product life cycle.

7. There is one major drawback to target costing. It is difficult to use with complex products that require many subassemblies, such as automobiles. This is because tracking costs becomes too complicated and tedious, and cost analysis must be performed at so many levels. However, because of the difficulty in tracking costs, the ease of incurring cost overruns, and the difficulty of finding the optimum manufacturing processes, traditional systems tend to fail miserably when applied to complex products. Target costing becomes even more useful as the opportunities for refining the process and reducing costs abound.

EXAMPLE OF TARGET COSTING: DESIGN FOR COST-EFFECTIVE MANUFACTURING

In practice, management focuses most of its efforts under target costing on ensuring that the designs for new products result in low-cost, high-quality products consistent with cost targets. Management has learned through TQM that upwards of 80 percent of production costs of many products are the result of design characteristics, many of which are not optimum. As a practical matter, cost targets cannot be achieved without appropriate focus on the concept and developmental process for the product. Design problems can cause the need for extra support costs, can complicate productions processes, can result in low yields, and can require high-cost specialized skill sets. Additionally, the design phase is the most reasonable focal point for new products, since all products must be designed.

The way to reduce these costs is to *design for cost-effective life cycle*, instead of attempting to force cost reductions in manufacturing after the product design is complete. Until recently, appropriate techniques did not exist to allow management to efficiently develop complex products by using cost targeting.

The following example illustrates the major differences between the application of target costing and less effective cost-reduction procedures.

Ace Electronics

Ace Electronics, a western U.S. producer of high-technology equipment for communications, has been producing a variety of products at moderate and low rates of production. Products range from custom hand-held communication units to local networks incorporating bar coding, optical sensing voice entry, and data storage devices. Customers use these communication networks to coordinate specific operations such as a dispatching, inventory control, or point-of-entry transactions.

Recently Ace, along with most of the electronics industry, began feeling the effects of increasing competitive pressures. The main product line produced in a local plant was equipment for a specialized local area network. Some of the components were purchased, but many were designed internally to exclusive specifications. Ace was being underpriced in the market for these products by competitors from Canada who were using assembly capabilities in Mexico. Competitive systems provided faster response time and increased interconnectivity with products from other manufacturers.

Ace management now recognized the need to reestablish themselves in their niche market as the low-cost, highest-functionality product leader. They believed they needed to aggressively lower market prices. Their strategy was to redesign their products to provide more capability at lower prices.

After a quarterly sales review meeting, the CEO invited the engineering director into his office and in a short meeting directed him to implement a strategy to regain business stature. The engineering director was at first unsure how to proceed. Then he remembered some discussions he had recently with one of his engineering managers about a target costing technique that had been applied successfully to the design process for another product.

After a meeting with his managers he decided to establish a design for cost-effective life-cycle (DCEL) team. The team's objective was to meet their established product specifications and cost requirements by concurrently redesigning both the product and associated processes. Although he had never used this technique, he was convinced a DCEL team could apply concurrent engineering tools in a multidisciplinary environment in a way that would meet his objectives.

The particular team he selected consisted of participants from program management, marketing, design engineering, test and integration, manufacturing management, and several potential customers.

The traditional approach to the design of an electronics system involved a sequential process. Marketing and systems engineering would first interact with the customer to determine customer needs. Then systems engineering would work with program management to define a set of requirements. Next, various design tasks would be assigned to personnel from mechanical design, electrical design, and software engineering. Each function would then carry out its task by the most locally efficient means.

Finally, as the design components were integrated, some attention was paid to manufacturability, testability and quality of the product. Unfortunately, at this point, most efforts were dedicated simply to integrating the separate design components into a functionally operational design. In addition, each engineering function was set in its ways, having invested substantial time and effort into its design; it was not ready to admit that their part of the overall design might require revision. This sequential design process usually resulted in the need for redesign as manufacturing proceeded to build the product to established cost objectives.

Cost targeting of the design using concurrent engineering methods such as DCEL approach the design process quite differently. Let's follow the activities engaged in by the Ace design-to-cost team. First, the multidisciplinary team selected by Ace management developed a shared vision for the product's intended use. This effort involved all disciplines but was primarily based on discussions with marketing and the customer. The team then developed a design-to-cost model for all cost elements, both recurring and nonrecurring, for the entire expected life cycle of the product. These cost elements were defined rather broadly. The emphasis was on capturing the cost of the product throughout its total life cycle. The cost elements were refined by the team in an ongoing manner throughout the design and manufacturing cycle.

In the next step, the team related cost elements to each customer requirement for the product as well as to each associated design requirement and to each production process requirement. This task would have been virtually impossible without the use of the quality function deployment (QFD) approach. QFD is a structured approach to design using a series of matrices to relate each product to its design and manufacturing requirements at all stages of the developmental process. For example, a two-dimensional matrix is developed which on one side lists each customer requirement—for example, rapid response time or ease of relocation of terminals. Across the top of the matrix, the specific design parameter that would ensure achievement of the requirement is listed. Below the first matrix, another matrix lists the design requirements on the left side and the specific processes required to meet the design requirement on the other side. The design team continues this process until each customer requirement is "flowed down" to a specific manufacturing process required to achieve that requirement.

Next, the team performed an analysis of risk and its management on the design. This task involved assessing both manufacturing and technical risk. The team used a decision-tree analysis to identify all possible outcomes of their design approach with the associated value of risk parameters, and probability of occurrence of each outcome. The following risk parameters were selected: cost of the product, development time, and functional response time of the completed network. Alternatives were then described which could minimize undesirable outcomes.

Following the risk analysis, the team performed an internal evaluation of the proposed design. This review ensured that the design and associated processes complied with performance and interface requirements. The team verified that the proposed design was adequate and that the proposed processes were sufficiently robust. In this step, the members considered trade-offs among cost, reliability, weight, volume, testability, maintainability, and other pertinent design factors. This process included peer reviews of each element of the design.

This internal evaluation yielded several innovative breakthroughs. Team members emphasized creativity and minimized defensive behavior in order to be most productive. This step was unique compared to the traditional design process. Team members were actually grasping the total design and associated processes before the actual design work was initiated.

The final step began the design process but in an accelerated fashion. It consisted of computer-aided design and rapid prototyping. Because the various disciplines were working together in a team effort, communication across disciplines had been enhanced sufficiently to carry out mechanical and electrical designs concurrently on a CAD system. Three-dimensional simulations were analyzed by the team as in the internal design review. Rapid-prototyping equipment allowed the team to fabricate high-risk structural components that needed further analysis. Finally, manufacturing began concurrently to design and build the required specialized production equipment and was ready to employ statistical control techniques to ensure that the processes achieved the desired high yields.

Results of the team's effort were excellent. They were able to reduce cost projections 55 percent from original cost estimates. The time required to design and produce the initial product was reduced by 40 percent from the previous design effort on a similar system. These results are representative of the relative improvement gained by using target costing and concurrent engineering methods over traditional design and costing methods.

The techniques used in this example are designed to achieve target costs, reduce time-to-market, and improve product value and quality. Management has found that these variables are all important in a successful target-costing effort. Additionally, cost targets must be derived from accurate estimates of the desired market price. The importance of remaining in close contact with market realities cannot be overemphasized. The basic tool used to perform market, operations, or process comparisons is *benchtrending* (or benchmarking), which is discussed next.

BENCHTRENDING AND BENCHMARKING

Benchmarking is the continuous process of comparing products and operations against the strongest competitors or the best practices in similar operations of the best-performing company.[2] Benchmarking is a process that is to be contrasted to the traditional method of establishing current goals based upon the past performance of the organization. Target costing is a specific form of benchmarking applied to product costs.

The benchmarking process consists of four subprocesses:

- Planning the variables to be benchmarked and selecting the companies that are to be used for comparison and the methods to be used to collect comparative data on these companies
- Establishing the current and projected gap in performance between the target company's operations and internal operations
- Communicating benchmark findings to operating personnel and establishing internal goals
- Developing implementation plans

The generic benchmarking process is shown in Exhibit 14-1.

PLANNING

The first step in planning is to ask: What product or service does the unit provide? Candidates for benchmarking include critical success factors, products manufactured, services provided, products or services purchased, and processes used. Of course, major cost variables are also benchmarked under target costing.

The next step in planning is to establish comparable companies on the outside whose performance constitutes best practices. These companies may be competitors, identical functions in the same company, or similar functions in companies out of the industry.

Exhibit 14-1
Generic Benchmarking Process

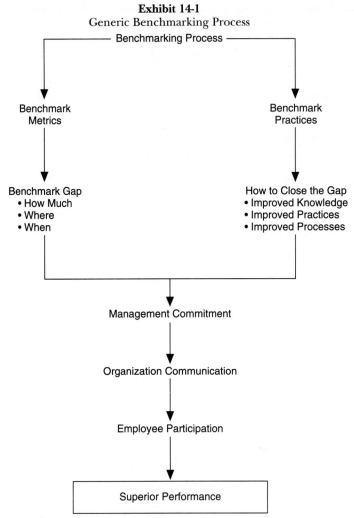

Adapted by permission from Robert C. Camp, *Benchmarking: The Search for Industry Best Practices that Lead to Superior Performance.* Milwaukee, Wis.: Quality Press, American Society for Quality Control, 1989, p. 5.

Firms with the best practices can be identified through both internal and external sources, including automated data bases, libraries, professional associations, industry studies, journals, universities, trade publications, consultants, contacts, professionals in the functions to be benchmarked, seminars, software vendors, and company-sponsored surveys.

DATA GATHERING

The purpose of the analysis phase is to determine the current gap in performance between current internal operations and best practices and to project the likely future gap if nothing is done. Best practices can be established based upon clear superiority, expert judgments, or repeated occurrences of best practices in many settings.

It is important to project the likely future gap, since practices change over time.

A chart showing the projection of the gap appears in Exhibit 14-2. The projected dynamics of the gap appear on Exhibit 14-3.

Exhibit 14-3 shows that the gap may be closed by two types of actions: *strategic actions* and *continuous operating actions.* Specific metrics must be used to measure the gap and to set goals for closing it.

The benchmarking studies usually provide useful information about the gaps in competitiveness for an operation or process at the time the study was conducted. The attractiveness of benchtrending is that the study includes a projection of the critical market and customer structural variables. That is, trending studies attempt to identify customer preference, innovation threats, new entrants, geopolitical impacts, and other market variables critical to the long-term success of the firm.

The techniques associated with benchtrending are similar to the techniques associated with benchmarking but with a new structural dimension. Hence the process is referred to as *benchtrending.* Current benchmarking does try to project gaps forward in time, but it tends to ignore other important variables. Also, current benchmarking techniques do not typically project company strengths and the impact of other market factors over time.

By the time the performance gaps have been closed by a company, the competition has moved forward to create new gaps in other areas. The benchmarking company can remain in a catch-up position indefinitely.

If a company tries to overshoot the gaps in anticipation of improved competitor performance, other factors can arise that affect competitiveness in still different ways. The best bet is to attempt to identify the important trends and appropriately address each as prescribed in benchtrending. For nonstrategic operations or process comparisons benchmarking may be sufficient.

Exhibit 14-2
The Current and Projected Gap

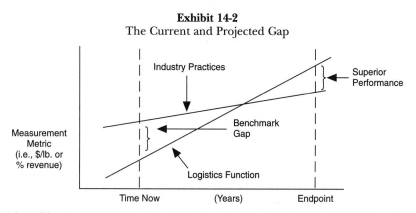

Adapted by permission from Robert C. Camp, *Benchmarking: The Search for Industry Best Practices that Lead to Superior Performance.* Milwaukee, Wis.: Quality Press, American Society for Quality Control, 1989, p. 151.

Exhibit 14-3
The Dynamics of the Gap

10-Year Logistics Productivity Trend

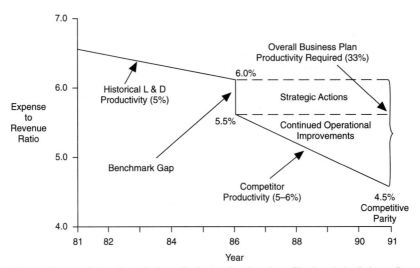

Adapted by permission from Robert C. Camp, *Benchmarking: The Search for Industry Best Practices that Lead to Superior Performance.* Milwaukee, Wis.: Quality Press, American Society for Quality Control, 1989, p. 152.

Management should decide when the extra effort required to perform benchtrending is advantageous and when benchmarking is sufficient. There are two distinct types of benchtrending: *strategic benchtrending* is used to set direction and actions for a business unit, and *operations* or *process benchtrending* is used to compare various functions, methods, processes, and operations to the competition.

Strategic Benchtrending Methods

The purpose of strategic benchtrending is to give direction for a business unit. The first step in planning is to ask: What are the long-term goals and objectives of the unit? Then ask next: Who are the key customers, and what is the market structure? Then ask: What product or service does the unit currently provide? Finally, what variables are candidates for benchtrending?

Strategic benchtrending provides focus for a business unit. Therefore selection of appropriate senior team members is important to the success of the effort. Usually, the study team consists of representatives from marketing, new business development, business management, engineering, and senior manufacturing management.

The first step is to define the market by determining its size, customer preferences, competitors, and relative business position of the company within the market.

The next step is to assess industry direction. This effort involves assessing technology shifts, geopolitical changes, competitor shifts, and consumer changes, as well as potential threats from outside sources.

After the industry structure and pertinent trends are evaluated, the team then determines the strongest current and potential future competitors. Then the study team gathers any performance data available relative to the competition and begins a comparison to current and future performance of the business unit versus the competition.

A performance baseline is established for the business unit, and gaps in performance are estimated relative to the strongest current and projected competition. Additionally, existing strengths of the business unit that need to be defended are identified.

Finally, a set of initiatives is identified which form the basis of an improvement plan to maintain strengths while reducing *projected gaps*.

Strategic Benchtrending: An Example

A company, which we will call P. Sensors Inc., produces an array of guidance and control systems primarily for marine applications. Currently, their main product is a line of sonar and radar units that have an ultrasensitive detector unit that can be programmed to minimize background noise and to present very accurate, high-quality pictures of nearby objects. Although water and air require different frequency ranges, the engineering staff at P. Sensors was able to adapt the principles of design to enhance an array of air and water products.

The basic electronics components for these products were manufactured in Dallas, Texas. Final integration and calibration was done in Santa Ana, California, where P. Sensor's sales force was located (close to a large boating market). Their yearly sales had grown from $20 million in 1974 to $90 million in 1989. Sales revenue leveled off through 1991 and dropped about 10 percent in 1992.

After-tax profits had averaged between 12 percent and 15 percent of revenues, but had dropped to 6 percent in 1992, partly as a result of the recession. Also, rebuilt units and low-cost units were gaining in market share as the technology gap appeared to be closing.

Mr. Parker, the CEO of P. Sensors, was concerned about the recession and was frankly surprised to see the rapid shift that was occurring in the market toward rebuilt and lower-cost units.

Parker did not want to conduct the yearly business and investment-planning process without having a better understanding of the industry, the competition, and any major trends that might create problems for the company in the future.

He therefore decided to perform a benchtrending analysis and selected a senior management team to conduct the study. The first task of the team was to gain an understanding of the market structure. Ten major customers were interviewed: five in California, two in Florida, one each in New York, Maryland, and Washington state.

Additionally, discrete interviews were conducted with direct competitors of new product lines, as well as with service facilities that rebuild units. Trade shows and key suppliers were visited. Finally, internal management was interviewed and a performance baseline was established. Next, the team carefully analyzed and compiled a report for the CEO.

The report listed: a summary of findings, the market structure and trends, key buying factors, competitive performance gaps, a projection of business activity in the event gaps were not closed or strategy was unchanged, suggested initiatives, and finally, market projections if the initiatives planned were implemented.

Let's review the results.

Results

The results of the market analysis are shown in Exhibit 14-4. We note that most competitors had both lower cost and lower performance, but competitor A has moved rapidly from lower to higher performance without increasing costs. This was increasing competitive pressure on the P. Sensors.

Exhibit 14-5 shows the projected market trends for rebuilt, high-cost–high-performance and low-cost–moderate-performance units. The trends show an increasingly cost-conscious customer who will readily opt for lower cost or rebuilt units.

Manufacturing costs were estimated by using pricing data contained in published financial reports and by estimating supplier costs. These estimates showed that competitors with products performing at very high levels were doing so at significantly lower costs than incurred by P. Sensors. This meant that competitors could reduce prices and increase competitive pressure on the company significantly if the company didn't take action quickly.

The total estimated costs for the major product line of P. Sensors is compared to competitor A in Exhibit 14-6. This chart shows the disadvantage for company P not only in manufacturing but also in support, engineering, and administration.

Exhibit 14-4
Market Analysis, P. Sensors Inc.

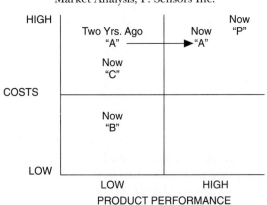

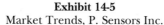

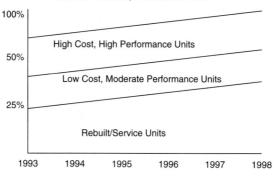

Exhibit 14-5
Market Trends, P. Sensors Inc.

Summary and Initiatives

The marine electronics market is changing rapidly. P. Sensor has relied heavily on technical advantage, but technological leveling is occurring. Customer service is becoming increasingly important. Major market forces are focusing on cost competition. Rebuilt units and prompt service are becoming more important to customers.

The company can continue to do well if it can adapt to the changes occurring in the market. This requires restructuring and a change in strategy. Current competitive gaps must be closed. They are

1. Manufacturing costs (that is, direct costs) are 55 percent more than competitors.
2. Overhead costs are much higher than the competitors.
3. Customer response time is too slow.
4. The company has lost its technical superiority.

Proposed initiatives include:

1. Establish small service center in major markets.
2. Relocate manufacturing to a low-cost site, such as Mexico.

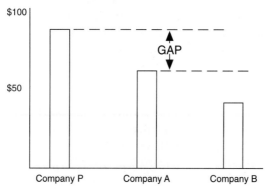

Exhibit 14-6
Estimated Manufacturing Costs
Per Unit, P. Sensors Inc.

3. Restructure ten departments into four market-focused departments and reduce redundant administration.
4. Implement a formal technical development planning process, including an investment plan, target return on investment, and a procedure for conducting risk analysis.

In summary, even though some of the cost data presented consisted of rough estimates it was important to the benchtrending study. When the team became aware that the customer was becoming increasingly more cost sensitive, they turned their attention to obtaining as much relative cost data as ethically possible. Benchtrending studies typically are carried out in this manner. As the team becomes more aware of critical market factors, more effort is expended to understand these specific factors.

If the company follows the recommendations of the study team, a major shift in company strategy and direction will occur.

Process Benchtrending Methods: An Example

In practice there are many occasions when management wants to improve a specific function or process. For example, a unit that produces electronic circuit boards might want to compare its process quality and productivity to several other facilities. This effort involves a process benchtrending study. We shall discuss the steps a typical process oriented unit would use to perform such a benchtrending study.

The most critical step involves gaining a full understanding of the requirements of the customers of the process that is to be benchtrended. These include the important features of the product, the intended use of the product, and any other specific needs of the customer. This step also involves describing the needs to be met from key suppliers.

The second most important step involves gaining a full understanding of process flow. Such an understanding occurs only after careful flow charting of steps of the process, and carefully describing cycle times, procedures, methods, equipment, and quality control parameters.

The third step involves identification and evaluation of the specific objectives of the benchtrending project. For example, the manager of the electronic circuit board department wants to benchmark productivity. The following questions should be asked: Is the variable measurable? Does it relate directly to the core business of the organization? Does the variable address one or more key success factors of the unit? Is the benchtrending project likely to receive support from upper management and the team's peers?

Therefore, the circuit board manager would probably select parameters such as cycle time to produce a unit if schedule is important. The manager might also want to compare test and assembly yields, and support cost per standard work hour if cost is important.

Next, benchtrending partners must be identified. The key to this step is to look for companies that appear to be very competitive even if they are in different markets. For example, the circuit board manager who produces commercial products could benchmark a defense supplier, or a computer supplier. This effort can be facilitated by trade magazine reviews, consulting experts in the field, or by contacting industry associations.

Then the study involves investigating the various practices, procedures, and processes used by competitors. The objective of this task is to determine which practices might be adaptable to your organization. Best practice information can be shared informally among partners, or obtained through investigation and research.

The specific measurement of each process, procedure, or practice is then related to the critical success factors previously determined in the initial steps of the study. Participants share visits and reports, and convert data to common metrics if possible. At this point, usually a relationship has been established with partners sufficiently to get an appreciation for which participants are most competitive and as a result which are worth additional investigation.

Determining specific process gaps and selling the resultant improvement plan to appropriate management personnel usually involve a careful evaluation of current business performance.

A Study of World-Class Operations

A major electronics company was recently interested in determining its relative position in using total quality techniques vis-à-vis other major global companies which all appeared to be worldwide leaders. The list of companies included both competitors and noncompetitors. The company had been making substantial progress in implementing total quality but wanted to better focus its near-term efforts. The company wanted to look for gaps in its own quest for world-class operations and believed that a comparison across several industries would enhance its program.

The following steps were taken:

1. A team of internal quality experts was formed. It involved representatives of different business units all interested in improving operations.
2. Objectives of the benchtrending study, the scope of work, and the time table required to complete the task were defined.
3. Criteria were established to measure world-class operations.
4. An industry survey was conducted to determine potential "best-in-class" candidates.
5. The team analyzed internal operations, using a rating questionnaire and follow-up interviews.
6. A survey was conducted on the processes of world-class companies.
7. Relative ranking of participants was done, and gaps were identified for each internal business unit. Improvement plans were identified by business unit.
8. Progress was compared, best practices were shared, and new surveys were conducted among consenting participants.

The team then decided to benchmark the use of world-class techniques at each of the implementation levels as well to assess which techniques were considered most important for the improvement of competitiveness.

The questionnaire was constructed to obtain answers in the following areas:

Questionnaire and Survey Structure

1. Estimated overall impact on performance from use of total quality techniques.
2. Who provided the leadership for total quality?

3. Improvement objectives.
4. Implementation status—from pilot phase to integrated planning approach.
5. People and team involvement.
6. Extent of total quality training and education.
7. Specific techniques being actively used.
8. Measurement of firms' performance and improvement.

The company was able to obtain agreement from nine external companies and ten internal business units to participate in the study. Here is a list of the characteristics of the companies participating:

Company	Market	Location
1. Company A	Defense electronics	Southeastern U.S.
2. Company B	Food ingredients	Midwestern U.S.
3. Company C	Chemical products	Eastern U.S.
4. Company D	Commercial electronics	Northeastern U.S.
5. Company E	Aircraft components	Northeastern U.S.
6. Company F	Telecommunications	Western U.S.
7. Company G	Engineering services	Southern U.S.
8. Company H	Automotive components	Northern U.S.
9. Company I	Agricultural equipment	Midwestern U.S.

Each company completed the questionnaire and participated in reciprocal visits to further assess the depth of their understanding of the total quality concepts in use, as well as to validate the extent of use of the methods. Additionally, best practices were shared among participants upon request. The functions examined by the team were engineering, manufacturing, all support functions, and information systems.

Rating Method

Each function was scored on a rating system from zero for no implementation, to 400 for complete systematic implementation and integration among all functions, where each function used appropriate quality techniques. Partial implementation such as pilot activities was rated 100. The objective was to get a maturity score and a performance score for each unit and to note which techniques were most successfully used.

Results

Exhibit 14-7 represents the composite ratings for the nine companies. Scores ranged from 250 for company A to 96.5 for company I. This information was used to direct attention toward company A and company B, which were the only firms that scored higher than the company conducting the study.

The next step was to examine the specific aspects of the scores between company A, B, and the company conducting the study to determine gaps in the maturity level of operations. Three areas were found that exhibited significant gaps. Exhibit 14-8 shows these results.

Therefore, the company could now focus the next year's improvement initiatives on these three areas with some confidence that investments made in these three areas would be beneficial.

Exhibit 14-7
External Partner Results
Composite Ratings by Maturity of World-Class Operations for External Partners

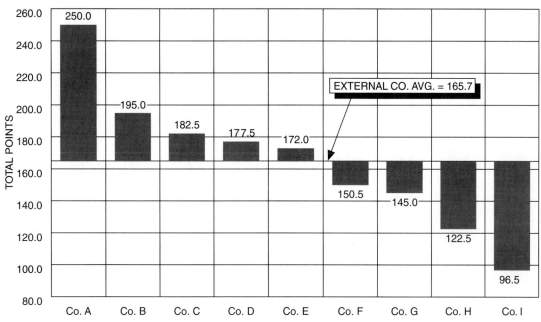

The team then examined the relative scores of the internal units of the organization to determine which units needed immediate assistance in improving its operations. These results are shown in Exhibit 14-9. We note that four of the 10 units scored very close to the two leading companies. One unit actually scored slightly higher than both leading companies. The company can now focus its efforts further by taking the internal gaps in maturity into account.

New Improvement Initiatives

As a result of the benchtrending study the following plans were initiated.

- The new yearly improvement initiative will focus on achieving three objectives. The first is to accelerate the implementation of strategic techniques, such as Hoshin planning and policy deployment.
- The second objective was to implement design of experiments and design to cost methods in the engineering function. The third was for each support function to develop and implement a plan to use appropriate total quality techniques throughout each unit.
- The third objective was to assemble a "red team" of company experts to review and facilitate the plans for the five lowest-rated units.

Summary

We can see that the process benchtrending effort provided valuable insight into the gaps present in an above average company. It is unlikely that the management would have focused on the same specific initiatives or offered help to those units needing assistance without the added visibility of the benchtrending study.

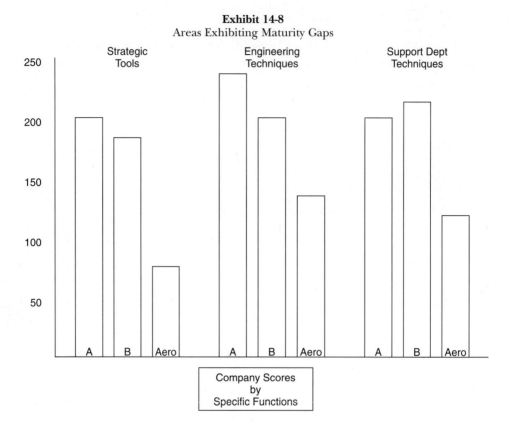

Exhibit 14-8
Areas Exhibiting Maturity Gaps

Benchtrending studies can be time consuming and costly. Therefore, it is important to ensure that the added information is used to actually implement improvement projects.

COMMUNICATION AND INTEGRATION

Formal and informal communications are used to introduce, gain acceptance, and sustain a benchmarking and benchtrending program. Formal methods must be used to acquaint the organization with the logic of the goals in terms of competitive necessity. Benchmark findings must be communicated to people involved and to their management. Informal networks should be established to share examples of successes, to discuss problems, and to provide assistance in attaining goals. Rewards should be established and informal recognition programs instituted to reinforce the need for change and to assist in attaining goals.

IMPLEMENTATION

Action plans are programs designed to attain the goals. Teams are established, tasks are specified and sequenced, resources are applied, responsibilities assigned, schedules established, and results monitored. The normal project control process is established for major goals.

Benchmarking becomes an essential part of both the budgeting and strategic planning processes. It is a method to bring the best practices of the marketplace directly into the long-range planning and budgeting processes. It forces each operation to act as the most efficient and effective market competitor in the industry. In this sense, benchmarking is the next best practice to making each unit a profit center and having it operate according to competitive standards of the marketplace.

Benchmarked goals can be implemented either through the line organization or through specifically organized project teams. When cross functional business processes are being benchmarked, cross functional teams are the most useful organization form.

QUALITY IMPROVEMENTS: PROCESS QUALITY TEAMING

The paradigm for improving quality has changed. Traditionally, quality was seen as requiring extra cost; if one wanted higher-quality products or service, then he or she must make the necessary expenditures to achieve it. Past efforts to better understand how these investments were made, such as the cost of quality method, which separated costs into prevention, appraisal, and failure costs, did little more

Exhibit 14-9
Maturity Rating for Internal Organizational Units

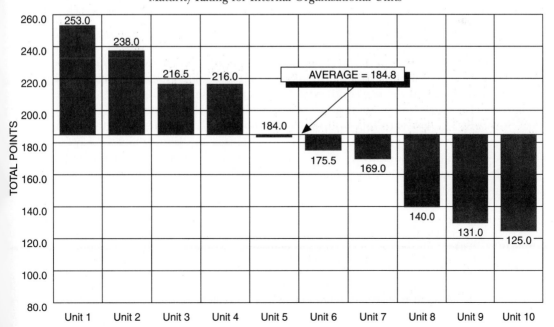

than show management where it was spending money to achieve higher quality, but did little or nothing to help reduce these costs.

> The implementation steps necessary to attain world-class operations tend to follow a pattern. After a company realizes that it is not world-class, members begin developing training programs to convince management that benefits can be achieved if total quality is implemented. Next, a few enterprising managers implement pilot programs to test out tools and techniques. For example, a manufacturing area might implement statistical process controls in a few areas and observe the output yields to determine improvement. The pilot phase continues as more and more isolated pilots are performed. The third step is to implement more sophisticated tools such as QFD, and DCEL on a pilot basis. Finally, the firm integrates all the various efforts into an integrated approach. Strategy is set and operations are carried out using the appropriate technique for each function.

Recently a concept that we shall call *process quality teaming* has become more popular with world-class operational management. The reason is that this method combines several successful total quality techniques into a cybernetic control system with cybernetic features such as feedback loops, action plans, and environmental scanning. We shall examine one common structure for process quality teaming that can be applied with minor modifications to various situations in practice. This method is very effective in improving yields as long as customer and supplier requirements are well established.

The generalized structure for a quality process team is shown in Exhibit 14-10. We note that the control loop involves:

1. Sensing the environment—either the customer or the current yields
2. Detecting the gap between expectations and results
3. Performing an analysis to determine appropriate action
4. Assigning the actions
5. Returning to step 1 by sensing the customer or observing the yields

This cybernetic cycle is repeated over and over, and each cycle usually results in an improvement. The advertised processes that have achieved extremely high yields usually employ some form of this methodology. Hence, we classify this method as one of the key continuous improvement methods.

The structure is applicable to almost any service, production, or support process. The key is to focus on improving the *processes* that are used to produce the output.

A typical response from service units is that the quality process team methodology is applicable only to manufacturers. The following exercise usually changes this perception:

> Services add value to the customer in some way; therefore, a careful examination of the specific attributes of service valuable to the customer, a review of ways to make it easier for the customer to obtain value, and a careful review of ways of improving the customer's pleasure in doing business with the particular unit, usually yield sufficient metrics to make a process quality team worthwhile. A straightforward way of performing this exercise is to ask the customer directly. The important feature of this method is that it facilitates quality improvement without incurring increased costs.

Exhibit 14-10
Quality Process Team Cybernetic Decision Structure

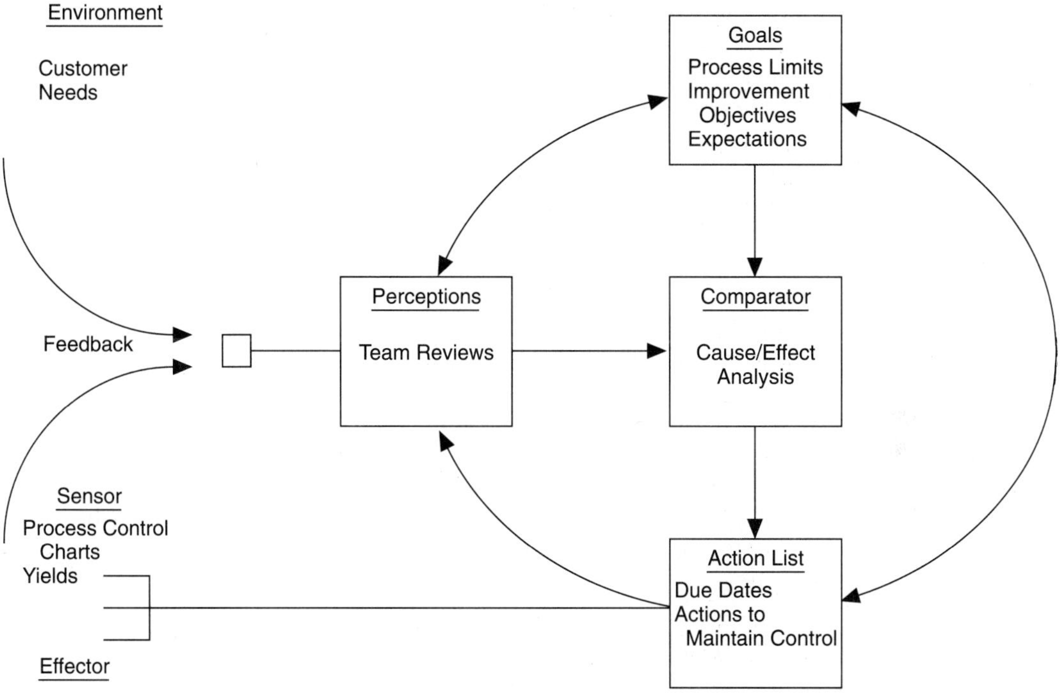

It is instructive at this point to discuss implementation of a process quality team in a specific application. We shall choose a manufacturing unit as an example.

The manufacturing process quality team involves the coordinated efforts of management, supervision, support personnel, and workers. Management first selects the unit, such as a manufacturing department, in which the quality improvement team will be implemented, determines the output to be improved, usually a product or service, and the inputs or suppliers to the process.

Next, the team members are selected. This process is important because it is necessary to select members who represent all key functions which have an impact on the success of the unit. For example, a production unit would select the production supervisor, key workers, process, quality and test engineers, as well as planning and materials personnel.

The next step is to clarify the responsibilities of each function. Too often, for example, the quality control department is held responsible for meeting quality specifications. But the responsibility for quality should lie with the production supervisor and with workers who actually build the product. The rule is: each person is responsible for the quality and value of his or her output to the customer.

The next four steps create a closed-loop corrective action system. The team starts by carefully finding out specific customer requirements, desires, and needs.

This step involves determining the relative importance of each requirement. In some cases, meeting schedule can be absolutely critical. In other cases reliability is extremely important. The goal is to meet all needs but to take extra actions to protect the critical ones.

Next, the process is flow charted. At each step, the product is documented and critical control parameters and associated measurements are documented.

Then appropriate process control limits are established for each step in the process. The output for each major step is inspected *after* actions are taken to ensure that the process is as productive as the system can be under good operating control. This is accomplished for this exercise by ensuring that only trained operators are used, all equipment is in appropriate shape, methods are followed accurately, and the material meets all requirements. Several product units are run, and yields relative to the key measurements are documented. This set of yields establishes the process control limit for each process. Next, the process is run as it normally does, and output yields are calculated for the major steps in the process. The most critical yield problems are then analyzed and ranked by occurrence.

The team then performs cause and effect analysis for the top problems and determines specific corrective action. The teams usually meet weekly to review the current yield losses and to determine if the corrective action works as well as potential new corrective action.

One of the daily actions of a team is to compare the current yields to the process control limits (PCL). This tells local supervision if a local problem has occurred with the operator, method, equipment, or material. Problems of a local nature should be immediately corrected by the supervisor or team as appropriate.

The team continues these actions over and over, continually analyzing low yields, taking actions, and reviewing results. The local supervisor concurrently analyzes any yield problems that exceed the current PCL to insure local statistical control is maintained. The supervisor uses all the appropriate statistical control techniques to accomplish this task. The quality process team then periodically lowers the PCL as system, procedure, or design improvements are implemented.

This combination of constantly improving the process and maintaining local control is the methodology that yields six sigma (near perfect) quality results—that is, complex production processes that function with losses of only a few defects per million chances. Exhibit 14-11 reflects a process quality team report for a typical manufacturing assembly process. This specific team focused on defects affecting an automated soldering process that attached electronic components to a circuit card.

In summary, we repeat the cautionary note that implementation of effective CPI methods can be complex. The implementation involves the liberal use of many total quality tools. Additionally, each tool has limitations to its effective application.

Management must have a good understanding of total quality, and must provide abundant personal support and recognition to achieve the sizable potential benefits from these methods. In the current competitive market, virtually all highly competitive companies practice some form of continuous process improvement.

Exhibit 14-11
Quality Process Team Report
Electronic Module Assembly
Wave Solder Yields

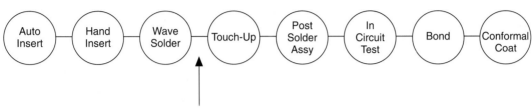

Defects Reduction Control Point (DRCP)

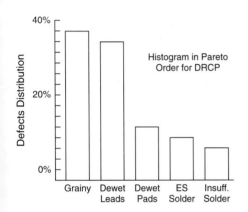

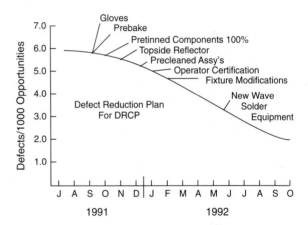

REFERENCES

1. BRINKER, BARRY J., ed., *Handbook of Cost Management*. Boston, Mass.: Warren, Gorham & Lambert, 1992.

2. CAMP, ROBERT C., *Benchmarking: The Search For Industry Best Practices That Lead to Superior Performance*. Milwaukee, Wis.: Quality Press, American Society for Quality Control, 1989.

3. COOPER, ROBIN, AND ROBERT S. KAPLAN, *The Design of Cost Management Systems: Text, Cases and Readings*. Englewood Cliffs, N.J.: Prentice Hall, 1991.

4. COOPER, ROBIN, AND ROBERT S. KAPLAN, *Solutions Manual and Teaching Notes, The Design of Cost Management Systems*. Englewood Cliffs, N.J.: Prentice Hall, 1991.

5. HORNGREN, CHARLES T., AND GEORGE FOSTER, *Cost Accounting: A Managerial Emphasis*, 7th ed., Englewood Cliffs, N.J.: Prentice Hall, 1991.

NOTES

1. We are grateful to our graduate assistant, Nadir Kanbani, for his assistance with the material in this section.
2. The section is adapted by permission from the book by Robert C. Camp entitled *Benchmarking: The Search For Industry Best Practices That Lead to Superior Performance*. Milwaukee, Wis.: Quality Press, American Society for Quality Control, 1989.

Case 14-1
Allrite Superior Interconnections [ALL-SI]: A Benchtrending Study

ALL-SI, a midwestern company supplying various types of connectors and custom-molded interconnects to major manufacturers, was under increasing competitive pressures. The demand for custom connectors had increased over the past several years and foreign competitors were increasingly turning attention to the U.S. custom connector market.

ALL-SI was formed in 1970 to meet a growing need for reliable specialty connectors in the commercial market. With increases in the DOD budget through the 1980 to 1990 time period, ALL-SI began supplying connectors to major defense contractors. Located near a very good midwestern university, ALL-SI management was able to hire good aggressive technical and management personnel.

William (Bill) Phillips, the CEO, was a progressive entrepreneur and invested in innovative techniques, such as plated pressure contacts and gold dot compression bonds, in order to provide the latest technology to the high end of the market. He also developed a bonding technique to form very complex shaped rigid-flex-rigid parts of high quality and reliability.

ALL-SI had reached $80 million in annual revenues in 1988, but revenues then remained flat or decreased somewhat in succeeding years. Profits also dropped because of investments in various technology development projects which were recently initiated to maintain a high-end product position in the market.

Major customers of ALL-SI included Boeing, General Dynamics, Loral, Delco, and Hughes, as well as approximately 100 smaller companies. Because ALL-SI supplied both commercial and DOD customers, they maintained two separate manufacturing departments. One specialized in providing appropriate military specification controls and procedures and the other concentrated on low overhead, fast time-to-market response to customer needs.

There are many suppliers of standard interconnections. ALL-SI does not try to compete with low-cost commodity producers, which usually use offshore manufacturing facilities.

Historically, ALL-SI's main competition came from other engineering-oriented companies which also provide interconnection design assistance to customers. Recently, however, a new source of competition had emerged. Two major high-volume foreign firms began supplying this niche market in order to gain insights into future product trends—seeking a head start on anticipated technology needs and trends.

The current forecast of the entire market projects a 30 percent decline in DOD sales volume and a 10 percent increase in commercial sales. Additionally, ALL-SI had entered the European market several years ago. Because specialty connectors were low volume, they were looked upon as a small commodity item. As a result, they encountered little pressure from foreign governments for local offsets. Foreign commercial sales forecasts were increasing 40 percent per year, but foreign sales accounted only for about 10 percent of ALL-SI's sales. Currently, commercial and DOD volumes were approximately equal.

As Mr. Phillips started his strategic planning process for the next five-year period, he had some doubts about maintaining the current business direction. He felt he had many "irons in the fire" and could have trouble maintaining adequate investment in each area. Therefore, he felt he needed to focus his investments. On the other hand, with the market uncertainties, he did not want to miss a growing opportunity. Thus he felt the need to step back and take a fresh look at both the current market situation and how his business and products fit competitively into the market.

After some reflection, Bill Phillips decided to perform a benchtrending study prior to beginning the planning and budgeting process for the next five-year period.

QUESTIONS

1. Describe how you (as Bill Phillips) would go about selecting the appropriate team members.
2. What initial objectives would you give the team?
3. Set up an action plan to define the current market and assess industry trends? Note that in practical situations markets sometimes are rather difficult to define clearly.
4. What are some of the sources of data you would consider?
5. From the facts in the case, what do you think the performance gaps might be? The strategic success factors?
6. Also, what changes in strategy might the team recommend to Phillips?
7. How well managed do you consider the company? Why?

15

CONTROL OF COMPLEX PROGRAMS I: PROGRAM PLANNING

INTRODUCTION: MUTUALLY SUPPORTIVE MANAGEMENT SYSTEMS FOR COMPLEX PROGRAMS

Complex programs are prevalent in many types of organizational work. They are especially prominent in aerospace and defense; construction; product development; public sector water, transportation, and urban development; strategic thrusts; and in all kinds of team-related activity.

Most of the control concepts and systems discussed in previous chapters are relevant to the control of complex programs. Our purpose in this and the next chapter is to demonstrate how these tools and concepts are applied to complex programs. Exhibit 15-1 identifies the key elements of the MSSM that are required to control complex programs. Many of the issues represented in Exhibit 15-1 have been discussed previously in this book, so we will simply summarize them here and dwell on those that are new.

Complex programs usually require the *matrix organization structure*. This comes about because of the need to maintain strong management oversight over two dimensions of projects: the *program dimension* and the *functional dimension*. Programs are complex and require the total coordination of program activities in order to bring about program control. On the other hand, technological complexity requires the organization to maintain strong functional specialties, and this requires close functional management. Therefore, organizations that are heavily involved in the management of complex programs almost always have some form of the matrix organization in place. The matrix organization was described extensively in Chapter 5.

Exhibit 15-1
MSSM for Complex Programs

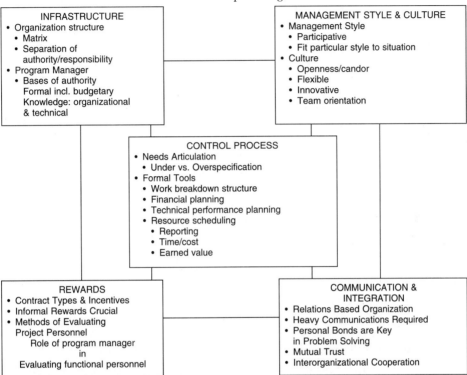

The responsibility of the program manager is much greater than his or her formal authority under the matrix structure, since the functional managers don't report directly to the program manager. The program manager has to make up for this gap by exercising formal authority fully through the use of budget authority. Next, the program manager has to develop informal authority through personal relationships with key functional personnel and through his or her knowledge of the organization and of the technical aspects of the program.

The management style of the program manager has to be participative, since the program manager lacks direct authority over functional personnel. Yet there are situations where the program manager must be more direct and authoritative. Management style should be adapted to the situation faced by the program manager.

Program managers should seek to maintain an open and candid culture. This is required because the number of problems to be solved on a complex program are numerous, and free and open communications are required. The cross disciplinary nature of many of the problems on programs require a team orientation throughout the duration of the entire project. The high-technology characteristics of complex programs create the need for a culture that is innovative and flexible.

The communication and integration subsystem reflects the heavy communications requirement for the successful management of complex programs.

Personal relationships that are related to flow of work and to problem solving are key elements in the management of complex programs. The culture of openness should go a long way toward creating mutual trust among the various parties in a matrix organization.

Many of the issues involving rewards are similar to the issues discussed in Chapter 7. In addition, we have to decide how the program and functional managers interrelate in the task of evaluating performance of functional personnel employed in program work. The most effective systems involve contributions from both functional and program managers in performance evaluation, but this has to be worked out in each organization.

Contracting methods on complex programs range from fixed price to cost plus profit. There are various incentive arrangements negotiated between the program organization and the customer. Incentive arrangements are varied but are usually negotiated based upon technical performance of program deliverables, schedule performance and cost performance.

Informal rewards bestowed among program and functional personnel are especially important in the relation-based organizations that characterize organizations that work on programs. Informal reward systems were also discussed in Chapter 7.

Many of the new dimensions of control systems that are required in the control of complex programs are found in the control process. The control process for complex programs requires a whole new set of new tools and concepts, because program activity tends to be more complex than more traditional activity and this complexity creates the demand for new tools. This and the next chapter are primarily concerned with the systematic development of these new process tools and concepts.

The *program control process* is a procedure for the management of a program that operates through the program control structure to achieve program goals. The process supports the formal relationships embodied within the matrix structure in that it provides information to program and functional personnel upon which their decisions are based. We will show that structure and process must be closely related if program goals are to be achieved.

Differences between processes required for program control and traditional management control occur because of the complexity of program activity and because of the difference in the organization structure employed. Complex programs require tools of equal complexity. Moreover, although each of the traditional functions of management are performed under program management, they are performed in a decentralized manner and are carried out through major changes in responsibility and authority relationships.

Planning and control requirements of complex programs create the need to achieve high levels of coordination without sacrificing efficiency, which in turn leads to the choice of the matrix organization, and this structure requires an information system to support it.[1] The program control process of an organization operates with the assistance of a formal and informal information system. This chapter and the next provide a detailed description of the formal information system and of the control process for the control of complex programs.

Throughout this chapter we shall have occasion to identify the interaction between elements of the process and the matrix organization structure.

THE PROGRAM CONTROL PROCESS

The program control process takes as given the objectives, strategies, and goals of the organization. These strategic choices result in certain quantitative profit goals for most programs, and these profit goals become the focus of the program control process. It is the purpose of the process to move the organization toward these goals.

Exhibit 15-2 summarizes the program control process. The process provides for planning according to goals and requirements and control by exception. As indicated by Exhibit 15-2, the process is initiated by establishing detailed program requirements. As these program requirements are met, we simultaneously achieve the profit goals of the program and of the organization.

Exhibit 15-2
Summary of Program Control Process

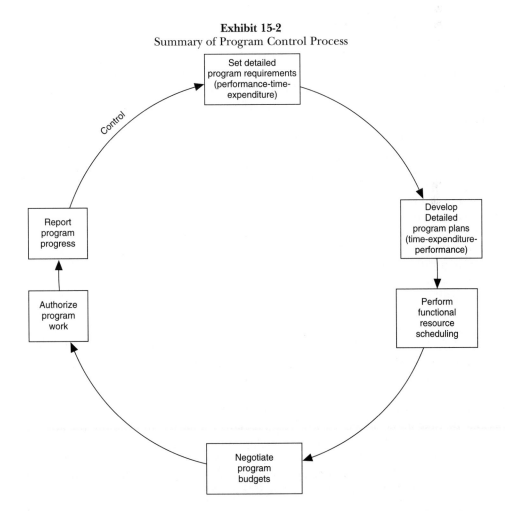

Detailed requirements are established by preparing a means–end breakdown of program work. The means–end analysis is carried out with the work breakdown structure (WBS), which is a hierarchical subdivision of a program. The WBS provides the framework within which we may establish program requirements and prepare detailed plans for the time, expenditures, and performance variables of the program.

Once all end items (purposes and subpurposes) of the program have been established, the next step of the process requires logical, consistent, and coordinated plans to achieve the end items of the program. Network analysis provides a tool for identifying functional activities that must be performed to achieve a lowest-level end on the WBS. That is, putting together the detailed plans for a complex program, we begin at a level of detail where we can identify functional activities with which we have had some prior experience and in this way break up the novel task into its known elements. This process tends to reduce the novelty of a complex program. The level of detail contained in the WBS depends upon the complexity and novelty of the program relative to those to which the organization is normally accustomed. Detail increases on the WBS until known functional activities may be grouped to accomplish lowest-level ends.

Once networks are constructed for all the lowest-end items of a WBS, they may be summarized to form a master program network. The cumulative time estimates so derived may not meet program requirements. Therefore, before leaving the planning process, adjustments must be made to the plan or to the goals and requirements, since a valid plan that meets the goals is the desired outcome. This process of adjusting a plan to meet requirements is called *optimizing* a plan and should be accomplished at minimum incremental cost.

Network plans and the WBS provide the basis for estimating the expenditures of a program. Labor, material, and overhead costs assigned to each lower-level item of a WBS may be derived from estimates of activities contained on networks. By summarizing vertically (that is, up the WBS) all expenditure estimates beginning at the lowest level of the WBS, we may arrive at expenditure estimates for any other level of the WBS. Standard costs do not exist for complex programs and must be established on an individual program basis.

From detailed network plans, constructed for each lowest-level end items of the WBS, detailed schedules are developed in *each* function with the goal of achieving the plans of the program. During the resource scheduling process, functional groups ensure that their contributions to each program are compatible in total with overall resource constraints. Functional managers must allocate their functional resources among competing programs to maximize compliance with all the program plans of the organization.

The crucial difference between the allocation function in complex programs and that of traditional management is that under the matrix structure, it is carried out by functional managers who do not have primary responsibility for any one program, but rather attempt to satisfy simultaneously multiple demands placed on limited resources by all the programs of the organization. Therefore, the *activating function* under the matrix structure is separated from the program planning function, the latter being carried out by program managers.

Financial planning must be done for the total program; yet the financial plan so derived cannot be utilized directly as a budget, since its construction assumes that activities will be accomplished in a manner considered optimum from the point of view of the program. In practice, tasks are rarely performed according to the optimum procedure contained in the plan. The need to balance resources among programs, observe institutional rules, and react to unexpected program change often requires us to accept less than optimum resource allocation. This means that *actual* resource allocation or scheduling decisions can be made only for those activities to be accomplished in a relatively short period of time, since long-range schedules would depend on long-range demands placed on a function by all programs, and these demands cannot be predicted with accuracy. Because resource allocation decisions involve committing resources, we want to ensure that the resources will be required before we commit expenditures to them. For these reasons budgets are established for only small portions of the work and, together with schedules and performance specifications from which they are derived, become the basis upon which program managers negotiate with the functions and authorize work.

It is at the budgeting stage of the program control process that the program manager recovers some of the authority he or she is forced to forgo under the matrix structure, for the manager has control of the resources and they cannot be spent without his or her authorization. The manager must therefore assure himself or herself that the program goals are being met by proposed budgets, schedules, and performance specifications.

Once these allocation decisions are made, a block of work represented on the network, derived from the WBS, is authorized. The program control process then turns to activities of control. Program office personnel are concerned with controlling actual performance to achieve a balance among expenditure, time, and quality variables of a program. Since we are required to achieve balance among these variables, our program control system must contain and process progress information on all three variables.

Unlike the variance analysis system of cost accounting, it is necessary both to calculate variances for expenditure, time, and quality goals and to derive measures of combined variable performance whenever possible. Techniques of variance analysis are available for combining the time and cost variables into planned and actual measures of *value of work performed.* Performance variables are usually introduced in a qualitative way, although in certain circumstances, quantitative performance variances may be defined. In any event the control system must report performance of these three variables versus plan.

The reporting structure should be designed to conform to the means–end breakdown of the program contained in the WBS. It should be possible to retrieve actual versus planned data on each of the three key program variables for any level of the WBS. In addition, it should be possible to summarize information horizontally to obtain detailed planned and actual data for functional organizations.

Program reporting, however, does not in itself produce program control, no matter how well the information system supports the matrix structure. Control is achieved through efforts of human beings. Personnel selection, motivation, and reward structures, together with other behavioral considerations, have as much to contribute to program control as do the detailed formal reporting systems. On the other hand, although formal reporting systems do not themselves produce control, the other structural and behavioral prerequisites for control may be present in the absence of these formal systems, and performance might still be unsatisfactory; well-intentioned and highly motivated but undirected performance usually fails to achieve program goals.

The reporting system is part of the contribution made in the program control process toward directing program effort to problem areas to resolve deviations that occur between program requirements and actual performance. It is not a substitute for a well-designed program control structure and proper organizational behavior; rather, it supports such a structure and behavior.

This brief overview of the program control process illustrates three characteristics of this process that distinguish it from management control processes found in traditional organizations. Planning is accomplished for each program under the assumption that functional resources required will be available upon demand; the plan is therefore a theoretical optimum procedure for accomplishing end items. In practice, each functional organization under the matrix structure must support many programs, which means that optimum plans of all programs can rarely be supported. The primary function of scheduling under the matrix structure is to reconcile these conflicting program demands so as to optimize functional resources.

The planning time horizon of a program is its entire duration, whereas the scheduling time horizon is very short. A short time horizon is necessary for scheduling, since actual resources must be allocated to specific tasks that must be accomplished at a specific time. Organizations undertaking complex program activity can rarely employ a time horizon for scheduling beyond one month because of the uncertainty associated with activities of complex programs.

The second distinguishing characteristic of the program control process is that financial planning is based on a longer time horizon than is budgeting. Financial planning is ordinarily accomplished by using the network plan as a basis for expenditure estimates. Yet, as we have seen previously, the network plan cannot be relied upon as a schedule for performing the work. The schedule may differ from the plan, and this difference may have significant budgeting implications. Budgeting therefore is based upon the financial plan, but it has a shorter time horizon and must be accomplished after resource scheduling decisions have been made.

The third distinguishing characteristic of the process results from the difference that exists under the matrix structure between the task of achieving an optimum plan and that of achieving an optimum allocation of resources. An optimum plan achieves program requirements in the least costly manner, whereas an optimum allocation of resources distributes functional resources, labor, and capital equipment in a way that best meets the needs of all programs while achieving an even distribution of demand for functional resources through time.

Each of these distinguishing characteristics of the process is necessitated by the unique distribution of authority and responsibility found in the matrix structure. The process, therefore, must be adapted to the needs of the structure to facilitate the work of program control.

Now that we have provided an overview of the program control process, we turn to defining each step in the process in detail with examples.

Work Breakdown Structure and Means–End Analysis

Work breakdown structures have been widely employed in defense and aerospace activities, but as with the development of the matrix structure, the WBS has been a pragmatic response to the needs posed by new and complex programs and has not drawn guidance from a body of theory. A broad outline of a theory for the WBS does exist, however, and is described by March and Simon (1978, pp. 31–32, 154, 190–191). Some of the questions regarding construction and the use of work breakdown structures for the elaboration of activities involved in new programs can be clarified by appealing to their work regarding means–end analysis (pp. 190–191):

> In the elaboration of new programs, the principal technique of successive approximations is mean–end analysis: (1) starting with the general goal to be achieved, (2) discovering a set of means, very generally specified, for accomplishing this goal, (3) taking each of these means, in turn as a new subgoal and discovering a set of more detailed means for achieving it, etc.

How much detail should the WBS contain? We again refer to Simon and March (p. 191):

> It proceeds until it reaches a level of concreteness where known, existing programs can be employed to carry out the remaining detail. Hence the process connects new general purposes with an appropriate subset of existing repertory of generalized means. When the new goal lies in a relatively novel area, this process may have to go quite far before it comes into contact with that which is already known and programmed; when the goal is of a familiar kind, only a few levels need to be constructed of the hierarchy before it can be fitted into available programmed sequences.

The objective of the WBS, therefore, is to take innovative output requirements of a complex program and proceed through a hierarchical subdivision of the program down to a level of detail at which groups of familiar activities can be identified. Familiar activities are those for which the functional organizations have had some experience. What is familiar to one organization may not be familiar to another, depending upon experience.

Program complexity is an organization-dependent variable, and the same program may require different levels of detail from different organizations. The primary determinant of complexity is organization-relevant technology. A program that is of relatively high technology for an organization requires more detailed analysis via the WBS than does a program that is of relatively low technology. A program can be complex, however, even if the technology is low relative to what the organization is accustomed to; that is, it may be ill structured with many design options available, organizationally interdependent with many interactions required among functional disciplines, or very large. Therefore, the degree of detail found in a WBS for a given program depends upon the relative level of technology required, the number of design options available, the interdependence of functional activities, and its size.

WBS and Project Management

Exhibit 15-3 provides an example of a WBS for a construction project. The objective of the project is to construct a television transmission tower and an associated building for housing television transmission equipment.[2] As a contractor for this project, we are given specifications for both the tower and building by our customer. We set out to prepare a proposal for this task that will be evaluated by the management of the television station.

As we see from the WBS, the main purpose or end item of the project (that is, level 0 of the WBS) is provision of the TV transmission system. The primary

Exhibit 15-3
WBS for TV Transmission System

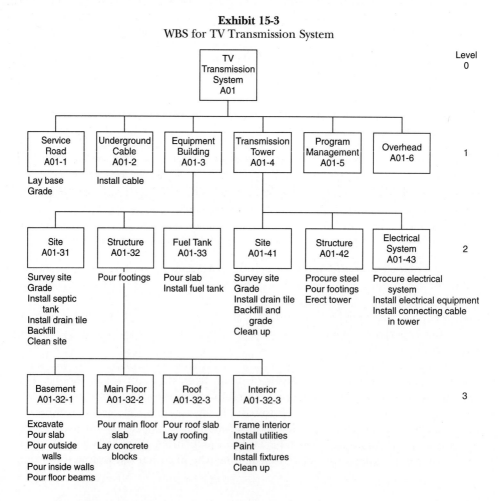

means for providing this system are shown in level 1 of the WBS. That is, to complete the system we must provide the TV tower, the equipment building, the cable connecting the two, and a service road between the building and the tower. These level 1 items are means for constructing the TV transmission system, but they are also ends unto themselves for the level 2 items. For example, to construct the tower, we must prepare the site, erect the structure, and install the electrical system. These level 2 items are means for accomplishing level 1 ends, which themselves were means for achieving the level 0 end.

Similarly, to provide an equipment building, we must prepare the site, provide a structure, and install a fuel tank. These level 2 WBS ends are also means for constructing the structure of the equipment building. Furthermore, to provide a structure for the equipment building, we must provide a basement, main floor, roof, and interior. These level 3 WBS items are means for accomplishing the building, but also ends unto themselves.

For each level 1 WBS item we proceed to elaborate means and ends until we arrive at means that are very familiar tasks, at which point we cease factoring the project into more detailed means. The amount of factoring done on a given end item and project therefore depends upon the relative novelty associated with the project. Notice that for the service road, we proceed immediately to final means (that is, lay the base and grade) to achieve that end. Those two means are familiar activities to the organization, and the factoring thus stops for that end item at level 1. Likewise for the level 1 WBS item "underground cable," we simply insert one activity ("install the cable") at level 2 and that ends the means–end chain for the cable.

Once we reach familiar means, we identify these as activities rather than ends, simply because they are final means, and, although our detailed planning may separate each of these activities into two or more tasks, there is no utility in identifying more detailed means. All other WBS elements except at level 0 serve as both means and ends. Our detailed network planning begins at the level of the WBS where these final means or activities are identified. Network planning thus begins at different levels of the WBS for various level 1 ends. For example, network planning will begin at level 2 for the service road, but at level 4 for the equipment building.

The elements of Exhibit 15-3 that remain to be explained are the level 1 ends "program management" and "overhead." Strictly speaking, we define our programs in terms of identifiable ends or outputs until we get down to the very last level, at which point we identify functions or activities; these latter activities are inputs rather than identifiable outputs. Because the input of project management is primarily that of planning, decision making, and control, it cannot be traced directly to any one WBS item, but rather must be assigned directly to the project itself. We accomplish this by making it a level 1 item so as to include within the WBS framework all the resource costs associated with the program. Similarly, when deriving the WBS, we initially trace only those means that are directly related to each end item. Yet we also want the WBS to provide an accounting framework for accumulating total project costs. Therefore, we assign all indirect resources to the level 1 item called "overhead."

Once the WBS is defined, we can assign an account code structure to it. The purpose of the account code structure is to provide unique identification for each end item of the WBS to serve as the basis for the cost accumulation and reporting system of the project.

Any combination of alphabetical and numerical characters may be used; the only real requirement for the identification system is that each end item contain in its identification the account letter and number of its parent. For example, the identification assigned to the TV transmission system is A01 at level 0 of the WBS. The equipment building is identified as A01-3, indicating that its parent is the TV transmission system and that it is the third, level 1, end item. The building structure is identified as A01-32, indicating that it is part of the equipment building (A01-3), which itself is part of the TV transmission system (A01). The account code structure proceeds down to the last end item of the WBS. Functional activities below lowest-level ends of the WBS are assigned resource code numbers or letters for purposes of estimating and reporting financial expenditures.

Planning to Achieve Program Goals

The means–end analysis represented by the work breakdown structure is carried to a level of detail where relatively familiar activities may be identified to accomplish each of the lower-level items on the WBS. That is, our means–end analysis proceeds to a level of detail where the lowest-level means for accomplishing ends are among the rather standard activities of functional organizations. Once these means have been classified in standard organizational terms, the ends that they serve can be accomplished with minimum difficulty. Each of the lowest-level ends usually requires the completion of a number of interrelated tasks or activities by multiple functional disciplines. Often these different functional disciplines of an organization engaged in complex programs interact more or less continuously with each other.

To plan and control these interrelated activities to achieve program goals, we must define each activity and identify their interrelationships for each of the lowest-level ends. After accomplishing this detailed planning for each lowest-level end, we must identify properly the interrelationships among these ends. Once these two tasks are complete, we have completed the task of identifying the activities required to achieve program goals together with their interrelationships. After we have identified the means for achieving lowest-level (that is, the most detailed) ends, it is only a matter of summarization to arrive at plans to achieve the higher-level ends.

In other words, the WBS and networks allow us to complete the definition of the means–end chain for our complex program. Without this detailed planning, program work is likely to be characterized by random activity and will lead to bottlenecks among functional resources. The resulting confusion is likely to occur regardless of the organization structure employed. The WBS and networks bring to the program tools of planning, coordination, and communication that are of a complexity equal to that of program needs.

The basic approach to detailed planning in the program control process is provided by network analysis. A network is a diagrammatic model of the procedure in which detailed activities of an end item are to be accomplished. Once constructed, it becomes the basis for estimating time and resource requirements.

Network Construction

To begin, let us refer to Exhibit 15-4, a typical network for an end item of a WBS. Notice that this simple network consists of interrelated lines, some related serially to one another and others proceeding simultaneously or in parallel. The lines of the network are called *activities*, and they represent the tasks or subtasks identified at the lowest level of the WBS. These activities consume functional resources.

Each activity of a network is identified uniquely by two circles or *events*. Each event represents a point in time only and therefore does not involve the use of resources in any way. The purpose of an event is to indicate the *start* or *completion* of an activity; it merely represents an instant in time.

Each activity, to be identified uniquely, requires a "start event" and an "end event," formally known as a *preceding* and a *succeeding* event, respectively. An activity may share either a preceding or succeeding event with other activities, but not both.

Detailed network analysis begins at the lowest-level means on the WBS. We proceed to establish a diagrammatic plan for accomplishing each of these lowest-level end items. Small projects may require only one network. Large projects often require a network for each of the lowest-level end items of the WBS.

The initial "pass" at network construction should proceed under ideal assumptions regarding the order and interrelationships among activities of the network. That is, if a given activity may be accomplished either in series or in parallel with another, it is customary during the network construction phase to use the more conservative approach, which ordinarily implies a serial relationship between the activities.

Each event on the network is numbered. Numbers are placed on the network consecutively beginning at the start of the network and proceeding toward

Exhibit 15-4
A Typical Network with Event Numbers

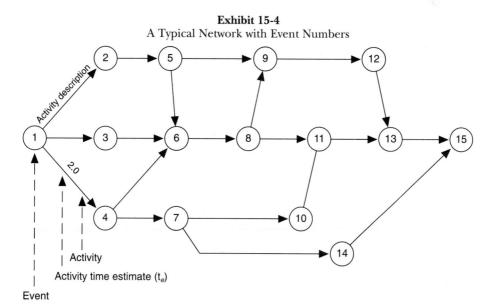

the end. The order of the numbering system of the network is left to right and top to bottom.

It is useful to distinguish two special types of events: *nodes* and *burst points*. A node is an event that serves as the succeeding event for two or more activities. Events 6, 9, 11, 13, and 15 of Exhibit 15-4 are therefore nodes or nodal events. Events that serve as preceding events for two or more activities are called burst points. Events 1, 4, 5, 7, and 8 are burst points. Although none appears in Exhibit 15-4, there are events that are both nodes and burst points.

A node represents the point of completion of multiple activities, any one of which may be complete without the node itself being complete. All activities of a node must be complete for the node to be complete and for the activity succeeding the node to begin. The node is considered complete, therefore, when the last activity of the node is complete.

A burst point represents the start event for multiple activities, which themselves proceed in parallel. Each activity for which the burst point serves as a start may proceed to completion while other parallel activities proceed at their own pace toward completion.

Events that are neither burst points nor nodes simply connect activities that must proceed serially or consecutively, one dependent upon the other. Events 2, 3, 12, and 14 are examples of these serial events. One activity precedes such an event and one activity succeeds it.

If all the activities of an end item in an optimum arrangement flow purely in series, there is hardly any need to consider network analysis as a planning tool. The task simply cannot be represented by a network. Therefore, burst points and nodes are the hallmark of networks and of any task for which accomplishment proceeds both in series and in parallel.

With this as background we can describe Exhibit 15-4 completely. Event 1 is the start event for the network. Activities 1–2, 1–3, and 1–4 may begin immediately and simultaneously. Activity 2–5 is serially dependent upon 1–2, and therefore cannot begin until event 2 is complete. Activity 5–6 is serially dependent upon 2–5 but may be completed without event 6 being complete, for event 6 is complete only when activities 5–6, 3–6, and 4–6 are *all* complete. Similarly, activity paths 1–3, 3–6, and 1–4, 4–6 proceed in series to node event 6.

Activities 4–7, 7–10 and 10–11 are serial. Activities 7–14 and 14–15 represent a path, parallel with 7–10 and 10–11 from burst event 7, which itself proceeds serially. Activity 6–8 may begin only after the completion of node event 6. Event 9 is a node that cannot be complete until both activities 5–9 and 8–9 are complete. Similarly event 11, a node, requires the completion of activities 8–11 and 10–11 for its completion.

Event 13 is a node requiring the completion of activities 12–13 and 11–13 for its completion. Activity 12–13 is serially dependent for its start on 9–12. Finally, the network is complete when event 15 is complete, which, since it is a node, requires the completion of activities 13–15 and 14–15.

Notice that activities of both nodes and burst points share a common event number. At burst points all activities have identical preceding event numbers; at nodes all activities share common succeeding event numbers.

A final consideration regarding the structure of networks is size. The amount of detail included in a network and the scope of the task modeled determine the size of the network. Although the question of size cannot be answered definitively for a given application, two principles may be used to support judgment regarding the question. First, the network is only a model of a complex program; as such, it should capture the essence of the task while not distorting reality in a significant manner. We must realize that the reality of program activity is too complex to be captured in its entirety by a network without the network's becoming unmanageable. The real test is: How significantly does the structure of the network distort program reality? If it captures the essence of the program, it is good enough.

The second principle involves the time duration of activities on the network. That is, how long should the average duration of activities be on our network? Time duration of an activity in general should be inversely related to its organizational familiarity. This principle follows directly from our discussion of the means–end approach to program definition. Unfamiliar tasks should be subdivided until relatively familiar subtasks appear. Therefore, the average duration of activity times should be inversely related to their familiarity.

Now that we have examined the structure of a network, we may proceed to establish time estimates for accomplishing the work represented on the network.

Network Calculations

Exhibit 15-5 is our sample network with time estimates included. For now, we deal only with single time estimates for each activity. Each of these estimates is called the expected completion time (t_e) for an activity.

Time estimates appearing below each activity in Exhibit 15-5 are given in weeks and tenths of weeks. They are established on the assumption that the proper resources will be available when necessary to perform the activity in the optimum manner. That is, in arriving at each time estimate, we assume not only that the proper level of resources will be available but also that the task will be accomplished at the minimum total cost.

This planning premise is necessary to avoid confusion in the planning process. It requires that we estimate the time requirements for each activity under the assumption that all scale economies or efficiencies will be achieved. This means that just the most efficient amount of labor, material, and facilities will be used. Although we know that complexities of the real world often prevent us from performing each activity in the most efficient way, there is no alternative standard assumption that will facilitate the planning process as well as this one.

The objective of the calculation procedure of network analysis is to compute expected times, scheduled completion times, and slack for each event of the network. In making these calculations, node and burst point events play the dominant role.

The expected completion time for an event is the sum of expected completion times (t_e) of individual activities on the longest path to that event. Therefore, at each node, we take the longest path to that node as the expected completion time T_E for the node event. The expected completion time becomes the basis for

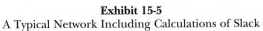

Exhibit 15-5
A Typical Network Including Calculations of Slack

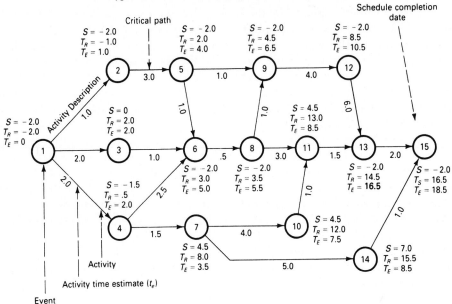

calculations of T_Es on succeeding events that are connected to it. The expected completion time for an event is also the expected start time for succeeding activities. For example, event 6 is a node. There are three paths flowing into event 6 (that is, 1–2, 2–5, 5–6; 1–3, 3–6; and 1–4, 4–6). The expected completion time for event 6 also is the longest of the three paths. The expected completion time for event 6 also is the *expected start time* for activity 6–8.

To find the T_E of each path leading to event 6 we simply sum t_e for all activities on that path. Notice that even though we defined T_E as the expected completion time of an event, at a node T_E is associated with the longest path leading to the node, which implies that we must calculate all path T_Es and compare them. The path calculations to a node event that are shorter than the longest path are ignored in calculating the T_E of the event, but they are used later to make slack calculations. The lower path has a T_E of 4.5 weeks; the middle, 3.0 weeks; and the upper, 5.0 weeks. Therefore, the longest path to event 6 is the upper path; event 6 thus has a T_E of 5.0. The events preceding 6 are all serial except event 1. All serial events have expected completion times equal to the sum of the T_E of the preceding event plus the t_e of the preceding activity.

Since we move forward in our calculations, burst points cause no difficulty in calculating T_Es; we simply take the T_E at the burst point and sum forward. The T_E at the initial event of a network is always zero.

To summarize, expected completion times for each event are the sum of the longest path leading to that event. The only difficulty created in calculating T_Es is at node events, since there we must choose the longest among alternative T_Es, which then becomes the basis for future forward calculations in the network. You should be sure that you can follow the calculations of T_Es to the end of our small sample network.

Once expected completion times have been calculated for each event of a network, we may compute required times for each event. To begin, we either must be supplied with a scheduled completion time for the entire network, or we must be willing to assume that the T_E for the end event is suitable as a scheduled completion date. Ordinarily we are supplied with a schedule completion date derived from customer or contractual requirements. Once we have a scheduled completion date, we proceed backward in our network to compute required dates for internal events (that is, all but the end event). We label the scheduled date T_s and internal required dates T_R.

Prior to immersing ourselves in the details of T_R calculations, it is useful to gain an intuitive feel for the overall process. Essentially, we begin with a scheduled end date for the last event and determine for internal events the required time at which we must start each one to arrive at the end event precisely on schedule, given the t_e of each activity on the path from each internal event to the end event.

In deciding how to arrive at the end event from a given internal event, we encounter a problem at burst events, such as event 1 or 8. At burst events we have two or more choices of paths to the end. This problem is resolved by choosing to follow the longest path from an internal event to the end event; this is quite logical, since to move from an internal event and reach the end event on time, we must make provision in our T_R calculations for the longest route from a given event to the end.

Required dates at each burst event should make provision for the longest path from them to the end to provide an accurate assessment of the date at which the activities on the longest path emanating from a burst event must begin to arrive at the end event on schedule. After all, a job cannot be complete until all its activities, even the most time consuming, are complete.

Required dates for internal events are therefore computed by subtracting the t_es of activities immediately succeeding a given internal event from the required date of the succeeding event of the activity, unless we are considering a burst event, in which case we must choose the earliest required date computed from the multiple activities emanating from it.

We turn again to Exhibit 15-5 to illustrate and gain practice in these calculations. Beginning as we must at the end event, we are given a T_S of 16.5 weeks for event 15. Therefore, the T_R of event 13 is 14.5. Similarly, once the T_R is computed for event 13, we proceed to compute T_R for events 12 and 11 by merely subtracting the respective t_e. The process continues as simple subtraction until we arrive at burst event, such as events 1, 7, and 8.

Consider event 7. The required start time for activity 7–14 is found by subtracting from the required date of event 14 the t_e of activity 7–14, producing a required time of 10.5 weeks. The required start time for activity 7–10 is found to be 8.0 weeks, again by subtracting its t_e of 4.0 weeks from the required date of 12.0 weeks of its succeeding event (that is, event 10). The T_R for burst event 7 is 8.0, the smaller of the two activity required times, and is determined by activity 7–10. The logic of this is straightforward. Event 7 must be complete at 8.0 weeks to provide just the time required by the longest path from event 7 to the end of the network. The longest path from event 7 is 7–10, 10–11, 11–13, 13–15, which has a cumulative expected completion time of 8.5 weeks; when this is added to the required completion time of event 7 of 8.0 weeks, it yields 16.5 weeks, precisely the scheduled completion time of the entire network.

To summarize this section, required completion times for internal events are derived from the scheduled completion date of the end event by subtracting from the scheduled date expected completion times of the longest path from that internal event to the end event. To implement this procedure, we simply subtract from the required date of an event the expected completion times of all activities flowing into it and assign the resultant required time to the *preceding* event. If a burst event is involved, we must choose the smallest required time of all activities for which the burst event serves as the predecessor as the required completion date for the burst event. You should trace through the calculations of all other required dates in the sample network.

Slack Calculations. Slack is the difference between the required T_R or scheduled T_S completion date of an event and its expected completion date. It is computed for each event on the network. Slack calculations provide a quantitative measure of how closely the plan represented by the network meets the time or schedule requirements of the program. Negative slack implies tardiness and positive slack, earliness; zero slack indicates that the event is expected to be completed on time.

The longest path of activities from the beginning of a network to the end is the one with the least amount of slack algebraically. That is, the longest path has either the smallest amount of positive slack or the largest amount in terms of absolute value of negative slack. This makes sense intuitively, since the longest path of activities from the beginning to the end determines the expected completion time of the end event, and there can be no path of greater length in the network. Each event off the longest path has more slack algebraically than each event on the longest path.

To find the longest path we simply trace back in the network those connected events that have identical slack, beginning at the end event. Since the T_E of event 15 is 18.5 weeks and the T_S is 16.5 weeks, event 15 has a slack of -2.0 weeks. We find that event 13 also has a slack of -2.0 and is connected with event 15 by activity 13–15; it too is on the longest path of the network. Proceeding backward, we find that events 12, 9, 8, 6, 5, 2, and 1 all have a slack of -2.0 and are connected to one another. Therefore, the activity path 1–2, 2–5, 5–6, 6–8, 8–9, 9–12, 12–13, and 13–15 is the longest path in the network. This path causes the plan to be 2.0 weeks late. It is therefore called the most limiting or *critical* path.

Slack on this most limiting path is constant, because the t_es that we accumulate to produce a T_E of 18.5 for event 15 are the same t_es we subtract from the T_S of 16.5 to arrive at T_Rs for each event on this longest path. The path that produced the greatest expected completion time on the network is also the one that produces the earliest required times. The slack on this path is therefore constant throughout.

Slack is only a meaningful measure given for a path, not a single event. For example, the events on the critical path have a slack of -2.0, indicating that the entire path is 2.0 weeks late. Given the T_S of event 15 and given the t_es of each activity *on the path*, each event may be said to be 2.0 weeks late, but only because the whole path is 2.0 weeks late. This aspect of slack will be very important to us later.

Although we have identified the most limiting path, other less limiting paths also must be identified, for if we are not careful, we may reduce the T_E on the most limiting path only to find that another path has become almost equally limiting and that our reductions were only partially beneficial.

To isolate the second most limiting path, we must look for an event with the next smallest (algebraic) amount of slack. We notice that event 4 has -1.5 weeks, and we now must identify the activities of this path, since it is the second most limiting.

Clearly activity 1–4 is on the second most limiting path, because it has a T_E of 2.0 and a T_R of 0.5, but does the path stop there? It does not. Notice that the T_E at node event 6 is 5.0 weeks. Recall also that the T_E at node 6 was caused by the upper path (1–2, 2–5, 5–6). The T_E of the lower path (that is, 1–4, 4–6) is 4.5 compared with a T_R at event 6 of 5.0, thus yielding slack of -1.5 for the entire path 1–4, 4–6. Therefore, to calculate slack at a node event for noncontrolling paths, we must compare the T_E of noncontrolling paths with the T_R at the node.

The importance of identifying secondary paths cannot be overestimated. For example, if any activity or series of activities on the critical path prior to node event 6 is expedited by 2.0 weeks in an attempt to eliminate all negative slack from the network, it will only reduce the T_E of the network by 0.5 of a week, simply because the path that was not reduced (that is, 1–4, 4–6) now becomes dominant at node event 6. The critical path forward of node event 6 will remain the same, but now with slack of -1.5 instead of -2.0. We can only eliminate two weeks of slack at node event 6 by cutting both the upper and lower paths, the upper by 2.0 weeks and the lower by 1.5 weeks.

In a similar manner, we can find the slack associated with each activity and event of the network. The slack for activities emanating from burst points is found by comparing the T_E of each activity with the T_R of its succeeding event. Normally at nodes, the slack of all but one activity differs from the slack at the event. It is a simple matter, however, to compute the slack of the other activities.

Although it is not crucial for purposes of network planning, it is useful at this point to differentiate between slack and free slack. For purposes of resource scheduling it is important to know if slack on an activity leading into a node is different (that is, greater) from slack at the node. If the slack of the activity is greater than that at the node, the difference represents free slack or, in the terminology employed by CPM, free float. Free slack is most useful for purposes of scheduling. It tells the functional manager by what amount he or she may extend an activity without affecting slack calculation on any activity or event that lies ahead of the node event.

An Application of Network Analysis

We illustrate the process of network planning by constructing a network for the TV transmission system whose work breakdown structure was illustrated in

Exhibit 15-3. We use that WBS as the basis for network construction. From the WBS we observe that most of the tasks to be performed are associated with either the equipment building or the transmission tower. Therefore, we shall draw two networks, one for the building and one for the tower. Since the cable and the service road involve only a few tasks, these activities will be integrated into the other two networks.

The network for the building is given in Exhibit 15-6. To draw the network plan for the building, it is necessary to identify the interrelationships among the lowest-level means on the WBS. We have assumed a set of interrelationships and have drawn the network accordingly. In this simple example, it is quite easy, although by no means trivial, to define optimum relationships among activities from the WBS. On more complex projects, the interrelationships must be ascertained by the planner from specialists in each functional discipline.

Notice the dashed lines that appear on this network for activities 5–6, 10–11, and 12–13. These dashed lines are called *dummy activities* and have two purposes in network analysis. First, the dummy activity is used to achieve unique numbering between parallel activities that originate at a common burst point and end at a common node. Dummy activity 5–6 is inserted for that reason. If it were not present, we would have two activities numbered identically (that is, 4–6), thereby violating the uniqueness requirement. Second, the dummy activity is used to show a dependent relationship between activities where this dependency *does not consume resources*. For example, before we can fill in the foundation and grade it, the roof must be on the building and the drain tiles must be installed. Activity 10–11 depicts the dependent relationship between the fill work on the building (activity 11–14) and the installation of the roof (activity 9–10). Yet no resources are consumed by this dummy relationship. Dummy activities should be kept to a minimum in network construction, but often they are essential. We turn now to the network for the transmission tower shown in Exhibit 15-7. The transmission network is quite straightforward with three notable exceptions. First, the dashed lines that flow into events 6 and 9 depict the interrelationships among the individual networks of the TV transmission system. Installation of the connecting cable between the tower and the building (activity 6–7) cannot begin until the tower is up (activity 5–6 of Exhibit 15-7) and until the foundation of the building is poured (activity 3–4 of Exhibit 15-6). Therefore, the dummy activity flowing into event 6 of Exhibit 15-7 starts from event 4 of Exhibit 15-6 and shows this physical dependency.

Second, final acceptance testing of the entire transmission system is shown on Exhibit 15-7. The start of acceptance testing not only requires the tower to be complete, it also requires the completion of the building and the service road. Therefore, we have two dummy activities showing these dependencies, one from Exhibit 15-6 and the other from Exhibit 15-8. Exhibit 15-8 contains the two serial activities involved in laying the service road.

To summarize, we have constructed networks for each of the level 1 ends of the WBS. Because the connecting cable is a single simple activity, we have included it on Exhibit 15-7 along with the tower. Moreover, the connecting road is a simple serial task, as shown in Exhibit 15-8.

Exhibit 15-6
Network for TV Transmission Building

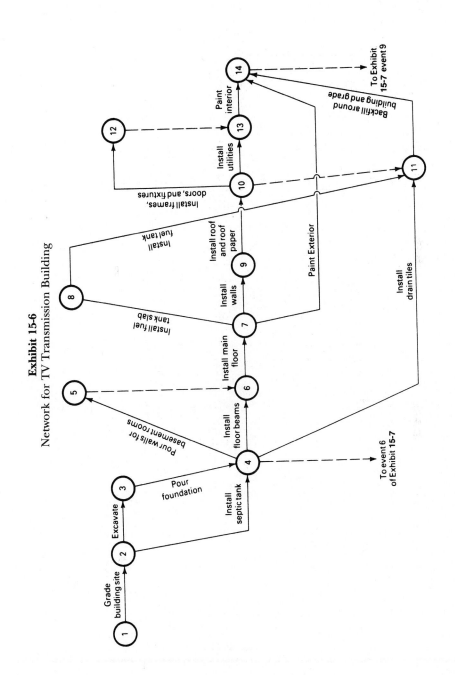

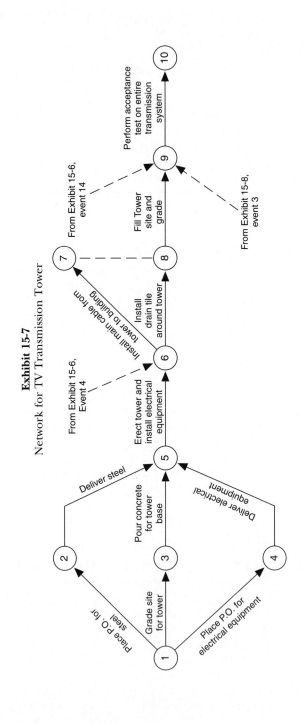

Exhibit 15-7
Network for TV Transmission Tower

Exhibit 15-8
Activities for Connecting Road

The networks constructed for this project are very simple, but realistic. Since they are quite simple, it is manageable to combine them into one integrated network for the project. An integrated network for the entire project should also contain an activity for contract negotiations with the customer. Exhibit 15-9 is such an integrated network, and we shall use this network as the basis for our time calculations. It is not always possible on large projects to combine individual networks into a complete project network. In those cases, we must let a computer program provide the integration of networks for us.

Network Calculations in the Integrated Network. Exhibit 15-9 contains time estimates and calculations for the integrated network. Time estimates are given in weeks and tenths of weeks. The entire network has an expected completion time of 24.0 weeks and a scheduled completion time of 20.0 weeks. The critical path has slack of −4.0 weeks and consists of activities 1–2, 2–6, 6–8, 8–13, 13–16, 16–18, 18–19, 19–21, 21–22, 22–23, and 23–24. Essentially, the critical path contains activities pertaining to the equipment building. Activity 8–11, another activity pertaining to the equipment building, has slack of −3.0 weeks and is therefore the second most critical path.

The electrical tower is not in much better shape, either. It contains the third most critical path of −2.5 weeks and includes activities 1–3, 3–7, 7–9, 9–15, and 15–23. You should trace through all other slack paths on the network before proceeding further.

Although we now have a network for the entire project, before we may consider this a valid plan for the TV transmission system, we must eliminate all the negative slack on the network in a nonarbitrary manner, so that the most limiting path has no less than zero slack. We turn now to procedures that may be employed to solve the problem of an invalid plan. We use a simple example to illustrate the principles.

Translating an Invalid Plan into a Valid One. Assuming that the time estimates provided on a network are correct, we may proceed in three ways to produce a valid plan. First, we may consider taking more risk in the way we carry out our activities. That is, we might evaluate the effects of performing certain serial activities in parallel. Let us return to the sample network of Exhibit 15-5, which contained slack of −2.0 weeks on its critical path. Exhibit 15-10 illustrates the effects of changing activities 12–13 and 13–15 from their present serial relationship to parallel construction. Since both these activities are on the critical path, we know that performing them in parallel will reduce the expected completion time of the final event by the t_e of activity 13–15, exactly 2.0 weeks, thus producing a valid plan! We know this *a priori* because, although event 13 is a node event, activity 11–3 has positive slack.

Exhibit 15-9

Integrated Network for TV Transmission System

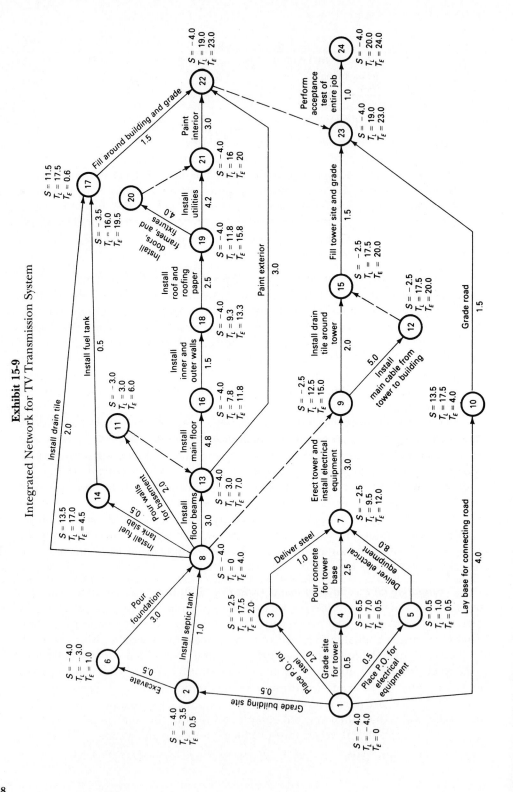

Exhibit 15-10
Validating a Typical Network

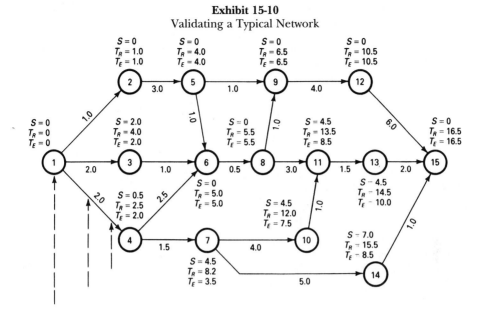

What does this kind of change imply? It implies that we are not going to wait for activity 12–13 (perhaps a test of some kind) prior to undertaking 13–15. Yet it may turn out that when we perform 12–13, we might have to alter the work represented by 13–15, based upon what we learn from 12–13. Therefore, if we alter the relationships of our otherwise optimum technological plan for performance, by definition we undertake additional risk. If no other acceptable way exists to achieve a valid plan, this course of action must be taken.

It is useful at this point to take a detour to provide a meaningful example of *free slack*. The critical path on our network passes through node event 6. At node event 6, there are two activities that have positive slack even though event 6 has zero slack. Activity 3–6 has a slack of 2.0 weeks and activity 4–6 has a slack of 0.5 week. The slack on both those activities is free slack, since it may be used up for those activities without affecting the slack in any part of the network *forward* of the node event. Knowledge of free slack is useful to functional managers during the resource scheduling process, as we shall see later.

The second procedure for producing a valid plan attempts to expedite certain activities in the network to save time while maintaining the optimum performance plan.

If the first two procedures are impossible, we can change only the schedule date, with the concurrence of our customer or management, or redefine the program.

One additional topic remains in this section; it concerns provision for uncertainty in our estimates of time and network relationships. It turns out that uncertainty is often the leading character in complex programs.

Provision for Uncertainty

PERT, an acronym for the program evaluation review technique, is a variant of network analysis, which was designed to deal with the problems of uncertainty associated with activities of complex programs. Under the PERT system, an option exists to provide three different time estimates for each activity. The beta distribution is then used to determine the expected completion time t_e for each activity. The formula for computation of the expected times from the beta distribution is

$$t_e = \frac{a + 4m + b}{6} \qquad (1)$$

where a is the optimistic estimate for the activity if everything goes well, b is the pessimistic completion time if everything goes wrong, and m is the most likely completion time of the activity. The three-time estimate is illustrated in Exhibit 15-11, assuming a beta distribution. If $a = 3$, $m = 4$, and $b = 11$ in equation (1), the expected completion time t_e is 5.0 weeks.

The expected completion time of 5.0 weeks is the mean of the distribution. The standard deviation of an activity is estimated to be one-sixth the total range of values between pessimistic and optimistic times of the activity given by

$$t_e = \frac{b - a}{6} = \frac{11 - 3}{6} = 1.3 \qquad (2)$$

The standard deviation of expected completion time for a given *event* is determined by calculating the square root of the sum of the squares of the standard deviations of the activities on the longest path (that is, the path determining the T_E) to the particular event or

$$\sigma T_E = \sqrt{\Sigma(\sigma + t_e)^2} \qquad (3)$$

The probability of completing a network on or before the scheduled completion date is then determined as follows:

$$Z = \frac{T_S - T_E}{T_E} \qquad (4)$$

Exhibit 15-11
Three-Time Estimate of PERT (a = optimistic time estimate,
m = most likely time estimate, b = pessimistic time estimate,
te = activity expected completion time)

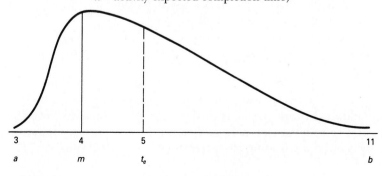

where T_S is the scheduled completion time in weeks from contract start and T_E is the expected completion time in weeks from contract start. The probability is then found by locating a Y value in a normal distribution table with Z.

If Z is positive, Y is added to 0.5. The resultant probability is the probability of completing the network on schedule. If negative slack exists (that is, $T_E > T_S$), Z will be negative and the probability of completing on schedule will be less than 0.5. If positive slack exists (that is, $T_E < T_S$) the probability of completing the network event on schedule would be greater than 0.5. We may calculate probabilities for any interior event by merely substituting the T_R of the interior event for T_S.

Although the initial goal of network analysis was to provide a probabilistic assessment of the uncertainty involved in completing a project on time, users soon found the three-time estimate procedure to be an administrative burden if done for each activity. Furthermore, other types of uncertainty, such as that associated with the network relationships themselves, were not considered by the three-time estimating procedure.

As a result of these limitations of the procedure provided by PERT for dealing with uncertainty, the three-time estimating procedure has been abandoned in practice. Special uses are made of the three-time estimating procedure for critical parts of complex programs, but it does not enjoy widespread use in even this limited form.

The use of single-time estimates rather than three-time estimates has not solved the problem associated with uncertainty. Uncertainty, which in most cases is not provided for, continues to be the main characteristic of complex programs.

When single-time estimates are provided for activities, the estimates are normally the m or most likely values. The most likely or modal value is the one that occurs most frequently, but it is certainly not the true average, or mean time. Using introspective reasoning, we may say that for many activities in complex programs, the "true" distribution of activity time values is probably skewed toward the right, as in Exhibit 15-11. Many things can go wrong for these activities, and few things can go much better than anticipated by the most likely estimate. All this suggests that when we have many such activities, some of the things that can go wrong, *will*! The most likely values, therefore, turn out to be quite optimistic.

The difficulty of making adequate provision for uncertainty within the context of a network is related to the difficulty of utilizing networks for the purpose of control. Briefly, however, we may say that if a program is of relatively low technology and well defined, single-time estimates are likely to prove quite accurate so that the problem of uncertainty that remains may be handled by a planning contingency (that is, a T_S 10 percent shorter than customer requirements) and a highly selective use of three-time estimates for critical activities.

On the other hand, for relatively high-technology and poorly defined programs, single-time estimates are likely to be notoriously inaccurate. In addition, the relationships in the network are likely to change so rapidly for complex programs that planners will be unable to provide up-to-date networks to "steer" or control program work. When rapid change occurs, we must introduce new mechanisms for planning and control that we shall call *control by feedback* rather than "control by plan," and these mechanisms will deal also with the uncertainty that is

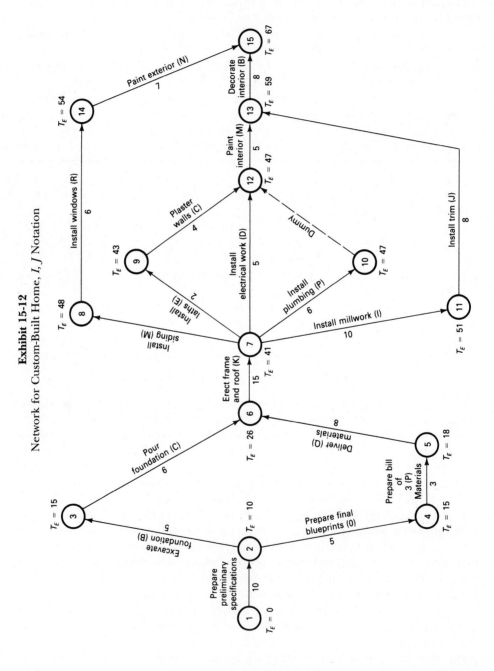

Exhibit 15-12

Network for Custom-Built Home, I, J Notation

associated with estimates of activity times. Even these new mechanisms, however, do not solve completely the problems posed by uncertainty, for in reality we have no perfect operational solution, only procedures for coping with it.

Precedence Networks

The method of network construction illustrated in the last section is not the only one possible. Many users prefer another network format that is called the *precedent format* and is contrasted to the previous format which we shall label the *I, J* format. In the *I, J* format, the activity takes place on the "line," whereas in a precedent network the activity takes place on the "node" or "event." In the *I, J* format each activity (or job) is described by a preceding event (*I*) and by a succeeding event (*J*). In a precedent formatted network, each job is described by an event number alone.

We proceed to illustrate the difference between *I, J* and precedent networks by an illustration of the construction of a custom-built home. Exhibit 15-12 presents a typical network in *I, J* notation for the custom home. This network is constructed by using the principles discussed previously in this chapter.

To convert from *I, J* to precedent networks, each event and its notation is laid out as shown in Exhibit 15-13.

Exhibit 15-14 presents the same network logic for the custom-built home but now in precedent notation.

Some users prefer precedent notation over *I, J* notation because networks are easier to construct and to understand. In the final analysis, it appears to be a matter of taste as to which one is used. So long as the logic of a network is correct, the form is of lesser importance, although it has been observed that users hold strong views as to one format over another. Therefore, the format should be adapted to the particular users.

This concludes our description of network analysis: a tool that allows us to complete the means-end chain for complex programs and provides a time plan for the program. It is a point of departure for estimating financial expenditures.

Exhibit 15-13
Precedence Notation

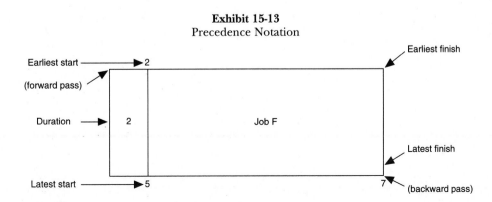

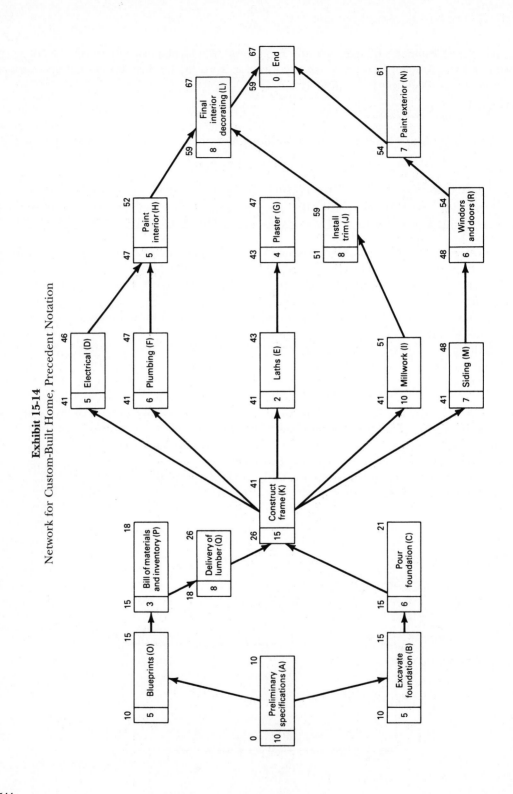

Exhibit 15-14
Network for Custom-Built Home, Precedent Notation

REFERENCES

CHANDLER, ALFRED D., *Strategy and Structure: Chapters in the History of American Enterprise.* Cambridge, Mass.: M.I.T. Press, 1962.

CLELAND, DAVID I., AND WILLIAM R. KING, eds., *Project Management Handbook*, 2nd ed. New York: Van Nostrand and Reinhold, 1988.

DAVIS, E. M., "Networks: Resource Allocation," *Industrial Engineering*, Vol. 6, no. 4 (1974), pp. 22–34.

FRAME, J. DAVIDSON, *Managing Projects in Organizations.* San Francisco, Jossey-Bass Publishers, 1990.

MACIARIELLO, J., *Program-Management Control Systems.* New York: John Wiley, 1978.

MARCH, J. G., AND H. A. SIMON, *Organizations.* New York: John Wiley, 1978.

MULVANEY, J., *Analysis Bar Charting, A Simplified Critical Path Analysis Technique.* Washington, D. C.: Management Planning and Control Systems, 1980.

SALYES, LEONARD R. AND MARGARET K. CHANDLER, *Managing Large Systems: Organizations for the Future.* New York: Harper and Row, 1971.

SHILLINGLAW, G., *Managerial Cost Accounting*, 5th ed. Homewood, Ill.: Richard D. Irwin, 1982.

NOTES

1. Although planning and control requirements have often necessitated changes to a firm's organization structure, as Chandler (1962, pp. 283–323) has shown, rarely in the past have these changes been based solely upon the requirements of planning and control.
2. This example is developed by permission of the publisher based upon the case study "Peterson General Contractors," reproduced in *The Theory and Management of Systems*, 3rd ed., by Richard A. Johnson, Fremont E. Kast, and James E. Rosenweig. New York: McGraw-Hill Book Company, pp. 268–273. The case was written by Albert N. Schreiber and first appeared in Albert N. Schrieber, et al., *Cases in Manufacturing Management.* New York: McGraw-Hill Book Company, 1965, pp. 262–268.

Case 15-1   General Aviation*

I've just received the results of a very extensive survey of my program managers concerning the effectiveness of the program-management systems in place in this division. The survey results look compelling. No key issue seems to have been ignored. Dave Shupp, the Assistant Controller of the Division, conducted the survey and has also attempted a number of explanations for the results. I am now trying to digest the results and the explanations in order to formulate a plan to correct the problems that have surfaced with regard to our program-management control systems.

Don Williams, General Manager
Life Support Division General Aviation
(in a discussion with the case writer)

General Aviation (GA) is a major subcontractor to commercial airframe manufacturers world wide. Its primary products are cabin air pressure and temperature control systems for commercial aircraft. GA develops proposals to design and manufacture these environmental control systems at the time the airframe manufacturer begins plans to design and manufacture a new model. Once a new plane has been built, GA then turns to the replacement parts and service and support side of the business.

THE SURVEY

David Shupp, the assistant controller and the most experienced management systems analyst in the life support division, was asked by Don Williams three months ago to conduct a systematic analysis of the management systems in place in the division with an eye toward improving the competitiveness of the division. General Aviation was under increasing pressure to become more competitive in light of the worldwide downturn in the environmental control systems business.

Shupp chose to survey the program managers systematically through the use of an instrument that contained questions about problems that he knew to be common to all programs in the division. The questions were arranged according to the MSSM framework. From four to twelve questions were developed for each sub system. The questions were phrased in the form of a statement; each question required two responses. The first response concerned the degree of agreement or disagreement with the statement. The second response concerned the degree of importance attached to the issue raised in the statement. Both responses were

*This case was prepared based upon an unpublished report written by Richard West, Executive Management Program, Claremont Graduate School, May 1992. It is used by permission.

requested in terms of a numerical scale arranged from 1 to 6 with a "6" ranking representing strong agreement and high importance and a "1" ranking representing low agreement and low importance. Appendix 15-A is the actual survey instrument administered by Shupp. Thirty-eight program managers participated in the survey.

RESULTS OF THE SURVEY

The average of the responses for each question is shown in Appendix 15-B. To make the results easier to interpret, Shupp assigned a positive or negative *valence* to the results depending upon whether the average of the responses represented a positive or negative state from the program managers' point of view. In order for high numbers to represent good states and low numbers poor states, Shupp inverted the numbers for unfavorable states. As a result, high average response rates always represent favorable states for the program managers, and low average numbers always represent unfavorable states. A "criticality quotient" was employed to highlight the responses where the average response was low, indicating an unfavorable state, and the average degree of importance was high. Shupp thought a criticality quotient above 1.7 was worthy of discussion.

CRITICAL ISSUES

The subsystem with the highest number of critical issues was the *infrastructure*. Five of the 14 critical issues were in the infrastructure. The other subsystems had the following number of critical issues:

Management style and culture	−3
Control processes	−2
Rewards	−2
Communications and integration	−2

DISCUSSION OF CRITICAL ISSUES

Each of the critical issues are discussed below together with Shupp's recommendations. Shupp also conducted some postsurvey discussions to probe his understanding of the rationale for the results.

Management Style and Culture

Three issues relating to style and structure were highlighted in the survey. The first dealt with customer focus, and the second and third dealt with change.

Customer Focus

Issues: Formal, #2
GA promotes a "customer first" way of doing things.
Agreement: 2.2   Importance: 4.6   Quotient: 2.1

Change

Issue: Informal, #4
The general perception at GA is that change is necessary and good.
Agreement: 2.2   Importance: 4.1   Quotient: 1.9

Issue: Informal, #5
When a change to a policy or support system is necessary, there is little resistance to that change.
Agreement: 1.9   Importance: 4.3   Quotient: 2.3

Plausible Explanations of Negative Findings

The program managers in the life support division do have a customer focus, but they do not believe that GA overall does. In fact, there is a standing joke at GA that "we ain't Burger King, you know," meaning that the customer can't have it his way—he gets it the GA way or he gets nothing at all. Recent threats to cancel existing programs appear to have begun improving responsiveness to customers.

In August 1990, the company reorganized to a matrix management system. GA was formerly organized by major program. As a result, program managers have not been able to fall back on old relationships and support systems. Shupp recommends patience and fortitude with an emphasis on building relationships across functional lines.

Other Findings

Program managers feel that GA promotes an open and informal atmosphere, and they clearly understand the vision and goals of the life support division. Also, they consider their management style highly participative, but they are probably closer to autocratic than they think.

Infrastructure

Five issues relating to infrastructure were highlighted in the survey. Three were concerned with the matrix structure, one with support organizations, and one with upper management support.

Matrix Structure

Issues: Formal, #1
   The matrix system employed by GA works well for my program.
Agreement: 2.1   Importance: 5.0   Quotient: 2.4

   Formal, #3
   The functional groups do not feel a sense of responsibility to meet cost or schedule goals on my program.
Agreement: 2.0   Importance: 4.9   Quotient: 2.5

   Informal, #3
   Politics and not true needs determine the priorities that functional groups use to make resource allocation decisions.
Agreement: 2.1   Importance: 4.4   Quotient: 2.1

Support Systems

Issues: Formal, #6
   In general, the support organizations at GA provide my project team and me with excellent service.
Agreement: 1.8   Importance: 4.6   Quotient: 2.6

Upper Management Support

Issues: Informal, #4
   I feel that GA management above our business unit supports us and gives us a fair share of its time, energy, and resources.
Agreement: 2.2   Importance: 4.4   Quotient: 2.0

Plausible Explanations of Negative Findings

The program managers will have to continue to work hard to build relationships with functional managers, provide contributors with a means of identifying with their programs, and insist on involvement in key functional resource allocation decisions. None of the issues raised here are peculiar to GA, but are a general problem with the matrix organization structure. Personal relationships are the only thing that prevents breakdown of the matrix structure.

The problematic support organizations are purchasing, shipping and receiving, configuration management, and quality.

On a per sales dollar basis, life support receives a smaller share of capital, proposal funds, overhead funds, and research and development funds than other GA divisions, even though it generates the largest share of GA profit.

Control Process

Two issues related to the control process were identified by the life support program managers. The first was related to the accuracy of the cost data provided to program managers. The second was related to long-term needs.

Cost Control

Issues: Formal, #4

The financial data that is reported to me is accurate and reliable.

Agreement: 2.2   Importance: 5.0   Quotient: 2.3

Formal, #11

Long-term needs for my program are integrated into the strategic and capital planning process.

Agreement: 2.2   Importance: 4.4   Quotient: 2.0

Plausible Explanations of Negative Findings

There are a number of shortcomings to the cost system at GA. A number of the program managers surveyed keep their own set of books to keep track of costs that the GA system can't track. In addition, no on-line financial system currently exists making it an arduous task to obtain information from the functional groups in order to update program budgets.

The strategic planning process within GA remains a mystery to program managers. They do not participate, nor do they see the results of the process.

Rewards

Two issues related to rewards were identified by the life support program managers. Both issues related to the relationship between rewards and performance.

Rewards and Performance

Issues: Formal, #2

The salary increases of those working on my program are closely tied to my program's success.

Agreement: 2.2   Importance: 4.6   Quotient: 2.1

Formal, #6

GA has a system of rewards that is tied to our business area's performance.

Agreement: 1.6   Importance: 4.1   Quotient: 2.6

Plausible Explanations of Negative Findings

Recent changes to GA's performance appraisal system may help to address the first one. Until last November, performance appraisals were conducted solely by functional managers. Now, the program managers have an opportunity to make a formal contribution to performance appraisal. This should make the functional contributors more responsive to program manager's needs.

The second issue probably relates to the rapid decline of the business in all but the life support division. Salary increments are averaged across GA regardless of overall divisional performance.

Communication and Integration

Two issues related to communication and integration were identified by the life support program managers. Both issues were related to the lack of integration with the functional departments that support the divisions programs.

Issues: Formal, #5

The interfaces among the various functional areas are clearly defined.

Agreement: 1.8   Importance: 3.8   Quotient: 2.1

Formal, #4

I have a good relationship with the functional managers whose departments support my program.

Agreement: 2.2   Importance: 3.8   Quotient: 1.7

Plausible Explanations of Negative Findings

Again, some program managers have developed good relationships with certain functions, whereas others demand good service, complain about results, and sit in their offices wondering why the system doesn't work. On the other hand, some functions appear to be impenetrable for many of the same reasons.

CONCLUSION

At the end of the interview with the case writer, Dave Shupp had some concluding observations.

> The MSSM served us well as a framework for evaluating the management systems in place in the life support division of GA. I can think of no key issue left unexamined. The framework could be applied equally well to the evaluation of program managers themselves. I only suggest that if it is used to evaluate program managers the model be expanded to incorporate continuous learning processes.

QUESTIONS

1. How should Don Williams proceed? Which items should he attack first? Provide a rationale for your plan of attack.
2. What is your overall evaluation of this approach to control systems redesign?

APPENDIX 15-A: MANAGEMENT SYSTEMS SURVEY

INSTRUCTIONS

Please review the whole survey before ranking any of the items.

Each statement on this survey requires two responses. In column A, please signify your agreement or disagreement with the statement by entering a number from six to one according to the following scale:

strongly agree	6
agree	5
somewhat agree	4
neutral or don't know	3
disagree	2
strongly disagree	1

In column B, signify the degree of importance that you currently associate with the issue addressed in the statement by entering a number from six to one according to the following scale:

extremely important	6
important	5
somewhat important	4
neutral or don't know	3
not important	2
not at all important	1

MANAGEMENT STYLE AND CULTURE

FORMAL

	A Agreement	B Importance
1. If the "GA Way" were expressed in one word, it would be integrity.	____	____
2. GA promotes a "customer first" way of doing things.	____	____
3. Management trusts me to make the right decisions on my program.	____	____
4. GA has formal systems and policies that encourage innovation.	____	____
5. I clearly understand the goals and vision of the business unit.	____	____
6. The management systems at GA are based on trust and respect for individual managers.	____	____

INFORMAL

	Agreement	Importance
1. GA management promotes an informal and open atmosphere.	____	____
2. My management will persecute me if I make a mistake.	____	____
3. I honestly report any problems on my program to management.	____	____
4. The general perception at GA is that change is necessary and good.	____	____

	Agreement	Importance
5. When a change to a policy or support system is necessary, there is little resistance to that change.	——	——
6. The upper management style at GA is highly participative.	——	——
7. My management style is highly participative.	——	——
8. The management style in our business area is highly participative.	——	——
9. I feel a strong sense of shared values with GA senior management.	——	——
10. I feel a strong sense of shared values with our business area management.	——	——
11. I consider myself a good leader.	——	——

INFRASTRUCTURE

FORMAL

	Agreement	Importance
1. The matrix system of organization that GA employs works well for my program.	——	——
2. I have the formal authority to accomplish my program's goals.	——	——
3. The functional groups do not feel a sense of responsibility to meet cost or schedule goals on my program.	——	——
4. I have a significant amount of technical knowledge about my product.	——	——
5. I really understand how this organization works.	——	——
6. In general, the support organizations at GA provide my project team and me with excellent service.	——	——
7. I visit all of my subcontractors frequently to solve problems and build team spirit.	——	——
8. Program staff meetings are held regularly.	——	——
9. Program staff meetings are very effective.	——	——

INFORMAL

	Agreement	Importance
1. I depend heavily on my personal contacts to accomplish my program goals	——	——
2. I often act in many capacities beyond my program management duties, such as marketing or counseling.	——	——
3. Politics, not true needs, determine the priorities that functional groups use to make resource allocation decisions.	——	——
4. I feel that GA management above our business unit supports us and gives us a fair share of its time, energy, and resources.	——	——
5. Ad hoc teams or task forces are an important part of the informal structure at GA.	——	——
6. I often get things done by the sheer force of my personality.	——	——
7. My program team is committed to making the program a success.	——	——
8. I have been working with the same project team for a long time; there have been very few changes.	——	——

CONTROL PROCESSES

FORMAL	Agreement	Importance
1. The goals of my program are clearly defined.	———	———
2. I clearly understand what my customer wants me to accomplish with my program.	———	———
3. My management and I agree on what the goals of my program are.	———	———
4. The financial data that are reported to me on program costs are accurate and reliable.	———	———
5. I run my program using a team structure.	———	———
6. I do benchmarking to determine where I stand in relationship to competitors.	———	———
7. My program applies techniques such as statistical process control to manage product quality.	———	———
8. I have a current financial plan that is consistent with my technical and delivery progress.	———	———
9. I use program planning tools, such as PERT charts and Gantt charts.	———	———
10. The functional organizations do additional planning and control activities to ensure that they meet their cost, schedule, and quality goals.	———	———
11. Long-term needs for my program are integrated into the strategic and capital planning process.	———	———
12. I have read and understand the strategic plan for GA.	———	———

INFORMAL	Agreement	Importance
1. I frequently conduct informal planning sessions with my program team.	———	———
2. I always seek collaborative decisions with my program team.	———	———
3. Events outside GA that I cannot control are the key determinant of my program's success or failure.	———	———
4. The feedback that I get informally often contradicts what the formal control systems tell me.	———	———

REWARDS

FORMAL	Agreement	Importance
1. My salary increases are closely tied to my program's success.	———	———
2. The salary increases of those working on my program are closely tied to my program's success.	———	———
3. My long-term success and promotion depends upon the success of my program.	———	———
4. I have discussed my career path with my boss, and I am optimistic about the future.	———	———
5. My yearly performance appraisal is strongly tied to my performance on my program.	———	———
6. GA has a system of rewards that is tied to our business area's performance.	———	———

INFORMAL   **Agreement**   **Importance**

1. I get frequent "atta boys" from management.   ———   ———
2. I give frequent "atta boys" to the people working on my
   program.   ———   ———
3. My peers recognize my accomplishments.   ———   ———
4. I receive frequent awards for my performance on my
   program.   ———   ———
5. I frequently give awards to those working on my
   program.   ———   ———
6. I feel that I have a stake in the success of GA as a whole.   ———   ———
7. I feel that I have a stake in the success of our business
   unit.   ———   ———
8. Rewards in general are distributed fairly at GA.   ———   ———

COMMUNICATION AND INTEGRATION

FORMAL   **Agreement**   **Importance**

1. I regularly report on my program's status to my
   customer.   ———   ———
2. The monthly program reviews held internally provide
   effective feedback to management on the health of my
   program.   ———   ———
3. I address problems with support on my program with
   the functional managers involved.   ———   ———
4. I have an opportunity to affect the operational plans of
   the functional organizations that support my program.   ———   ———
5. The interfaces among the various functional areas are
   clearly defined.   ———   ———

INFORMAL   **Agreement**   **Importance**

1. I talk to my customer frequently.   ———   ———
2. My customer and I like and trust one another.   ———   ———
3. The people working on my program and I like and trust
   one another.   ———   ———
4. I have a good relationship with the functional managers
   whose departments support my program.   ———   ———
5. I understand the roles and many of the problems of the
   functional managers.   ———   ———
6. Our business area does a good job of managing conflict.   ———   ———
7. Each member of my project team feels a responsibility
   well beyond his immediate specialty to improve the
   product, meet schedules, and reduce cost.   ———   ———

APPENDIX 15-B: MANAGEMENT SYSTEMS SURVEY RESULTS

Category	Question Number	Valence	Agreement Average Response	Importance Average Response	Criticality Quotient Import/Agree
Management Style and Culture					
Formal	1	+	2.9	3.2	1.1
	2	+	2.6	4.6	1.8
	3	+	4.1	5.1	1.2
	4	+	3.1	3.6	1.2
	5	+	4.8	3.1	0.6
	6	+	3.0	4.0	1.3
Informal	1	+	3.8	3.1	0.8
	2	−	2.8	4.0	1.4
	3	+	4.6	4.6	1.0
	4	+	2.2	4.1	1.9
	5	+	1.9	4.3	2.3
	6	+	1.9	3.0	1.6
	7	+	3.6	2.8	0.8
	8	+	5.1	5.0	1.0
	9	+	2.3	3.1	1.3
	10	+	5.2	4.8	0.9
	11	+	4.3	5.1	1.2
Infrastructure					
Formal	1	+	2.1	5.0	2.4
	2	+	2.3	3.3	1.4
	3	−	2.0	4.9	2.5
	4	+	4.6	3.6	0.8
	5	+	2.9	3.2	1.1
	6	+	1.8	4.6	2.6
	7	+	3.3	3.4	1.0
	8	+	4.6	3.1	0.7
	9	+	3.2	3.2	1.0
Informal	1	+	3.3	3.1	0.9
	2	+	3.4	4.3	1.3
	3	−	2.1	4.4	2.1
	4	+	2.2	4.4	2.0
	5	+	2.0	2.2	1.1
	6	+	3.4	3.8	1.1
	7	+	4.6	5.1	1.1
	8	+	3.4	4.9	1.4
Control Processes					
Formal	1	+	4.8	4.4	0.9
	2	+	4.6	5.3	1.2
	3	+	4.4	3.3	0.8
	4	+	2.2	5.0	2.3
	5	+	3.6	3.9	1.1
	6	+	3.1	3.8	1.2
	7	+	3.3	4.1	1.2
	8	+	3.9	4.2	1.1
	9	+	5.2	4.8	0.9

Continued

APPENDIX 15-B *(Continued)*

Category	Question Number	Valence	Agreement Average Response	Importance Average Response	Criticality Quotient Import/Agree
	10	+	3.1	4.6	1.5
	11	+	2.2	4.4	2.0
	12	+	2.6	3.4	1.3
Informal	1	+	2.4	3.3	1.4
	2	+	3.1	3.1	1.0
	3	−	4.0	3.3	0.8
	4	−	3.6	4.4	1.2
Rewards					
Formal	1	+	4.4	3.3	0.8
	2	+	2.2	4.6	2.1
	3	+	4.6	2.9	0.6
	4	+	3.1	4.8	1.5
	5	+	4.8	3.9	0.8
	6	+	1.6	4.1	2.6
Informal	1	+	3.2	4.2	1.3
	2	+	4.1	4.3	1.0
	3	+	3.4	3.6	1.1
	4	+	2.4	3.6	1.5
	5	+	2.9	3.8	1.3
	6	+	3.8	4.1	1.1
	7	+	5.1	4.9	1.0
	8	+	4.3	4.8	1.1
Communication and Integration					
Formal	1	+	5.1	4.6	0.9
	2	+	3.2	3.1	1.0
	3	+	2.6	2.8	1.1
	4	+	3.1	3.6	1.2
	5	+	1.8	3.8	2.1
Informal	1	+	5.2	4.6	0.9
	2	+	3.6	4.2	1.2
	3	+	3.8	4.3	1.1
	4	+	2.2	3.8	1.7
	5	+	3.4	2.9	0.9
	6	+	2.9	3.3	1.1
	7	+	3.6	4.6	1.3

16

CONTROL OF COMPLEX PROGRAMS II: FINANCIAL PLANNING, RESOURCE SCHEDULING, BUDGETING, AND REPORTING

INTRODUCTION

A close relationship exists among the work breakdown structure, networks, and financial expenditure plans of a program. Since complex programs are characterized by the same uncertainty in the cost dimension, whatever forces extend the time dimension of a program ordinarily extend its expenditure dimension also.

In an organization concerned predominantly with large complex projects, the project cost accounting system must be different in some fundamental respects from more traditional cost accounting systems. On the other hand, a product or service organization employing the matrix organization structure may often utilize a traditional cost accounting system for financial expenditure planning, with very few variations. In all cases, activity-based costing may be applied to overhead allocations for complex programs.

Systems for financial planning on complex programs have been developed most extensively in the area of complex projects. The requirements for financial expenditure planning have been more stringent, as a rule, for complex projects than for complex products and services simply because the most complex programs of the past have been projects. For these reasons, we concentrate in this chapter on financial expenditure planning for complex projects, while recognizing that all the tools and concepts are directly transferable to other complex programs, usually in somewhat reduced form, always reflecting the managerial requirements of a program.

PROJECT COST ACCOUNTING SYSTEMS

Each project is a unique undertaking, which implies that it follows the cost accounting procedures used for job-order production. Furthermore, the planning and control needs of complex projects require that we provide a system for estimating and controlling project expenditures. This implies a need for both estimated (that is, standard) and actual costs.

Cost accounting systems for complex projects utilize standard costs for purposes of planning and actual costs for purposes of reporting, evaluating, and control. The characteristics of project cost accounting systems that distinguish them from traditional standard cost accounting systems result from the need (1) to develop standards almost from scratch for each project and (2) to develop combined measures of cost and time performance for purposes of project reporting and control.

Project cost accounting systems should be designed for three managerial purposes. First, and perhaps most important, the system should provide an expenditure plan or standard for the project. Since a complex project is a unique undertaking, it is necessary to establish standards for each "job." Past experience regarding identical activities does not exist. Second, a project cost accounting system should be designed to motivate good project performance by utilizing a number of behavioral practices that produce challenging but realistic expenditure plans. Third, the project accounting system should be used for evaluation of performance.

An expenditure plan for a complex project is usually prepared during the proposal phase of project activity. Such a plan consists of a time-phased summary of each element of cost for the project. The three elements of costs that must be accounted for are (1) direct labor, (2) direct materials, and (3) overhead. Direct labor consists of those expenditures that can be traced to a specific work breakdown structure element of the project. That is, the expenditures they represent are identifiable with an end item of the WBS, and they contribute directly to the completion of an end item. Direct labor benefits only one end item and does not spill over to benefit other end items at the same level of the WBS. Direct material costs for a project are those costs that are incurred for material that becomes identifiable with a given end item. Direct costs for each end item of the WBS consist of the sum of direct labor and direct material costs. These costs are caused by or causally related to a given end item of the project.

Indirect, or overhead, costs are those costs that cannot be traced directly to a single end item but rather help many end items in a real but untraceable manner. These cannot be traced either because it is impossible to do so (for example, tracing program management costs to each end item) or because it is impractical to do so (for example, tracing office supplies to each end item). Moreover, even if an element of cost may be traced directly to an end item, management may not believe it worthwhile to do so.

Given all the reasons for treating a cost item as indirect, it is still desirable to treat as many of the total costs as possible as direct, without being arbitrary or impractical. All methods of allocating indirect costs tend to be at least somewhat imprecise.

In addition to the three principal elements of costs, project proposals generally contain a catchall category of costs called "general and administrative costs." These are overhead items that are considered to be even more remote from the project than are those items included in overhead. Examples include research and development activities, public relations, corporate executive office costs, and so on. Generally, these costs are allocated to projects as a percentage (for example, 15 percent) of total costs.

FINANCIAL EXPENDITURE PLANNING: TV TRANSMISSION SYSTEM PROJECT

Exhibit 16-1 is a reproduction of the WBS transmission system, but now with expenditure estimates attached. Each activity of the network is estimated and placed under the appropriate WBS item. Each WBS item has a code number to identify it uniquely. Below each WBS item is an estimate of cost broken down by each element of cost. It is important for our reporting and evaluation procedure to have cost estimates segregated by type.

Notice that the WBS includes an account code structure. Each end item in the means–end chain has a unique account number assigned to it. Each means is linked to its parent end item by this hierarchical numbering system. The code structure is very useful in the financial estimation phase of the program control process.

For example, the account code number for the overall project is A01 (that is, level 0 of the WBS). Each level 1 WBS item carries the number of its end (that is, A01) plus a unique suffix to identify it. For example, the equipment building number is A01-3. Each level 2 item carries the number of its parent plus a suffix to uniquely identify it. The building structure is numbered A01-3-2 to signify that it belongs to the overall system (A01) and to the equipment building A01-3.

The WBS of Exhibit 16-1 has three levels. The means for achieving the levels' ends are activities on the network. To estimate standard costs for each end item of the WBS, we estimate each of the lowest-level items and accumulate the standard costs up the WBS.

From the network of the TV system we estimate direct labor and material cost for each of the lowest-level end items of the WBS. Since this is a relatively small project, each of the lowest-level end items is equal to one work package, and we develop *planned value of work* estimates for each of the lowest-level end items. We identify direct labor and direct material costs separately under each end item.

The standard overhead rate for this organization is 65 percent of labor costs. Labor cost is therefore the overhead driver. The organization has determined that indirect expenditures vary more directly with labor costs than with any other input or output variable. The overhead rate is thus computed by estimating overhead expenditures over the accounting period (normally a year) and dividing these expenditures by the expected or normal volume of labor costs for that same period.

Once we have arrived at the overhead rate, we simply apply it at each lowest-level end item to the standard assigned to the variable that serves as the overhead cost driver. This gives us the standard overhead charge for that end item. We then

Exhibit 16-1
WBS for TV Transmission System

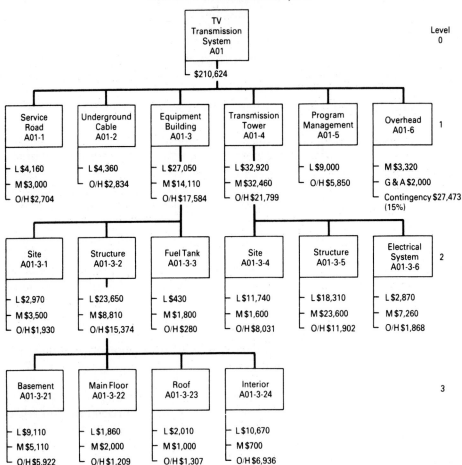

sum the three elements of cost to arrive at standard costs for an end item. Since we can relate a lowest-level end item to the network, we shall be in a position in the reporting phase to collect actual costs for work performed and compare them with the planned value of work performed. Finally, we sum standard costs for each end item to its parent to find successively higher levels of project costs until we arrive at the standard cost for the entire system (that is, A01 on the WBS).

Notice that there are costs for project management and certain other overhead items that we choose not to allocate to project end items, but rather we identify these separately at level 1 of the WBS. Of course, they too become part of our total estimated costs for the project. The estimated costs for the project may also be displayed by month as in Exhibit 16-2. Exhibit 16-2 becomes a control document; it does not contain profit or contingency, thus displaying a total cost that is $44,579 lower than the costs appearing on the WBS in Exhibit 16-1.

Exhibit 16-2

Financial Expenditure Plan According to Expected Completion Dates

Element of Cost	Week											
	(1-22) 1-3	(22-44) 4-6	(44-66) 7-9	(66-88) 10-12	(88-110) 13-15	(110-132) 16-18	(132-154) 19-21	(154-176) 22-24	(176-198) 25-27	(198-220) 28-30	Total
Labor	$17,200	$8,570	$5,220	$2,660	$15,100	$3,600	$14,110	$2,300			$68,760
Material expenditures	$30,860	$21,730									$52,590
Applied overhead (65% of labor)	$11,180	$5,571	$3,383	$1,729	$9,815	$2,340	$9,172	$1,495			$44,695
Project total cost	$59,240	$35,871	$8,613	$4,389	$24,915	$5,940	$23,382	$3,795			$166,045
Cumulative total cost	$59,240	$95,111	$103,724	$108,113	$133,028	$138,968	$162,250	$166,045			
Activities	A, B, C, D, G	X, AA, BB, M, N, W	L, Y, P, Z	O, Q	R, I, T, H	J	B, Y	U, K, CC, DD, EE			

The work package, because it connects the WBS, the network, and the cost accounting system for a meaningful segment of work, is the basic instrument for integrating the time and cost variables of a project. It is the lowest level of detail at which it is feasible to devise a combined measure of performance for time and cost.

The combined measure of performance is ordinarily called the budgeted value of work planned (BVWP), and it is arrived at simply by estimating the budgeted value of work represented on the network for each work package. Each work package thus contains estimates of its planned value, so that any major part of the work package is accorded a corresponding planned value.

Once work progresses, we collect data on actual expenditures and progress and assign *actual cost for work actually accomplished* (ACWA) for each work package. We then compare the *budgeted value of work actually accomplished* (BVWA) with the actual cost of work accomplished and compute the variance. The variance thus represents a measure of cost performance versus plan for the work actually accomplished. It integrates expenditures with schedule performance, thus achieving the joint measure of performance we seek. We shall discuss this integrated reporting measure further, later in this chapter.

RESOURCE ALLOCATION VERSUS PROGRAM PLANNING

Program plans represented by networks and financial plans provide functional management with the requirements, resources, and priorities for their function on each of the organization's programs. Although network plans provide a schedule for accomplishing the work, this schedule is not always practical or feasible when all other constraints placed upon the function are considered.

Six specific requirements excluded during the planning process must be considered during the resource allocation process:

1. Sufficient personnel to perform each activity in an optimum manner is assumed to be available when formulating and optimizing plans. Limited availability of personnel and the competition among programs for the same workers must be taken into account during the resource allocation process.
2. The pattern of resource demands from all of the program plans must be considered not only in the light of resources available but also in terms of the distribution of demand placed upon resources over time. Functional management cannot be expected continuously to increase and reduce functional personnel in light of the fluctuating demands of each program. Functional worker levels are determined based upon long-term organizational demands, and utilization must be relatively even from one period to the next.
3. Common facilities (for example, computer time and test rigs) are often required simultaneously by activities of the same program or by activities of different programs. The allocation process must resolve these conflicts.
4. Cash flow requirements of the programs are not always feasible for the organization, and these limitations enter into the allocation function.
5. State work laws and regulations must be observed in allocation decisions when overtime is being considered.

6. The nature of the contract negotiated between contractor and customer with regard to the relative value of various programs to the organization, as well as the long-term objectives of the organization, affect the relative priority that should be accorded various programs by the organization. This is a consideration of the resource allocation process.

Not only must we recognize scheduling as a distinct activity in the program control process separate from, yet related to, planning, but we must also establish different time horizons for these two activities. Program planning must be carried out for the entire duration of the program. Scheduling, on the other hand, ordinarily may be done profitably only on a short-term time horizon.

Scheduling requires commitment of resources on the part of functional management to specific tasks of the many programs of the organization. As the network relationships indicate, however, activities of one functional organization are dependent upon the completion of activities of other functional organizations. Because of the dynamic, constantly changing nature of complex programs, we cannot expect network relationships and time estimates to be very precise. Expected start and completion times of activities become more tenuous as time elapses from the present. Therefore, functional organizations cannot establish realistic long-term schedules for carrying out the work of multiple programs. It is usually futile to allocate resources to specific jobs unless they are to be performed in the near term. More accurate scheduling can be done for these near-term activities since most of the activities that limit their start are either in progress or are complete.

For the examples presented later in this chapter, we have selected a time horizon of 10 weeks for scheduling and have assumed that the scheduling process takes place on a monthly basis. This time horizon and scheduling interval appear to be realistic.

Start dates for activities that are scheduled by the functional organizations must find their way back to appropriate program plans. Scheduled start dates are superimposed upon network calculations, and they supersede early expected start dates in calculation of the network so long as they are equal to or greater than expected start dates. Scheduled start dates that are earlier than expected start dates are invalid. Program office personnel must check the consistency of functional schedules and approve their implications. The portion of a program plan that has been scheduled is called a *scheduled plan.*

Although distant activities cannot be scheduled, it is important to preserve a valid plan for distant work, since the time estimates and interrelationships of the entire plan determine the time requirements (required dates) of work that can be scheduled.

To summarize this section, we may say that resource allocation or scheduling is a function with different purposes than planning. A network plan cannot ordinarily be utilized as a schedule for a project, yet it must serve as the basis for the schedule. Moreover, once activities are scheduled, these data must be incorporated into network plans. Thus there is a feedback in both directions between these two important functions. If the plan alone is used as a schedule for performing the work, with slack used without considering other activities and competing programs, the ability to optimize performance in the organization is restricted, and the value of the program control system is lessened.

The resource allocation process consists of three distinct but interrelated tasks: *resource loading, resource leveling,* and *constrained resource scheduling.* Resource loading is concerned with deriving the total demands of all programs placed upon the resources of a function during a specified period of time. Resource leveling attempts to "smooth out" the demands to eliminate major peaks and troughs. Constrained resource scheduling is concerned with achieving all demands of the programs of an organization within the resource constraints of the function at minimum disruption to the plans of each of the organization's programs.

The next section of this chapter is concerned with the three elements of resource allocation. We turn first to the resource loading process, next to resource leveling, and finally to constrained resource scheduling.

RESOURCE LOADING

To understand the resource loading process, it is convenient to view the problem in matrix form. The various programs of an organization place demands on resources during a particular period of time, and the functional organizations supply these resources. A matrix illustrating this process appears in Exhibit 16-3. The matrix represents the total demands placed upon each of five functions by each program. These demands, however, are not time-phased in this exhibit. The resource demands in the matrix are taken from the work packages that are expected to be performed during the scheduling period.

Each work package consists of a group of activities for a program. In addition, they contain time-phased estimates of the resources required to accomplish the work. These time-phased estimates for each function for the scheduling horizon must then be summed across all programs to produce a work force loading report.

Information on demands placed upon each functional group during the scheduling horizon is only part of the information required in the resource loading process. In addition we require slack information from each of the program plans.

Exhibit 16-4 is an example of a computer output report for one function, drafting, for one program for a 10-week period. This information is derived from program plans. The activities represented on the report have start dates, expected completion dates, required dates, and slack calculations.

Loading information from work packages, together with calculations of slack from program plans, are then combined into the work force loading report for one functional organization. Exhibit 16-5 presents an example of a time-phased loading plan based upon expected start and completion times for each of the activities. Where positive or negative slack exists, it is indicated by an extension of each bar to its right (for positive slack) or left (for negative slack). Within each bar we have placed the number of workers per week required to achieve each task and have summed the total demands placed upon the function vertically by week. The

Exhibit 16-3
Resource Loading in Matrix Form*

Functions	Programs					Total Functional Workers Hours
	1	2	3	4	5	
A	20	40	8	5	0	73
B	30	30	15	0	0	75
C	25	25	20	8	20	98
D	10	15	20	14	30	89
E	40	10	12	10	0	72
Total program worker hours	125	120	75	37	50	407

*Resource allocation matrix: three-month period based on earliest expected start dates.

row on the bottom of the chart therefore contains an estimate of the total demands in terms of person-weeks of effort placed upon the function of drafting by all programs. Exhibit 16-6 presents the loading plan graphically.

From Exhibit 16-6 we note that there is an uneven distribution of demand for drafting resources over the 10-week period, with very high demands occurring in weeks 6–7 and 7–8. Even if labor is in good supply in the drafting organization, it is usually undesirable to have these large variations in the demand for workers. The *resource leveling process* attempts to remedy this situation by leveling or smoothing personnel demands within the constraints of required dates for the various activities.

Exhibit 16-4
Planned Activities of Functional Organization Resource Loading in Matrix Form

Function
Program: XXX
Responsibility: John Smith

Preceding/ Succeeding Event Numbers	Activity	Time Estimate	Start Date	Expected Completion Date	Required Completion Date	Slack
001–002	Prepare detail drawings — 101	2.0	01/01/89	01/15/89	01/29/89	2.0
011–012	Prepare detail drawings — 105	4.0	01/15/89	02/15/89	02/15/89	0.0
021–022	Prepare detail drawings — 208	3.0	02/01/89	02/22/89	02/15/89	−1.0
031–032	Prepare detail drawings — 304	1.5	02/01/89	02/11/89	02/04/89	−1.0
051–052	Prepare detail drawings — 508	2.5	02/15/89	03/03/89	03/01/89	−0.4

Exhibit 16-5
Time-Phased Work Force Loading Plan

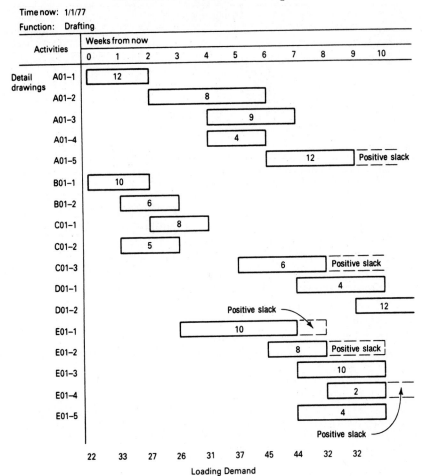

RESOURCE LEVELING

The resource leveling process begins with the resource loading and slack calculations of Exhibit 16-5 and the work force profile of Exhibit 16-6. It proceeds to level
the demands for resources without exceeding the required dates of programs. The
process is constrained by its leveling objectives and by the overall time requirements of the programs, not by available resources.

By utilizing slack calculations some start times of activities may be adjusted to
begin later than their earlier expected start date, thus shifting the demand for
resources to a latter point in time, without exceeding the original expected comple-

Exhibit 16-6
Profile for Demands for Personnel

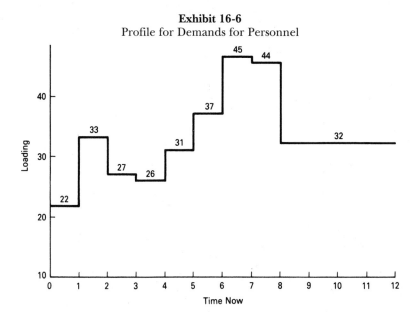

tion date of the network. Therefore, the resource leveling process requires us to adjust performance times of activities according to slack calculations to produce a pattern of demand for resources that is as stable as possible over the scheduling horizon.

The resource requirements of the valid plan are taken as a beginning point for resource leveling. Required completion dates are treated as constraints so that we maintain valid plans. Adjustments are made by each functional manager; these adjustments are coordinated with personnel assigned to the various program management offices to ensure that each functional organization does not frustrate the schedules of the other. That is, the utilization of slack by the various functions must be coordinated by the various program offices.

Free slack (or float), which we defined to be that part of activity slack that if used does not affect slack calculations forward of the activity in the network, may be utilized immediately without approval of the program office, since its use cannot affect any other activity in the program. Normal slack, however, is identified with a path and, although we may utilize it during resource leveling, its use must be coordinated with program office personnel whose program is affected. Coordination is necessary, since only one activity on a path may utilize its positive slack; if all functions represented by activities on a single path utilize the slack, the combined network calculations would produce a negative slack path.

The resource leveling function may be carried out manually unless the networks are large and involve multiple resources. Computer programs are available for more complex networks, including those which operate on microcomputers.

Resource leveling for our sample programs results in the revised loading plan of Exhibit 16-7 and the personnel profile of Exhibit 16-8. Notice that in the

Exhibit 16-7
Resource-Leveled Plan

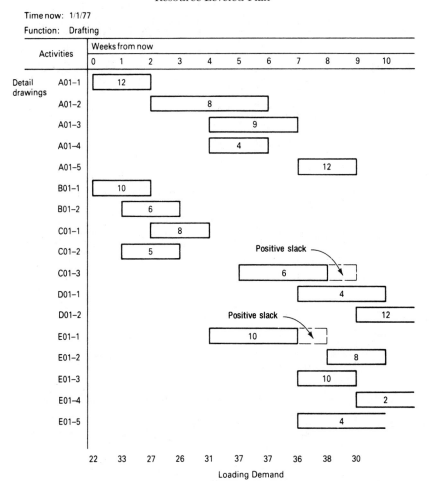

Time now: 1/1/77

Function: Drafting

leveling process we were able to reduce peak demands of weeks 6–7 and 7–8 significantly. This was accomplished by the selective use of positive slack that was available on the program. Assuming that this utilization of slack meets the approval of the proper program office personnel, the leveling procedure results in a definite improvement in the distribution of resources of the drafting organization. The personnel profile produced by the resource leveling procedure, however, may not be feasible in light of known worker levels. The next problem, therefore, involves scheduling all these drafting tasks within the limits of available draftspersons. This is the task of scheduling subject to personnel constraints, to which we turn now.

Exhibit 16-8
Revised Profile of Demand for Personnel

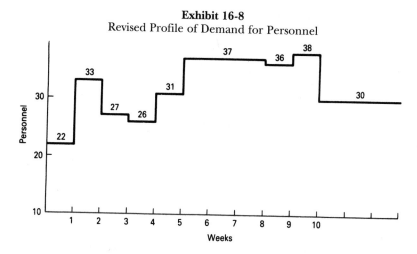

Resource Scheduling Subject to Personnel Constraints

If the resource leveling process produces a loading profile within the personnel limitations of the function, all is well. If, however, the loading demands of the leveling process produce personnel requirements that exceed worker availability, including the use of overtime, then we must relax schedules until they "fit" within resource limits. This relaxation process must be done in such a way as to minimize the extensions required to the critical path while maintaining a reasonably smooth distribution of demand for resources.

When the resource leveling procedure does not produce a feasible schedule under otherwise optimal planning conditions, we are forced to increase the duration of schedules of at least some programs of the organization. To determine which activities should be prolonged, we require a priority system. Two types of systems exist: optimal procedures and rule-of-thumb, or heuristic procedures. We examine each category in turn.

Optimal Procedures for Constrained Resource Allocation

Optimal procedures for the allocation of resources involve mathematical procedures that lead to selection of the best schedule under assumed resource constraints. The optimization tool of linear programming would seem to be appropriate here, since we have an objective function, which is to minimize schedule slippage on all programs, subject to the constraints of available resources. The problem with the linear programming approach, however, is that realistic network and resource conditions require an enormous amount of computation. Davis (1974, p. 30) reports that a 55-activity network with four different types of resources would require 5000 equations. The technique clearly is impractical for any large network even with a computer program.

Other optimization procedures include attempts to enumerate all possible sequences of schedules for a given type of resource, from which the optimal one is chosen. This technique has proved to be computationally impractical, except for small networks or medium-sized networks with a single-resource type.

There is another even more fundamental objection to these optimal techniques. As we have observed throughout, there is a good deal of uncertainty in complex programs concerning even the best estimates of time, relationships, and resources for activities. To devise optimal schedules, after elaborate calculations, based upon these uncertain estimates seems not to be worth the cost. Less optimal rule-of-thumb procedures would seem to be good enough for most cases and well worth the cost of the exercise. We now turn to these so-called "heuristic" procedures.

HEURISTIC SCHEDULING PROCEDURES

Heuristic procedures are rules-of-thumb for solving problems; they are used to develop satisfactory but usually not optimal schedules. Such procedures are widely employed to solve the constrained resource scheduling problem. Starting from the optimum plan, these procedures lead us to schedule activities on the basis of certain rules to produce good resource-feasible schedules.

A heuristic procedure for scheduling within resource constraints must contain decision rules for extending activities so that total resource requirements are within resource constraints. There are two common decision rules:

> Accord priorities to activities based upon their required completion dates with activities having the earliest required completion dates scheduled ahead of those with later required completion dates.

> Rank activities in order of duration, and perform activities with the shortest duration first.

These two rules-of-thumb are given as examples of procedures that may be used to solve the constrained scheduling problem, given a leveled loading plan. All heuristic procedures proceed to extend activities that cannot be accommodated by available levels of personnel through the use of one of these rules. A heuristic procedure must also have secondary rules for breaking ties. For example, if two activities have identical required dates yet cannot be performed simultaneously because of resource constraints, we might decide to perform the one with the shortest duration first.

It is important to realize that these rules-of-thumb are not likely to produce optimal schedules. They are designed to produce satisfactory feasible schedules. When placed in the context of the uncertainties found in organizations engaged in complex programs, however, rules-of-thumb such as these are operational and flexible enough to respond to the inevitable changes brought about by these uncertainties. Optimal scheduling procedures are not only currently nonoperational but are not dynamic enough to respond to the numerous changes that are likely in the atmosphere of complex programs.

We should note that although we have described the resource allocation process as three distinct but interrelated tasks, in practice they are often performed informally and simultaneously, depending on the magnitude of the task and the sophistication of the program control process.

THE BUDGET PROCESS

A close parallel exists in the relationship between expenditure planning and budgeting to the relationship we described between network planning and resource scheduling. The resource scheduling process begins with the activities, time requirements, and calculations of the network and proceeds to load personnel, smooth resources, and construct schedules that are resource feasible for a short period of time into the future. The portion of a network plan that has been scheduled for performance by functional groups is called a *scheduled plan.*

Similarly, the budgeting process begins with plans established during the financial planning process and proceeds to authorize expenditure limits within which, *on balance*, budgets are expected to adhere. The budget for a work package, however, is likely to differ in some important aspects from the financial plan, since the authorized work package must reflect decisions made in the resource allocation process. The portion of the financial expenditure plan for which we have a budget is called a *budgeted plan.*

WORK-PACKAGE AND OPERATING BUDGETS

As in all organizations, each responsibility center of an organization engaged in complex programs requires an operating budget. For organizations engaged in complex programs, however, it is almost impossible to prepare an annual operating budget for a functional organization with any degree of confidence that it will be followed closely. Yet each organizational unit must perform resource and expenditure planning over a longer horizon than that which it can forecast perfectly.

This apparent budgeting dilemma is resolved by requiring both work-package and operating budgets. Work-package budgets, covering a short period of time, serve as work authorization documents, whereas approved operating budgets serve to guide decisions regarding resource levels in each of the functional departments.

Financial data on work packages prepared during the expenditure planning process are far from ready to serve as budgets for the program. These financial plans were derived from estimates of network activities. As we saw previously, network plans ordinarily cannot be converted directly into schedules, but rather must be considered in light of available resources and other competing demands. Therefore, the financial plans of a given work package cannot be converted into budgets until the activities included in the work package have been scheduled, for only then do we know precisely when activities will be done and by whom and what resources will be utilized. Only a small portion of the financial plan is eligible to serve as a budget, for only a small portion of the network plan upon which the expenditure plan is based has been scheduled. The budget for the portion of the network plan that has been scheduled is negotiated between program and functional personnel. The approved budget then serves as the document that authorizes functional work.

THE BUDGET AS AN AUTHORIZATION DOCUMENT

We have seen that to achieve both scale economies and coordination, the matrix structure causes us to violate the classical principle of *unity of command.* The stresses produced by the dual sources of command to which functional personnel must respond are nowhere potentially more divisive than in the budgeting and authorization process. This process, however, if performed correctly, also possesses opportunities to enhance identification with program goals, improve performance, and reduce or eliminate these natural tensions caused by dual lines of command.

Since the management function of directing program work formally lies with functional managers under the matrix structure, the program manager should use the budget and related authorizing documents to exert control over functional performance.

Once the schedule is prepared for functional work, the budget implications may be derived by applying rates for each cost element as established in the program cost accounting system. The schedule for functional work and its supporting budget serve as authorizing documents for functional work. By reviewing and approving the schedules and budgets of these work packages, the program manager begins to assert control over his or her program. Thus a major portion of a program manager's time is spent negotiating budgets with functional managers in light of original financial planning for the work, current schedules, past performance by the various functions, and overall program status.

Program office personnel should have the following questions regarding proposed work-package budgets:

Does the schedule as presented by the functional groups validate our program plans?

Will the work schedule meet technical specifications?

Is the budget for the work consistent with planning estimates?

If each of these questions is answered in the affirmative, the program manager simply approves the budget and authorizes performance. He or she may authorize performance for the entire scheduling horizon, 10 weeks in our examples, for the duration of the work package, or for the scheduling period, assumed to be one month in our examples. The time limit set for the work authorization period is controlled by specifying the time period during which the program manager will accept charges against the account number assigned to a given work package.

AUTHORIZATION DOCUMENT

The characteristics of complex programs require that we integrate time and expenditure plans into a measure of *budgeted value of work planned* (BVWP). Once a schedule and budget are prepared and approved, budgeted value may be established for each work package, or we may decide to integrate expenditure and time plans at a level somewhat higher on the WBS. The tightest control is achieved when planned values are established at the work-package level.

If the integration is done at the work-package level, the planned value of work becomes the approved budget for the work package. Later in the reporting process, actual costs for work performed on a work package can be compared with planned value for work to monitor in an integrated way time and cost performance.

The authorization document is a work package approved by the program manager or by his or her representative. It should contain detailed information on time, cost, planned value, and expected performance on that segment of work. When approved by both program and functional management, it becomes the agreement, or performance contract, between program and functional personnel. Exhibit 16-9 provides an illustration of an authorizing document.

Exhibit 16-9
Sample Work-Package Authorization Document

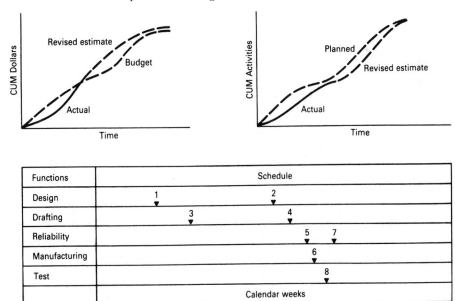

Functions	Schedule					
Design	1		2			
Drafting		3		4		
Reliability				5	7	
Manufacturing				6		
Test					8	
	Calendar weeks					

Planned Value of Work Scheduled

Milestones:
1. Complete preliminary design
2. Complete final design
3. Prepare preliminary drawings
4. Prepare final detail drawings

5. Reliability summary
6. Manufacture
7. Reliability summary
8. Test

Work Package Description: The purpose of this task is to design and fabricate air inlet valve according to specification xxx. WBS No. xxx–xxx–xxx.

Exhibit 16-9 contains a summary description of the work embodied in the work package, a milestone chart indicating scheduled completion dates for work-package activities, a time-phased financial expenditure plan, and a time-phased work plan. Finally, it contains planned value of work calculations for major milestones.

If the process leading to the issuance of the authorizing document is properly organized, the standards established should induce sufficient motivation on the part of functional personnel to perform the task and achieve or exceed the standards established.

THE BUDGET PROCEDURE

Operating budgets are ordinarily prepared for each program and functional organization on an annual basis. Each program prepares an operating budget for each period, and the budget normally represents a portion of the overall budget for the entire program. Each program budget contains an estimate of revenue and expenses. Expenses are ordinarily derived from a combination of approved work-package budgets and program expenditure plans for the period and normally include some funds for contingency. Estimating annual revenue for programs that are expected to extend over many budgeting periods is a difficult problem.

Operating budgets are prepared for each functional group for the budget period. If these functional budgets are tight and challenging, we must expect many functions to require some contingency funds for inevitable overexpenditures. These funds may be provided either through an appeal process to program managers, and a corresponding revision to the operating budget, or through a partial allocation of contingency funds from program budgets to functional organizations during the expenditure planning process. The latter procedure is likely to lead to goal-congruent behavior if functional organizations are treated as profit centers. The former procedure is likely to be most effective if functional organizations are treated as cost centers, which is the typical responsibility center designation for these organizational units.

Operating budgets for functional disciplines are prepared by summing approved work-package budgets pertaining to a function with planned expenditures derived from approved program expenditure plans for the portion of the budget period not covered by authorized work packages.

Contingency funds are required in these operating budgets to allow for some overexpenditures that are expected with tight budgets as well as unanticipated but inevitable differences that occur between financial expenditure plans and approved work-package plans. That is, annual operating budgets for each function must be approved largely on the basis of expenditure plans of the organization. Later, approved costs of work packages usually will deviate from the costs included in the original operating budget because of changes that occur between the planning process and the resource allocation process.

If differences between approved work packages and operating budgets are large, revisions are called for in operating budgets; if differences are small, they should be absorbed into a contingency account, which itself may be treated as an overhead account, along with all other nonprogram work. The responsibility center overhead account should also include idle time, company-sponsored research and development, proposal effort, indirect functional supplies, and functional supervision.

FUNCTIONAL OVERHEAD BUDGETS

Functional overhead budgets normally contain estimates for all functional expenditures that cannot be traced directly to a funded program. If functional organizations are cost centers, they are held responsible for performance regarding these overhead budgets. Under these circumstances, functional managers will attempt to keep their personnel employed on either a contractual program or an approved company-funded project, such as a proposal or a research project. Otherwise, the time of functional personnel must be charged to a special account called "idle time," and although some charges are expected to this account because of resource allocation problems and because of normal transitions from one program to another that often involve delays, these charges must be kept to a minimum for the functional manager to achieve good performance regarding his or her overhead budget.

Program managers, on the other hand, seek to remove functional personnel from their programs as quickly as possible, since the performance of these managers is often evaluated on the basis of profit. Functional managers must be able to employ these personnel on other programs for the organization as a whole to achieve the cost reduction that is attributed to the program office. If the organization cannot employ personnel so released, their time must be charged to idle time, which may cause functional managers to overextend their overhead budgets. If functional overhead budgets are in jeopardy, the temptation is always present to mischarge functional time to contracts that appear to be able to absorb such charges and to prolong existing problem work longer than necessary.

Because many organizations treat their level of functional resources as essentially fixed during the short term, an unplanned underexpenditure on a program ordinarily shifts an equivalent amount of costs somewhere else in the organization and does not result in a comparable organization saving *unless* these resources may be absorbed profitably on another contract or approved internally funded program.

These facts of organizational life lead us to place a premium upon planning and flexibility on the part of functional managers. Functional planning must always include provision for contingencies, whether this takes the form of pre-planned effort on internally approved programs or plans to shift resources to new programs if they are released prematurely.

If this kind of contingency planning is not done within functional disciplines, pressures will build to mischarge contracts, overrun overhead budgets, and adjust the level of personnel in the organization at an undesirable rate.

Moreover, it is a mistake to place too much emphasis on performance regarding overhead budgets in the evaluation of functional managers to the exclusion of performance regarding cost, schedule, and quality on all programs that are supported by the function. In addition, the quality of planning for the utilization of functional resources should play an important role in performance evaluation.

SYSTEMS OF REPORTING FOR PROGRAM CONTROL

To put the general requirements of a reporting system for complex programs into perspective, it is necessary to remember that we are describing a system that replaces the cost accounting system in the management control process. The program cost accounting system, however, does have similarities with conventional cost accounting systems (for example, account code structure, standards, variances, and overhead allocations), as we have seen. Therefore, when it comes to designing program reporting systems, it is useful to begin by reviewing the reporting system established in conventional cost accounting for each element of cost. It turns out that each of the variances used in conventional cost accounting may be used in program cost accounting, but they must be supplemented with combined cost and schedule variances.

The labor variances of conventional cost accounting are subdivided into time and rate variances. The time variance is found for a task as follows:

$$\text{(standard hours} - \text{actual hours)} \times \text{standard rate} = \text{time variance} \qquad (1)$$

The rate variance for labor is found by

$$\text{(standard rate} - \text{actual rate)} \times \text{actual hours} = \text{rate variance} \qquad (2)$$

The total labor variance for a task is

$$\begin{array}{ccc} \text{standard} & - & \text{actual} & = & \text{total} \\ \text{labor cost} & & \text{labor cost} & & \text{labor variance} \end{array} \qquad (3)$$

Material variances are similarly subdivided into quantity and price variances. The quantity variance is computed as follows:

$$\begin{array}{ccc} \text{(standard} & - & \text{actual} & \times & \text{standard} & = & \text{quantity} \\ \text{quantity} & & \text{quantity)} & & \text{price} & & \text{variance} \end{array} \qquad (4)$$

The price variance is given by

$$\begin{array}{ccc} \text{(standard} & - & \text{actual} & \times & \text{actual} & = & \text{price} \\ \text{price} & & \text{price)} & & \text{quantity} & & \text{variance} \end{array} \qquad (5)$$

The total material variance is

$$\begin{array}{ccc} \text{standard} & - & \text{actual} & = & \text{total} \\ \text{material cost} & & \text{material cost} & & \text{material variance} \end{array} \qquad (6)$$

We omit the overhead variances, since our reporting system is normally concerned with controllable variable costs.

Now the difference between the requirements for program reporting and conventional cost reporting systems develops because the labor and material variances are only cost or spending variances. They essentially assume that the scheduled work was completed in the process of spending funds for labor and materials. This is a realistic assumption in most manufacturing operations. Not so, however, in the management of complex programs.

For any WBS item, we are interested in the relationship between *budgeted value of work* for a given time period and *actual cost of work* for the same time period. This will tell us our total variance for the task, and we seek, by the computation of more detailed variances, to trace its causes.

There are five potential causes for any total variance:

- We did more or less work than scheduled.
- We used more or less labor than budgeted for the actual work we did.
- We paid more or less than budgeted for the actual labor used.
- We used more or less material than budgeted for the work we accomplished.
- We paid more or less than budgeted for the material we actually used.

The portion of the total variance attributable to (1) is called the *schedule variance,* and the portion attributable to (2) through (5) is called the *spending variance.* Therefore, the total variance for a given task or end item of a program is:

$$\underset{a}{\text{budgeted value of work planned}} - \underset{b}{\text{actual cost of work accomplished}} = \text{total variance} \qquad (7)$$

The schedule variance is given by

$$\underset{a}{\text{budgeted value of work planned}} - \underset{c}{\text{budgeted value of work accomplished}} = \text{schedule variance} \qquad (8)$$

The spending variance is

$$\underset{c}{\text{budgeted value of work accomplished}} - \underset{b}{\text{actual cost of work accomplished}} = \text{spending variance} \qquad (9)$$

The spending variance is then subdivided into labor and material variances according to equations (3) and (6). Labor and material variances may be subdivided further into rate and quantity variances according to equations (1), (2), (4), and (5).

These nine variances may be computed for each level of the WBS and for each functional organization at regular intervals throughout the life of a program. The total variance for a WBS end item tells the responsible manager whether there is a problem or not regarding cost and schedule performance. If a problem exists, the manager can request more detailed reporting information for the next level of the WBS and find exactly where the problem is and whether

Exhibit 16-10
Integrated Time-Cost Reporting System

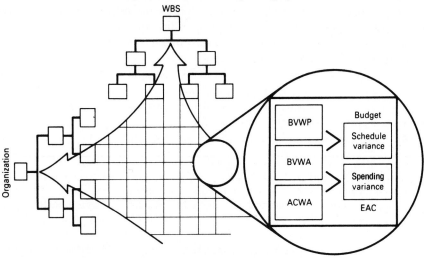

The variance terms in the diagram are defined as follows:
BVWP–budget value of work planned; BVWA–budget value of work
accomplished; ACWA–actual cost of work accomplished; EAC–Estimate
of costs at completion.

the problem is concerned with schedule slippage or with a labor or material spending variance.

Notice that the only variance that is new is the schedule variance. Each of the other variances appears in conventional cost accounting systems. The schedule variance requires for its computation data on planned and actual schedule performance together with normal cost data for each level of the WBS. The fact that there is only one new variance required should dispel any mystery surrounding the schedule and cost reporting requirements for complex programs.

Conceptually the time and cost reporting system for complex programs may be represented by Exhibit 16-10. We should be capable of calculating a schedule variance and a spending variance for any level of the WBS. We should be able to divide the spending variance into its labor and material elements. And we should be able to trace the schedule variance to a scheduled plan.

The reporting system should also contain the capability to provide program information for each functional organization that is performing work on the program by WBS end item. This information should follow the same format as that for the program.

These, then, are the broad outlines that the formal reporting system should take, although we recognize that the systems should be flexible and adaptable to each organization.

Let us look at an example of an application of our variance system. Let us assume that we are considering a work package for the structure (A01-3-2) of our TV transmission building. Moreover, let us assume that we placed the material orders at the estimated price and that we have chosen not to include overhead in our project control reports, since the project manager has little or no control over it. Therefore, our primary control variance is the estimated $23,650 of labor costs for this work package.

Approximately six weeks into the project we have an integrated progress chart drawn up for us. It is shown in Exhibit 16-11. The chart shows that work on the structure is currently three weeks ahead of schedule, but that is not the whole story. The schedule variance is positive, and we have done more in the first six weeks than was originally planned (that is, BVWA > BVWP). Yet we have spent more than budgeted for the work accomplished (that is, ACWA > BVWA). Projecting these trends to completion, we will spend approximately $2,000 more than estimated, but we will finish three weeks early. Our conclusion at first glance might be that the schedule gain was accomplished by spending more labor resources, and further investigation might show that to be true. Nevertheless, unless there are some changes made, the work package will overrun by approxi-

Exhibit 16-11
Integrated Progress Chart for the Structure of the TV
Transmission Building A01-3-2

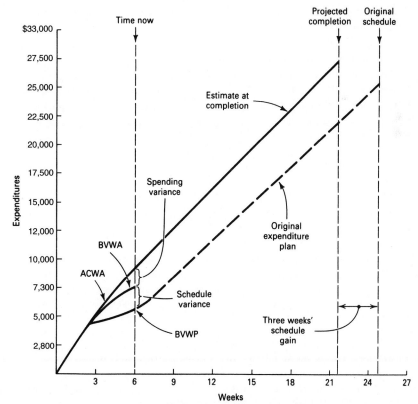

Source: Adapted by permission from G. Shillinglaw, *Managerial Cost Accounting,* 4th ed., Richard D. Irwin, Homewood, Illinois, 1982, p. 763.

mately $2,000 at completion, and that is bad news! The integrated report gives us a rather complete picture. It is much clearer than independent budget versus actual expenditure and schedule progress reports.

REPORTING DELAYS AND BIAS

There always must be some delay between actual program progress and problems and their reporting, since the reporting process consumes time. All program status must be ascertained from the performing organizations. These data then must be processed. After processing, these reports must be analyzed to ensure that the processing was done correctly and to analyze progress and problems. It is not unusual for this processing and analysis work to consume two weeks or more on a complex program.

Moreover, the subsequent meetings and recommendations for action may take still another week or two. When action is finally taken, it may be to remedy a problem that existed a month ago. To complicate the reporting problem further, bias may creep into the reports.

If functional supervision is evaluated on the basis of its rate of progress alone, then we should expect bias to enter into the reporting system. Bias can be prevented to some extent by explicit definition of activities that then become standard for the organization.

Often standardization of activity descriptions manifests itself in the preparation of a dictionary of terms and activities. The dictionary serves to identify accurately completed activities and improves communication within the program group while providing the basis for a historical file of time and cost data. This file becomes useful for estimating future programs containing similar activities.

Finally, the frequency of reporting should vary from one program to the next, depending upon the nature of the contract, the importance of the program to the organization, and customer reporting requirements.

REFERENCES

ARCHIBALD, RUSSELL D., *Managing High-Technology Programs and Projects.* New York: John Wiley, 1976.

CLELAND, DAVID I., AND WILLIAM R. KING, eds., *Project Management Handbook,* 2nd ed. New York: Van Nostrand and Reinhold, 1988.

DAVIS, E. M., "Networks: Resource Allocation," *Industrial Engineering,* Vol. 6, no. 4 (1974), pp. 22–34.

FERGUSON, DAVID W., *Public Works Program Management Using Owner-Consultant Partnerships: Organizational Factors Influencing Effectiveness,* Ph.D. dissertation, Claremont Graduate School, Clarement, CA., 1993.

MACIARIELLO, JOSEPH A., *Program-Management Control Systems.* New York: John Wiley, 1978.

MARCH, JAMES G., AND HERBERT A. SIMON, *Organizations.* New York: John Wiley, 1958.

ROBERTS, EDWARD B., *The Management of R&D.* New York: Harper & Row, 1964.

SHILLINGLAW, GORDON G., *Managerial Cost Accounting,* 5th ed. Homewood, Ill.: Richard D. Irwin, 1982.

Northwest Research Laboratory:
Case 16-1 The Local Area Network (LAN) Project*

The LAN project is typical of all the software development projects undertaken in this department in the seven years that I have been department manager. These projects seem to exceed their schedule and their budget—not by a little but by a lot. I am not sure that anybody knows how to manage them successfully. The LAN project is typical but on top of schedule and cost problems, we didn't even get the system we thought we were going to get. I would welcome any help you can give us in managing these kind of projects. I am not sure that standard program management techniques are adequate to manage software development projects like the LAN.

Max Siegel, Manager,
Contracts Department,
Northwest Reasearch Laboratory
(in an interview with the case writer)

INTRODUCTION

In mid-1988, the contracts department of a large research laboratory located in the northwestern United States chose to invest in the development of a local area network (LAN)—a networked computer software program to integrate the department's word-processing and data-reporting activities. The program was expanding, the number of proposals and contracts requiring contract administration was increasing, and the overall workload exceeded the capacity of the six-person contracts department.

The firm's automation support group (ASG) was chosen to perform the system development work. At the time this case was investigated, the intended six-month effort was four months behind schedule and more than 100 percent in excess of budget. It was estimated that an additional two months of effort and another 50 percent of the original budget would be required to make operational only 75 percent of the proposed specifications.

CASE HISTORY: THE CONTRACT ADMINISTRATION DEPARTMENT

The contract administration department (hereafter referred to as the "department" or the "user") is charged with the responsibility of providing the interface between the customer and the firm and with providing information regarding the business aspects of the program to upper management.

At the time of the case, the department consisted of six people. Three additional personnel had been hired and were awaiting security clearance—a process that involved six to ten months to complete. The anticipated organization of the department when fully staffed is shown below. The personnel designated to work the LAN project are indicated by asterisks.

*This case was prepared by Edie Levenson with the assistance of Professor Joseph A. Maciariello and Peter Zalkind.

Even with an eventual total of nine employees, the department would be understaffed in relation to planned work. Since the security aspects of the program precluded near-term availability of additional personnel, achieving greater efficiencies was considered essential to accomplishing the department's responsibilities and objectives.

Contract Administration Department

1 Dept. Manager**		
2 Secretaries		
Aplied Research Contracts	**Pure Research Contracts**	**Prototype Contracts**
1 Manager	1 Section Head**	1 Contract
1 Section Head	1 Contract	Negotiator
1 Contract	Analyst	
Analyst**		

OPERATIONS OF THE DEPARTMENT PRIOR TO LAN

The department is responsible for all proposal, negotiation, and ongoing administration activities associated with multiple complex project contracts. The data needed to perform these operations may be required by any member of the department at any time during the process of the program. It is essential, therefore, that the management system provide a means for everyone in the department to quickly generate, access, and manipulate all required data.

The volume of correspondence going into and out of the department is high, consisting of approximately 150 incoming letters and 100 outgoing letters per month. Personal computers were introduced into the department in 1984. The PCs were used to assist in tracking specific contractual information which must be readily available to perform contract administration and to answer queries from other program personnel. This type of information was maintained on individual,

**LAN Project

stand-alone files using standard file management programs. Because each of these files was independent, each piece of information was entered manually wherever it was required.

There was no standardization of the word-processing programs or formats to generate the documents produced by department personnel. Whether document drafts were prepared by using word processors or in longhand, the secretary retyped the texts into the Wang word processing system, using either a Wang system terminal or a stand-alone work station, adhering to company correspondence format and archive procedures. Since the Wang system did not interface with any of the personal computers, information about each letter generated on the Wang had to be entered a second time into the PC file program that tracked correspondence.

The PC usage described above provided the department with a means to access and report information that had been entered into individual files. Procedures to guide the entry of data evolved informally and were eventually consolidated into a department instruction.

The control system to ensure adherence to the instruction was informal. On the many occasions when the computer files did not contain desired information, employees spent considerable time searching for source documents which were located in various places, such as employees' offices, the central contracts files, or in the program's data center.

THE LOCAL AREA NETWORK

A review of existing management systems revealed that considerable time was spent accessing, reviewing, and updating various unrelated tracking systems associated with the numerous documents involved with proposal preparation, contract negotiation, and daily contract administration activities. The ability to conduct these activities effectively and efficiently had a direct impact on the ability to obtain contract awards and achieve program success.

It was suggested that an investment in automation would:

1. Solve the understaffing problem.
2 Favorably improve the department's ability to obtain and administer contracts.
3. Result in significant long-term cost savings in the area of human resources for the department.

The project involved development of an integrated word and data generation and processing system to be operated on a local area network within the department. The department envisioned that the LAN system would:

1. Centralize and integrate all information generation, processing, and storage.
2. Require only one entry of any piece of data no matter where the data are needed in the system.
3. Provide capability for simultaneous access of all information by all Department personnel.
4. Provide required routine reporting.
5. Provide capability for ad hoc reporting.

The contract analyst, a person recently recruited from another division of the same company, coordinated the LAN project for the department. She had five years of engineering experience but was new to PC systems and contracts administration. Her responsibilities for the LAN project involved:

1. defining system requirements
2. interfacing with ASG
3. converting existing data to the new system
4. training department personnel to operate the new system

The section head had designed the existing systems and was most familiar with both the methods and work to be processed through the LAN. She therefore provided assistance in both defining department requirements and reviewing ASG's design solutions. The department manager was available to resolve management problems as required.

The ASG proposal was based upon a six-month effort (July through December) and included costs for required hardware, commercial software, development of custom software, system integration, user training, documentation, and project management. The proposal identified an ASG project manager, project leader, and various programming and consulting personnel. Pertinent portions of the proposed ASG tasks extracted from the proposal include:

1. *Management and reports.* Project planning, coordination reporting, and periodic meetings with user. Monthly status report of finances, manpower, 30-day summary of activities and milestones.
2. *Systems analysis.* Examine system inputs, outputs, and necessary processing. Analyze data relationships and define file structures.
3. *Systems design.* Prepare narrative description of the functions to be programmed. Design screen and report layouts. Develop data dictionary. Update systems requirements specification as necessary to reflect changes affecting project total cost or schedule.
4. *Coding and testing.* Write program code based on information compiled during systems analysis and design. Fully test each module.
5.–8. *Systems test, Implementation, Documentation, and Training.*

PROJECT DIARY

Biweekly status meetings were begun in July. Project managers and key personnel from both the contracts department and ASG attended these meetings. At the first meeting, ASG submitted a program status summary that indicated, "No major variation in funding or schedule at this time." ASG also submitted a task list containing start and end dates for design, implementation, coding, and training for each system element. At the request of the department manager, the ASG project management and reporting process were upgraded to the procedures required by a commercially available project management software package. The intent was to obtain a more specific level of both planning and reporting to enable the managers to quickly focus on any schedule or budget variance.

Certain project ground rules were established at this first coordination meeting. The five key integrative features (enumerated above) which the department wanted to design into the system were reviewed. The department manager stated that he understood ASG's eagerness to develop a useful and marketable product and its willingness to make adjustments as the understanding of requirements grew. However, he cautioned that if at any time such adjustments would cause any cost growth or schedule delay, he wanted the opportunity for approval or rejection prior to initiating the action.

At the first meeting in August, ASG advised that due to problems in acquiring the LAN hardware and operating system, the installation date would slip from December 11, 1988 to January 8, 1989. All of the other communications at this meeting were routine.

ASG provided a functional requirements specification at the first September meeting. The document restated the department's business problem and need, the generalized benefits to be realized from the resulting system, and a descriptive list of categories of transactions that the system would process. The document did not describe the project's end-product or address key features which would enable the product to meet department needs. To be sure that department goals were communicated, the manager reiterated the purpose of the project, citing the ground rules established at the July meeting. ASG reported that submittal of this specification completed the review of contracts' office automation requirements. The next task was to specify the functional design.

At the second September meeting, ASG again reported that there were "no major variations in cost or schedule." ASG provided a functional design specification. The specification was purported to be an "essential system model." It contained rather esoteric computer terminology. Although ASG provided an explanation of the specification, the department manager made reference to the ground rules established at the first coordination meeting, reiterating that ASG was considered to be the expert in program design. Contract's contribution to the project would be explanations of the department's requirements so that ASG could design the integrated system that was the objective of the project. There was no further discussion relative to acceptability, concurrence, or approval of the functional design specification. No action items resulted from the meeting.

At the first meeting in October, the project management report indicated that there was a delay in development of the software routine to convert existing department data to the new system, but there was "no impact on the overall schedule at this time." ASG presented an executive control function specification. The specification contained a breakdown of the internal system structure descending from the main menu through five modules and associated detail functions. ASG also presented a screen design specification. Like the functional design specification, these documents were written in "computerese" and not particularly meaningful to the user. The department manager again made reference to the still valid project goal, namely to develop an integrated system.

In the first November meeting, ASG advised that the coding effort was behind schedule. To recover, two more people had been added to the project. ASG stated they would start using money from management reserves but since the effort was proposed on a fixed-price basis, ASG would absorb any cost overruns. The overall impact would be a slip of the installation date to January 21.

At the second November meeting, ASG gave the first demonstration of correspondence processing on the system. The demonstration revealed that many more control features were built into the system than were either requested or desired by the department. The department did not want to build a system to control each step of a contract administrator's work. Therefore, the excessive control features were identified for removal from the system. The objectives of the system were again reviewed for ASG. The department manager also reminded ASG that changes to the original requirements which would result in cost impact or schedule delay needed to be addressed as soon as they were identified.

At the December meeting additional pieces of the system were presented for review. It continued to be necessary to request that the screen wording be revised to reflect actual department requirements. The LAN was now scheduled to be installed during the week of February 1. To meet this revised date, ASG scheduled programming time during the holiday break period. ASG again advised that since the project was bid on a fixed-price basis and since customer satisfaction was considered important, costs that exceeded the original price would not be billed to the department.

The first meeting in January was, in a word, disastrous. The purpose of the meeting was to review approximately twenty screens which had been prepared by the ASG systems analyst and which represented the core of the user interface with the overall system. The systems analyst opened the meeting with the caveat: "You may not see the immediate use of these screens now, but we are trying to build for the long haul." The first screen was a "components catalogue" which called for input of data not related to contract administration work. The second screen addressed contract change orders. When asked about the interrelationship of this file to the proposal and correspondence files, the systems analyst advised that there were no such interrelationships. Required information would have to be entered into each individual file. The third screen presented a financial form

that had been deleted from the requirements on October 16. The fourth screen addressed a company organizational hierarchy file which also was of no particular interest to the department. There were problems with nearly all of the screens presented at that meeting. It was apparent that a serious problem existed, but since neither manager was at the meeting, the problem was not dealt with at that time.

The overall communication at the first January meeting was that the system did not address the initial objective of integrating all information generation, processing, and storage activities such that any piece of data needed to be entered only one time, notwithstanding the number of places in which it would eventually be required. A management meeting was convened the next week to address this fundamental project issue. ASG presented a chart addressing five areas believed to cause development problems:

1. Time span. Design is six months old and environments have changed.
2. Education. Change in user requirements.
3. Specifications. System specs evolved from generic to specific.
4. New technology. Misjudged effort to link database/word processor.
5. Security. Department's security requirements not understood.

In addition, ASG presented a three-page document addressing features which in ASG's opinion were not outlined in the original proposal but had been designed into the current system. These features addressed relationships between elements of the database as well as specific means to access information. The department maintained that the project objective remained as it was originally envisioned and repeated at several biweekly meetings. It did not concur with the statements that the user environment and user requirements had changed. ASG explained that the change involved the extent of required data file integration, which had not been understood at the time of the proposal. Furthermore, ASG had substantially underestimated the technology development effort that was required to enable transport of data back and forth between the word processor and the database software. As a final point, ASG stated that interface with a team of three representatives from the user department was resulting in conflict of direction. ASG asked for one designated point of contact. Discussion of these points did not alter the current failure of the system to satisfy the department's requirements. ASG was requested to present its assessment of remaining tasks. The result was a slip in the planned installation date to March 18.

The section head of the department believed that a portion of the discrepancies in system design might stem from misunderstandings about how work actually flows through the department. She asked to review a schematic of planned work flow through the LAN system. ASG advised that such schematics are not utilized in PC development projects. The systems analyst explained that PC development projects are based upon diagrams of file relationships and a prototyping process wherein user feedback is solicited throughout the project. In lieu of the requested schematic, a chart of file relationships was presented by ASG. It was not possible for the department to determine from the chart whether work would properly flow through the system or whether the system in fact integrated the department's work as desired.

ASG removed the system analyst from the project and substituted a development programmer who had more closely related PC experience. (The system analyst's background primarily involved mainframe program development). To partially address the department's concern for a work flow schematic, a WBS-type chart was prepared showing the hierarchy of the system's user screens.

While this WBS appeared to indicate proper file relationships, work flow or integration of data was not addressed. ASG advised it would take two weeks and $20,000 to produce the requested schematic. The department did not authorize the expenditure. During the next several weeks, significant progress was made in revising the screens to reflect the initial requirements. However, no information was available to determine whether the screen changes were cosmetic only or whether the files were indeed interrelated as requested.

On March 17, the day before installation was scheduled to take place, ASG advised that installation would slip to the week of April 25. There were no new problems cited as a cause for the delay. On March 23, a staff person from the office of the division director of contract administration telephoned the contracts department to advise that ASG had charged the Departments' directorate account more than 100 percent in excess of the project authorization. Several meetings were held to move through the line of authority at ASG—ASG is run by a staff vice president, who reports to the firm's corporate controller. Although ASG had repeatedly said that it would absorb the overrun, there was no ASG overhead account within which overrun charges could be accumulated. Failing to agree upon a means to resolve the funding problem within a very short time, the department issued a stop work order on April 7.

QUESTIONS

1. Appendix 16-A gives a list of potential failure modes for projects arranged according to cybernetic categories. Evaluate the LAN project in terms of these failure modes.
2. Where were the key control problems in the LAN project? How could they have been avoided?
3. Is there any modification you would make to the cybernetic diagram to incorporate your findings in this case?

APPENDIX 16-A:
POTENTIAL FAILURES IN STEERING

Potential failures in the task of successfully steering a project toward its objectives include those *external* to the decision maker(s) and those *internal* to the decision maker and the organization. The vertical line on Exhibit 16-12 depicts the division.

Steerability may be impeded as a result of four potential environmental failures as defined in Exhibit 16-12. *Lack of data* implies that a manager lacks information about the project environment which is necessary to achieve goals. A variant of the lack of data is the *lack of predictability* regarding environmental disturbances that impact performance towards a goal. *Overwhelming events* are environmental disturbances that overwhelm the manager's ability to cope. *Interference* occurs when factors or persons in the environment constrain the behavior of the manager in a way that prevents goal attainment.

Feedback is critical to steering an organization towards its goal. Feedback frustrations occur when data for evaluating the effectiveness of past decisions are insufficient. If feedback is insufficient a manager does not know which actions to repeat and which to delete in the future. That is, there can be no organizational learning. *Erroneous feedback* as to the success of various actions can lead to decision error and goal failure. *Conflict feedback* leaves the decision maker confused as to the state of goal achievement. *Confounded feedback* occurs when the results of an action are mixed up with the results of other actions and with environmental changes so the decision maker is confused as to the ultimate effects of a past decision. Finally, feedback may be *untimely* so far as necessary corrective decisions are concerned.

Perceptual frustration includes many of the same frustrations that are external to the decision maker, but these involve perceptual processes. *Uncertainty* occurs when a manager doesn't understand that a goal that is being pursued is in danger of being missed. *Inaccurate perceptions* may be based upon inaccurate information concerning the environment or incorrect interpretation of the data that are available. *Inconsistent information* involves different interpretations of the same event or conflicting interpretations of multiple events. *Failure to forecast* is a failure to forecast the implications of trends that are at least partially visible. *Information overload* is a condition where accurate perception breaks down because of the inability to process environmental information effectively. *Lack of data* is the same frustration as discussed above for environmental variables, except that this one pertains to perceptions that data are inadequate for making the necessary inferences. Similarly, *erroneous data* are data perceived to contain errors. *Irrelevant data* are those perceived as being inapplicable for necessary inferences. *Confounded data* may lead to spurious perceptions.

Goal frustrations are among the most serious impediments to steerability. *Ambiguous goals* are those for which criteria for achievement are not clear, thus frustrating the measurement process. *Unrealistic goals* are those that are simply beyond the individual's ability to achieve them. *Conflicting goals* are those individual and organizational goals that are incompatible and cannot be attained simultaneously because of the trade-offs required for the accomplishment of each goal. *Bland goals* are those that are simply not highly valued, thus providing low motivation for their achievement. *Goal overload* occurs when the complexity of goals overwhelms the decision maker's ability to sequence or prioritize them.

Comparator frustrations include the *failure to compare*, which is a case in which relevant perceptions are simply not compared to goals to determine if a gap exists. *Incomparable measures* are found where goals and measurements of progress toward goals are conceptualized differently and incorrect surrogates for

Exhibit 16-12
Cybernetic Failure Modes in Project Manager

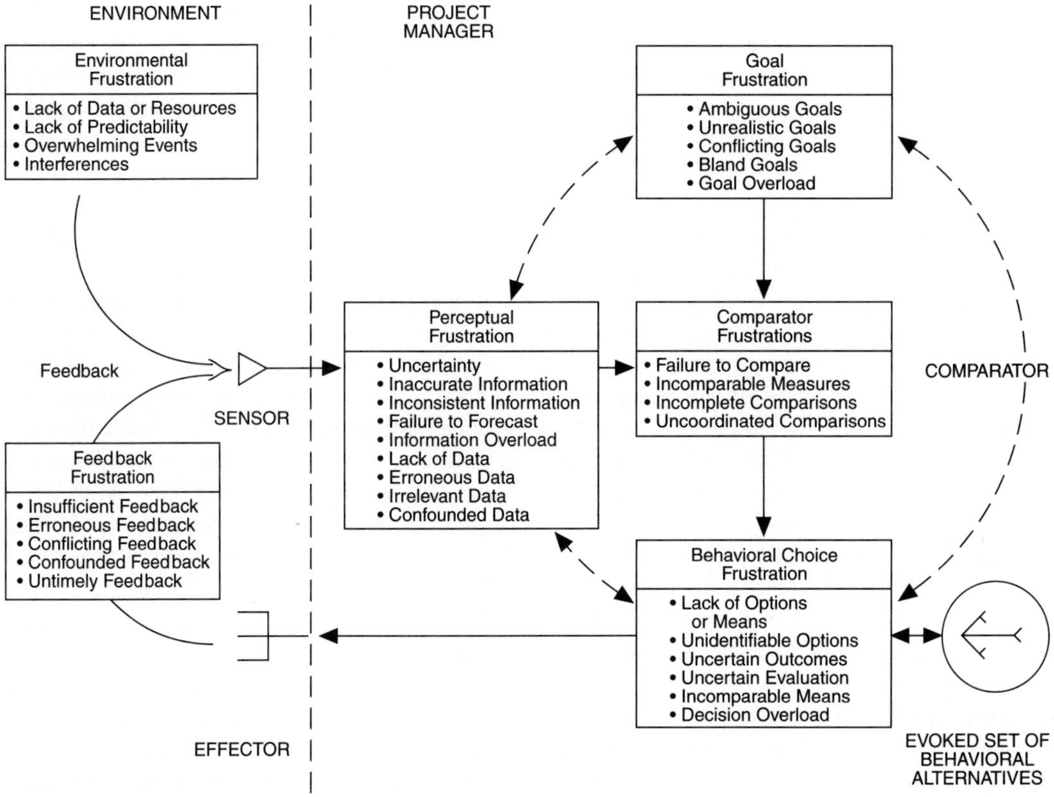

goals are measured. *Incomplete measures* are found where the measure is a valid one for the goal but is incomplete as an assessment of performance towards the goal. *Uncoordinated comparisons* are failure to compare perceptions and goals at the same point in time. This commonly occurs when there are long processing delays in preparing relevant information.

Behavioral choice frustrations are those involving the decision-making process itself. *Lack of options* is the frustration that occurs when because of lack of ability, experience, or free will, the decision maker is unable to solve a problem and steer the organization toward its goal. Related, *unidentifiable options* are frustrations produced when appropriate

behaviors, although known, are simply not accessed by the decision maker as a result of inappropriate search procedures. *Uncertain evaluations and outcomes* occurs when the decision maker is uncertain about predictions of the impact of alternatives upon the goal, thus making it difficult to choose effective remedies. *Incomparable means* involve two or more alternatives that are believed to make a contribution toward the goal but whose impacts upon the goal are not strictly comparable, thus frustrating rational choice. Finally, *decisional overload* occurs when too many decisions must be made in a given period of time, not allowing enough time for analysis of each decision.

17

CONTROL OF MULTINATIONAL OPERATIONS

CONTROL ISSUES IN THE MULTINATIONAL CORPORATION

One of the most dramatic changes that has taken place in American corporations during the past three decades has been the rapid internationalization of their operations. This strategy has led to changes in organization structure, which were discussed in Chapter 5. In addition, it has created a number of additional control challenges. Some of these challenges are related to the control structure, whereas others are related to the control process. This chapter is concerned with these additional issues.

Before we discuss the specific issues that are peculiar to the control of foreign operations, we will review the central role of strategy in determining the design of control systems for foreign operations.

CENTRAL ROLE OF STRATEGY IN CONTROL SYSTEMS DESIGN
FOR FOREIGN OPERATIONS

In determining the methods to use to control foreign operations, we must first focus on the strategy the parent has adopted for the foreign operation. Then we must determine the relevant key success factors under that strategy. Once the key success factors are determined, we are then in a position to decide upon the appropriate degree of autonomy for the foreign operation as well as the management systems that are appropriate for the control of these operations.

A country within which the multinational corporation (MNC) does business is called the host country. The country within which it is headquartered is called the home country.

Let's illustrate the effects of strategy upon management systems by assuming two widely employed generic strategies of a parent for its foreign operations:

1. To penetrate a host country market with new and innovative products that are appropriate for the host market.
2. To more fully utilize production capacity in the home country by producing additional product in the home country for sale in the host market.

Strategy number one requires much closer attention to the host market characteristics than strategy number two. It requires much more innovation in product development.

Strategy number one requires significant decentralization of decision making and relatively high levels of autonomy for the foreign operation. It follows from this that the management systems should be designed to reflect this autonomy in order to successfully implement this strategy.

In organizing a foreign unit under strategy one, the parent might consider designating the foreign marketing unit as a *profit or investment center*. A production facility might also be established in the host country if the volume of production warrants it. The production operation, in this case, might be designated a *cost and quality responsibility center*.

The foreign division would be designated as a profit or investment center under strategy one. Transfers from the parent to the foreign operations would be at prices that would aid in successfully implementing the strategy of the parent.

Under strategy number two, a different tack would be taken. Since achieving economies of scale is a key success factor for strategy two, production of goods for the foreign market would be done where it could be done most efficiently, which would probably be at home. In that case there would be no host market production facility.

The marketing organization in the host market would probably be designated a *revenue center*, since it is merely selling a standard product in a new market. The entire foreign operation would probably be a *revenue center*, since it has limited responsibility for new product development and no responsibility for the production cost of the product.

Transfers from the domestic to the foreign market would probably be at standard cost, since all the profits are recorded by the parent. The autonomy of the foreign operation would be very limited, and the design of the remaining management systems would be expected to reflect this limited autonomy.

Many other strategies exist for entering foreign markets besides the two illustrated. Some specific additional strategies are (Carr, 1989, pp. 3–4)

1. To seek low-cost production of existing products.
2. To follow original equipment makers to their foreign operations.
3. To seek a global strategy for the products of the firm.
4. To supply an existing market with locally produced goods.

5. To participate in a market that is experiencing continuous product innovation.
6. To expand closer to sources of raw material.
7. To seek acquisitions in an attractive foreign market.

Each one of these different strategies has associated with it slightly different key success factors. In turn, each may have a slightly different set of management systems that are appropriate for the implementation of the strategy. It simply has to be thought through on a case-by-case basis.

ADDITIONAL ISSUES IN THE CONTROL OF FOREIGN OPERATIONS

Since most of the additional issues involved in the control of foreign operations are concerned with adjustments to the control process, we shall merge the one additional structural item (that is, transfer pricing) with the process items in this chapter without any further distinction.

We shall deal in order with the following issues:

1. Analysis of foreign investment projects (that is, programming)
2. Empirical findings concerning methods used to evaluate foreign affiliates
3. Transfer pricing for affiliates of a multinational corporation
4. Budgeting for foreign affiliates of a multinational corporation

ANALYSIS OF FOREIGN INVESTMENT PROJECTS BY MULTINATIONAL CORPORATIONS (MNCs)

The analysis of foreign projects is full of surprises for the unwary analyst who has only a domestic orientation. We will consider a number of refinements to the net present value model that are necessary in order to evaluate foreign investments properly.

Many of these new considerations may be incorporated within the NPV model, yet they complicate the analysis considerably. In this section we consider each of the principal differences between domestic and foreign investments.

Taxes on Income Associated with Foreign Projects

The host country ordinarily levies taxes on the income of an MNC earned in that country. These rates differ from country to country and are sometimes offset by tax concessions granted to the MNC in return for some desirable service provided the host country by the MNC, such as employment, training, or the transfer of technology.

Furthermore, many host countries levy an additional tax on that portion of profits that is repatriated to the home country in the form of dividends. In addition, many home countries (including the United States) tax profits repatriated from foreign operations. Income taxes and withholding taxes on dividends, interest, and royalties paid by United States firms to foreign governments are deductible from United States corporate income taxes.

While it is beyond the scope of this chapter to treat the subject of taxation of MNCs exhaustively, it is important to note some of the major variations that occur from country to country. The major variations are as follows:

1. Unlike the current practice in the United States, many countries rely heavily upon indirect taxes such as value added, excise, and turnover taxes. The value added tax, a sales tax at each stage of production of consumer goods, is the main source of revenue in the European Economic Community (EEC) and in Scandinavian countries.
2. Definitions of taxable income differ. Rates allowed for depreciation differ from one country to the next. For example, Peru and Brazil allow depreciation to be computed on the basis of asset values restated to account for inflation.
3. Some countries allow tax exemptions or reduced taxation on income from certain "desirable" investment projects. Tax concessions may be granted to motivate employment, induce certain categories of investment, train the labor force, and transfer technology. Tax exemptions include special "tax holidays" (that is, exemption from taxes for a certain number of years), exemptions from import and export duties, and investment allowances that permit extra depreciation allowances on plant and equipment.
4. Presently, 35 tax treaties exist among the United States and other industrialized nations, and many more are in the process of negotiation. The primary purpose of these tax treaties is the avoidance of double taxation on income earned abroad. Many of the treaties reduce taxes on dividends, interest, and royalties paid by a foreign subsidiary to its parent. Since these treaties reduce the tax on repatriated income, they materially affect the prospects of an investment.
5. A number of countries in an attempt to attract foreign investment offer *tax havens*. At present 44 countries offer very low or zero corporate tax rates for income earned in those countries.

Therefore, while it is usually easy to calculate an effective tax rate for domestic investment projects, the effective tax rate applied to foreign projects of a United States firm is a function of the host country tax rate, the U.S. tax rate, applicable withholding taxes, foreign tax credits on U.S. taxes, and tax concessions.

Actual taxes paid on funds remitted from foreign projects depend also upon the *transfer mechanism* used. There are numerous methods of repatriating funds from foreign operations that are subjected to varying rates of host and home country taxes. Funds may be repatriated through the use of relatively high transfer prices for goods and services provided the foreign affiliate by the company, by levying management fees and royalty charges upon the subsidiary, by repayment of loans and debt, and by dividend flows. The Internal Revenue Service, however, under Section 482 of the IRS Code retains authority to allocate income between parent and foreign subsidiary to reflect the true income of the parent and subsidiary. Foreign governments also place restrictions on the latitude for setting transfer prices.

Finally, also within limits, net profits from foreign projects may be reinvested locally without U.S. taxes and repatriated at the end of the project's life rather than at periodic intervals throughout the life of the project.

The complications in evaluating foreign projects of MNCs arising from taxes may be incorporated into the NPV model directly. Summing the Rs of all periods, our NPV model in summation notation now becomes

$$\text{NPV} = -C_0 + \sum_{t=1}^{n} \frac{R_t}{(1+i)^t} \tag{1}$$

We look at each project as it affects the incremental cost and revenue stream of the corporation as a whole. That is, we take the perspective of headquarters management and ask, "What are the incremental returns of the project to the home office?" Therefore, we count incremental repatriated income net of host country income taxes, foreign withholding taxes, and home country taxes. This is how we arrive at each R term in the summation.

The next question is: "What about profits that are not repatriated?" To take unremitted profits into account, we must add another term to the equation that shows the reinvestment of unremitted profits after taxes (host and home country taxes), to a terminal date (for example, project completion) at the local reinvestment rate, and discount these reinvestment profits back to the present. Our model then becomes

$$\text{NPV} = -C_0 + \sum_{t=1}^{n} \frac{R_t}{(1+i)^t} + \sum_{t=1}^{n} \frac{S_t(1+r)^n}{(1+i)^n} \tag{2}$$

where the last term of the equation takes that part of the incremental return (S) that is reinvested to the terminal date (n) at the local reinvestment rate (r) and discounts the terminal value to time now by $1/(1+i)^n$.

The third question is: "What do we do with true profits from the project that were repatriated by (legal) means other than by dividend payment or profit consolidation?" To account for these profits, we must add still another term that takes into account the "true profits" of a project that are repatriated by these other means. Our model then becomes

$$\text{NPV} = -C_0 + \sum_{t=1}^{n} \frac{R_t}{(1+i)^t} + \sum_{t=1}^{n} \frac{S_t(1+r)^n}{(1+i)^n} + \sum_{t=1}^{n} \frac{U_t}{(1+i)^t} \tag{3}$$

where the last U attempts to capture these other transfers which are incremental returns of the project.

Some combination of the equations (1), (2), and (3) may be required to fit the true circumstances of a particular foreign investment project.

Political Risks

The most extreme risk of doing business overseas is expropriation of foreign investments by host governments. This can occur in two forms: seizure of property or official socialization of industry. Examples of the former were the 1971 takeover by the government of Chile of Kennecott, Anaconda, Cerro, Ford, and IT&T and the 1969 takeover by the government of Bolivia of Gulf Oil. An example of the latter was the nationalization of all industry in Cuba in 1960. Some countries have past records of expropriating capital goods without full compensation to the corporation, and this risk must be considered in capital investment decisions.

There are other more subtle methods of interference with the operations of a foreign subsidiary, which although less dramatic in their effects, pose risks to investment projects. Seven such restrictions are as follows:

1. Additional taxes may be levied against profits of the subsidiary, or new exchange controls blocking the flow of funds may be imposed.
2. Restrictions may be placed upon the entry of foreign managerial and technical personnel.
3. Restrictions may be placed upon imports of supplies and raw materials.
4. Domestic consumers may be "advised" to boycott products of a foreign subsidiary.
5. Employees may be encouraged by government to strike their foreign employer.
6. Government may attempt to interfere with labor negotiations or arbitrations.
7. Regulations may be enacted requiring joint ventures with majority ownership resting within the host country.

Each of these potential restrictions will tend to reduce the profitability of foreign investment and may be designed either to force the subsidiary to leave the foreign country or to expropriate gradually the assets of a subsidiary.

Numerous analytical methods exist for evaluating the risk of expropriation together with some more intuitive methods. It is possible to insure an investment at book value against expropriation and include the insurance premiums as a charge against the project. The United States government through the Overseas Private Insurance Corporation (OPIC) sells insurance for various categories of political risk. Private insurers (for example, Lloyd's of London) will also sell political risk insurance. The MNC may also self-insure and charge the project an insurance premium approximately equal to that charged by government or private insurance carriers.

Many companies deal with political risk by adopting a "go, no-go" approach. They simply refuse to consider investments in nations deemed to have an unfavorable investment climate or nations where unstable political conditions exist or where the courts cannot be relied upon to uphold contractual relationships. Between 1960 and 1976, Latin American countries had the largest number of expropriations [144] but the Arab states had the highest percentage of expropriations as a percentage of total U.S. companies in the region (Bradley, 1977, p. 78).

We may also use the NPV model in various ways to evaluate directly the risk of expropriation upon the acceptability of a project. Estimates may be made of the probabilities of the occurrence of various events, and these estimates may be used to calculate expected cash flows. The resultant expected net present value may be subjected to extensive sensitivity analyses to determine the sensitivity of the project evaluation decision to changes in the probabilities of expropriation or of other hostile events.

Another use of the NPV model is to find the *discounted payback period* for the project. The discounted payback period, as we discussed in Chapter 10, is the time period necessary to earn just the minimum acceptable return on the project. One might conclude that the shorter the discounted payback period, the less the risk of capital loss. At least it is easier to judge the political climate in the short term than in the more distant future.

In many unstable countries, it is almost impossible to quantify the magnitude of political risk in the longer term. However, the *minimum discounted payback period* is a practical guide to investment decision making when one is considering doing business in politically unstable nations. This criterion coupled with the purchase of political risk insurance should lead companies to satisfactory decisions. We should also recognize the value of tax deductions in the home country for realized capital losses incurred as a result of expropriation or nationalization as well as possible partial compensation from the local governments that are expropriating capital assets. Moreover, it may be possible to manage any political risk by borrowing locally to finance a project as a hedge in a politically unstable country. This tends to minimize potential losses if a host government expropriates assets; it is always possible to cease repayment of funds borrowed in the host country.

In evaluating foreign investment projects, it may be possible legally to circumvent political controls that limit the repatriation of funds through transfers. Firms may maximize these "nondividend" transfers by structuring projects in such a way that there are many trade links established with other affiliates, thus maximizing the firms' ability to repatriate funds through the use of "adjustments" to transfer prices. They may also structure the project so that it utilizes many of the companies' trademarks, patents, and management services and collect royalties and fees for these services. In addition, debt financing permits the parent to recover its capital investment in the presence of exchange controls that limit dividends.

If, when the project is structured, it is possible to repatriate funds by methods other than dividends, these other funds should be incorporated into the NPV model as follows:

$$\text{NPV} = -C_0 + \sum_{t=1}^{n} \frac{R_t}{(1 + i)^t} + \sum_{t=1}^{n} \frac{U_t}{(1 + i)^t} \tag{4}$$

where U_t represents profits repatriated by means other than dividends.

If a project is found to be sensitive to the magnitude of U_t, the investment can be structured initially to maximize U_t. This can be done by setting high transfer prices into the subsidiary, where legally possible, while purchasing goods from the foreign subsidiary at relatively low transfer prices. The point is, however, that the presence of political exchange controls means that the organization must design the project to optimize its cash flows from the subsidiary.

Economic Risks

Although it is difficult to draw a neat distinction between political and economic risk, it is useful to examine economic risk separately because these risks can be managed to a far greater extent than can political controls.

The two principal economic risks that can influence the success of a project are exchange rate changes and inflation. Although these two risks are in many respects opposite sides of the same coin (that is, if allowed to seek their own level, exchange rates will move in the opposite direction of relative rates of inflation), it is useful to analyze each one separately, because in practice the exchange rate is under political influence and local price controls often prevent market forces from working.

Exchange Rate Risk

The exchange rate not only influences the dollar cash flows from foreign investment, but because it is a price, it influences the revenue of a project denominated in local currency. In the event of devaluation, prices for output will fall relative to the prices charged by competitors. Therefore, revenues from the project should rise because of relatively lower prices in both foreign and domestic markets.

Not only are local revenues affected by exchange rate changes but so are costs. In a country experiencing a devaluation, the prices of raw materials imported from countries against which the local currency has been devalued will rise. Moreover, domestic inflation often accompanies a devaluation, so prices of raw materials purchased locally will rise also. As costs and prices rise locally, so will wages.

Therefore, if risk exists of exchange rate changes, these risks should be reflected in estimates of project costs and benefits to the extent that it is possible to do so. To make appropriate adjustments, however, we must estimate in terms of the local currency the impact of exchange rate changes upon incremental revenue and upon each element of incremental cost. Only after net returns (R) are computed in local currency should we convert the net returns to dollars (in the case of a U.S. headquartered firm).

The crucial lesson from this discussion of exchange rate risk is that we cannot forecast the effects of exchange rate change upon the net returns of a project without estimating its effects upon at least the major elements of costs and revenues. Moreover, certain portions of the incremental returns and incremental costs of a project may be fixed either contractually in terms of the home or local currency or by accounting convention. For example, depreciation is an expense based upon the original book value of an asset. In the case of devaluation of a local currency, depreciation will ordinarily remain the same in the home currency. Furthermore, the firm may negotiate long-term contracts to purchase raw materials at prices fixed in terms of local currency.

Let us now turn to an analysis of the effects of an anticipated devaluation of a local currency by 10 percent at the end of the first year of operations of a new foreign investment upon the cash flows of a company headquartered in the United States.[1] We assume the following estimates:

1. Sales of the output of the new plant are expected to be in both domestic and foreign markets.
2. Domestic as well as imported raw materials are used in the production process.
3. Prices of raw materials purchased domestically are expected to increase by 5 percent as a result of increased demand caused by the expected currency devaluation.
4. Prices of raw materials purchased in foreign markets are expected to rise in terms of local currency by 10 percent.

5. Domestic wages will rise by 5 percent as a result of the inflation set off by the devaluation.
6. Fixed costs excluding depreciation are expected to rise by 5 percent.
7. Prices of products sold from the new plant to domestic and foreign markets are expected to rise by 5 percent in terms of local currency.
8. Total sales volume to export and local markets is expected to increase by 5 percent as a result of the devaluation.
9. Since the initial dollar price of the produce is $2.50, a 10 percent devaluation reduces the price to $2.25, and then the subsequent inflation in the foreign country results in a price increase of 5 percent, raising the dollar price to $2.36.

Taking all these factors into account, local currency (LC) cash flows will change in the second year of the project from LC 125,000 to LC 133,150 and dollar-dominated cash flows will change from $62,500 to $59,977. These results are shown in Exhibit 17-1.

Inflation

In a world of perfectly flexible exchange rates, changes in the relative rates of inflation in local and home countries would be automatically reflected in exchange rates, so we could ignore inflation, since its effects would be incorporated into exchange rates.

Exhibit 17-1
Cash Flow Effects of a 10 Percent Devaluation

	Exchange Rate	
	Year 1 **$LC_1 = \$.50$**	**Year 2** **$LC_1 = \$.45$**
Revenues (local currency)		
Sales volume (units)		
Domestic	100,000	105,000
Foreign	100,000	105,000
Unit selling price	5.00	5.25
Gross revenue	LC 1,000,000	LC 1,102,500
Costs (local currency)		
Raw material costs per unit		
Domestic	1.25	1.31
Imported	1.00	1.10
Labor per unit	1.25	1.31
Variable costs per unit	3.50	3.72
Total variable cost	LC 700,000	LC 781,200
Fixed costs	100,000	105,000
Depreciation	50,000	50,000
Total costs	LC 850,000	LC 936,200
Profit before taxes	150,000	166,300
Tax 50%	75,000	83,150
Net profit after taxes	75,000	83,150
Depreciation	50,000	50,000
Cash flow	LC 125,000	LC 133,150
Dollar cash flow	$ 62,500	$ 59,977

In practice, there is at minimum a lag between relative rates of inflation and adjustment of exchange rates. We do not currently have a regime of freely flexible exchange rates, but rather one that may be characterized as a *managed float.* Moreover, local governments may impose wage and price controls that prevent latent inflation from manifesting itself. Simultaneously, it may impose import controls and export subsidies to bolster its exchange rate. For all these reasons, we should estimate separately the effects of inflation and exchange rate changes upon our projects. Adjustments for inflation for foreign investment projects must be carried out on an item-by-item basis. The procedure is, however, identical to the one we would follow for domestic investment projects, and was illustrated in the previous example for exchange rate risk.

This ends our review of the principal differences in the evaluation of capital investment projects in foreign affiliates. As we turn next to the differences in the budgeting and performance evaluation processes, we are fortunate to have a extensive survey of the performance evaluation practices and problems of 125 of the largest United States-based multinational corporations. The study was conducted by William Persen and Van Lessig for the Financial Executives Research Foundation and was published in 1979 under the title *Evaluating the Financial Performance of Overseas Operations.* Data for the study were gathered by a combination of interview and questionnaire techniques. We shall summarize the empirical results of this study in the next part of this chapter. Then we shall turn to the specific issues of budgeting, performance evaluation, and transfer pricing.

EMPIRICAL FINDINGS CONCERNING METHODS USED TO EVALUATE FOREIGN AFFILIATES

Control Systems for Foreign Affiliates[2]

With regard to the general approach to the control of foreign operations, Persen and Lessig (1979, pp. 11–12) conclude, "almost without exception, the procedures used in measuring domestic profitability were expanded and modified to apply to foreign units when the firm expanded overseas." Firms attempt to "export" their control systems to their overseas operation with appropriate adjustments for the new demands of foreign operations. Ninety percent (p. 46) of the respondents reported using the identical format for budgeting of international operations as used for domestic operations.

When asked for the main difference between the financial evaluation of domestic and foreign operation, 106 respondents gave replies that fell within the following five categories (p. 114):

Responses

Differences in currencies, exchange rate fluctuations	45
Translation of currencies	20
Variances in inflation rates	18
Variation in financial and economic conditions	12
Multiplicity of government regulations and controls	11

You should notice that most of the respondents indicated the principal difference to be currency exchange rates and the related problem of making translations from one currency to another.

Currency Translation, Budgeting, and Performance Evaluation

One of the major issues in the evaluation of foreign operations concerns translation of the results of foreign affiliates whose business is carried out in currencies other than the United States dollar. Only 4 percent of the United States parent companies in the above study evaluate foreign operations in terms of the local currency alone (p. 89). The remaining 96 percent evaluate foreign operations in either the parent company's currency alone or use both the parent and local currencies to evaluate foreign operations. Sixty-five percent of those using the parent's currency to evaluate results use a projected exchange rate for purpose of budgeting, whereas 26 percent use the exchange rate that exists at the time of budget preparation (p. 58). This result implies that the budget is prepared in terms of the parent's currency by using a forecast of either an average exchange rate for the budget period or a forecast of the exchange rate for the end of the budget period. Fifty-five percent of those who use a projected exchange rate do not alter the budget, regardless of actual movements in exchange rates (p. 59).

Those who use the parent's currency for budgeting were further asked about the exchange rate used for performance evaluation. Fifty percent reported (p. 90) using the actual exchange rate at the end of the budget period for performance evaluation. Sixty-eight percent of the respondents use a different rate for budgeting than for performance evaluation. Moreover, 37 percent of those respondents using a different rate for budgeting than for evaluation purposes indicated that they hold managers of foreign operations responsible for variances from budget that are due to *exchange rate fluctuations*. The larger firms were more likely to hold affiliates responsible for the exchange rate variance.

Sixty-two percent (p. 48) of the respondents in the study reported preparing income, balance sheet, and cash flow statements in the budget process. The remainder usually omitted the cash flow statement.

With regard to the other principal differences between the control systems for domestic and foreign operations, almost 70 percent of the respondents said that they did not attempt to make adjustment for inflation in the evaluation process (p. 110), although most adjust for inflation in making budget projections. The survey results also indicated that companies by and large do attempt to take other economic and political trends of the local market into account in the evaluation process of the overseas operation. These other factors are included in evaluations in a qualitative manner and do not cause a great deal of difficulty in the evaluation process.

Transfer Pricing

Transfer pricing is one of the most difficult internal issues for the multinational firm to deal with, but some recognition must be given to the firm's need to sell goods and services among its affiliates located in different countries. Ideally, international companies would set high transfer prices for goods going to high-tax countries, so as to minimize taxes there, and low transfer prices to low-tax countries, so as to show higher profits in the low-tax areas. Of course, taxing authorities have an interest in transfer prices and through legislation attempt to define fair or arm's-length transfer prices among foreign affiliates.

Persen and Lessig found that, while firms often use more than one basis of transfer pricing, the most common bases of transfer pricing are (p. 118) cost plus markup (32%), market price (27%), and market less a discount (22%). A more recent study by Tang (1993) reporting on the most widely used methods for international transfer pricing among Fortune 500 firms in 1990, indicates a continued preference for cost plus markup (26.8%) and market price (26.1%). Little seems to have changed!

Perhaps the more interesting question, however, is What factors determine how transfer prices are set between the parent and its foreign affiliates? Using case study methods, Carr (May, 1989) investigated the transfer pricing practices of 15 multinational corporations, including a number of the very largest MNCs from the United States, Japan, and West Germany. He found that factors outside of the need to measure performance were dominant in the decision as to how to establish transfer prices. The most important factor determining transfer prices in these firms was *corporate strategy*. The reasons firms enter a foreign market in the first place has a lot to do with how they set transfer prices. His work, although limited to 15 companies, strongly suggests that transfer pricing in a MNC is a tool that management uses to support strategic goals and that the principal problem in transfer pricing is to establish *strategic congruence* between corporate strategy for the affiliate and the related transfer price. When congruence does not exist, the foreign affiliate is out of sync with the parent.

Reporting Requirements for Foreign Affiliates

Most firms (87 percent) in the Persen van Lessig study used the same reporting format for international operations as for domestic operations (p. 34). The major reporting differences between domestic and foreign operations were in the following three areas (pp. 34–35):

1. Reports on gains and losses in foreign exchange and foreign exchange exposure are required only for foreign affiliates.
2. Fifty-two percent of the firms require overseas operations to submit borrowing schedules, whereas most borrowing for domestic operations is carried out by the central headquarters.
3. Reports to central headquarters for foreign operations are less frequent and are prepared in somewhat less detail.

Exhibit 17-2 is a tabulation of the evaluation criterion used by the 125 firms in evaluating performance of their foreign operations. We see from Exhibit 17-2 that the most widely used method of performance evaluation involves comparison

Exhibit 17-2
Techniques for Evaluating Foreign Operations

Focus	Current	Past	Future
Operating budget comparisons	62%	50%	59%
Contributions to earnings per share	44	45	42
Return on investment	40	45	42
Contribution to corporate cash flow	35	14	55
Return on sales	34	32	34
Return on assets	34	21	41
Asset/liability management	30	9	50
Nonaccounting data	16	13	22
Long-term plan comparison	12	6	23
Return on investment (inflation adjusted)	8	3	31

Source: This exhibit has been reproduced by permission from William Persen and Van Lessig, *Evaluating the Financial Performance of Overseas Operations,* Financial Executives Research Foundation, New York, 1979, p. 68.

of actual versus planned performance as represented by the operating budget. It is important to note from the exhibit that ROI is also widely used as an evaluation criterion for multinational operations.

With this extensive background of empirical data regarding control systems used by United States firms for their foreign operations, we now examine in some detail the important normative issues concerning transfer pricing and budgeting. Most of the differences in the control of foreign affiliates can be grouped into these two categories.

TRANSFER PRICING FOR AFFILIATES OF A MNC

The transfer pricing problem for the multinational firm is similar to the transfer pricing problem for the domestic firm with one very important difference. For the domestic firm, transfer prices mainly affect the allocation of the firm's total profit among the various profit centers. They do not directly affect taxes paid by the corporation. They do create strong motivational effects, and they may have an impact upon the total profit level of the firm, but for a given level of income before taxes, they do not affect the total tax bill. For the multinational, transfer prices do affect the level of taxes paid for a given level of income before taxes. Therefore, they are important not only to the firm but also to the government of the parent company as well as to the government of the host country.

The Potential for the Manipulation of Global Income

The potential for the manipulation (or maximization, if we choose) of income by the multinational through the use of transfer pricing may occur through the following devices:

1. Transfer prices may be set relatively high for affiliates in relatively high-tax countries that purchase inputs from affiliates located in relatively low-tax countries.
2. Transfer prices to affiliates in countries subject to import duties for goods and services purchased may be set low so as to avoid host country taxes.
3. Transfer prices to an affiliate in a country that is encountering relatively high inflation may be set relatively high to avoid some of the adverse effects of local currency devaluations that are related to the high inflation.
4. Transfer prices may be set high for goods and services purchased by an affiliate operating in a country that has imposed restrictions on the repatriation of income to foreign countries.

In addition to these four methods of manipulating taxes, transfer prices may be set low for an affiliate that is trying to establish a competitive advantage over a local company either to break into a market or to establish a higher share of the country's business.

Given the opportunities for manipulation and the high stakes for both host and home countries, the taxing authorities have established rules and regulations governing the transfer pricing practices of parent and affiliate companies. The objective of these regulations is to achieve "arm's-length pricing" practices in transfer pricing. We now turn to an examination of these regulations in the United States.

Section 482 of the Internal Revenue Code

The idea behind Section 482 of the IRS Code is to ensure parity (that is, arm's-length pricing) between uncontrolled taxpayers and controlled taxpayers. Controlled taxpayers are affiliates of a multinational corporation. Uncontrolled affiliates are independent entities not under the control of a multinational parent. The idea of the legislation is to encourage multinational companies to develop transfer prices for affiliates of the company that are comparable to prices that are paid in an uncontrolled transaction in which at least one of the parties to the transaction is not an affiliate of the multinational.

The legislation specifies three acceptable ways, in order of preference to the IRS, in which acceptable transfer prices among affiliates may be determined. These three are as follows:

Market-Price Method. Under this method the firm sets transfer prices among its affiliates to conform to market prices for comparable goods and services as determined in market transactions where at least one of the parties was not an affiliate of the parent company. The reference transaction should not be a distress sale that represents unrealistically low or marginal pricing. This is the most preferred method, according to the IRS, for determining arm's-length transfer prices.

If there is no ready market for comparable goods, the firm must choose one of the remaining two methods in order of priority.

Resale Price Method. This method requires the firm to estimate an appropriate transfer price for a product if that product becomes an input to a final transaction within a reasonable period of time after the transfer from one affiliate to another. The transfer price is arrived at by subtracting any further processing costs plus profit markup from the selling price of the market transaction. The resultant figure is the transfer price.

The appropriate markup is the percentage of sales earned in an uncontrolled sale by either the affiliate or another company. This method may be used when there are no comparable sales for the goods transferred between affiliates. If this method is not practical because of the passage of a relatively long period of time between purchase and sale or for any other reason, the third method may be used.

Cost Method. This method is a nonmarket method that requires a knowledge of the cost structure of the selling affiliate to compute a full-cost-based transfer price. The method must be supported by a sound cost accounting structure.

Under Section 482, the burden of proof is placed upon the multinational corporation to prove that the transfers have in fact taken place under arm's-length conditions. In other words, once the IRS brings a tax adjustment claim on a multinational based in the United States, the burden of proof shifts to the defendant corporation to prove its compliance with Section 482. The firm may agree with the IRS or adjudicate the matter in tax court.

It should be noted that Section 482 also allows a multinational to establish lower transfer prices to break into new foreign markets.

Transfer Pricing and the Control of Multinational Operations

We began this section on transfer pricing by elaborating some of the possible manipulations that are possible by multinationals to minimize global taxes and maximize global income. We then described the tax law in the United States that operates as a constraint on the ability of the multinationals to manipulate transfer prices.

Even though Section 482 and similar tax laws in other countries limit the discretion of management over transfer prices, it should be obvious that when a firm operates within the law it has considerable discretion in establishing "comparable prices," "appropriate markups," and "costs." Here we should find that experts will disagree on just what is appropriate and comparable. Nevertheless, management is constrained in a real way from using negotiable transfer prices for purposes of management control.

The need to establish arm's-length prices limits the discretion of decentralized divisions in negotiating with sister affiliates in different countries. Moreover, to the extent that the firm attempts to minimize taxes worldwide through its transfer pricing mechanism, it is forced either to keep a different set of books for management control or to limit the autonomy of its managers of foreign affiliates to bring about the desired tax effects. One might question the independence of an affiliate whose input prices are determined or whose input prices are influenced by the tax minimization needs of the parent.

BUDGETING FOR FOREIGN AFFILIATES OF A MNC

As we have seen from the empirical data, comparison of actual versus planned financial performance in the context of the operating budget is the most common method of evaluating performance of foreign affiliates. The budget is also one of the principal tools used for communication in the multinational firm. It helps to knit together the heterogeneous subunits of the MNC.

The complexities encountered in budgeting for overseas operations revolve around exchange rate considerations. We should recall that the empirical work reported indicated that currency fluctuations are at the heart of the differences between control of domestic operations and control of foreign operations.

We noted that almost all the firms in the sample used the parent company's currency alone, or they used both the parent and local currencies to evaluate foreign operations. We also observed that 65 percent of those using the parent's currency to evaluate results used a projected exchange rate for purpose of budgeting. Sixty-eight percent of the respondents used a different rate for budgeting than they did for performance evaluation. However, only 37 percent of those respondents using a different rate for budgeting than for evaluation purpose indicated that they held the managers of the foreign operation responsible for those variances from budget that were due to exchange rate fluctuations.

This raises a number of questions about budgeting and performance evaluation in the MNC. These questions are as follows:

1. Which exchange rates should be used for budgetary planning?
2. Which exchange rates should be used for reporting performance?
3. Should managers of foreign affiliates be held responsible for the effects of exchange rate fluctuation, that is, for any foreign exchange variance?

We shall examine these issues by applying the criteria of *goal congruence* and *controllability* (or fairness). These criteria are the same as those applied throughout this volume for the design of management control systems. We turn first to look at goal congruence and take the parent's perspective.

Goal Congruence—The Parent's Point of View

The parent is primarily concerned with earnings and return on invested capital as translated into the parent's currency. If the parent is a United States corporation, it shall be preparing consolidated statements in terms of dollars. It shall be paying dividends in terms of United States dollars. Its objectives and goals for foreign operations are therefore best stated in terms of United States dollars.

Therefore, from a perspective of goal congruence, the parent would like to budget using projected exchange rates at the end of the period. This is most reflective of the interests of the parent. Moreover, following the same criterion, the parent would like results reported in terms of actual exchange rates, since this reflects the actual translated sums received by the parent.

Whether it is goal congruent to hold the subsidiary responsible for the foreign exchange variances depends on the extent to which it is even desirable to have affiliates making decisions with regard to foreign exchange, given their local perspective.

Controllability—The Affiliate's Point of View

Clearly, exchange rate fluctuations are not controllable by local management. The exchange rate is an example of a key success factor that is completely outside the control of the manager of the affiliate. But the question is: Can local management exert sufficient influence over other internal variables so as to mitigate the negative effects of exchange rate fluctuations on earnings as translated into the parent's currency?

Local management, for example, may manipulate credit policy so as not to offer extended credit to customers in the local currency if the local currency appears weak and ready for a sizable devaluation. Local management may minimize exchange rate fluctuations by shifting liquid funds into stronger currencies. Pricing policies may be adopted that protect the firm against inflation and exchange rate fluctuations. Moreover, in dealing with suppliers, local management may negotiate purchases in advance in local currency so as to protect against devaluation. Yet clearly, these actions will affect only the income statement. They are *transaction effects.*

The more difficult matter for the local management concerns the so-called translation effects, namely, the effects of currency devaluation upon balance sheet items such as long-term assets and liabilities. Unless the local management has control over its capital structure, it probably has very little influence over these so-called translation effects. Normally these are handled by the parent. Moreover, it may not wish to allow local management the discretion to hedge in other currencies, since this too may best be accomplished on a global basis.

To summarize this section to this point, local management may be given the latitude by the parent to exert control over the size of the transaction effects, and if it is, it should be held accountable for these "income statement effects." It would be more unusual to hold local management responsible for the translation or "balance sheet effects."

Concerning the appropriate exchange rates to use for budgeting the operations of a local affiliate, we saw that the empirical results reported by Persen and Lessig indicate that most firms use *projected exchange rates for budgeting* and *actual exchange rates for reporting performance* of affiliates.

The format of projected rates for budgeting and actual rates for performance evaluation assumes that local managers have reasonable control over the transaction effects. If this is a fair assumption, this combination of rates is fair for planning and for performance evaluation. Whenever the same rate, actual or projected, is used for planning and performance evaluation, the presumption is that local management does not have control over exchange rate fluctuations.

From the point of view of *controllability*, it is best to budget and report performance using the same set of exchange rates: *current, forecasted,* or *actual.* But clearly, there may be a trade-off here in order to achieve *goal congruence.*

THE IMPACT OF FINANCIAL ACCOUNTING ON PERFORMANCE EVALUATION: FASB 52

Financial accounting provides the data base upon which budgeting and reporting systems are built. It is reasonable, therefore, to expect that accounting regulations will have a significant impact upon the format of management planning and performance evaluation. We now examine the effect of a pronouncement of the financial Accounting Standards Board as it impacts performance planning and evaluation.

FASB 52[3]

FASB 52, which became effective for fiscal years beginning on or after December 15, 1982 in the United States, attempts to redress the problems created by earlier regulation. It does so by requiring that *all* assets and liabilities be translated at current exchange rates at the balance sheet date [the current rate method]. It requires that all income statement accounts be translated at a *weighted average* exchange rate for the period rather than at ending exchange rates. Exhibits 17-3, 17-4, and 17-5 illustrate the effect of FASB 52 on the financial statements of a United States parent firm.

From a control point of view, FASB 52 should motivate firms toward using projected rates for budget planning and weighted average rates for performance evaluation. The translation adjustment is reported as income or loss at the time of *sale or complete liquidation* of the foreign enterprise. Foreign exchange gains and losses resulting from foreign currency transactions are to be reported in current income.

The current rate method is the most frequently used translation method throughout the world.

Exhibit 17-3
Balance Sheet Translation Under FASB 52

	Local Currency	Exchange Rate	United States
Assets			
Cash	LC 1,500	1.5*	$2,251
Receivables	2,000	1.5	3,000
Inventory	3,000	1.5	4,500
Fixed assets	5,000	1.5	7,500
Total assets	LC 11,500		$17,250
Liabilities and shareholders' equity			
Notes payable	LC 3,000	1.5	$4,500
Accounts payable	2,550	1.5	3,750
Capital stock	5,000	1.75†	8,750
Retained earnings	1,000	‡	2,500
Accumulated translation adjustments	0	§	(2,250)
Total liabilities and shareholders' equity	LC 11,500		$17,250

*Current exchange rate.
†Historical exchange rate.
‡Combination of historical retained earnings and exchange gains.
§See reconciliation of translation adjustment in Exhibit 17-5.

Exhibit 17-4
Income Statement Translation Under FASB 52

	Local Currency	Weighted Average Rate	Dollars
Sales	LC 10,000	2.5	$25,000
Expenses			
Cost of sales	6,000	2.5	15,000
Depreciation	900	2.5	2,250
General selling	1,000	2.5	2,500
Income taxes	500	2.5	1,250
Net income	LC 1,600		$4,000
Dividends	600	2.5	1,500
Net increase in R/E	LC 1,000		$2,500
R/E beginning	0		0
R/E ending	LC 1,000		$ 2,500

Exhibit 17-5
Reconciliation of Translation Adjustment Under FASB 52

Net increase in total assets (local currency)	$6,000	
Current exchange rate	× 1.5	$9,000
Less: capital stock (Exhibit 17-3)		8,750
ending R/E (Exhibit 17-4)		2,500
Translation adjustment		$(2,250)

REFERENCES

ANTHONY, ROBERT N., JOHN DEARDEN, AND VIJAY GOVINDARAJAN, *Management Control Systems*, 7th ed. Homewood, Ill.: Richard D. Irwin, 1992, Chapter 16.

ARPAN, JEFFREY S., AND DHIA D. ALHASHIM, *International Accounting*. Boston, Mass.: Kent Publishing Company, 1984.

BRADLEY, DAVID G., "Managing Against Expropriation," *Harvard Business Review,* July–August 1977, p. 78.

CARR, LAWRENCE P., Multinational Transfer Pricing: A Management Systems Framework, Ph.D. dissertation, Schenectady, N.Y.: Union College, May 1989.

CARR, LAWRENCE P., "Multinational Transfer Pricing: Patterns of Policy Formulation," unpublished draft, Babson College, Boston, Mass., 1989.

DELOITE, HASKINS AND SELLS, *Foreign Currency Translation: FASB Statement No. 52*, December 1981.

KRADER, EUGENE M., Part H2 in Paul J. Wendell, ed., *Corporate Controller's Manual*, Volume 2. Boston, Mass.: Warren Gorham Lamont, 1993.

LESSARD, DONALD R, "Transfer Prices, Taxes, and Financial Markets: Implications of Internal Financial Transfers Within the Multinational Firm." Working paper, Massachusetts Institute of Technology, Cambridge, Mass., 1977.

PERSEN, WILLIAM, AND VAN LESSIG, *Evaluating the Financial Performance of Overseas Operations*. New York: Research Foundation of Financial Executives Institute, 1979.

PORTER, MICHAEL E., *The Competitive Advantage of Nations*, New York: The Free Press, 1990.

SERVICE, WILLIAM W., "Evaluation and Control System Design for Multinational Enterprises," Unpublished senior thesis, Economics Department, Claremont McKenna College, Claremont, Calif., 1982.

SHAPIRO, ALAN C., "Capital Budgeting for the Multinational Corporation," *Financial Management*, Spring 1978.

SHAPIRO, ALAN C., *Multinational Financial Management*, 3rd ed. Boston, Mass.: Allyn and Bacon, 1989, Chapter 19.

SONDHI, ASHWINPAUL C., "International Taxation," Part H1 in Paul J. Wendell, ed., *Corporate Controller's Manual*, Vol. 2. Boston, Mass.: Warren Gorham Lamont, 1993.

TANG, ROGER Y. W., *Transfer Pricing in the 1990's: Tax and Management Perspective*. Westport, Conn.: Quorum Books, 1993.

NOTES

1. This example has been adapted by permission from "Capital Budgeting for the Multinational Corporation," *Financial Management*, Spring 1978, by Alan C. Shapiro.
2. This discussion draws heavily on William Persen and Van Lessig, *Evaluating the Financial Performance of Overseas Operations* (New York: Research Foundation of Financial Executives Institute, 1979).
3. This section, including the exhibits, is based upon the work of William Service (1982). The exhibits are used by permission.

Case 17-1 AB Thorsten (A)*

This case deals with an investment proposal made by Anders Ekstrom, President of AB Thorsten, a firm engaged in the production and sale of chemicals, with headquarters in Stockholm, Sweden. This proposal was made to the management of Roget S.A. in Brussels, Belgium. AB Thorsten is a 100 percent owned subsidiary of Roget S.A.[1]

SUMMARY OF OPERATIONS: ROGET S.A.

Roget S.A. is one of the largest industrial companies in Belgium. Founded forty years ago, the company originally produced a line of simple products for sale in Belgium. Today it has expanded to produce 208 complex chemical products in 21 factories.

Mr. André Juvet, President of Roget, states that the organization of the Company (Exhibit A1) is the result of careful planning. "Until five years ago, we were organized with one large manufacturing division here in Belgium, and one large sales division. One department of the sales division was devoted to export sales. However, exports grew so fast, and domestic markets became so complex, that we created three main product divisions, each with its own manufacturing plants and sales organizations. In addition, we have created foreign subsidiaries to take over the business in certain areas. For example, in Industrial Chemicals we have two subsidiaries—one in the U.K. and one in Sweden which serves all Scandinavia. At the same time, the domestic department of the Industrial Chemicals Division exports to the rest of Europe. The U.K. and Sweden account for 9 percent and 5 percent of sales in that division, but 14 percent added to total sales is very important."

"Another thing we achieve in the new organization is individual profit responsibility of all executives at all levels. Mr. Gillot is responsible for profits for all industrial chemicals, Mr. Lambert is responsible for profits from domestic operations (manufacturing and sales) and export sales to countries where we do not have subsidiaries or factories, and Mr. Ekstrom is responsible for profits in Scandinavia. We also utilize a rather liberal bonus system to reward executives at each level, based on the profits of their divisions.

"This, together with a policy of promotion from within, helps stimulate managers in Roget to a degree not enjoyed by some of our competitors. It also helps to keep men

This case was prepared by Professors Gordon Shillinglaw and Charles Summer as a basis for class discussion rather than to illustrate either effective or ineffective handling of an administrative situation.

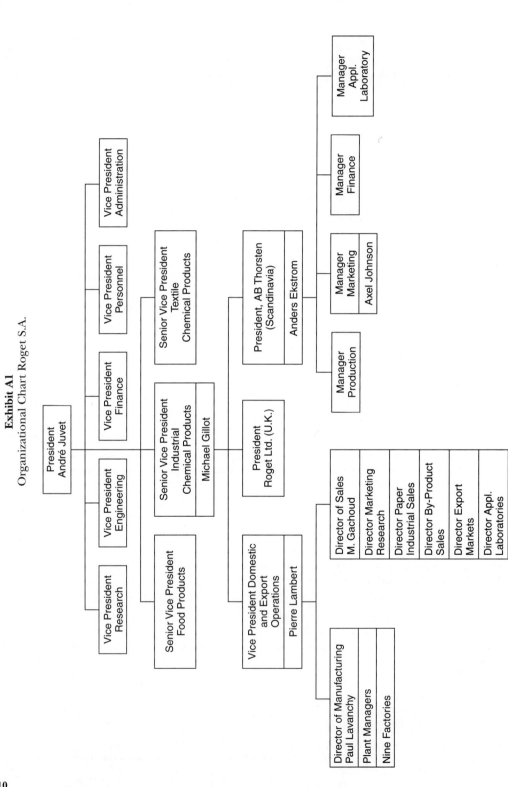

Exhibit A1
Organizational Chart Roget S.A.

in an industry where experience is of great importance. Most of our executives have been in the starch chemicals business all of their lives. It is a complex business, and we feel that it takes many years to learn in.

"We have developed certain policies—rules of the game—which govern relationships with our subsidiary company Presidents. These are intended to maintain efficiency of the whole Roget complex, while at the same time to give subsidiary managers autonomy to run their own businesses. For example a subsidiary manager can determine what existing Roget products he wants to sell in his part of the world market. Export sales will quote him the same price as they quote agents in all countries. He is free to bargain, and if he doesn't like the price he needn't sell the product. Second, we encourage subsidiaries to propose to division management in Brussels the development of new products. If these are judged feasible we manufacture them in Belgium for supply to world markets. Third, the subsidiary President can build his own manufacturing plants if he can justify the investment in his own market."

COMPANY BACKGROUND: AB THORSTEN

AB Thorsten was purchased by Roget S.A. eight years ago. Since that time the same four men have constituted Thorsten's Board of Directors: Ekstrom; Mr. Michael Gillot, Senior Vice President in charge of Roget's Industrial Chemical Products Division; Mr. Ingve Norgren, a Swedish banker; and Mr. Ove Svensen, a Stockholm industrialist. Swedish corporation law requires any company incorporated in Sweden to have Swedish directors, and the Roget management felt fortunate in finding two men as prominent as Norgren and Svensen to serve on the Thorsten Board.

During the first four years of Roget's ownership, Thorsten's sales fluctuated between Skr. 5 and 7 million, but hit a low at the end of that period.[2] The Board of AB Thorsten decided at that time that the company was in serious trouble, and that the only alternative to selling the company was to hire a totally different management to overhaul and streamline the entire company operation.

On advice of the Swedish directors, Mr. Anders Ekstrom, a 38-year-old graduate of the Royal Institute of Technology, was hired. He had had sixteen years of experience in production engineering for a large machinery company, as marketing manager of a British subsidiary in Sweden, and as division manager responsible for profits in a large paper company.

Ekstrom has been President of AB Thorsten for the past four years. In that time, sales have increased to Skr. 20 million and profits have reached levels that Roget's management finds highly satisfactory. Both Ekstrom and Norgren (a Director) attribute this performance to: (a) an increase in industrial activity in Scandinavia; (b) changes in production methods, marketing strategy and organization structure made by Ekstrom; (c) the hiring of competent staff; and (d) Ekstrom's own ambition and hard work. To these reasons the case writer also adds Ekstrom's knowledge of modern planning techniques—rather sophisticated market research methods, financial planning by use of discounted cash flows and incremental analysis, and, as Ekstrom puts it, "all those things my former company had learned from the American companies."

Ekstrom says that at the time he joined Thorsten, he knew it was a risk. "I like the challenge of building a company. If I do a good job here I will have the confidence of Norgren and Svenson as well as of the Roget management in Brussels. Deep down inside, succeeding in this situation will teach me things that will make me more competent as a top executive. So I chose this job even though I had at the time (and still have) offers from other companies."

INITIAL PROPOSAL FOR MANUFACTURE OF XL-4

Two years ago, Ekstrom informed the Thorsten Board of Directors that he proposed to study the feasibility of constructing a factory in Sweden for the manufacture of XL-4, a product used in paper converting. He explained that he and his customer engineers had discovered a new way of helping large paper mills convert their machines at little cost so that they could use XL-4 instead of competitors' products. Large paper mill customers would be able to realize dramatic savings in material handling and storage costs and to shorten drying time substantially. In his judgment, Thorsten could develop a market in Sweden almost as big as Roget's present worldwide market for XL-4. XL-4 was then being produced in Roget's Domestic Division at the rate of 600 tons a year, but none of this was going to Sweden.

"At that meeting," Ekstrom states, "Mr. Gillot and the other Directors seemed enthusiastic. Gillot said, 'Of course—go ahead with your study and when you have a proposed plan, with the final return on investment, send it in and we will consider it thoroughly.'

"During the next six months, we did the analysis. My market research department estimated the total potential in Sweden at 800 tons of XL-4 per year. We interviewed important customers and conducted trials in the factories of three big companies which proved that with the introduction of our machine designs the large cost saving would indeed materialize. We determined that if we could sell the product for Skr. 1,850 per ton, we could capture one half of the market within a three year period, or 400 tons a year.

"At the same time, I called the head of the Corporate Engineering Division in Brussels (see Exhibit A1) asking his help in designing a plant to produce 400 tons per year, and in estimating the cost of the investment. This is a routine thing. The central staff divisions are advisory and always comply with requests for help. He assigned a project manager and four other engineers to work on the design of factory and machinery, and to estimate the cost. At the same time I assigned three men from my staff to work on the project. In three months this joint task group reported that the necessary plant could be built for Skr. 700,000.

"All of this we summarized in a pro forma calculation (Exhibits A2 through A5). This calculation, together with a complete written explanation, was mailed 18 months ago to Mr. Gillot. I felt rather excited, as did most of my staff. We all know that introduction of new products is one of the keys to continued growth and profitability. The yield of this investment (15 percent) was well above the minimum 8 percent established as a guideline for new investment by the Roget Vice President of Finance. We also knew that it was a *good* analysis, done by modern tools of management. In the covering letter, I asked that it be put on the agenda for the next Board meeting."

The minutes of the next Board meeting held in Stockholm three weeks later show on the agenda "A Proposal for Investment in Sweden" to be presented by Mr. Ekstrom, using a series of charts (Exhibits A2 through A5). The minutes also quote his remarks as he explained the proposal to other directors:

"You will see from the summary table (Exhibit A2) that this project is profitable. On an initial outlay of Skr. 700,000 for equipment and Skr. 56,000 for working capital, we get a rate of return of 15 percent and a present value of Skr. 246,000.

"Let me explain some of the figures underlying this summary table. My second

Exhibit A2
AB Thorsten: Proposal for Manufacture of XL-4 in Sweden
Financial Summary (all figures in Skr.)

Year	Description	After-Tax Cash Flows*	Present Value at 8%
0	Equipment	−700,000	
	Working capital	− 56,000	
	Total	−756,000	−756,000
1	Cash operating profit	+105,000	
	Working capital	− 2,000	
	Total	+103,000	+ 95,000
2	Cash operating profit	+160,000	
	Working capital	− 7,000	
	Total	+153,000	+131,000
3	Cash operating profit	+215,000	+171,000
4	Cash operating profit	+215,000	+158,000
5	Cash operating profit	+215,000	+146,000
6	Cash operating profit	+145,000	+ 91,000
7	Cash operating profit	+145,000	
	Recovery value of equipment and working capital	+215,000	
	Total	+360,000	+210,000
	Grand Total	+650,000	+246,000

Net present value	Skr. 246,000
Payback period (before tax)	4 years
Internal rate of return	15%

*From Exhibits A3, A4, and A5

chart (Exhibit A3) summarizes the operating cash flows that we expect to get from the XL-4 project. The sales forecast for the first 7 years is shown in column two. The forecast was not extended beyond seven years because our engineers estimate that the technology of starch manufacture will improve gradually, so that major plant renovations will become economical at about the end of the seventh year. Actually, we see no reason why this particular product, XL-4, will decline in demand after seven years.

"The estimated variable cost of Skr. 1,000 per ton shown in column three is our estimate of the full operating cost of manufacturing XL-4 in Sweden, including out-of-pocket fixed costs such as plant management salaries, but excluding depreciation. These fixed costs must of course be included because they are incremental to the decision.

"As column four shows, we feel certain that we can enter the market initially with a selling price of Skr. 2,000 a ton, but full market penetration will require a price reduction to Skr. 1,850 at the beginning of the second year.

"The variable profit resulting from these figures is shown in columns five and six. Column seven then lists the market development and promotion expenditures that are needed to launch the product and achieve the forecasted sales levels. Column eight contains the net operating cash flows before tax, based on figures in the preceding columns.

"The cost of the plant can be written off for tax purposes over a five-year period, at

Exhibit A3

AB Thorsten: Estimated Operating Cash Flows from Manufacture and Sale of XL-4 in Sweden

(1)	(2)	(3)	(4)	(5)	(6)	(7)	(8)	(9)	(10)	(11)
Year	Sales (in Tons)	Var. Costs per Ton	Sales Price per Ton	Var. Profit Margin per Ton (4) − (3)	Total Var. Profit Margin (2)×(5)	Promotion Costs	Profit Contrib. (6) − (7)	Tax Depreciation	Tax 50% of [(8) − (9)]	Net Cash Flow After Tax (8) − (10)
		(Skr. per ton)					(figures in thousands of Skr.)			
1	200	1,000	2,000	1,000	200	130	70	140	(35)	105
2	300	1,000	1,850	850	255	75	180	140	20	160
3	400	1,000	1,850	850	340	50	290	140	75	215
4	400	1,000	1,850	850	340	50	290	140	75	215
5	400	1,000	1,850	850	340	50	290	140	75	215
6	400	1,000	1,850	850	340	50	290	—	145	145
7	400	1,000	1,850	850	340	50	290	—	145	145
Total	2,500				2,155	455	1,700	700	500	1,200

the rate of 20 percent of original cost each year. Subtracting this amount from the before-tax cash flow yields the taxable income figures summarized in column nine. The tax in column ten is then subtracted from the before-tax cash flow to yield the after-tax cash flow in column eleven.

"A proposal of this kind also requires some investment in working capital. My third chart (Exhibit A4) summarizes our estimates on this element. We'll need about Skr. 80,000 to start with, but some of this can be deducted immediately from our income taxes. Swedish law permits us to deduct 60 percent of the cost of inventories from taxable income. For this reason, we can get an immediate reduction of Skr. 24,000 in the taxes we have to pay on our other income in Sweden. This is shown in column five. The net investment in working capital is thus only Skr. 56,000, the figure we show in column six.

"We'll need small additional amounts of working capital in the next two years, and these amounts are also shown in column six. Altogether, our working capital requirements will add up to Skr. 65,000 by the end of our second full year of operations.

"Now let's look at one last chart (Exhibit A5). Seven years is a very conservative estimate of the life of the product. If we limit the analysis to seven years, we'll be overlooking the value of our assets at the end of that time. At the very worst, the plant itself should be worth Skr. 300,000 after seven years. We'd have to pay tax on that, of course, because the plant would be fully depreciated, but this would still leave us with Skr. 150,000 for the plant.

"The working capital should be fully recoverable, too. After paying the deferred tax on inventories, we'd still get Skr. 65,000 back on that. The total value at the end of seven years would thus be Skr. 215,000."

Mr. Ekstrom ended this opening presentation by saying, "Gentlemen, it seems clear from these figures that we can justify this investment in Sweden on the basis of sales to the Swedish market. The group Vice President for Finance has laid down the policy that any new investment should yield at least 8 percent. This particular proposal shows a return of 15 percent. My management and I strongly recommend this project." (The Thorsten vice presidents for production, sales, and finance had been called into the Board meeting to be present when this proposal was made.)

Ekstrom told the casewriter that while he was making this proposal he was sure that it would be accepted.

Exhibit A4
AB Thorsten: Estimated Working Capital Required for Manufacture and Sale of XL-4 in Sweden*
(Skr. 000)

	(1)	(2)	(3)	(4)	(5)	(6)
	Inventory at Cost	Other Curr. Assets less Curr. Liab.	Working Capital (1)+(2)	Change from Previous Year	Tax Credit (30% of Change in (1))	Net Funds Required (4)−(5)
Year 0	80	0	80	+80	24	56
Year 1	90	−5	85	+ 5	3	2
Year 2	100	−5	95	+10	3	7
Year 3 & later	100	−5	95	0	0	0
Total	100	−5	95	95	30	65

*These figures are in addition to the estimated equipment cost of Skr. 700,000.

Exhibit A5
AB Thorsten: Estimated End-of-Life Value of Swedish Assets

Plant	Skr. 300,000	
Less tax on gain if sold at this price	150,000	
Net value of plant		Skr. 150,000
Working capital	Skr. 95,000	
Less payment of deferred tax on special inventory reserves	30,000	
Net value of working capital		65,000
Net Value of Swedish Assets After 7 Years		Skr. 215,000

QUESTIONS

1. Evaluate the financial analysis of the investment proposal to construct a factory in Sweden for the manufacture of XL-4. To which variables are the NPV and IRR most sensitive? How accurate do you believe these estimates to be? Do you think the proposal should be approved?
2. Is the construction of the new factory in Sweden in the best interests of Thorsten's parent company?

NOTES

1. The letters "AB" and "S.A." are the equivalent designations in Sweden and Belgium of "Corp." or "Inc." in the U.S. and "Ltd." in the U.K.
2. In round numbers, the Skr. is approximately equivalent to U.S.$0.20, or ten Belgian francs (BFr.). To avoid confusion, all monetary figures in this case series are stated in Swedish kroner, even though some of the actual transactions are made in Belgian francs.

Case 17-2 AB Thorsten (B)*

Mr. Ekstrom's proposal for the construction of a factory to manufacture XL-4 in Sweden was presented to Mr. Gillot, Roget S.A.'s Senior Vice President in charge of Industrial Chemicals. The proposal was placed on the agenda for the next meeting of the Board of Directors.

"When the Board met in Stockholm three weeks later," Mr. Ekstrom recalled, "I presented the plan along with my Directors of Sales, Finance and Production. We took only an hour, since I was sure Gillot had checked it thoroughly with various corporate staff departments (Finance, Engineering) as well as with the Sales and Manufacturing managers in the Domestic and Export Operations Department within his own Division.

"Gillot said that it seemed to him to be a clear case. He asked interesting questions, mainly about the longer-term likelihood that we could see more than 400 tons a year, and about how we would get the money. I explained that we in Sweden were very firm in our judgment that we would reach 400 tons a year even before one year, but felt constrained to show a conservative estimate of a three-year transition period. We also showed him how we could finance any expansion by borrowing in Sweden. That is, if Roget would furnish the initial capital, and if our 400 tons were reached quickly, any further expansion would easily be lent by banks. The two Swedish Directors confirmed this. The Board voted unanimously to construct the plant."

DISAGREEMENT BETWEEN PARENT AND SUBSIDIARY

About a week later, Gillot telephoned Ekstrom. "Since my return to Brussels I have been through some additional discussions with the production and marketing people here in the Domestic Department. They think the engineering design and plant cost is accurate, but that you are too optimistic on your sales forecast. It looks like you will have to justify this more."

"I pushed him to set up a meeting the following week," Ekstrom says. "This meeting was attended by myself and my marketing and production Directors, from Sweden, and four people from Belgium—Gillot, Lavanchy (Director of Manufacturing), Gachoud (Director of Sales), and Lambert (Vice President for Domestic and Export).[1]

"That was one of the worst meetings of my life. It lasted all day. Gachoud said that they had sales experience from other countries and that in his judgment the market potential and our share were too optimistic. I told him over and over how we arrived at this figure but he just kept repeating the over-optimism argument. Then Lavanchy said that the production of this product is complicated, and that he had difficulties producing it in Belgium, even with trained workers who have long experience. I told him I only needed five trained production workers and that he could send me two men for two months to train Swedes to do the job. I impressed on him that 'if you can manufacture it in Belgium you can manufacture it for us in Sweden until we learn if you don't have confidence in Swedish technology.' He repeated that the difficulties in manufacturing were great. I stressed that we were prepared to learn and take the risk. Somehow I just couldn't get through to him.

"Lavanchy then said that the whole world market for Roget was only 600 tons a year, that it was being produced in Belgium at this level, and that it was inconceivable that Sweden alone could take 400 tons.

"At 6 p.m. everyone was tired. Lambert had backed up his two production and sales officials all day, repeating their arguments. Gillot seemed to me to just sit there and listen, occasionally asking questions. I cannot understand why he didn't back me up. He seemed so easy to get along with at the prior Board meeting in Stockholm—and he seemed decisive. Not so at this meeting. He seemed distant, indecisive, and an ineffective executive.

"He stopped the meeting without a solution, and said that he hoped all concerned would do more investigation of this subject. He vaguely referred to the fact that he would think about it himself and let us know when another meeting would be held."

OBJECTION FROM A SWEDISH DIRECTOR

Ekstrom states that he returned to Stockholm and reported the meeting to his own staff,

and to the two Swedish members of his Board. "They, like I, were really disgusted. Here we were operating with initiative and with excellent financial techniques. Roget management had often made talks in which they emphasized the necessity for decentralized profit responsibilities, authority and initiative on the part of foreign subsidiary Presidents. One of my men told me that they seem to talk decentralization and act like tin gods at the same time."

Mr. Norgren, the Swedish banker on Thorsten's board, expressed surprise. "I considered this carefully. It is sound business for AB Thorsten, and XL-4 will help to build one more growth company in the Swedish economy. Somehow, the management in Brussels has failed to study this, or they don't wish the Swedish subsidiary to produce it. I have today dictated a letter to Mr. Gillot telling him that I don't know why the project is rejected, that Roget has a right to its own reasons, but that I am prepared to resign as a director. It is not that I am angry, or that I have a right to dictate decisions for the whole world-wide Roget S.A. It is simply that, if I spend my time studying policy decisions, and those decisions do not serve the right function for the business, then it is a waste of time to continue."

Finally, Ekstrom states, "while I certainly wouldn't bring these matters out in a meeting, I think those Belgian production and sales people simply want to build the empire and make the money in Roget Belgium. They don't care about Thorsten and Sweden. That's a smooth way to operate. We have the ideas and initiative, and they take them and get the payoff."

FURTHER STUDY

After Mr. Gillot received Norgren's letter, he contacted Messrs. Lavanchy, Gachoud, and Bols (V.P. Finance, Roget Corporate Staff). He told them that the Swedish XL-4 project had become a matter of key importance for the whole Roget Group, because of its implications for company profits, and for the morale and autonomy of the subsidiary management. He asked them to study the matter and report their recommendations in one month. Meanwhile, he wrote Ekstrom, "Various members of the Corporate Headquarters are studying the proposal. You will hear from me within about six weeks regarding my final decision."

QUESTION

1. What questions are raised about the strategy of Roget in the industrial chemical business? Do the control systems support the strategy?

NOTES

1. See the first case in this series, AB Thorsten (A), Exhibit A1, for a chart of Roget's organization structure and roster of top executives.

Case 17-3 AB Thorsten (C)*

Anders Ekstrom, Managing Director of AB Thorsten, spent a busy eight months after requesting and receiving permission from the management of his parent company in Belgium, Roget S.A., to study the feasibility of building a factory in Sweden to make XL-4, an industrial adhesive. Previous cases in this series have focused on the events of this eight-month period. This case picks up the story at that point and presents the reactions of Roget's headquarters staff during the ensuing month.

SUMMARY OF PREVIOUS CASES

1. During the first six months, Ekstrom and his staff studied the XL-4 project and prepared a report, recommending construction of the factory.
2. At the end of that time, Ekstrom mailed his report to Mr. Gillot, the head of Roget's Industrial Chemical Products Division.
3. Three weeks later, the proposal was approved unanimously by AB Thorsten's Board of Directors, meeting in Stockholm. Gillot attended this meeting in his capacity as one of Roget's representatives on the Thorsten Board.
4. One week later, Gillot telephoned Ekstrom to say that production and marketing officials in Belgium would not endorse the pro-

posal unless Ekstrom could present a stronger case for it. Ekstrom requested a meeting to defend the proposal.
5. One week after that, Ekstrom and the Thorsten directors of marketing and production met in Brussels with Gillot and three other Roget executives: Mr. Lambert (vice president for domestic and export), Mr. Lavanchy (director of manufacturing), and Mr. Gachoud (director of sales). No decision was reached at this meeting.
6. One week after this meeting, Ekstrom reported back to his executives in Sweden that the project was being turned down. Mr. Norgren, a Swedish Director, wrote to Roget that he was prepared to resign from the Thorsten Board if the proposal was not approved.
7. A few days after receiving this letter, Gillot told the production and marketing executives in Belgium that the XL-4 project was of key importance, and asked them to study it and report to him in one month.

REPORT OF ROGET'S DIRECTOR OF MANUFACTURING

A month after he was asked to study the XL-4 project, Lavanchy gave Gillot a memorandum explaining his reasons for opposing the proposal:

"At your request, I have reexamined thoroughly all of the cost figures that bear on

*Copyright © 1969 by IMEDE, Lausanne, Switzerland. The International Institute for Management Development (IMD), resulting from the merger between IMEDE, Lausanne, and IMI, Geneva, acquires and retains all rights. Not to be used or reproduced without written permission from IMD, Lausanne, Switzerland.

This case was prepared by Professors Gordon Shillinglaw and Charles Summer as a basis for class discussion rather than to illustrate either effective or ineffective handling of an administrative situation.

the XL-4 proposal. I find that manufacture of this product in Sweden would be highly uneconomical, for two reasons: (1) overhead costs would be higher; and (2) variable costs would be greater.

"As to the first, we can produce XL-4 in Belgium with less overhead cost. Suppose that Thorsten does sell 400 tons a year so that our total worldwide sales rise to 1,000 tons. We can produce the whole 1,000 tons in Belgium with essentially the same capital investment we have now. If we produce 1,000 tons, our fixed costs will decrease by Skr. 120 a ton.[1] That means Skr. 72,000 in savings on production for domestic and export to countries other than Sweden (600 tons a year), and Skr. 120,000 for worldwide production including Sweden (1,000 tons).

"Second, we could save on variable costs. If we were to produce the extra 400 tons in Belgium, the total production of 1,000 tons a year would give us longer production runs, lower set-up costs, and larger raw material purchases, thus allowing mass purchasing and material handling and lower purchase prices. My accounting department has studied this and concludes that our average variable costs will decrease from Skr. 950 a ton to Skr. 930 (Exhibit C1). This Skr. 20 per ton difference means a saving of Skr. 12,000 on Belgian domestic production or Skr. 20,000 for total worldwide production, assuming that Sweden takes 400 tons a year.

Exhibit C1
AB Thorsten: Estimated Variable Cost
of Manufacturing XL-4 in Belgium
for Shipment to Sweden

Variable costs per ton:		
Manufacturing	Skr.	930
Shipping from Belgium to Sweden		50
Swedish import duty		400
Total Variable Cost per Ton	Skr.	1,380
Total Variable Cost, 400 tons to Sweden	Skr.	552,000

"Taxes on these added profits are about the same in Belgium as in Sweden—about 50 percent of taxable income.

"In conclusion, that plant should not be built. Ekstrom is a bright young man, but he does not know the adhesives business. He would be head over heels in costly production mistakes from the very beginning. I recommend that you inform the Thorsten management that it is in the Company's interest, and therefore it is Roget policy, that he must buy from Belgium."

REPORT OF VICE PRESIDENT— FINANCE

The same day, Gillot received the following memorandum from Eric Bols, Roget's financial vice president:

"I am sending you herewith estimates of the working capital requirements if Roget increases its production of XL-4 in our Belgian plant from 600 to 1,000 tons a year (Exhibit C2). Initially, we will need Skr. 54,000, mostly for additional inventories. By the end of the second year, this will have increased to Skr. 74,000. Incidentally, the tax credits shown in column five of the exhibit are based on a Swedish law which permits businesses to deduct 60 percent of inventory costs from taxable income.

"I have also looked at Lavanchy's calculations for the fixed and variable manufacturing costs, and am in full agreement with them."

EKSTROM'S THOUGHTS AT THIS TIME

In an interview about this same time, Ekstrom expressed some impatience with "the way things are going. I have other projects that need developing for Thorsten, and this kind of long-range planning takes much time and energy. Also, just keeping on top of

Exhibit C2
AB Thorsten: Estimated Working Capital Required for Manufacture
of XL-4 in Belgium for Sale in Sweden (Skr. 000)

	(1) Inventory at Cost	*(2)* Other Curr. Assets less Curr. Liab.	*(3)* Working Capital (1)+(2)	*(4)* Change from Previous Year	*(5)* Tax Credit (30% of Change in (1))	*(6)* Net Funds Required (4)−(5)
Year 0	50	10	60	+60	6*	54
Year 1	55	15	70	+10	0	10
Year 2	60	20	80	+10	0	10
Year 3 & later	60	20	80	0	0	0
Total	60	20	80	80	6	74

*Based on finished goods inventory of Skr. 20,000 in Sweden.

the normal operating problems of the business we already have takes up a lot of my time. Sometimes I feel like telling them to go and sell XL-4 themselves."

QUESTION

1. Why was the investment proposal rejected by Roget S.A.?

2. What is the appropriate transfer price for XL-4?

NOTES

1. Total fixed cost in Belgium is the equivalent of Skr. 180,000 a year. Divided by 600, this equals Skr. 300 a ton. If it were spread over 1,000 tons, the average fixed cost would be Skr. 180.

Exhibit C3

AB Thorsten: Estimated Operating Cash Flows from Manufacture of XL-4 in Belgium for Shipment to Sweden

(1) Year	(2) Sales (in Tons)	(3) Variable Costs per Ton	(4) Sales Price per Ton	(5) Variable Profit Margin per Ton (4)−(3)	(6) Direct Variable Profit Margin (2)×(5)	(7) Sales Promotion Costs	(8) Savings on Variable Costs for Other Markets (600×20)	(9) Cash Profit Contribution (6)−(7)+(8)	(10) Tax 50% of (9)	(11) Net Cash Flow After Tax (9)−(10)	(12) Present Value at 8%
		(Skr. per Ton)					*(figures in thousands of Skr.)*				
1	200	1,380	2,000	620	124	130	12	6	3	3	3
2	300	1,380	1,850	470	141	75	12	78	39	39	33
3	400	1,380	1,850	470	188	50	12	150	75	75	
4	400	1,380	1,850	470	188	50	12	150	75	75	
5	400	1,380	1,850	470	188	50	12	150	75	75	257
6	400	1,380	1,850	470	188	50	12	150	75	75	
7	400	1,380	1,850	470	188	50	12	150	75	75	
Total	2,500				1,205	455	84	834	417	417	293

Case 17-4 Granadia's Power Gadgets

In early 1993, the manager of Risky Enterprises in Granadia submitted the following new product proposal for approval to the parent company in New York. Granadia is a developing country and Risky Enterprises operates there as a fully owned subsidiary.

Product: Power Gadgets. Risky Enterprises had been manufacturing gadgets in Granadia. The proposed project will allow the company to produce more powerful gadgets, Power Gadgets.

Investment. It is estimated that an investment of 300,000 Granadia peso (GP) in plant and equipment will be required for the new product. However, 50,000 GP of the 300,000 GP required could be provided by the parent from its inventory of fully depreciated and technologically obsolete equipment held in various U.S. factories. Moreover, the government of Granadia has agreed that the plant and equipment for this project can be depreciated for the full 300,000 GP by the straight-line method over a five-year period.

Product Life. Although the market for Power Gadgets was expected to continue expanding as Granadia continued to build its industrial infrastructure, Granadia's government, as a precondition for its approval of the new plant, demanded the right to purchase the new super-gadget plant in December of 1998 for a price of 200,000 GP.

Demand. At the price of 800 GP per unit, demand for Power Gadgets is estimated as follows:

	Domestic	Exports
	(units)	
1994	200	100
1995	300	150
1996	400	200
1997	400	200
1998	400	200

Domestic demand is considered to be price inelastic. That is, for the relevant range of future prices, the quantity demanded appears to be independent of the price charged. However, this is not the case for exports. Export demand is considered to be price elastic. It is estimated that for each 1 percent increase in prices, the export demand for Power Gadgets will decrease by 1.3 percent.

Prices. Industrial engineers at Risky estimate that the new gadgets can be sold competitively for 800 GP per unit. This price is expected to inflate at 15 percent per year given the historical rates of inflation experienced in Granadia. The price of 800 GP for 1994 already incorporates the rate of inflation between 1993 and 1994.

Variable Costs. These costs have been estimated by the industrial engineering department as follows:

Raw material	Domestic	100 GP per unit
	Imported	50 GP per unit
Labor		50 GP per unit

Recent inflation of labor and raw material costs in Granadia has been averaging 17 percent per annum. There appears to be no let up in sight. Imported raw material costs are expected to fluctuate with movements in the rate of exchange of the GP in relationship to the U.S. dollar.

Fixed Costs. The annual fixed expenses associated with the new product are estimated as follows:

Depreciation on plant and equipment	60,000 GP
Executive management fees	20,000 GP
Selling and administrative expenses	60,000 GP

The executive fees are to be paid to the parent and are not expected to change from year to year. Depreciation is fixed in terms of GP. Selling and administrative expenses, however, are expected to inflate at the rate of domestic cost inflation.

Exchange Rates. The controller's de–partment in New York projects the following GP exchange rates with respect to the dollar for the next five years:

	GP per $
1994	8.00
1995	8.80
1996	9.00
1997	9.50
1998	9.50

There are no government controls in Granadia on repatriation of earnings to parent companies.

Taxes:

Granadia's taxes:	30% income tax and no deductions for previous losses
	30% withholding taxes on dividends
Parent country taxes:	Income: 48%, with deductions for income and withholding taxes paid abroad
	Capital gains: 20%

Profit Remittances. All profits from the new product are to be remitted to the parent company.

Cost of Capital Applicable to Granadia. Risky Enterprises was required by the parent to impose a 30 percent after-tax discount rate on investments in this risk category.

QUESTIONS

1. Evaluate this project from the point of view of the parent, using the NPV method. Assume that all the withholding taxes on dividends in Granadia are tax deductible in the United States. In addition, assume that local taxes paid in Granadia are deductible according to the ratio of gross dividends (dividends remitted plus withholding tax) to profits before taxes and that the tax basis for foreign earnings in the United States is gross dividends.

2. Would you accept this product? To which variables, in addition to projections of demand and costs, is the success of this product sensitive?

Case 17-5 EMC: Strategic Multinational Transfer Pricing*

EMC is a well-established capital equipment corporation. They manufacture, market, and service medical apparatus for the global market. This European-based company has a century-old history of contribution to the medical profession. Business leaders recognize EMC for their active and often leading role in the development of medical technology. The company enjoys an excellent reputation for product quality and leading-edge technology. They enjoy a close working relationship with the medical community, which often leads to a number of proprietary devices. EMC has experienced rapid growth during the post-World War II economic boom.

FOREIGN OPERATIONS

EMC expansion concentrated first on the home market and quickly moved to the total European market, South America, and Africa. The U.S. market size, growth, and technology known throughout the world was extremely attractive for EMC. The United States, the world leader in medical research, had the largest medical care capacity. It also was a very formidable market. There exists a lengthy process for government agency approvals (primarily the FDA) and a very competent domestic market leader (GE). Despite these unattractive obstacles, EMC felt a strong need to initiate a presence in the largest market segment of the world market.

A select group of managers from the home office started the U.S. operations over twenty years ago. Understanding the U.S. culture and product technical competence were the prime factors for this assignment. These managers established a subsidiary staffed with local personnel wherever possible. Their main interest was to create access to the emerging medical techniques and technology. The home research and development facility looked forward to strong feedback.

The U.S. subsidiary was initially treated as an expense center with a very modest expectation for sales gain and market penetration. The primary assignment of the U.S. operation was to support the home company with market and industry intelligence. The U.S. managers formed relationships at the cutting edge of medical technology. In addition, home management learned more about the U.S. culture and business style. After an initial start-up phase, the U.S. operations began to grow very quickly. The local management demonstrated an aggressive entrepreneurial spirit and began to see expansion opportunities in the market. They understood market needs and matched this [understanding] with EMC equipment or technology to meet those needs.

*This case was written by Lawrence P. Carr, Associate Professor, Babson College, as a basis for class discussion rather than to illustrate either an effective or ineffective handling of an administrative situation. Copyright 1992 by Lawrence P. Carr (617) 239-5138. It is reproduced here by permission.

Conflicts arose quickly over the charter for the U.S. operation. The United States sought growth and profit opportunity, while the home facilities found U.S. product modification cumbersome and expensive. This negatively influenced production capacities and product availability.

TRANSFER PRICING METHODS

The corporate transfer pricing policy was then and is today a negotiated method. All billing was done in the home currency. The negotiation was between the business manager of the U.S. operation and the plant manager of the appropriate home production facility. Transfer pricing decisions were important. Both the home plant managers and the U.S. general manager have profit and loss responsibility for their operations. The negotiated transfer price influences the targeted results. For EMC, transfer pricing was a full-cost system. All overhead and special costs for adapting standard products for the U.S. market were part of the price. There was little flexibility in the system, and corporate managers did not expect profit from the U.S. operation. Home management operated as if the world were still on a fixed exchange rate system.

Though slow initially, the U.S. operation grew quite rapidly. At the time of the case, sales were over 1 billion dollars, with eight U.S. operating companies covering a full range of medical products for the market. They locally manufacture over 50 percent of the products sold. EMC has carved out a solid market share (over 10 percent) in the United States and continues to grow and gain share.

STRATEGY AND TRANSFER PRICING

The strategic perception changed about 12 years ago as EMC management became more confident with the U.S. operation. They realized they had the technology and industry knowledge to penetrate the formidable market barriers of the United States. Although the transfer pricing did not change in method, the various home production facilities became more flexible in their negotiation. The products transferred to the United States no longer carried all of the additional costs for electrical and regulation adaptation. The home factories realized the positive effect the U.S. operations had on factory loading and its impact on the factory profit performance. The home company was beginning to realize the favorable influence the U.S. operations had on the consolidated results. The strategic attractiveness of the United States began to change.

A major modification in the transfer pricing system did take place six years ago. EMC management switched the currency for transfer pricing from the home currency to U.S. dollars. Thus, the home company absorbed the full currency risk. The United States is the only foreign subsidiary of EMC to pay in local currency, but also the largest single operation outside the home country. They were growing at double the consolidated corporate growth rate in both sales and profits. The reason for the change in currency valuation was that the home production facility added over 50 percent of the value to the products. EMC also realized that the United States was their dominant growth opportunity. EMC management said, "We need to have a reasonable market share in the world's largest market if we want to be a global player." EMC financed and supported the growth of the U.S. subsidiary and now accepted the currency risks.

The current U.S. business manager believes that the transfer pricing system is quite fair. The "constructive conflict" of negotiations was very healthy for the company. He spends more than 40 percent of his time working on transfer pricing issues. He knows the field managers drive the system backed by corporate management's willingness to make pricing exceptions for market success (buy market share). Interviews with the field sales personnel fully supported the positive perception of the transfer pricing process. The switch to dollar billing for the U.S. subsidiaries reflects a major strategic commitment to the U.S. market.

Senior EMC management resolved conflicts or impasses in transfer pricing negotiation. Taking the issue to a higher level of management, however, was rarely done. It was not career enhancing and viewed as a weak management trait. Senior management wanted a consensus decision and a sharing of goals among managers. The U.S. market success bred an increased flexibility in the transfer pricing process. It was very obvious throughout EMC that the U.S. growth (double the consolidated rate) was making the company a much stronger global competitor. EMC had a sense of pride and accomplishment. It was extremely important, from a motivational point of view, for the local work force to have a clearly signaled and openly stated strategy.

DECISION PROCESS

The U.S. business manager and the home central department routinely handled transfer pricing negotiations. The home department coordinated pricing, home factory loading, and logistics for sales to foreign operations. A transferee from the home country served as the U.S. subsidiary representative. Management recognized the power of personal relationships in easing tensions and building mutual trust. This is critical to smooth transfer pricing negotiations. The U.S. business manager worked with the various division managers to verify local price claims and identify possible strategic market gains. Indeed, the price elas-

ticity of the local market was continually tested. In the medical equipment market, better prices do not easily buy market share. He, however, knew that EMC treated the U.S. [operation] far better than other foreign operations. He also felt the pressure of additional performance expectations. The possible changes in regulations or the issuance of additional laws governing the lengthy approval process concerned EMC. This factor was one of the reasons for the slow market penetration. They were not going to make a significant financial commitment in a market where they had little control. Experience, better knowledge, and a U.S. government lobbying activity improved the perception. All parties realized a major commitment in resources was necessary to be successful in the United States. The commitment had to be clear and tangible. The U.S. subsidiary needed to attract talented people and maintain a positive motivation to sustain the market share gain.

Both home and local operations were acutely aware of the budgeted exchange rate, which served as a reference point in transfer price negotiations. During the annual operating budget preparation management set the dollar-denominated transfer price. Achieving budgeted targets was very important to the local operation management. The bonus program tied directly to sales and profit attainment. There was a demonstrated flexibility in the transfer pricing because home management clearly made the U.S. market a key global target. EMC did not permit product outsourcing. All products came from EMC facilities. There were many occasions where customer needs could not be filled. This situation also required flexibility from the home facilities.

Today, the U.S. operation is no longer viewed as an expense center. They are an independent operating entity, an investment center, with full profit, loss, and balance sheet responsibility. A sound understanding of the U.S. principles of business learned during the exploratory phase of their market involvement has enabled EMC management to become comfortable with the market. They, however, remain concerned with the hostile nature of the market and the aggressive behavior of the competitors.

QUESTIONS

1. What were the causes of the conflicts in determining the appropriate transfer price?
2. What signals were sent to the foreign affiliate by the change to transfer pricing in terms of the host country's currency?
3. How can mutual frustration between the parent and the foreign affiliate be avoided in transfer pricing?
4. What role did corporate strategy play in the transfer pricing decision?

18

CONTROL OF NONPROFIT INSTITUTIONS

CONTROL OF NONPROFIT INSTITUTIONS*

A nonprofit institution is one that is chartered by the state to operate in the interest of society. It operates free of any obligation to pay income taxes. It is restricted, by definition, from participation in equity markets, since it has no shareholders. Its sources of funds are derived from contributions, grants, operating surplus, and debt instruments of various types. The principal goal of nonprofits is defined by their mission. Unlike for-profit institutions, profit does not enter into their mission.

The nonprofit segment of society is large in terms of its impact. Drucker (1990) estimates that 6 percent of the employed population in the United States is employed in the nonprofit sector. But this significantly underestimates involvement in these institutions. Approximately 30 percent of the population in the United States, or 80 million people, participate as volunteer workers in these institutions.

Nonprofit institutions may be classified into two groups: governmental organizations and private, tax-exempt organizations. Private organizations can be further divided into commercial organizations and charitable groups; the former includes unions, trade associations, and clubs, and the latter includes hospitals, religious groups, research, educational, and social service organizations.

It is the latter group that has experienced exponential growth in recent years as a result of the increased recognition of human need. And it is this latter group that will be our focus in this chapter.

*We are grateful for the assistance of Dan Braun, Elizabeth Hall, and John Joyce with the material in this chapter.

The term *nonprofit* is a term used in this chapter to refer to human service organizations that are not operated for a profit nor are they governmental agencies. Examples include universities, hospitals, churches and other religious organizations, charitable organizations, community service organizations, and foundations. The term "nonprofit" tends to have negative connotations because it tells us what these organizations don't do, not what they do.

These organizations also may be referred to as "mission" organizations. They are driven primarily by their mission, which is their purpose. They are human change agents. Their mission is not financial gain.

Nonprofits receive tax-free status and are restricted from distributing excess revenues over costs or from having shareholders. Tax-free status is granted these organizations because they perform a function that benefits society. The absence of equity and shareholders prevents a potential conflict of interest from developing between serving shareholders' needs and performing a service that benefits society.

The importance of this sector should not be underestimated. The United States has approximately one million nonprofit organizations that receive approximately $104 billion annually in contributions.[1] Nearly 80 million people volunteer at least five hours per week to these institutions.[2]

Designing control systems for nonprofit institutions is different from designing them for profit-seeking institutions. The principal characteristics of these institutions that cause differences in their control systems are[3]

1. The absence of a profit measure.   Performance evaluation is more difficult.
2. Different tax and legal status.   These institutions are not taxed and no stockholders exist.
3. The tendency of nonprofit institutions to be service organization.   This makes it difficult to measure the quantity and quality of service provided.
4. Greater constraints on goals and strategies.   Donors may restrict the use of funds to predetermined purposes.
5. Less dependence on clients for financial support.   Many depend on endowed sources of support, thus making them less dependent upon customers for support.
6. The dominance of professionals.   Potentially dysfunctional pressures on the goals of an organization can be created, since these personnel have dual allegiances, to the organization and to their profession.
7. Differences in governance.   There are more numerous sources of influence and power, thus creating fragmentary governance processes.
8. Differences in senior management.   Often these institutions are run by professionals trained in another field besides management, such as college professors, musical artists, ministers and priests, and doctors.
9. A tradition of inadequate management controls.   This too is derived from a tendency in these organizations for management to be made up of professionals who value professional goals but who undervalue managerial skills.

The two largest sectors within the nonprofit category in terms of full-time employment and expenditures are health services and education. The largest number of volunteer employment in this sector is in religious organizations.[4]

The two largest sectors have grown dramatically and are very likely to continue to grow relative to GNP because of their characteristics. Let's look at these growth dynamics in detail.

Growth Dynamics of Key Nonprofits: Health Services and Education

In 1989 medical outlays comprised 12 percent of GNP, whereas education expenditures were 7 percent.[5] If real prices of medical and education services continue to rise at their past growth rates (2.9 and 2.2 percent per annum, respectively), and there are compelling reasons why they may, medical outlays will constitute more than 35 percent of GNP in the year 2039 and education more than 29 percent. Let us examine the reasons why.

Quality in both medical care and education is believed to be related to the amount of labor services in them. Patient care cannot be rushed and must be tailored to the patient. Patients do not believe they are receiving good care when they are rushed in and out of the doctor's office. Class size in elementary education is believed by both parents of children and teachers to be related to the quality of education.

In these very labor-intensive services, it is very hard to sustain the rates of growth in productivity that are sustained in other more productivity "progressive" sectors of society, such as manufacturing or agriculture. The upshot is that as salaries rise they are passed on as higher costs in these sectors. As wages and salaries rise in the more progressive sectors, their impact on costs is reduced by increases in productivity. Over time, these "progressive" sectors get smaller in relation to GNP whereas the "nonprogressive" sectors get larger. In an expanding economy, both sectors can increase in absolute terms, but the nonprogressive sector will get relatively larger.

This explains why the many attempts to control health care costs in the United States have been so frustrating. Health care costs have grown from one percent of GNP in the 1920s to over 14 percent of GNP at present in spite of numerous attempts by government, industry, and medical organizations to control costs. Efforts to control costs, such as the establishment of diagnostic related groups (DRGs) as the basis for medicare reimbursements and the encouragement of health maintenance organizations, for-profit health care organizations, and competition have slowed down the trend of increasing costs, but only temporarily with the cost trend eventually resuming and actually gathering more momentum. The story in education is the same.

Obviously, these segments of the economy are important and are likely, together with the other segments of the nonprofit sector, to be of increasing importance in developed economies. The challenge is to develop good control systems to manage these activities because of their explosive cost tendencies and because of their importance to the economy.

The Mission of Nonprofits

Nonprofits are organized so as to pursue and accomplish a mission. The accomplishment of the mission is its purpose. That mission could be a well-adjusted child in the case of a welfare agency or a healed patient in the case of a hospital. Drucker (1989) emphasizes that a mission statement should contain the following three elements:

1. The opportunities that the organization can exploit or needs that it can meet
2. The strengths of the organization
3. What members of the organization believe in.

We repeat as an example the mission statement for Central Hospital (Case 1-2):

> Central Hospital has been founded to meet human needs. We contribute to the physical, psychological, and social well-being of the patients and community we serve. We adhere to the highest ethical standards of the healing professions. Central Hospital seeks to communicate and collaborate with private and public agencies and organizations of the people we serve. We are a nonprofit, acute care hospital offering generalized and specialized inpatient and outpatient health care services within the limits of our resources. We respect all persons, including the medical staff, employees, and volunteers who serve in any capacity in our hospital. Quality of care is continuously monitored and evaluated. To perpetuate the institution and to fulfill our mission, we utilize principles of sound management.

Based on the overall institution's mission statement, each department of the hospital should in turn develop its mission statement. Here is an example of a mission statement for an emergency room of a hospital:

> Our mission is to provide quality emergency medical care in a compassionate and cost-effective manner to all who need it. We shall endeavor to serve the best interest of the patient through the utilization of qualified, credentialed emergency physicians. To the maximum extent possible, quality emergency medicine shall be provided to all without any financial barriers.

Here is a mission statement for a residential treatment program for abused and battered children:

> This society is dedicated to:[6]
>
> * Treating and educating abused and neglected children and their families
> * Promoting the prevention of child abuse and neglect
> * Creating an atmosphere in which children can grow and heal
> * Advocating for children in developing new treatment techniques
> * Setting the highest standards for developing effective programs
> * Combining the talents and experience of professionals and volunteers from many different fields
> * Acting as a leader in making its research and experience available.

STAKEHOLDERS

All organizations have multiple stakeholders. Yet the ultimate stakeholder in a public corporation is the stockholder (that is, the owner), and in government the ultimate stakeholder is the voter. In a nonprofit organization, there often is no dominant stakeholder but a multiplicity of key stakeholders. A school board, a church, or a child care agency ordinarily has multiple key stakeholders.

Boards of trustees are often major stakeholders in nonprofit organizations because they are the key donors and contributors of time and effort. The boards of nonprofit institutions represent a real opportunity for these institutions, so long as they focus on achieving the mission of the institution and stay out of operational details. The purpose of the board is to guide and direct the mission of the institution by evaluating major strategies; to select the CEO; to provide and secure funds; to provide outside professional perspective on governance; and to make the CEO accountable for the accomplishment of the mission. They should resist the temptation to micromanage the institution and leave the operational details to the staff.

In addition to the board, each nonprofit has *mission* stakeholders to serve: to save the lost, to heal the sick, to protect abused children, to educate children, and so on. In addition, there are often external parties who do not participate directly in the affairs of the institution that have a vital interest in the institution, such as the public in the work of a school district.

Many employees and volunteers in nonprofit organizations participate because they believe in the mission of the organization. But they may believe in different aspects of that mission. For example, hospitals are interested in healing, but hospital administrators are also interested in maintaining the financial viability of the institution. They want to heal, but they also want and need to cover cost and earn a surplus. Physicians, in contrast, look upon hospitals as a place to provide service for patients. They want beds to be available when needed for their patients. They want services for patients to be readily available at all times and to be performed rapidly, regardless of the cost. They are not concerned about hospital finances, and they resist contractual arrangements that interfere with their practices. The result is often a conflict between hospital administrators and the physicians employed at the hospital. Physicians are as much customers of the hospital as are the patients.

In formulating stakeholder goals, the executive must try to integrate all of the stakeholder goals around the mission of the organization. But the mission must not be seen as the sum of the stakeholder goals. If that becomes the case, the institution will lose its social reason for functioning. Rather, the mission has to be implemented in such a way as to satisfy the particular goals of the critical stakeholders. For example, in the mission of a primary-grade school, the principal must see to it that the school satisfies the students, parents, teachers, taxpayers, government officials, and the school board. Each has different interests, but they must be made compatible with the overall mission of the organization, which is to educate students.

Still another example of merging the overall mission of an organization with stakeholder goals occurs in churches. The overall mission may be to save the lost and to make disciples. This mission is translated in terms of the goals of the various stakeholders. The trustees are concerned with fund development and the maintenance of the financial integrity of the institution. The youth are interested in youth activities. Singles are interested in singles ministries. The sick are interested in care, nurturing, and prayer for wellness. The grieved are interested in solace. The deacons and deaconnesses may be most interested in programs to feed and clothe the poor and homeless. Many churchgoers are most interested in teaching and moral development for themselves and their families. All of these goals can be melded into the overall mission of the church. Balance in the allocation of resources is required here, but it can be accomplished.

KEY SUCCESS FACTORS

As we have seen previously, in the design of control systems we move from overall mission to stakeholder goals to key success factors. So here we ask what are the key success factors for nonprofit institutions? Each goal has key success factors associated with it; variables which, if not held at specified levels, will threaten the attainment of the goal and therefore the mission of the institution. Here we concentrate on some key success factors that are quite common to this class of institution.

A key success factor for many nonprofit institutions is the *number of volunteers* that it is able to attract and the number of volunteers it is able to train at various levels of quality. Are we attracting and holding the right kind of volunteers? Of paid staff?

A critical variable for all nonprofit institutions is *fund development,* since most rely heavily on the support of people, especially the volunteers, for contributions to support its paid staff and its programs.

Another generic critical variable is the ability to attract the *quantity and quality of board member* it needs.

As far as each goal is concerned, we should be attempting to see the reality of the institution and what is important to achieve these goals for a particular institution. We should be brutally frank in identifying the reality behind the achievement of each goal.

PERFORMANCE MEASURES

There are numerous problems in measuring performance of nonprofit institutions. Outputs are often difficult to measure. Is it healed patients? Patients seen? Souls saved? Functioning adults? Time spent with clients? The result is that these institutions often don't attempt to measure performance, and as a result they underperform. This should not be.

Performance measures should be established for each critical success factor for each goal. Reports on these performance measures should be prepared and distributed to those responsible for their management.

We should attempt to quantify as many measurements as possible. Some are quite easy to quantify (for example, the number of patients attended to by a physician during a specified period of time). Others (for example, the quality of care) are not so easy to measure but are nevertheless critical. But even those critical variables that are not easily quantified may have quantitative surrogates. Still others, however, such as the productivity of physicians, may be quantified in a misleading manner. Comparing the number of patients that physicians see may have relevance only when one is comparing similar departments. Judgment must always be applied to these quantitative measures when one is interpreting them.

Although measurement is often difficult and surrogates are prone to all kinds of problems, requiring judgment in interpretation, the only thing worse than attempting to develop good surrogates for performance is not doing so. As Drucker states:[7]

> Nonprofits are prone to become inward looking. People are so convinced they are doing the right thing, and are so committed to the cause, that they see the institution as an end in itself. But that's a bureaucracy. Soon people in the organization no longer ask: Does it serve our mission? They ask: Does it fit our rules? And that only inhibits performance; it destroys vision and dedication.

UNCONTROLLABLE KEY SUCCESS FACTORS

A number of variables external to the nonprofit institution may be very critical to its success. These are variables the institution must monitor but can do nothing about. Their impact on the organization must be assessed and actions taken to capitalize upon them or mitigate their affects.

Examples of potentially uncontrollable key success factors are demographic shifts and changes in the mindset of large segments of the population. The women's movement of recent decades and the increased awareness of all kinds of health-related problems illustrate dramatic shifts in the mindset of the population that has had a significant effect upon many nonprofit institutions.

CULTURE OF NONPROFIT INSTITUTIONS

There are many cultural characteristics of nonprofits that affect their management, and they are not all positive. These institutions are dominated by professionals, such as clergy, physicians, musicians, or professors. These professionals have historically had little regard for management and have preferred to concentrate on what they know and do best—their profession. As a result, management has been undervalued. Many times professional objectives are pursued to the detriment of the mission of the organization.

Because historically there has been little incentive for good management in these institutions and poor definition of goals and performance measures, these institutions have not always attracted the best managerial talent, nor have they performed at their potential. Compounding the problem has been a disdain for management by professionals. A recent piece in a scientific research journal in chemistry illustrates this perception:[8]

> The heaviest element known to science was recently discovered—tentatively named administratium. Administratium is inert. Nonetheless it can be detected chemically because it seems to impede every reaction in which it takes part. Administratium has a half-life of approximately 3 years at which time it does not actually decay. Instead, it undergoes an internal reorganization in which associates to neutron, deputy associ-

ates to the neutron, and assistant deputy associates to the neutron all exchange places. Some studies have indicated that the atomic mass actually increases after each reorganization. Dare we speculate that this is the principal constituent of black holes, which suck in surrounding energy and admit nothing?

Although this piece was written in fun and it identifies bureaucratic tendencies, it also reflects a cultural attitude that is widely prevalent in nonprofit institutions which makes management suspect and increases the difficulty of bringing good management practice to bear upon these institutions.

The good news is that this attitude is changing. The American Academy of Physician Executives has been formed to correct this problem in medicine. An organization consisting of some 60,000 doctors, it is devoted to raising the professional management standards in medicine. Robert Buford has founded Leadership Network to work with large evangelical churches in the United States to improve their management. Both are welcomed trends that should affect the cultural attitudes toward management in these institutions.

THE MUTUALLY SUPPORTIVE SUBSYSTEM MODEL APPLIED TO NONPROFIT INSTITUTIONS

Infrastructure

Nonprofits tend to have flatter organizational structures. Organizations tend to be functional, and the functions are headed by professionals (for example, doctors, social workers, ministers, professors). Moreover, funding is usually in short supply and senior-level management is expensive and therefore, often considered expendable.

Typical responsibility centers in a child care agency are social work, operations, administration, and education. These tend to be cost centers unless revenue is generated, in which case they are either revenue centers or contribution centers.

The Hospital

The modern hospital has a dual organization structure: one for the medical side of the institution and one for hotel services. The medical side is dominated by physicians and a broad range of technical and support staff. All the hospital needs that are not medically related are under hotel services: housekeeping, food service, maintenance, billing, and accounting. With the increased concern for cost control in the health care system, there has been increased administrative attention on the medical side of the organization.

A good deal of autonomy is usually granted to the hospital departments headed by professionals, such as nursing, laboratory, pathology, radiology, surgery, and so on. Most of these departments are cost centers, where quality of care and overall cost performance are the key performance measures.

Many hospitals have created SBUs for identifiable segments of the hospital. Examples of units that have been given SBU status are outpatient surgery, obstetrics, pharmacy, emergency room, physical medicine, imaging, chemical dependency, and women's diagnostic units. These units are profit centers and are established for strategic planning and implementation purposes.

Hospital boards, mostly part-time and volunteers, are often very strong participants in the governance of hospitals, since they are usually composed of individuals who have significant commitments to these institutions and make large financial contributions.

MANAGEMENT STYLE AND CULTURE

Of course, institutions differ markedly, but many of these institutions, especially the small and mid-sized ones, tend to take on the particular personality traits of the executive director. If the executive director is a professional, there is a tendency for him or her to place primary attention upon his or her area of interest or training.

THE HOSPITAL

Institutions differ widely in specifics, but there are many common generalities that can be stated. The dual structure of the hospital often results in an adversarial, but co-dependent style. To manage the institution effectively, control must be maintained on the medical side of the organization. Physicians fiercely resist any attempt on the part of the administration to reduce their autonomy. While this is changing somewhat, this fierce independence of physicians is part of the culture of medicine.

There is a deep co-dependency between the physicians and hospital administration. The hospital serves the physician, but the physician cannot generate revenue without the hospital.

Many hospitals have developed an "us versus them" attitude in dealing with their many low- to non-skilled, often unionized, employees.

A general theme that seems to be pervasive in all departments of hospitals is the belief that they are trying to deliver health care of the highest quality possible. This cultural dimension is generally present among the entire staff, including union members, physicians, and the administration. Each of these associates gains a sense of satisfaction and pride in providing patient care. This value serves as a very powerful incentive to participate in the institution and should be promoted.

FORMAL CONTROL PROCESSES

The most widely used formal control tool in nonprofits is the budget.[9] As government support is cut and as competition among nonprofits intensifies, the budgeting process becomes increasingly critical as a major tool in the resource allocation process.

The budgeting process is complicated in nonprofits by the absence of clear, quantifiable performance objectives for evaluating programs. Many nonprofits are beginning to establish more definitive goals and quantifiable surrogates to guide the resource allocation process.

Program evaluation is a very critical function in nonprofit institutions. Programs that are no longer bearing fruit must be abandoned. Those that are bearing fruit should be pruned and expanded. As a part of program evaluation, it is necessary to determine program costs. Unfortunately, cost accounting systems in nonprofit institutions are woefully inadequate to answer some of the basic questions raised in program evaluation. These are questions of cost/benefit relating to various programs and cost effectiveness of various approaches to the delivery of services.

Program costs are usually subdivided into two categories: direct and indirect. In most nonprofits, if overhead is allocated to programs it is done so on the basis of direct labor costs. The difficulty in program costing is twofold:

1. What is the program? Is it: Children attended to? Healed patients? Clients served?
2. How should indirect costs be allocated?

THE HOSPITAL

Control within the medical side of the hospital is pervasive and necessary for quality patient care. Many people of diverse disciplines interact with the patient; as a result, there is a need for a well-established mechanism so that adequate information is passed from one individual to another. This is done by using the patient record chart, which is divided into many segments containing progress notes, reports, and requests for all diagnostic and therapeutic procedures performed. Within each department, there are many levels of control related to the patient care mission to ensure the highest-quality care.

Outside of the medical control system, the formal control systems of most hospitals are underdeveloped, although this is changing rapidly. Controllers have traditionally been concerned with fiduciary accounting and ensuring proper reimbursement. Growth in the area of management control has been in response to external pressure from government and competitors.

Labor costs are the greatest lever on cost control in these organizations. To exert major leverage over labor costs, patterns of physician practice must be changed, and hospitals are now engaged in the task of changing physician practices. We turn now to an illustration.

Program Costing

Within a hospital there are many mission centers, departments that work with patients directly. Examples of mission centers are inpatient care, laboratory, and radiology. These departments provide services to patients directly. Service centers, in turn, provide support to each of the mission centers. Service centers include services such as housekeeping, laundry, and medical records. In addition, there are many other categories of support costs that are indirect costs, such as supplies, depreciation, and insurance, that serve both service and mission centers.

Program costing then involves choosing the *final cost objective:* a day of care, an admission, an event of care, or the costs associated with a particular diagnostic category. To do this, all the direct costs associated with the final cost objective are traced to that cost objective. Then it becomes necessary to allocate the indirect costs. This is where the difficulty arises.

The best of standard practice would take the costs of support pools and allocate them to both service and mission centers based upon allocation criteria that had the closest bearing on how the costs were incurred. Once the indirect costs have been allocated to service and mission centers, the next step is to allocate service center costs to mission centers by using allocation bases that most nearly reflect the demand for service activities in mission centers.

The final step in the cost procedure is to assign the costs traced and allocated to mission centers to final cost objectives. Let us assume that the final cost objective is DRG 123. The cost objective receives direct costs from each mission center, along with some indirect or overhead costs assigned previously to the mission center. Ideally, the indirect cost of the mission center should be assigned to the DRG on the basis of criteria that most nearly reflects the incidence of these costs.

It should be apparent that it is a most difficult job to arrive at accurate product costs. Even the most sophisticated costing systems provide only approximations to product or program costs. The move to ABC costing described in Chapter 13 should improve the accuracy of these costs, but the nonprofit sector is far behind the profit sector in applying this more accurate costing method, and the problems of applying these more accurate methods are formidable. Nevertheless, we should expect a movement in the direction of ABC in some of the more managerially advanced nonprofit institutions.

Using Costing to Influence Behavior

The following case study[10] is an example of how good cost data can be developed to pinpoint cost variances, identify aberrant costs, and use these data to effect changes of behavior in members of a nonprofit institution, in this case a medical staff of a nonprofit hospital.

> The director of surgical inpatient units at a metropolitan hospital was evaluating a recently completed study of costs incurred for various drugs. The study group had investigated DRG, which had incurred net losses in the 1988–89 fiscal year. Two subcommittees had been formed, each with multidisciplinary representation to address the financial losses observed within some diagnostic groups.
>
> One subgroup had analyzed DRG 154 (stomach, esophageal, and duodenal surgery). This subgroup was headed by the administrative director of the department of pathology and included the director of surgical services, the director of surgical inpatients unit, and a clinical services manager of the pharmacy.
>
> Medical records had been reviewed on 13 patients. These records revealed a broad spectrum of cases. The average patient was 67.2 years, with a span from 51 to 87. Costs per patient ranged from $4,600 to $32,500. Length of stay ranged from 3 to 41 days,

with an average of 13.3 days. The hospital had been reimbursed for only 40 percent of their estimated actual costs.

After examining five of these cases in detail, the committee came to three specific conclusions. First, the intensity of service and length of stay varied tremendously. Second, customary physician practice patterns significantly influenced costs. Third, organizational practice patterns maintained by hospital personnel also influenced costs. The following recommendations were made for bringing costs under control:

1. Reduce intensity of service and length of stay through aggressive clinical management by the nursing team.
2. Reduce daily diagnostics.
3. Reduce routine cross-matching of blood.
4. Review laboratory panels and promote standardization of use.
5. Review antibiotic therapy and promote standardization of use.

The question facing the committee was: How can management influence both physicians and hospital personnel to alter their behavior patterns in order to reduce costs? Changing behavior of the hospital personnel would probably be easier. Training programs can be developed and their progress monitored, but how do you secure the cooperation of the physicians?

The first step in the process to reduce physician costs had already been taken. The direct physician charges had been documented. The second step would be to enlist the support of key formal and informal leaders of the medical staff department and to get them to agree on what are reasonable tests and procedures. The third step would be to release data on the direct charges but not to give the names of the physicians involved. The fourth step would be to send the data, in confidence, to each physician whose charges seemed to be out of line, indicating which patients were his or hers and to ask for help in controlling costs.

A number of the other aspects of the MSSM can be used in order to gain the cooperation of the physicians in bringing costs under control. One is to appeal to shared beliefs of the institution and how cost control fulfills these beliefs. The second is to try to offer rewards to the physicians in return for their cooperation. Examples of potential rewards are to offer assistance to physicians in marketing their services, or to offer to negotiate with payers for joint physician–hospital contracted services.

In summary, a cost system should be designed to measure the cost of an activity within the health care institution as a whole or within a mission or service center. The documentation of costs is the first step for controlling costs. Once costs have been documented, methods of influencing behavior must then be devised to correct those items whose costs are out of line.

REWARDS

Formal rewards are significantly below what similar people would reap in the profit sector. Most do not work for nonprofits because of the financial rewards. Mission is a major reward. Consequently, the paid staff as well as the volunteer staff are committed to the mission. The mission could be clean air or combatting AIDS.

Promotion opportunities are infrequent in nonprofits. When they occur, they usually are found outside the institution.

There is a clear message for the profit sector in these nonprofit institutions. Most volunteers find the nonprofit sector more rewarding because of the sense of purpose and the challenge. Drucker reports:[11] "When I ask them why they do it [that is, work for nonprofits], far too many give the same answer: Because in my job there isn't enough challenge, not enough responsibility; and there is no mission, there is only expediency." Many who work for nonprofits find the reward of working toward a goal or mission that they believe in to be sufficient reward!

THE HOSPITAL

The primary rewards in a hospital are derived from the satisfaction received from fulfillment of the mission to provide high-quality health care. Physicians are well paid, but most other professionals are paid at 80 to 90 percent of what their counterparts earn in the for-profit sector of the economy. Promotion possibilities in hospitals are few, given the flat organization structure. Management careers are advanced by moving from one institution to an other. There is little crossover from the medical side to the administrative side. This leaves legions of medical technical personnel, with advanced degrees, with few career growth opportunities.

COMMUNICATION SYSTEMS

Board members, if organized properly, can provide a very valuable contribution to the communication systems of the nonprofit institution. If their strategic work is organized by committee and each committee meets regularly with the relevant operating committee to add vision and perspective, the board can play a very strong function in furthering the mission of the organization.

Efficient communication methods are expensive. It is here that the competition for limited resources is acutely felt, with many operations that could easily be computerized being carried out on a manual basis. For example, in order to access a client's file, a person might have to check the filing cabinets in different departments rather than making an inquiry into an integrated data base. The result is inefficiency: in order to become fully informed about a client, the investigator would have to go through the laborious task of checking files in different departments.

THE HOSPITAL

There is a plethora of communication mechanisms within both the medical and administrative sides of hospitals. On the medical side, there is usually a computerized hospital information system that provides up-to-date patient information at nursing stations and contributes to the patient control process. The medical committees are comprised of physicians trying to work out the best course of treatment for a particular patient. These committees are a place to begin to alter physician behavior to achieve better cost performance while continuing to provide the highest quality of care.

It should also be noted that computerized systems for management reporting are proliferating and are becoming the basis for extensive planning and reporting capability in hospitals.

INFORMAL CONTROL

INTERPERSONAL RELATIONSHIPS

Because of fewer hard measurements, informal communications, networking, and politics tend to be important organizational processes for making resource allocation decisions.

Within given disciplines informal relations are usually rich. However, the danger here is that it can create functional fixation with a sense of superiority of one group over another. Cross disciplinary teams, as described above under the program costing section, should be used extensively to raise quality and reduce costs.

INFORMAL CONTROL PROCESSES

Medical management of patients tends to be very adaptable to the progression and resolution of diseases. Management flexibility, on the other hand, has historically been much less demonstratable.

INFORMAL REWARDS

The strong culture of concern and pride in patient care is rewarded with a sense of accomplishment, providing strong informal rewards. These are the strongest rewards hospitals have in motivating performance.

Many positions provide a fair degree of status within a hospital. Certainly, the physicians and administrators are in positions of high status.

INFORMAL COMMUNICATIONS

Informal communications tend to be very prevalent and natural among peers but more restricted laterally between departments.

REFERENCES

ANTHONY, ROBERT N., AND DAVID W. YOUNG, *Management Control in Nonprofit Organizations*, 4th ed., Homewood, Ill.: Richard D. Irwin, 1988.

ASAY, LYAL D., AND JOSEPH A. MACIARIELLO, *Executive Leadership in Health Care*. San Francisco: Jossey-Bass Publishers, 1991.

BRAUN, DAN, "The Design of Cost Systems for Operational and Strategic Decision Making for the Nonprofit," unpublished research paper, Claremont Graduate School, Spring 1992.

BAUMOL, WILLIAM J., "A Growing Economy Can Pay its Bills," *Wall Street Journal*, May 19, 1992.

DRUCKER, PETER F., *The Nonprofit Drucker* (audiotape series), Volumes I–IV. Tyler, Texas: Leadership Network, 1989.

———, *Managing the Nonprofit Organization*, New York: Harper Collins, 1990.

———, "What Business Can Learn from Nonprofits," *Harvard Business Review*, July–August 1990.

HALL, ELIZABETH, "Control Systems in Nonprofit Organizations," unpublished research paper, Claremont Graduate School, Fall 1990.

JOYCE, JOHN P., "Control Systems in Non-profits," unpublished research paper, Claremont Graduate School, December 1990.

NOTES

1. John B. Byrne, "Profiting from the Non-profit," *Business Week*, March 26, 1990, p. 68.
2. Peter F. Drucker, "What Business Can Learn from Nonprofits," *Harvard Business Review*, July–August 1990, p. 88.
3. These characteristics are discussed in detail in Chapter 1 of *Management Control in Nonprofit Institutions*, by Robert N. Anthony and David Young (Homewood, Ill.: Richard D. Irwin, 4th ed., 1988, pp. 54–70). They are used by permission. Anthony and Young consider government organizations to be nonprofit. We make a distinction between profit, governmental, and nonprofit organizations and consider only the latter in this chapter.
4. Anthony and Young, p. 54.
5. The analysis of this section is based upon a model of economic growth called the *unbalanced growth model.* It has been a very reliable predictor of the growth rates of services that are considered necessities. A clear nontechnical explanation of this model is contained in an editorial by William J. Baumol, "A Growing Economy Can Pay its Bills," *Wall Street Journal*, May 19, 1992. This section is based on the conclusions that one draws from the unbalanced productivity growth model and his nontechnical exposition of this model.
6. Five Acres, *1991 Annual Report*, 760 West Mountain View Street, Altadena, California.
7. Peter F. Drucker, *Managing the Nonprofit Organization.* New York: HarperCollins, 1990, p. 113.
8. Burtis, "New Element," *Cal Chemistry*, 1990, p. 827.
9. Anthony Gambino and Thomas Reardon, "Financial Planning and Evaluation for the Nonprofit Organization," National Association of Accountants, 1981, p. 3.
10. This case was written by Joseph A. Maciariello and is adapted by permission from Asay, Lyal D., and Joseph A., *Executive Leadership in Health Care*, pp. 97–98. Copyright 1991 by Jossey-Bass, Inc., Publishers.
11. Peter F. Drucker, "What Business Can Learn from Nonprofits," *Harvard Business Review*, July–August 1990, p. 93.

Case 18-1 City Hospital*

I have worked hard at developing the new cost accounting system at City Hospital. I think it works reasonably well in all nonphysician departments. But the principal driver of our costs is physician behavior and we still do not have control over this driver.

> Miles Vanderman, Manager,
> Cost Accounting
> (in an interview with the case writer)

City Hospital is a 250-bed tertiary care hospital specializing in the treatment of many forms of cancer. Founded in 1913 as a center for the treatment of tuberculosis patients, it has evolved to become a major research and treatment institution. Many experimental therapies have been pioneered at City Hospital, and patients with advanced disease find treatments here that are unavailable anywhere else. From its inception until 1960, City Hospital was an eleemosynary institution, providing care to patients free of charge. In 1960, it began to bill patients and insurers for care provided. Because most funds were obtained through fund raising, City Hospital made no effort to compute cost per patient prior to 1988.

The medical staff at City contains several world-famous physicians and is of high caliber and noteworthy reputation. The medical staff is for the most part full-time hospital staff unlike most hospitals, where the medical staff is independent of the hospital. The administrative staff is professional and is determined to bring professional management practices to hospital operations. To this end, the staff is committed to developing sound cost accounting and control procedures.

This case focuses upon recent attempts at City Hospital to design a new cost accounting system to help the hospital control costs.

COST ACCOUNTING

Traditionally, hospitals have done little or no cost accounting. In the past cost reimbursement was based upon "actual costs incurred" for patients. All that changed in 1983, when the federal government adopted a prospective payment system for medicare patients.

Through a method of establishing the severity of diagnosis known as diagnosis related groups (DRGs), medicare set reimbursement levels for patients in 467 different diagnosis categories. This has resulted in tremendous pressure on hospitals, including City Hospital, to determine their "true" costs for each relevant diagnosis category so that costs can be reduced below the reimbursement level in order to provide subsidies for those services in which costs cannot be reduced.

---

*This case was prepared by John P. Joyce with the assistance of Joseph Maciariello. It is reproduced here by permission.

THE NEW COST SYSTEM

City Hospital hired a cost accounting manager in 1987 to install a new cost accounting system that could be used for budgeting and cost control at the hospital. In 1988 the cost accounting manager identified the top revenue-producing procedures and concentrated upon developing standard costs for those DRGs first. With full approval of management but without introduction or appointment, he appeared at the offices of the supervisors of various medical departments responsible for the charges. He interviewed each department head and related technicians to determine the actual cost of each procedure performed in the department. The interviews identified the direct input of departmental labor, single-use expendable supplies, reusable supplies, equipment, and expenses related to equipment use, such as service contracts, for each procedure.

Departmental personnel were then given a form to fill out allocating the time each employee spent on a given task. Material costs were established by estimating the use of disposable supplies per procedure, reusable supply consumption was determined by estimating the average number of uses of each piece of equipment over its expected lifetime to develop an average rate per procedure.

All costs not directly related to billable procedures incurred in the department and institutional overhead were allocated to sub-units of the department by using 15 allocation criteria, such as admitting (total revenue), environmental services (square feet), and administration (accumulated total expenses). The rationale used in allocation was to relate each expenditure to the most logical allocation base. For example, admitted patients produced the greatest source of revenue; the cost of environmental services was a function of the area of the unit served; administration was

related to the amount of activity in a unit. Indirect costs allocated to units were then divided by the actual number of procedures to arrive at the rate per procedure.

Next, the process was repeated for the medical group. The direct labor input of physicians was estimated separately to reinforce to the medical staff that the administration considers them apart from the remainder of the hospital. Although this was the process used for developing estimates of physician labor for each procedure, it was subsequently dropped from the ongoing control process.[1]

The cost data developed per procedure were then used to develop the annual operating budget. Each department head was expected to forecast a volume of procedures for the next year. When new procedures were added, the department head was expected to estimate its cost based upon similarities with and differences from previous procedures. This was in contrast with past practice where historical data plus a negotiated incremental increase was used.

Besides actual volume of procedures, case mix was also forecasted by each department head. Here departments estimated the kinds of patients they were expecting to treat over the next year. A standard treatment plan was identified in order to identify what it took to treat an average patient with a given disease. Therefore, an approximate treatment cost to the hospital for a particular diagnosis and therapy was developed. In this way the hospital could gain insight into which procedures were more cost effective as well as the costs of treating specific diseases.

With an understanding of expected total hospital expenses per patient diagnostic category, the hospital then developed its operating budget. The budget was a function of the expected volume of patients. The budget also became the basis for comparison of actual costs versus budget for the actual number of patients treated.

EXPERIENCE WITH THE
NEW COST SYSTEM

A great disparity exists in the quality of cost estimates that are made in each department. Most department managers take the job seriously. Others simply make educated "guesses." They all feel pressure from the short time available for making estimates. Many of the poor estimates are corrected by cost accounting personnel in the process, since in many cases the required time to perform the functions does not correlate well with time available. The managers responsible are then pressured to renegotiate their estimates to more accurate levels.

Since the process of developing operating budgets in relationship to patient volume is a new concept to many medical managers, a considerable amount of time had to be spent on explanations of the process. It is only when managers understand how to analyze their areas to eliminate unfavorable variances that a modicum of acceptance emerges. Even now, however, department managers cringe at the site of the manager of cost accounting, since he is confronting them with a problem that is outside of their area of competence and not directly related to the mission of their organization, which is to provide the highest-quality health care to patients.

A monthly cost report is used to determine productivity levels for all nonphysician personnel. A number of cost items are monitored monthly, such as wage rates, overtime utilization, and supplies using variations from standards developed in the study. Physicians have refused to use monthly cost reports to control their behavior.

QUESTIONS

1. Using the City Hospital case as an example, what kind of steps are necessary for top management to take to gain control over hospital expenses through the use of control systems?
2. What light does the MSSM and our work on the design of control systems shed on this problem (*Hint:* the problem of managing professionals in nonprofit organizations)?

NOTES

1. Physician estimates were not subsequently updated. Only new procedures were estimated.

19

MANAGEMENT CONTROL OF THE ETHICAL DIMENSION OF ORGANIZATIONS

This chapter deals with two issues that pertain to the ethical dimension of organizations and control systems used within them. It is not concerned with the narrow question of personal morality in the organization. That question, for the most part, is beyond the scope of this book.

Here our concerns are broader. The first concern is the need organizations have to design control systems to ensure compliance with ethical codes, ethical policies, and various laws impinging upon their operation. The second concern has to do with the ethical properties of a control system in general.

DESIGNING CONTROL SYSTEMS TO REGULATE ETHICAL CONDUCT

In Chapter 1, following the work of Packer (1978, pp. 19–38), we made five basic assumptions about human behavior that were important to the work of control system design. These five assumptions are

1. Basic rationality—human beings are *rational.*
2. Creativity—human beings are *creative.*
3. Mastery—human beings seek *mastery.*
4. Morality—human beings have strong *moral instincts,* although these instincts do not always control behavior.
5. Community—human beings have strong desires for *human association.*

Assumption 4 deals with the moral dimension of human conduct. It implies that although individuals as a rule have strong instincts to do what is right, they are also capable of engaging in unethical and illegal acts. All organizations should establish formal and informal control mechanisms to induce ethical behavior and to prevent unethical behavior.

The pressures to achieve organizational goals and the incentives to do so are often very strong. This may lead managers and other employees to take measures that are expedient under the circumstances but which are unethical, either because they break a law of the country in which the firm is operating or because they are against the code of ethics of the organization.

For example, assume that a manager is responsible for building electrical components for which the customer has contracted for a lengthy and costly set of electrical tests, and that he is currently behind schedule. Further assume he is under intense pressure from his boss to "meet the schedule or else." This might lead him to order a reduced set of tests on the components, which represents a violation of the contract with the customer.

Ethical cases such as this one might seem straightforward, but upon closer examination are very difficult to resolve equitably. If the components fail, what disciplinary action should be administered on the manager who ordered the reduction in testing? Also, how about the test engineer who followed the order, but knew better? What about associate workers who knew the violation took place but looked the other way? Finally, what about the top manager who put pressure on the manager responsible for the components? This manager virtually forced the component manager to "do something" to reduce time.

This example illustrates the need to have a well-designed ethics program, followed by clear policies, that are consistently and fairly carried out. Actions must be carried out appropriately and feedback loops must be established properly.

As a result, organizations, often develop *codes of conduct* to govern behavior of individuals in the organization. Then the task is to train managers in the behaviors expected and to periodically monitor that behavior to ensure that employees are conforming to the codes. Ethical behavior is first a moral problem, but it is also a control problem.

This section contains an approach that may be taken to the design of a control system to help the organization conduct its operations in an ethical manner. First, we look at the cybernetic dimensions of the control problem. Next, we develop the aspects of the formal MSSM that are required to support the control process so as to achieve ethical behavior. Ethical problems are embedded within the normal operations of the organization. As a result, the control of ethical behavior must also be embedded within the organization.

Exhibit 19-1 is a representation of the cybernetic dimensions of a program to control ethical behavior.[1] First the goal: *to achieve compliance with all laws, ethical codes, and policies of the organization.* Next, perceptions: *to sensitize all managers and employees as to what kind of behavior constitutes improper behavior.* The second step is necessary because managers and employees come to the organization with their own codes of conduct, which may or may not lead to the desired ethical behavior.

The third step in the ethics program is to *audit the behavior of employees* on activities with all stakeholders. Next is to *report significant deviations* from desired ethical conduct. The fifth step is to *investigate alleged violations,* and the sixth step is to *implement decisions to correct improper behavior.*

The ethics program takes place in an environment in which there are various laws regulating business activity. In addition, employees are influenced by various ethical codes, including personal codes and professional codes of conduct. Included are regulations governing generally acceptable accounting procedures (GAAP). Moreover, the cultural values of the organization together with the entire informal control system create pressures towards or against ethical behavior.

Numerous reports are usually produced in an ethics program. These are indicated under the Sensor in Exhibit 19-1. These reports are intended to influence employee perceptions as to what constitutes ethical behavior in the organization. They include policies and procedures, ethical guidelines for dealing with various stakeholders, and numerous documents used in training employees up and down the hierarchy.

CONTROL SYSTEMS SUPPORTING THE ETHICS PROGRAM

The control process for the ethics program was described in Exhibit 19-1. That process is supported by a formal control structure that is represented in Exhibit 19-2.

The style of management and the culture of the organization have a major influence over the attitude that develops in the organization regarding what is acceptable and what is not. Our examples of style and culture in Chapter 4 illustrate how both can be used to enhance ethical conduct in the organization. An

Exhibit 19-1
Cybernetic Control Process
Ethics Program

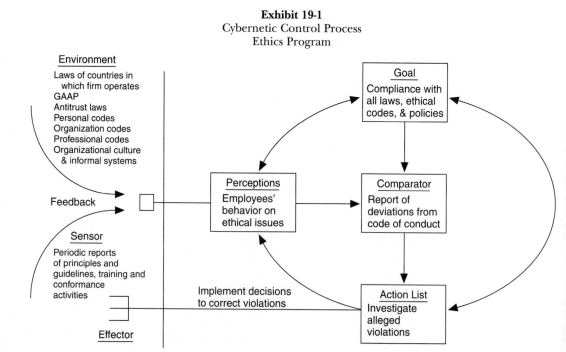

Exhibit 19-2
Control System for Ethics Program

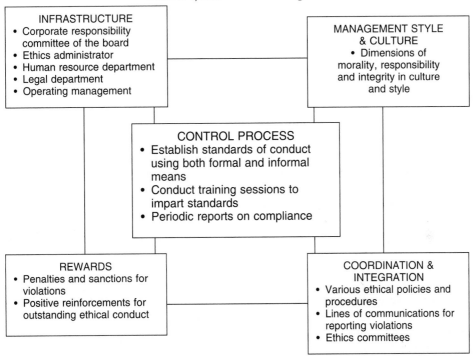

external style, where heavy emphasis is placed upon formal measurement and evaluation, and where rewards are strongly linked to formal measurement systems, has the tendency to create pressures toward cheating and unethical behavior. When the external management style is used, it must be infused with well developed procedures to prevent unethical behavior and to detect its occurrence. The internal style, which relies more heavily upon informal control mechanisms, is also sensitive to ethical abuses in certain circumstances. For example, if products or services must follow detailed manufacturing or administration procedures precisely, an overly informal system may lack discipline and control to follow these steps time after time. Therefore, while we may say that the internal style is less sensitive to ethical abuses, management must be careful to adapt the style that is appropriate to the situation at hand.

The culture instituted by Thomas Watson, the founder of IBM, which was reported on in Chapter 4, relied heavily upon the Golden Rule with respect to the treatment of customers. A pervasive cultural attitude that included an emphasis on the Golden Rule regarding behavior with all stakeholders would certainly minimize but not eliminate the possibility of unethical behavior.

Normally, the overall oversight of the ethics program is with a committee of the board of directors. Sometimes, organizations establish ethics committees at various levels in the organization such as the CEO level. Ethics programs must be broad enough to have jurisdiction over cases involving the highest-ranking members of the organization. For these cases, ethics programs usually employ independent, external, legal assistance.

An ethics administrator may be appointed and may report to the board directly or to a high-ranking executive of the firm. The ethics administrator is a staff person responsible for writing and distributing various ethical policies and for monitoring conformance to ethical guidelines. The legal department is a staff department that consults with operating managers and employees on both the spirit and the letter of various laws governing corporate behavior. The human resource department conducts various training programs and plays a major role in implementing ethical guidelines in the recruiting, promotion, and retention process. Operating management is expected to carry out the ethical guidelines in their organizational unit. When product integrity is involved, it is important that the ethics program make provision for the involvement of appropriate technical, engineering, and quality experts to resolve the issues raised.

The coordination and communications dimension of the ethical control system involves establishing formal communication channels for reporting ethical violations. These channels should be established so as to protect those employees who report violations from punitive actions by their superiors or by their fellow employees. For example, anonymous "ethics hot lines" can be established and made available to all employees. They may be answered by relatively high-level executives. We might expect many calls to be received when these lines are first established due to the existence of pent-up problems, but the activity tends to slow down after a time and the hot lines become very effective tools.

Rewards and punishments are critical to the effective enforcement of ethical behavior. Ethical behavior should be highly regarded by top management and should be used in evaluation of promotion decisions. This is one of the most effective strategies an organization can use to encourage ethical behavior. Strong negative penalties, including dismissal, should exist for willful unethical or illegal behavior. The combination of strong positive and strong negative incentives should increase the likelihood of ethical behavior dramatically.

THE ETHICAL PRINCIPLE OF FAIRNESS
IN THE DESIGN OF CONTROL SYSTEMS

As we have seen throughout the book, a control system is designed to assist managers in reaching the goals and objectives of their organization. A control system in which all the subsystems are designed to achieve goals and objectives is a *goal-congruent subsystem*. The criterion of goal congruence is central to the design of all subsystems as well as to the design of managerial controls.

The foundation for a control system that is ethical requires a business and operating environment conducive to ethical conduct. It is better to foster ethical behavior than to police, catch, and punish unethical behavior. The idea is to align with each stakeholder an environment that is congruent with ethical behavior, business objectives, and stakeholder objectives. We stress the concept of *fairness* to achieve this environment.

We do not believe that in the long run the criterion of fairness is at odds with the criterion of goal congruence. In the short run, however, it often is. For example, managers are sometimes held responsible for variables whose values are significantly out of their control in the hope that it will generate behavior on the part of the manager to influence other managers in a way that is in total goal congruent. We maintain that while this may accomplish short-term results, it is a practice that is best avoided and one which we predict will lead to long-term problems.

Subsystems and managerial controls that are unfair create stress and resentment. They result in the loss of goodwill to the organization. Morale falls, and manipulative behavior ensues. Given enough time, unfairly designed subsystems undermine the efforts of the organization to achieve its goals. Since these subsystems lack ethical support, they often result in unethical countermeasures on the part of employees. The result is a distortion of control information, poor decisions, and a misallocation of resources.

Accordingly, it is very important that adequate disciplinary records be kept and used to insure that the ethics program is perceived as fair by the organization at large. To illustrate, if a manager fills a time card in order to get more overtime than actually worked and as a result receives a five-day suspension and a line worker does the same thing and is discharged, the program will be perceived as biased and low morale will likely occur.

Unfair control systems (including ethical control systems) and controls undermine trust in and between organizations. If trust is lost, it is replaced by all kinds of defensive, bureaucratic, dysfunctional behavior. Without trust, the control systems must become more elaborate to achieve the same level of previous performance. This raises costs and reduces efficiency.

A control system that is ethical is a control system that has the fairness criterion built in throughout. Fairness should extend to all of the activities of all stakeholders. Although the criterion of fairness is subjective, stakeholders do have opinions as to fairness, at least as to what within a range of behavior toward them constitutes fairness. Aside from personal interactions, fairness may also be assessed through formal interviews and surveys. Let us look at some of the fairness issues with respect to stakeholders.[2]

It is in the long-run interests of the firm to treat customers fairly. What does this mean? It certainly means high-quality goods and services at reasonable prices. But it also means genuinely trying to determine and meet customer needs. Moreover, advertising should be truthful, not only to help the customer make wise decisions, but because stretching the truth has a negative effect upon the perceptions of current employees regarding the ethical character of the organization. Employees may become cynical about the organization's intent.

The first obligation to shareholders is financial solvency. Next, shareholders should be able through their investment in the organization to earn a fair return on their investment; here fairness is defined in relation to similar firms in the industry.

Employees should be informed of the true financial condition of the organization and its plans for the future. The firm should seek to pay fair wages and salaries and provide opportunities for growth of individual talent. In times of economic recession, the firm should assist displaced employees in finding other suitable employment.

Compensation to management is a key ethical issue for organizations. If highly visible management bonuses increase dramatically during periods in which shareholders and employees are asked to retrench, this creates obvious cynical reactions to management and the organization. Salaries should be in line with the competition, and every effort should be made to reduce salaries and bonuses that have no good rationale in terms of the competition for executive talent or in terms of the profits of the firm.

Suppliers are often key stakeholders. The organization owes its loyal suppliers consideration during periods of downturn. This may come in the form of loans or in the form of agreements to continue purchases during the downturn at a certain levels. Key suppliers should be advised as to prospective business plans so far as they impact the supplier.

The organization should seek to obey both the letter and the spirit of various local laws and regulations. It should seek in all ways to be a good neighbor, including making contributions to worthy civic projects in the community.

Often the interests of various stakeholders conflict in decision making. For example, to maintain current dividends to shareholders management may have to reduce employment or salaries. These conflicts often present ethical dilemmas: having to choose between two courses of action, each one of which has negative consequences to a stakeholder. These decisions take much wisdom on the part of management and cannot be arrived at in the abstract.

REFERENCES

BENSON, GEORGE C. S., "To Whom Does the Corporation Owe a Duty?", Robert W. McGee, ed., *Business Ethics & Common Sense.* Westport, Connecticut: Quorum Books, 1992, pp. 115–136.

HARVARD BUSINESS SCHOOL. "H. J. Heinz Company," (A)–(D), Case Numbers 382-034 through 382-037. Cambridge, Mass.: HBS Case Services, 1981.

PACKER, JAMES I., *Knowing Man.* Westchester, Ill.: Cornerstone Books, 1978, pp. 19–38.

NOTES

1. This chapter draws upon published policy elements that support the administration of the Hughes Aircraft Ethics Program, publicly recognized as an excellent program.
2. The material in this section on fairness to stakeholders summarizes many of the arguments made by George C. S. Benson in "To Whom Does the Corporation Owe a Duty?" Robert W. McGee, ed., *Business Ethics & Common Sense.* Westport, Connecticut: Quorum Books, 1992, pp. 115–136.

Case 19-1 The Case of Double Standards

A senior manager has been told by top management to relocate a small engineering and manufacturing department to a lower-cost state. He tells the department manager, "Make the move in three months and don't miss any schedules."

The department manager wants to reduce risk, so he offers a higher than allowed relocation package to three technicians. Two accept without questioning his generosity, but they both believe that the relocation allowances violate company policy. A third technician accepts but doesn't check company policy.

The department manager, tired of working double shifts during the time of the move, rents a home at the new location, moves his girl friend, and writes off all these expenses as business-related relocation expenses.

The senior manager hears some "rumblings" that some strange things are happening during the move. Before he can respond, he receives a call from an irate customer relating to the work of the department involved in the move. He attends to the customer problem and decides to ignore the rumblings.

Two months into the move, it is discovered that some manufacturing equipment which runs a sensitive bonding process on some of the top-selling products of the department "isn't quite right." An inexperienced machine operator, recently hired during the move, runs the parts anyway, not bothering to ask the supervisor for the go-ahead.

Finally, one of the technicians, whose high relocation allowance was rejected by the human resource department, calls the ethics hotline to log a formal complaint about the violations of the machine operator and the technicians and department manager who received high relocation allowances.

QUESTIONS

1. Describe an ethics policy that would be appropriate to cover this situation. Does your policy satisfy all stakeholder needs?
2. What is the appropriate discipline for each of the individuals involved in ethical violations?

INDEX